A Guide to Modern Econometrics

A Guide to Modern Econometrics

Marno Verbeek

KU Leuven
and
Tilburg University

JOHN WILEY & SONS, LTD

Chichester · New York · Weinheim · Brisbane · Toronto · Singapore

Other Wiley Editorial Offices

John Wiley & Sons, Inc., 605 Third Avenue,
New York, NY 10158-0012, USA

VCH Verlagsgesellschaft mbH, Pappelallee 3,
D-69469 Weinheim, Germany

Jacaranda Wiley Ltd, 33 Park Road, Milton,
Queensland 4064, Australia

John Wiley & Sons (Canada) Ltd, 22 Worcester Road,
Rexdale, Ontario M9W 1L1, Canada

John Wiley & Sons (Asia) Pte Ltd, 2 Clementi Loop #02-01,
Jin Xing Distripark, Singapore 129809

Library of Congress Cataloging-in-Publication Data

Verbeek, Marno.
    A guide to modern econometrics / by Marno Verbeek.
        p. cm.
    Includes bibliographical references and index.
    ISBN 0-471-89982-8 (alk. paper)
      1. Econometrics.   2. Regression analysis.   I. Title.

    HB139.V465 2000
    330'.01'5195–dc21   99-059518

British Library Cataloguing in Publication Data

A catalogue record for this book is available from the British Library

ISBN 0-471-89982-8

Typeset in 10/12 pt Times by C.K.M. Typesetting, Salisbury, Wiltshire.
Printed and bound in Great Britain by Antony Rowe, Chippenham, Wiltshire.
This book is printed on acid-free paper responsibly manufactured from sustainable forestry,
in which at least two trees are planted for each one used for paper production.

Contents

Preface

The field of econometrics has developed rapidly in the last two decades, while the use of up-to-date econometric techniques has become more and more standard practice in empirical work in many fields of economics. Typical topics include unit root tests, cointegration, estimation by the generalized method of moments, heteroskedasticity and autocorrelation consistent standard errors, modelling conditional heteroskedasticity, models based on panel data, and models with limited dependent variables, endogenous regressors and sample selection. At the same time econometrics software has become more and more user friendly and up-to-date. As a consequence, users are able to implement fairly advanced techniques even without a basic understanding of the underlying theory and without realizing potential drawbacks or dangers. In contrast, many introductory econometrics textbooks pay a disproportionate amount of attention to the standard linear regression model under the strongest set of assumptions. Needless to say that these assumptions are hardly satisfied in practice (but not really needed either). On the other hand, the more advanced econometrics textbooks are often too technical or too detailed for the average economist to grasp the essential ideas and to extract the information that is needed. This book tries to fill this gap.

The goal of this book is to familiarize the reader with a wide range of topics in modern econometrics, focusing on what is important for doing and understanding empirical work. This means that the text is a guide to (rather than an overview of) alternative techniques. Consequently, it does not concentrate on the formulae behind each technique (although the necessary ones are given) nor on formal proofs, but on the intuition behind the approaches and their practical relevance. The book covers a wide range of topics that is usually not found in textbooks at this level. In particular, attention is paid to cointegration, the generalized method of moments, models with limited dependent variables and panel data models. As a result, the book discusses developments in time series analysis, cross-sectional methods as well as panel data modelling. Throughout, a few dozen full-scale empirical examples and illustrations are provided, taken from fields like labour economics, finance, international economics, consumer behaviour, environmental economics and macro-economics. In addition, a number of exercises are of an empirical nature and require the use of actual data.

The present text originates from lecture notes used for courses in Applied Econometrics in the M.Sc. programs in Economics at K. U. Leuven and Tilburg University. It is written for an intended audience of economists and economics students that would like to become familiar with up-to-date econometric approaches and techniques, important for doing, understanding and evaluating empirical work. It is very well suited for courses in applied econometrics at the masters or graduate level. At some schools this book will be suited for one or more courses at the under-graduate level, provided students have a sufficient background in statistics. Some of the later chapters can be used in more advanced courses covering particular topics, for example, panel data, limited dependent variable models or time series analysis. In addition, this book can serve as a guide for managers, research economists and practitioners who want to update their insufficient or outdated knowledge of econo-metrics. Throughout, the use of matrix algebra is limited.

I am very much indebted to Arie Kapteyn, Bertrand Melenberg, Theo Nijman, and Arthur van Soest, who all have contributed to my understanding of econometrics and have shaped my way of thinking about many issues. The fact that some of their ideas have materialized in this text, is a tribute to their efforts. I also owe many thanks to several generations of students who helped me to shape this text into its current form, by commenting upon previous versions and by providing me with questions they could not find an answer to. A wide range of practical and empirical problems con-cerning econometrics posed to me by students and colleagues was an important motivation to finish this text. A large number of people read through parts of the manuscript and made corrections or suggestions. I am very grateful to Peter de Goeij, Ben Jacobsen, Wim Koevoets, Marco Lyrio, Konstantijn Maes, Wessel Marquering, Bertrand Melenberg, Paulo Nunes, Anatoly Peresetsky, Max van de Sande Bakhuyzen, Erik Schokhaert, Arthur van Soest, Frederic Vermeulen, Kuo-chun Yeh and a number of anonymous reviewers. Of course I retain sole responsibility for any remaining errors. Special thanks go to Jef Flechet for his help with many empirical illustrations and his constructive comments on many previous versions. Finally, I want to thank my wife Marcella and my two children, Timo and Thalia, for their patience and understanding for all the times that my mind was with this book, while it should have been with them.

1 Introduction

1.1 About Econometrics

Economists are frequently interested in relationships between different quantities, for example between individual wages and the level of schooling. The most important job of econometrics is to quantify these relationships on the basis of available data and using statistical techniques, and to interpret, use or exploit the resulting outcomes appropriately. Consequently, econometrics is the interaction of economic theory, observed data and statistical methods. It is the interaction of these three that makes econometrics interesting, challenging and, perhaps, difficult. In the words of a seminar speaker, several years ago: 'Econometrics is much easier without data'.

Traditionally econometrics has focused upon aggregate economic relationships. Macro-economic models consisting of several up to many hundreds equations were specified, estimated and used for policy evaluation and forecasting. The recent theoretical developments in this area, most importantly the concept of cointegration, have generated increased attention to the modelling of macro-economic relationships and their dynamics, although typically focusing on particular aspects of the economy. Since the 1970s econometric methods are increasingly employed in micro-economic models describing individual, household or firm behaviour, stimulated by the development of appropriate econometric models and estimators which take into account problems like discrete dependent variables and sample selection, by the availability of large survey data sets, and by the increasing computational possibilities. More recently, the empirical analysis of financial markets has required and stimulated many theoretical developments in econometrics. Currently econometrics plays a major role in empirical work in all fields of economics, almost without exception, and in most cases it is no longer sufficient to be able to run a few regressions and interpret the results. As a result, introductory econometrics textbooks usually provide insufficient coverage for applied researchers. On the other hand, the more advanced econometrics textbooks are often too technical or too detailed for the average economist to grasp the essential ideas and to extract the information that is needed. Thus there is a need for an accessible textbook that discusses the recent and relatively more advanced developments.

The relationships that economists are interested in are formally specified in mathematical terms, which lead to econometric or statistical models. In such models there is room for deviations from the strict theoretical relationships due to, for example, measurement errors, unpredictable behaviour, optimization errors or unexpected events. Broadly, econometric models can be classified in a number of categories.

A first class of models describes relationships between present and past. For example, how does the short-term interest rate depend on its own history? This type of models, typically referred to as time series models, usually lacks any economic theory and is mainly built to get forecasts for future values and the corresponding uncertainty or volatility.

A second type of models considers relationships between economic quantities over a certain time period. These relationships give us information on how (aggregate) economic quantities fluctuate over time in relation to other quantities. For example, what happens to the long-term interest rate if the monetary authority adjusts the short-term one? These models often give insight into the economic processes that are operating.

Third, there are models that describe relationships between different variables measured at a given point in time for different units (for example households or firms). Most of the time, this type of relationships is meant to explain why these units are different or behave differently. For example, one can analyse to what extent differences in household savings can be attributed to differences in household income. Under particular conditions, these cross-sectional relationships can be used to analyse 'what if' questions. For example, how much more would a given household, or the average household, save if income would increase by 1%?

Finally, one can consider relationships between different variables measured for different units over a longer time span (at least two periods). These relationships simultaneously describe differences between different individuals (why does person 1 save much more than person 2?), and differences in behaviour of a given individual over time (why does person 1 save more in 1992 than in 1990?). This type of model usually requires panel data, repeated observations over the same units. They are ideally suited for analysing policy changes on an individual level, provided that it can be assumed that the structure of the model is constant into the (near) future.

The job of econometrics is to specify and quantify these relationships. That is, econometricians formulate a statistical model, usually based on economic theory, confront it with the data, and try to come up with a specification that meets the required goals. The unknown elements in the specification, the parameters, are *estimated* from a sample of available data. Another job of the econometrician is to judge whether the resulting model is 'appropriate'. That is, check whether the assumptions made to motivate the estimators (and their properties) are correct, and check whether the model can be used for what it is made for. For example, can it be used for prediction or analysing policy changes? Often, economic theory implies that certain restrictions apply to the model that is estimated. For example, (one version of) the efficient market hypothesis implies that stock market returns are not predictable from their own past. An important goal of econometrics is to formulate such hypotheses in terms of the parameters in the model and to test their validity.

The number of econometric techniques that can be used is numerous and their validity often depends crucially upon the validity of the underlying assumptions. This book attempts to guide the reader through this forest of estimation and testing procedures, not by describing the beauty of all possible trees, but by walking through this forest in a structured way, skipping unnecessary side-paths, stressing the similarity of the different species that are encountered, and by pointing out dangerous pitfalls. The resulting walk is hopefully enjoyable and prevents the reader from getting lost in the econometric forest.

1.2   The Structure of this Book

The first part of this book consists of Chapters 2, 3 and 4. Like most textbooks, it starts with discussing the linear regression model and the OLS estimation method. Chapter 2 presents the basics of this important estimation method, with some emphasis on its validity under fairly weak conditions, while Chapter 3 focuses on the interpretation of the models and the comparison of alternative specifications. Chapter 4 considers two particular deviations from the standard assumptions of the linear model: autocorrelation and heteroskedasticity of the error terms. It is discussed how one can test for these phenomena, how they affect the validity of the OLS estimator and how this can be corrected. This includes a critical inspection of the model specification, the use of adjusted standard errors for the OLS estimator and the use of alternative (GLS) estimators. These three chapters are essential for the remaining part of this book and should be the starting point in any course.

In Chapter 5 another deviation from the standard assumptions of the linear model is discussed which is, however, fatal for the OLS estimator. As soon as the error term in the model is correlated with one or more of the explanatory variables all good properties of the OLS estimator disappear and we necessarily have to use alternative estimators. The chapter discusses instrumental variables (IV) estimators and, more generally, the generalized method of moments (GMM). This chapter, at least its earlier sections, is also recommended as an essential part of any econometrics course.

Chapter 6 is mainly theoretical and discusses maximum likelihood (ML) estimation. Because in empirical work maximum likelihood is often criticized for its dependence upon distributional assumptions, it is not discussed in the earlier chapters where alternatives are readily available that are either more robust than maximum likelihood or (asymptotically) equivalent to it. Particular emphasis in Chapter 6 is on misspecification tests based upon the Lagrange multiplier principle. While many empirical studies tend to take the distributional assumptions for granted, their validity is crucial for consistency of the estimators that are employed and should therefore be tested. Often these tests are relatively easy to perform, although most software does not routinely provide them (yet). Chapter 6 is crucial for understanding Chapter 7 on limited dependent variable models and for a small number of sections in Chapters 8 to 10.

The last part of this book contains four chapters. Chapter 7 presents models that are typically (though not exclusively) used in micro-economics, where the dependent variable is discrete (e.g. zero or one), or partly discrete (e.g. zero or positive). It also includes a discussion of sample selection problems that goes further than its typical textbook treatment. It is stressed that the sample selection problem is a potentially important problem in empirical work for which no standard solution exists.

Chapters 8 and 9 discuss time series modelling including unit roots, cointegration and error-correction models. These chapters can be read immediately after Chapter 4 or 5, with the exception of a few parts that relate to maximum likelihood estimation. The theoretical developments in this area over the last 15 years have been substantial and many recent textbooks seem to focus upon it almost exclusively. Univariate time series models are covered in Chapter 8. In this case models are developed that explain an economic variable from its own past. This includes ARIMA models, as well as GARCH models for the conditional variance of a series. Multivariate time series modes that consider several variables simultaneously are discussed in Chapter 9. This includes vector autoregressive models, cointegration and error-correction models.

Finally, Chapter 10 covers models based on panel data. Panel data are available if we have repeated observations of the same units (for example households, firms or countries). The last decade the use of panel data has become important in many areas of economics. Micro-economic panels of households and firms are readily available and, given the increase in computing resources, more manageable than in the past. In addition, it is more and more common to pool time series of several countries. One of the reasons for this may be that researchers believe that a cross-sectional comparison of countries provides interesting information, in addition to a historical comparison of a country with its own past.

At the end of the book the reader will find two short appendices discussing mathematical and statistical results that are used at several places in the book. This includes a discussion of some relevant matrix algebra and distribution theory. In particular, a discussion of properties of the (bivariate) normal distribution, including conditional expectations, variances and truncation is provided.

In my experience the material in this book is too much to be covered in a single course. Different courses can be scheduled on the basis of the chapters that follow. For example, a typical graduate course in applied econometrics would cover Chapters 2, 3, 4, parts of Chapter 5, and then continue with selected parts of Chapters 8 and 9 if the focus is on time series analysis, or continue with Section 6.1 and Chapter 7 if the focus is on cross-sectional models. A more advanced undergraduate or graduate course may focus attention to the time series chapters (Chapters 8 and 9), the micro-econometric chapters (Chapters 6 and 7) or panel data (Chapter 10 with some selected parts from Chapters 6 and 7).

Given the focus and length of this book, I had to make many choices of which material to present or not. As a general rule I did not want to bother the reader with details that I considered not essential or do not have empirical relevance. The main goal was to give a general and comprehensive overview of the different methodologies and approaches, focusing on what is relevant for doing and understanding empirical work. Some topics are only very briefly mentioned and no attempt is made to discuss them at any length. To compensate for this I have tried to give references at appropriate places to other, often more advanced, textbooks that do cover these issues.

1.3   Illustrations and Exercises

In most chapters a variety of empirical illustrations is provided in separate sections or subsections. While it is possible to skip these illustrations essentially without losing continuity, these sections do provide important aspects concerning the implementation of the methodology discussed in the preceding text. In addition, I have attempted to provide illustrations that are of economic interest in itself, using data that are typical for current empirical work and covering a wide range of different areas. This means that most data sets are used in recently published empirical work and are fairly large, both in terms of number of observations and number of variables. Given the current state of computing facilities, it is usually not a problem to handle such large data sets empirically.

Learning econometrics is not just a matter of studying a textbook. Hands-on experience is crucial in the process of understanding the different methods and how and when to implement them. Therefore, readers are strongly encouraged to get their hands dirty and to estimate a number of models using appropriate or inappropriate methods, and to perform a number of alternative specification tests. With modern software becoming more and more user-friendly, the actual computation of even the more complicated estimators and test statistics is often surprisingly simple, sometimes dangerously simple. That is, even with the wrong data, the wrong model and the wrong methodology, programs may come up with results that are seemingly all right. At least some expertise is required to prevent the practitioner from such situations and this book plays an important role in this.

To stimulate the reader to use actual data and estimate some models, almost all data sets used in this text are available through the internet via the K.U. Leuven page http://www.econ.kuleuven.ac.be/GME. Readers are encouraged to re-estimate the models reported in this text and check whether their results are the same, as well as to experiment with alternative specifications or methods. Some of the exercises make use of the same or additional data sets and provide a number of specific issues to consider. It should be stressed that for estimation methods that require numerical optimization, alternative programs, algorithms or settings may give slightly different outcomes. However, you should get results that are close to the ones reported.

I do not advocate the use of any particular software package. For the linear regression model any package will do, while for the more advanced techniques each package has its particular advantages and disadvantages. There is typically a trade off between user-friendliness and flexibility. Menu driven packages often do not allow you to compute anything else than what's on the menu, but if the menu is sufficiently rich that may not be a problem. Command driven packages require somewhat more input from the user, but are typically quite flexible. For the illustrations in this text I made use of Eviews 2.0, GAUSS 3.2, LIMDEP 7.0, MicroFit 4.0, SAS 6.12, Stata 5.0 and TSP 4.3. Several alternative econometrics programs are available, including ET, PcGive, RATS and SHAZAM. Journals like the *Journal of Applied Econometrics* and the *Journal of Economic Surveys* regularly publish software reviews.

The exercises included at the end of each chapter consist of a number of questions that are primarily intended to check whether the reader has grasped the most important concepts. Therefore, they typically do not go into technical details nor ask for derivations or proofs. In addition, several exercises are of an empirical nature and require the reader to use actual data.

2 An Introduction to Linear Regression

One of the cornerstones of econometrics is the so-called **linear regression model** and the **ordinary least squares (OLS)** estimation method. In the first part of this book we shall review the linear regression model with its assumptions, how it can be estimated, how it can be used for generating predictions and for testing economic hypotheses.

Unlike many textbooks, I do not start with the statistical regression model with the standard, Gauss–Markov, assumptions. In my view the role of the assumptions underlying the linear regression model is best appreciated by first treating the most important technique in econometrics, ordinary least squares, as an algebraic tool rather than a statistical one. This is the topic of Section 2.1. The linear regression model is then introduced in Section 2.2, while Section 2.3 discusses the properties of the OLS estimator in this model under the so-called Gauss–Markov assumptions. Section 2.4 discusses goodness-of-fit measures for the linear model, and hypothesis testing is treated in Section 2.5. In Section 2.6, we move to cases where the Gauss–Markov properties are not necessarily satisfied and the small sample properties of the OLS estimator are unknown. In such cases, the limiting behaviour of the OLS estimator when – hypothetically – the sample size becomes infinitely large, is commonly used to approximate its small sample properties. An empirical example concerning the capital asset pricing model (CAPM) is provided in Section 2.7. Sections 2.8 and 2.9 discuss multicollinearity and prediction, respectively. Throughout, an empirical example concerning individual wages is used to illustrate the main issues. Additional discussion on how to interpret the coefficients in the linear model, how to test some of the model's assumptions and how to compare alternative models, is provided in Chapter 3.

2.1   Ordinary Least Squares as an Algebraic Tool

2.1.1   Ordinary Least Squares

Suppose we have a sample with N observations on individual wages and some background characteristics. Our main interest lies in the question how *in this sample* wages are related to the other observables. Let us denote wages by y and the other $K - 1$ characteristics by $x_2, \ldots, x_K$. It will become clear below why this numbering of variables is convenient. Now we may ask the question: which linear combination of $x_2, \ldots, x_K$ and a constant gives a good approximation of y? To answer this question, first consider an arbitrary linear combination, including a constant, which can be written as

$$\tilde{\beta}_1 + \tilde{\beta}_2 x_2 + \cdots + \tilde{\beta}_K x_K, \tag{2.1}$$

where $\tilde{\beta}_K$s are constants to be chosen. Let us index the observations by i such that $i = 1, \ldots, N$. Now, the difference between an observed value y_i and its linear approximation is

$$y_i - \left[\tilde{\beta}_1 + \tilde{\beta}_2 x_{i2} + \cdots + \tilde{\beta}_K x_{iK} \right]. \tag{2.2}$$

To simplify the derivations we shall introduce some short-hand notation. Appendix A provides additional details for readers unfamiliar with the use of vector notation. First, we collect the x-values for individual i in a vector x_i, which includes the constant. That is,

$$x_i = (1 \ x_{i2} \ x_{i3} \ldots x_{iK})'.$$

Collecting the $\tilde{\beta}$ coefficients in a K-dimensional vector $\tilde{\beta} = (\tilde{\beta}_1, \ldots, \tilde{\beta}_K)'$, we can briefly write (2.2) as

$$y_i - x_i' \tilde{\beta}. \tag{2.3}$$

Clearly, we would like to choose values for $\tilde{\beta}_1, \ldots, \tilde{\beta}_K$ such that these differences are small. Although different measures can be used to define what we mean by 'small', the most common approach is to choose $\tilde{\beta}$ such that the sum of squared differences is as small as possible. That is, we determine $\tilde{\beta}$ to minimize the following objective function

$$S(\tilde{\beta}) \equiv \sum_{i=1}^{N} (y_i - x_i' \tilde{\beta})^2. \tag{2.4}$$

This approach is referred to as the **ordinary least squares** or **OLS** approach. Taking squares makes sure that positive and negative deviations do not cancel out when taking the summation.

To solve the minimization problem, we can look at the first order conditions, obtained by differentiating $S(\tilde{\beta})$ with respect to the vector $\tilde{\beta}$. (Appendix A discusses some rules on how to differentiate a scalar expression, like (2.4), with respect to a vector.) This gives the following system of K conditions:

$$-2 \sum_{i=1}^{N} x_i (y_i - x_i' \tilde{\beta}) = 0 \tag{2.5}$$

or

$$\left(\sum_{i=1}^{N} x_i x_i'\right)\tilde{\beta} = \sum_{i=1}^{N} x_i y_i. \tag{2.6}$$

These equations are sometimes referred to as **normal equations**. As this system has K unknowns, one can obtain a unique solution for $\tilde{\beta}$ provided that the symmetric matrix $\sum_{i=1}^{N} x_i x_i'$, which contains sums of squares and cross products of the regressors x_i, can be inverted. For the moment, we shall assume that this is the case. The solution to the minimization problem, which we shall denote by b, is then given by

$$b = \left(\sum_{i=1}^{N} x_i x_i'\right)^{-1}\sum_{i=1}^{N} x_i y_i. \tag{2.7}$$

By checking the second order conditions, it is easily verified that b indeed corresponds to a minimum.

The resulting linear combination of x_i is thus given by

$$\hat{y}_i = x_i' b,$$

which is the **best linear approximation** of y from $x_2, \ldots, x_K$ and a constant. The phrase 'best' refers to the fact that the sum of squared differences (approximation errors) is minimal for the least squares solution b.

In deriving the linear approximation we have not used any economic or statistical theory. It is simply an algebraic tool and it holds irrespective of the way the data are generated. That is, given a set of variables we can always determine the best linear approximation of one variable using the other variables. The only assumption that we had to make (which is directly checked from the data) is that the $K \times K$ matrix $\sum_{i=1}^{N} x_i x_i'$ is invertible. This says that none of the x_{ik}s is an *exact* linear combination of the other ones and thus redundant. This is usually referred to as the **no-multi-collinearity assumption**. It should be stressed that the linear approximation is an *in-sample* result (that is, in principle it does not give information about observations (individuals) that are not in the sample) and, in general, there is no direct interpretation of the coefficients.

Despite these limitations, the algebraic results on the least squares method are very useful. Defining a **residual** e_i as the difference between the observed and the approximated value, $e_i = y_i - \hat{y}_i = y_i - x_i' b$, we can decompose the observed y_i as

$$y_i = \hat{y}_i + e_i = x_i' b + e_i. \tag{2.8}$$

This allows us to write the minimum value for the objective function as

$$S(b) = \sum_{i=1}^{N} e_i^2, \tag{2.9}$$

which is referred to as the **residual sum of squares**. It can be shown that the approximated value $x_i' b$ and the residual e_i satisfy certain properties by construction. For example, if we rewrite (2.5), substituting the OLS solution b, we obtain

$$\sum_{i=1}^{N} x_i(y_i - x_i' b) = \sum_{i=1}^{N} x_i e_i = 0. \tag{2.10}$$

This means that the vector $e = (e_1, \ldots, e_N)'$ is orthogonal[1] to each vector of observations on an x-variable. For example, if x_i contains a constant, it implies that $\sum_{i=1}^{N} e_i = 0$. That is, the average residual is zero. This is an intuitively appealing result. If the average residual were nonzero, this would mean that we could improve upon the approximation by adding or subtracting the same constant for each observation, i.e. by changing b_1. Consequently, for the average observation it follows that

$$\bar{y} = \bar{x}'b, \qquad (2.11)$$

where $\bar{y} = (1/N) \sum_{i=1}^{N} y_i$ and $\bar{x} = (1/N) \sum_{i=1}^{N} x_i$, a K-dimensional vector of sample means. This shows that for the average observation there is no approximation error. Similar interpretations hold for the other x-variables: if the derivative of the sum of squared approximation errors with respect to $\tilde{\beta}_K$ is positive, that is if $\sum_{i=1}^{N} x_{ik} e_i > 0$ it means that we can improve the objective function by decreasing $\tilde{\beta}_K$.

2.1.2 Simple Linear Regression

In the case where $K = 2$ we only have one regressor and a constant. In this case, the observations[2] (y_i, x_i) can be drawn in a two-dimensional graph with x-values on the horizontal axis and y-values on the vertical one. This is done in Figure 2.1 for a data set that is used in Section 2.7 below. The best linear approximation of y from x

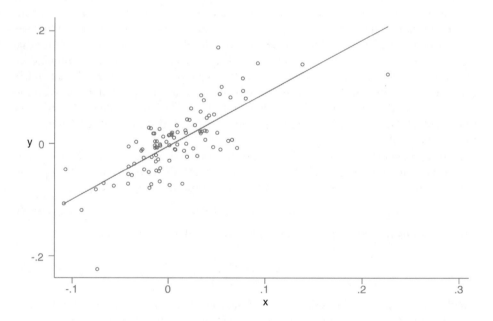

Figure 2.1   Simple linear regression: fitted line and observation points

---

[1] Two vectors x and y are said to be orthogonal if $x'y = 0$, that is if $\sum_i x_i y_i = 0$ (see Appendix A).
[2] In this subsection x_i will be used to denote the single regressor, so that it does not include the constant.

and a constant is obtained by minimizing the sum of squared residuals, which – in this two-dimensional case – equal the vertical distance between an observation and the fitted value. All fitted values are on a straight line, the **regression line**.

Because a 2×2 matrix can be inverted analytically we can derive solutions for b_1 and b_2 in this special case from the general expression for b above. Equivalently, we can minimize the residual sum of squares with respect to the unknowns directly. Thus we have,

$$S(\tilde{\beta}_1, \tilde{\beta}_2) = \sum_{i=1}^{N} (y_i - \tilde{\beta}_1 - \tilde{\beta}_2 x_i)^2. \tag{2.12}$$

The basic elements in the derivation of the OLS solutions are the first order conditions:

$$\frac{\partial S(\tilde{\beta}_1, \tilde{\beta}_2)}{\partial \tilde{\beta}_1} = -2 \sum_{i=1}^{N} (y_i - \tilde{\beta}_1 - \tilde{\beta}_2 x_i) = 0, \tag{2.13}$$

$$\frac{\partial S(\tilde{\beta}_1, \tilde{\beta}_2)}{\partial \tilde{\beta}_2} = -2 \sum_{i=1}^{N} x_i(y_i - \tilde{\beta}_1 - \tilde{\beta}_2 x_i) = 0. \tag{2.14}$$

From (2.13) we can write

$$b_1 = \frac{1}{N} \sum_{i=1}^{N} y_i - b_2 \frac{1}{N} \sum_{i=1}^{N} x_i = \bar{y} - b_2 \bar{x}, \tag{2.15}$$

where b_2 is solved from combining (2.14) and (2.15). First, from (2.14) write

$$\sum_{i=1}^{N} x_i y_i - b_1 \sum_{i=1}^{N} x_i - \left(\sum_{i=1}^{N} x_i^2 \right) b_2 = 0$$

and then substitute (2.15) to obtain

$$\sum_{i=1}^{N} x_i y_i - N\bar{x}\bar{y} - \left(\sum_{i=1}^{N} x_i^2 - N\bar{x}^2 \right) b_2 = 0$$

such that we can solve for the slope coefficient b_2 as

$$b_2 = \frac{\sum_{i=1}^{N} (x_i - \bar{x})(y_i - \bar{y})}{\sum_{i=1}^{N} (x_i - \bar{x})^2}. \tag{2.16}$$

Through adding a factor $1/(N-1)$ to numerator and denominator it appears that the OLS solution b_2 is the ratio of the sample covariance between x and y and the sample variance of x. From (2.15), the intercept is determined so as to make the average approximation error (residual) equal to zero.

2.1.3 Example: Individual Wages

An example that will appear frequently in this chapter, is based on a sample of individual wages with background characteristics, like gender, race and years of schooling. We use a subsample of the US National Longitudinal Survey (NLS) that relates to 1987 and we have a sample of 3296 young working individuals, of which 1569 are female.[3] The average hourly wage rate in this sample equals $6.42 for males and $5.15 for females. Now suppose we try to approximate wages by a linear combination of a constant and a 0–1 variable denoting whether the individual is male or not. That is, $x_i = 1$ if individual i is male and zero otherwise. Such a variable, which can only take on the values of zero and one, is called a **dummy variable**. Using the OLS approach the result is

$$\hat{y}_i = 5.15 + 1.28 x_i.$$

This means that for females our best approximation is $5.15 and for males it is $5.15 + $1.28 = $6.42. It is not a coincidence that these numbers are exactly equal to the sample means in the two subsamples. It is easily verified from the results above that

$$b_1 = \bar{y}_f$$

$$b_2 = \bar{y}_m - \bar{y}_f,$$

where $\bar{y}_m = \sum_i x_i y_i / \sum_i x_i$ is the sample average of the wage for males, and $\bar{y}_f = \sum_i (1 - x_i) y_i / \sum_i (1 - x_i)$ is the average for females.

2.1.4 Matrix Notation

Because econometricians make frequent use of matrix expressions as shorthand notation, some familiarity with this matrix 'language' is a prerequisite to reading the econometrics literature. In this text, we shall regularly rephrase results using matrix notation, and occasionally, when the alternative is extremely cumbersome, restrict attention to matrix expressions only. Using matrices, deriving the least squares solution is faster, but it requires some knowledge of matrix differential calculus. We introduce the following notation:

$$X = \begin{pmatrix} 1 & x_{12} & \cdots & x_{1K} \\ \vdots & \vdots & & \vdots \\ 1 & x_{N2} & \cdots & x_{NK} \end{pmatrix} = \begin{pmatrix} x_1' \\ \vdots \\ x_N' \end{pmatrix}, \quad y = \begin{pmatrix} y_1 \\ \vdots \\ y_N \end{pmatrix}.$$

So, in the $N \times K$ matrix X the i-th row refers to observation i, and the k-th column refers to the k-th explanatory variable (regressor). The criterion to be minimized, as given in (2.4), can be rewritten in matrix notation using that the inner product of a vector with itself $(x'x)$ is the sum of its squared elements (see Appendix A). That is,

$$S(\tilde{\beta}) = (y - X\tilde{\beta})'(y - X\tilde{\beta}) = y'y - 2y'X\tilde{\beta} + \tilde{\beta}'X'X\tilde{\beta}, \tag{2.17}$$

from which the least squares solution follows from differentiating[4] with respect to $\tilde{\beta}$ and setting the result to zero:

$$\frac{\partial S(\tilde{\beta})}{\partial \tilde{\beta}} = -2(X'y - X'X\tilde{\beta}) = 0. \tag{2.18}$$

---

[3] The data for this example are available as WAGES1.
[4] See Appendix A for some rules for differentiating matrix expressions with respect to vectors.

Solving (2.18) gives the OLS solution

$$b = (X'X)^{-1}X'y, \tag{2.19}$$

which is exactly the same as the one derived in (2.7) but now written in matrix notation. Note that we again have to assume that $X'X = \sum_{i=1}^{N} x_i x_i'$ is invertible, i.e. that there is no exact (or perfect) multicollinearity.

As before, we can decompose y as

$$y = Xb + e, \tag{2.20}$$

where e is an N-dimensional vector of residuals. The first order conditions imply that $X'(y - Xb) = 0$ or

$$X'e = 0, \tag{2.21}$$

which means that each column of the matrix X is orthogonal to the vector of residuals. With (2.19) we can also write (2.20) as

$$y = Xb + e = X(X'X)^{-1}X'y + e = \hat{y} + e \tag{2.22}$$

so that the predicted value for y is given by

$$\hat{y} = Xb = X(X'X)^{-1}X'y = P_X y. \tag{2.23}$$

In linear algebra, the matrix $P_X \equiv X(X'X)^{-1}X'$ is known as a projection matrix (see Appendix A). It projects the vector y upon the columns of X (the column space of X). This is just the geometric translation of finding the best linear approximation of y from the columns (regressors) in X. The residual vector of the projection $e = y - Xb = (I - P_X)y = M_X y$ is the orthogonal complement. It is a projection of y upon the space orthogonal to the one spanned by the columns of X. This interpretation is sometimes useful. For example, projecting twice on the same space should leave the result unaffected, so that it holds that $P_X P_X = P_X$ and $M_X M_X = M_X$. More importantly, it holds that $M_X P_X = 0$ as the column space of X and its orthogonal complement do not have anything in common (except the null vector). This is an alternative way to interpret the result that $\hat{y}$ and e and also X and e are orthogonal. The interested reader is referred to Davidson and MacKinnon (1993, Chapter 1) for an excellent discussion on the geometry of least squares.

2.2 The Linear Regression Model

Usually, economists want more than just finding the best linear approximation of one variable given a set of others. They want economic relationships that are more generally valid than the sample they happen to have. They want to draw conclusions about what happens if one of the variables actually changes. That is: they want to say something about things that are not observed (yet). In this case, we want the relationship that is found to be more than just a historical coincidence; it should reflect a fundamental relationship. To do this it is assumed that there is a general relationship that is valid for all possible observations from a well-defined population (for example all US households, or all firms in a certain industry). Restricting attention to linear relationships, we specify a **statistical model** as

$$y_i = \beta_1 + \beta_2 x_{i2} + \cdots + \beta_K x_{iK} + \varepsilon_i \tag{2.24}$$

or

$$y_i = x_i'\beta + \varepsilon_i, \tag{2.25}$$

where y_i and x_i are observable variables and ε_i is unobserved and referred to as an **error term** or disturbance term. The equality in (2.25) is supposed to hold for any possible observation, while we only observe a **sample** of N observations. We shall consider this sample as one realization of all potential samples of size N that could have been drawn from the same population. In this way we can view y_i and ε_i (and often x_i) as **random variables**. Each observation corresponds to a realization of these random variables. Again we can use matrix notation and stack all observations to write

$$y = X\beta + \varepsilon, \tag{2.26}$$

where y and ε are N-dimensional vectors and X, as before, is of dimension $N \times K$. Notice the difference between this equation and (2.20).

In contrast to (2.20), equations (2.25) and (2.26) are population relationships, where β is a vector of unknown parameters characterizing the population. The **sampling process** describes how the sample is taken from the population and, as a result, determines the randomness of the sample. In a first view, the x_i variables are considered as fixed and non-stochastic, which means that every new sample will have the same X matrix. In this case one refers to x_i as being **deterministic**. A new sample only implies new values for ε_i, or – equivalently – for y_i. The only relevant case where the x_is are truly deterministic is in a laboratory setting, where a researcher can set the conditions of a given experiment (e.g. temperature, air pressure). In economics we will typically have to work with non-experimental data. Despite this, it is convenient and in particular cases appropriate in an economic context to treat the x_i variables as deterministic. In this case, we will have to make some assumptions about the sampling distribution of ε_i. A convenient one corresponds to **random sampling** where each error ε_i is a random drawing from the population distribution, independent of the other error terms. We shall return to this issue below.

In a second view, a new sample implies new values for both x_i and ε_i, so that each time a new set of N observations for (y_i, x_i) is drawn. In this case random sampling means that each set (x_i, ε_i) or (y_i, x_i) is a random drawing from the population distribution. In this context, it will turn out to be important to make assumptions about the joint distribution of x_i and ε_i, in particular regarding the extent to which the distribution of ε_i is allowed to depend upon X. The idea of a (random) sample is most easily understood in a cross-sectional context, where interest lies in a large and fixed population, for example all UK households in January 1999, or all stocks listed at the New York Stock Exchange on a given date. In a time series context, different observations refer to different time periods and it does not make sense to assume that we have a random sample of time periods. Instead, we shall take the view that the sample we have is just one realization of what could have happened in a given time span and the randomness refers to alternative states of the world. In such a case we will need to make some assumptions about the way the data are generated (rather than the way the data are sampled).

It is important to realize that without additional restrictions the *statistical* model in (2.25) is a tautology: for any value for β one can always define a set of ε_is such that

(2.25) holds exactly for each observation. We thus need to impose some assumptions to give the model a meaning. A common assumption is that the expected value of ε_i given all the explanatory variables in x_i is zero, that is $E\{\varepsilon_i|x_i\} = 0$. Usually, people refer to this as the assumption saying that the x-variables are **exogenous**. Under this assumption it holds that

$$E\{y_i|x_i\} = x_i'\beta, \tag{2.27}$$

so that the regression line $x_i'\beta$ describes the conditional expectation of y_i given the values for x_i. The coefficients β_k measure how the expected value of y_i is changed if the value of x_{ik} is changed, keeping the other xs constant (the **ceteris paribus** condition). Economic theory, however, often suggest that the model in (2.25) describes a causal relationship, in which the β coefficients measure the changes in y_i *caused* by a ceteris paribus change in x_{ik}. In such cases, ε_i has an economic interpretation (not just a statistical one) and imposing that it is uncorrelated with x_i, as we do by imposing $E\{\varepsilon_i|x_i\} = 0$, may not be justified. As in many cases it can be argued that unobservables in the error term are related to observables in x_i, we should be cautious interpreting our regression coefficients as measuring causal effects. We shall come back to these issues in Chapter 5.

Now that our β coefficients have a meaning, we can try to use the sample (y_i, x_i), $i = 1, \ldots, N$ to say something about it. The rule which says how a given sample is translated into an approximate value for β is referred to as an **estimator**. The result for a given sample is called an **estimate**. The *estimator* is a vector of random variables, because the sample may change. The *estimate* is a vector of numbers. The most widely used estimator in econometrics is the **ordinary least squares (OLS)** estimator. This is just the ordinary least squares rule described in Section 2.1 applied to the available sample. The OLS estimator for β, is thus given by

$$b = \left(\sum_{i=1}^{N} x_i x_i' \right)^{-1} \sum_{i=1}^{N} x_i y_i. \tag{2.28}$$

Because we have assumed an underlying 'true' model (2.25), combined with a sampling scheme, b is now a vector of random variables. Our interest lies in the true unknown parameter vector β, and b is considered an approximation to it. While a given sample only produces a single estimate, we evaluate the quality of it through the properties of the underlying estimator. The estimator b has a sampling distribution because its value depends upon the sample that is taken (randomly) from the population.

2.3 Small Sample Properties of the OLS Estimator

2.3.1 The Gauss–Markov Assumptions

In this section we shall discuss several important properties of the OLS estimator b. To do so, we need to make some assumptions about the error term and the explanatory variables x_i. The first set of assumptions we consider are the so-called Gauss–Markov assumptions. These assumptions are usually standard in the first chapters of econometrics textbooks, although – as we shall see below – they are not all strictly needed to justify the use of the ordinary least squares estimator. They just constitute a simple case in which the small sample properties of b are easily derived.

The standard set of **Gauss–Markov assumptions** is given by

$$E\{\varepsilon_i\} = 0, \quad i = 1, \ldots, N \tag{A1}$$

$$\{\varepsilon_1, \ldots, \varepsilon_N\} \text{ and } \{x_1, \ldots, x_N\} \text{ are independent} \tag{A2}$$

$$V\{\varepsilon_i\} = \sigma^2, \quad i = 1, \ldots, N \tag{A3}$$

$$\mathrm{cov}\{\varepsilon_i, \varepsilon_j\} = 0, \quad i, j = 1, \ldots, N, \ i \neq j. \tag{A4}$$

Assumption (A1) says that the expected value of the error term is zero, which means that, *on average*, the regression line should be correct. Assumption (A3) states that all error terms have the same variance, which is referred to as **homoskedasticity**, while assumption (A4) imposes zero correlation between different error terms. This excludes any form of **autocorrelation**. Taken together, (A1), (A3) and (A4) imply that the error terms are uncorrelated drawings from a distribution with expectation zero and constant variance σ^2. Using the matrix notation from above, it is possible to rewrite these three conditions as

$$E\{\varepsilon\} = 0 \text{ and } V\{\varepsilon\} = \sigma^2 I_N, \tag{2.29}$$

where I_N is the $N \times N$ identity matrix. This says that the covariance matrix of the vector of error terms ε is a diagonal matrix with σ^2 on the diagonal. Assumption (A2) implies that X and ε are independent. This is a fairly strong assumption, which can be relaxed somewhat (see below). It implies that

$$E\{\varepsilon|X\} = E\{\varepsilon\} = 0 \tag{2.30}$$

and

$$V\{\varepsilon|X\} = V\{\varepsilon\} = \sigma^2 I_N. \tag{2.31}$$

That is, the matrix of regressor values X does not provide any information about the expected values of the error terms or their (co)variances. The two conditions (2.30) and (2.31) combine the necessary elements from the Gauss–Markov assumptions needed for the results below to hold. Often, assumption (A2) is stated as: the regressor matrix X is a deterministic nonstochastic matrix. The reason for this is that the outcomes in the matrix X can be taken as given without affecting the properties of ε, that is, one can derive all properties conditional upon X. For simplicity, we shall take this approach in this section and Section 2.5. Under the Gauss–Markov assumptions (A1) and (A2), the linear model can be interpreted as the conditional expectation of y_i given x_i, i.e. $E\{y_i|x_i\} = x_i'\beta$. This is a direct implication of (2.30).

2.3.2 Properties of the OLS Estimator

Under assumptions (A1)–(A4), the OLS estimator b for β has several desirable properties. First of all, it is **unbiased**. This means that, in repeated sampling, we can expect that our estimator is on average equal to the true value β. We formulate this as

$E\{b\} = \beta$. It is instructive to see the proof:

$$E\{b\} = E\{(X'X)^{-1}X'y\} = E\{\beta + (X'X)^{-1}X'\varepsilon\}$$
$$= \beta + E\{(X'X)^{-1}X'\varepsilon\} = \beta.$$

The latter step here is essential and it follows from

$$E\{(X'X)^{-1}X'\varepsilon\} = E\{(X'X)^{-1}X'\}E\{\varepsilon\} = 0,$$

because X and ε are independent and $E\{\varepsilon\} = 0$. Note that we did not use assumptions (A3) and (A4) in the proof. This shows that the OLS estimator is unbiased as long as the error terms are mean zero and independent of all explanatory variables, even if heteroskedasticity or autocorrelation are present. We shall come back to this issue in Chapter 4.

In addition to knowing that we are, on average, correct, we would also like to make statements about how (un)likely it is to be far off in a given sample. This means we would like to know the distribution of b. First of all, the variance of b (conditional upon X) is given by

$$V\{b|X\} = \sigma^2(X'X)^{-1} = \sigma^2\left(\sum_{i=1}^{N} x_i x_i'\right)^{-1}, \tag{2.32}$$

which, for simplicity, we shall denote by $V\{b\}$. Implicitly, this means that we treat X as deterministic. The proof is fairly easy and goes as follows:

$$V\{b\} = E\{(b - \beta)(b - \beta)'\} = E\{(X'X)^{-1}X'\varepsilon\varepsilon'X(X'X)^{-1}\}$$
$$= (X'X)^{-1}X'(\sigma^2 I_N)X(X'X)^{-1} = \sigma^2(X'X)^{-1}.$$

Without using matrix notation the proof goes as follows:

$$V\{b\} = V\{(\sum_i x_i x_i')^{-1} \sum_i x_i \varepsilon_i\} = (\sum_i x_i x_i')^{-1} V\{\sum_i x_i \varepsilon_i\}(\sum_i x_i x_i')^{-1}$$
$$= (\sum_i x_i x_i')^{-1} \sigma^2 (\sum_i x_i x_i')(\sum_i x_i x_i')^{-1} = \sigma^2(\sum_i x_i x_i')^{-1}. \tag{2.33}$$

The last result is collected in the **Gauss–Markov Theorem**, which says that under assumptions (A1)–(A4) the OLS estimator b is the **best linear unbiased estimator** for β. In short we say that b is BLUE for β. To appreciate this result, consider the class of linear unbiased estimators. A linear estimator is a linear function of the elements in y and can be written as $\tilde{b} = Ay$, where A is a $K \times N$ matrix. The estimator is unbiased if $E\{Ay\} = \beta$. (Note that the OLS estimator is obtained for $A = (X'X)^{-1}X'$.) Then the theorem states that the difference between the covariance matrices of $\tilde{b} = Ay$ and the OLS estimator b is always positive semi-definite. What does this mean? Suppose we are interested in some linear combination of β coefficients, given by $d'\beta$ where d is a K-dimensional vector. Then the Gauss–Markov result implies that the variance of the OLS estimator $d'b$ for $d'\beta$ is not larger than the variance of any other linear unbiased estimator $d'\tilde{b}$, that is

$$V\{d'\tilde{b}\} \geq V\{d'b\} \text{ for any vector } d.$$

As a special case this holds for the k-th element and we have that

$$V\{\tilde{b}_k\} \geq V\{b_k\}.$$

Thus, under the Gauss–Markov assumptions, the OLS estimator is the most accurate (linear) unbiased estimator for β. More details on the Gauss–Markov result can be found in Greene (1997, 2000,[5] Section 6.6) or Stewart and Gill (1998, Section 2.4).

So far, we made no assumption about the shape of the distribution of the error terms ε_i, except that they were mutually uncorrelated, independent of X, had zero mean and a constant variance. For exact statistical inference from a given sample of N observations, explicit distributional assumptions have to be made.[6] The most common assumption is that the errors are jointly normally distributed.[7] In this case the uncorrelatedness of (A4) is equivalent to independence of all error terms. The precise assumption is as follows

$$\varepsilon \sim \mathcal{N}(0, \sigma^2 I_N), \tag{A5}$$

saying that ε has an N-variate normal distribution with mean vector 0 and covariance matrix $\sigma^2 I_N$. Assumption (A5) thus replaces (A1), (A3) and (A4). An alternative way of formulating (A5) is

$$\varepsilon_i \sim NID(0, \sigma^2), \tag{A5'}$$

which is a shorthand way of saying that the error terms ε_i are independent drawings from a normal distribution (n.i.d.) with mean zero and variance σ^2. Even though error terms are unobserved, this does not mean that we are free to make any assumptions we like. For example, if error terms are assumed to follow a normal distribution this means that y_i (for a given value of x_i) also follows a normal distribution. Clearly, we can think of many variables whose distribution (conditional upon a given set of x_i variables) is not normal, in which case the assumption of normal error terms is inappropriate. Fortunately, not all assumptions are equally crucial for the validity of the results that follow and, moreover, the majority of the assumptions can be tested empirically; see Chapters 3, 4 and 6 below.

To make things simpler let us consider the X matrix as fixed and deterministic or, alternatively, let us work conditional upon the outcomes X. Now the following result holds. Under assumptions (A2) and (A5) the OLS estimator b is normally distributed with mean vector β and covariance matrix $\sigma^2 (X'X)^{-1}$, i.e.

$$b \sim \mathcal{N}(\beta, \sigma^2 (X'X)^{-1}). \tag{2.34}$$

The proof of this follows directly from the result that b is a linear combination of all ε_i and is omitted here. From this it also follows that each element in b is normally distributed, for example

$$b_k \sim \mathcal{N}(\beta_k, \sigma^2 c_{kk}), \tag{2.35}$$

where c_{kk} is the (k, k) element in $(X'X)^{-1}$. These results provide the basis for statistical tests based upon the OLS estimator b.

---

[5] Unless indicated otherwise, all references below are equally appropriate for the third edition (Greene, 1997) and the fourth one (Greene, 2000).

[6] Later we shall see that for approximate interference in large samples this is not necessary.

[7] The distributions used in this text are explained in Appendix B.

To estimate the variance of b we need to replace the unknown error variance σ^2 by an estimate. An obvious candidate is the sample variance of the **residuals** $e_i = y_i - x_i'b$, that is

$$\tilde{s}^2 = \frac{1}{N-1} \sum_{i=1}^{N} e_i^2 \tag{2.36}$$

(recalling that the average residual is zero). However, because e_i is different from ε_i, it can be shown that this estimator is biased for σ^2. An unbiased estimator is given by

$$s^2 = \frac{1}{N-K} \sum_{i=1}^{N} e_i^2. \tag{2.37}$$

This estimator has a degrees of freedom correction as it divides by the number of observations minus the number of regressors (including the intercept). An intuitive argument for this is that K parameters were chosen so as to minimize the residual sum of squares and thus to minimize the sample variance of the residuals. The proof that s^2 is unbiased is not given and can be found in several econometrics textbooks (for example Greene, 2000, Section 6.6, or Judge *et al.*, 1988, Section 5.8). The variance of b can thus be estimated by

$$\hat{V}\{b\} = s^2 (X'X)^{-1} = s^2 \left(\sum_{i=1}^{N} x_i x_i' \right)^{-1}. \tag{2.38}$$

The estimated variance of an element b_k is given by $s^2 c_{kk}$. The square root of this estimated variance is usually referred to as the **standard error** of b_k. It is the *estimated* standard deviation of b_k and is a measure for the accuracy of the estimator.

2.3.3 Example: Individual Wages (Continued)

Let us now turn back to our wage example. We can formulate a statistical model as

$$wage_i = \beta_1 + \beta_2 male_i + \varepsilon_i, \tag{2.39}$$

where $wage_i$ denotes the hourly wage rate of individual i and $male_i = 1$ if i is male and 0 otherwise. Imposing that $E\{\varepsilon_i\} = 0$ and $E\{\varepsilon_i|male_i\} = 0$ gives β_1 the interpretation of the expected wage rate for females, while $E\{wage_i|male_i = 1\} = \beta_1 + \beta_2$ is the expected wage rate for males. These are unknown population quantities and we may wish to estimate them. Assume that we have a random sample, implying that different observations are independent. Also assume that ε_i is independent of the regressors, in particular, that the variance of ε_i does not depend upon gender ($male_i$). Then the OLS estimator for β is unbiased and its covariance matrix is given by (2.32). The estimation results are given in Table 2.1. In addition to the OLS estimates, identical to those presented before, we now also know something about the accuracy of the estimates, as reflected in the reported standard errors. We can now say that our estimate of the expected hourly wage differential β_2 between males and females is $1.28 with a standard error of $0.14. Combined with the normal distribution, this allows us to make statements about β_2. For example, we can test the

Table 2.1 OLS results wage equation

Dependent variable: *wage*		
Variable	Estimate	Standard error
constant	5.1469	0.1011
male	1.2777	0.1397

$s = 4.0048 \quad R^2 = 0.0248 \quad F = 83.68$

hypothesis that $\beta_2 = 0$. If this is the case, the wage differential between males and females in our sample is nonzero only by chance. Section 2.5 discusses how to test hypotheses regarding β.

2.4 Goodness-of-fit

Having estimated a particular linear model, a natural question that comes up is: how well does the estimated regression line fit the observations? A popular measure for the goodness-of-fit is the proportion of the (sample) variance of y that is explained by the model. This variable is called the R^2 (R squared) and is defined as

$$R^2 = \frac{\hat{V}\{\hat{y}_i\}}{\hat{V}\{y_i\}} = \frac{1/(N-1)\sum_{i=1}^{N}(\hat{y}_i - \bar{y})^2}{1/(N-1)\sum_{i=1}^{N}(y_i - \bar{y})^2}, \tag{2.40}$$

where $\hat{y}_i = x_i'b$ and $\bar{y} = (1/N)\sum_i y_i$ denotes the sample mean of y_i. Note that $\bar{y}$ also corresponds with the sample mean of $\hat{y}_i$, because of (2.11).

From the first order conditions (compare (2.10)) it follows directly that

$$\sum_{i=1}^{N} e_i x_{ik} = 0, \quad k = 1, \ldots, K.$$

Consequently, we can write $y_i = \hat{y}_i + e_i$ where $\sum_i e_i \hat{y}_i = 0$. In the most relevant case where the model contains an intercept term, it holds that

$$\hat{V}\{y_i\} = \hat{V}\{\hat{y}_i\} + \hat{V}\{e_i\}, \tag{2.41}$$

where $\hat{V}\{e_i\} = \tilde{s}^2$. Using this, the R^2 can be rewritten as

$$R^2 = 1 - \frac{\hat{V}\{e_i\}}{\hat{V}\{y_i\}} = 1 - \frac{1/(N-1)\sum_{i=1}^{N} e_i^2}{1/(N-1)\sum_{i=1}^{N}(y_i - \bar{y})^2}. \tag{2.42}$$

Equation (2.41) shows how the sample variance of y_i can be decomposed into the sum of the sample variances of two orthogonal components: the predictor $\hat{y}_i$ and the residual e_i. The R^2 thus indicates which proportion of the sample variation in y_i is explained by the model.

If the model of interest contains an intercept term, the two expressions for R^2 in (2.40) and (2.42) are equivalent. Moreover, in this case it can be shown that $0 \leq R^2 \leq 1$. Only if all $e_i = 0$ it holds that $R^2 = 1$, while the R^2 is zero if the model does not explain anything in addition to the sample mean of y_i. That is, the R^2 of a model with just an intercept term is zero by construction. In this sense, the R^2

indicates how much better the model performs than a trivial model with only a constant term.

From the results in Table 2.1, we see that the R^2 of the very simple wage equation is only 0.0248. This means that only approximately 2.5% of the variation in individual wages can be attributed to gender differences. Apparently, many other observable and unobservable factors affect a person's wage besides gender. This does not automatically imply that the model that was estimated in Table 2.1 is incorrect or useless: it just indicates the relative (un)importance of gender in explaining individual wage variation.

In the exceptional cases that the model does *not* contain an intercept term, the two expressions for R^2 are not equivalent. The reason is that (2.41) is violated because $\sum_{i=1}^{N} e_i$ is no longer equal to zero. In this situation it is possible that the R^2 computed from (2.42) becomes negative. An alternative measure, which is routinely computed by some software packages if there is no intercept, is the uncentred R^2, which is defined as

$$\text{uncentred } R^2 = \frac{\sum_{i=1}^{N} \hat{y}_i^2}{\sum_{i=1}^{N} y_i^2} = 1 - \frac{\sum_{i=1}^{N} e_i^2}{\sum_{i=1}^{N} y_i^2}. \tag{2.43}$$

Generally, the uncentred R^2 is higher than the standard R^2.

Because the R^2 measures the explained variation in y_i it is also sensitive to the definition of this variable. For example, explaining wages is something different than explaining log wages, and the R^2s will be different. Similarly, models explaining consumption, changes in consumption or consumption growth will not be directly comparable in terms of their R^2s. It is clear that some sources of variation are much harder to explain than others. For example, variation in aggregate consumption for a given country is usually easier to explain than the cross-sectional variation in consumption over individual households. Consequently, there is no absolute benchmark to say that an R^2 is 'high' or 'low'. A value of 0.2 may be high in certain applications but low in others, and even a value of 0.95 may be low in certain contexts.

Sometimes the R^2 is interpreted as a measure of quality of the *statistical* model, while in fact it measures nothing more than the quality of the linear approximation. As the OLS approach is developed to give the best linear approximation, irrespective of the 'true' model and the validity of its assumptions, estimating a linear model by OLS will always give the best R^2 possible. Any other estimation method, and we will see several below, will lead to lower R^2 values even though the corresponding estimator may have much better statistical properties under the assumptions of the model. Even worse, when the model is not estimated by OLS the two definitions (2.40) and (2.42) are not equivalent and it is not obvious how an R^2 should be defined. For later use, we shall present an alternative definition of the R^2, which for OLS is equivalent to (2.40) and (2.42), and for any other estimator is guaranteed to be between zero and one. It is given by

$$R^2 = \text{corr}^2\{y_i, \hat{y}_i\} = \frac{\left(\sum_{i=1}^{N}(y_i - \bar{y})(\hat{y}_i - \bar{y})\right)^2}{\left(\sum_{i=1}^{N}(y_i - \bar{y})^2\right)\left(\sum_{i=1}^{N}(\hat{y}_i - \bar{y})^2\right)}, \tag{2.44}$$

which denotes the squared (sample) correlation coefficient between the actual and fitted values. Using (2.41) it is easily verified that for the OLS estimator (2.44) is equivalent to (2.40). Written in this way, the R^2 can be interpreted to measure how well the variation in $\hat{y}_i$ relates to variation in y_i. Despite this alternative definition, the R^2 reflects the quality of the linear approximation and not necessarily that of the statistical model we are interested in. As a result, the R^2 is typically not the most important aspect of our estimation results.

Another drawback of the R^2 is that it will never decrease if the number of regressors is increased, even if the additional variables have no real explanatory power. A common way to solve this is to correct the variance estimates in (2.42) for the degrees of freedom. This gives the so-called **adjusted** R^2, or $\bar{R}^2$, defined as

$$\bar{R}^2 = 1 - \frac{1/(N-K)\sum_{i=1}^N e_i^2}{1/(N-1)\sum_{i=1}^N (y_i - \bar{y})^2}. \tag{2.45}$$

This goodness-of-fit measure has some punishment for the inclusion of additional explanatory variables in the model and, therefore, does not automatically increase when regressors are added to the model (see Chapter 3). In fact, it may decline when a variable is added to the set of regressors. Note that, in extreme cases, the $\bar{R}^2$ may become negative. Also note that the adjusted R^2 is strictly smaller than R^2 unless the model only includes a constant term and both measures are zero.

2.5   Hypothesis Testing

Under the Gauss–Markov assumptions (A1)–(A4) and normality of the error terms (A5), we saw that the OLS estimator b has a normal distribution with mean β and covariance matrix $\sigma^2(X'X)^{-1}$. We can use this result to develop tests for hypotheses regarding the unknown population parameters β. Starting from (2.35), it follows that the variable

$$z = \frac{b_k - \beta_k}{\sigma\sqrt{c_{kk}}} \tag{2.46}$$

has a standard normal distribution (i.e. a normal distribution with mean 0 and variance 1). If we replace the unknown σ by its estimate s, this is no longer exactly true. It can be shown[8] that the unbiased estimator s^2 defined in (2.37) is independent of b and has a Chi-squared distribution with $N - K$ degrees of freedom. In particular,[9]

$$(N-K)s^2/\sigma^2 \sim \chi^2_{N-K}. \tag{2.47}$$

Consequently, the following random variable

$$t_k = \frac{b_k - \beta_k}{s\sqrt{c_{kk}}} \tag{2.48}$$

is the ratio of a standard normal variable and the square root of an independent Chi-squared variable and therefore follows Student's t distribution with $N - K$ degrees of freedom. The t distribution is close to the standard normal distribution except that it

---

[8] The proof of this is beyond the scope of this text. The basic idea is that a sum of squared normals is Chi-squared distributed (see Appendix B).

[9] See Appendix B for details about the distributions in this section.

has fatter tails, particularly when the number of degrees of freedom $N - K$ is small. The larger $N - K$ the closer the t distribution resembles the standard normal, and for sufficiently large $N - K$, the two distributions are identical.

2.5.1 A Simple t-test

The result above can be used to construct test statistics and confidence intervals. The general idea of hypothesis testing is as follows. Starting from a given hypothesis, the **null hypothesis**, a **test statistic** is computed that has a known distribution *under the assumption that the null hypothesis is valid*. Next, it is decided whether the computed value of the test statistic is unlikely to come from this distribution, which indicates that the null hypothesis is unlikely to hold. Let us illustrate this with an example. Suppose we have a null hypothesis that specifies the value of β_k, say H_0: $\beta_k = \beta_k^0$, where β_k^0 is a specific value chosen by the researcher. If this hypothesis is true we know that the statistic

$$t_k = \frac{b_k - \beta_k^0}{s\sqrt{c_{kk}}} \tag{2.49}$$

has a t distribution with $N - K$ degrees of freedom. If the null hypothesis is not true, the alternative hypothesis H_1: $\beta_k \neq \beta_k^0$ holds. As there are no unknown values in t_k, it becomes a **test statistic** that can be computed from the estimate b_k and its standard error $s\sqrt{c_{kk}}$. The usual testing strategy is to reject the null hypothesis if t_k realizes a value that is very unlikely if the null hypothesis is true. In this case this means very large absolute values for t_k. To be precise, one rejects the null hypothesis if the probability of observing a value of $|t_k|$ or larger is smaller than a given **significance level** α, often 5%. From this, one can define the **critical values** $t_{N-K;\alpha/2}$ using

$$P\{|t_k| > t_{N-K;\alpha/2}\} = \alpha.$$

For $N - K$ not too small, these critical values are only slightly larger than those of the standard normal distribution, for which the two-tailed critical value for $\alpha = 0.05$ is 1.96. Consequently, at the 5% level the null hypothesis will be rejected if

$$|t_k| > 1.96.$$

The above test is referred to as a **two-sided test** because the alternative hypothesis allows for values of β_k on both sides of β_k^0. Occasionally, the alternative hypothesis is one-sided, for example: the expected wage for a man is larger than that for a woman. Formally, we define the null hypothesis as H_0: $\beta_k \leq \beta_k^0$ with alternative H_1: $\beta_k > \beta_k^0$. Next we consider the distribution of the test statistic t_k at the boundary of the null hypothesis (i.e. under $\beta_k = \beta_k^0$, as before) and we reject the null hypothesis if t_k is too large (note that large values for b_k lead to large values for t_k). Large negative values for t_k are compatible with the null hypothesis and do not lead to its rejection. Thus for this **one-sided test**, the critical value is determined from

$$P\{t > t_{N-K;\alpha}\} = \alpha.$$

Using the standard normal approximation again, we reject the null hypothesis at the 5% level if

$$t_k > 1.64.$$

Regression packages typically report the following t-value,

$$t_k = \frac{b_k}{s\sqrt{c_{kk}}},$$

sometimes referred to as the t-ratio, which is simply the point estimate divided by its standard error. The t-ratio is simply the t-statistic one would compute to test the null hypothesis that $\beta_k = 0$, which may be an hypothesis that is of economic interest as well. If it is rejected, it is said that 'b_k differs significantly from zero', or that the corresponding variable 'x_{ik} has a significant impact on y_i'. Often we simply say that (the effect of) 'x_{ik} is significant'.

A **confidence interval** can be defined as the interval of all values for β_k^0 for which the null hypothesis that $\beta_k = \beta_k^0$ is not rejected by the t-tests. Loosely speaking, a confidence interval gives a range of values for the true β_k that are not unlikely given the data, i.e. given the estimate b_k and the associated standard error. This implies the following inequalities that hold with probability $1 - \alpha$

$$-t_{N-K;\alpha/2} < \frac{b_k - \beta_k}{s\sqrt{c_{kk}}} < t_{N-K;\alpha/2}, \tag{2.50}$$

or

$$b_k - t_{N-K;\alpha/2}s\sqrt{c_{kk}} < \beta_k < b_k + t_{N-K;\alpha/2}s\sqrt{c_{kk}}. \tag{2.51}$$

Consequently, using the standard normal approximation, a 95% confidence interval for β_k is given by the interval

$$[b_k - 1.96s\sqrt{c_{kk}}, \ b_k + 1.96s\sqrt{c_{kk}}]. \tag{2.52}$$

In repeated sampling, 95% of these intervals will contain the true value β_k which is a fixed but unknown number (and thus not stochastic).

2.5.2 Example: Individual Wages (Continued)

From the results in Table 2.1 we can compute t-ratios and perform simple tests. For example, if we want to test whether $\beta_2 = 0$, we construct the t-statistic as the estimate divided by its standard error to get $t = 9.15$. Given the large number of observations, the appropriate t distribution is virtually identical to the standard normal one, so the 5% two-tailed critical value is 1.96. This means that we clearly have to reject the null hypothesis that $\beta_2 = 0$. We thus have to reject that in the population the expected wage differential between males and females is zero. We can also compute a confidence interval, which has bounds $1.28 \pm 1.96 \times 0.14$. This means that with 95% confidence we can say that over the entire population the expected wage differential between males and females is between \$1.00 and \$1.56 per hour.

2.5.3 Testing One Linear Restriction

The test discussed above involves a restriction on a single coefficient. Often, an hypothesis of economic interest implies a linear restriction on more than one coefficient, such as[10] $\beta_2 + \beta_3 + \cdots + \beta_K = 1$. In general, we can formulate such a linear hypothesis as

$$H_0: r_1\beta_1 + \cdots + r_K\beta_K = r'\beta = q, \tag{2.53}$$

for some scalar value q and a K-dimensional vector r. We can test the hypothesis in (2.53) using the result that $r'b$ is the BLUE for $r'\beta$ with variance $V\{r'b\} = r'V\{b\}r$. As b is K-variate normal, $r'b$ is normal as well (see Appendix B), so that we have

$$\frac{r'b - r'\beta}{s\sqrt{r'(X'X)^{-1}r}} \sim t_{N-K}, \tag{2.54}$$

which is a straightforward generalization of (2.48).[11] The test statistic for H_0 follows as

$$t = \frac{r'b - q}{s\sqrt{r'(X'X)^{-1}r}}, \tag{2.55}$$

which has a t_{N-K} distribution *under the null hypothesis*. At the 5% level, absolute values of t in excess of 1.96 (the normal approximation) lead to rejection of the null. This represents the most general version of the ***t*-test**.

Sometimes a more convenient way to obtain the same test statistic is by a reparametrization of the original model, such that the linear restriction in H_0 corresponds to a restriction of the usual form, say $\beta_k^* = 0$. For example, consider

$$y_i = \beta_1 + \beta_2 x_{i2} + \beta_3 x_{i3} + \varepsilon_i$$

and suppose the restriction of interest is $\beta_2 = \beta_3$. Then, we can rewrite the model as[12]

$$y_i = \beta_1 + (\beta_2 - \beta_3)x_{i2} + \beta_3(x_{i3} + x_{i2}) + \varepsilon_i$$

or

$$y_i = \beta_1 + \beta_2^* x_{i2} + \beta_3(x_{i3} + x_{i2}) + \varepsilon_i.$$

From the definition of OLS as minimizing the residual sum of squares, it follows that it is invariant to linear reparametrizations. Consequently, the OLS estimator for β_3 in both formulations of the model will be identical, and the estimator for β_2^* is identical to $b_2 - b_3$. The advantage of the reparametrization is that the null hypothesis can be written as a zero restriction on one of the regression coefficients, i.e. $H_0: \beta_2^* = 0$. Consequently, it can be tested using the standard t-ratio for β_2^* in the reparametrized model. The denominator of the test statistic (or the entire test statistic) is automatically provided by the regression package.

A reparametrization is not always possible and may be inconvenient if many hypotheses have to be tested. In such cases, one can use the t-test as discussed

---

[10] For example, in a Cobb–Douglas production function, written as a linear regression model in logs, constant returns to scale corresponds to the sum of all slope parameters (the coefficients for all log inputs) being equal to one.

[11] The statistic is the same if r is a K-dimensional vector of zeroes with a 1 on the k-th position.

[12] This reparametrization is not unique.

above, or – if a joint test of more than one restriction is required – use one of the
approaches below.

2.5.4 A Joint Test of Significance of Regression Coefficients

A standard test that is often automatically supplied by a regression package as well, is
a test for the joint hypothesis that all coefficients, except the intercept β_1, are equal to
zero. We shall discuss this procedure slightly more generally by testing the null that J
of the K coefficients are equal to zero. Without loss of generality, assume that these
are the last J coefficients in the model,

$$H_0: \beta_{K-J+1} = \cdots = \beta_K = 0. \tag{2.56}$$

The alternative hypothesis in this case is that H_0 is not true, i.e. that at least one of
these J coefficients is not equal to zero.

   The easiest test procedure in this case is to compare the sum of squared residuals of
the full model with the sum of squared residuals of the restricted model (which is the
model with the last J regressors omitted). Denote the residual sum of squares of the
full model by S_1 and that of the restricted model by S_0. If the null hypothesis is correct
one would expect that the sum of squares with the restriction imposed is only slightly
larger than that in the unrestricted case. A test statistic can be obtained by using the
following result, which we present without proof. Under the null hypothesis and
assumptions (A1)–(A5) it holds that

$$\frac{S_0 - S_1}{\sigma^2} \sim \chi_J^2. \tag{2.57}$$

From earlier results we know that $(N - K)s^2/\sigma^2 = S_1/\sigma^2 \sim \chi_{N-K}^2$. Moreover, under
the null hypothesis it can be shown that $S_0 - S_1$ and s^2 are independent. Consequently,
we can define the following test statistic,

$$f = \frac{(S_0 - S_1)/J}{S_1/(N - K)}. \tag{2.58}$$

Under the null hypothesis f has an F distribution with J and $N - K$ degrees of
freedom, denoted F_{N-K}^J. If we use the definition of the R^2 from (2.42), we can also
write this f statistic as

$$f = \frac{(R_1^2 - R_0^2)/J}{(1 - R_1^2)/(N - K)}, \tag{2.59}$$

where R_1^2 and R_0^2 are the usual goodness-of-fit measures for the unrestricted and the
restricted model, respectively.

   It is clear that in this case only very large values for the test statistic imply rejection
of the null hypothesis. Despite the two-sided alternative hypothesis, the critical values
$F_{N-K;\alpha}^J$ for this so-called F-**test** are one-sided, and defined by the following equality

$$P\{f > F_{N-K;\alpha}^J\} = \alpha,$$

where α is the significance level of the test. For example, if $N - K = 60$ and $J = 3$ the
critical value at the 5% level is 2.76.

In most applications the estimators for different elements in the parameter vector will be correlated, which means that the explanatory powers of the explanatory variables overlap. Consequently, the marginal contribution of each explanatory variable, when added last, may be quite small. Hence, it is perfectly possible for the t-tests on each variable's coefficient not to be significant, while the F-test for a number of these coefficients is highly significant. That is, it is possible that the null hypothesis $\beta_1 = 0$ is as such not unlikely, that the null $\beta_2 = 0$ is not unlikely, but that the joint null $\beta_1 = \beta_2 = 0$ is quite unlikely to be true. As a consequence, in general, t-tests on each restriction separately may not reject, while a joint F-test does. The converse is also true: it is possible that individual t-tests do reject the null, while the joint test does not. The section on multicollinearity below illustrates this point.

A special case of this F-test is sometimes misleadingly referred to as the model test,[13] where one tests the significance of all regressors, i.e. one tests H_0: $\beta_2 = \beta_2 = \cdots = \beta_K = 0$, meaning that all partial slope coefficients are equal to zero. The appropriate test statistic in this case is

$$f = \frac{(S_0 - S_1)/(K - 1)}{S_1/(N - K)}, \qquad (2.60)$$

where S_1 is the residual sum of squares of the model, that is $S_1 = \sum_i e_i^2$, and S_0 is the residual sum of squares of the restricted model containing only an intercept term, that is $S_0 = \sum_i (y_i - \bar{y})^2$.[14] Because the restricted model has an R^2 of zero by construction the test statistic can also be written as

$$F = \frac{R^2/(K - 1)}{(1 - R^2)/(N - K)}, \qquad (2.61)$$

where we used the convention to denote this statistic as F. Note that it is a simple function of the R^2 of the model. If the test based on F does not reject the null hypothesis, one can conclude that the model performs rather badly: a 'model' with just an intercept term would not do statistically worse. However, the converse is certainly not true: if the test does reject the null, one cannot conclude that the model is good, perfect, valid or the best. An alternative model may perform much better. Chapter 3 pays more attention to this issue.

2.5.5 Example: Individual Wages (Continued)

The fact that we concluded above that there was a significant difference between expected wage rates for males and females does not necessarily point to discrimination. It is possible that working males and females differ in terms of their characteristics, for example, their years of schooling. To analyse this, we can extend the regression model with additional explanatory variables, for example $school_i$, which

---

[13] This terminology is misleading as it does not in any way test whether the restrictions imposed by the model are correct. The only thing tested is whether all coefficients, excluding the intercept, are equal to zero, in which case one would have a trivial model with an R^2 of zero. As shown in (2.61), the test statistic associated with the model test is simply a function of the R^2.

[14] Using the definition of the OLS estimator, it is easily verified that the intercept term in a model without regressors, is estimated as the sample average $\bar{y}$. Any other choice would result in a high S value.

denotes the years of schooling, and $exper_i$, which denotes experience in years. The model is now interpreted to describe the conditional expected wage of an individual given his gender, years of schooling and experience. The coefficient β_2 for $male_i$ now measures the difference in expected wage between a male and a female *with the same schooling and experience*. Similarly, the coefficient β_3 for $school_i$ gives the expected wage difference between two individuals with the same experience and gender where one has one additional year of schooling. In general, the coefficients in a multiple regression model can only be interpreted under a **ceteris paribus condition**, which says that the other variables that are included in the model are constant.

Estimation by OLS produces the results given in Table 2.2. The coefficient for $male_i$ now suggests that if we compare an arbitrary male and female with the same years of schooling and experience, the expected wage differential is $1.47 compared to $1.28 before. With a standard error of $0.14, this difference is still statistically highly significant. The null hypothesis that schooling has no effect on a person's wage, given gender and experience, can be tested using the t-test described above, with a test statistic of 14.86. Clearly the null hypothesis has to be rejected. The estimated wage increase from one additional year of schooling, keeping years of experience fixed, is $0.62. It should not be surprising, given these results, that the joint hypothesis that all three partial slope coefficients are zero, that is wages are not affected by gender, schooling or experience, has to be rejected as well. The F-statistic takes the value of 103.4, the appropriate 5% critical value being 2.60.

Finally, we can use the above results to compare this model with the simpler one in Table 2.1. The R^2 has increased from 0.0248 to 0.0861, which means that the current model is able to explain 8.6% of the within sample variation in wages. We can perform a joint test on the hypothesis that the two additional variables, schooling and experience, both have zero coefficients, by performing the F-test described above. The test statistic in (2.59) can be computed from the R^2s reported in Tables 2.1 and 2.2 as

$$f = \frac{(0.0861 - 0.0248)/2}{(1 - 0.0861)/(3296 - 4)} = 110.41.$$

With a 5% critical value of 3.00, the null hypothesis is obviously rejected. We can thus conclude that the model that includes gender, schooling and experience performs significantly better than the model which only includes gender.

Table 2.2   OLS results wage equation

Dependent variable: *wage*

Variable	Estimate	Standard error	t-ratio
constant	−2.8901	0.5916	−4.884
male	1.4702	0.1370	10.729
school	0.6204	0.0417	14.861
exper	0.0896	0.0302	2.964

$s = 4.00476$ $R^2 = 0.0861$ $\bar{R}^2 = 0.0853$ $F = 103.387$

2.5.6 The General Case

The most general linear null hypothesis is a combination of the previous two cases and comprises a set of J linear restrictions on the coefficients. We can formulate these restrictions as

$$R\beta = q,$$

where R is a $J \times K$ matrix, assumed to be of full row rank,[15] and q is a J-dimensional vector. An example of this is the set of restrictions $\beta_2 + \beta_3 + \cdots + \beta_K = 1$ and $\beta_2 = \beta_3$, in which case $J = 2$ and

$$R = \begin{pmatrix} 0 & 1 & 1 & \cdots & \cdots & 1 \\ 0 & 1 & -1 & 0 & \cdots & 0 \end{pmatrix}, \quad q = \begin{pmatrix} 1 \\ 0 \end{pmatrix}.$$

In principle it is possible to estimate the model imposing the above restrictions, such that the test procedure of the Subsection 2.5.4 can be employed. However, in many cases these restrictions are such that it is hard to estimate under the null hypothesis (i.e. imposing $R\beta = q$). In such a case, one can use the result that

$$Rb \sim \mathcal{N}(R\beta, \sigma^2 R(X'X)^{-1}R'), \tag{2.62}$$

such that a quadratic form can be constructed that has a Chi-squared distribution under the null hypothesis, i.e.

$$\xi = \frac{(Rb - q)'(R(X'X)^{-1}R')^{-1}(Rb - q)}{\sigma^2} \sim \chi_J^2. \tag{2.63}$$

As σ^2 is unknown we have to replace it by its estimator s^2. There are two ways to continue. The first one simply replaces σ^2 in (2.63) by s^2 and uses that the resulting statistic is approximately χ^2 distributed (under the null, of course).[16] Often, one refers to this as a **Wald test**. The second way of going on uses (2.47) again such that a test statistic can be defined as the ratio of two independent χ^2 variables, i.e.

$$
\begin{aligned}
f &= \frac{(Rb - q)'(\sigma^2 R(X'X)^{-1}R')^{-1}(Rb - q)/J}{[(N - K)s^2/\sigma^2]/(N - K)} \\
&= \frac{(Rb - q)'(R(X'X)^{-1}R')^{-1}(Rb - q)}{Js^2},
\end{aligned} \tag{2.64}
$$

which, under H_0, follows an F distribution with J and $N - K$ degrees of freedom. As before, large values of f lead to rejection of the null. It can be shown that the f statistic in (2.64) is algebraically identical to the ones in (2.58) and (2.59) given above. It is simply a matter of computational ease which one to use.

It is also possible to construct joint confidence regions for two or more elements in β. As this is hardly used in empirical work, we shall skip this here and refer the interested reader to Greene (2000, Section 7.2) or Judge et al. (1988, Section 6.3) for details.

---

[15] Full row rank implies that the restrictions do not exhibit any linear dependencies.

[16] The approximate result is obtained from the asymptotic distribution, and also holds if normality of the error terms is not imposed (see below). The approximation is more accurate if the sample size is large.

2.5.7 Size, Power and p-Values

When an hypothesis is statistically tested two types of errors can be made. The first one is that we reject the null hypothesis while it is actually true, and is referred to as a **type I error**. The second one, a **type II error** is that the null hypothesis is not rejected while the alternative is true. The probability of a type I error is directly controlled by the researcher through his choice of the significance level α. When a test is performed at the 5% level, the probability of rejecting the null hypothesis while it is true is exactly 5%. This probability (significance level) is often referred to as the **size** of the test. The probability of a type II error depends upon the true parameter values. Intuitively, if the truth deviates much from the stated null hypothesis, the probability of such an error will be relatively small, while it will be quite large if the null hypothesis is close to the truth. The reversal probability, that is, the probability of rejecting the null hypothesis when it is false, is known as the **power** of the test. It indicates how 'powerful' a test is in finding deviations from the null hypothesis (depending upon the true parameter value). In general, reducing the size of a test will decrease its power, so that there is a trade off between type I and type II errors.

Suppose that we are testing the hypothesis that $\beta_2 = 0$, while its true value is in fact 0.1. It is clear that the probability that we reject the null hypothesis depends upon the standard error of our OLS estimator b_2 and thus, among other things, upon the sample size. The larger the sample the smaller the standard error and the more likely we are to reject. This implies that type II errors become increasingly unlikely if we have large samples. To compensate for this, researchers typically reduce the probability of type I errors (that is of incorrectly rejecting the null hypothesis) by lowering the size α of their tests. This explains why in large samples it is more appropriate to choose a size of 1% or less rather than the 'traditional' 5%. Similarly, in very small samples we may prefer to work with a significance level of 10%.

Commonly, the null hypothesis that is chosen is assumed to be true unless there is convincing evidence of the contrary. This suggests that if a test does not reject, for whatever reason, we stick to the null hypothesis. This view is not completely appropriate. A range of alternative hypotheses could be tested (for example $\beta_2 = 0$, $\beta_2 = 0.1$ and $\beta_2 = 0.5$), with the result that none of them is rejected. Obviously, concluding that these three null hypotheses are simultaneously true would be ridiculous. The only appropriate conclusion is that we *cannot reject* that β_2 is 0, nor that it is 0.1 or 0.5. Sometimes, econometric tests are simply not very powerful and very large sample sizes are needed to reject a given hypothesis.

A final probability that plays a role in statistical tests is usually referred to as the ***p*-value**. This p or probability value denotes the minimum size for which the null hypothesis would still be rejected. It is defined as the probability, under the null, to find a test statistic that (in absolute value) exceeds the value of the statistic that is computed from the sample. If the p-value is smaller than the significance level α, the null hypothesis is rejected. Many modern software packages supply such p-values and in this way allow researchers to draw their conclusions without consulting or computing the appropriate critical values. It also shows the sensitivity of the decision to reject the null hypothesis, with respect to the choice of significance level.

2.6 Asymptotic Properties of the OLS Estimator

In many cases, the small sample properties of the OLS estimator may deviate from those discussed above. For example, if the error terms in the linear model ε_i do not follow a normal distribution, it is no longer the case that the sampling distribution of the OLS estimator b is normal. If assumption (A2) of the Gauss–Markov conditions is violated, it can no longer be shown that b has an expected value of β. In fact, the linear regression model under the Gauss–Markov assumptions and with normal error terms is one of the very few cases in econometrics where the exact sampling distribution of the parameter estimators is known. As soon as we relax some of these assumptions or move to alternative models, the small sample properties of our estimators are typically unknown. In such cases we use an alternative approach to evaluate the quality of our estimators, which is based on asymptotic theory. Asymptotic theory refers to the question what happens if, hypothetically, the sample size grows infinitely large. Asymptotically, econometric estimators usually have nice properties, like normality, and we use the asymptotic properties to approximate the properties in the finite sample that we happen to have. This section presents a first discussion of the asymptotic properties of the OLS estimator.

2.6.1 Consistency

Let us start with the linear model under the Gauss–Markov assumptions. In this case we know that the OLS estimator b has the following first two moments

$$E\{b\} = \beta \tag{2.65}$$

$$V\{b\} = \sigma^2 \left(\sum_{i=1}^{N} x_i x_i' \right)^{-1} = \sigma^2 (X'X)^{-1}. \tag{2.66}$$

Unless we assume that the error terms are normal, the shape of the distribution of b is unknown. It is, however, possible to say something about the distribution of b, at least approximately. A first starting point is the so-called **Chebycheff inequality**, which says that the probability that a random variable z deviates more than a positive number δ from its mean, is bounded by its variance divided by δ^2, that is

$$P\{|z - E\{z\}| > \delta\} < \frac{V\{z\}}{\delta^2}, \quad \text{for all } \delta > 0. \tag{2.67}$$

For the OLS estimator this implies that each k-th element satisfies

$$P\{|b_k - \beta_k| > \delta\} < \frac{V\{b_k\}}{\delta^2} = \frac{\sigma^2 c_{kk}}{\delta^2} \quad \text{for all } \delta > 0, \tag{2.68}$$

where c_{kk}, as before, is the (k, k) element in $(X'X)^{-1} = (\sum_{i=1}^{N} x_i x_i')^{-1}$. In most applications, the above inequality is not very useful as the upper bound on the probability is larger than one. Let us, however, look at this inequality keeping δ fixed and letting, in our mind, the sample size N grow to infinity. Then what happens? It is clear that $\sum_{i=1}^{N} x_i x_i'$ increases as the number of terms grows, so that the variance of b decreases as the sample size increases. If we assume that[17]

$$\frac{1}{N}\sum_{i=1}^{N} x_i x_i' \text{ converges to a finite nonsingular matrix } \Sigma_{xx} \qquad (A6)$$

if the sample size N becomes infinitely large, it follows directly from the above inequality that

$$\lim_{N\to\infty} P\{|b_k - \beta_k| > \delta\} = 0 \text{ for all } \delta > 0. \qquad (2.69)$$

This says that, asymptotically, the probability that the OLS estimator deviates more than δ from the true parameter value, is zero. We usually refer to this property as 'the probability limit of b is β', or 'b converges in probability to β', or just[18]

$$\text{plim } b = \beta. \qquad (2.70)$$

Note that b is a vector of random variables, whose distribution depends on N, and β is a vector of fixed (unknown) numbers. When an estimator for β converges to the true value, we say that it is a **consistent estimator**. Any estimator that satisfies (2.69) is a consistent estimator for β, even if it is biased.

Consistency is a so-called large sample property and, loosely speaking, says that if we obtain more and more observations, the probability that our estimator is some positive number away from the true value β becomes smaller and smaller. Values that b may take that are not close to β become increasingly unlikely. In many cases, one cannot prove that an estimator is unbiased, and it is possible that no unbiased estimator exists (for example in nonlinear or dynamic models). In these cases, a minimum requirement for an estimator to be useful appears to be that it is consistent. In the sequel we shall therefore mainly be concerned with consistency of our estimators, not with their (un)biasedness.

A useful property of probability limits (plims) is the following. If plim $b = \beta$ and $g(.)$ is a continuous function (at least in the true value β), it also holds that

$$\text{plim } g(b) = g(\beta). \qquad (2.71)$$

This guarantees that, for example, the parametrization employed is irrelevant for consistency. For example, if s^2 is a consistent estimator for σ^2, then s is a consistent estimator for σ. Note that this result does not hold for unbiasedness, as $E\{s\}^2 \neq E\{s^2\}$ (see Appendix B).

The OLS estimator is consistent under substantially weaker conditions than the ones employed above. To see this, let us write the OLS estimator as

$$b = \left(\frac{1}{N}\sum_{i=1}^{N} x_i x_i'\right)^{-1} \frac{1}{N}\sum_{i=1}^{N} x_i y_i = \beta + \left(\frac{1}{N}\sum_{i=1}^{N} x_i x_i'\right)^{-1} \frac{1}{N}\sum_{i=1}^{N} x_i \varepsilon_i. \qquad (2.72)$$

---

[17] The nonsingularity of Σ_{xx} requires that, asymptotically, there is no multicollinearity. The requirement that the limit is finite is a 'regularity' condition, that will be satisfied in most empirical applications. A sufficient condition is that the x-variables are independent drawings from the same distribution with a finite variance. Violations typically occur in time series contexts where one or more of the x-variables may be trended. We shall return to this issue in Chapters 8 and 9.

[18] Unless indicated otherwise, lim and plim refer to the (probability) limit for the sample size N going to infinity ($N \to \infty$).

In this expression, the sample averages of $x_i x_i'$ and $x_i \varepsilon_i$ play a role. If the sample size increases the sample averages are taken over increasingly more observations. It seems reasonable to assume, and it can be shown to be true under very weak conditions,[19] that in the limit these samples averages converge to the corresponding population means. Now, under assumption (A6), we have that

$$\text{plim}(b - \beta) = \Sigma_{xx}^{-1} E\{x_i \varepsilon_i\}, \tag{2.73}$$

which shows that the OLS estimator is consistent if it holds that

$$E\{x_i \varepsilon_i\} = 0. \tag{A7}$$

This simply says that the error term is mean zero and uncorrelated with any of the explanatory variables. Note that $E\{\varepsilon_i | x_i\} = 0$ implies (A7), while the converse is not necessarily true.[20] Thus we can conclude that the OLS estimator b is consistent for β under conditions (A6) and (A7). Typically, these conditions are much weaker than the Gauss–Markov conditions (A1)–(A4) required for unbiasedness. We shall discuss the relevance of this below.

Similarly, the least squares estimator s^2 for the error variance σ^2 is consistent under conditions (A6), (A7) and (A3) (and some weak regularity conditions). The intuition is that with b converging to β the residuals e_i become asymptotically equivalent to the error terms ε_i, so that the sample variance of e_i will converge to the error variance σ^2, as defined in (A3).

2.6.2 Asymptotic Normality

If the small sample distribution of an estimator is unknown, the best we can do is try to find some approximation. In most cases, one uses an asymptotic approximation (for N going to infinity) based on the **asymptotic distribution**. Most estimators in econometrics can be shown to be asymptotically normally distributed (under weak regularity conditions). By the asymptotic distribution of a consistent estimator $\hat{\beta}$ we mean the distribution of $\sqrt{N}(\hat{\beta} - \beta)$ as N goes to infinity. The reason for the factor $\sqrt{N}$ is that asymptotically $\hat{\beta}$ is equal to β with probability one for all consistent estimators. That is, $\hat{\beta} - \beta$ has a degenerate distribution for $N \to \infty$ with all probability mass at zero. If we multiply by $\sqrt{N}$ and consider the asymptotic distribution of $\sqrt{N}(\hat{\beta} - \beta)$, this will usually be a nondegenerate normal distribution. In that case $\sqrt{N}$ is referred to as the rate of convergence and it is sometimes said that the corresponding estimator is root-N-consistent. In later chapters we shall see a few cases where the rate of convergence differs from root N.

For the OLS estimator it can be shown that under the Gauss–Markov conditions (A1)–(A4) combined with (A6) we have that

$$\sqrt{N}(b - \beta) \to \mathcal{N}(0, \sigma^2 \Sigma_{xx}^{-1}), \tag{2.74}$$

---

[19] The result that sample averages converge to population means is provided in several versions of the **law of large numbers** (see Greene, 2000, Section 9.4; Greene, 1997, Section 6.7; or Davidson and MacKinnon, 1993, Section 4.5).

[20] To be precise, $E\{\varepsilon_i | x_i\} = 0$ implies that $E\{\varepsilon_i g(x_i)\} = 0$ for *any* function g (see Appendix B).

where $\rightarrow$ means 'is asymptotically distributed as'. Thus, the OLS estimator b is asymptotically normally distributed with variance–covariance matrix $\sigma^2 \Sigma_{xx}^{-1}$. In practice, where we necessarily have a finite sample, we can use this result to approximate the distribution of b as

$$b \sim \mathcal{N}\left(\beta, \sigma^2 \Sigma_{xx}^{-1}/N\right). \tag{2.75}$$

Because the unknown matrix Σ_{xx} will be consistently estimated by the sample mean $(1/N)\sum_{i=1}^{N} x_i x_i'$, this approximate distribution is estimated as

$$b \sim \mathcal{N}\left(\beta, s^2 \left(\sum_{i=1}^{N} x_i x_i'\right)^{-1}\right). \tag{2.76}$$

In (2.76) we have a distributional result for the OLS estimator b based upon the asymptotic results, which is approximately valid in small samples. The quality of the approximation increases as the sample size grows and typically it is hoped that the sample size is sufficiently large for the approximation to be reasonably accurate. Because the result in (2.76) corresponds exactly to what is used in the case of the Gauss–Markov assumptions combined with the assumption of normal error terms, it follows that all the distributional results for the OLS estimator reported above, including those for t- and F-statistics, are approximately valid, *even if the errors are not normally distributed.*

Because asymptotically, a t_{N-K} distributed variable converges to a standard normal one, it is not uncommon to use the critical values from a standard normal distribution (like the 1.96 at the 5% level) for all inferences, while not imposing normality of the errors. Similarly, if f has an F_{N-K}^J distribution then asymptotically $\xi = Jf$ has a χ^2 distribution with J degrees of freedom. To test a set of J linear restrictions on β, we can thus use J times the f statistics and use the critical values from the asymptotic Chi-squared distribution (compare (2.63) and (2.64)).

It is possible to further relax the assumptions without affecting the validity of the results in (2.74) and (2.76). In particular, we can relax assumption (A2) to

$$x_i \text{ and } \varepsilon_i \text{ are independent.} \tag{A8}$$

This condition does not rule out dependence between x_i and ε_j for $i \neq j$, which is of interest for models with lagged dependent variables. Note that (A8) implies (A7). Further discussion on the asymptotic distribution of the OLS estimator and how it can be estimated, is provided in Chapters 4 and 5.

2.7 Illustration: the Capital Asset Pricing Model

One of the most important models in finance is the Capital Asset Pricing Model (CAPM). The CAPM is an equilibrium model which assumes that all investors compose their asset portfolio on the basis of a trade off between the expected return and the variance of the return on their portfolio. This implies that each investor holds a so-called **mean variance efficient** portfolio, a portfolio that gives maximum expected return for a given variance (level of risk). If all investors hold the same beliefs about expected returns and (co)variances of individual assets, and in the absence of transaction costs, taxes and trading restrictions of any kind, it is also the case that the aggregate of all individual portfolios, the **market portfolio**, is mean variance efficient. In this case, it can be shown that expected returns on individual assets are linearly related to the expected return on the market portfolio. In particular, it holds that[21]

$$E\{r_{jt} - r_f\} = \beta_j E\{r_{mt} - r_f\}, \tag{2.77}$$

where r_{jt} is the risky return on asset j in period t, r_{mt} the risky return on the market portfolio, and r_f denotes the riskless return, which we assume to be time-invariant for simplicity. The proportionality factor β_j is given by

$$\beta_j = \frac{\text{cov}\{r_{jt}, r_{mt}\}}{V\{r_{mt}\}} \tag{2.78}$$

and indicates how strong fluctuations in the returns on asset j are related to movements of the market as a whole. As such, it is a measure of systematic risk (or market risk). Because it is impossible to eliminate systematic risk through a diversification of one's portfolio without affecting the expected return, investors are compensated for bearing this source of risk through a risk premium $E\{r_{mt} - r_f\} > 0$.

In this section, we consider the CAPM and see how it can be rewritten as a linear regression model, which allows us to estimate and test it. A more extensive discussion of empirical issues related to the CAPM can be found in Berndt (1991) or, more technically, in Campbell, Lo and MacKinlay (1997). More details on the CAPM can be found in finance textbooks, for example Elton and Gruber (1995).

2.7.1 The CAPM as a Regression Model

The relationship in (2.77) is an *ex ante* equality in terms of unobserved expectations. Ex post, we only observe realized returns on the different assets over a number of periods. If, however, we make the usual assumption that expectations are rational, so that expectations of economic agents correspond to mathematical expectations, we can derive a relationship from (2.77) that involves actual returns. To see this, let us define the unexpected returns on asset j as

$$u_{jt} = r_{jt} - E\{r_{jt}\},$$

and the unexpected returns on the market portfolio as

$$u_{mt} = r_{mt} - E\{r_{mt}\}.$$

Then, it is possible to rewrite (2.77) as

$$r_{jt} - r_f = \beta_j(r_{mt} - r_f) + \varepsilon_{jt,} \tag{2.79}$$

where

$$\varepsilon_{jt} = u_{jt} - \beta_j u_{mt}.$$

Equation (2.79) is a regression model, without an intercept, where ε_{jt} is treated as an error term. This error term is not something that is just added to the model, but it has a meaning, being a function of unexpected returns. It is easy to show, however, that it

---

[21] Because the data correspond to different time periods, we index the observations by t, $t = 1, 2, \ldots, T$, rather than i.

satisfies some minimal requirements for a regression error term, as given in (A7). For example, it follows directly from the definitions of u_{mt} and u_{jt} that it is mean zero, i.e.

$$E\{\varepsilon_{jt}\} = E\{u_{jt}\} - \beta_j E\{u_{mt}\} = 0. \tag{2.80}$$

Furthermore, it is uncorrelated with the regressor $r_{mt} - r_f$. This follows from the definition of β_j, which can be written as

$$\beta_j = \frac{E\{u_{jt}u_{mt}\}}{V\{u_{mt}\}},$$

(note that r_f is not stochastic) and the result that

$$E\{\varepsilon_{jt}(r_{mt} - r_f)\} = E\{(u_{jt} - \beta_j u_{mt})u_{mt}\} = E\{u_{jt}u_{mt}\} - \beta_j E\{u_{mt}^2\}.$$

From the previous section, it then follows that the OLS estimator provides a consistent estimator for β_j. If, in addition, we impose assumption (A8) that ε_{jt} is independent of $r_{mt} - r_f$ and assumptions (A3) and (A4) stating that ε_{jt} does not exhibit autocorrelation or heteroskedasticity, we can use the asymptotic result in (2.74) and the approximate distributional result in (2.76). This implies that routinely computed OLS estimates, standard errors and tests are appropriate, by virtue of the asymptotic approximation.

2.7.2 Estimating and Testing the CAPM

The CAPM describes the expected returns on any asset, as a function of the (expected) return on the market portfolio. In this subsection, we consider the returns on three different stocks listed at the Brussels stock exchange, while approximating the return on the market portfolio by the return on the Belgian All Share index. Stock returns are available for the period January 1988 to February 1996 (98 months) for the following companies: Petrofina (petrochemical industry), General Bank (one of the largest Belgian banks) and CBR (concrete and cement works).[22] Note that the sample period excludes the October 1987 stock market crash. While theoretically, the market portfolio should include all tradeable assets, we shall assume that the Belgian All Share index, containing stocks of the majority of Belgian firms, is a good approximation. The riskless rate is approximated by the return on 3-month treasury bills. Although this return is time-varying, it is known to investors when making their decisions.

First, we estimate the CAPM relationship (2.79) for these three stocks. That is, we regress excess returns on the stocks (returns in excess of the riskless rate) upon excess returns on the market index proxy, not including an intercept. This produces the results presented in Table 2.3. The estimated beta coefficients indicate how sensitive the value of the companies' stocks are to general market movements. This sensitivity is relatively low for the General Bank, but fairly high for CBR: an excess return on the market of, say, 10%, corresponds to an expected excess return on the General Bank and CBR stocks of 7.3% and 11.0%, respectively. Assuming that the conditions required for the distributional results of the OLS estimator are satisfied, we can

---

[22] The data for this illustration are available as CAPM.

Table 2.3　CAPM regressions (without intercept)

Dependent variable: *excess stock returns*

Company:	Petrofina	General Bank	CBR
excess market return	0.940	0.725	1.101
	(0.082)	(0.077)	(0.105)
uncentred R^2	0.575	0.477	0.534
s	0.0384	0.0360	0.0488

Note: standard errors in parentheses.

directly test the hypothesis (which is of limited economic interest) that $\beta_j = 1$ for each of the three stocks. This results in *t*-values of -0.73, -3.57 and 0.96, respectively, so that we reject the null hypothesis for General Bank only.

As the CAPM implies that the only relevant variable in the regression is the excess return on the market portfolio, any other variable (known to the investor when making his decisions) should have a zero coefficient. This also holds for a constant term. To check whether this is the case, we can re-estimate the above models while including an intercept term. This produces the results in Table 2.4. From these results, we can test the validity of the CAPM by testing whether the intercept term is zero. Clearly, we do not find any statistical evidence that allows us to reject the CAPM in this way: none of the constant terms is significantly different from zero. This also explains why the estimated beta coefficients are very similar to those in Table 2.3 and why the R^2s are close to the uncentred R^2s.

The R^2 in these regressions has an interesting economic interpretation. Equation (2.79) allows us to write that

$$V\{r_{jt}\} = \beta_j^2 V\{r_{mt}\} + V\{\varepsilon_{jt}\},$$

which shows that the variance of the return on a stock consists of two parts: a part related to the variance of the market index and an idiosyncratic part. In economic terms this says that total risk equals market risk plus idiosyncratic risk. Market risk is determined by β_j and is rewarded: stocks with a higher β_j provide higher expected returns because of (2.77). Idiosyncratic risk is not rewarded because it can be eliminated by diversification: if we construct a portfolio that is well diversified it will consist of a great number of assets, with different characteristics, so that most

Table 2.4　CAPM regressions (with intercept)

Dependent variable: *excess stock returns*

Company:	Petrofina	General Bank	CBR
constant	-0.005	0.003	0.005
	(0.004)	(0.004)	(0.005)
excess market return	0.943	0.723	1.099
	(0.082)	(0.077)	(0.105)
R^2	0.580	0.477	0.535
s	0.0382	0.0361	0.0488

Note: standard errors in parentheses.

Table 2.5 CAPM regressions (with intercept and January dummy)

Dependent variable: *excess stock returns*

Company:	Petrofina	General Bank	CBR
constant	−0.005	0.002	0.005
	(0.004)	(0.004)	(0.005)
January dummy	−0.003	0.007	−0.000
	(0.014)	(0.013)	(0.017)
excess market return	0.945	0.716	1.099
	(0.083)	(0.079)	(0.106)
R^2	0.580	0.479	0.535
s	0.0384	0.0362	0.0491

Note: standard errors in parentheses.

of the idiosyncratic risk will cancel out and mainly market risk matters. The R^2, being the proportion of explained variation in total variation, is an estimate of the relative importance of market risk for each of the stocks. For example, it is estimated that 58% of the risk (variance) of the Petrofina stock is due to the market as a whole, while 42% is idiosyncratic risk.

Finally, we consider one deviation from the CAPM that is often found in empirical work: the existence of a January effect. There is some evidence that, ceteris paribus, returns in January are higher than in any of the other months. We can test this within the CAPM framework by including a dummy in the model for January and testing whether it is significant. Doing this, we obtain the results in Table 2.5. Computing the *t*-statistics corresponding to the January dummy clearly shows that for none of the stocks we can reject the absence of a January effect. As the January effect is typically found for small firms, this result is not very surprising given that the three firms we consider are among the largest in Belgium.

2.8   Multicollinearity

In general, there is nothing wrong with including variables in your model that are correlated. In an individual wage equation, for example, we may want to include both age and experience, although it can be expected that older persons, on average, have more experience. However, if the correlation between two variables is too high, this may lead to problems. Technically, the problem is that the matrix $X'X$ is close to being not invertible. This may lead to unreliable estimates with high standard errors and of unexpected sign or magnitude. Intuitively, the problem is also clear. If age and experience are highly correlated it may be hard for the model to identify the *individual* impact of these two variables, which is exactly what we are trying to do. In such a case, a large number of observations with sufficient variation in both age and experience may help us to get sensible answers. If this is not the case and we do get poor estimates (for example: *t*-tests show that neither age nor experience are individually significant), we can only conclude that there is insufficient information in the sample to identify the effects we would like to identify. In the wage equation, we are trying to identify the effect of age, keeping experience and the other included variables constant, as well as the effect of experience, keeping age and the other variables constant (the ceteris paribus condition). It is clear that in the extreme case that people with the same age would have the same level of experience we would not be able to identify these effects. In the case where age and experience are highly but not perfectly correlated, the estimated effects are likely to be highly inaccurate.

In general, the term **multicollinearity** is used to describe the problem when an approximate linear relationship among the explanatory variables leads to unreliable regression estimates. This approximate relationship is not restricted to two variables but can involve more or even all regressors. In the wage equation, for example, the problems may be aggravated if we include years of schooling in addition to age and years of experience. In the extreme case, one explanatory variable is an exact linear combination of one or more other explanatory variables (including the intercept). This is usually referred to as **exact multicollinearity**, in which case the OLS estimator is not uniquely defined from the first order conditions of the least squares problem (the matrix $X'X$ is not invertible).

The use of too many dummy variables (which are either zero or one) is a typical cause for exact multicollinearity. Consider the case where we would like to include a dummy for males ($male_i$), a dummy for females ($female_i$) as well as a constant. Because $male_i + female_i = 1$ for each observation (and 1 is included as the constant), the $X'X$ matrix becomes singular. Exact multicollinearity is easily solved by excluding one of the variables from the model and estimating the model including either $male_i$ and a constant, $female_i$ and a constant, or both $male_i$ and $female_i$ but no constant. The latter approach is not recommended because standard software tends to compute statistics like the R^2 and the F-statistic in a different way if the constant is suppressed; see the illustration in the next subsection. Another useful example of exact multicollinearity in this context is the inclusion of the variables age, years of schooling and potential experience, defined as age minus years of schooling minus six. Clearly, this leads to a singular $X'X$ matrix if a constant is included in the model (see Section 5.4 for an illustration).

To illustrate the effect of multicollinearity on the OLS estimator in more detail, consider the following example. Let the following regression model be estimated,

$$y_i = \beta_1 x_{i1} + \beta_2 x_{i2} + \varepsilon_i,$$

where it is assumed that the sample means $\bar{y} = \bar{x}_1 = \bar{x}_2 = 0$.[23] Moreover, assume that the sample variances of x_{i1} and x_{i2} are equal to 1, while the sample covariance (correlation coefficient) is r_{12}. Then the variance of the OLS estimator can be written as

$$V\{b\} = \sigma^2 \frac{1}{N} \begin{pmatrix} 1 & r_{12} \\ r_{12} & 1 \end{pmatrix}^{-1} = \frac{\sigma^2/N}{1 - r_{12}^2} \begin{pmatrix} 1 & -r_{12} \\ -r_{12} & 1 \end{pmatrix}.$$

It is clear that the variances of both b_1 and b_2 increase if the absolute value of the correlation coefficient between x_1 and x_2 increases.[24] Due to the increased variance of

---

[23] This can be achieved by deducting the sample mean from all variables. In this case, there is no need for a constant term because the OLS estimator of the intercept will be equal to zero.

[24] Note that this also holds if the true value of one of the regression coefficients is zero. Thus, including unnecessary regressors in a model decreases the precision of the OLS estimator for the other coefficients (see Chapter 3).

the OLS estimator, t-statistics will be smaller. If x_{i1} and x_{i2} show a strong positive correlation ($r_{12} > 0$), the estimators b_1 and b_2 will be *negatively* correlated.

Another consequence of multicollinearity is that some linear combinations of the parameters are pretty accurately estimated, while other linear combinations are highly inaccurate. Usually, when regressors are positively correlated, the sum of the regression coefficients can be rather precisely determined, while the difference cannot. In the above example we have for the variance of $b_1 + b_2$ that

$$V\{b_1 + b_2\} = \frac{\sigma^2/N}{1 - r_{12}^2}(2 - 2r_{12}) = 2\frac{\sigma^2/N}{1 + r_{12}},$$

while for the variance of the difference we have

$$V\{b_1 - b_2\} = \frac{\sigma^2/N}{1 - r_{12}^2}(2 + 2r_{12}) = 2\frac{\sigma^2/N}{1 - r_{12}}.$$

So if r_{12} is close to 1, the variance of $b_1 - b_2$ is many times higher than the variance of $b_1 + b_2$. For example, if $r_{12} = 0.95$ the ratio of the two variances is 39. An important consequence of this result is that for prediction purposes, in particular the accuracy of prediction, multicollinearity typically has little impact. This is a reflection of the fact that the 'total impact' of all explanatory variables is accurately identified.

In summary, high correlations between (linear combinations of) explanatory variables may result in multicollinearity problems. If this happens, one or more parameters we are interested in are estimated highly inaccurately. Essentially, this means that our sample does not provide sufficient information about these parameters. To alleviate the problem, we are therefore forced to use more information, for example by imposing some a priori restrictions on the vector of parameters. Commonly, this means that one or more variables are omitted from the model. Another solution, which is typically not practical, is to extend the sample size. As illustrated by the above example all variances decrease as the sample size increases. An extensive and critical survey of the multicollinearity problem and the (in)appropriateness of some mechanical procedures to solve it, is provided in Maddala (1992, Chapter 7).

2.8.1 Example: Individual Wages (Continued)

Let us go back to the simple wage equation of Subsection 2.3.3. As explained above, the inclusion of a female dummy in the model would cause exact multicollinearity. Intuitively, it is also obvious that with only two groups of people one dummy variable and a constant are sufficient to capture them. The choice of whether to include the male or the female dummy is arbitrary. The fact that the two dummy variables add up to one for each observation does not imply multicollinearity if the model does not contain an intercept term. Consequently, it is possible to include both dummies while excluding the intercept term. To illustrate the consequences of these alternative choices, consider the estimation results in Table 2.6.

As specification C does not contain an intercept term, the uncentred R^2 is provided rather than the R^2, which explains its high value. As before, the coefficient for the male dummy in specification A denotes the expected wage differential between men

Table 2.6 Alternative specifications with dummy variables

Dependent variable: *wage*

Specification	A	B	C
constant	5.147 (0.101)	6.425 (0.096)	—
male	1.278 (0.140)	—	6.425 (0.096)
female	—	−1.278 (0.140)	5.147 (0.101)
R^2, uncentred R^2	0.0248	0.0248	0.6811

Note: standard errors in parentheses.

and women. Similarly, the coefficient for the female dummy in the second specification denotes the expected wage differential between women and men. For specification C, however, the coefficients for *male* and *female* reflect the expected wage for men and women, respectively. It is quite clear that all three specifications are equivalent, while their parametrization is somewhat different.

2.9 Prediction

The econometrician's work does not end after having produced the coefficient estimates and corresponding standard errors. A next step is to interpret the results and to use the model for the goals it was intended. One of these goals, particularly with time series data, is prediction. In this section we consider prediction using the regression model, that is, we want to predict the value for the dependent variable at a given value for the explanatory variables, x_0. Given that the model is assumed to hold for all potential observations, it will also hold that

$$y_0 = x_0'\beta + \varepsilon_0,$$

where ε_0 satisfies the same properties as all other error terms. The obvious predictor for y_0 is $\hat{y}_0 = x_0'b$. As $E\{b\} = \beta$ it is easily verified that this is an **unbiased predictor**, i.e.[25] $E\{\hat{y}_0 - y_0\} = 0$. Under assumptions (A1)–(A4), the variance of the predictor is given by

$$V\{\hat{y}_0\} = V\{x_0'b\} = x_0'V\{b\}x_0 = \sigma^2 x_0'(X'X)^{-1}x_0. \tag{2.81}$$

This variance, however, is only an indication of the variation in the predictor if different samples would be drawn, that is the variation in the predictor due to variation in b. To analyse how accurate the predictor is, we need the variance of the **prediction error**, which is defined as

$$y_0 - \hat{y}_0 = x_0'\beta + \varepsilon_0 - x_0'b = \varepsilon_0 - x_0'(b - \beta). \tag{2.82}$$

---

[25] In this expectation both $\hat{y}_0$ and y_0 are treated as random variables.

The prediction error has variance

$$V\{y_0 - \hat{y}_0\} = \sigma^2 + \sigma^2 x_0'(X'X)^{-1}x_0 \qquad (2.83)$$

provided that it can be assumed that b and ε_0 are uncorrelated. This is usually not a problem because ε_0 is not used in the estimation of β. In the simple regression model (with one explanatory variable x_i), one can rewrite the above expression as (see Maddala, 1992, Section 3.7)

$$V\{y_0 - \hat{y}_0\} = \sigma^2 + \sigma^2 \left(\frac{1}{N} + \frac{(x_0 - \bar{x})^2}{\sum_i (x_i - \bar{x})^2} \right).$$

Consequently, the further the value of x_0 is from the sample mean $\bar{x}$, the larger the variance of the prediction error. This is a sensible result: if we want to predict y for extreme values of x we cannot expect it to be very accurate.

Finally, we can compute a so-called **prediction interval**. A 95% prediction interval for y_0 is given by

$$\left[x_0'b - 1.96s\sqrt{1 + x_0'(X'X)^{-1}x_0}, \ x_0'b + 1.96s\sqrt{1 + x_0'(X'X)^{-1}x_0} \right], \qquad (2.84)$$

where, as before, 1.96 is the critical value of a standard normal distribution. It can be said that with a probability of 95%, this interval contains the true unobserved value y_0.

As one of the important goals of dynamic models is forecasting, we shall return to the prediction issue in Chapter 8.

Exercises

Exercise 2.1 (Regression)

Consider the following linear regression model:

$$y_i = \beta_1 + \beta_2 x_{i2} + \beta_3 x_{i3} + \varepsilon_i = x_i'\beta + \varepsilon_i.$$

a. Explain how the ordinary least squares estimator for β is determined and derive an expression for b.

b. Which assumptions are needed to make b an unbiased estimator for β?

c. Explain how a confidence interval for β_2 can be constructed. Which additional assumptions are needed?

d. Explain how one can test the hypothesis that $\beta_3 = 1$.

e. Explain how one can test the hypothesis that $\beta_2 + \beta_3 = 0$.

f. Explain how one can test the hypothesis that $\beta_2 = \beta_3 = 0$.

g. Which assumptions are needed to make b a consistent estimator for β?

h. Suppose that $x_{i2} = 2 + 3x_{i3}$. What will happen if you try to estimate the above model?

i. Suppose that the model is estimated with $x_{i2}^* = 2x_{i2} - 2$ included rather than x_{i2}. How are the coefficients in this model related to those in the original model? And the R^2s?

j. Suppose that $x_{i2} = x_{i3} + u_i$, where u_i and x_{i3} are uncorrelated. Suppose that the model is estimated with u_i included rather than x_{i2}. How are the coefficients in this model related to those in the original model? And the R^2s?

Exercise 2.2 (Individual Wages)

Using a sample of 545 full-time workers in the USA, a researcher is interested in the question whether women are systematically underpaid compared to men. First, she estimates the average hourly wages in the sample for men and women, which are \$5.91 and \$5.09, respectively.

a. Do these numbers give an answer to the question of interest? Why not? How could one (at least partially) correct for this?

The researcher also runs a simple regression of an individual's wage on a male dummy, equal to 1 for males and 0 for females. This gives the results reported in Table 2.7.

Table 2.7   Hourly wages explained from gender: OLS results

Variable	Coefficient	Standard error	t-ratio
constant	5.09	0.58	8.78
male	0.82	0.15	5.47

$N = 545$ $s = 2.17$ $R^2 = 0.26$

b. How can you interpret the coefficient estimate of 0.82? How do you interpret the estimated intercept of 5.09?

c. How do you interpret the R^2 of 0.26?

d. Explain the relationship between the coefficient estimates in the table and the average wage rates of males and females.

e. A student is unhappy with this model as 'a female dummy is omitted from the model'. Comment upon this criticism.

f. Test, using the above results, the hypothesis that men and women have, on average, the same wage rate, against the *one-sided* alternative that women earn less. State the assumptions required for this test to be valid.

g. Construct a 95% confidence interval for the average wage differential between males and females in the population.

Subsequently, the above 'model' is extended to include differences in age and education, by including the variables *age* (age in years) and *educ* (education level, from 1 to 5). Simultaneously, the endogenous variable is adjusted to be the *natural logarithm* of the hourly wage rate. The results are reported in Table 2.8.

Table 2.8 Log hourly wages explained from gender, age and education level: OLS results

Variable	Coefficient	Standard error	t-ratio
constant	−1.09	0.38	2.88
male	0.13	0.03	4.47
age	0.09	0.02	4.38
educ	0.18	0.05	3.66

$N = 545$ $s = 0.24$ $R^2 = 0.691$ $\bar{R}^2 = 0.682$

h. How do you interpret the coefficients of 0.13 for the male dummy, and 0.09 for age?

i. Test the joint hypothesis that gender, age and education do no affect a person's wage.

j. A student is unhappy with this model as 'the effect of education is rather restrictive'. Can you explain this criticism? How could the model be extended or changed to meet the above criticism? How can you test whether the extension has been useful?

The researcher re-estimates the above model including age^2 as an additional regressor. The t-value on this new variable becomes -1.14, while $R^2 = 0.699$ and the $\bar{R}^2$ increases to 0.683.

k. Could you give a reason why the inclusion of age^2 might be appropriate?

l. Would you retain this new variable given the R^2 and the $\bar{R}^2$ measures? Would you retain age^2 given its t-value? Explain this apparent conflict in conclusions.

Exercise 2.3 (Asset Pricing – Empirical)

In the recent finance literature it is suggested that asset prices are fairly well described by a so-called factor model, where excess returns are linearly explained from excess returns on a number of 'factor portfolios'. As in the CAPM, the intercept term should be zero, just like the coefficient for any other variable included in the model the value of which is known in advance (e.g. a January dummy). The data set *assets* contains excess returns on four factor portfolios (see Carhart, 1997) for July 1963 to October 1993:

> *rm*: excess return on a value-weighted market proxy
> *rsize*: return on a zero-investment factor-mimicking portfolio for size
> *rbm*: ditto for book-to-market equity
> *rmom*: ditto for one-year momentum.

All data are for the USA. Each of the last three variables denotes the difference in returns on two hypothetical portfolios of stocks. These portfolios are re-formed each month on the basis of the most recent available information on firm size, book-to-market value of equity and historical returns, respectively. For example, *rsize* reflects the difference in returns on a portfolio of small firms and one of large firms. The factors are motivated by empirically found anomalies of the CAPM (for example, small firms appear to have higher returns than large ones, even after the CAPM risk correction).

In addition to the excess returns on these four factors, we have observations on the returns on ten different 'assets' which are ten portfolios of stocks, maintained by the Center for Research in Security Prices (CRSP). These portfolios are size-based, which means that portfolio 1 contains the 10% smallest firms listed at the New York Stock Exchange and portfolio 10 contains the 10% largest firms that are listed. Excess returns (in excess of the riskfree rate) on these portfolios are denoted by $r1$ to $r10$, respectively.

In answering the following questions use $r1$, $r10$ and the returns on two additional portfolios that you select.

a. Regress the excess returns on your four portfolios upon the excess return on the market portfolio (proxy), noting that this corresponds to the CAPM. Include a constant in these regressions.

b. Give an economic interpretation of the estimated β coefficients.

c. Give an economic and a statistical interpretation of the R^2s.

d. Test the hypothesis that $\beta_j = 1$ for each of the four portfolios. State the assumptions you need to make for the tests to be (asymptotically) valid.

e. Test the validity of the CAPM by testing whether the constant terms in the four regressions are zero.

f. Test for a January effect in each of the four regressions.

g. Next, estimate the four-factor model

$$r_{jt} = \alpha_j + \beta_{j1}rm_t + \beta_{j2}rsize_t + \beta_{j3}rbm_t + \beta_{j4}rmom_t + \varepsilon_t$$

by OLS. Compare the estimation results with those obtained from the one-factor (CAPM) model. Pay attention to the estimated partial slope coefficients and the R^2s.

h. Perform F-tests for the hypothesis that the coefficients for the three new factors are jointly equal to zero.

i. Test the validity of the four-factor model by testing whether the constant terms in the four regressions are zero. Compare your conclusions with those obtained from the CAPM.

3 Interpreting and Comparing Regression Models

In the previous chapter attention was paid to the estimation of linear regression models. In particular, the ordinary least squares approach was discussed, including its properties under several sets of assumptions. This allowed us to estimate the vector of unknown parameters β and to test parametric restrictions, like $\beta_k = 0$. In the first section of this chapter we pay additional attention to the interpretation of regression models and their coefficients. In Section 3.2, we discuss how we can select the set of regressors to be used in our model and what the consequences are if we misspecify this set. This also involves comparing alternative models. Section 3.3 discusses the assumption of linearity and how it can be tested. To illustrate the main issues, this chapter is concluded with two empirical examples. Section 3.4 describes a model to explain house prices, while Section 3.5 discusses the estimation and specification of an individual wage equation.

3.1 Interpreting the Linear Model

As already stressed in the previous chapter, the linear model

$$y_i = x_i'\beta + \varepsilon_i \tag{3.1}$$

has little meaning unless we complement it with additional assumptions on ε_i. It is common to state that ε_i has expectation zero and that the x_is are taken as given. A formal way of stating this is that it is assumed that the expected value of ε_i given X, or the expected value of ε_i given x_i, is zero, that is

$$E\{\varepsilon_i|X\} = 0 \quad \text{or} \quad E\{\varepsilon_i|x_i\} = 0, \tag{3.2}$$

respectively, where the latter condition is implied by the first. Under $E\{\varepsilon_i|x_i\} = 0$, we can interpret the regression model as describing the conditional expected value of y_i given values for the explanatory variables x_i. For example, what is the expected wage for an *arbitrary* woman of age 40, with a university education and 14 years of experience? Or, what is the expected unemployment rate given wage rates, inflation and total output in the economy? The first consequence of (3.2) is the interpretation of the individual β coefficients. For example, β_k measures the expected change in y_i if x_{ik} changes with one unit but all the other variables in x_i do not change. That is

$$\frac{\partial E\{y_i|x_i\}}{\partial x_{ik}} = \beta_k. \tag{3.3}$$

It is important to realize that we had to state explicitly that the other variables in x_i did not change. This is the so-called **ceteris paribus condition**. In a multiple regression model single coefficients can only be interpreted under ceteris paribus conditions. For example, β_k could measure the effect of age on the expected wage of a woman, if the education level and years of experience are kept constant. An important consequence of the ceteris paribus condition is that *it is not possible to interpret a single coefficient in a regression model without knowing what the other variables in the model are.*

Sometimes these ceteris paribus conditions are hard to maintain. For example, in the wage equation case, it may be very common that a changing age almost always corresponds to changing years of experience. Although the β_k coefficient in this case still measures the effect of age keeping years of experience (and the other variables) fixed, it may not be very well identified from a given sample, due to the collinearity between the two variables. In some cases, it is just impossible to maintain the ceteris paribus condition, for example if x_i includes both age and age-squared. Clearly, it is ridiculous to say that a coefficient β_k measures the effect of age given that age-squared is constant. In this case, one should go back to the derivative (3.3). If $x_i'\beta$ includes, say, $age_i\beta_2 + age_i^2\beta_3$, we can derive

$$\frac{\partial E\{y_i|x_i\}}{\partial age_i} = \beta_2 + 2age_i\beta_3, \tag{3.4}$$

which can be interpreted as the marginal effect of a changing age if the other variables in x_i (excluding age_i^2) are kept constant. This shows how the marginal effects of explanatory variables can be allowed to vary over the observations by including additional terms involving these variables (in this case age_i^2). For example, we can allow the effect of age to be different for men and women by including an interaction term $age_i male_i$ in the regression, where $male_i$ is a dummy for males. Thus, if the model includes $age_i\beta_2 + age_i male_i\beta_3$ the effect of a changing age is

$$\frac{\partial E\{y_i|x_i\}}{\partial age_i} = \beta_2 + male_i\beta_3, \tag{3.5}$$

which is β_2 for females and $\beta_2 + \beta_3$ for males. Sections 3.4 and 3.5 will illustrate the use of such interaction terms.

Frequently, economists are interested in elasticities rather than marginal effects. An **elasticity** measures the *relative* change in the dependent variable due to a *relative* change in one of the x_i variables. Often, elasticities are estimated directly from a linear regression model involving the logarithms of most explanatory variables (excluding dummy variables), that is

$$\log y_i = (\log x_i)'\gamma + v_i, \tag{3.6}$$

where $\log x_i$ is shorthand notation for a vector with elements $(1, \log x_{i2}, \ldots, \log x_{iK})'$ and it is assumed that $E\{v_i| \log x_i\} = 0$. We shall call this a **loglinear model**. In this case,

$$\frac{\partial E\{y_i|x_i\}}{\partial x_{ik}} \cdot \frac{x_{ik}}{E\{y_i|x_i\}} \approx \frac{\partial E\{\log y_i| \log x_i\}}{\partial \log x_{ik}} = \gamma_k, \tag{3.7}$$

where the $\approx$ is due to the fact that $E\{\log y_i| \log x_i\} = E\{\log y_i|x_i\} \neq \log E\{y_i|x_i\}$. Note that (3.3) implies that in the linear model

$$\frac{\partial E\{y_i|x_i\}}{\partial x_{ik}} \cdot \frac{x_{ik}}{E\{y_i|x_i\}} = \frac{x_{ik}}{x_i'\beta} \beta_k, \tag{3.8}$$

which shows that the linear model implies that elasticities are *nonconstant* and vary with x_i, while the loglinear model imposes *constant* elasticities. While in many cases the choice of functional form is dictated by convenience in economic interpretation, other considerations may play a role. For example, explaining $\log y_i$ rather than y_i may help reducing heteroskedasticity problems, as illustrated in Section 3.5 below. In Section 3.3 we shall briefly consider statistical tests for a linear versus a loglinear specification.

If x_{ik} is a dummy variable (or another variable that may take nonpositive values) we cannot take its logarithm and we include the original variable in the model. Thus we estimate

$$\log y_i = x_i'\beta + \varepsilon_i. \tag{3.9}$$

Of course, it is possible to include some explanatory variables in logs and some in levels. In (3.9) the interpretation of a coefficient β_k is the *relative* change in y_i due to an *absolute* change of one unit in x_{ik}. So if x_{ik} is a dummy for males, β_k is the (ceteris paribus) relative wage differential between men and women. Again this holds only approximately, see Subsection 3.5.2.

The inequality of $E\{\log y_i|x_i\}$ and $\log E\{y_i|x_i\}$ also has some consequences for prediction purposes. Suppose we start from the loglinear model (3.6) with $E\{v_i| \log x_i\} = 0$. Then, we can determine the predicted value of $\log y_i$ as $(\log x_i)'\gamma$. However, if we are interested in predicting y_i rather than $\log y_i$, it is not the case that $\exp\{(\log x_i)'\gamma\}$ is a good predictor for y_i in the sense that it corresponds to the expected value of y_i, given x_i. That is, $E\{y_i|x_i\} \neq \exp\{E\{\log y_i|x_i\}\} = \exp\{(\log x_i)'\gamma\}$. The reason is that taking logarithms is a nonlinear transformation, while the expected value of a nonlinear function is not this nonlinear function of the expected value. The only way to get around this problem is to make distributional assumptions. If, for example, it can be assumed that v_i in (3.6) is normally distributed with mean zero and variance σ_v^2, it implies that the conditional distribution of y_i is lognormal (see Appendix B) with mean

$$E\{y_i|x_i\} = \exp\{E\{\log y_i|x_i\} + \tfrac{1}{2}\sigma_v^2\} = \exp\{(\log x_i)'\gamma + \tfrac{1}{2}\sigma_v^2\}. \tag{3.10}$$

Sometimes, the additional half-variance term is also added when the error terms are not assumed to be normal. Often, it is simply omitted.

It should be noted that the assumption that $E\{\varepsilon_i|x_i\} = 0$ is also important, as it says that changing x_i should not lead to changes in the expected error term. There are many cases in economics where this is hard to maintain and the models we are interested in do not correspond to conditional expectations. We shall come back to this issue in Chapter 5.

Another consequence of (3.2) is often overlooked. If we change the set of explanatory variables x_i to z_i, say, and estimate another regression model,

$$y_i = z_i'\gamma + v_i \tag{3.11}$$

with the interpretation that $E\{y_i|z_i\} = z_i'\gamma$, there is no conflict with the previous model that said that $E\{y_i|x_i\} = x_i'\beta$. Because the conditioning variables are different, both conditional expectations could be correct in the sense that both are linear in the conditioning variables. Consequently, if we interpret the regression models as describing the conditional expectation given the variables that are included there can never be any conflict between them. It is just two different things we might be interested in. For example, we may be interested in the expected wage as a function of gender only, but also in the expected wage as a function of gender, education and experience. Note that, because of a different ceteris paribus condition, the coefficients for gender in these two models do not have the same interpretation. Often, researchers implicitly or explicitly make the assumption that the set of conditioning variables is larger than those that are included. Sometimes, it is suggested that the model contains all relevant observable variables (implying that observables that are not included are in the conditioning set but irrelevant). If it would be argued, for example, that the two linear models above should be interpreted as

$$E\{y_i|x_i, z_i\} = z_i'\gamma$$

and

$$E\{y_i|x_i, z_i\} = x_i'\beta,$$

respectively, then the two models *are* typically in conflict and at most one of them can be correct.[1] Only in such cases, it makes sense to compare the two models statistically and to test, for example, which model is correct and which one is not. We come back to this issue in Subsection 3.2.3.

3.2　Selecting the Set of Regressors

3.2.1　Misspecifying the Set of Regressors

If one is (implicitly) assuming that the conditioning set of the model contains more variables than the ones that are included, it is possible that the set of explanatory variables is 'misspecified'. This means that one or more of the omitted variables are relevant, i.e. have nonzero coefficients. This raises two questions: what happens

---

[1] We abstract from trivial exceptions, like $x_i = -z_i$ and $\beta = -\gamma$.

when a relevant variable is excluded from the model and what happens when an irrelevant variable is included in the model? To illustrate this, consider the following two models

$$y_i = x_i'\beta + z_i'\gamma + \varepsilon_i, \qquad (3.12)$$

and

$$y_i = x_i'\beta + v_i, \qquad (3.13)$$

both interpreted as describing the conditional expectation of y_i given x_i, z_i (and may be some additional variables). The model in (3.13) is nested in (3.12) and implicitly assumes that z_i is irrelevant ($\gamma = 0$). What happens if we estimate model (3.13) while in fact model (3.12) is the correct model? That is, what happens when we omit z_i from the set of regressors?

The OLS estimator for β based on (3.13), denoted b_2, is given by

$$b_2 = \left(\sum_{i=1}^{N} x_i x_i' \right)^{-1} \sum_{i=1}^{N} x_i y_i. \qquad (3.14)$$

The properties of this estimator under model (3.12) can be determined by substituting (3.12) into (3.14) to obtain

$$b_2 = \beta + \left(\sum_{i=1}^{N} x_i x_i' \right)^{-1} \sum_{i=1}^{N} x_i z_i' \gamma + \left(\sum_{i=1}^{N} x_i x_i' \right)^{-1} \sum_{i=1}^{N} x_i \varepsilon_i. \qquad (3.15)$$

Depending upon the assumptions made for model (3.12), the last term in this expression will have an expectation or probability limit of zero.[2] The second term on the right hand side, however, corresponds to a bias (or asymptotic bias) in the OLS estimator due to estimating the incorrect model (3.13). This is referred to as an **omitted variable bias**. As expected, there will be no bias if $\gamma = 0$ (implying that the two models are identical), but there is one more case in which the estimator for β will not be biased and that is when $\sum_{i=1}^{N} x_i z_i' = 0$, or, asymptotically, when $E\{x_i z_i'\} = 0$. If this happens we say that x_i and z_i are **orthogonal**. This does not happen very often in economic applications. Note, for example, that the presence of an intercept in x_i implies that $E\{z_i\}$ should be zero.

The converse is less of a problem. If we estimate model (3.12) while in fact model (3.13) is appropriate, that is, we needlessly include the irrelevant variables z_i, we would simply be estimating the γ coefficients, which are zero. In this case, however, it would be preferable to estimate β from the restricted model (3.13) rather than from (3.12) because the latter estimator for β will usually have a higher variance and thus be less reliable. While the derivation of this result requires some tedious matrix manipulations, it is intuitively obvious: model (3.13) imposes more information, so that we can expect that the estimator that exploits this information is, on average, more accurate than one which does not. Thus, including irrelevant variables in your model, even though they have a zero coefficient, will typically increase the variance of the estimators for the other model parameters. Including as many variables as possible in a model is thus not a good strategy, while including too few variables

---

[2] Compare the derivations of the properties of the OLS estimator in Chapter 2.

has the danger of biased estimates. This means we need some guidance on how to select the set of regressors.

3.2.2 Selecting Regressors

Again, it should be stressed that if we interpret the regression model as describing the conditional expectation of y_i given the *included* variables x_i, there is no issue of a misspecified set of regressors, although there might be a problem of functional form (see the next section). This implies that statistically there is nothing to test here. The set of x_i variables will be chosen on the basis of what we find interesting and often economic theory or common sense guides us in our choice. Interpreting the model in a broader sense implies that there may be relevant regressors that are excluded or irrelevant ones that are included. To find potentially relevant variables we can use economic theory again. For example, when specifying an individual wage equation we may use the human capital theory which essentially says that everything that affects a person's productivity will affect his or her wage. In addition, we may use job characteristics (blue or white collar, shift work, public or private sector, etc.) and general labour market conditions (e.g. sectorial unemployment).

It is good practice to select the set of *potentially* relevant variables on the basis of economic arguments rather than statistical ones. Although it is sometimes suggested otherwise, statistical arguments are never certainty arguments. That is, there is always a small (but not ignorable) probability of drawing the wrong conclusion. For example, there is always a probability (corresponding to the size of the test) of rejecting the null hypothesis that a coefficient is zero, while the null is actually true. Such type I errors are rather likely to happen if we use a sequence of many tests to select the regressors to include in the model. This process is referred to as **data snooping** or **data mining** (see Leamer, 1978; Lovell, 1983; or Charemza and Deadman, 1992, Chapter 2), and in economics it is not a compliment if someone accuses you of doing it. In general, data snooping refers to the fact that a given set of data is used more than once to choose a model specification and to test hypotheses. You can imagine, for example, that if you have a set of 20 potential regressors and you try each one of them, that it is quite likely to conclude that one of them is significant, even though there is no true relationship between any of these regressors and the variable you are explaining. Although statistical software packages sometimes provide mechanical routines to select regressors, these are *not recommended* in economic work. The probability of making incorrect choices is high and it is not unlikely that your 'model' captures some peculiarities in the data that have no real meaning outside the sample. In practice however, it is hard to avoid that some amount of data snooping enters your work. Even if you do not perform your own specification search and happen to 'know' which model to estimate, this 'knowledge' may be based upon the successes and failures of past investigations. Nevertheless, it is important to be aware of the problem. In recent years, the possibility of data snooping biases plays an important role in empirical studies that model stock returns. Lo and MacKinlay (1990), for example, analyse such biases in tests of financial asset pricing models, while Sullivan, Timmermann and White (1998) analyse to what extent the presence of calendar effects in stock returns, like the January effect discussed in Section 2.7, can be attributed to data snooping.

The danger of data mining is particularly high if the specification search is from simple to general. In this approach, you start with a simple model and you include additional variables or lags of variables until the specification appears adequate. That is, until the restrictions imposed by the model are no longer rejected and you are happy with the signs of the coefficient estimates and their significance. Clearly, such a procedure may involve a very large number of tests. An alternative approach is the **general-to-specific modelling** approach advocated by Professor David Hendry and some of his colleagues from the London School of Economics. This approach starts by estimating a general and fairly unrestricted model, which is subsequently reduced in size and complexity by testing for restrictions that can be imposed. See Charemza and Deadman (1992) for an extensive treatment. In practice, most applied researchers will start somewhere 'in the middle' with a specification that could be appropriate and, ideally, then test (1) whether restrictions imposed by the model are correct and test (2) whether restrictions not imposed by the model could be imposed. In the first category are misspecification tests for omitted variables, but also for autocorrelation and heteroskedasticity (see Chapter 4). In the second category are tests of parametric restrictions, for example that one or more explanatory variables have zero coefficients.

In presenting your estimation results, it is not a 'sin' to have insignificant variables included in your specification. The fact that your results do not show a significant effect on y_i of some variable x_{ik} is informative to the reader and there is no reason to hide it by re-estimating the model while excluding x_{ik}. Of course, you should be careful including many variables in your model that are multicollinear so that, in the end, almost none of the variables appears individually significant.

Besides formal statistical tests there are other criteria that are sometimes used to select a set of regressors. First of all, the R^2, discussed in Section 2.4 measures the proportion of the sample variation in y_i that is explained by variation in x_i. It is clear that if we were to extend the model by including z_i in the set of regressors, the explained variation would never decrease, so that also the R^2 will never decrease if we include additional variables in the model. Using the R^2 as criterion would thus favour models with as many explanatory variables as possible. This is certainly not optimal, because with too many variables we will not be able to say very much about the model's coefficients, as they may be estimated rather inaccurately. Because the R^2 does not 'punish' the inclusion of many variables, one would better use a measure which incorporates a trade off between goodness-of-fit and the number of regressors employed in the model. One way to do this, is to use the adjusted R^2 (or $\bar{R}^2$), as discussed in the previous chapter. Writing it as

$$\bar{R}^2 = 1 - \frac{1/(N-K)\sum_{i=1}^{N} e_i^2}{1/(N-1)\sum_{i=1}^{N}(y_i - \bar{y})^2} \tag{3.16}$$

and noting that the denominator in this expression is unaffected by the model under consideration, shows that the adjusted R^2 provides a trade-off between goodness-of-fit, as measured by $\sum_{i=1}^{N} e_i^2$, and the simplicity or parsimony of the model, as measured by the number of parameters K. There exist a number of alternative criteria that

provide such a trade-off, the most common ones being **Akaike's Information Criterion**
(*AIC*), proposed by Akaike (1973), given by

$$AIC = \log \frac{1}{N} \sum_{i=1}^{N} e_i^2 + \frac{2K}{N} \tag{3.17}$$

and the **Schwarz Bayesian Information Criterion** (*BIC*), proposed by Schwarz (1978),
which is given by

$$BIC = \log \frac{1}{N} \sum_{i=1}^{N} e_i^2 + \frac{K}{N} \log N. \tag{3.18}$$

Models with a lower *AIC* or *BIC* are typically preferred. Note that both criteria add a
penalty that increases with the number of regressors. Because the penalty is larger for
BIC, the latter criterion tends to favour more parsimonious models than *AIC*. The
use of either of these criteria is usually restricted to cases where alternative models are
not nested (see Subsection 3.2.3) and economic theory provides no guidance on
selecting the appropriate model. A typical situation is the search for a parsimonious
model that describes the dynamic process of a particular variable (see Chapter 8).

Alternatively, it is possible to test whether the increase in R^2 is statistically significant. Testing this is exactly the same as testing whether the coefficients for the newly
added variables z_i are all equal to zero, and we have seen a test for that in the previous
chapter. Recall from (2.59) that the appropriate *F*-statistic can be written as

$$f = \frac{(R_1^2 - R_0^2)/J}{(1 - R_1^2)/(N - K)}, \tag{3.19}$$

where R_1^2 and R_0^2 denote the R^2 in the model with and without z_i, respectively, and J is
the number of variables in z_i. Under the null hypothesis that z_i has zero coefficients,
the f statistic has an F distribution with J and $N - K$ degrees of freedom, provided we
can impose conditions (A1)–(A5) from Chapter 2. The *F*-test thus provides a statistical answer to the question whether the increase in R^2 due to including z_i in the model
was significant or not. It is also possible to rewrite f in terms of adjusted R^2s. This
would show that $\bar{R}_1^2 > \bar{R}_0^2$ if and only if f exceeds a certain threshold. In general, these
thresholds do not correspond to 5% or 10% critical values of the F distribution, but
are substantially smaller. In particular, it can be shown that $\bar{R}_1^2 > \bar{R}_0^2$ if and only if the
f statistic is larger than one. For a single variable ($J = 1$) this implies that the adjusted
R^2 will increase if the additional variable has a t-ratio with an absolute value larger
than unity. (Recall that for a single restriction $t^2 = f$.) This reveals that the adjusted
R^2 would lead to the inclusion of more variables than standard t or *F*-tests.

Direct tests of the hypothesis that the coefficients γ for z_i are zero can be obtained
from the t and *F*-tests discussed in the previous chapter. Compared to f above, a test
statistic can be derived which is more generally appropriate. Let $\hat{\gamma}$ denote the OLS
estimator for γ and let $\hat{V}\{\hat{\gamma}\}$ denote an estimated covariance matrix for $\hat{\gamma}$. Then, it can
be shown that under the null hypothesis that $\gamma = 0$ the test statistic

$$\xi = \hat{\gamma}' \hat{V}\{\hat{\gamma}\}^{-1} \hat{\gamma} \tag{3.20}$$

has an asymptotic χ^2 distribution with J degrees of freedom. This is similar to the
Wald test described in Chapter 2 (compare (2.63)). The form of the covariance matrix

of $\hat{\gamma}$ depends upon the assumptions we are willing to make. Under the Gauss–Markov assumptions we would obtain a statistic that satisfies $\xi = Jf$.

It is important to recall that two single tests are not equivalent to one joint test. For example, if we are considering the exclusion of two single variables with coefficients γ_1 and γ_2, the individual t-tests may not reject both $\gamma_1 = 0$ and $\gamma_2 = 0$, while the joint F-test (or Wald test) does reject the joint restriction $\gamma_1 = \gamma_2 = 0$. The message here is that if we want to drop two variables from the model *at the same time*, we should be looking at a joint test rather than at two separate tests. Once the first variable is omitted from the model, the second one may appear significant. This is particularly of importance if collinearity exists between the two variables.

3.2.3 Comparing Non-nested Models

Sometimes econometricians want to compare two different models that are not nested. In this case neither of the two models is obtained as a special case of the other. Such a situation may arise if two alternative economic theories lead to different models for the same phenomenon. Let us consider the following two alternative specifications:

$$\text{Model A: } y_i = x_i'\beta + \varepsilon_i \tag{3.21}$$

and

$$\text{Model B: } y_i = z_i'\gamma + v_i, \tag{3.22}$$

where both are interpreted as describing the conditional expectation of y_i given x_i and z_i. The two models are non-nested if z_i includes a variable that is not in x_i and vice versa. Because both models are explaining the same endogenous variable, it is possible to use the $\bar{R}^2$, *AIC* or *BIC* criteria, discussed in the previous subsection. An alternative and more formal idea that can be used to compare the two models is that of **encompassing** (see Mizon, 1984; Mizon and Richard, 1986): if model A is believed to be the correct model it must be able to encompass model B, that is, it must be able to explain model B's results. If model A is unable to do so, it has to be rejected. Vice versa, if model B is unable to encompass model A, it should be rejected as well. Consequently, it is possible that both models have to be rejected, not because of type I errors, but because neither of them is correct. If model A is not rejected, we can test it against another rival model and maintain it as long as it is not rejected.

The encompassing principle is very general and it is legitimate to require a model to encompass its rivals. If these rival models are nested within the current model, they are automatically encompassed by it, because a more general model is always able to explain results of simpler models (compare (3.15) above). If the models are not nested encompassing is nontrivial. Unfortunately, encompassing tests for general models are fairly complicated, but for the regression models above things are relatively simple.

We shall consider two alternative tests. The first is the **non-nested F-test** or encompassing F-test. Writing $x_i' = (x_{1i}' \; x_{2i}')$ where x_{1i} is included in z_i (and x_{2i} is not), model B can be tested by constructing a so-called artificial nesting model as

$$y_i = z_i'\gamma + x_{2i}'\delta_A + v_i. \tag{3.23}$$

This model typically has no economic rationale, but reduces to Model B if $\delta_A = 0$. Thus, the validity of model B (model B encompasses model A) can be tested using an F-test for the restrictions $\delta_A = 0$. In a similar fashion, we can test the validity of Model A by testing $\delta_B = 0$ in

$$y_i = x_i'\beta + z_{2i}'\delta_B + \varepsilon_i, \tag{3.24}$$

where z_{2i} contains the variables from z_i that are not included in x_i. The null hypotheses that are tested here state that one model encompasses the other. The outcome of the two tests may be that both models have to be rejected. On the other hand, it is also possible that neither of the two models is rejected. Thus the fact that model A is rejected should not be interpreted as evidence in favour of model B. It just indicates that something is captured by model B which is not adequately taken into account in model A.

A more parsimonious non-nested test is the **J-test**. Let us start again from an artificial nesting model that nests both model A and model B, given by

$$y_i = (1 - \delta)x_i'\beta + \delta z_i'\gamma + u_i, \tag{3.25}$$

where δ is a scalar parameter and u_i denotes the error term. If $\delta = 0$, equation (3.25) corresponds to model A and if $\delta = 1$ it reduces to model B. Unfortunately, the nesting model (3.25) cannot be estimated because in general β, γ and δ cannot be separately identified. One solution to this problem (suggested by Davidson and MacKinnon, 1981) is to replace the unknown parameters γ by $\hat{\gamma}$, the OLS estimates from model B, and to test the hypothesis that $\delta = 0$ in

$$y_i = x_i'\beta^* + \delta z_i'\hat{\gamma} + u_i = x_i'\beta^* + \delta \hat{y}_{iB} + u_i, \tag{3.26}$$

where $\hat{y}_{iB}$ is the predicted value from model B and $\beta^* = (1 - \delta)\beta$. The J-test for the validity of model A uses the t-statistic for $\delta = 0$ in this last regression. Computationally, it simply means that the fitted value from the rival model is added to the model that we are testing and that we test whether its coefficient is zero using a standard t-test. Compared to the non-nested F-test, the J-test involves only one restriction. This means that the J-test may be more attractive (have more power) if the number of additional regressors in the non-nested F-test is large. If the non-nested F-test involves only one additional regressor, it is equivalent to the J-test. More details on non-nested testing can be found in Davidson and MacKinnon (1993, Sect. 11.3) and the references therein.

Another relevant case with two alternative models that are non-nested is the choice between a linear and loglinear functional form. Because the dependent variable is different (y_i and $\log y_i$, respectively) a comparison on the basis of goodness-of-fit measures, including AIC and BIC, is inappropriate. One way to test the appropriateness of the linear and loglinear models involves nesting them in a more general model using the so-called Box–Cox transformation (see Davidson and MacKinnon, 1993, Sect. 14.6), and comparing them against this more general alternative. Alternatively, an approach similar to the encompassing approach above can be chosen by making use of an artificial nesting model. A very simple procedure is the PE test, suggested by MacKinnon, White and Davidson (1983). First, estimate both the linear and loglinear models by OLS. Denote the predicted values by $\hat{y}_i$ and $\log \tilde{y}_i$, respectively. Then the linear model can be tested against its loglinear alternative by testing the null hypothesis that $\delta_{LIN} = 0$ in the test regression

$$y_i = x_i'\beta + \delta_{LIN}(\log \hat{y}_i - \log \tilde{y}_i) + u_i.$$

Similarly, the loglinear model corresponds to the null hypothesis $\delta_{LOG} = 0$ in

$$\log y_i = (\log x_i)'\gamma + \delta_{LOG}(\hat{y}_i - \exp\{\log \tilde{y}_i\}) + u_i.$$

Both tests can simply be based on the standard t-statistics, which under the null hypothesis have an approximate standard normal distribution. If $\delta_{LIN} = 0$ is not rejected, the linear model may be preferred. If $\delta_{LOG} = 0$ is not rejected, the loglinear model is preferred. If both hypotheses are rejected, neither of the two models appears to be appropriate and a more general model should be considered, for example by generalizing the functional form of the x_i variables in either the linear or the loglinear model.[3] An empirical illustration using the PE test is provided in Section 3.4.

3.3 Misspecifying the Functional Form

Although the assumptions made in interpreting the models are fairly weak, there is one important way in which the models may be misspecified and that is in their linearity. The interpretation that $E\{y_i|x_i\} = x_i'\beta$ implies that no other functions of x_i are relevant in explaining the expected value of y_i. This *is* restrictive and the main motivation for linear specifications is their convenience.

3.3.1 Nonlinear Models

Nonlinearities can arise in two different ways. In a first case, the model is still linear in the parameters but nonlinear in its explanatory variables. This means that we include nonlinear functions of x_i as additional explanatory variables, for example the variables age_i^2 and $age_i male_i$ could be included in an individual wage equation. The resulting model is still linear in the parameters and can still be estimated by ordinary least squares. In a second case, the model is nonlinear in its parameters and estimation is less easy. In general, this means that $E\{y_i|x_i\} = g(x_i, \beta)$, where $g(.)$ is a regression function nonlinear in β. For example, for a single x_i we could have that

$$g(x_i, \beta) = \beta_1 + \beta_2 x_i^{\beta_3} \tag{3.27}$$

or for a two-dimensional x_i

$$g(x_i, \beta) = \beta_1 x_{i1}^{\beta_2} x_{i2}^{\beta_3}, \tag{3.28}$$

which corresponds to a Cobb–Douglas production function with two inputs. As the second function is linear in parameters after taking logarithms (assuming $\beta_1 > 0$), it is

---

[3] It may be noted that with sufficiently general functional forms it is possible to obtain models for y_i and $\log y_i$ that are both correct in the sense that they represent $E\{y_i|x_i\}$ and $E\{\log y_i|x_i\}$, respectively. It is not possible, however, that both specifications have a homoskedastic error term (see the example in Section 3.5).

a common strategy in this case to model $\log y_i$ rather than y_i. This does not work for the first example.

Nonlinear models can also be estimated by a nonlinear version of the least squares method, by minimizing the objective function

$$S(\tilde{\beta}) = \sum_{i=1}^{N} (y_i - g(x_i, \tilde{\beta}))^2 \qquad (3.29)$$

with respect to $\tilde{\beta}$. This is called **nonlinear least squares** estimation. Unlike in the linear case, it is generally not possible to analytically solve for the value of $\tilde{\beta}$ that minimizes $S(\tilde{\beta})$ and we need to use numerical procedures to obtain the nonlinear least squares estimator. A necessary condition for consistency is that there exists a *unique* global minimum for $S(\tilde{\beta})$, which means that the model is identified. An excellent treatment of such nonlinear models is given in Davidson and MacKinnon (1993) and we will not pursue it here.

It is possible to rule out functional form misspecifications completely, by saying that one is interested in the *linear* function of x_i that approximates y_i as well as possible. This goes back to the initial interpretation of ordinary least squares as determining the linear combination of x-variables that approximates a variable y as well as possible. We can do the same thing in a statistical setting by relaxing the assumption that $E\{\varepsilon_i|x_i\} = 0$ to $E\{\varepsilon_i x_i\} = 0$. Recall that $E\{\varepsilon_i|x_i\} = 0$ implies that $E\{\varepsilon_i g(x_i)\} = 0$ for any function g (provided expectations exist), so that it is indeed a relaxation of assumptions. In this case, we can interpret the linear regression model as describing the best linear approximation of y_i from x_i. In many cases, we would interpret the linear approximation as an estimate for its population equivalent rather than just an in-sample result. Note that the condition $E\{\varepsilon_i x_i\} = 0$ corresponds to condition (A7) from Chapter 2 and is necessary for consistency of the OLS estimator.

3.3.2 Testing the Functional Form

A simple way to test the functional form of

$$E\{y_i|x_i\} = x_i'\beta \qquad (3.30)$$

would be to test whether additional nonlinear terms in x_i are significant. This can be done using standard t-tests, F-tests, or, more generally, Wald tests. This only works if one can be specific about the alternative. If the number of variables in x_i is large the number of possible tests is also large.

Ramsey (1969) has suggested a test based upon the idea that under the null hypothesis nonlinear functions of $\hat{y}_i = x_i'b$ should not help explaining y_i. In particular, he tests whether powers of $\hat{y}_i$ have nonzero coefficients in the auxiliary regression

$$y_i = x_i'\beta + \alpha_2\hat{y}_i^2 + \alpha_3\hat{y}_i^3 + \cdots + \alpha_Q\hat{y}_i^Q + v_i. \qquad (3.31)$$

An **auxiliary regression**, and we shall see several below, is typically used to compute a test statistic only, and is not meant to represent a meaningful model. In this case we can use a standard F-test for the $Q - 1$ restrictions in H_0: $\alpha_2 = \cdots = \alpha_Q = 0$, or a more general Wald test (with an asymptotic χ^2 distribution with $Q - 1$ degrees of freedom). These tests are usually referred to as **RESET tests** (regression equation specification error tests). Often, a test is performed for $Q = 2$ only. It is not unlikely that a RESET test rejects because of the omission of relevant variables from the model (in the sense defined earlier) rather than just a functional form misspecification. That is, the inclusion of an additional variable may capture the nonlinearities indicated by the test.

3.4 Illustration: Explaining House Prices

In this section we consider an empirical illustration concerning the relationship between sale prices of houses and their characteristics. The resulting price function can be referred to as a **hedonic price function**, because it allows the estimation of hedonic prices (see Rosen, 1974). A hedonic price refers to the implicit price of a certain attribute (e.g. the number of bedrooms) as revealed by the sale price of a house. In this context, a house is considered as a bundle of such attributes. Typical products for which hedonic price functions are estimated are computers, cars and houses. For our purpose, the important conclusion is that a hedonic price function describes the expected price (or log price) as a function of a number of characteristics. Berndt (1990, Chapter 4) discusses additional economic and econometric issues relating to the use, interpretation and estimation of such price functions.

The data we use[4] are taken from a recent study by Anglin and Gençay (1996) and contain sale prices of 546 houses, sold during July, August and September of 1987, in the city of Windsor, Canada, along with their important features. The following characteristics are available: the lot size of the property in square feet, the numbers of bedrooms, full bathrooms and garage places, and the number of stories. In addition there are dummy variables for the presence of a driveway, recreational room, full basement and central air conditioning, for being located in a preferred area and for using gas for hot water heating. To start our analysis, we shall first estimate a model that explains the log of the sale price from the log of the lot size, the numbers of bedrooms and bathrooms and the presence of air conditioning. OLS estimation produces the results in Table 3.1. These results indicate a reasonably high R^2 of 0.57 and fairly high t-ratios for all coefficients. The coefficient for the air conditioning dummy indicates that a house that has central air conditioning is expected to sell at a 21% higher price than a house without it, both houses having the same number of bedrooms and bathrooms and the same lot size. A 10% larger lot, ceteris paribus, increases the expected sale price by about 4%, while an additional bedroom is estimated to raise the price by almost 8%. The expected log sale price of a house with four bedrooms, one full bathroom, a lot size of 5000 sq. ft and no air conditioning can be computed as

$$7.094 + 0.400 \log(5000) + 0.079 \times 4 + 0.216 = 11.028,$$

which corresponds to an expected price of $\exp\{11.028 + 0.5 \times 0.2456^2\} = 63\,460$ Canadian dollars. The latter term in this expression corresponds to one half of the estimated error variance (s^2) and is based upon the assumption that the error term is normally distributed (see (3.10)). Omitting this term produces an expected price of

---

[4] The data are available as HOUSING.

Table 3.1   OLS results hedonic price function

Dependent variable: log(*price*)

Variable	Estimate	Standard error	t-ratio
constant	7.094	0.232	30.636
log(*lot size*)	0.400	0.028	14.397
bedrooms	0.078	0.015	5.017
bathrooms	0.216	0.023	9.386
air conditioning	0.212	0.024	8.923

$s = 0.2456$ $R = 0.5674$ $\bar{R}^2 = 0.5642$ $F = 177.41$

only 61 575 dollars. To appreciate the half-variance term, consider the fitted values of our model. Taking the exponential of these fitted values produces predicted prices for the houses in our sample. The average predicted price is 66 679 dollars, while the sample average of actual prices is 68 122. This indicates that without any corrections we would systematically underpredict prices. When the half-variance term is added, the average predicted price based on the model explaining log prices increases to 68 190, which is fairly close to the actual average.

To test the functional form of this simple specification, we can use the RESET test. This means that we generate predicted values from our model, take powers of them, include them in the original equation and test their significance. Note that these latter regressions are run for testing purposes only and are not meant to produce a meaningful model. Including the squared fitted value produces a t-statistic of 0.514 ($p = 0.61$), and including the squared and cubed fitted values gives an F-statistic of 0.56 ($p = 0.57$). Both tests do not indicate particular misspecifications of our model. Nevertheless, we may be interested in including additional variables in our model because prices may also be affected by characteristics like the number of garage places or its geographical location. To this end, we include all other variables in our model to obtain the specification that is reported in Table 3.2. Given that the R^2 increases to 0.68 and that all the individual t-statistics are larger than 2 this extended specification

Table 3.2   OLS results hedonic price function, extended model

Dependent variable: log(*price*)

Variable	Estimate	Standard error	t-ratio
constant	7.745	0.216	35.801
log(*lot size*)	0.303	0.027	11.356
bedrooms	0.034	0.014	2.410
bathrooms	0.166	0.020	8.154
air conditioning	0.166	0.021	7.799
driveway	0.110	0.028	3.904
recreational room	0.058	0.026	2.225
full basement	0.104	0.022	4.817
gas for hot water	0.179	0.044	4.079
garage places	0.048	0.011	4.178
preferred area	0.132	0.023	5.816
stories	0.092	0.013	7.268

$s = 0.2104$ $R^2 = 0.6865$ $\bar{R}^2 = 0.6801$ $F = 106.33$

appears to perform significantly better in explaining house prices than the previous one. A joint test on the hypothesis that all seven additional variables have a zero coefficient is provided by the F-test, where the test statistic is computed on the basis of the respective R^2s as

$$f = \frac{(0.6865 - 0.5674)/7}{(1 - 0.6865)/(546 - 12)} = 28.99,$$

which is highly significant for an F distribution with 7 and 532 degrees of freedom ($p = 0.000$). Looking at the point estimates, the ceteris paribus effect of a 10% larger lot size is now estimated to be only 30%. This is almost certainly due to the change in ceteris paribus condition, for example because houses with larger lot sizes tend to have a driveway relatively more often.[5] Similarly, the estimated impact of the other variables is reduced compared to the estimates in Table 3.1. As expected, all coefficient estimates are positive and relatively straightforward to interpret. Ceteris paribus, a house in a preferred neighbourhood of the city is expected to sell at a 13% higher price than a house located elsewhere.

As before we can test the functional form of the specification by performing one or more RESET tests. With a t-value of 0.06 for the squared fitted values and an F-statistic of 0.04 for the squared and cubed terms, there is again no evidence of misspecification of the functional form. It is possible though to consider more specific alternatives when testing the functional form. For example, one could hypothesize that an additional bedroom implies a larger price increase when the house is in a preferred neighbourhood. If this is the case, the model should include an interaction term between the location dummy and the number of bedrooms. If the model is extended to include this interaction term, the t-test on the new variable produces a highly insignificant value of -0.131. Overall, the current model appears surprisingly well specified.

The model allows us to compute the expected log sale price of an arbitrary house in Windsor. If you would own a 2-story house on a lot of 10 000 square feet, located in a preferred neighbourhood of the city, with 4 bedrooms, 1 bathroom, 2 garage places, a driveway, recreational room, air conditioning and a full and finished basement, using gas for water heating, the expected log price is 11.87. This indicates that the hypothetical price of your house, if sold in the summer of 1987, is estimated to be 179 000 Canadian dollars.

Instead of modelling log prices, we could also consider explaining prices. Table 3.3 reports the results of a regression model where prices are explained as a linear function of lot size and all other variables. Compared to the previous model the coefficients now reflect absolute differences in prices rather than relative differences. For example, the presence of a driveway (ceteris paribus) is expected to increase the house price by 6 688 dollars, while Table 3.2 implies an estimated increase of 11%. It is not directly clear from a comparison of the results in Tables 3.2 and 3.3 which of the two specifications is preferable. Recall that the R^2 does not provide an appropriate means of comparison. As discussed in Subsection 3.2.3, it is possible to test these two non-nested models against each other. Using the PE test we can test the two hypotheses that the linear model is appropriate and that the loglinear model is appropriate. When

---

[5] The sample correlation coefficient between log lot size and the driveway dummy is 0.29.

Table 3.3 OLS results hedonic price function, linear model

Dependent variable: *price*

Variable	Estimate	Standard error	t-ratio
constant	−4038.35	3409.47	−1.184
lot size	3.546	0.350	10.124
bedrooms	1832.00	1047.00	1.750
bathrooms	14335.56	1489.92	9.622
air conditioning	12632.89	1555.02	8.124
driveway	6687.78	2045.25	3.270
recreational room	4511.28	1899.96	2.374
full basement	5452.39	1588.02	3.433
gas for hot water	12831.41	3217.60	3.988
garage places	4244.83	840.54	5.050
preferred area	9369.51	1669.09	5.614
stories	6556.95	925.29	7.086

$s = 15423 \quad R^2 = 0.6731 \quad \bar{R}^2 = 0.6664 \quad F = 99.97$

testing the linear model we obtain a test statistic of −6.196. Given the critical values of a standard normal distribution, this implies that the specification in Table 3.3 has to be rejected. This does not automatically imply that the specification in Table 3.2 is appropriate. Nevertheless, when testing the loglinear model (where only price and lot size are in logs) we find a test statistic of −0.569, so that it is not rejected.

3.5   Illustration: Explaining Individual Wages

It is a well-known fact that the average hourly wage rates of males are higher than those of females for almost all industrialized countries. In this section, we analyse this phenomenon for Belgium. In particular, we want to find out whether factors such as education level and experience can explain the wage differential. For this purpose we use a data set consisting of 1472 individuals, randomly sampled from the working population in Belgium for the year 1994. The data set, taken from the Belgian part of the European Community Household Panel, contains 893 males and 579 females.[6] The analysis is based on the following four variables:

wage	before tax hourly wage rate, in Belgian francs (Bef) per hour
male	1 if male, 0 if female
educ	education level, 1 = primary school,
	2 = lower vocational training, 3 = intermediate level,
	4 = higher vocational training, 5 = university level
exper	experience in years

Some summary statistics of these variables are given in Table 3.4. We see, for example, that the average wage rate for men is Bef 466.42 per hour (11.56 euro[7]), while for women it is only Bef 413.95 per hour, which corresponds to a difference of

---

[6] The data for this illustration are available as BWAGES.
[7] Conversion rate: 40.3399 Bef = 1 euro.

Table 3.4 Summary statistics, 1472 individuals

	Males		Females	
	Mean	Standard dev.	Mean	Standard dev.
wage	466.42	191.77	413.95	153.64
educ	3.24	1.26	3.59	1.09
exper	18.52	10.25	15.20	9.70

Bef 52.47 or almost 13%. Because the average years of experience in the sample is lower for women than for men, this does not necessarily imply that there is wage discrimination against women.

3.5.1 Linear Models

A first model to estimate the effect of gender on the hourly wage rate, correcting for differences in experience and education level, is obtained by regressing *wage* upon *male*, *exper* and *educ*, the results of which are given in Table 3.5. If we interpret this model as describing the expected wage given gender, experience and education level, the ceteris paribus effect of gender is virtually identical to the average wage differential. Apparently, adjusting for differences in education and experience does not change the expected wage differential between males and females. Note that the difference is statistically highly significant, with a *t*-ratio of 6.984. As expected, the effect of experience, keeping the education level fixed, is positive: an additional year of experience increases the expected wage by somewhat less than Bef 8 per hour. Similarly, higher education levels substantially increase the expected wage. If we compare two people with two adjacent education levels but of the same gender and having the same experience, the expected wage differential is approximately Bef 80 per hour. Given the high *t*-ratios, both the effects of *exper* and *educ* are statistically highly significant. The R^2 of the estimated model is 0.3656, which implies that more than 36% of the variation in individual wages can be attributed (linearly) to differences in gender, experience and education.

It could be argued that experience affects a person's wage nonlinearly: after many years of experience, the effect of an additional year on one's wage may become increasingly smaller. To model this, we can include the square of experience in the model, which we expect to have a negative coefficient. The results of this are given in Table 3.6. The additional variable $exper^2$ has a coefficient that is estimated to be negative, as expected. With a *t*-ratio of -5.487 we can safely reject the null hypothesis

Table 3.5 OLS results specification 1

Dependent variable: *wage*

Variable	Estimate	Standard error	t-ratio
constant	8.620	15.607	0.552
male	54.303	7.775	6.984
educ	80.119	3.253	24.629
exper	7.756	0.387	20.064

$s = 143.14$ $R = 0.3656$ $\bar{R}^2 = 0.3643$ $F = 281.98$

Table 3.6   OLS results specification 2

Dependent variable: *wage*

Variable	Estimate	Standard error	t-ratio
constant	−36.003	17.463	−2.062
male	53.801	7.700	6.988
educ	80.201	3.221	24.897
exper	14.442	1.277	11.309
exper^2	−0.176	0.032	−5.487

$s = 141.75$ $R^2 = 0.3783$ $\bar{R}^2 = 0.3766$ $F = 223.20$

that squared experience has a zero coefficient and we can conclude that including *exper*^{2} significantly improves the model. Note that the adjusted R^2 has increased from 0.3643 to 0.3766. Given the presence of both experience and its square in the specification, we cannot interpret their coefficients in isolation. One way to describe the effect of experience is to say that the expected wage difference through a marginal increase of experience, is, ceteris paribus, given by (differentiate with respect to experience as in (3.4)):

$$14.44 - 0.18 \times 2 \times exper_i,$$

which shows that the effect of experience differs with its level. Initially, it is as big as Bef 14.44 per hour, but it reduces to Bef 3.87 for a person with 30 years of experience. Alternatively, we can simply compare predicted wages for a person with, say, 30 years of experience and one with 31 years. The estimated wage difference is then given by

$$14.44 - 0.18(31^2 - 30^2) = 3.69,$$

which produces a slightly lower estimate. The difference is caused by the fact that the first number is based on the effect of a 'marginal' change in experience (it is a derivative), while an increase of 1 year is not really marginal.

   Before continuing our statistical analysis, it is important to analyse to what extent the assumptions regarding the error terms are satisfied in this example. Recall that for the standard errors and statistical tests to be valid, we need to exclude both autocorrelation and heteroskedasticity. Given that there is no natural ordering in the data and individuals are randomly sampled, autocorrelation is not an issue, but heteroskedasticity could be problematic. While we shall see some formal tests for heteroskedasticity in Chapter 4, a quick way to get some insight into the likelihood of the failure of the homoskedasticity assumption is to make a graph of the residuals of the model against the predicted values. If there is no heteroskedasticity, we can expect that the dispersion of residuals does not vary with different levels of the fitted values. For the model in Table 3.6, we present such a graph in Figure 3.1.

   Figure 3.1 clearly shows an increased variation in the residuals for higher fitted values and thus casts serious doubt on the assumption of homoskedasticity. This implies that the routinely computed standard errors and corresponding t-tests are not appropriate.

   One way to eliminate or reduce the heteroskedasticity problem is provided by changing the functional form and use log wages rather than wages as the explanatory

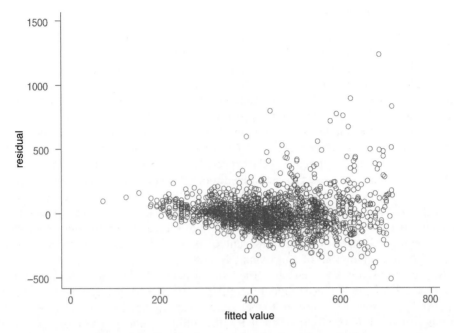

Figure 3.1 Residuals versus fitted values, linear model

variable. Why this may help solving the problem can be seen as follows. Let us denote the current model as

$$w_i = g(x_i) + \varepsilon_i, \tag{3.32}$$

where $g(x_i)$ is a function of x_i that predicts the wage w_i (e.g. $x_i'\beta$) and ε_i is an error term that has mean zero (conditional upon x_i). This is an additive model in the sense that the error term is added to the predicted value. It is also possible to consider a multiplicative model of the form

$$w_i = g(x_i) \exp\{\eta_i\}, \tag{3.33}$$

where η_i is an error term that has mean zero (conditional upon x_i). It is easily verified that the two models are equivalent if $g(x_i)[\exp\{\eta_i\} - 1] = \varepsilon_i$. If η_i is homoskedastic, it is clear that ε_i is heteroskedastic with a variance that depends upon $g(x_i)$. If we thus find heteroskedasticity in the additive model, it could be the case that a multiplicative model is appropriate with a homoskedastic error term. The multiplicative model can easily be written as an additive model, with an additive error term, by taking logarithms. This gives

$$\log w_i = \log g(x_i) + \eta_i = f(x_i) + \eta_i. \tag{3.34}$$

In our case $g(x_i) = x_i'\beta$. Estimation of (3.34) becomes simple if we assume that the function f is such that $\log g(x_i)$ is a linear function of the parameters. Typically, this involves the inclusion of logs of the x-variables (excluding dummy variables), so that we obtain a loglinear model (compare (3.6)).

3.5.2 Loglinear Models

In our next specification, we estimate a loglinear model that explains the log of the hourly wage rate from gender, the log of experience, the squared log of experience and the log of education. (Note that the log of experience squared is perfectly collinear with the log of experience.) This gives the results in Table 3.7. Because the endogenous variable is different, the R^2 is not really comparable to those for the models that explain the hourly wage rate, but it happens to be almost the same. The interpretation of the coefficient estimates is also different from before. The coefficient of *male* now measures the *relative* difference in expected wages for males and females. In particular, the ceteris paribus difference of the expected log wage between men and women is 0.118. If a woman is expected to earn an amount w^*, a comparable man is expected to earn $\exp\{\log w^* + 0.118\} = w^* \exp\{0.118\} = w^*1.125$, which corresponds to a difference of approximately 12%. Because $\exp(a) \approx 1 + a$ if a is close to zero, it is common in loglinear models to make the direct transformation from the estimated coefficients to percentage changes. Thus a coefficient of 0.118 for males is interpreted as an expected wage differential of approximately 11.8%.

Before continuing, let us consider the issue of heteroskedasticity again. A plot of the residuals of the loglinear model against the predicted log wages is provided in Figure 3.2. While there appear to be some traces of heteroskedasticity still, the graph is much less pronounced than for the additive model. Therefore, we shall continue to work with specifications that explain log wages rather than wages and, where needed, assume that the errors are homoskedastic. In particular, we shall assume that standard errors and routinely computed t and F-tests are appropriate. Chapter 4 provides some additional discussion on tests for heteroskedasticity and how it can be handled.

The coefficients for log experience and its square are somewhat hard to interpret. If $\log^2(exper)$ were excluded, the estimated coefficient for $\log(exper)$ would simply imply an expected wage increase of approximately 11% for an experience increase of 1%. In the current case, we can estimate the elasticity as

$$0.110 + 2 \times 0.026 \log(exper).$$

It is surprising to see that this elasticity is increasing with experience. This, however, is not in conflict with our earlier finding that suggested that the effect of experience is positive but decreasing with its level. The effects of $\log(exper)$ and $\log^2(exper)$ are, individually, marginally significant at the 5% level but insignificant at the 1% level. (Note that given the large number of observations a size of 1% may be considered

Table 3.7 OLS results specification 3

Dependent variable: log(*wage*)

Variable	Estimate	Standard error	t-ratio
constant	4.960	0.066	74.765
male	0.118	0.016	7.574
$\log(educ)$	0.442	0.018	24.306
$\log(exper)$	0.110	0.054	2.019
$\log^2(exper)$	0.026	0.011	2.266

$s = 0.286$ $R^2 = 0.3783$ $\bar{R}^2 = 0.3766$ $F = 223.13$

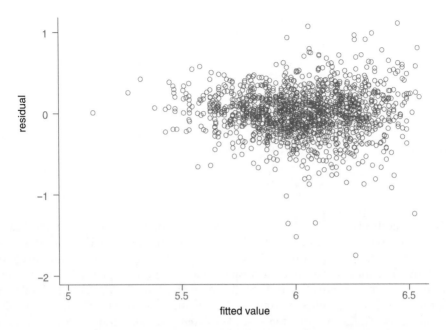

Figure 3.2 Residuals against fitted values, loglinear model

more appropriate.) This does not necessarily mean that experience has no significant effect upon wages. To that end, we need to consider a joint test for the two restrictions. The test statistic can be computed from the R^2s of the above model and a restricted model that excludes both $\log(exper)$ and $\log^2(exper)$. This restricted model has an R^2 of only 0.1798, such that an F-statistic can be computed as

$$f = \frac{(0.3783 - 0.1798)/2}{(1 - 0.3783)/(1472 - 5)} = 234.2,$$
(3.35)

which indicates a remarkable strong rejection. We could consider dropping one of the two variables that involve experience. If we drop $\log^2(exper)$, we obtain the results in Table 3.8, which show that the resulting model only has a slightly worse fit.

Let us consider this reduced specification in more detail. Because the effect of education is restricted to be linear in the log of the education level, the ceteris paribus difference in expected log wages between two persons with education levels *educ*1 and

Table 3.8 OLS results specification 4

Dependent variable: log(*wage*)

Variable	Estimate	Standard error	*t*-ratio
constant	4.842	0.041	117.581
male	0.120	0.016	7.715
log(*educ*)	0.437	0.018	24.188
log(*exper*)	0.231	0.011	21.488

$s = 0.287$ $R^2 = 0.3761$ $\bar{R} = 0.3748$ $F = 294.96$

Table 3.9   OLS results specification 5

Dependent variable: log(*wage*)

Variable	Estimate	Standard error	t-ratio
constant	4.969	0.045	110.835
male	0.118	0.015	7.610
educ = 2	0.114	0.033	4.306
educ = 3	0.305	0.033	9.521
educ = 4	0.474	0.032	14.366
educ = 5	0.639	0.033	19.237
log(*exper*)	0.230	0.011	21.804

$s = 0.282$ $R^2 = 0.3976$ $\bar{R}^2 = 0.3951$ $F = 161.14$

*educ*2, respectively, is $0.437(\log(educ1) - \log(educ2))$. So compared to the lowest education level 1, the effects of levels 2–5 are estimated as 0.30, 0.48, 0.61 and 0.70, respectively. It is also possible to unrestrictedly estimate these four effects by including four dummy variables corresponding to the four higher education levels. The results of this are provided in Table 3.9. Note that with five educational levels, the inclusion of four dummies is sufficient to capture all effects. By including five dummies, we would fall into the so-called **dummy variable trap**, and exact multi-collinearity would arise. Which of the five dummy variables is excluded is immaterial; it only matters for the economic interpretation of the other dummies' coefficients. The omitted category acts as reference group and all effects are relative to this group. In this example, the reference category has education level one.

Looking at the results in Table 3.9, we see that each of the four dummy variables is individually highly significant, with coefficients that deviate somewhat from the effects estimated on the basis of the restricted model. In fact, the previous model is nested within the current model and imposes three restrictions. While it is somewhat complicated to determine analytical expressions for these three restrictions, we can easily test them using the R^2 version of the F-test. This gives

$$f = \frac{(0.3976 - 0.3761)/3}{(1 - 0.3976)/(1472 - 7)} = 17.358. \tag{3.36}$$

As the 1% critical value for an F distribution with 3 and 1465 degrees of freedom is given by 3.78, the null hypothesis has to be rejected. That is, specification 5 with educational dummies is a significant improvement over specification 4 with the log education level.

3.5.3   The Effects of Gender

Until now the effect of gender was assumed to be constant, irrespective of a person's experience or education level. As it is possible, for example, that men are differently rewarded than women for having more education, this may be restrictive. It is possible to allow for such differences by interacting each of the explanatory variables with the gender dummy. One way to do so is to include the original regressor variables as well as the regressors multiplied by *male*. This way the coefficients for the latter set of variables measure to what extent the effect is different for males.

Table 3.10   OLS results specification 6

Dependent variable: log(*wage*)

Variable	Estimate	Standard error	*t*-ratio
constant	4.913	0.078	63.251
male	0.154	0.095	1.615
educ = 2	0.224	0.068	3.316
educ = 3	0.433	0.063	6.851
educ = 4	0.602	0.063	9.585
educ = 5	0.755	0.065	11.673
log(*exper*)	0.207	0.017	12.535
educ = 2 × *male*	−0.097	0.078	−1.242
educ = 3 × *male*	−0.167	0.073	−2.272
educ = 4 × *male*	−0.172	0.074	−2.317
educ = 5 × *male*	−0.146	0.076	−1.935
log(*exper*) × *male*	0.041	0.021	1.891

$s = 0.281$ $R^2 = 0.4032$ $\bar{R}^2 = 0.3988$ $F = 89.69$

Including interactions for all five variables produces the results in Table 3.10. An exactly equivalent set of results would have been obtained if we estimate the model separately for the two subsamples of males and females. The only advantage of estimating over the subsamples is the fact that in computing the standard errors it is assumed that the error terms are homoskedastic *within each subsample*, while the pooled model in Table 3.10 imposes homoskedasticity over the entire sample. This explains why estimated standard errors will be different, a large difference corresponding to strong heteroskedasticity. The coefficient estimates are exactly identical. This follows directly from the definition of the OLS estimator: minimizing the sum of squared residuals with different coefficients for two subsamples is exactly equivalent to minimizing for each subsample separately.

The results in Table 3.10 do not indicate important significant differences between men and women in the effect of experience. There are some indications, however, that the effect of education is lower for men than for women, as two of the four education dummies interacted with male are significant at the 5% level, though not at the 1% level. Note that the coefficient for *male* no longer reflects the gender effect, as the other variables are a function of gender as well. The estimated wage differential between a male and female of, say, 20 years of experience and education level 2 can be computed as

$$0.154 + 0.041 \log(20) - 0.097 = 0.180,$$

corresponding to somewhat more than 18%. To statistically test the joint hypothesis that each of the five coefficients of the variables interacted with *male* are zero, we can easily compute an *F*-test from the R^2s in Tables 3.10 and 3.9. This results in

$$f = \frac{(0.4032 - 0.3976)/5}{(1 - 0.4032)/(1472 - 12)} = 2.7399,$$

which does not exceed the 1% critical value of 3.01, but does reject at the 5% level. As a more general specification test, we can perform Ramsey's RESET test. Including the

Table 3.11 OLS results specification 7

Dependent variable: log(wage)

Variable	Estimate	Standard error	t-ratio
constant	5.186	0.212	24.460
male	0.116	0.015	7.493
educ = 2	0.067	0.226	0.297
educ = 3	0.135	0.219	0.618
educ = 4	0.205	0.219	0.934
educ = 5	0.341	0.218	1.565
log(exper)	0.163	0.065	2.494
log(exper) × educ = 2	0.019	0.070	0.274
log(exper) × educ = 3	0.050	0.068	0.731
log(exper) × educ = 4	0.088	0.069	1.277
log(exper) × educ = 5	0.100	0.068	1.465

$s = 0.281$ $R^2 = 0.4012$ $\bar{R}^2 = 0.3971$ $F = 97.90$

square of the fitted value to the specification in Table 3.10, produces a t-statistic of 3.989, which implies rejection at both the 5% and 1% level.

A final specification that we explore involves interaction terms between experience and education, which allows the effect of education to be different across education levels and at the same time allows the effects of different education levels to vary with experience. To do so, we interacted log(exper) with each of the four education dummies. The results are reported in Table 3.11. The coefficient for log(exper) interacted with educ = 2 measures to what extent the effect of experience is different for education level 2 in comparison with the reference category, being education level 1. The results do not indicate any important interaction effects between experience and education. Individually, each of the four coefficients does not differ significantly from zero, and jointly, the F-test produces the insignificant value of 2.196.

Apparently, this last specification suffers from multicollinearity. Almost none of the individual coefficients is significant, while the R^2 is reasonably large. Note that a joint test on all coefficients, except the intercept, being zero produces the highly significant value of 97.90. Finally, we perform a RESET test (with $Q = 2$) on this model, which produces a t-value of 2.13, which is insignificant at the 1% level. Nevertheless, specification 6 in Table 3.10 seems more appropriate than the current one.

3.5.4 Some Words of Warning

Despite our relatively careful statistical analysis, we still have to be cautious in interpreting the resulting estimates economically. The educational level, for example, will to a large extent capture differences in the type of jobs people are employed in. That is, the effect of education, as measured by the models' coefficients, will typically operate through a person's job characteristics. Thus the educational effect cannot be interpreted to hold for people *that have the same job*, besides having the same experience and gender. Of course, this is a direct consequence of not including 'job type' in the model, such that it is not captured by our ceteris paribus condition.

Another issue is that the model is only estimated for the subpopulation of working males and females. There is no reason why it would be valid to extend the estimation results to also explain wages of non-workers that consider entering the labour market. It may well be the case that selection into the labour market is nonrandom and depends upon potential wages, which would lead to a so-called selection bias in the OLS estimator. To take this into account, it is possible to model wages jointly with the decision to join the labour market and we shall discuss a class of models for such problems in Chapter 7.

We should also be careful of interpreting the coefficient for education as measuring the *causal* effect. That is, if we would increase the education level of an arbitrary person in the sample, the expected effect upon his or her wage may not correspond to the estimated coefficient. The reason is that education is typically correlated with unobserved characteristics (intelligence, ability) that also determine a person's wage. In this sense, the effect of education as estimated by OLS is partly due to differences in unobserved characteristics of people attaining the different education levels. Chapter 5 comes back to this problem.

Exercises

Exercise 3.1 (Specification Issues)

a. Explain what is meant by 'data mining'.

b. Explain why it is inappropriate to drop two variables from the model at the same time on the basis of their t-ratios only.

c. Explain the usefulness of the $\bar{R}^2$, AIC and BIC criteria to compare two models that are nested.

d. Consider two non-nested regression models explaining the same variable y_i. How can you test one against the other?

e. Explain why a functional form test (like Ramsey's RESET test) may indicate an omitted variable problem.

Exercise 3.2 (Regression – Empirical)

In the data set CLOTHING information is contained on sales, size and other characteristics of 400 Dutch men's fashion stores. The goal is to explain sales per square metre (*sales*) from the characteristics of the shop (number of owners, full-time and part-time workers, number of hours worked, shop size, etc.).

a. Estimate a linear model (model A) that explains *sales* from total number of hours worked (*hoursw*), shop size in square metres (*ssize*) and a constant. Interpret the results.

b. Perform Ramsey's RESET test with $Q = 2$.

c. Test whether the number of owners (*nown*) affects shop sales, conditional upon *hoursw* and *ssize*.

d. Also test whether the inclusion of the number of part-time workers (*npart*) improves the model.

e. Estimate a linear model (model B) that explains *sales* from the number of owners, full-time workers (*nfull*), part-time workers and shop size. Interpret the results.

f. Compare model A and model B on the basis of $\bar{R}^2$, *AIC* and *BIC*.

g. Perform a non-nested F-test of model A against model B. Perform a non-nested F-test of model B against model A. What do you conclude?

h. Repeat the above test using the J-test. Does your conclusion change?

i. Include the numbers of full-time and of part-time workers in model A to obtain model C. Estimate this model. Interpret the results and perform a RESET test. Are you satisfied with this specification?

Exercise 3.3 (Regression – Empirical)

The data set HOUSING contains the data of the models estimated in Section 3.4.

a. Create four dummy variables relating to the number of bedrooms, corresponding to 2 or less, 3, 4, and 5 or more. Estimate a model for log prices that includes log lot size, the number of bathrooms, the air conditioning dummy and three of these dummies. Interpret the results.

b. Why is the model under **a** not nested in the specification that is reported in Table 3.1?

c. Perform two non-nested F-tests to test these two specifications against each other. What do you conclude?

d. Include all four dummies in the model and re-estimate it. What happens? Why?

e. Suppose that lot size would be measured in square metres rather than square feet. How would this affect the estimation results in Table 3.2? Pay attention to the coefficient estimates, the standard errors and the R^2. How would the results in Table 3.3 be affected by this? Note: the conversion is $1m^2 = 10.76ft^2$.

4 Heteroskedasticity and Autocorrelation

In many empirical cases, the Gauss–Markov conditions (A1)–(A4) from Chapter 2 will not all be satisfied. As we have seen in Subsection 2.6.1, this is not necessarily fatal for the OLS estimator in the sense that it is consistent under fairly weak conditions. In this chapter we will discuss the consequences of heteroskedasticity and autocorrelation, which imply that the error terms in the model are no longer independently and identically distributed. In such cases, the OLS estimator may still be unbiased or consistent, but its covariance matrix is different from that derived in Chapter 2. Moreover, the OLS estimator may be relatively inefficient and no longer have the BLUE property.

In Section 4.1, we discuss the general consequences for the OLS estimator of an error covariance matrix that is not a constant times the identity matrix, while Section 4.2 presents, in a general matrix notation, an alternative estimator that is best linear unbiased in this more general case. Heteroskedasticity is treated in Sections 4.3–4.5, while the remaining sections of this chapter are devoted to autocorrelation. Examples of heteroskedasticity and its consequences are discussed in Section 4.3, while Section 4.4 describes a range of alternative tests. An empirical illustration involving hetero-skedastic error terms is presented in Section 4.5.

The basics of autocorrelation are treated in Sections 4.6 and 4.7, while a fairly simple illustration is given in Section 4.8. In Sections 4.9 and 4.10 attention is paid to some additional issues concerning autocorrelation, which includes a discussion of moving average error terms and so-called Newey–West standard errors. Finally, Section 4.11 has an extensive illustration on uncovered interest rate parity, which involves autocorrelation due to a so-called overlapping samples problem.

4.1   Consequences for the OLS Estimator

The model of interest is unchanged and given by

$$y_i = x_i'\beta + \varepsilon_i, \tag{4.1}$$

which can be written as

$$y = X\beta + \varepsilon. \tag{4.2}$$

The essential Gauss–Markov assumptions from (A1)–(A4) can be summarized as

$$E\{\varepsilon|X\} = E\{\varepsilon\} = 0 \tag{4.3}$$

$$V\{\varepsilon|X\} = V\{\varepsilon\} = \sigma^2 I, \tag{4.4}$$

which say that the conditional distribution of the errors given the matrix of explanatory variables has zero means, constant variances and zero covariances. In particular this means that each error has the same variance and that two different error terms are uncorrelated. These assumptions imply that $E\{\varepsilon_i|x_i\} = 0$, so that the model corresponds to the conditional expectation of y_i given x_i. Moreover, it was shown that the OLS estimator was the best linear unbiased estimator for β.

Both heteroskedasticity and autocorrelation imply that (4.4) no longer holds. Heteroskedasticity arises if different error terms do not have identical variances, so that the diagonal elements of the covariance matrix are not identical. For example, it is possible that different groups in the sample have different variances. It can also be expected that the variation of unexplained household savings increases with income, just as the level of savings will increase with income. Autocorrelation almost exclusively arises in cases where the data have a time dimension. It implies that the covariance matrix is nondiagonal such that different error terms are correlated. The reason could be persistence in the unexplained part of the model. Both of these problems will be discussed in more detail below, but for the moment it is important to note that they both violate (4.4). Let us assume that the error covariance matrix can more generally be written as

$$V\{\varepsilon|X\} = \sigma^2 \Psi, \tag{4.5}$$

where Ψ is a positive definite matrix, which, for the sake of argument, we will sometimes assume to be known. It is clear from the above that it may depend upon X.

If we reconsider the proof of unbiasedness of the OLS estimator, it is immediately clear that only assumption (4.3) was used. As this assumption is still imposed, assuming (4.5) instead of (4.4) will not change the result that the OLS estimator b is an unbiased estimator for β. However, the simple expression for the covariance matrix of b is no longer valid. In the more general case, we obtain (for a given matrix X)

$$V\{b|X\} = V\{(X'X)^{-1}X'\varepsilon|X\} = (X'X)^{-1}X'V\{\varepsilon|X\}X(X'X)^{-1}$$
$$= \sigma^2(X'X)^{-1}X'\Psi X(X'X)^{-1}, \tag{4.6}$$

which only reduces to the simpler expression $\sigma^2(X'X)^{-1}$ if Ψ is an identity matrix. Consequently, although the OLS estimator is still unbiased, its routinely computed variance and standard errors will be based on the wrong expression. Thus, standard t- and F-tests will no longer be valid and inferences will be misleading. In addition, the proof of the Gauss–Markov result that the OLS estimator is BLUE also breaks down, so that the OLS estimator is unbiased, but no longer best.

These consequences indicate two ways of handling the problems of heteroskedasticity and autocorrelation. The first implies the derivation of an alternative estimator that is best linear unbiased. The second implies sticking to the OLS estimator but somehow adjust the standard errors to allow for heteroskedasticity and/or autocorrelation. In fact, there is also a third way of eliminating the problems. The reason is that in many cases you may find heteroskedasticity and (particularly) autocorrelation because the model you are estimating is misspecified in one way or the other. If this is the case, detecting heteroskedasticity or autocorrelation should lead you to reconsider the model to evaluate to what extent you are confident in its specification. Examples of this will be discussed below.

For pedagogical purposes we shall first, in the next section, consider the derivation of an alternative estimator. It should be stressed, however, that this is in many cases not the most natural thing to do.

4.2   Deriving an Alternative Estimator

In this section we shall derive the best linear unbiased estimator for β under assumption (4.5) assuming that Ψ is completely known. The idea behind the derivation is that we know the best linear unbiased estimator under the Gauss–Markov assumptions (A1)–(A4), so that we transform the model such that it satisfies the Gauss–Markov conditions again, i.e. such that we obtain error terms that are homoskedastic and exhibit no autocorrelation. We start this by writing

$$\Psi^{-1} = P'P, \tag{4.7}$$

for some square, nonsingular matrix P, not necessarily unique. For the moment, it is not important how to find such a matrix P. It suffices to note that because Ψ is positive definite there will always exist a matrix P that satisfies (4.7). Using (4.7) it is possible to write

$$\Psi = (P'P)^{-1} = P^{-1}(P')^{-1}$$

$$P\Psi P' = PP^{-1}(P')^{-1}P' = I.$$

Consequently, it holds for the error term vector ε premultiplied by the transformation matrix P that

$$E\{P\varepsilon|X\} = PE\{\varepsilon|X\} = 0$$

$$V\{P\varepsilon|X\} = PV\{\varepsilon|X\}P' = \sigma^2 P\Psi P' = \sigma^2 I.$$

In other words, $P\varepsilon$ satisfies the Gauss–Markov conditions. Consequently, we can transform the entire model by this P matrix to obtain

$$Py = PX\beta + P\varepsilon \quad \text{or} \quad y^* = X^*\beta + \varepsilon^*, \tag{4.8}$$

where the error term vector ε^* satisfies the Gauss–Markov conditions. We know that applying ordinary least squares in this transformed model produces the best linear unbiased estimator for β.[1] This, therefore, is automatically the best linear unbiased estimator for β in the original model with assumptions (4.3) and (4.5). The resulting estimator is given by

$$\hat{\beta} = (X^{*\prime}X^*)^{-1}X^{*\prime}y^* = (X'\Psi^{-1}X)^{-1}X'\Psi^{-1}y. \tag{4.9}$$

This estimator is referred to as the **generalized least squares (GLS) estimator**. It is easily seen that it reduces to the OLS estimator if $\Psi = I$. Moreover, the choice of P is irrelevant for the estimator; only Ψ^{-1} matters. We shall see several examples of GLS estimators below which are easier to interpret than this general formula. The point to remember from this expression is that all the GLS estimators that we will see below are special cases of (4.9).

Clearly, we can only compute the GLS estimator if the matrix Ψ is known. In practice this will typically not be the case and Ψ will have to be estimated first. Using an estimated version of Ψ in (4.9) results in a **feasible generalized least squares** estimator for β, typically referred to as **FGLS** or **EGLS** (with the 'E' for estimated). This raises some additional issues that we will consider below.

The fact that the GLS estimator can be obtained as the OLS estimator in some transformed model not only has theoretical interest. On the contrary, it is fairly common to transform the observable variables yourself and apply standard OLS routines. The advantage of deriving the GLS estimator in this way is also that we do not have to derive a new covariance matrix or a new estimator for σ^2: we can simply use all the standard OLS results after replacing the original variables by their transformed counterparts. For example, the covariance matrix of $\hat{\beta}$ (for a given X) is given by

$$V\{\hat{\beta}\} = \sigma^2(X^{*\prime}X^*)^{-1} = \sigma^2(X'\Psi^{-1}X)^{-1}, \tag{4.10}$$

where σ^2 can be estimated by dividing the residual sum of squares by the number of observations minus the number of regressors, i.e.

$$\hat{\sigma}^2 = \frac{1}{N-K}(y^* - X^*\hat{\beta})'(y^* - X^*\hat{\beta}) = \frac{1}{N-K}(y - X\hat{\beta})'\Psi^{-1}(y - X\hat{\beta}). \tag{4.11}$$

The fact that $\hat{\beta}$ is BLUE implies that it has a smaller variance than the OLS estimator b. Indeed, it can be shown that the OLS covariance matrix (4.6) is larger than the GLS covariance matrix (4.10), in the sense that the matrix difference is positive semi-definite.

4.3 Heteroskedasticity

4.3.1 Introduction

The case where $V\{\varepsilon|X\}$ is diagonal, but not equal to σ^2 times the identity matrix, is referred to as **heteroskedasticity**. It means that the error terms are mutually uncorrelated, while the variance of ε_i may vary over the observations. This problem is

---

[1] Alternative transformation matrices P can be found such that the vector $P\varepsilon$ does not exhibit autocorrelation or heteroskedasticity. The requirement that P is nonsingular guarantees that no information is lost in the transformation.

frequently encountered in cross-sectional models. For example, consider the case where y_i denotes expenditure on food and x_i consists of a constant and disposable income DPI_i. An Engel curve for food is expected to be upward sloping (with decreasing slope). Thus, on average higher income corresponds with higher expenditure on food. In addition, one can expect that the variation of food expenditures among high-income households is much larger than the variation among low-income households. If this is the case, the variance of ε_i increases with income. This kind of heteroskedasticity could be modelled as

$$V\{\varepsilon_i | DPI_i\} = \sigma_i^2 = \sigma^2 \exp\{\alpha_2 DPI_i\} = \exp\{\alpha_1 + \alpha_2 DPI_i\} \tag{4.12}$$

for some α_2 and $\alpha_1 = \log \sigma^2$. For the moment, we will not make additional assumptions about the form of heteroskedasticity. We just assume that

$$V\{\varepsilon_i | X\} = V\{\varepsilon_i | x_i\} = \sigma^2 h_i^2, \tag{4.13}$$

where all h_i^2s *are known*. Combining this with the assumed absence of autocorrelation, we can formulate the new assumption as

$$V\{\varepsilon | X\} = \sigma^2 Diag\{h_i^2\} = \sigma^2 \Psi, \tag{A9}$$

where $Diag\{h_i^2\}$ is a diagonal matrix with elements $h_1^2, \ldots, h_N^2$. Assumption (A9) replaces assumptions (A3) and (A4) from Chapter 2. Clearly, if the variances of our error terms depend upon the explanatory variables, we can no longer assume independence, as in (A2). Therefore, we replace assumptions (A1) and (A2) by

$$E\{\varepsilon | X\} = 0, \tag{A10}$$

which is weaker. Note that (A10) is still substantially stronger than (A7) which says that $E\{\varepsilon_i x_i\} = 0$.

We are interested in the best linear unbiased estimator for β in the model

$$y_i = x_i' \beta + \varepsilon_i, \quad i = 1, \ldots, N \tag{4.14}$$

under assumptions (A9) and (A10). To this end, we can use the general matrix expressions from above. From the structure of Ψ it is easily seen that an appropriate transformation matrix P is given by

$$P = Diag\{h_i^{-1}\}, \tag{4.15}$$

which is a diagonal matrix with elements $h_1^{-1}, \ldots, h_N^{-1}$. Typical elements in the transformed data vector Py are thus $y_i^* = y_i / h_i$ (and similar for the elements in x_i and ε_i). The GLS estimator for β is thus obtained by running OLS on the following transformed model

$$y_i^* = x_i^{*\prime} \beta + \varepsilon_i^* \tag{4.16}$$

or

$$\frac{y_i}{h_i} = \left(\frac{x_i}{h_i}\right)' \beta + \frac{\varepsilon_i}{h_i}. \tag{4.17}$$

It is easily seen that the transformed error term is homoskedastic. The resulting least squares estimator is given by

$$\hat{\beta} = \left(\sum_{i=1}^{N} h_i^{-2} x_i x_i'\right)^{-1} \sum_{i=1}^{N} h_i^{-2} x_i y_i. \tag{4.18}$$

(Note that this is a special case of (4.19).) This GLS estimator is sometimes referred to as a **weighted least squares** estimator, because it is a least squares estimator in which each observation is weighted by (a factor proportional to) the inverse of the error variance. It can be derived directly from minimizing the residual sum of squares in (2.4) after dividing each element in the sum by h_i^2. Under assumptions (A9) and (A10), the GLS estimator is the best linear unbiased estimator for β. The use of weights implies that observations with a higher variance get a smaller weight in estimation. Loosely speaking, the greatest weights are given to observations of the highest quality and the smallest weights to those of the lowest quality. It is important to note that in the transformed model all variables are transformed, including the intercept term. This implies that the new model does not contain an intercept term. It should also be stressed that the transformed regression is only employed to easily determine the GLS estimator and not necessarily has an interpretation of itself. That is, *the parameter estimates are to be interpreted in the context of the original untransformed model.*

4.3.2 Estimator Properties and Hypothesis Testing

Because the GLS estimator is simply an OLS estimator in a transformed model that satisfies the Gauss–Markov properties, we can immediately determine the properties of $\hat{\beta}$ from the standard properties of the OLS estimator, after replacing all variables by their transformed counterparts. For example, the covariance matrix of $\hat{\beta}$ is given by

$$V\{\hat{\beta}\} = \sigma^2 \left(\sum_{i=1}^{N} h_i^{-2} x_i x_i' \right)^{-1}, \tag{4.19}$$

where the unknown error variance σ^2 can be estimated unbiasedly by

$$\hat{\sigma}^2 = \frac{1}{N-K} \sum_{i=1}^{N} h_i^{-2} (y_i - x_i'\hat{\beta})^2. \tag{4.20}$$

If, in addition to assumptions (A9) and (A10), we assume normality of the error terms as in (A5), it also follows that $\hat{\beta}$ has a normal distribution with mean zero and variance (4.19). This can be used to derive tests for linear restrictions on the β coefficients. For example, to test the hypothesis H_0: $\beta_2 = 1$ against H_1: $\beta_2 \neq 1$, we can use the t-statistic given by

$$t_2 = \frac{\hat{\beta}_2 - 1}{\sqrt{\hat{V}\{\hat{\beta}_2\}}}. \tag{4.21}$$

Because we assumed that all h_i^2s are known, estimating the error variance by $\hat{\sigma}^2$ has the usual consequence of changing the standard normal distribution into a t_{N-K} distribution. If normality of the errors is not assumed, the normal distribution is only asymptotically valid. The null hypothesis would be rejected at the 5% level if $|t_2|$ is larger than the critical value of the standard normal distribution, which is 1.96.

As before, the F-test can be used to test a number of linear restrictions on β, summarized as H_0: $R\beta = q$, where R is of dimension $J \times K$. For example, we could test $\beta_2 + \beta_3 + \beta_4 = 1$ and $\beta_5 = 0$ simultaneously $(J = 2)$. The alternative is H_1: $R\beta \neq q$ (which means that the equality sign does not hold for at least one element). The test statistic is based upon the GLS estimator $\hat{\beta}$ and requires the (estimated) variance of $R\hat{\beta}$, which is given by $V\{R\hat{\beta}\} = RV\{\hat{\beta}\}R'$. It is given by

$$\xi = (R\hat{\beta} - q)'(R\hat{V}\{\hat{\beta}\}R')^{-1}(R\hat{\beta} - q). \tag{4.22}$$

Under H_0 this statistic has an asymptotic χ^2 distribution with J degrees of freedom. This test is usually referred to as a **Wald test** (compare Chapters 2 and 3). Because $\hat{V}\{\hat{\beta}\}$ is obtained from $V\{\hat{\beta}\}$ by replacing σ^2 by its estimate $\hat{\sigma}^2$, we can also construct a version of this test that has an exact F-distribution (imposing normality of the error terms), as in the standard case (compare Subsection 2.5.6). The test statistic is given by $f = \xi/J$, which under the null hypothesis has an F distribution with J and $N - K$ degrees of freedom.

4.3.3 When the Variances are Unknown

Obviously, it is hard to think of any economic example in which the variances of the error terms would be known up to a proportionality factor. Probably the only relevant case arises when the heteroskedasticity is related to one observed variable only, for example

$$V\{\varepsilon_i | x_i\} = \sigma^2 x_{i2}^2, \tag{4.23}$$

where x_{i2} is an observed exogenous variable (satisfying $x_{i2} > 0$). In this case $h_i = x_{i2}$ and the transformed regression is given by

$$\frac{y_i}{x_{i2}} = \left(\frac{x_i}{x_{i2}}\right)' \beta + \frac{\varepsilon_i}{x_{i2}}, \tag{4.24}$$

while the variance of the new disturbance term is

$$V\left\{\frac{\varepsilon_i}{x_{i2}} \middle| x_i\right\} = \frac{\sigma_i^2}{x_{i2}^2} = \sigma^2. \tag{4.25}$$

If the h_i^2s are *unknown*, it is no longer possible to compute the GLS estimator. In this case $\hat{\beta}$ is only of theoretical interest. The obvious solution seems to be to replace the unknown h_i^2s by unbiased or consistent estimates and hope that this does not affect the properties of the (pseudo) GLS estimator. This is not as simple as it seems. The main problem is that there are N unknown h_i^2s and only N observations to estimate them. In particular, for any observation i there is only one residual e_i to estimate the variance of ε_i. As a consequence, we cannot expect to find consistent estimators for the h_i^2s unless additional assumptions are made. These assumptions relate to the form of heteroskedasticity and will usually specify the N unknown variances as a function of observed (exogenous) variables and a small number of unknown parameters.

Often the variance of the error term may be related to more than just a single exogenous variable. In addition, the relationship between σ_i^2 and x_{ik}^2 may not be proportional. Therefore, more general forms than (4.23) are often employed. For example,

$$V\{\varepsilon_i\} = \sigma^2 x_{ik}^\alpha \tag{4.26}$$

or

$$V\{\varepsilon_i\} = \sigma^2(x_{ik}^{\alpha_1} + x_{i\ell}^{\alpha_2}), \tag{4.27}$$

where $(x_{ik}, x_{i\ell})$ are two observed exogenous variables. The specifications in (4.26) and (4.27) contain additional unknown parameters that have to be estimated first to apply the GLS procedure with estimated values of h_i^2. Suppose for the moment that we have consistent estimates for α_1 and α_2. Then, we can compute $\hat{h}_i^2$, which is a consistent estimator for h_i^2, and subsequently compute the estimator

$$\hat{\beta}^* = \left(\sum_{i=1}^{N} \hat{h}_i^{-2} x_i x_i' \right)^{-1} \sum_{i=1}^{N} \hat{h}_i^{-2} x_i y_i. \tag{4.28}$$

This estimator is a **feasible** (or estimated) **generalized least squares estimator** (FGLS, EGLS), because it is based on estimated values for h_i^2. Provided the unknown parameters in h_i^2 are consistently estimated it holds (under some weak regularity conditions) that the EGLS estimator $\hat{\beta}^*$ and the GLS estimator $\hat{\beta}$ are asymptotically equivalent. This just means that asymptotically we can ignore the fact that the unknown weights are replaced by consistent estimates. Unfortunately, the EGLS estimator does not share the small sample properties of the GLS estimator, so that we cannot say that $\hat{\beta}^*$ is BLUE. In fact, $\hat{\beta}^*$ will usually be a nonlinear estimator as $\hat{h}_i^2$ is a nonlinear function of y_is. Thus, although we can expect that in reasonably large samples the behaviour of the EGLS and the GLS estimator are fairly similar, there is no guarantee that the EGLS estimator outperforms the OLS estimator in small samples (although usually it does).

What we can conclude is that under assumptions (A8) and (A9), together with an assumption about the form of heteroskedasticity, the feasible GLS estimator is consistent for β and asymptotically best (asymptotically efficient). Its covariance matrix can be estimated by

$$\hat{V}\{\hat{\beta}^*\} = \hat{\sigma}^2 \left(\sum_{i=1}^{N} \hat{h}_i^{-2} x_i x_i' \right)^{-1}, \tag{4.29}$$

where $\hat{\sigma}^2$ is the standard estimator for the error variance from the transformed regression (based on (4.20) but replacing $\hat{\beta}$ by $\hat{\beta}^*$.)

In the remaining part of our discussion on heteroskedasticity, we shall pay attention to three issues. First, we shall see that we can apply ordinary least squares and adjust its standard errors for heteroskedasticity, without making any assumptions about its form. Second, we shall see how assumptions on the form of heteroskedasticity can be exploited to consistently estimate the unknown parameters in h_i^2 in order to determine the EGLS estimator. Third, in Section 4.4, we discuss a range of alternative tests for the detection of heteroskedasticity.

4.3.4 Heteroskedasticity-consistent Standard Errors for OLS

Reconsider the model with heteroskedastic errors,

$$y_i = x_i'\beta + \varepsilon_i, \tag{4.30}$$

with $E\{\varepsilon_i|X\} = 0$ and $V\{\varepsilon_i|X\} = \sigma_i^2$. In matrix notation this can be written as

$$y = X\beta + \varepsilon,$$

with $V\{\varepsilon|X\} = \sigma^2 \Psi = Diag\{\sigma_i^2\}$. If we apply ordinary least squares in this model, we know from the general results above that this estimator is unbiased and consistent for β. The appropriate covariance matrix is given by

$$V\{b|X\} = (X'X)^{-1}X'Diag\{\sigma_i^2\}X(X'X)^{-1}. \tag{4.31}$$

It seems that to estimate this covariance matrix we also need to estimate all σ_i^2s, which is impossible without additional assumptions. However, in an important paper, White (1980) argues that only a consistent estimator of the $K \times K$ matrix

$$\Sigma \equiv \frac{1}{N}X'Diag\{\sigma_i^2\}X = \frac{1}{N}\sum_{i=1}^{N}\sigma_i^2 x_i x_i' \tag{4.32}$$

is required. Under very general conditions, it can be shown that

$$S \equiv \frac{1}{N}\sum_{i=1}^{N}e_i^2 x_i x_i', \tag{4.33}$$

where e_i is the OLS residual, is a consistent[2] estimator for Σ. Therefore,

$$\hat{V}\{b\} = (X'X)^{-1}\sum_{i=1}^{N}e_i^2 x_i x_i'(X'X)^{-1}$$

$$= \left(\sum_{i=1}^{N}x_i x_i'\right)^{-1}\sum_{i=1}^{N}e_i^2 x_i x_i'\left(\sum_{i=1}^{N}x_i x_i'\right)^{-1} \tag{4.34}$$

can be used as an estimate of the true variance of the OLS estimator. This result shows that we can still make appropriate inferences based upon b without actually specifying the type of heteroskedasticity. All we have to do is replace the standard formula for computing the OLS covariance matrix with the one in (4.34), which is a simple option in most modern software packages. Standard errors computed as the square root of the diagonal elements in (4.34) are usually referred to as **heteroskedasticity-consistent standard errors** or simply White standard errors.[3] It is common to report them within square brackets.

4.3.5 *A Model with Two Unknown Variances*

In this subsection we consider a simple case where the sample consists of two separate groups which can have a different error variance. As examples, consider samples of developed and developing countries, single-person and multi-person households, male and female workers, etc. A linear wage equation for this latter sample could be specified as

$$y_i = x_i'\beta + \varepsilon_i,$$

where $E\{\varepsilon_i|x_i\} = 0$ and $V\{\varepsilon_i|x_i\} = \sigma_A^2$ if i belongs to group A (males) and $V\{\varepsilon_i|x_i\} = \sigma_B^2$ if i belongs to group B (females). If we would know[4] σ_A^2 and σ_B^2,

---

[2] To be precise, the probability limit of $S - \Sigma$ equals a null matrix.

[3] This covariance matrix estimate is also attributed to Eicker (1967), so that some authors refer to the corresponding standard errors as the Eicker–White standard errors.

[4] To compute the GLS estimator, it is actually sufficient to know the ratio σ_A^2/σ_B^2.

GLS estimation would be straightforward. When σ_A^2 and σ_B^2 are unknown, they can be estimated fairly simply. Just split the sample into the two groups (males/females) and run separate regressions. Using the residuals from these regressions, the error variance can be estimated in the usual way, because within each subsample the error term is homoskedastic.

Assume that there are N_A observations in the first group and N_B in the second group. The OLS estimator for β based on group A observations is given by

$$b_A = \left(\sum_{i \in A} x_i x_i' \right)^{-1} \sum_{i \in A} x_i y_i$$

where the summations are over all observations in group A. Similarly, we obtain b_B. The error variance is estimated in the standard way, viz.

$$s_A^2 = \frac{1}{N_A - K} \sum_{i \in A} (y_i - x_i' b_A)^2 \tag{4.35}$$

and similarly for s_B^2. These are unbiased and consistent estimators for σ_A^2 and σ_B^2. The EGLS estimator for β is given by

$$\hat{\beta}^* = \left(\sum_{i \in A} s_A^{-2} x_i x_i' + \sum_{i \in B} s_B^{-2} x_i x_i' \right)^{-1} \left(\sum_{i \in A} s_A^{-2} x_i y_i + \sum_{i \in B} s_B^{-2} x_i y_i \right). \tag{4.36}$$

It is easily seen that (4.36) is a special case of (4.28). Moreover, it can be shown that (4.36) is a matrix-weighted average of the two least squares estimators b_A and b_B. In particular, $\hat{\beta}^* = W b_A + (I - W) b_B$, where I is the K-dimensional identity matrix and

$$W = \left(\sum_{i \in A} s_A^{-2} x_i x_i' + \sum_{i \in B} s_B^{-2} x_i x_i' \right)^{-1} \sum_{i \in A} s_A^{-2} x_i x_i'. \tag{4.37}$$

The weighting matrices W and $I - W$ are inversely related to the (estimated) variance matrices of the respective estimators. Thus the more accurate estimate gets a higher weight than the less accurate (higher variance) one.

4.3.6 Multiplicative Heteroskedasticity

A common form of heteroskedasticity employed in practice is that of **multiplicative heteroskedasticity**. Here it is assumed that the error variance is related to a number of exogenous variables, gathered in a J-dimensional vector z_i (not including a constant). To guarantee positivity of the error variance for all parameter values, an exponential function is used. In particular, it is assumed that

$$V\{\varepsilon_i | x_i\} = \sigma_i^2 = \sigma^2 \exp\{\alpha_1 z_{i1} + \cdots + \alpha_J z_{iJ}\} = \sigma^2 \exp\{z_i' \alpha\} \tag{4.38}$$

where z_i is a vector of observed variables that is a function of x_i (usually a subset of x_i variables or a transformation thereof). In this model the error variance is related to one or more exogenous variables, as in the Engel curve example above. Note that in the special case when $J = 1$ and z_{i1} is a dummy variable (e.g. a dummy for males), we obtain the model with two unknown variances.

To be able to compute the EGLS estimator, we need consistent estimators for the unknown parameters in $h_i^2 = \exp\{z_i'\alpha\}$, that is for α, which can be based upon the OLS residuals. To see how, first note that $\log \sigma_i^2 = \log \sigma^2 + z_i'\alpha$. One can expect that the OLS residuals $e_i = y_i - x_i'b$ have something to tell about σ_i^2. Indeed it can be shown that

$$\log e_i^2 = \log \sigma^2 + z_i'\alpha + v_i, \tag{4.39}$$

where $v_i = \log(e_i^2/\sigma_i^2)$ is an error term which is (asymptotically) homoskedastic and uncorrelated with z_i. One problem is that it does not have zero expectation (not even asymptotically). However, this will only affect the estimation of the constant $\log \sigma^2$, which is irrelevant. Consequently, the EGLS estimator for β can be obtained along the following steps.

1. Estimate the model with OLS. This gives the least squares estimator b.
2. Compute $\log e_i^2 = \log(y_i - x_i'b)^2$ from the least square residuals.
3. Estimate (4.39) with least squares, i.e. regress $\log e_i^2$ upon z_i and a constant. This gives consistent estimators $\hat{\alpha}$ for α.
4. Compute $\hat{h}_i^2 = \exp\{z_i'\hat{\alpha}\}$ and transform all observations to obtain

$$y_i/\hat{h}_i = (x_i/\hat{h}_i)'\beta + (\varepsilon_i/\hat{h}_i),$$

   and run OLS on the transformed model. Do not forget to transform the constant. This yields the EGLS estimator $\hat{\beta}*$ for β.
5. The scalar σ^2 can be estimated consistently by

$$\hat{\sigma}^2 = \frac{1}{N-K} \sum_{i=1}^{N} \frac{(y_i - x_i'\hat{\beta}*)^2}{\hat{h}_i^2}.$$

6. Finally, a consistent estimator for the covariance matrix of $\hat{\beta}*$ is given by

$$\hat{V}\{\hat{\beta}*\} = \hat{\sigma}^2 \left(\sum_{i=1}^{N} \frac{x_i x_i'}{\hat{h}_i^2} \right)^{-1}.$$

This corresponds to the least squares covariance matrix in the transformed regression that is automatically computed in regression packages.

4.4   Testing for Heteroskedasticity

In order to judge whether in a given model the OLS results are misleading because of inappropriate standard errors due to heteroskedasticity, a number of alternative tests are available. If these tests do not reject the null, there is no need to suspect our least squares results. If rejections are found, we may consider the use of an EGLS estimator, a White covariance matrix for the OLS estimator, or we may revise the specification of our model. In this section, we discuss several tests that are designed to test the null hypothesis of homoskedasticity against a variety of alternative hypotheses of heteroskedasticity.

4.4.1 Testing Equality of Two Unknown Variances

The first test we consider concerns the situation of two unknown variances as discussed above, i.e. the variance of ε_i equals σ_A^2 if observation i belongs to group A and equals σ_B^2 if observation i belongs to group B. The null hypothesis is the hypothesis that the variance is constant, i.e. H_0: $\sigma_A^2 = \sigma_B^2$. A test for H_0 can be derived by using the result that (approximately or exactly if we assume normality of the errors)

$$(N_j - K) \frac{s_j^2}{\sigma_j^2} \sim \chi_{N_j - K}^2, \quad j = A, B. \tag{4.40}$$

Moreover, s_A^2 and s_B^2 are independent, so we have that (see Appendix B)

$$\frac{s_A^2/\sigma_A^2}{s_B^2/\sigma_B^2} \sim F_{N_B - K}^{N_A - K}. \tag{4.41}$$

Under the null hypothesis this reduces to

$$\lambda = s_A^2/s_B^2 \sim F_{N_B - K}^{N_A - K}. \tag{4.42}$$

In the case of a two-sided alternative, H_1: $\sigma_A^2 \neq \sigma_B^2$, the null hypothesis of homoskedasticity is thus rejected if the ratio of the two estimated variances is either too small or too large. For a one-sided alternative, H_1: $\sigma_A^2 > \sigma_B^2$, we reject if λ is too large. If the alternative hypothesis specifies that $\sigma_A^2 < \sigma_B^2$ we can simply interchange the role of groups A and B in computing the test statistic. This test is a special case of the Goldfeld–Quandt test (Goldfeld and Quandt, 1965; see Greene, 2000, Sect. 12.3).

4.4.2 Testing for Multiplicative Heteroskedasticity

For this test, the alternative hypothesis is well-specified and is given by (4.38), i.e.

$$\sigma_i^2 = \sigma^2 \exp\{z_i' \alpha\}, \tag{4.43}$$

where z_i is a J-dimensional vector as before. The null hypothesis of homoskedasticity corresponds with $\alpha = 0$, so the problem under test is

$$H_0: \alpha = 0 \quad \text{versus} \quad H_1: \alpha \neq 0.$$

This hypothesis can be tested using the results of the least squares regression in (4.39). There are several (asymptotically equivalent) ways to perform this test, but the simplest one is based on the standard F-test in (4.39) for the hypothesis that all coefficients, except the constant, are equal to zero. This statistic is usually automatically provided in a regression package. Because the error term in (4.39) does not satisfy the Gauss–Markov conditions exactly, the F-distribution (with J and $N - J - 1$ degrees of freedom) holds only by approximation. Another approximation is based on the asymptotic χ^2-distribution (with J degrees of freedom) of the test statistic after multiplication by J (compare Subsection 2.5.6).

4.4.3 The Breusch–Pagan Test

In this test, proposed by Breusch and Pagan (1980), the alternative hypothesis is less specific and generalizes (4.38). It is given by

$$\sigma_i^2 = \sigma^2 h(z_i' \alpha), \tag{4.44}$$

where h is an unknown, continuously differentiable function (that does not depend on i), such that $h(.) > 0$ and $h(0) = 1$. As a special case (if $h(t) = \exp\{t\}$) we obtain (4.38). A test for H_0: $\alpha = 0$ versus H_1: $\alpha \neq 0$ can be derived independently of the function h. The simplest variant of the Breusch–Pagan test can be computed as the number of observations multiplied by the R^2 of an auxiliary regression, in particular the R^2 of a regression of e_i^2 (the squared OLS residuals) on z_i and a constant. The resulting test statistic, given by $\xi = NR^2$ is asymptotically χ^2 distributed with J degrees of freedom. The Breusch–Pagan test is a **Lagrange multiplier test** for heteroskedasticity. The main characteristics of Lagrange multiplier tests are that they do not require that the model is estimated under the alternative and that they are often simply computed from the R^2 of some auxiliary regression (see Chapter 6).

4.4.4 The White Test

All tests for heteroskedasticity above test for deviations from the null of homoskedasticity in particular directions. That is, it is necessary to specify the nature of heteroskedasticity one is testing for. The White test (White, 1980) does not require additional structure on the alternative hypothesis and exploits further the idea of a heteroskedasticity-consistent covariance matrix for the OLS estimator. As we have seen, the correct covariance matrix of the least squares estimator is given by (4.31), which can be estimated by (4.34). The conventional estimator is

$$\hat{V}\{b\} = s^2 \left(\sum_{i=1}^{N} x_i x_i' \right)^{-1}. \tag{4.45}$$

If there is no heteroskedasticity, (4.45) will give a consistent estimator of $V\{b\}$, while if there is, it will not. White has devised a statistical test based on this observation. A simple operational version of this test is carried out by obtaining NR^2 in the regression of e_i^2 on a constant and all (unique) first moments, second moments and cross products of the original regressors. The test statistic is asymptotically distributed as Chi-squared with P degrees of freedom, where P is the number of regressors in the auxiliary regression, excluding the intercept.

The White test is a generalization of the Breusch–Pagan test, which also involves an auxiliary regression of squared residuals, but excludes any higher order terms. Consequently, the White test may detect more general forms of heteroskedasticity than the Breusch–Pagan test. In fact, the White test is extremely general. Although this is a virtue, it is, at the same time, a potentially serious shortcoming. The test may reveal heteroskedasticity, but it may instead simply identify some other specification error (such as an incorrect functional form). On the other hand, the power of the White test may be rather low against certain alternatives, particularly if the number of observations is small.

4.4.5 Which Test?

In practice, the choice of an appropriate test for heteroskedasticity is determined by how explicit we want to be about the form of heteroskedasticity. In general, the more explicit we are, e.g. $\sigma_i^2 = \sigma^2 x_{ik}^2$, the more powerful the test will be, i.e. the more likely it is that the test will correctly reject the null hypothesis. However, if the true hetero-skedasticity is of a different form, the chosen test may not indicate the presence of heteroskedasticity at all. The most general test, the White test, has limited power against a large number of alternatives, while a specific test, like the one for multi-plicative heteroskedasticity, has more power but only against a limited number of alternatives. In some cases, a visual inspection of the residuals (e.g. a plot of OLS residuals against one or more exogenous variables) or economic theory can help us in choosing the appropriate alternative. You may also refer to the graphs presented in Section 3.5.

4.5 Illustration: Explaining Labour Demand

In this section we consider a simple model to explain labour demand of Belgian firms. To this end, we have a cross-sectional data set of 569 firms that includes information for 1996 on the total number of employees, their average wage, the amount of capital and a measure of output. The following four variables play a role:[5]

labour: total employment (number of workers);
capital: total fixed assets (in million Bef);[6]
wage: total wage costs divided by number of workers (in million Bef);
output: value added (in million Bef);

To set ideas, let us start from a simple production function[7]

$$Q = f(K, L),$$

where Q denotes output and K and L denote the capital and labour input, respec-tively. The total production costs are $rK + wL$, where r denotes the costs of capital and w denotes the wage rate. Taking r and w and the output level Q as given, mini-mizing total costs (with respect to K and L) subject to the production function, results in demand functions for capital and labour. In general form, the labour demand function can be written as

$$L = g(Q, r, w)$$

for some function g. Because observations on the costs of capital are not easily available and typically do not exhibit much cross-sectional variation, we will, in estimation, approximate r by the capital stock K.

First, we shall assume that the function g is linear in its arguments and add an additive error term. Estimating the resulting linear regression model using the sample of 569 firms yields the results reported in Table 4.1. The coefficient estimates all have the expected sign: higher wages ceteris paribus lead to a reduction of labour input, while more output requires more labour.

Before interpreting the associated standard errors and other statistics, it is useful to check for the possibility of heteroskedasticity. We do this by performing a

---

[5] The data are available in LABOUR.
[6] Conversion rate: 1 million Bef = 24789 euro.
[7] An excellent overview of production functions with cost minimization, in an applied econometrics context, is given in Wallis (1979).

Table 4.1 OLS results linear model

Dependent variable: *labour*

Variable	Estimate	Standard error	t-ratio
constant	287.72	19.64	14.648
wage	−167.13	12.43	−13.446
output	0.382	0.009	43.304
capital	−0.114	0.007	−17.067

$s = 156.26$ $R^2 = 0.9352$ $\bar{R}^2 = 0.9348$ $F = 2716.02$

Table 4.2 Auxiliary regression Breusch–Pagan test

Dependent variable: e_i^2

Variable	Estimate	Standard error	t-ratio
constant	−22719.51	11838.88	−1.919
wage	5673.13	7491.66	0.757
output	132.92	5.31	25.015
capital	−87.840	4.019	−21.858

$s = 94182$ $R^2 = 0.5818$ $\bar{R}^2 = 0.5796$ $F = 262.05$

Breusch–Pagan test using the alternative hypothesis that the error variance depends upon the three explanatory variables. Running an auxiliary regression of the squared OLS residuals upon *wage*, *output* and *capital*, including a constant, leads to the results in Table 4.2. The high t-ratios as well as the relatively high R^2 are striking and indicate that the error variance is unlikely to be constant. We can compute the Breusch–Pagan test statistic by computing $N = 569$ times the R^2 of this auxiliary regression, which gives 331.0. As the asymptotic distribution under the null hypothesis is a Chi-squared with three degrees of freedom, this implies a very sound rejection of homoskedasticity.

It is actually quite common to find heteroskedasticity in situations like this, in which the size of the observational units differs substantially. For example, our sample contains firms with one employee and firms with over 1000 employees. We can expect that large firms have larger absolute values of all variables in the model, including the unobservables collected in the error term. A common approach to alleviate this problem is to use logarithms of all variables rather than their levels (compare Section 3.5). Consequently, our first step in handling the heteroskedasticity problem is to consider a loglinear model. It can be shown that the loglinear model is obtained if the production function is of the Cobb–Douglas type, i.e. $Q = AK^{\alpha}L^{\beta}$.

The OLS estimation results for the loglinear model are given in Table 4.3. Recall that in the loglinear model the coefficients have the interpretation of elasticities. The wage elasticity of labour demand is estimated to be −0.93, which is fairly high. It implies that a 1% increase in wages, ceteris paribus, results in almost 1% decrease in labour demand. The elasticity of the demand for labour with respect to output has an estimate of approximately unity, so that 1% more output requires 1% more labour input.

If the error term in the loglinear model is heteroskedastic, the standard errors and t-ratios in Table 4.3 are not appropriate. We can perform a Breusch–Pagan test in a

Table 4.3 OLS results loglinear model

Dependent variable: log(*labour*)

Variable	Estimate	Standard error	*t*-ratio
constant	−0.448	0.093	−4.806
log(*wage*)	−0.928	0.071	−12.993
log(*output*)	0.990	0.026	37.487
log(*capital*)	−0.004	0.019	−0.197

$s = 0.465$ $R^2 = 0.8430$ $\bar{R}^2 = 0.8421$ $F = 1011.02$

similar way as before: the auxiliary regression of squared OLS residuals upon the three explanatory variables (in logs) leads to an R^2 of 0.0136. The resulting test statistic is 7.74, which is on the margin of being significant at the 5% level. A more general test is the White test. To compute the test statistic we run an auxiliary regression of squared OLS residuals upon all original regressors, their squares and all their interactions. The results are presented in Table 4.4. With an R^2 of 0.1029, the test statistic takes the value of 58.6, which is highly significant for a Chi-squared variable with 9 degrees of freedom. Looking at the *t*-ratios in this regression, the variance of the error term appears to be significantly related to output and capital.

As the White test strongly indicates the presence of heteroskedasticity, it seems appropriate to compute heteroskedasticity-consistent standard errors for the OLS estimator. This is a standard option in most modern software packages and the results are presented in Table 4.5. Clearly, the adjusted standard errors are larger than the incorrect ones, reported in Table 4.3. Note that the *F*-statistic is also adjusted and uses the heteroskedasticity-consistent covariance matrix. Qualitatively, the conclusions are not changed: wages and output are significant in explaining labour demand, capital is not.

If we are willing to make assumptions about the form of heteroskedasticity, the use of the more efficient EGLS estimator is an option. Let us consider the multiplicative form in (4.38), where we choose $z_i = x_i$. That is, the variance of ε_i depends upon log(*wage*), log(*output*) and log(*capital*). We can estimate the parameters of the multiplicative heteroskedasticity by computing the log of the squared OLS residuals and

Table 4.4 Auxiliary regression White test

Dependent variable: e_i^2

Variable	Estimate	Standard error	*t*-ratio
constant	1.324	0.458	2.891
log(*wage*)	0.359	0.556	0.646
log(*output*)	−0.774	0.242	−3.194
log(*capital*)	0.380	0.146	2.607
$\log^2(wage)$	0.193	0.259	0.744
$\log^2(output)$	0.138	0.036	3.877
$\log^2(capital)$	0.090	0.014	6.401
log(*wage*)log(*output*)	0.138	0.163	0.849
log(*wage*)log(*capital*)	−0.252	0.105	−2.399
log(*output*)log(*capital*)	−0.192	0.037	−5.197

$s = 0.851$ $R^2 = 0.1029$ $\bar{R}^2 = 0.0884$ $F = 7.12$

Table 4.5   OLS results loglinear model with White standard errors

Dependent variable: log(*labour*)

Variable	Estimate	Heteroskedasticity-consistent Standard error	*t*-ratio
constant	−0.448	0.133	−3.362
log(*wage*)	−0.928	0.087	−10.706
log(*output*)	0.990	0.047	21.159
log(*capital*)	−0.004	0.038	−0.098

$s = 0.465$ $R^2 = 0.8430$ $\bar{R}^2 = 0.8421$ $F = 544.73$

then running a regression of $\log e_i^2$ upon z_i and a constant. This gives the results in Table 4.6. The variables log(*capital*) and log(*output*) appear to be important in explaining the variance of the error term. Also note that the *F*-value of this auxiliary regression leads to rejection of the null hypothesis of homoskedasticity. To check whether this specification for the form of heteroskedasticity is not too restrictive, we estimated a version where the three squared terms are also included. An *F*-test on the three restrictions implied by the model presented in Table 4.6 produced an *f*-statistic of 1.85 ($p = 0.137$), so that the null hypothesis cannot be rejected.

Recall that the previous regression produces consistent estimates for the parameters describing the multiplicative heteroskedasticity, excluding the constant. The exponential of the predicted values of the regression can be used to transform the original data. As the inconsistency of the constant affects all variables equiproportionally, it does not affect the estimation results based on the transformed data. Transforming all variables and using an OLS procedure on the transformed equation yields the EGLS estimates presented in Table 4.7. If we compare the results in Table 4.7 with the OLS results with heteroskedasticity-consistent standard errors in Table 4.5 we see that the efficiency gain is substantial. The standard errors for the

Table 4.6   Auxiliary regression multiplicative heteroskedasticity

Dependent variable: $\log e_i^2$

Variable	Estimate	Standard error	*t*-ratio
constant	−3.214	0.449	−7.160
log(*wage*)	−0.061	0.344	−0.178
log(*output*)	0.267	0.127	2.099
log(*capital*)	−0.331	0.090	−3.659

$s = 2.241$ $R^2 = 0.0245$ $\bar{R}^2 = 0.0193$ $F = 4.73$

Table 4.7   EGLS results loglinear model

Dependent variable: log(*labour*)

Variable	Estimate	Standard error	*t*-ratio
constant	−0.466	0.091	−5.145
log(*wage*)	−0.856	0.072	−11.903
log(*output*)	1.035	0.027	37.890
log(*capital*)	−0.057	0.022	−2.636

$s = 2.509$ $R^2 = 0.9903$ $\bar{R}^2 = 0.9902$ $F = 14401.3$

EGLS approach are substantially smaller. Note that a comparison with the results in Table 4.3 is not appropriate, as the standard errors in the latter table are only valid in the absence of heteroskedasticity. The EGLS coefficient estimates are fairly close to the OLS ones. A remarkable difference is that the effect of capital is now significant at the 5% level, while we did not find statistical evidence for this effect before. We can test the hypothesis that the wage elasticity equals minus one by computing the t-statistic $(-0.856 + 1)/0.072 = 2.01$, which implies a (marginal) rejection at the 5% level.

The fact that the R^2 in Table 4.7 is larger than in the OLS case is misleading for two reasons. First, the transformed model does not contain an intercept term so that the uncentred R^2 is computed. Second, the R^2 is computed for the transformed model with a transformed endogenous variable. If one would compute the implied R^2 for the original model, it would be smaller than the one obtained by running OLS. It is known from Chapter 2 that the alternative definitions of the R^2 do not give the same outcome if the model is not estimated by OLS. Using the definition that

$$R^2 = \mathrm{corr}^2\{y_i, \hat{y}_i\}, \tag{4.46}$$

where $\hat{y}_i = x_i'\hat{\beta}^*$, the above example produces an R^2 of 0.8403, which is only slightly lower than the OLS value. Because OLS is defined to minimize the residual sum of squares, it automatically maximizes the R^2. Consequently, the use of any other estimator will never increase the R^2, and the R^2 is not a good criterion to compare alternative estimators. (Of course, there are more important things in an econometrician's life than a high R^2.)

4.6   Autocorrelation

We will now look at another case where $V\{\varepsilon\} = \sigma^2 I$ is violated, viz. when the covariances between different error terms are not all equal to zero. The most relevant example of this occurs when two or more consecutive error terms are correlated, and we say that the error term is subject to **autocorrelation** or **serial correlation**. Given our general discussion above, as long as it can be assumed that $E\{\varepsilon|X\} = 0$ (assumption (A9)), the consequences of autocorrelation are similar to those of heteroskedasticity: OLS remains unbiased, but it becomes inefficient and its standard errors are estimated in the wrong way.

Autocorrelation normally occurs only when using time series data. To stress this, we shall follow the literature and index the observations from $t = 1, 2, \ldots, T$ rather than from $i = 1, 2, \ldots, N$. The most important difference is that now the order of the observations does matter and the index reflects a natural ordering. In general, the error term ε_t picks up the influence of those variables affecting the dependent variables that have not been included in the model. Persistence of the effects of excluded variables is therefore a frequent cause of positive autocorrelation. If such excluded variables are observed and could have been included in the model, we can also interpret the resulting autocorrelation as an indication of a misspecified model. This explains why tests for autocorrelation are very often interpreted as misspecification tests. Incorrect functional forms, omitted variables and an inadequate dynamic specification of the model may all lead to findings of autocorrelation.

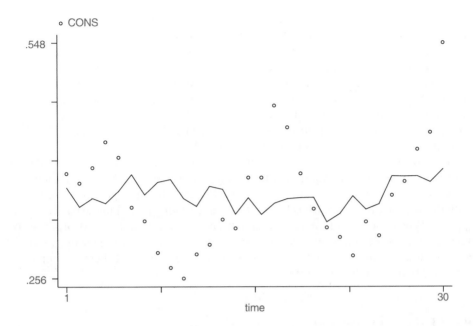

Figure 4.1   Actual and fitted consumption of ice cream, March 1951–July 1953

Suppose you are using monthly data to estimate a model that explains the demand for ice cream. Typically, the state of the weather will be an important factor hidden in the error term ε_t. In this case, you are likely to find a pattern of observations that is like the one in Figure 4.1. In this figure we plot ice cream consumption against time, while the connected points describe the fitted values of a regression model that explains ice cream consumption from aggregate income and a price index.[8] Clearly, positive and negative residuals group together. In macro-economic analyses, business cycle movements may have very similar effects. In most economic applications, auto-correlation is positive, but sometimes it will be negative: a positive error for one observation is likely to be followed by a negative error for the next, and vice versa.

4.6.1   First Order Autocorrelation

There are many forms of autocorrelation and each one leads to a different structure for the error covariance matrix $V\{\varepsilon\}$. The most popular form is known as the first-order autoregressive process. In this case the error term in

$$y_t = x_t'\beta + \varepsilon_t \tag{4.47}$$

is assumed to depend upon its predecessor as follows

$$\varepsilon_t = \rho\varepsilon_{t-1} + v_t, \tag{4.48}$$

---

[8] The data used in this figure are taken from Hildreth and Lu (1960) and are available in ICECREAM; see also Section 4.8.

where $v_t \sim IID(0, \sigma_v^2)$. This assumes that the value of the error term in any observation is equal to ρ times its value in the previous observation plus a fresh component v_t. This fresh component is assumed to have zero mean and constant variance, and to be independent over time. Furthermore, assumption (A2) from Chapter 2 is imposed which implies that all explanatory variables are independent of all error terms. The parameters ρ and σ_v^2 are typically unknown, and, along with β we may wish to estimate them. Note that the statistical properties of v_t are the same as those assumed for ε_t in the standard case: thus if $\rho = 0$, $\varepsilon_t = v_t$ and the standard Gauss–Markov conditions (A1)–(A4) from Chapter 2 are satisfied.

To derive the covariance matrix of the error term vector ε, we need to make an assumption about the distribution of the initial period error, ε_1. Most commonly, it is assumed that ε_1 is mean zero with the same variance as all other ε_ts. This is consistent with the idea that the process has been operating for a long period in the past and that $|\rho| < 1$. When the condition $|\rho| < 1$ is satisfied we say that the first-order autoregressive process is **stationary**. A stationary process is such that the mean, variances and covariances of ε_t do not change over time (see Chapter 8 below). Imposing stationarity it easily follows from

$$E\{\varepsilon_t\} = \rho E\{\varepsilon_{t-1}\} + E\{v_t\}$$

that $E\{\varepsilon_t\} = 0$. Further, from

$$V\{\varepsilon_t\} = V\{\rho\varepsilon_{t-1} + v_t\} = \rho^2 V\{\varepsilon_{t-1}\} + \sigma_v^2,$$

we obtain that the variance of ε_t, denoted as σ_ε^2, is given by

$$\sigma_\varepsilon^2 = V\{\varepsilon_t\} = \frac{\sigma_v^2}{1 - \rho^2}. \tag{4.49}$$

The nondiagonal elements in the variance–covariance matrix of ε follow from

$$\text{cov}\{\varepsilon_t, \varepsilon_{t-1}\} = E\{\varepsilon_t \varepsilon_{t-1}\} = \rho E\{\varepsilon_{t-1}^2\} + E\{\varepsilon_{t-1} v_t\} = \rho \frac{\sigma_v^2}{1 - \rho^2}. \tag{4.50}$$

The covariance between error terms two periods apart is

$$E\{\varepsilon_t \varepsilon_{t-2}\} = \rho E\{\varepsilon_{t-1} \varepsilon_{t-2}\} + E\{\varepsilon_{t-2} v_t\} = \rho^2 \frac{\sigma_v^2}{1 - \rho^2}, \tag{4.51}$$

and in general we have, for non-negative values of s,

$$E\{\varepsilon_t \varepsilon_{t-s}\} = \rho^s \frac{\sigma_v^2}{1 - \rho^2}. \tag{4.52}$$

This shows that for $0 < |\rho| < 1$ all elements in ε are mutually correlated with a decreasing covariance if the distance in time gets large (i.e. if s gets large). The covariance matrix of ε is thus a full matrix (a matrix without zero elements). From this matrix an appropriate transformation matrix can be derived, as discussed in Section 4.2. However, looking at (4.47) and (4.48) directly, it is immediately apparent which transformation is appropriate. Because $\varepsilon_t = \rho\varepsilon_{t-1} + v_t$, where v_t satisfies the Gauss–Markov conditions, it is obvious that a transformation like $\varepsilon_t - \rho\varepsilon_{t-1}$ will generate homoskedastic non-autocorrelated errors. That is, all observations should be transformed as $y_t - \rho y_{t-1}$ and $x_t - \rho x_{t-1}$. Consequently, the transformed model is given by

$$y_t - \rho y_{t-1} = (x_t - \rho x_{t-1})'\beta + v_t, \quad t = 2, 3, \ldots, T. \tag{4.53}$$

Because the model in (4.53) satisfies the Gauss–Markov conditions, estimation with OLS yields the GLS estimator (assuming ρ is known). However, this statement is not entirely correct, since the transformation in (4.53) cannot be applied to the first observation (because y_0 and x_0 are not observed). The information in this first observation is lost and OLS in (4.53) produces only an approximate GLS estimator.[9] Of course, when the number of observations is large, the loss of a single observation will typically not have a large impact on the results.

The first observation can be rescued by noting that the error term for the first observation, ε_1, is uncorrelated with all v_ts, $t = 2, \ldots, T$. However, the variance of ε_1 (given in (4.49)) is much larger than the variance of the transformed errors $(v_2, \ldots, v_T)$, particularly when ρ is close to unity. To obtain homoskedastic and non-autocorrelated errors in a transformed model (which includes the first observation), this first observation should be transformed by multiplying it by $\sqrt{1 - \rho^2}$. The complete transformed model is thus given by

$$\sqrt{1 - \rho^2}y_1 = \sqrt{1 - \rho^2}x_1'\beta + \sqrt{1 - \rho^2}\varepsilon_1, \tag{4.54}$$

and by (4.53) for observations 2 to T. It is easily verified that the transformed error in (4.54) has the same variance as v_t. OLS applied on (4.53) and (4.54) produces the GLS estimator $\hat{\beta}$, which is the best linear unbiased estimator (BLUE) for β.

In early work (Cochrane and Orcutt, 1949) it was common to drop the first (transformed) observation and to estimate β from the remaining $T - 1$ transformed observations. As said, this yields only an approximate GLS estimator and it will not be as efficient as the estimator using all T observations. However, if T is large the difference between the two estimators is negligible. Estimators not using the first transformed observations are often referred to as Cochrane–Orcutt estimators. Similarly, the transformation not including the first observation is referred to as the Cochrane–Orcutt transformation. The estimator that uses all transformed observations is sometimes called the Prais–Winsten (1954) estimator.

4.6.2 Unknown ρ

In practice it is of course highly uncommon that the value of ρ is known. In that case we will have to estimate it. Starting from

$$\varepsilon_t = \rho\varepsilon_{t-1} + v_t, \tag{4.55}$$

where v_t satisfies the usual assumptions, it seems natural to estimate ρ from a regression of the OLS residual e_t on e_{t-1}. The resulting OLS estimator for ρ is given by

$$\hat{\rho} = \left(\sum_{t=2}^{T} e_{t-1}^2\right)^{-1} \left(\sum_{t=2}^{T} e_t e_{t-1}\right). \tag{4.56}$$

---

[9] Technically, the implicit transformation matrix P that is used here is not a square matrix and thus not invertible.

While this estimator for ρ is typically biased, it is a consistent estimator for ρ under weak regularity conditions. If we use $\hat{\rho}$ instead of ρ to compute the feasible GLS (EGLS) estimator $\hat{\beta}^*$, the BLUE property is no longer retained. Under the same conditions as before, it holds that the EGLS estimator $\hat{\beta}^*$ is asymptotically equivalent to the GLS estimator $\hat{\beta}$. That is, for large sample sizes we can ignore the fact that ρ is estimated.

A related estimation procedure is the so-called iterative Cochrane–Orcutt procedure, which is applied in many software packages. In this procedure ρ and β are recursively estimated until convergence, i.e. having estimated β with EGLS (by $\hat{\beta}^*$), the residuals are recomputed and ρ is estimated again using the residuals from the EGLS step. With this new estimate of ρ, EGLS is applied again and one obtains a new estimate of β. This procedure goes on until convergence, i.e. until both the estimate for ρ and the estimate for β do not change anymore. One can expect that this procedure increases the efficiency (i.e. decreases the variance) of the estimator for ρ. However, there is no guarantee that it will increase the efficiency of the estimator for β as well. We know that asymptotically it does not matter that we estimate ρ, and – consequently – it does not matter (asymptotically) how we estimate it either, as long as it is estimated consistently. In small samples, however, iterated EGLS typically performs somewhat better than its two-step variant.

4.7 Testing for First Order Autocorrelation

When $\rho = 0$ no autocorrelation is present and OLS is BLUE. If $\rho \neq 0$ inferences based on the OLS estimator will be misleading because standard errors will be based on the wrong formula. Therefore, it is common practice with time series data to test for autocorrelation in the error term. Suppose interest lies in the hypothesis H_0: $\rho = 0$ versus H_1: $\rho \neq 0$ (or a one-sided alternative). We will present a few tests for the model in (4.47) with (4.48). The first two tests are relatively simple, but only asymptotically valid, while the last test has a known small sample distribution.

4.7.1 Asymptotic Tests

Under suitable assumptions (including $|\rho| < 1$), it can be shown that

$$\sqrt{T}(\hat{\rho} - \rho) \rightarrow \mathcal{N}(0, 1 - \rho^2),$$

i.e. the estimator $\hat{\rho}$ is consistent and asymptotically normal. Thus, in finite samples, it holds approximately that $\hat{\rho}$ is normal with mean ρ and variance $(1 - \rho^2)/T$. Thus

$$z = \frac{\sqrt{T}(\hat{\rho} - \rho)}{\sqrt{1 - \rho^2}}$$

is approximately standard normal. If H_0 is true we have that

$$z = \sqrt{T}\hat{\rho} \tag{4.57}$$

is approximately standard normal and we can use z as a test statistic. Consequently, at the 5% significance level, we reject H_0 (against H_1) if

$$|\sqrt{T}\hat{\rho}| > 1.96.$$

Alternatively, a test statistic can be computed by considering the regression of OLS residuals e_t upon their lags e_{t-1} again. If we take the R^2 of this regression and multiply it by the effective number of observations $T - 1$ we obtain a test statistic that, under the null hypothesis, has a χ^2 distribution with one degree of freedom. Clearly an R^2 close to zero in this regression implies that lagged residuals are not explaining current residuals and a simple way to test $\rho = 0$ is by computing $(T - 1)R^2$. This test is a special case of the Breusch (1978)–Godfrey (1978) Lagrange multiplier test (see Chapter 6) and is easily extended to higher orders of autocorrelation (by including additional lags of the residual and adjusting the degrees of freedom accordingly) and to models that include lagged dependent variables (by including the regressors x_t in the auxiliary regression).

Note that both of these tests are asymptotic tests and the asymptotic approximation may not be very good when T is small. An alternative test based on small sample theory is the Durbin–Watson test.

4.7.2   The Durbin–Watson Test

One of the most popular tests in econometrics is the Durbin–Watson test (Durbin and Watson, 1950). Two important assumptions underlying this test are that we can treat the x_ts as deterministic and that x_t contains an intercept term. The first assumption is important because it requires that all error terms are independent of *all* explanatory variables (assumption (A2)). Most importantly, this excludes the inclusion of lagged dependent variables in the model.

The Durbin–Watson test statistic is given by

$$dw = \frac{\sum_{t=2}^{T}(e_t - e_{t-1})^2}{\sum_{t=1}^{T} e_t^2},$$ (4.58)

where e_t is the OLS residual (notice the different indices for the summations). By writing

$$\sum_{t=2}^{T}(e_t - e_{t-1})^2 = \sum_{t=1}^{T} e_t^2 - e_1^2 - 2\sum_{t=2}^{T} e_t e_{t-1} + \sum_{t=2}^{T+1} e_{t-1}^2 - e_T^2,$$

we can rewrite

$$dw = 2 - 2\hat{\rho}\left(\frac{\sum_{t=2}^{T} e_t^2}{\sum_{t=1}^{T} e_t^2}\right) - \left(\frac{e_1^2 + e_T^2}{\sum_{t=1}^{T} e_t^2}\right) \approx 2 - 2\hat{\rho}.$$ (4.59)

The $\approx$-sign in (4.59) is due to the fact that the first term in brackets tends to one if T gets large, while the second term in brackets tends to zero for large T. From this we can derive an alternative estimator for ρ given by

$$\tilde{\rho} = 1 - \tfrac{1}{2}dw,$$ (4.60)

which is also consistent.

Under the null hypothesis of no autocorrelation ($\rho = 0$), the distribution of dw can be shown to be symmetric around 2. So if dw is close to two, this indicates that ρ is close to zero. If dw is 'much smaller' than 2, this is an indication for positive

Table 4.8 Lower and upper bounds for 5% critical values of the Durbin–Watson test (Savin and White, 1977)

Number of observations	Number of regressors (incl. intercept)							
	$K = 3$		$K = 5$		$K = 7$		$K = 9$	
	d_L	d_U	d_L	d_U	d_L	d_U	d_L	d_U
$T = 25$	1.206	1.550	1.038	1.767	0.868	2.012	0.702	2.280
$T = 50$	1.462	1.628	1.378	1.721	1.291	1.822	1.201	1.930
$T = 75$	1.571	1.680	1.515	1.739	1.458	1.801	1.399	1.867
$T = 100$	1.634	1.715	1.592	1.758	1.550	1.803	1.506	1.850
$T = 200$	1.748	1.789	1.728	1.810	1.707	1.831	1.686	1.852

autocorrelation ($\rho > 0$); if dw is much larger than 2 then $\rho < 0$. Even under H_0: $\rho = 0$, the distribution of dw depends not only upon the sample size T and the number of variables K in x_t, but also upon the actual values of the x_ts. Consequently, critical values cannot be tabulated for general use. Fortunately, it is possible to compute upper and lower limits for the critical values of dw that depend only upon sample size T and number of variables K in x_t. These values, d_L and d_U, were tabulated by Durbin and Watson (1950) and Savin and White (1977), and are partly reproduced in Table 4.8. The true critical value d_{crit} is between the bounds that are tabulated, that is $d_L < d_{crit} < d_U$. Under H_0 we thus have that (at the 5% level)

$$P\{dw < d_L\} \leq P\{dw < d_{crit}\} = 0.05 \leq P\{dw < d_U\}.$$

For a one-sided test against positive autocorrelation ($\rho > 0$), there are three possibilities:

a. dw is less than d_L. In this case, it is certainly lower than the true critical value d_{crit}, so you would reject H_0;

b. dw is larger than d_U. In this case, it is certainly larger than d_{crit} and you would not reject H_0;

c. dw lies between d_L and d_U. In this case it might be larger or smaller than the critical value. Because you cannot tell which, you are unable to accept or reject H_0. This is the so-called 'inconclusive region'.

The larger the sample size, the smaller the inconclusive region. For $K = 5$ and $T = 25$ we have $d_{L;5\%} = 1.038$ and $d_{U;5\%} = 1.767$; for $T = 100$ these numbers are 1.592 and 1.758.

In case **c** there is not much you can do. There are some approximations possible, as discussed in Judge *et al.* (1988, pp. 398–399), but these are hardly used in practice. Fortunately, some computer packages, like SHAZAM, provide exact critical values, computed numerically. Despite its disadvantages the Durbin–Watson test is one of the most often used tests in practice: it is based on small sample distributions, although in some cases the result may be 'inconclusive'.

In the less common case where the alternative hypothesis is the presence of negative autocorrelation ($\rho < 0$), the symmetry of the distribution of dw (around 2) implies that the true critical value is between $4 - d_U$ and $4 - d_L$, so that no additional tables are required.

4.8 Illustration: The Demand for Ice Cream

This empirical illustration is based on one of the founding articles on autocorrelation, viz. Hildreth and Lu (1960). The data used in this study are time series data with 30 four-weekly observations from 18 March 1951 to 11 July 1953 on the following variables:[10]

cons: consumption of ice cream per head (in pints);
income: average family income per week (in US Dollars);
price: price of ice cream (per pint);
temp: average temperature (in Fahrenheit).

A graphical illustration of the data is given in Figure 4.2, where we see the time series patterns of consumption, price and temperature (divided by 100). The graph clearly suggests that the temperature is an important determinant for the consumption of ice cream, which supports our expectations.

The model used to explain consumption of ice cream is a linear regression model with *income*, *price* and *temp* as explanatory variables. The results of a first OLS regression are given in Table 4.9. While the coefficient estimates have the expected signs, the Durbin–Watson statistic is computed as 1.0212. For a one-sided Durbin–Watson test for H_0: $\rho = 0$, against the alternative of positive autocorrelation, we have at the 5% level ($\alpha = 0.05$) that $d_L = 1.21$ ($T = 30$, $K = 4$) and $d_U = 1.65$. The value of 1.02 clearly implies that the null hypothesis should be rejected against the alter-

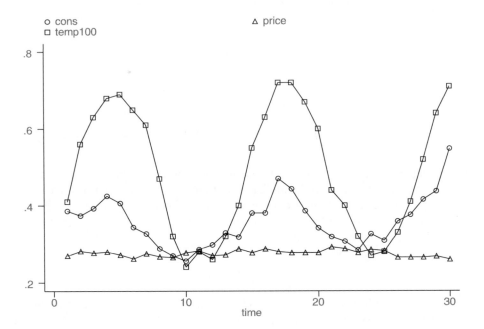

Figure 4.2   Ice cream consumption, price and temperature/100

[10] Data available in ICECREAM.

Table 4.9   OLS results

Dependent variable: *cons*

Variable	Estimate	Standard error	*t*-ratio
constant	0.197	0.270	0.730
price	−1.044	0.834	−1.252
income	0.00331	0.00117	2.824
temp	0.00345	0.00045	7.762

$s = 0.0368$ $R^2 = 0.7190$ $\bar{R}^2 = 0.6866$ $F = 22.175$ $dw = 1.0212$

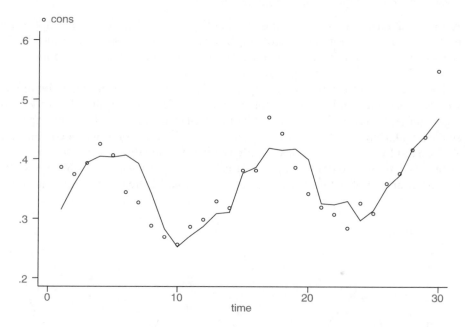

Figure 4.3   Actual and fitted values (connected) ice cream consumption

native of positive autocorrelation. When we plot the true values of *cons* and the predicted values according to the model, as in Figure 4.3, we see that positive (negative) values for the error term are more likely to be followed by positive (negative) values. Apparently, the inclusion of *temp* in the model is insufficient to capture the seasonal fluctuation in ice cream consumption.

The first order autocorrelation coefficient in

$$\varepsilon_t = \rho \varepsilon_{t-1} + v_t$$

is easily estimated by saving the residuals from the previous regression and running a least squares regression of e_t on e_{t-1} (without a constant).[11] This gives an estimate $\hat{\rho} = 0.401$ with an R^2 of 0.149. The asymptotic test for H_0: $\rho = 0$ against first order autocorrelation is based on $\sqrt{T}\hat{\rho} = 2.19$. This is larger than the 5% critical value from

---

[11] There is no need to include a constant because the average OLS residual is zero.

Table 4.10 EGLS (iterative Cochrane–Orcutt) results

Dependent variable: *cons*

Variable	Estimate	Standard error	*t*-ratio
constant	0.157	0.300	0.524
price	−0.892	0.830	−1.076
income	0.00320	0.00159	2.005
temp	0.00356	0.00061	5.800
$\hat{\rho}$	0.401	0.2079	1.927

$s = 0.0326^*$ $R^2 = 0.7961^*$ $\bar{R}^2 = 0.7621^*$ $F = 23.419$ $dw = 1.5486^*$

the standard normal distribution given by 1.96, so again we have to reject the null hypothesis of no serial correlation. The Breusch–Godfrey test produces a test statistic of $(T - 1)R^2 = 4.32$, which exceeds the 5% critical value of 3.84 of a Chi-squared distribution with one degree of freedom.

These rejections imply that OLS is no longer the best linear unbiased estimator for β and, most importantly, that the routinely computed standard errors are not correct. It is possible to make correct and more accurate statements about the price elasticity of ice cream if we choose a more efficient estimation method, like (estimated) GLS. The iterative Cochrane–Orcutt method yields the results presented in Table 4.10. Note that the EGLS results confirm our earlier results which indicate that income and temperature are important determinants in the consumption function. It should be stressed that the statistics in Table 4.10 that are indicated by an asterisk correspond to the transformed model and are not directly comparable to their equivalents in Table 4.9 that reflect the untransformed model. This also holds for the Durbin–Watson statistic, which is no longer appropriate in Table 4.10.

As mentioned before, the finding of autocorrelation may be an indication that there is something wrong with the model, like the functional form or the dynamic specification. A possible way to eliminate the problem of autocorrelation is to change the specification of the model. It seems natural to consider including one or more lagged variables in the model. In particular, we will include the lagged temperature $temp_{t-1}$ in the model. OLS in this extended model produces the results in Table 4.11.

Compared to Table 4.9, the Durbin–Watson test statistic has increased to 1.58, which is in the inconclusive region ($\alpha = 0.05$) given by (1.14, 1.74). As the value is fairly close to the upper bound, we may choose not to reject the null of no autocorrelation. Apparently lagged temperature has a significant negative effect on ice cream

Table 4.11 OLS results extended specification

Dependent variable: *cons*

Variable	Estimate	Standard error	*t*-ratio
constant	0.189	0.232	0.816
price	−0.838	0.688	−1.218
income	0.00287	0.00105	2.722
temp	0.00533	0.00067	7.953
$temp_{t-1}$	−0.00220	0.00073	−3.016

$s = 0.0299$ $R^2 = 0.8285$ $\bar{R}^2 = 0.7999$ $F = 28.979$ $dw = 1.5822$

consumption, while the current temperature has a positive effect. This may indicate an increase of demand when the temperature rises, which is not fully consumed and reduces expenditures one period later.[12]

4.9 Alternative Autocorrelation Patterns

4.9.1 Higher Order Autocorrelation

First order autoregressive errors are not uncommon in macro-economic time series models and in most cases allowing for first order autocorrelation will eliminate the problem. However, when we have quarterly or monthly data for example, it is possible that there is a periodic (quarterly or monthly) effect that is causing the errors across the same periods but in different years to be correlated. For example, we could have (in the case of quarterly data) that

$$\varepsilon_t = \gamma \varepsilon_{t-4} + v_t, \tag{4.61}$$

or, more generally,

$$\varepsilon_t = \gamma_1 \varepsilon_{t-1} + \gamma_2 \varepsilon_{t-2} + \gamma_3 \varepsilon_{t-3} + \gamma_4 \varepsilon_{t-4} + v_t, \tag{4.62}$$

which is known as fourth order autocorrelation. Essentially, this is a straightforward generalization of the first order process and estimation by EGLS follows along the same lines. As long as the explanatory variables are uncorrelated with all error terms, EGLS is based on a first step OLS estimation of (4.61) or (4.62) where the errors are replaced by least squares residuals e_t. The appropriate transformation to derive the EGLS estimator for β will be clear from (4.61) or (4.62). Note that the first four observations will be lost in the transformation.

4.9.2 Moving Average Errors

As discussed, an autoregressive specification of the errors, as in (4.48), (4.61) or (4.62), implies that all error terms are mutually correlated, although the correlation between terms that are many periods apart will be negligibly small. In some cases, (economic) theory suggests a different form of autocorrelation, in which only particular error terms are correlated, while all others have a zero correlation. This can be modelled by a so-called **moving average** error process. Moving average structures often arise when the sampling interval (e.g. one month) is smaller than the interval for which the variables are defined. Consider the problem of estimating an equation to explain the value of some financial instrument such as 90-day treasury bills or 3-month forward contracts on foreign exchange. If one uses monthly data, then any innovation occurring in month t would affect the value of instruments maturing in months $t, t + 1$ and $t + 2$ but would not affect the value of instruments maturing later, because the latter would not yet have been issued. This suggests correlation between the error terms one and two months apart, but zero correlation between terms further apart.

Another example is the explanation of the yearly change in prices (inflation), observed every 6 months. Suppose we have observations on the change in consumer prices compared to the level one year ago, at 1 January and 1 July. Also suppose that

---

[12] What is measured by *cons* is expenditures on ice cream, not actual consumption.

background variables (for example money supply) included in x_t are observed half-yearly. If the 'true' model is given by

$$y_t = x_t'\beta + v_t, \quad t = 1, 2, \ldots, T \text{ (half-yearly)}, \tag{4.63}$$

where y_t is the half-yearly change in prices and the error term v_t satisfies the Gauss–Markov conditions, it holds for the change on a yearly level, $y_t^* = y_t + y_{t-1}$ that

$$y_t^* = (x_t + x_{t-1})'\beta + v_t + v_{t-1}, \quad t = 1, 2, \ldots, T, \tag{4.64}$$

or

$$y_t^* = x_t^{*\prime}\beta + \varepsilon_t, \quad t = 1, 2, \ldots, T, \tag{4.65}$$

where $\varepsilon_t = v_t + v_{t-1}$ and $x_t^* = x_t + x_{t-1}$. If we assume that v_t has a variance σ_v^2, the properties of the error term in (4.65) are the following

$$E\{\varepsilon_t\} = E\{v_t\} + E\{v_{t-1}\} = 0$$

$$V\{\varepsilon_t\} = V\{v_t + v_{t-1}\} = 2\sigma_v^2$$

$$\text{cov}\{\varepsilon_t, \varepsilon_{t-1}\} = \text{cov}\{v_t + v_{t-1}, v_{t-1} + v_{t-2}\} = \sigma_v^2$$

$$\text{cov}\{\varepsilon_t, \varepsilon_{t-s}\} = \text{cov}\{v_t + v_{t-1}, v_{t-s} + v_{t-1-s}\} = 0, \quad s = 2, 3, \ldots$$

Consequently, the covariance matrix of the error term vector contains a large number of zeros. On the diagonal we have $2\sigma_v^2$ (the variance) and just below and above the diagonal we have σ_v^2 (the first order autocovariance), while all other covariances are equal to zero. We call this a first order moving average process (for ε_t). In fact, this is a restricted version because the correlation coefficient between ε_t and ε_{t-1} is a priori fixed at 0.5. A general first order moving average process would be specified as

$$\varepsilon_t = v_t + \alpha v_{t-1}$$

for some α, $|\alpha| < 1$; see the discussion in Chapter 8 on time series models.

It is generally somewhat harder to estimate regression models with moving average errors than with autoregressive errors. This is because the transformation generating 'Gauss–Markov errors' is complicated. Some software packages have specialized procedures available, but if appropriate software is lacking, estimation can be quite difficult. A possible solution is to apply ordinary least squares while correcting standard errors for the presence of autocorrelation (of whatever nature) in ε_t. This will be discussed in the next section. An empirical example involving moving average errors is provided in Section 4.11.

4.10 What to do When you Find Autocorrelation?

In many cases the finding of autocorrelation is an indication that the model is mis-specified. If this is the case, the most natural route is *not* to change your *estimator* (from OLS to EGLS) but to change your *model*. Typically, three (interrelated) types of misspecification may lead to a finding of autocorrelation in your OLS residuals: dynamic misspecification, omitted variables and functional form misspecification.

If we leave the case where the error term is independent of all explanatory variables, there is another reason why GLS or EGLS may be inappropriate. In particular, it is possible that the GLS estimator is inconsistent because the transformed model does not satisfy the minimal requirements for the OLS estimator to be consistent. This situation can arise even if OLS applied to the original equation *is* consistent. Section 4.11 provides an empirical example of this issue.

4.10.1 Misspecification

Let us start with functional form misspecification. Suppose that the true linear relationship is between y_t and $\log x_t$ as

$$y_t = \beta_1 + \beta_2 \log x_t + \varepsilon_t$$

and suppose, for illustrative purposes, that x_t increases with t. If we nevertheless estimate a linear model that explains y_t from x_t we could find a situation as depicted in Figure 4.4. In this figure, based upon simulated data with $x_t = t$ and $y_t = 0.5 \log x_t$ plus a small error, the fitted values of a linear model are connected while the actual values are not. Very clearly, residuals of the same sign group together. The Durbin–Watson statistic corresponding to this example is as small as 0.193. The solution in this case is not to re-estimate the linear model using feasible generalized least squares but to change the functional form and include $\log x_t$ rather than x_t.

As discussed above, the omission of a relevant explanatory variable may also lead to a finding of autocorrelation. For example, in Section 4.8 we saw that excluding sufficient variables that reflect the seasonal variation of ice cream consumption resulted in such a case. In a similar fashion, an incorrect dynamic specification may

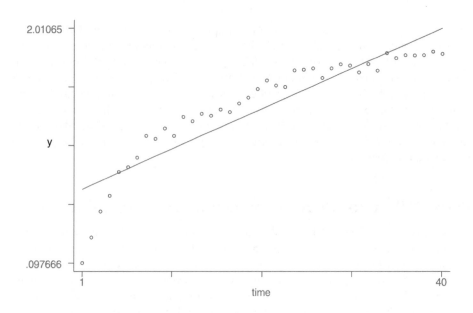

Figure 4.4   Actual and fitted values when true model is $y_t = 0.5 \log t + \varepsilon_t$

result in autocorrelation. In such cases, we have to decide whether the model of interest is supposed to be static or dynamic. To illustrate this, start from the (static) model

$$y_t = x_t'\beta + \varepsilon_t \tag{4.66}$$

with first order autocorrelation $\varepsilon_t = \rho\varepsilon_{t-1} + v_t$. We can interpret the above model as describing $E\{y_t|x_t\} = x_t'\beta$. However, we may also be interested in forecasting on the basis of current x_t values as well as lagged observations on x_{t-1} or y_{t-1}, that is $E\{y_t|x_t, x_{t-1}, y_{t-1}\}$. For the above model, we obtain

$$E\{y_t|x_t, x_{t-1}, y_{t-1}\} = x_t'\beta + \rho(y_{t-1} - x_{t-1}'\beta) \tag{4.67}$$

and we can write a dynamic model as

$$y_t = x_t'\beta + \rho y_{t-1} - \rho x_{t-1}'\beta + v_t, \tag{4.68}$$

the error term in which does not exhibit any autocorrelation. The model in (4.68) shows that the inclusion of a lagged dependent variable and lagged exogenous variables results in a specification that does not suffer from autocorrelation. Conversely, we may find autocorrelation in (4.66) if the dynamic specification is similar to (4.68) and includes, for example, only y_{t-1} or some elements of x_{t-1}. In such cases, the inclusion of these 'omitted' variables will resolve the autocorrelation problem.

The static model (4.66) with first order autocorrelation provides us with $E\{y_t|x_t\}$ as well as the dynamic forecast $E\{y_t|x_t, x_{t-1}, y_{t-1}\}$ and may be more parsimonious compared to a full dynamic model with several lagged variables included (with unrestricted coefficients). It is a matter of choice whether we are interested in $E\{y_t|x_t\}$ or $E\{y_t|x_t, x_{t-1}, y_{t-1}\}$ or both. For example, explaining a person's wage from his wage in the previous year may be fairly easy, but may not provide answers to the questions we are interested in. In many applications, though, the inclusion of a lagged dependent variable in the model will eliminate the autocorrelation problem. It should be emphasized, though, that the Durbin–Watson test is inappropriate in a model where a lagged dependent variable is present. In Subsection 5.2.1 particular attention is paid to models with both autocorrelation and a lagged dependent variable.

4.10.2 Heteroskedasticity-and-autocorrelation-consistent Standard Errors for OLS

Let us reconsider our basic model

$$y_t = x_t'\beta + \varepsilon_t, \tag{4.69}$$

where ε_t is subject to autocorrelation. If this is the model we are interested in, for example because we want to know the conditional expectation of y_t given a well-specified x_t, we can choose to apply the GLS approach or apply ordinary least squares while adjusting its standard errors. This last approach is particularly useful when the correlation between ε_t and ε_{t-s} can be argued to be (virtually) zero after some lag length H and/or when the conditions for consistency of the GLS estimator happen to be violated.

If $E\{x_t\varepsilon_t\} = 0$ and $E\{\varepsilon_t\varepsilon_{t-s}\} = 0$ for $s = H, H+1, \ldots$, the OLS estimator is consistent and its covariance matrix can be estimated by

$$\hat{V}^*\{b\} = \left(\sum_{t=1}^{T} x_t x_t'\right)^{-1} TS^* \left(\sum_{t=1}^{T} x_t x_t'\right)^{-1}, \tag{4.70}$$

where

$$S^* = \frac{1}{T}\sum_{t=1}^{T} e_t^2 x_t x_t' + \frac{1}{T}\sum_{j=1}^{H-1} w_j \sum_{s=j+1}^{T} e_s e_{s-j}\left(x_s x_{s-j}' + x_{s-j} x_s'\right). \tag{4.71}$$

Note that we obtain the White covariance matrix, as discussed in Subsection 4.3.4, if $w_j = 0$, so that (4.70) is a generalization. In the standard case $w_j = 1$, but this may lead to an estimated covariance matrix in finite samples that is not positive definite. To prevent this, it is common to use Bartlett weights, as suggested by Newey and West (1987). These weights decrease linearly with j as $w_j = 1 - j/H$. The use of such a set of weights is compatible with the idea that the impact of the autocorrelation of order j diminishes with $|j|$. Standard errors computed from (4.70) are referred to as **hetero-skedasticity-and-autocorrelation-consistent (HAC) standard errors** or simply **Newey–West standard errors**. Sometimes HAC standard errors are also used when the auto-correlation is strictly speaking not restricted to H lags, for example with an autoregressive structure. Theoretically, this can be justified by applying an asymptotic argument that H increases with T as T goes to infinity (but not as fast as T). Empirically, this may not work very well in small samples.

To obtain some intuition for the expression in (4.71), it is instructive to note that S^* is an estimator for the asymptotic covariance matrix of the sample mean $(1/T)\sum_{t=1}^{T} x_t \varepsilon_t$ (compare (2.33) in Chapter 2). Suppose that ε_t would be observable, then one could think of estimating this covariance matrix as

$$\frac{1}{T}\sum_{s,t} \varepsilon_t \varepsilon_s x_t x_s',$$

where the summation is over all relevant elements (symmetric in s and t). This estimator is actually inconsistent, because, for example, the covariance between $x_1 \varepsilon_1$ and $x_T \varepsilon_T$ is estimated from one data point. This explains why we need to restrict the autocorrelation structure. With zero autocorrelation at lag length H or more, the summation is over $|s - t| \leq H - 1$ only and the above estimator becomes consistent.

The Bartlett weights guarantee that the estimator S^* is positive definite in every sample. This can be understood by looking at the covariance matrix of a short-run sum $\sum_{j=0}^{H-1} x_{t-j}\varepsilon_{t-j}$, which is given by

$$\begin{aligned}
V\left\{\sum_{j=0}^{H-1} x_{t-j}\varepsilon_{t-j}\right\} &= HE\{\varepsilon_t^2 x_t x_t'\} \\
&\quad + (H-1)\left[E\{\varepsilon_t \varepsilon_{t-1} x_t x_{t-1}'\} + E\{\varepsilon_{t-1}\varepsilon_t x_{t-1} x_t'\}\right] + \cdots \\
&\quad + \left[E\{\varepsilon_t \varepsilon_{t-H+1} x_t x_{t-H+1}'\} + E\{\varepsilon_{t-H+1}\varepsilon_t x_{t-H+1} x_t'\}\right] \\
&= H\sum_{j=0}^{H-1}(1-j/H)\left[E\{\varepsilon_t \varepsilon_{t-j} x_t x_{t-j}'\} + E\{\varepsilon_{t-j}\varepsilon_t x_{t-j} x_t'\}\right],
\end{aligned}$$

which is positive definite by construction. Dividing by H, and replacing the expectation operators by sample averages and ε_t by e_t, produces the S^* matrix. Because with one sample there is only one sample mean $(1/T) \sum_{t=1}^{T} x_t \varepsilon_t$ to look at, we estimate its variance by looking at the variance, within the sample, of short-run averages, $(1/H) \sum_{j=0}^{H-1} x_{t-j} \varepsilon_{t-j}$ and divide this by the sample size T. Because S^* is estimating an *asymptotic* covariance matrix, i.e. the covariance matrix of $\sqrt{T}$ times the sample average, this $(1/T)$ factor disappears again in (4.71). Note that in the absence of autocorrelation we would estimate the variance of the sample mean as the sample variance of $x_t \varepsilon_t$, divided by T. Finally, the fact that the estimator uses the OLS residuals e_t rather than the unobservable ε_t has no asymptotic consequences.

4.11   Illustration: Risk Premia in Foreign Exchange Markets

A trader who orders goods abroad that have to be paid at some later date can settle his required payments in different ways. As an example, consider a German trader who at the end of the current month buys an amount of coffee at the price of US\$100 000, to be paid by the end of next month. A first strategy to settle his account is to buy dollars now and hold these in deposit until the end of next month. This has the obvious consequence that the trader does not get the German (one month) interest rate during this month, but the US one (assuming he holds the dollar amount in a US deposit). A second strategy is to buy dollars at the so-called forward market. There a price (exchange rate) is determined, that has to be paid for dollars when delivered at the end of next month. This **forward rate** is agreed upon in the current period and has to be paid at delivery (one month from now). Assuming that the forward contract is riskless (ignoring default risk, which is usually very small), the trader will be indifferent between the two strategies. Both possibilities are without risk and therefore it is expected that both yield the same return at the end of next month. If not, arbitrage possibilities would generate riskless profits. The implied equality of the interest rate differential (German and US rates) and the difference between the forward rate and the spot rate is known as the **covered interest rate parity** condition (CIP).

   A third possibility for the trader to pay his bill in dollars is simply to wait until the end of next month and then buy US dollars at a yet unknown exchange rate. If the usual assumption is made that the trader is risk-averse, it will only be attractive to take the additional exchange rate risk if it can be expected that the future spot rate (expressed in Deutsch Mark per dollar) is lower than the forward rate. If this is the case, we say that the market is willing to pay a **risk premium**. In the absence of a risk premium (the forward rate equals the expected spot rate), the covered interest rate parity implies the **uncovered interest rate parity** (UIP), which says that the interest rate differential between two countries equals the expected relative change in the exchange rate. In this section we consider tests for the existence of risk premia in the forward exchange market, based upon regression models. Background reading on these issues can be found in, for example, Frankel (1993), Isard (1995) and Stoll and Whaley (1993), where the latter is orientated to a finance context.

4.11.1 Notation

For a German investor it is possible to hedge against currency risk by buying at time t the necessary amount of US dollars for delivery at time $t + 1$ against a known rate F_t, the forward exchange rate. Thus, F_t is the rate at time t against which dollars can be bought and sold (through a forward contract) at time $t + 1$. The riskless interest rates for Germany and the US are given by $R^D_{f,t+1}$ and $R^{US}_{f,t+1}$, respectively. For the German investor, the investment in US deposits can be made riskless through hedging on the forward exchange market. That is, a riskless investment for the German investor would give return

$$R^{US}_{f,t+1} + \log F_t - \log S_t, \tag{4.72}$$

where S_t is the current spot (exchange) rate. To avoid riskless arbitrage opportunities (and unlimited profits for investors), this return should equal the riskless return on German deposits, i.e. it should hold that

$$R^D_{f,t+1} - R^{US}_{f,t+1} = \log F_t - \log S_t. \tag{4.73}$$

The right hand side of (4.73) is known as the (negative of the) forward discount, while the left hand side is referred to as the interest differential. Condition (4.73) is known as covered interest rate parity and is a pure no-arbitrage condition which is therefore almost surely satisfied in practice (if transaction costs are negligible).

An alternative investment corresponds to an investment in US deposits without hedging the currency risk. The return on this risky investment is

$$R^{US}_{f,t+1} + \log S_{t+1} - \log S_t, \tag{4.74}$$

the expected value of which equals (4.72) if

$$E_t\{\log S_{t+1}\} = \log F_t \quad \text{or} \quad E_t\{s_{t+1}\} = f_t,$$

where small letters denote the log of capital letters, and $E_t\{.\}$ denotes the conditional expectation given all available information at time t. The equality $E_t\{s_{t+1}\} = f_t$ together with covered interest rate parity implies the uncovered interest rate parity condition, which says that the interest differential between two countries equals the expected exchange rate change, i.e.

$$R^D_{f,t+1} - R^{US}_{f,t+1} = E_t\{\log S_{t+1}\} - \log S_t. \tag{4.75}$$

Many macro-economic models employ this UIP condition. One of its consequences is that a small country cannot both control its domestic interest rate level and its exchange rates. In the sequel attention will be paid to the question whether uncovered interest rate parity holds, i.e. whether risk premia on the forward exchange markets exist.

The reason why the expected future spot rate $E_t\{s_{t+1}\}$ may differ from the forward rate f_t is the existence of a risk premium. It is possible that the market is willing to pay a risk premium for taking the exchange rate risk in (4.74). In the absence of a risk premium, hedging against currency risk is free and any investor can eliminate his exchange rate risk completely without costs.

Note that the risk premium is defined as the difference between the expected *log* of the future spot rate and the *log* of the forward rate. Dropping the logarithm has the important objection that expressing exchange rates in one or the other currency is no longer irrelevant. In the logarithmic case this is irrelevant because $E_t\{\log S_{t+1}^{-1}\} - \log F_t^{-1} = -E_t\{\log S_{t+1}\} + \log F_t$.

4.11.2 Tests for Risk Premia in the One-month Market

One approach to test for the presence of risk premia is based on a simple regression framework. In this subsection we shall discuss tests for the presence of a risk premium in the 1-month forward market using monthly data. That is, the sampling frequency corresponds exactly with the length of the term contract. Empirical results will be presented for 1-month forwards on the DM/US\$ and US\$/£Sterling exchange rates, using monthly data from January 1979 to August 1994. The use of monthly data to test for risk premia on the 3-month forward market is discussed in the next subsection.

The hypothesis that there is no risk premium can be written as

$$H_0: E_{t-1}\{s_t\} = f_{t-1}. \tag{4.76}$$

A simple way to test this hypothesis exploits the well known result that the difference between a random variable and its conditional expectation given a certain information set is uncorrelated with any variable from this information set, i.e.

$$E\{(s_t - E_{t-1}\{s_t\})x_{t-1}\} = 0 \tag{4.77}$$

for any x_{t-1} that is known at time $t-1$. From this we can write the following regression model

$$s_t - f_{t-1} = x_{t-1}'\beta + \varepsilon_t, \tag{4.78}$$

where $\varepsilon_t = s_t - E_{t-1}\{s_t\}$. If H_0 is correct and if x_{t-1} is known at time $t-1$, it should hold that $\beta = 0$. Consequently, H_0 is easily tested by testing whether $\beta = 0$ for a given choice of x_{t-1} variables. Below we shall choose as elements in x_{t-1} a constant and the forward discount $s_{t-1} - f_{t-1}$.

Because $s_{t-1} - f_{t-2}$ is observed in period $t-1$, ε_{t-1} is also an element of the information set at time $t-1$. Therefore, (4.77) also implies that under H_0 the error terms in (4.78) exhibit no autocorrelation. Autocorrelation in ε_t is thus an indication for the existence of a risk premium. Note that the hypothesis does not imply anything about the variance of ε_t, which suggests that imposing homoskedasticity may not be appropriate and heteroskedasticity-consistent standard errors could be employed.

The data employed[13] are taken from DATASTREAM and cover the period January 1979–August 1994. The exchange rates employed are the DM/US\$ rate and the US\$/£Sterling rate, where – following standard conventions – the first rate is expressed in Deutsch Mark per US\$, while the second rate is expressed in US\$ per £Sterling. The two exchange rates are visualized in Figure 4.5. From this figure we can infer the weakness of the dollar relative to both the Deutsch Mark and the pound Sterling in the beginning of the eighties and the late 1980s/early 1990s.

In Figure 4.6 the monthly forward discount $s_t - f_t$ is plotted for both exchange rates. For the Deutsch Mark the spot rate is in almost all months above the forward

---

[13] The data for this illustration are available in FORWARD.

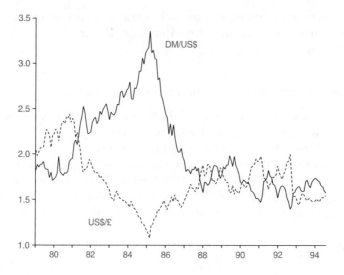

Figure 4.5   DM/US$ and US$/£Sterling exchange rates, January 1979–August 1994

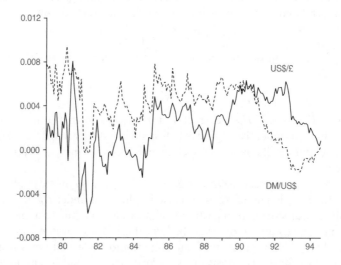

Figure 4.6   Forward discount, DM/US$ and US$/£Sterling, January 1979–August 1994

rate, which implies, given the covered interest rate parity argument, that the US nominal interest rate exceeds the German one. Only for the last two years the converse seems to be the case.

Next, equation (4.78) is estimated by OLS taking $x_{t-1} = (1, s_{t-1} - f_{t-1})'$. The results for the US$/£Sterling rate are given in Table 4.12. Because the forward discount has the properties of a lagged dependent variable ($s_{t-1} - f_{t-1}$ is correlated with

---

[14] Below we use the effective number of observations in the auxiliary regressions to determine T in TR^2.

Table 4.12   OLS results US$/£Sterling

Dependent variable: $s_t - f_{t-1}$

Variable	Estimate	Standard error	t-ratio
constant	−0.0078	0.0035	−2.266
$s_{t-1} - f_{t-1}$	3.8131	1.0163	3.752

$s = 0.0355$ $R^2 = 0.0707$ $\bar{R}^2 = 0.0657$ $F = 14.076$

ε_{t-1}), the Durbin–Watson test is not appropriate. The simplest alternative is to use the Breusch–Godfrey test, which is based upon an auxiliary regression of e_t upon e_{t-1}, $s_{t-1} - f_{t-1}$ and a constant (see above) and then taking[14] TR^2. We can test for higher order autocorrelations by including additional lags, like e_{t-2} and e_{t-3}. This way, the null hypothesis of no autocorrelation can be tested against the alternatives of 1st and (up to) 12th order autocorrelation, with test statistics of 0.54 and 12.06. With 5% critical values of 3.84 and 21.0 (for a χ_1^2 and χ_{12}^2, respectively), this does not imply rejection of the null hypotheses. The t-statistics in the regression indicate that the intercept term is significantly different from zero, while the forward discount has a significantly positive coefficient. A joint test on the two restrictions $\beta = 0$, results in an f-statistic of 7.08 ($p = 0.001$), so that the null hypothesis of no risk premium is rejected. The numbers imply that if the nominal UK interest rate exceeds the US interest rate such that the forward discount $s_{t-1} - f_{t-1}$ exceeds 0.002 (e.g. since 1988), it is found that $E_{t-1}\{s_t\} - f_{t-1}$ is positive. Thus, UK investors can sell their pounds on the forward market at a rate of, say, $1.75, while the expected spot rate is, say, $1.77. UK importers that want to hedge against exchange rate risk for their orders in the US have to pay a risk premium. On the other hand, US traders profit from this; they can hedge against currency risk and cash (!) a risk premium at the same time.[15]

The t-tests employed above are only asymptotically valid if ε_t exhibits no auto-correlation, which is guaranteed by (4.77), and if ε_t is homoskedastic. The Breusch–Pagan test statistic for heteroskedasticity can be computed as TR^2 of an auxiliary regression of e_t^2 upon a constant and $s_{t-1} - f_{t-1}$, which yields an insignificant value of 3.03. Apparently, there is no reason to suspect the usual OLS standard errors.

In a similar way we can test for a risk premium in the DM/US$ forward rate. The results of this regression are as follows:

$$s_t - f_{t-1} = 0.0024 + 0.176 (s_{t-1} - f_{t-1}) + e_t, \quad R^2 = 0.0002,$$
$$\quad\quad\quad (0.0047) \quad (1.007)$$
$$BG(1) = 0.02, \quad BG(12) = 10.48.$$

Here $BG(h)$ denotes the Breusch–Godfrey test statistic for up to h-th order autocorrelation. For the DM/US$ rate no risk premium is found: both the regression coefficients are not significantly different from zero and the hypothesis of no autocorrelation is not rejected.

---

[15] There is no fundamental problem with the risk premium being negative. While this means that the expected return is lower than that of a riskless investment, the actual return may still exceed the riskless rate in situations that are particularly interesting to the investor. For example, a fire insurance on your house typically has a negative expected return, but a large positive return in the particular case that your house burns down.

4.11.3 Tests for Risk Premia Using Overlapping Samples

The previous subsection was limited to an analysis of the one-month forward market for foreign exchange. Of course, forward markets exist with other maturities, for example 3 months or 6 months. In this subsection we shall pay attention to the question to what extent the techniques discussed in the previous section can be used to test for the presence of a risk premium in the 3-month forward market. The frequency of observation is, still, one month.

Let us denote the log price of a 3-month forward contract by f_t^3. The null hypothesis of no risk premium can then be formulated as

$$H_0: E_{t-3}\{s_t\} = f_{t-3}^3. \tag{4.79}$$

Using similar arguments as before, a regression model similar to (4.78) can be written as

$$s_t - f_{t-3}^3 = x_{t-3}'\beta + \varepsilon_t, \tag{4.80}$$

where $\varepsilon_t = s_t - E_{t-3}\{s_t\}$. If x_{t-3} is observed at time $t - 3$, the vector β in (4.80) should equal zero under H_0. Simply using OLS to estimate the parameters in (4.80) with $x_{t-3} = (1, s_{t-3} - f_{t-3})'$ gives the following results for the US\$/£Sterling rates:

$$s_t - f_{t-3}^3 = -0.020 + 3.509 \ (s_{t-3} - f_{t-3}^3) + e_t, \quad R^2 = 0.1319,$$
$$\phantom{s_t - f_{t-3}^3 =} (0.006) \ \ (0.665)$$

$$BG(1) = 81.59, \ \ BG(12) = 112.92,$$

and for the DM/US\$ rates:

$$s_t - f_{t-3}^3 = 0.011 - 0.243 \ (s_{t-3} - f_{t-3}^3) + e_t, \quad R^2 = 0.0007,$$
$$\phantom{s_t - f_{t-3}^3 =} (0.009) \ \ (0.661)$$

$$BG(1) = 87.51, \ \ BG(12) = 113.64.$$

These results seem to suggest the clear presence of a risk premium in both markets: the Breusch–Godfrey tests for autocorrelation indicate strong autocorrelation, while the regression coefficients for the US\$/£Sterling exchange market are highly significant. *These conclusions are, however, incorrect.*

The assumption that the error terms exhibit no autocorrelation was based on the observation that (4.77) also holds for $x_{t-1} = \varepsilon_{t-1}$ such that ε_{t+1} and ε_t were uncorrelated. However, this result is only valid if the frequency of the data coincides with the maturity of the contract. In the present case, we have monthly data for 3-month contracts. The analogue of (4.77) now is

$$E\{(s_t - E_{t-3}\{s_t\})x_{t-3}\} = 0 \text{ for any } x_{t-3} \text{ known at time } t - 3. \tag{4.81}$$

Consequently, this implies that ε_t and ε_{t-j} $(j = 3, 4, 5, \ldots)$ are uncorrelated but does not imply that ε_t and ε_{t-1} or ε_{t-2} are uncorrelated. On the contrary, these errors are likely to be highly correlated.

Consider an illustrative case where (log) exchange rates are generated by a so-called random walk[16] process, i.e. $s_t = s_{t-1} + \eta_t$ where the η_t are independent and identically

---

[16] More details on random walk processes are provided in Chapter 8.

distributed with mean zero and variance σ_η^2 and where no risk premia exist, i.e. $f_{t-3}^3 = E_{t-3}\{s_t\}$. Then it is easily shown that

$$\varepsilon_t = s_t - E_{t-3}\{s_t\} = \eta_t + \eta_{t-1} + \eta_{t-2}.$$

Consequently, the error term ε_t is described by a moving average autocorrelation pattern or order 2. When log exchange rates are not random walks, the error term ε_t will comprise 'news' from periods $t, t-1$ and $t-2$, and therefore ε_t will be a moving average even in the more general case. This autocorrelation problem is due to the so-called overlapping samples problem, where the frequency of observation (monthly) is higher than the frequency of the data (quarterly). If we test whether the autocorrelation goes beyond the first two lags, that is whether ε_t is correlated with ε_{t-3} up to ε_{t-12}, we can do so by running a regression of the OLS residual e_t upon $e_{t-3}, \ldots, e_{t-12}$ and x_t. This results in Breusch–Godfrey test statistics of 8.01 and 6.04, respectively, both of which are insignificant for a Chi-squared distribution with 10 degrees of freedom.

The fact that the first two autocorrelations of the error terms in the regressions above are nonzero, implies that the regression results are not informative about the existence of a risk premium: standard errors are computed in an incorrect way and, moreover, the Breusch–Godfrey tests for autocorrelation may have rejected because of the first two autocorrelations being nonzero, which is not in conflict with the absence of a risk premium. Note that the OLS estimator is still consistent, even with a moving average error term.

One way to 'solve' the problem of autocorrelation is simply dropping two-thirds of the information by using the observations from three-month intervals only. This is unsatisfactory, because of the loss of information and therefore the potential loss of power of the tests. Two alternatives may come to mind: (i) using GLS to (hopefully) estimate the model more efficiently, and (ii) using OLS while computing corrected (Newey–West) standard errors. Unfortunately, the first option is not appropriate here because the transformed data will not satisfy the conditions for consistency and GLS will be inconsistent. This is due to the fact that the regressor $s_{t-3} - f_{t-3}^3$ is correlated with lagged error terms. It is possible to use alternative estimators that are more efficient than OLS, but their discussion is beyond the scope of this text (see Nijman, 1990).

We shall therefore consider the OLS estimation results again, but compute HAC standard errors. Note that $H = 3$ is sufficient. Recall that these standard errors also allow for heteroskedasticity. The results can be summarized as follows. For the US\$/£Sterling rates we have

$$s_t - f_{t-3}^3 = -0.020 + 3.509 \ (s_{t-3} - f_{t-3}^3) + e_t, \quad R^2 = 0.1319,$$
$$[0.008] \quad [1.133]$$

and for the Deutsch Mark/dollar rates:

$$s_t - f_{t-3}^3 = 0.011 - 0.243 \ (s_{t-3} - f_{t-3}^3) + e_t, \quad R^2 = 0.0007,$$
$$[0.012] \quad [0.919]$$

where the standard errors within square brackets are the Newey–West standard errors with $H = 3$. Note that these are substantially larger than those estimated in the conventional way. Qualitatively, however, the conclusions do not change: for the

3-month US\$/£Sterling market, uncovered interest rate parity has to be rejected. Because covered interest rate parity implies that

$$s_t - f_t = R^*_{f,t+1} - R_{f,t+1},$$

where * denotes the foreign country and the exchange rates are measured, as before, in units of home currency for one unit of foreign currency, the results imply that at times when the US interest rate is high relative to the UK one, UK investors pay a risk premium to US traders. For the German/US market, the existence of a risk premium was not found in the data.

Exercises

Exercise 4.1 (Heteroskedasticity – Empirical)

The data set AIRQ contains observations for 30 standard metropolitan statistical areas (SMSAs) in California for 1972 on the following variables:

airq: indicator for air quality (the lower the better);
vala: value added of companies (in 1000 US\$);
rain: amount of rain (in inches);
coas: dummy variable, 1 for SMSAs at the coast; 0 for others;
dens: population density (per square mile);
medi: average income per head (in US\$).

a. Estimate a linear regression model that explains *airq* from the other variables using ordinary least squares. Interpret the coefficient estimates.

b. Test the null hypothesis that average income does not effect the air quality. Test the joint hypothesis that none of the variables has an effect upon air quality.

c. Test whether the variance of the error term is different for coastal and non-coastal areas, using the test of Subsection 4.4.1. In view of the outcome of the test, comment upon the validity of the test from **b**.

d. Perform a Breusch–Pagan test for heteroskedasticity related to all five explanatory variables.

e. Perform a White test for heteroskedasticity. Comment upon the appropriateness of the White test in light of the number of observations and the degrees of freedom of the test.

f. Assuming that we have multiplicative heteroskedasticity related to *coas* and *medi*, estimate the coefficients by running a regression of $\log e_i^2$ upon these two variables. Test the null hypothesis of homoskedasticity on the basis of this auxiliary regression.

g. Using the results from **f**, compute an EGLS estimator for the linear model. Compare your results with those obtained under **a**. Redo the tests from **b**.

h. Comment upon the appropriateness of the R^2 in the regression of **g**.

Exercise 4.2 (Autocorrelation – Empirical)

Consider the data and model of Section 4.8 (the demand for ice cream). Extend the model by including lagged consumption (rather than lagged temperature). Perform a test for first order autocorrelation in this extended model.

Exercise 4.3 (Autocorrelation Theory)

a. Explain what is meant by the 'inconclusive region' of the Durbin–Watson test.

b. Explain why autocorrelation may arise as the result of an incorrect functional form.

c. Explain why autocorrelation may arise because of an omitted variable.

d. Explain why adding a lagged dependent variable and lagged explanatory variables to the model, eliminates the problem of first order autocorrelation. Give at least two reasons why this is not necessarily a preferred solution.

e. Explain what is meant by an 'overlapping samples' problem. What is the problem?

f. Give an example where first order autocorrelation leads to an inconsistent OLS estimator.

g. Explain when you would use Newey–West standard errors.

h. Describe in steps how you would compute the feasible GLS estimator for β in the standard model with (second order) autocorrelation of the form $\varepsilon_t = \rho_1 \varepsilon_{t-1} + \rho_2 \varepsilon_{t-2} + v_t$. (You do not have to worry about the initial observation(s).)

5 Endogeneity, Instrumental Variables and GMM

Until now, it was assumed that the error terms in the linear regression model were contemporaneously uncorrelated with the explanatory variables, or even that they were *independent* of *all* explanatory variables.[1] As a result, the linear model could be interpreted as describing the conditional expectation of y_t given a set of variables x_t. In this chapter we shall discuss cases in which it is unrealistic or impossible to treat the explanatory variables in a model as given or exogenous. In such cases, it can be argued that some of the explanatory variables are correlated with the equation's error term, such that the OLS estimator is biased and inconsistent. There are different reasons why one may argue that error terms are contemporaneously correlated with one or more of the explanatory variables, but the common aspect is that the linear model no longer corresponds to a conditional expectation or a best linear approximation.

In Section 5.1, we start with a review of the properties of the OLS estimator in the linear model under different sets of assumptions. Section 5.2 discusses cases where the OLS estimator cannot be shown to be unbiased or consistent. In such cases, we need to look for alternative estimators. The instrumental variables estimator is considered in Sections 5.3 and 5.5, while in Section 5.6 we generalize this class of instrumental variables estimators to the generalized method of moments (GMM), which also allows estimation of nonlinear models. Empirical illustrations concerning the returns to schooling and the estimation of intertemporal asset pricing models are provided in Sections 5.4 and 5.7, respectively.

---

[1] Recall that independence is stronger than uncorrelatedness (see Appendix B).

5.1 A Review of the Properties of the OLS Estimator

Let us consider the linear model again

$$y_t = x_t'\beta + \varepsilon_t, \quad t = 1, 2, \ldots, T, \tag{5.1}$$

or, in matrix notation,

$$y = X\beta + \varepsilon. \tag{5.2}$$

In Chapters 2 and 4 we saw that the OLS estimator b is unbiased for β if it can be assumed that ε is mean zero and conditional mean independent of X, i.e. if $E\{\varepsilon|X\} = 0$ (assumption (A10) from Chapter 4). This says that knowing any of the explanatory variables is uninformative about the expected value of any of the error terms. Independence of X and ε with $E\{\varepsilon\} = 0$ (assumptions (A1) and (A2) from Section 2.3) implies that $E\{\varepsilon|X\} = 0$ but is stronger, as it does not allow the variance of ε to depend upon X either.

In many cases, the assumption that ε is conditionally mean independent of X is too strong. To illustrate this, let us start with a motivating example. The efficient market hypothesis (under constant expected returns) implies that the returns on any asset are unpredictable from any publicly available information. Under the so-called weak form of the efficient market hypothesis asset returns cannot be predicted from their own past (see the seminal paper by Fama, 1970). This hypothesis can be tested statistically using a regression model and testing whether lagged returns explain current returns. That is, in the model

$$y_t = \beta_1 + \beta_2 y_{t-1} + \beta_3 y_{t-2} + \varepsilon_t, \tag{5.3}$$

where y_t denotes the return in period t, the null hypothesis of weak form efficiency implies that $\beta_2 = \beta_3 = 0$. Because the explanatory variables are lagged dependent variables (which are a function of lagged error terms), the assumption $E\{\varepsilon|X\} = 0$ is inappropriate. Nevertheless, we can make weaker assumptions under which the OLS estimator is consistent for $\beta = (\beta_1, \beta_2, \beta_3)'$.

In the notation of the more general model (5.1), consider the following set of assumptions:

$$x_t \text{ and } \varepsilon_t \text{ are independent (for each } t) \tag{A8}$$

$$\varepsilon_t \sim IID(0, \sigma^2), \tag{A11}$$

where the notation in (A11) is shorthand for saying that the error terms ε_t are independent and identically distributed (i.i.d.) with mean zero and variance σ^2. Under some additional regularity conditions,[2] the OLS estimator b is consistent for β and asymptotically normally distributed with covariance matrix $\sigma^2 \Sigma_{xx}^{-1}$, where as before

$$\Sigma_{xx} = \plim_{T \to \infty} \frac{1}{T} \sum_{t=1}^{T} x_t x_t'.$$

Formally it holds that

---

[2] We shall not present any proofs or derivations here. The interested reader is referred to more advanced textbooks, like Hamilton (1994, Chapter 8). The most important 'regularity condition' is that Σ_{xx} is finite and invertible (compare assumption (A6) from Section 2.6).

$$\sqrt{T}(b - \beta) \to \mathcal{N}(0, \sigma^2 \Sigma_{xx}^{-1}), \tag{5.4}$$

which corresponds to (2.74) from Chapter 2. In small samples, it thus holds *approximately* that

$$b \sim \mathcal{N}\left(\beta, \sigma^2 \left(\sum_{t=1}^{T} x_t x_t'\right)^{-1}\right). \tag{5.5}$$

This distributional result for the OLS estimator is the same as that obtained under the Gauss–Markov assumptions (A1)–(A4), combined with normality of the error terms in (A5), albeit that (5.5) only holds approximately by virtue of the asymptotic result in (5.4). This means that *all standard tests in the linear model (t-tests, F-tests, Wald tests) are valid by approximation, provided assumptions (A8) and (A11) are satisfied*. For the asymptotic distribution in (5.4) to be valid we have to assume that x_t and ε_t are independent (for each t). This means that x_s is allowed to depend upon ε_t as long as $s \neq t$. The inclusion of a lagged dependent variable is the most important example of such a situation. The current result shows that as long as the error terms are independently and identically distributed, the presence of a lagged dependent variable in x_t only affects the small sample properties of the OLS estimator but not the asymptotic distribution. Under assumptions (A8) and (A11) the OLS estimator is consistent and asymptotically efficient.

Assumption (A11) excludes autocorrelation and heteroskedasticity in ε_t. In the example above, autocorrelation can be excluded as it is a violation of market efficiency (returns should be unpredictable). The homoskedasticity assumption is more problematic. Heteroskedasticity may arise when the error term is more likely to take on extreme values for particular values of one or more of the regressors. In this case the variance of ε_t depends upon x_t. Similarly, shocks in financial time series are usually clustered over time, i.e. big shocks are likely to be followed by big shocks, in either direction. An example of this is that after a stock market crash, it is hard to predict whether stock prices will go up or down in subsequent periods, but it is clear that there is much more uncertainty in the market than in other periods. In this case, the variance of ε_t depends upon historical innovations $\varepsilon_{t-1}, \varepsilon_{t-2}, \dots$. Such cases are referred to as conditional heteroskedasticity, or sometimes just as ARCH or GARCH, which are particular specifications to model this phenomenon.[3]

When assumption (A11) is dropped, it can no longer be claimed that $\sigma^2 \Sigma_{xx}^{-1}$ is the appropriate covariance matrix nor that (5.5) holds by approximation. In general however, consistency and asymptotic normality of b are not affected. Moreover, asymptotically valid inferences can be made if we estimate the covariance matrix in a different way. Let us relax assumptions (A8) and (A11) to

$$E\{x_t \varepsilon_t\} = 0 \text{ for each } t \tag{A7}$$

ε_t are serially uncorrelated with expectation zero. (A12)

Assumption (A7) imposes that x_t is uncorrelated[4] with ε_t, while (A12) allows for heteroskedasticity in the error term, but excludes autocorrelation. Under some addi-

---

[3] ARCH is short for AutoRegressive Conditional Heteroskedasticity, and GARCH is a Generalized form of that. We shall discuss this in more detail in Chapter 8.

tional regularity conditions, it can be shown that the OLS estimator b is consistent for β and asymptotically normal, according to

$$\sqrt{T}(b - \beta) \to \mathcal{N}\left(0, \Sigma_{xx}^{-1}\Sigma\Sigma_{xx}^{-1}\right), \tag{5.6}$$

where

$$\Sigma \equiv \text{plim} \frac{1}{T}\sum_{t=1}^{T} \varepsilon_t^2 x_t x_t'.$$

In this case, the asymptotic covariance matrix can be estimated following the method of White (see Chapter 4). Consequently,

$$\hat{V}\{b\} = \left(\sum_{t=1}^{T} x_t x_t'\right)^{-1} \sum_{t=1}^{T} e_t^2 x_t x_t' \left(\sum_{t=1}^{T} x_t x_t'\right)^{-1}, \tag{5.7}$$

where e_t denotes the OLS residual, is a consistent estimator for the true covariance matrix of the OLS estimator under assumptions (A6), (A7) and (A12). Consequently, all standard tests for the linear model are asymptotically valid in the presence of heteroskedasticity of unknown form if the test statistics are adjusted by replacing the standard estimate for the OLS covariance matrix with the heteroskedasticity-consistent estimate from (5.7).

In several cases, people are interested in predictability of long-horizon returns, for example over a horizon of several years. In principle, tests of long-term predictability can be carried out along the same lines as short-term predictability tests. However, for horizons of five years, say, this would imply that only a limited number of 5-year returns can be analysed, even if the sample period covers several decades. Therefore, tests of predictability of long-horizon returns have typically tried to make more efficient use of the available information by using overlapping samples (compare Subsection 4.11.3); see Fama and French (1988) for an application. In this case, 5-year returns are computed over all periods of five consecutive years. Ignoring second order effects, the return over five years is simply the sum of five annual returns, so that the return over 1990–1994 partly overlaps with, for example, the returns over 1991–1995 and 1992–1996. Denoting the return in year t as y_t, the 5-year return over the years t to $t+4$ is given by $Y_t = \sum_{j=0}^{4} y_{t+j}$. To test the predictability of these 5-year returns, suppose we estimate a model that explains Y_t from its value in the previous 5-year period (Y_{t-5}) using data for every year, that is

$$Y_t = \delta_5 + \theta_5 Y_{t-5} + \varepsilon_t, \quad t = 1, \ldots, T \text{ years}. \tag{5.8}$$

All T *annual* observations in the sample on *5-year* returns are regressed on a constant and the 5-year return *lagged five years*. In this model the error term exhibits *auto-correlation* because of the overlapping samples problem. In order to explain this issue, assume that the following model holds for annual returns

$$y_t = \delta_1 + \theta_1 y_{t-1} + u_t, \tag{5.9}$$

where u_t exhibits no autocorrelation. Under the null hypothesis that $\theta_1 = 0$, it can be shown that $\delta_5 = 5\delta_1$ and $\theta_5 = 0$, while $\varepsilon_t = \sum_{j=0}^{4} u_{t+j}$. Consequently, the covariance

---

[4] Note that $E\{x_t z_t\} = \text{cov}\{x_t, z_t\}$ if either x_t or z_t has a zero mean (see Appendix B).

between ε_t and ε_{t-j} is nonzero as long as $j < 5$. From Chapter 4 we know that the presence of autocorrelation invalidates routinely computed standard errors, including those based on the heteroskedasticity consistent covariance matrix in (5.7). However, if we can still assume that the regressors are contemporaneously uncorrelated with the error terms (condition (A7)), and the autocorrelation is zero after H periods, it can be shown that all results based on assumptions (A7) and (A12) hold true if the covariance matrix of the OLS estimator is estimated by the Newey–West (1987) estimator presented in Section 4.10.2

$$\hat{V}^*\{b\} = \left(\sum_{t=1}^{T} x_t x_t'\right)^{-1} TS^* \left(\sum_{t=1}^{T} x_t x_t'\right)^{-1}, \tag{5.10}$$

where

$$S^* = \frac{1}{T}\sum_{t=1}^{T} e_t^2 x_t x_t' + \frac{1}{T}\sum_{j=1}^{H-1} w_j \sum_{s=j+1}^{T} e_s e_{s-j}\left(x_s x_{s-j}' + x_{s-j} x_s'\right) \tag{5.11}$$

with $w_j = 1 - j/H$. Note that in the above example H equals 5. As a consequence, the standard tests from the linear model are asymptotically valid in the presence of heteroskedasticity and autocorrelation (up to a finite number of lags), if we replace the standard covariance matrix estimate by the heteroskedasticity and autocorrelation consistent estimate from (5.10).

5.2 Cases Where the OLS Estimator Cannot be Saved

The previous section shows that we can go as far as assumption (A7) and impose $E\{\varepsilon_t x_t\} = 0$, essentially without affecting the consistency of the OLS estimator. If the autocorrelation in the error term is somehow restricted, it is still possible to make appropriate inferences in this case, using the White or Newey–West estimates for the covariance matrix. The assumption that $E\{\varepsilon_t x_t\} = 0$ says that error terms and explanatory variables are *contemporaneously uncorrelated*. Sometimes there are statistical or economic reasons why we would not want to impose this condition. In such cases, we can no longer argue that the OLS estimator is unbiased or consistent, and we need to consider alternative estimators. Some examples of such situations are: the presence of a lagged dependent variable and autocorrelation in the error term, **measurement errors** in the regressors, and **simultaneity** or **endogeneity** of regressors. Let us now consider examples of these situations in turn.

5.2.1 Autocorrelation with a Lagged Dependent Variable

Suppose the model of interest is given by

$$y_t = \beta_1 + \beta_2 x_t + \beta_3 y_{t-1} + \varepsilon_t, \tag{5.12}$$

where x_t is a single variable. Recall that as long as we can assume that $E\{x_t \varepsilon_t\} = 0$ and $E\{y_{t-1}\varepsilon_t\} = 0$ for all t, the OLS estimator for β is consistent (provided that some regularity conditions are met). However, suppose that ε_t is subject to first order autocorrelation, that is

$$\varepsilon_t = \rho \varepsilon_{t-1} + v_t. \tag{5.13}$$

Now, we can rewrite the model as

$$y_t = \beta_1 + \beta_2 x_t + \beta_3 y_{t-1} + \rho \varepsilon_{t-1} + v_t. \tag{5.14}$$

But it also holds that

$$y_{t-1} = \beta_1 + \beta_2 x_{t-1} + \beta_3 y_{t-2} + \varepsilon_{t-1}, \tag{5.15}$$

from which it follows immediately that the error term ε_t is correlated with y_{t-1}. Thus, if $\rho \neq 0$ OLS no longer yields consistent estimators for the regression parameters in (5.12). Neither does GLS or EGLS in this case. A possible solution is the use of maximum likelihood or instrumental variables techniques that will be discussed below; Stewart and Gill (1998, Sect. 7.4) provide additional discussion and details. Note that the Durbin–Watson test is not valid to test for autocorrelation in model (5.12), because the condition that the explanatory variables can be treated as deterministic is violated. An alternative test is provided by the Breusch–Godfrey Lagrange Multiplier test for autocorrelation (see Section 4.7, or Chapter 6 for a general discussion on Lagrange Multiplier tests). This test statistic can be computed as T times the R^2 of a regression of the least squares residuals e_t on e_{t-1} and all included explanatory variables (including the relevant lagged values of y_t). Under H_0, the test statistic asymptotically has a Chi-squared distribution with 1 degree of freedom.

It can be noted that in the above example the linear regression model does not correspond with the conditional expectation of y_t given x_t and y_{t-1}. Because knowledge of y_{t-1} tells us something about the expected value of the error term ε_t, it will be the case that $E\{\varepsilon_t | x_t, y_{t-1}\}$ is a function of y_{t-1}. Consequently the last term in

$$E\{y_t | x_t, y_{t-1}\} = \beta_1 + \beta_2 x_t + \beta_3 y_{t-1} + E\{\varepsilon_t | x_t, y_{t-1}\} \tag{5.16}$$

will be nonzero. As we know that OLS is generally consistent when estimating a conditional expectation, we may suspect that OLS is inconsistent whenever the model we are estimating does not correspond to a conditional expectation. A lagged dependent variable, combined with autocorrelation of the error term, is such a case.

5.2.2 An Example with Measurement Error

Another illustration where the OLS estimator is likely to be inconsistent arises when an explanatory variable is subject to measurement error. Suppose that a variable y_t depends upon a variable w_t according to

$$y_t = \beta_1 + \beta_2 w_t + v_t, \tag{5.17}$$

where v_t is an error term with zero mean and variance σ_v^2. It is assumed that $E\{v_t | w_t\} = 0$, such that the model describes the expected value of y_t given w_t,

$$E\{y_t | w_t\} = \beta_1 + \beta_2 w_t.$$

As an example, we can think of y_t denoting household savings and w_t denoting disposable income. We shall suppose that w_t cannot be measured absolutely accurately (for example, because of misreporting) and denote the *measured* value for w_t by x_t. For each observation, x_t equals – by construction – the true value w_t plus the

measurement error u_t, that is

$$x_t = w_t + u_t. \tag{5.18}$$

Let us consider the following set of assumptions, which may be reasonable in certain applications. First, it is assumed that the measurement error u_t is mean zero with constant variance σ_u^2. Second, u_t is assumed to be independent of the error term v_t in the model. Third, and most importantly, the measurement error is independent of the underlying true value w_t. This means that the true level of disposable income (in our example) does not reveal any information about the size, sign or value of the measurement error. Substituting (5.18) into (5.17) we obtain

$$y_t = \beta_1 + \beta_2 x_t + \varepsilon_t, \tag{5.19}$$

where $\varepsilon_t = v_t - \beta_2 u_t$.

Equation (5.19) presents a linear model in terms of the observables y_t and x_t with an error term ε_t. If we use the available data on y_t and x_t, and unsuspectingly regress y_t upon x_t and a constant, the OLS estimator b is inconsistent for $\beta = (\beta_1, \beta_2)'$, because x_t depends on u_t and so does ε_t. That is, $E\{x_t\varepsilon_t\} \neq 0$ and one of the necessary conditions for consistency of b is violated. Suppose that $\beta_2 > 0$. When the measurement error in an observation is positive two things happen: x_t has a positive component u_t, and ε_t has a negative component $-\beta_2 u_t$. Consequently, x_t and ε_t are negatively correlated, $E\{x_t\varepsilon_t\} = \text{cov}\{x_t, \varepsilon_t\} < 0$, and it follows that the OLS estimator is inconsistent for β. When $\beta_2 < 0$, x_t and ε_t are positively correlated.

To illustrate the inconsistency of the OLS estimator, write the estimator for β_2 as (compare Subsection 2.1.2)

$$b_2 = \frac{\sum_{t=1}^{T}(x_t - \bar{x})(y_t - \bar{y})}{\sum_{t=1}^{T}(x_t - \bar{x})^2}, \tag{5.20}$$

where $\bar{x}$ denotes the sample mean of x_t. Substituting (5.19), this can be written as

$$b_2 = \beta_2 + \frac{(1/T)\sum_{t=1}^{T}(x_t - \bar{x})(\varepsilon_t - \bar{\varepsilon})}{(1/T)\sum_{t=1}^{T}(x_t - \bar{x})^2}. \tag{5.21}$$

As the sample size increases to infinity, sample moments converge to population moments. Thus

$$\text{plim } b_2 = \beta_2 + \frac{\text{plim }(1/T)\sum_{t=1}^{T}(x_t - \bar{x})(\varepsilon_t - \bar{\varepsilon})}{\text{plim }(1/T)\sum_{t=1}^{T}(x_t - \bar{x})^2} = \beta_2 + \frac{E\{x\varepsilon_t\}}{V\{x_t\}}. \tag{5.22}$$

The last term in this probability limit is not equal to zero. First,

$$E\{x_t\varepsilon_t\} = E\{(w_t + u_t)(v_t - \beta_2 u_t)\} = -\beta_2\sigma_u^2,$$

and, second,

$$V\{x_t\} = V\{w_t + u_t\} = \sigma_w^2 + \sigma_u^2,$$

where $\sigma_w^2 = V\{w_t\}$. Consequently,

$$\text{plim } b_2 = \beta_2\left(1 - \frac{\sigma_u^2}{\sigma_w^2 + \sigma_u^2}\right). \tag{5.23}$$

So, b_2 is consistent only if $\sigma_u^2 = 0$, that is, if there is no measurement error. It is asymptotically biased towards zero if σ_u^2 is positive, with a larger bias if the measurement error is large relative to the variance in the true variable w_t. The ratio σ_u^2/σ_w^2 may be referred to as a noise-to-signal ratio, because it gives the variance of the measurement error (the noise) in relation to the variance of the true values (the signal). If this ratio is small, we have a small bias, if it is large, the bias is also large. In general, the OLS estimator underestimates the effect of true disposable income if reported disposable income is subject to measurement error unrelated to the true level.

It is important to note that the inconsistency of b_2 carries over to the estimator b_1 for the constant term $\beta_1 = E\{y_t - \beta_2 x_t\}$. In particular,

$$\text{plim}(b_1 - \beta_1) = \text{plim}(\bar{y} - b_2\bar{x} - E\{y_t\} + \beta_2 E\{x_t\})$$

$$= -\text{plim}(b_2 - \beta_2)E\{x_t\}, \tag{5.24}$$

So, if $E\{x_t\} > 0$ an overestimation of the slope parameter corresponds to an underestimated intercept. This is a general result: *inconsistency of one element in* b *usually carries over to all other elements.*

Again, let us stress that the model of interest in this case does not correspond to the conditional expectation of y_t given x_t. From (5.19) we can derive that

$$E\{y_t|x_t\} = \beta_1 + \beta_2 x_t - \beta_2 E\{u_t|x_t\},$$

where the latter term is nonzero because of (5.18). If we assume normality of u_t, w_t and x_t, it follows that (see Appendix B)

$$E\{u_t|x_t\} = \frac{\sigma_u^2}{\sigma_w^2 + \sigma_u^2}(x_t - E\{x_t\}).$$

Combining the last two equations and using (5.23) shows that the OLS estimator, though inconsistent for β_2, is consistent for the coefficients in the conditional expectation of savings y_t given *reported* disposable income x_t, but this is not what we are interested in![5]

5.2.3 Simultaneity: the Keynesian Model

Another important situation where we are not interested in a conditional expectation arises when the model of interest contains behavioural parameters, usually measuring the causal effects of changes in the explanatory variables, and one or more of these explanatory variables are jointly determined with the left-hand side variable. For example, if we write down a Keynesian consumption function

$$C_t = \beta_1 + \beta_2 Y_t + \varepsilon_t, \tag{5.25}$$

where C_t denotes a country's real per capita consumption and Y_t is real per capita income, we want to interpret the coefficient β_2 as the marginal propensity to consume $(0 < \beta_2 < 1)$. This means that β_2 has a causal interpretation reflecting the impact of income upon consumption: how much more will people consume if their income

---

[5] This result may be useful as it implies that we can ignore the measurement error problem if we interpret the coefficients in terms of the effects of reported variables rather their true underlying values. This would often not make sense economically but statistically there is no problem.

increases by one unit? However, aggregate income Y_t is not exogenously given as it will be determined by the identity

$$Y_t = C_t + I_t, \tag{5.26}$$

where I_t is real per capita investment. This equation is a definition equation for a closed economy without government and says that total consumption plus total investment should equal total income. We assume that this relationship holds in the sample.

Let us assume that assumption (A11) holds, which says that ε_t is i.i.d. over time with mean zero and variance σ^2. In addition, it is assumed that

$$I_t \text{ and } \varepsilon_t \text{ are independent (for each } t) \tag{5.27}$$

This last assumption says that investment I_t is **exogenous** and determined independently of the error term (that is, determined outside the model). In contrast, both C_t and Y_t are **endogenous** variables, which are *jointly* (*simultaneously*) determined in the model. The model in (5.25)–(5.26) is a very simple simultaneous equations model in **structural form** (or in short: a structural model).

The fact that Y_t is endogenous has its consequences for the estimation of the consumption function (5.25). Because C_t influences Y_t through (5.26) we can no longer argue that Y_t and ε_t are uncorrelated. Consequently, the OLS estimator for β_2 will be biased and inconsistent. To elaborate upon this, it is useful to consider the **reduced form** of this model, in which the endogenous variables C_t and Y_t are expressed as a function of the exogenous variable I_t and the error term. Solving (5.25)–(5.26) for C_t and Y_t, we obtain the reduced form equations

$$Y_t = \frac{\beta_1}{1 - \beta_2} + \frac{1}{1 - \beta_2} I_t + \frac{1}{1 - \beta_2} \varepsilon_t, \tag{5.28}$$

$$C_t = \frac{\beta_1}{1 - \beta_2} + \frac{\beta_2}{1 - \beta_2} I_t + \frac{1}{1 - \beta_2} \varepsilon_t. \tag{5.29}$$

From the first of these two equations it follows that

$$\text{cov}\{Y_t, \varepsilon_t\} = \frac{1}{1 - \beta_2} \text{cov}\{I_t, \varepsilon_t\} + \frac{1}{1 - \beta_2} V\{\varepsilon_t\} = \frac{\sigma^2}{1 - \beta_2}. \tag{5.30}$$

Consequently, equation (5.25) presents a linear model where the regressor Y_t is correlated with the error term ε_t. As a result, OLS applied to (5.25) will be biased and inconsistent. Similar to the earlier derivation, it holds that

$$\text{plim } b_2 = \beta_2 + \frac{\text{cov}\{Y_t, \varepsilon_t\}}{V\{Y_t\}}, \tag{5.31}$$

where

$$V\{Y_t\} = V\left\{ \frac{1}{1 - \beta_2} I_t + \frac{1}{1 - \beta_2} \varepsilon_t \right\} = \frac{1}{(1 - \beta_2)^2} \left(V\{I_t\} + \sigma^2 \right),$$

so that we finally find that

$$\text{plim } b_2 = \beta_2 + (1 - \beta_2) \frac{\sigma^2}{V\{I_t\} + \sigma^2}. \tag{5.32}$$

As $0 < \beta_2 < 1$, and $\sigma^2 > 0$, the OLS estimator will *overestimate* the true marginal propensity to consume β_2. While we have only shown the inconsistency of the estimator for the slope coefficient, the intercept term will in general also be estimated inconsistently (compare (5.24)).

The simple model in this subsection illustrates a common problem in macro- and micro-economic models. If we consider an equation where one or more of the explanatory variables is jointly determined with the left-hand side variable, the OLS estimator will typically provide inconsistent estimators for the behavioural parameters in this equation. Statistically, this means that the equation we have written down does not correspond to a conditional expectation so that the usual assumptions on the error term cannot be imposed.

In the next sections we shall consider alternative approaches to estimating a single equation with endogenous regressors, using so-called instrumental variables. While relaxing the exogeneity assumption in (A7), we shall stress that these approaches require the imposition of alternative assumptions, like (5.27), which may or may not be valid in practice. Such assumptions can be motivated by presenting a complete system of structural equations, explaining all the endogenous variables and stating all the relevant exogenous variables. It will be shown that if there are sufficient exogenous variables in the system that can act as instruments, it is possible to identify and consistently estimate the structural parameters of interest.

The reduced form equations (5.28) and (5.29) express the two endogenous variables in terms of the exogenous variable and an error term. Consequently, we can estimate the *reduced form parameters* consistently by applying ordinary least squares to (5.28) and (5.29). The reduced form parameters are, however, nonlinear functions of the structural form parameters (which is what we are really interested in) and it is the question whether the reduced form parameters give us sufficient information to identify all structural parameters. This is the famous issue of **identification** in simultaneous equations models. We shall not, in this text, discuss identification in the context of deriving structural parameters from the reduced form. Interested readers are referred to Judge *et al.* (1988, Chapter 14) or Greene (2000, Chapter 16). Instead, we consider the identification problem as one of finding sufficient instruments for the endogenous variables in the model. Strictly speaking, this only gives necessary conditions for identification.

5.3   The Instrumental Variables Estimator

In macro-economics there is a wide range of models that consists of a system of equations that simultaneously determine a number of endogenous variables. Consider, for example, a demand and a supply equation, both depending upon prices, and an equilibrium condition that says that demand and supply should be equal. The resulting system simultaneously determines quantities and prices and it can typically not be said that prices determine quantities or quantities determine prices. An even simpler example is the Keynesian model discussed in the previous section. It is becoming more and more common that a researcher's interest is in just one of the equations in such a system and that the remaining equations are not explicitly formulated. In this case there is need for an estimator that can consistently estimate such an equation, even if one or more of the explanatory variables are not exogenous. In this section we shall consider such an estimator, where we use a motivating example from micro-economics.

5.3.1 Estimation with a Single Endogenous Regressor and a Single Instrument

Suppose we explain an individual's log wage y_i by a number of personal characteristics, x_{1i}, as well as the number of hours person i is working (x_{2i}) by means of a linear model

$$y_i = x'_{1i}\beta_1 + x_{2i}\beta_2 + \varepsilon_i. \tag{5.33}$$

We know from Chapter 2 that this model has no interpretation unless we make some assumptions about ε_i. Otherwise, we could just set β_1 and β_2 to arbitrary values and define ε_i such that the equality in (5.33) holds for every observation. The most common interpretation so far is that (5.33) describes the conditional expectation or the best linear approximation of y_i given x_{1i} and x_{2i}. This requires us to impose that

$$E\{\varepsilon_i x_{1i}\} = 0 \tag{5.34}$$

$$E\{\varepsilon_i x_{2i}\} = 0, \tag{5.35}$$

which are the necessary conditions for consistency of the OLS estimator. As soon as we relax any of these conditions, the model no longer corresponds to the conditional expectation of y_i given x_{1i} and x_{2i}.

In the above wage equation, ε_i includes all unobservable factors that affect a person's wage, including things like 'ability' or 'intelligence'. Typically, it is argued that the number of hours a person is working partly also depends on these unobserved characteristics. If this is the case, OLS is *consistently* estimating the conditional expected value of a person's wage given, among other things, how many hours he or she is working, but *not consistently* estimating the causal effect of hours of work. That is, the OLS estimate for β_2 would reflect the difference in the expected wage of two arbitrary persons with the same observed characteristics in x_{1i}, but working x_2 and $x_2 + 1$ hours, respectively. It does not, however, measure the expected wage difference if an arbitrary person (for some exogenous reason) decides to increase his hours from x_2 to $x_2 + 1$. The reason is that in the first interpretation the unobservable factors affecting a person's wage are not assumed to be constant across the two persons, while in the second interpretation the unobservables are kept unchanged. Put differently, *when we interpret the model as a conditional expectation, the ceteris paribus condition only refers to the included variables, while for a causal interpretation it also includes the unobservables (omitted variables) in the error term.*

Quite often, coefficients in a regression model are interpreted as measuring causal effects. In such cases, it makes sense to discuss the validity of conditions like (5.34) and (5.35). If $E\{\varepsilon_i x_{2i}\} \neq 0$, we say that x_{2i} is **endogenous** (with respect to the causal effect β_2). For micro-economic wage equations, it is often argued that many explanatory variables are potentially endogenous, including education level, union status, sickness, industry, and marital status. To illustrate this, it is not uncommon (for USA data) to find that expected wages are about 10% higher if a person is married. Quite clearly, this is not reflecting the causal effect of being married, but the consequence of differences in unobservable characteristics of married and unmarried people.

If it is no longer imposed that $E\{\varepsilon_i x_{2i}\} = 0$, the OLS method produces a biased and inconsistent estimator for the parameters in the model. The solution requires an alternative estimation method. To derive a consistent estimator, it is necessary that we make sure that our model is statistically identified. This means that we need to impose additional assumptions; otherwise the model is not identified and any estimator is necessarily inconsistent. To see this, let us go back to the conditions (5.34)–(5.35). These conditions are so-called **moment conditions**, conditions in terms of expectations (moments) that are implied by the model. These conditions should be sufficient to identify the unknown parameters in the model. That is, the K parameters in β_1 and β_2 should be such that the following K equalities hold:

$$E\{(y_i - x_{1i}'\beta_1 - x_{2i}\beta_2)x_{1i}\} = 0 \tag{5.36}$$

$$E\{(y_i - x_{1i}'\beta_1 - x_{2i}\beta_2)x_{2i}\} = 0. \tag{5.37}$$

When estimating the model by OLS we impose these conditions on the estimator through the corresponding sample moments. That is, the OLS estimator $b = (b_1', b_2)'$ for $\beta = (\beta_1', \beta_2)'$ is solved from

$$\frac{1}{N}\sum_{i=1}^{N}(y_i - x_{1i}'b_1 - x_{2i}b_2)x_{1i} = 0 \tag{5.38}$$

$$\frac{1}{N}\sum_{i=1}^{N}(y_i - x_{1i}'b_1 - x_{2i}b_2)x_{2i} = 0. \tag{5.39}$$

In fact, these are the first-order conditions for the minimization of the least squares criterion. The number of conditions exactly equals the number of unknown parameters, so that b_1 and b_2 can be solved from (5.38) and (5.39). However, as soon as (5.35) is violated, condition (5.39) drops out and we can no longer solve for b_1 and b_2. This means that β_1 and β_2 are no longer identified.

So to identify β_1 and β_2 in the more general case, we need at least one additional moment condition. Such a moment condition is usually derived from the availability of an **instrument** or **instrumental variable**. An instrumental variable z_{2i}, say, is a variable that can be assumed to be uncorrelated with the models error ε_i but correlated with the endogenous variable x_{2i}.[6] If such an instrument can be found, condition (5.37) can be replaced by

$$E\{(y_i - x_{1i}'\beta_1 - x_{2i}\beta_2)z_{2i}\} = 0. \tag{5.40}$$

Provided this moment condition is not a combination of the other ones (z_{2i} is not a linear combination of x_{1i} s), this is sufficient to identify the K parameters β_1 and β_2.

---

[6] The assumption that the instrument is correlated with x_{2i} is needed for identification. If there would be no correlation the additional moment does not provide any (identifying) information on β_2.

The **instrumental variables estimator** $\hat{\beta}_{IV}$ can then be solved from

$$\frac{1}{N}\sum_{i=1}^{N}(y_i - x_i'\hat{\beta}_{1,IV} - x_{2i}\hat{\beta}_{2,IV})x_{2i} = 0 \tag{5.41}$$

$$\frac{1}{N}\sum_{i=1}^{N}(y_i - x_i'\hat{\beta}_{1,IV} - x_{2i}\hat{\beta}_{2,IV})z_{2i} = 0. \tag{5.42}$$

The solution can be determined analytically and leads to the following expression for the IV estimator

$$\hat{\beta}_{IV} = \left(\sum_{i=1}^{N} z_i x_i'\right)^{-1} \sum_{i=1}^{N} z_i y_i, \tag{5.43}$$

where $x_i' = (x_{1i}', x_{2i})$ and $z_i' = (x_{1i}', z_{2i})$. Clearly, if $z_{2i} = x_{2i}$, this expression reduces to the OLS estimator.

Under assumptions (5.36) and (5.40) and some regularity conditions, the instrumental variables estimator is consistent and asymptotically normal. The most important of these regularity conditions is that the $K \times K$ matrix

$$\text{plim} \frac{1}{N}\sum_{i=1}^{N} z_i x_i' = \Sigma_{zx}$$

is finite and invertible. A necessary condition for this is that the instrument z_{2i} is correlated with x_{2i} and not a linear combination of the elements in x_{1i}. The asymptotic covariance matrix of $\hat{\beta}_{IV}$ depends upon the assumptions we make about the distribution of ε_i. In the standard case where ε_i is $IID(0, \sigma^2)$, independent of z_i, it can be shown that

$$\sqrt{N}(\hat{\beta}_{IV} - \beta) \rightarrow \mathcal{N}(0, \sigma^2(\Sigma_{xz}\Sigma_{zz}^{-1}\Sigma_{zx})^{-1}), \tag{5.44}$$

where the symmetric $K \times K$ matrix

$$\Sigma_{zz} \equiv \text{plim} \frac{1}{N}\sum_{i=1}^{N} z_i z_i'$$

is assumed to be invertible, and $\Sigma_{zx} = \Sigma_{xz}'$. Nonsingularity of Σ_{zz} requires that there is no multicollinearity among the K elements in the vector z_i. In finite samples we can estimate the covariance matrix of $\hat{\beta}_{IV}$ by

$$\hat{V}\{\hat{\beta}_{IV}\} = \hat{\sigma}^2\left(\left(\sum_{i=1}^{N} x_i z_i'\right)\left(\sum_{i=1}^{N} z_i z_i'\right)^{-1}\left(\sum_{i=1}^{N} z_i x_i'\right)\right)^{-1}, \tag{5.45}$$

where $\hat{\sigma}^2$ is a consistent estimator for σ^2 based upon the residual sum of squares, for example,

$$\hat{\sigma}^2 = \frac{1}{N}\sum_{i=1}^{N}(y_i - x_i'\hat{\beta}_{IV})^2. \tag{5.46}$$

As in the least squares case, it is possible to adjust for degrees of freedom and divide by $N - K$ rather than N.

The problem for the practitioner is that it is sometimes far from obvious which variables could act as appropriate instruments. In the above example we need a variable that is correlated with hours of work x_{2i} but uncorrelated with the unobserved 'ability' factors that are included in ε_i. It can be argued that variables relating to the composition of one's family *may* serve as instrumental variables.

It is important to realize that the assumptions captured in the moment conditions are identifying. *That is, they cannot be tested statistically.* The only case where the moment conditions are partially testable is when there are more conditions than actually needed for identification. In this case, one can test the so-called overidentifying restrictions, without, however, being able to specify which of the moment conditions corresponds to these restrictions (see below).

5.3.2 Back to the Keynesian Model

The problem for the practitioner is thus to find suitable instruments. In most cases, this means that somehow our knowledge of economic theory has to be exploited. In a complete simultaneous equations model (that specifies relationships for all endogenous variables), this problem can be solved because any exogenous variable in the system that is not included in the equation of interest can be used as an instrument. More precisely, any exogenous variable that has an effect on the endogenous regressor can be used as an instrument, provided it is excluded from the equation that is estimated.[7] Information on this is obtained from the reduced form for the endogenous regressor. For the Keynesian model, this implies that investments I_t provide a valid instrument for income Y_t. The resulting instrumental variable estimator is then given by

$$\hat{\beta}_{IV} = \left[\sum_{t=1}^{T} \binom{1}{I_t} (1 \quad Y_t) \right]^{-1} \sum_{t=1}^{T} \binom{1}{I_t} C_t, \tag{5.47}$$

which we can solve for $\hat{\beta}_{2,IV}$ as

$$\hat{\beta}_{2,IV} = \frac{\sum_{t=1}^{T} (I_t - \bar{I})(C_t - \bar{C})}{\sum_{t=1}^{T} (I_t - \bar{I})(Y_t - \bar{Y})}, \tag{5.48}$$

where $\bar{I}$, $\bar{C}$, and $\bar{Y}$ denote the sample averages.

An alternative way to see that the estimator (5.48) works, is to start from (5.25) and take the covariance with our instrument I_t on both sides of the equality sign. This gives

$$\text{cov}\{C_t, I_t\} = \beta_2 \, \text{cov}\{Y_t, I_t\} + \text{cov}\{\varepsilon_t, I_t\}. \tag{5.49}$$

Because the last term in this equality is zero (I_t is assumed to be exogenous) and $\text{cov}\{Y_t, I_t\} \neq 0$, we can solve β_2 from this as

$$\beta_2 = \frac{\text{cov}\{I_t, C_t\}}{\text{cov}\{I_t, Y_t\}}. \tag{5.50}$$

---

[7] This explains why choosing instruments can be interpreted as imposing exclusion restrictions.

This relationship suggests an estimator for β_2 by replacing the population covariances by their sample counterparts. This gives the instrumental variables estimator we have seen above:

$$\hat{\beta}_{2,IV} = \frac{(1/T) \sum_{t=1}^{T} (I_t - \bar{I})(C_t - \bar{C})}{(1/T) \sum_{t=1}^{T} (I_t - \bar{I})(Y_t - \bar{Y})}. \tag{5.51}$$

Consistency follows directly from the general result that sample moments converge to population moments.

5.3.3 Back to the Measurement Error Problem

The model is given by

$$y_t = \beta_1 + \beta_2 x_t + \varepsilon_t,$$

where (as an interpretation) y_t denotes savings and x_t denotes *observed* disposable income, which equals true disposable income plus a random measurement error. The presence of this measurement error induces correlation between x_t and ε_t.

Given this model, no obvious instruments arise. In fact, this is a common problem in models with measurement errors due to inaccurate recording. The task is to find an observed variable that is (1) correlated with income x_t, but (2) not correlated with u_t, the measurement error in income (nor with ε_t). If we can find such a variable, we can apply instrumental variables estimation. Mainly due to the problem of finding suitable instruments, the problem of measurement error is often ignored in empirical work.

5.3.4 Multiple Endogenous Regressors

If more than one explanatory variable is considered to be endogenous, the dimension of x_{2i} is increased accordingly and the model reads

$$y_i = x_{1i}'\beta_1 + x_{2i}'\beta_2 + \varepsilon_i.$$

To estimate this equation we need an instrument for each element in x_{2i}. This means that if we have five endogenous regressors we need at least five different instruments. Denoting the instruments by the vector z_{2i}, the instrumental variables estimator can again be written as in (5.43),

$$\hat{\beta}_{IV} = \left(\sum_{i=1}^{N} z_i x_i' \right)^{-1} \sum_{i=1}^{N} z_i y_i,$$

where now $x_i' = (x_{1i}', x_{2i}')$ and $z_i' = (x_{1i}', z_{2i}')$.

It is sometimes convenient to refer to the entire vector z_i as the vector of instruments. If a variable in x_i is assumed to be exogenous, we do not need to find an instrument for it. Alternatively and equivalently, this variable is used as its own instrument. This means that the vector of exogenous variables x_{1i} is included in the K-dimensional vector of instruments z_i. If all the variables are exogenous, $z_i = x_i$ and we obtain the OLS estimator, where 'each variable is instrumented by itself'.

In a simultaneous equations context, the exogenous variables from elsewhere in the system are candidate instrumental variables. The so-called 'order condition for identification' (see Greene, 2000, Sect. 16.3) essentially says that sufficient instruments should be available in the system. If, for example, there are five exogenous variables in the system that are not included in the equation of interest, we can have up to five endogenous regressors. If there is only one endogenous regressor, we have five different instruments to choose from. It is also possible and advisable to estimate more efficiently by using all the available instruments simultaneously. This is discussed in Section 5.5. First, however, we shall discuss an empirical illustration concerning the estimation of the causal effect of schooling on earnings.

5.4   Illustration: Estimating the Returns to Schooling

It is quite clear that, on average, people with more education have higher wages. It is less clear, however, whether this positive correlation reflects a causal effect of schooling, or that individuals with a greater earnings capacity have chosen for more years of schooling. If the latter possibility is true, the OLS estimates on the returns to schooling simply reflect differences in unobserved characteristics of working individuals and an increase in a person's schooling due to an exogenous shock will have no effect on this person's wage. The problem of estimating the causal effect of schooling upon earnings has therefore attracted substantive attention in the literature; see Card (1999) for a survey.

Most studies are based upon the human capital earnings function, which says that

$$w_i = \beta_1 + \beta_2 S_i + \beta_3 E_i + \beta_4 E_i^2 + \varepsilon_i,$$

where w_i denotes the log of individual earnings, S_i denotes years of schooling and E_i denotes years of experience. In the absence of information on actual experience, E_i is sometimes replaced by 'potential experience', measured as $age_i - S_i - 6$, assuming people start school at the age of 6. This specification is usually augmented with additional explanatory variables that one wants to control for, like regional, gender and racial dummies. In addition, it is sometimes argued that the returns to education vary across individuals. With this in mind, let us reformulate the wage equation as

$$w_i = z_i'\beta + \gamma_i S_i + u_i$$

$$= z_i'\beta + \gamma S_i + \varepsilon_i, \tag{5.52}$$

where $\varepsilon_i = u_i + (\gamma_i - \gamma)S_i$, and z_i includes all observable variables (except S_i), including the experience variables and a constant. It is assumed that $E\{\varepsilon_i z_i\} = 0$. The coefficient γ has the interpretation of the average return to (an additional year of) schooling $E\{\gamma_i\} = \gamma$ and is our parameter of interest. In addition, we specify a reduced form for S_i as

$$S_i = z_i'\pi + v_i, \tag{5.53}$$

where $E\{v_i z_i\} = 0$. This reduced form is simply a best linear approximation of S_i and not necessarily has an economic interpretation. OLS estimation of β and γ in (5.52) is consistent only if $E\{\varepsilon_i S_i\} = E\{\varepsilon_i v_i\} = 0$. This means that there are no unobservable characteristics that both affect a person's choice of schooling and his (later) earnings.

As discussed in Card (1995), there are different reasons why schooling may be correlated with ε_i. An important one is 'ability bias' (see Griliches, 1977). Suppose that some individuals have unobserved characteristics (ability) that enables them to get higher earnings. If these individuals also have above average schooling levels, this implies a positive correlation between ε_i and v_i and an OLS estimator that is *upward* biased. Another reason why ε_i and v_i may be correlated is the existence of measurement error in the schooling measure. As discussed in Subsection 5.2.2 this induces a negative correlation between ε_i and v_i and, consequently a *downward* bias in the OLS estimate of γ. Finally, if the individual specific returns to schooling (γ_i) are higher for individuals with low levels of schooling, the unobserved component $(\gamma_i - \gamma)S_i$ will be negatively correlated with S_i, which, again, induces a *downward* bias in the OLS estimator.

In the above formulation there are no instruments available for schooling as all potential candidates are included in the wage equation. Put differently, the number of moment conditions in

$$E\{\varepsilon_i z_i\} = E\{(w_i - z_i'\beta - \gamma S_i)z_i\} = 0$$

is one short to identify β and γ. However, if we can think of a variable in z_i (z_{2i}, say) that affects schooling but not wages, this variable can be excluded from the wage equation so as to reduce the number of unknown parameters by one, thereby making the model exactly identified. In this case the instrumental variables estimator for[8] β and γ, using z_{2i} as an instrument, is a consistent estimator.

A continuing discussion in labour economics is the question which variable can legitimately serve as an instrument. Typically, an instrument is thought of as a variable that affects the costs of schooling (and thus the choice of schooling) but not earnings. There is a long tradition of using family background variables, e.g. parents' education, as instrument. As Card (1999) notes, the interest in family background is driven by the fact that children's schooling choices are highly correlated with the characteristics of their parents. More recently, institutional factors of the schooling system are exploited as potential instruments. For example, Angrist and Krueger (1991) use an individual's quarter of birth as an instrument for schooling. Using an extremely large data set of men born from 1930 to 1959 they find that people with birth dates earlier in the year have slightly less schooling than those born later in the year. Assuming that quarter of birth is independent of unobservable taste and ability factors, it can be used as an instrument to estimate the returns to schooling. In a more recent paper, Card (1995) uses the presence of a nearby college as an instrument that can validly be excluded from the wage equation. Students who grow up in an area without a college face a higher cost of college education, while one would expect that higher costs, on average, reduce the years of schooling, particularly in low-income families.

In this section we use data[9] on 3010 men taken from the US National Longitudinal Survey of Young Men, also employed in Card (1995). In this panel survey, a group of individuals is followed since 1966 when they were aged 14–24, and interviewed in a number of consecutive years. The labour market information that we use covers 1976.

---

[8] Note that z_{2i} is excluded from the wage equation so that the element in β corresponding to z_{2i} is set to zero.
[9] Available in SCHOOLING.

In this year, the average years of schooling in this sample is somewhat more than 13 years, with a maximum of 18. Average experience in 1976, when this group of men was between 24 and 34 years old, is 8.86 years, while the average hourly raw wage is $5.77.

Table 5.1 reports the results of an OLS regression of an individual's log hourly wage upon years of schooling, experience and experience squared and three dummy variables indicating whether the individual was black, lived in a metropolitan area (SMSA) and lived in the south. The OLS estimator implies estimated average returns to schooling of approximately 7.4% per year.[10] The inclusion of additional variables, like region of residence in 1966 and family background characteristics in some cases significantly improved the model but hardly affected the coefficients for the variables reported in Table 5.1 (see Card, 1995), so that we shall continue with this fairly simple specification.

If schooling is endogenous then experience and its square are by construction also endogenous, given that age is not a choice variable and therefore unambiguously exogenous. This means that our linear model may suffer from three endogenous regressors so that we need (at least) three instruments. For experience and its square, age and age squared are obvious candidates. As discussed above, for schooling the solution is less trivial. Card (1995) argues that the presence of a nearby college in 1966 may provide a valid instrument. A necessary (but not sufficient) condition for this is that college proximity in 1966 affects the schooling variable, conditional upon the other exogenous variables. To see whether this is the case, we estimate a reduced form, where schooling is explained by age and age squared, the three dummy variables from the wage equation and a dummy indicating whether an individual lived near a college in 1966. The results, by OLS, are reported in Table 5.2. Recall that this reduced form is not an economic or causal model to explain schooling choice. It is just a statistical reduced form, corresponding to the best linear approximation of schooling.

The fact that the lived near college dummy is significant in this reduced form is reassuring. It indicates that, ceteris paribus, students who lived near a college in 1966 have on average 0.35 years more schooling. Recall that a necessary condition for a

Table 5.1   Wage equation estimated by OLS

Dependent variable: log(*wage*)

Variable	Estimate	Standard error	*t*-ratio
constant	4.7337	0.0676	70.022
schooling	0.0740	0.0035	21.113
exper	0.0836	0.0066	12.575
exper^2	−0.0022	0.0003	−7.050
black	−0.1896	0.0176	−10.758
smsa	0.1614	0.0156	10.365
south	−0.1249	0.0151	−8.259

$s = 0.374$ $R^2 = 0.2905$ $\bar{R}^2 = 0.2891$ $F = 204.93$

---

[10] Because the dependent variable is in logs, a coefficient of 0.074 corresponds to a relative difference of approximately 7.4%; see Chapter 3.

Table 5.2 Reduced form for schooling, estimated by OLS

Dependent variable: *schooling*

Variable	Estimate	Standard error	*t*-ratio
constant	−1.8695	4.2984	−0.435
age	1.0614	0.3014	3.522
age²	−0.0188	0.0052	−3.386
black	−1.4684	0.1154	−12.719
smsa	0.8354	0.1093	7.647
south	−0.4597	0.1024	−4.488
lived near college	0.3471	0.1070	3.244

$s = 2.5158$ $R^2 = 0.1185$ $\bar{R}^2 = 0.1168$ $F = 67.29$

valid instrument was that the candidate instrument is correlated with schooling but not a linear combination of the other variables in the model. The crucial condition for a valid instrument, viz. that it is uncorrelated with the error term in the wage equation, cannot be tested. It would only be possible to test for such a correlation if we have a consistent estimator for β and γ first, but we can only find a consistent estimator if we impose that our instrument is valid. The validity of instruments can only be tested, to some extent, if the model is overidentified; see Section 5.5 below. In this case we thus need to trust economic arguments, rather than statistical ones, to rely upon the instrument that is chosen.

Using age, age squared and the lived near college dummy as instruments for experience, experience squared and schooling,[11] we obtain the estimation results reported in Table 5.3. The estimated returns to schooling are over 13% with a relatively large standard error of somewhat more than 5%. While the estimate is substantially higher than the OLS one, its inaccuracy is such that this difference could just be due to sampling error. Nevertheless, the value of the IV estimate is fairly robust to changes in the specification (for example, the inclusion of regional indicators or family background variables). The fact that the IV estimator suffers from such large standard errors is due to the fairly low correlation between the instruments and the endogenous regressors. This is reflected in the R^2 of the reduced form for schooling, which is only 0.1185.[12] While in general the instrumental variables estimator is less accurate than the OLS estimator (which may be inconsistent), the loss in efficiency is particularly large if the instruments are only weakly correlated with the endogenous regressors.

Table 5.3 does not report any goodness-of-fit statistics. The reason is that there is no unique definition of an R^2 or adjusted R^2 if the model is not estimated by ordinary least squares. More importantly, the fact that we estimate the model by instrumental variables methods indicates that goodness-of-fit is not what we are after. Our goal was to consistently estimate the causal effect of schooling upon earnings and that is exactly what instrumental variables is trying to do. Again this reflects that the R^2 plays no role whatsoever in comparing alternative estimators.

---

[11] Although the formulation suggests otherwise, it is not the case that instruments have a one-to-one correspondence with the endogenous regressors. Implicitly, all instruments are jointly used for all variables.

[12] The R^2s for the reduced forms for experience and experience squared (not reported) are both larger than 0.60.

Table 5.3   Wage equation estimated by IV

Dependent variable: log(*wage*)

Variable	Estimate	Standard error	*t*-ratio
constant	4.0656	0.6085	6.682
schooling	0.1329	0.0514	2.588
exper	0.0560	0.0260	2.153
exper^2	−0.0008	0.0013	−0.594
black	−0.1031	0.0774	−1.333
smsa	0.1080	0.0050	2.171
south	−0.0982	0.0288	−3.413

Instruments: *age*, *age*^{2}, *lived near college*
used for: *exper*, *exper*^{2} and *schooling*

If college proximity is to be a valid instrument for schooling it has to be the case that it has no direct effect on earnings. As with most instruments, this is a point of discussion (see Card, 1995). For example, it is possible that families that place a strong emphasis on education choose to live near a college, while children of such families have a higher 'ability' or are more motivated to achieve labour market success (as measured by earnings). Unfortunately, as said before, the current, exactly identified, specification does not allow us to test the validity of the instruments.

The fact that the IV estimate of the returns to schooling is higher than the OLS one suggests that OLS underestimates the true causal effect of schooling. This is at odds with the most common argument against the exogeneity of schooling, namely 'ability bias', but in line with the more recent empirical studies on the returns to schooling (including, for example, Angrist and Krueger, 1991). The downward bias of OLS could be due to measurement error, or – as argued by Card (1995) – to the possibility that the true returns to schooling vary across individuals, negatively related to schooling.

5.5   The Generalized Instrumental Variables Estimator

In Section 5.3 we considered the linear model where for each explanatory variable exactly one instrument was available, which could equal the variable itself if it was assumed exogenous. In this section we generalize this by allowing the use of an arbitrary number of instruments.

5.5.1   Multiple Endogenous Regressors with an Arbitrary Number of Instruments

Let us, in general, consider the following model

$$y_i = x_i'\beta + \varepsilon_i, \tag{5.54}$$

where x_i is of dimension K. The OLS estimator is based upon the K moment conditions

$$E\{\varepsilon_i x_i\} = E\{(y_i - x_i'\beta)x_i\} = 0.$$

More generally, let us assume that there are R instruments available in the vector z_i, which may overlap with x_i. The relevant moment conditions are then given by the following R restrictions

$$E\{\varepsilon_i z_i\} = E\{(y_i - x_i'\beta)z_i\} = 0. \tag{5.55}$$

If $R = K$ we are back in the previous situation and the instrumental variables estimator can be solved from the sample moment conditions

$$\frac{1}{N}\sum_{i=1}^{N}(y_i - x_i'\hat{\beta}_{IV})z_i = 0$$

and we obtain

$$\hat{\beta}_{IV} = \left(\sum_{i=1}^{N} z_i x_i'\right)^{-1} \sum_{i=1}^{N} z_i y_i.$$

If the model is written in matrix notation

$$y = X\beta + \varepsilon$$

and the matrix Z is the $N \times R$ matrix of values for the instruments, this instrumental variables estimator can also be written as

$$\hat{\beta}_{IV} = (Z'X)^{-1}Z'y. \tag{5.56}$$

If $R > K$ there are more instruments than regressors. In this case it is not possible to solve for an estimate of β by replacing (5.55) with its sample counterpart. The reason for this is that there would be more equations than unknowns. Instead of dropping instruments (and losing efficiency), one therefore chooses β in such a way that the R sample moments

$$\frac{1}{N}\sum_{i=1}^{N}(y_i - x_i'\beta)z_i$$

are as close as possible to zero. This is done by minimizing the following quadratic form

$$Q_N(\beta) = \left[\frac{1}{N}\sum_{i=1}^{N}(y_i - x_i'\beta)z_i\right]' W_N \left[\frac{1}{N}\sum_{i=1}^{N}(y_i - x_i'\beta)z_i\right] \tag{5.57}$$

where W_N is an $R \times R$ positive definite symmetric matrix. This matrix is a weighting matrix and tells us how much weight to attach to which (linear combinations of the) sample moments. In general it may depend upon the sample size N, because it may itself be an estimate. For the asymptotic properties of the resulting estimator for β, the probability limit of W_N, denoted $W = \text{plim } W_N$, is important. This matrix W should be positive definite and symmetric. Using matrix notation for convenience, we can rewrite (5.57) as

$$Q_N(\beta) = \left[\frac{1}{N}Z'(y - X\beta)\right]' W_N \left[\frac{1}{N}Z'(y - X\beta)\right]. \tag{5.58}$$

Differentiating this with respect to β (see Appendix A) gives as first order conditions:

$$-2X'ZW_N Z'y + 2X'ZW_N Z'X\hat{\beta}_{IV} = 0,$$

which in turn implies

$$X'ZW_NZ'y = X'ZW_NZ'X\hat{\beta}_{IV}. \tag{5.59}$$

This is a system with K equations and K unknown elements in $\hat{\beta}_{IV}$, where $X'Z$ is of dimension $K \times R$ and $Z'y$ is $R \times 1$. Provided the matrix $X'Z$ is of rank K, the solution to (5.59) is

$$\hat{\beta}_{IV} = (X'ZW_NZ'X)^{-1}X'ZW_NZ'y, \tag{5.60}$$

which, in general, depends upon the weighting matrix W_N.

If $R = K$ the matrix $X'Z$ is square and (by assumption) invertible. This allows us to write

$$\hat{\beta}_{IV} = (Z'X)^{-1}W_N^{-1}(X'Z)^{-1}X'ZW_NZ'y$$
$$= (Z'X)^{-1}Z'y,$$

which corresponds to (5.56), the weighting matrix being irrelevant. In this situation, the number of moment conditions is exactly equal to the number of parameters to be estimated. One can think of this as a situation where β is 'exactly identified' because we have just enough information (i.e. moment conditions) to estimate β. An immediate consequence of this is that the minimum of (5.58) is zero, implying that all samples moments can be set to zero by choosing β appropriately. That is, $Q_N(\hat{\beta}_{IV})$ is equal to zero. In this case $\hat{\beta}_{IV}$ does not depend upon W_N and the same estimator is obtained regardless of the choice of weighting matrix.

If $R < K$, the number of parameters to be estimated exceeds the number of moment conditions. In this case β is 'underidentified' (not identified) because there is insufficient information (i.e. moment conditions) from which to estimate β uniquely. Technically, this means that the inverse in (5.60) does not exist and an infinite number of solutions satisfy the first order conditions in (5.59). Unless we can come up with additional moment conditions, this identification problem is fatal in the sense that no consistent estimator for β exists. Any estimator is necessarily inconsistent.

If $R > K$, then the number of moment conditions exceeds the number of parameters to be estimated, and so β is 'overidentified' because there is more information than is necessary to obtain a consistent estimate of β. In this case we have a range of estimators for β, corresponding to alternative choices for the weighting matrix W_N. As long as the weighting matrix is (asymptotically) positive definite, the resulting estimators are all consistent for β. The idea behind the consistency result is that we are minimizing a quadratic loss function in a set of sample moments that asymptotically converge to the corresponding population moments, while these population moments are equal to zero for the true parameter values. This is the basic principle behind the so-called method of moments, which will be discussed in more detail in the next section.

Different weighting matrices W_N lead to different consistent estimators with generally different asymptotic covariance matrices. This allows us to choose an optimal weighting matrix that leads to the most efficient instrumental variables estimator. It can be shown that the optimal weighting matrix is proportional to the inverse of the covariance matrix of the sample moments. Intuitively, this means that sample moments with a small variance which – consequently – provide accurate information about the parameters in β, get more weight in estimation than the sample moments with a large variance. Essentially, this is the same idea as the weighted least squares approach discussed in Chapter 4, albeit that the weights now reflect different sample moments rather than different observations.

Of course the covariance matrix of the sample moments

$$\frac{1}{N} \sum_{i=1}^{N} \varepsilon_i z_i$$

depends upon the assumptions we make about ε_i and z_i. If, as before, we assume that ε_i is $IID(0, \sigma^2)$ and independent of z_i, the asymptotic covariance matrix of the sample moments is given by

$$\sigma^2 \Sigma_{zz} = \sigma^2 \operatorname{plim} \frac{1}{N} \sum_{i=1}^{N} z_i z_i'.$$

Consequently, an optimal weighting matrix is obtained as

$$W_N^{opt} = \left(\frac{1}{N} \sum_{i=1}^{N} z_i z_i' \right)^{-1} = \left(\frac{1}{N} Z'Z \right)^{-1},$$

and the resulting IV estimator is

$$\hat{\beta}_{IV} = \left(X'Z(Z'Z)^{-1}Z'X \right)^{-1} X'Z(Z'Z)^{-1}Z'y. \qquad (5.61)$$

This is the expression that is found in most textbooks (see, e.g. Greene, 2000, Sect. 16.5). The estimator is sometimes referred to as the **generalized instrumental variables estimator** (GIVE). It is also known as the two-stage least squares or 2SLS estimator (see below). If ε_i is heteroskedastic or exhibits autocorrelation, the optimal weighting matrix should be adjusted accordingly. How this is done follows from the general discussion in the next section.

The asymptotic distribution of $\hat{\beta}_{IV}$ is given by

$$\sqrt{N}(\hat{\beta}_{IV} - \beta) \rightarrow \mathcal{N}(0, \sigma^2(\Sigma_{xz}\Sigma_{zz}^{-1}\Sigma_{zx})^{-1}),$$

which is the same expression as given in Section 5.3. The only difference is in the dimensions of the matrices Σ_{xz} and Σ_{zz}. An estimator for the covariance matrix is easily obtained by replacing the asymptotic limits with their small sample counterparts. This gives

$$\hat{V}\{\hat{\beta}_{IV}\} = \hat{\sigma}^2 \left(X'Z(Z'Z)^{-1}Z'X \right)^{-1} \qquad (5.62)$$

where the estimator for σ^2 is obtained from the IV-residuals $\hat{\varepsilon}_i = y_i - x_i'\hat{\beta}_{IV}$ as

$$\hat{\sigma}^2 = \frac{1}{N} \sum_{i=1}^{N} \hat{\varepsilon}_i^2.$$

The results on consistency and the asymptotic distribution of the generalized instrumental variables estimator are based on the assumption that the model is correctly specified. As the estimator is only based on the model's moment conditions, it is required that the moment conditions are correct. It is therefore important to test whether the data are consistent with these moment conditions. In the 'exactly identified' case, $(1/N)\sum_i \hat{\varepsilon}_i z_i = 0$ by construction, regardless of whether or not the population moment conditions are true. Consequently, one cannot derive a useful test from the corresponding sample moments. Put differently, these $K = R$ identifying restrictions are not testable. However, if β is overidentified it is clear that only K (linear combinations) of the R elements in $(1/N)\sum_i \hat{\varepsilon}_i z_i$ are set equal to zero. If the population moment conditions are true one would expect that the elements in the vector $(1/N)\sum_i \hat{\varepsilon}_i z_i$ are all sufficiently close to zero (as they should converge to zero asymptotically). This provides a basis for a test of the model specification. It can be shown that (under (5.55)) the statistic (based on the GIV estimator with optimal weighting matrix)[13]

$$\xi = N Q_N(\hat{\beta}_{IV}) = \left(\sum_{i=1}^{N} \hat{\varepsilon}_i z_i \right)' \left(\hat{\sigma}^2 \sum_{i=1}^{N} z_i z_i' \right)^{-1} \left(\sum_{i=1}^{N} \hat{\varepsilon}_i z_i \right) \qquad (5.63)$$

has an asymptotic Chi-squared distribution with $R - K$ degrees of freedom. Note that the degrees of freedom equals the number of moment conditions minus the number of parameters to be estimated. This is the case because only $R - K$ of the sample moment conditions $(1/N)\sum_i \hat{\varepsilon}_i z_i$ are free on account of the K restrictions implied by the first-order conditions for $\hat{\beta}_{IV}$ in (5.59). A test based on (5.63) is usually referred to as an **overidentifying restrictions test**. If the test rejects, the specification of the model is rejected in the sense that the sample evidence is inconsistent with the joint validity of all R moment conditions. Note that it is not possible to determine which of the moments are incorrect, i.e. which of the instruments are invalid.[14]

5.5.2 Two-stage Least Squares and the Keynesian Model Again

The estimator in (5.61) is often used in the context of a simultaneous equations system and then has the name of the **two-stage least squares (2SLS) estimator**. This is due to Theil (1953). Essentially, this interpretation says that the same estimator can be obtained in two steps, both of which can be estimated by least squares. In the first step the reduced form is estimated by OLS (that is: a regression of the endogenous regressors upon all instruments). In the second step the original structural equations are estimated by OLS, while replacing all endogenous variables on the right hand side with their predicted values from the reduced form.

To illustrate this, let the reduced form of the k-th explanatory variable be given by (in vector notation)

$$x_k = Z \pi_k + v_k.$$

OLS in this equation produces predicted values $\hat{x}_k = Z(Z'Z)^{-1}Z'x_k$. If x_k is a column in Z we will automatically have that $\hat{x}_k = x_k$. Consequently, the matrix of explanatory variables in the second step can be written as $\hat{X}$ which has the columns $\hat{x}_k, k = 1, \ldots, K$, where

$$\hat{X} = Z(Z'Z)^{-1}Z'X.$$

---

[13] Note that all terms involving N cancel out.

[14] Suppose a pub allows you to buy three beers but pay for only two. Can you tell which of the three beers is the free one?

The OLS estimator in the second step is thus given by

$$\hat{\beta}_{IV} = (\hat{X}'\hat{X})^{-1}\hat{X}'y, \tag{5.64}$$

which can easily be shown to be identical to (5.61). The advantage of this approach is that the estimator can be computed using standard OLS software. In the second step OLS is applied to the original model where all endogenous regressors are replaced by their predicted values on the basis of the instruments.[15] It should be stressed, although this is often overlooked, that the second stage does not automatically provide the correct standard errors (see Maddala, 1992, pp. 374–376, for details).

The use of $\hat{X}$ also allows us to write the generalized instrumental variables estimator in terms of the standard formula in (5.56) if we redefine our matrix of instruments. If we use the K columns of $\hat{X}$ as instruments in the standard formula (5.56) we obtain

$$\hat{\beta}_{IV} = (\hat{X}'X)^{-1}\hat{X}'y,$$

which is identical to (5.61). It shows that one can also interpret $\hat{X}$ as the matrix of instruments (which is sometimes done).

To go back to our Keynesian model, let us now assume that the economy includes a government and a private sector, with government expenditures G_t and private investment I_t, both of which are assumed exogenous. The definition equation now reads

$$Y_t = C_t + G_t + I_t.$$

This implies that both G_t and I_t are now valid instruments to use for income Y_t in the consumption function. Although it is possible to define simple IV estimators similar to (5.51) using either G_t or I_t as instrument, the most efficient estimator uses both instruments simultaneously. The generalized instrumental variables estimator is thus given by

$$\hat{\beta}_{IV} = \left(X'Z(Z'Z)^{-1}Z'X\right)^{-1}X'Z(Z'Z)^{-1}Z'y.$$

where the rows in Z, X and y are given by $z_t' = (1, G_t, I_t)$, $x_t' = (1, Y_t)$ and $y_t = C_t$, respectively.

5.6 The Generalized Method of Moments

The approaches sketched above are special cases of an approach proposed by Hansen (1982), usually referred to as the Generalized Method of Moments (GMM). This approach estimates the model parameters directly from the moment conditions that are imposed by the model. These conditions can be linear in the parameters (as in the above examples) but quite often are nonlinear. To enable identification, the number of moment conditions should be at least as large as the number of unknown parameters. The present section provides a fairly intuitive discussion of the Generalized Method of Moments. First, in the next subsection, we start with a motivating example that illustrates how economic theory can imply nonlinear moment conditions. An extensive, not too technical, overview of GIVE and GMM methodology is given in Hall (1993).

---

[15] Note that the predicted values from the instruments rather than the instruments themselves should be included in the equation of interest to replace the endogenous regressors.

5.6.1 Example

The following example is based on Hansen and Singleton (1982). Consider an individual agent who maximizes the expected utility of current and future consumption by solving

$$\max E_t \left\{ \sum_{s=0}^{S} \delta^s U(C_{t+s}) \right\}, \tag{5.65}$$

where C_{t+s} denotes consumption in period $t+s$, $U(C_{t+s})$ is the utility attached to this consumption level, which is discounted by the discount factor δ ($0 < \delta \leq 1$), and where E_t is the expectation operator conditional upon all information available at time t. Associated with this problem is a set of intertemporal budget constraints of the form

$$C_{t+s} + q_{t+s} = w_{t+s} + (1 + r_{t+s})q_{t+s-1}, \tag{5.66}$$

where q_{t+s} denotes financial wealth at the end of period $t+s$, r_{t+s} is the return on financial wealth (invested in a portfolio of assets), and w_{t+s} denotes labour income. The budget constraint thus says that labour income plus asset income should be spent on consumption C_{t+s} or saved in q_{t+s}. This maximization problem is hard to solve analytically. Nevertheless, it is still possible to estimate the unknown parameters involved through the first order conditions. The first order conditions of (5.65) subject to (5.66) imply that

$$E_t \{ \delta U'(C_{t+1})(1 + r_{t+1}) \} = U'(C_t),$$

where U' is the first derivative of U. The right-hand side of this equality denotes the marginal utility of one additional dollar consumed today, while the left-hand side gives the expected marginal utility of saving this dollar until the next period (so that it becomes $1 + r_{t+1}$ dollars) and consuming it then. Optimality thus implies that (expected) marginal utilities are equalized.

As a next step, we can rewrite this equation as

$$E_t \left\{ \frac{\delta U'(C_{t+1})}{U'(C_t)} (1 + r_{t+1}) - 1 \right\} = 0. \tag{5.67}$$

Essentially, this is a (conditional) moment condition which can be exploited to estimate the unknown parameters if we make some assumption about the utility function U. We can do this by transforming (5.67) into a set of unconditional moment conditions. Suppose z_t is included in the information set. This implies that z_t does not provide any information about the expected value of

$$\frac{\delta U'(C_{t+1})}{U'(C_t)} (1 + r_{t+1}) - 1$$

so that it also holds that[16]

$$E \left\{ \left(\frac{\delta U'(C_{t+1})}{U'(C_t)} (1 + r_{t+1}) - 1 \right) z_t \right\} = 0. \tag{5.68}$$

---

[16] We use the general result that $E\{x_1 | x_2\} = 0$ implies that $E\{x_1 g(x_2)\} = 0$ for any function g (see Appendix B).

Thus we can interpret z_t as a vector of instruments, valid by the assumption of optimal behaviour (rational expectations) of the agent. For simplicity, let us assume that the utility function is of the power form, that is

$$U(C) = \frac{C^{1-\gamma}}{1-\gamma},$$

where γ denotes the (constant) coefficient of relative risk aversion, where higher values of γ correspond to a more risk averse agent. Then we can write (5.68) as

$$E\left\{\left(\delta\left(\frac{C_{t+1}}{C_t}\right)^{-\gamma}(1+r_{t+1}) - 1\right)z_t\right\} = 0. \tag{5.69}$$

We now have a set of moment conditions which identify the unknown parameters δ and γ, and given observations on C_{t+1}/C_t, r_{t+1} and z_t allow us to estimate them consistently. This requires an extension of the earlier approach to nonlinear functions.

5.6.2 The Generalized Method of Moments

Let us, in general, consider a model that is characterized by a set of R moment conditions as

$$E\{f(w_t, z_t, \theta)\} = 0, \tag{5.70}$$

where f is a vector function with R elements, θ is a K-dimensional vector containing all unknown parameters, w_t is a vector of observable variables that could be endogenous or exogenous, and z_t is the vector of instruments. In the example of the previous subsection $w_t' = (C_{t+1}/C_t, \ r_{t+1})$; in the linear model of Section 5.5 $w_t' = (y_t, x_t')$.

To estimate θ we take the same approach as before and consider the sample equivalent of (5.70) given by

$$g_T(\theta) \equiv \frac{1}{T}\sum_{t=1}^{T} f(w_t, z_t, \theta). \tag{5.71}$$

If the number of moment conditions R equals the number of unknown parameters K, it would be possible to set the R elements in (5.71) to zero and to solve for θ to obtain a unique consistent estimator. If f is nonlinear in θ an analytical solution may not be available. If the number of moment conditions is less than the number of parameters, the parameter vector θ is not identified. If the number of moment conditions is larger, we cannot solve uniquely for the unknown parameters by setting (5.71) to zero. Instead, we choose our estimator for θ such that the vector of sample moments is as close as possible to zero, in the sense that a quadratic form in $g_T(\theta)$ is minimized. That is,

$$\min_{\theta} Q_T(\theta) = \min_{\theta} g_T(\theta)' W_T g_T(\theta), \tag{5.72}$$

where, as before, W_T is a positive definite matrix with $\mathrm{plim}\, W_T = W$. The solution to this problem provides the **generalized method of moments** or GMM estimator $\hat{\theta}$. Although we cannot obtain an analytical solution for the GMM estimator in the general case, it can be shown that it is consistent and asymptotically normal under some weak regularity conditions. The heuristic argument presented for the generalized instrumental variables estimator in the linear model extends to this more general setting. Because sample averages converge to population means, which are zero for the true parameter values, an estimator chosen to make these sample moments as close to zero as possible (as defined by (5.72)) will converge to the true value and will thus be consistent. In practice, the GMM estimator is obtained by numerically solving the minimization problem in (5.72), for which a variety of algorithms is available; see Greene (2000, Chapter 5) for a general discussion.

As before, different weighting matrices W_T lead to different consistent estimators with different asymptotic covariance matrices. The optimal weighting matrix, which leads to the smallest covariance matrix for the GMM estimator, is the inverse of the covariance matrix of the sample moments. In the absence of autocorrelation it is given by

$$W^{opt} = \left(E\{f(w_t, z_t, \theta)f(w_t, z_t, \theta)'\}\right)^{-1}.$$

In general this matrix depends upon the unknown parameter vector θ, which presents a problem which we did not encounter in the linear model. The solution is to adopt a multi-step estimation procedure. In the first step we use a suboptimal choice of W_T which does not depend upon θ (for example the identity matrix), to obtain a first consistent estimator $\hat{\theta}_{[1]}$, say. Then, we can consistently estimate the optimal weighting matrix by[17]

$$W_T^{opt} = \left(\frac{1}{T}\sum_{t=1}^{T} f(w_t, z_t, \hat{\theta}_{[1]})f(w_t, z_t, \hat{\theta}_{[1]})'\right)^{-1}. \tag{5.73}$$

In the second step one obtains the asymptotically efficient (optimal) GMM estimator $\hat{\theta}_{GMM}$. Its asymptotic distribution is given by

$$\sqrt{T}(\hat{\theta}_{GMM} - \theta) \rightarrow \mathcal{N}(0, V), \tag{5.74}$$

where the asymptotic covariance matrix V is given by

$$V = (DW^{opt}D')^{-1}, \tag{5.75}$$

where D is the $K \times R$ derivative matrix

$$D = E\left\{\frac{\partial f(w_t, z_t, \theta)}{\partial \theta'}\right\}. \tag{5.76}$$

Intuitively, the elements in D measure how sensitive a particular moment is with respect to small changes in θ. If the sensitivity with respect to a given element in θ is large, small changes in this element lead to relatively large changes in the objective function $Q_T(\theta)$ and the particular element in θ is relatively accurately estimated. As usual, the covariance matrix in (5.75) can be estimated by replacing the population moments in D and W^{opt} by their sample equivalents, evaluated at $\hat{\theta}_{GMM}$.

---

[17] If there is autocorrelation in $f(w_t, z_t, \theta)$ up to a limited order, the optimal weighting matrix can be estimated using a variant of the Newey–West estimator discussed in Section 5.1; see Greene (2000, Subsection 11.5.5).

The great advantage of the generalized method of moments is that (1) it does not require distributional assumptions, like normality, (2) it can allow for heteroskedasticity of unknown form and (3) it can estimate parameters even if the model cannot be solved analytically from the first order conditions. Unlike most of the cases we discussed before, the validity of the instruments in z_t is beyond doubt if the model leads to a conditional moment restriction (as in (5.67)) and z_t is in the conditioning set. For example, if at time t the agent maximizes expected utility given all publicly available information then any variable that is observed (to the agent) at time t provides a valid instrument.

Finally, we consider the extension of the **overidentifying restrictions test** to nonlinear models. Following the intuition from the linear model, it would be anticipated that if the population moment conditions $E\{f(w_t, z_t, \theta)\} = 0$ are correct then $g_T(\hat{\theta}_{GMM}) \approx 0$. Therefore, the sample moments provide a convenient test of the model specification. Provided that all moment conditions are correct, the test statistic

$$\xi = Tg_T(\hat{\theta}_{GMM})' W_T^{opt} g_T(\hat{\theta}_{GMM}),$$

where $\hat{\theta}_{GMM}$ is the optimal GMM estimator and W_T^{opt} is the optimal weighting matrix given in (5.73) (based upon a consistent estimator for θ), is asymptotically Chi-squared distributed with $R - K$ degrees of freedom. Recall that for the exactly identified case, there are zero degrees of freedom and there is nothing that can be tested.

In Section 5.7 we present an empirical illustration using GMM to estimate intertemporal asset pricing models. In Section 10.5 we shall consider another example of GMM, where it is used to estimate a dynamic panel data model. First, we consider a few simple examples.

5.6.3 Some Simple Examples

As a very simple example, assume we are interested in estimating the population mean μ of a variable y_i on the basis of a sample of N observations ($i = 1, 2, \ldots, N$). The moment condition of this 'model' is given by

$$E\{y_i - \mu\} = 0,$$

with sample equivalent

$$\frac{1}{N} \sum_{i=1}^{N} (y_i - \mu).$$

By setting this to zero and solving for μ we obtain a method of moments estimator

$$\hat{\mu} = \frac{1}{N} \sum_{i=1}^{N} y_i,$$

which is just the sample average.

If we consider the linear model

$$y_i = x_i'\beta + \varepsilon_i$$

again, with instrument vector z_i, the moment conditions are

$$E\{\varepsilon_i z_i\} = E\{(y_i - x_i'\beta)z_i\} = 0.$$

If ε_i is i.i.d. the optimal GMM is the instrumental variables estimator given in (5.43) and (5.56). More generally, the optimal weighting matrix is given by

$$W^{opt} = \left(E\{\varepsilon_i^2 z_i z_i'\} \right)^{-1},$$

which is estimated unrestrictedly as

$$W_N^{opt} = \left(\frac{1}{N} \sum_{i=1}^{N} \hat{\varepsilon}_i^2 z_i z_i' \right)^{-1},$$

where $\hat{\varepsilon}_i$ is the residual based upon an initial consistent estimator. When it is imposed that ε_i is i.i.d. we can simply use

$$W_N^{opt} = \left(\frac{1}{N} \sum_{i=1}^{N} z_i z_i' \right)^{-1}.$$

The $K \times R$ derivative matrix is given by

$$D = E\{x_i z_i'\},$$

which we can estimate consistently by

$$D_N = \frac{1}{N} \sum_{i=1}^{N} x_i z_i'.$$

In general, the covariance matrix of the *optimal* GMM or GIV estimator $\hat{\beta}$ for β can be estimated as

$$\hat{V}\{\hat{\beta}\} = \left(\sum_{i=1}^{N} x_i z_i' \right)^{-1} \sum_{t=1}^{T} \hat{\varepsilon}_t^2 z_t z_t' \left(\sum_{i=1}^{N} z_i x_i' \right)^{-1}. \tag{5.77}$$

This estimator generalizes (5.62) just as the White heteroskedasticity consistent covariance matrix generalizes the standard OLS expression. Thus, the general GMM set-up allows for heteroskedasticity of ε_i automatically.

5.7 Illustration: Estimating Intertemporal Asset Pricing Models

In the recent finance literature, the GMM framework is frequently used to estimate and test asset pricing models. An asset pricing model, for example the CAPM discussed in Section 2.7, should explain the variation in expected returns for different risky investments. Because some investments are more risky than others, investors may require compensation for bearing this risk by means of a risk premium. This leads to variation in expected returns across different assets.

In this section we consider the consumption-based asset pricing model. This model is derived from the framework sketched in Subsection 5.6.1 by introducing a number of alternative investment opportunities for financial wealth. Assume that there are J alternative risky assets available that the agent can invest in, with returns $r_{j,t+1}$, $j = 1, \ldots, J$, as well as a riskless asset with certain return $r_{f,t+1}$. Assuming that the agent optimally chooses his portfolio of assets, the first order conditions of the problem now imply that

$$E_t\{\delta U'(C_{t+1})(1 + r_{f,t+1})\} = U'(C_t)$$

$$E_t\{\delta U'(C_{t+1})(1 + r_{j,t+1})\} = U'(C_t), \quad j = 1, \ldots, J.$$

This says that the expected marginal utility of investing one additional dollar in asset j is equal for all assets and equal to the marginal utility of consuming this additional dollar today. Assuming power utility, as before, and restricting attention to unconditional expectations[18] the first order conditions can be rewritten as

$$E\left\{\delta\left(\frac{C_{t+1}}{C_t}\right)^{-\gamma}(1 + r_{f,t+1})\right\} = 1 \tag{5.78}$$

$$E\left\{\delta\left(\frac{C_{t+1}}{C_t}\right)^{-\gamma}(r_{j,t+1} - r_{f,t+1})\right\} = 0, \quad j = 1, \ldots, J, \tag{5.79}$$

where the second set of conditions is written in terms of excess returns, i.e. returns in excess of the riskfree rate.

Let us, for convenience, define the intertemporal marginal rate of substitution

$$m_{t+1}(\theta) \equiv \delta\left(\frac{C_{t+1}}{C_t}\right)^{-\gamma},$$

where θ contains all unknown parameters. In finance, $m_{t+1}(\theta)$ is often referred to as a stochastic discount factor or a pricing kernel (see Campbell, Lo and MacKinlay, 1997, Chapter 8). Alternative asset pricing models are described by alternative specifications for the pricing kernel $m_{t+1}(\theta)$. To see how a choice for $m_{t+1}(\theta)$ provides a model that describes expected returns, we use that for two arbitrary random variables $E\{xy\} = \text{cov}\{x, y\} + E\{x\}E\{y\}$ (see Appendix B), from which it follows that

$$\text{cov}\{m_{t+1}(\theta), r_{j,t+1} - r_{f,t+1}\} + E\{m_{t+1}(\theta)\}E\{r_{j,t+1} - r_{f,t+1}\} = 0.$$

This allows us to write

$$E\{r_{j,t+1} - r_{f,t+1}\} = -\frac{\text{cov}\{m_{t+1}(\theta), r_{j,t+1} - r_{f,t+1}\}}{E\{m_{t+1}(\theta)\}}, \tag{5.80}$$

which says that the expected excess return on any asset j is equal to a risk premium that depends linearly upon the covariance between the asset's excess return and the stochastic discount factor. Knowledge of $m_{t+1}(\theta)$ allows us to describe or explain the cross-sectional variation of expected returns across different assets. In the consumption-based model, this tells us that an asset has a high expected return if the covariance between its return and consumption growth is large and negative. This means that an asset is more rewarded when it has a high return in times when consumption growth is small.[19]

The moment conditions in (5.78)–(5.79) can be used to estimate the unknown parameters δ and γ. In this section we use data[20] that cover monthly returns over

---

[18] This means that we restrict attention to moments using instrument $z_t = 1$ only.

[19] For example, you may reward a particular asset if it delivers a high return in the situation where you happen to get unemployed.

[20] The data are available in PRICING.

the period February 1959–November 1993. The basic assets we consider are ten portfolios of stocks, maintained by the Center for Research in Security Prices at the University of Chicago. These portfolios are size-based, which means that port-folio 1 contains the 10% smallest firms listed at the New York Stock Exchange, while portfolio 10 contains the 10% largest firms that are listed. The riskless return is approximated by the monthly return on a 3 month US Treasury Bill, which does not vary much over time. For consumption we use total US personal consumption expenditures on nondurables and services. It is assumed that the model is valid for a representative agent, whose consumption corresponds to this measure of aggregate per capita consumption. Data on size-based portfolios are used because most asset pricing models tend to underpredict the returns on the stocks of small firms. This is the so-called small firm effect (see Banz, 1981; or Campbell, Lo and MacKinlay, 1997, p. 211).

With one riskless asset and ten risky portfolios, (5.78)–(5.79) provide 11 moment conditions with only two parameters to estimate. These parameters can be estimated using the identity matrix as a suboptimal weighting matrix, using the efficient two-step GMM estimator that was presented above, or using a so-called iterated GMM estimator. This estimator has the same asymptotic properties as the two-step one, but is sometimes argued to have a better small-sample performance. It is obtained by computing a new optimal weighting matrix using the two-step estimator, and using this to obtain a next estimator, $\hat{\theta}_{[3]}$, say, which in turn is used in a weighting matrix to obtain $\hat{\theta}_{[4]}$. This procedure is repeated until convergence.

Table 5.4 presents the estimation results on the basis of the monthly returns from February 1959–November 1993, using one-step GMM (using the identity matrix as weighting matrix) and iterated GMM.[21] The γ estimates are huge and rather impre-cise. For the iterated GMM procedure, for example, a 95% confidence interval for γ based upon the approximate normal distribution is as large as $(-10.21, 124.09)$. The estimated risk aversion coefficients of 56.9 and 91.6 are much higher than what is considered economically plausible. This finding illustrates the so-called equity premium puzzle (see Mehra and Prescott, 1985), which reflects that the high risk premia on risky assets (equity) can only be explained in this model if agents are extremely risk averse (compare Campbell, Lo and MacKinlay, 1997, Section 8.2). If we look at the overidentifying restrictions tests, we see, somewhat surprisingly, that they do not reject the joint validity of the imposed moment conditions. This means

Table 5.4 GMM estimation results consumption-based asset pricing model

	One-step GMM		Iterated GMM	
	Estimate	s.e.	Estimate	s.e.
δ	0.7025	0.1438	0.8337	0.1163
γ	91.6393	38.1066	56.9363	34.2604
$\xi\,(df = 9)$	5.674	$(p = 0.77)$	5.692	$(p = 0.77)$

---

[21] For the one-step GMM estimator the standard errors and the overidentifying restrictions test are com-puted in a non-standard way. The formulae given in the text do not apply because the optimal weighting matrix is not used. See Cochrane (1996) for the appropriate expressions.

that the consumption-based asset pricing model is statistically not rejected by the data. This is solely due to the high imprecision of the estimates. Unfortunately this is only a statistical satisfaction and certainly does not imply that the model is economically valuable. The gain in efficiency from the use of the optimal weighting matrix appears to be fairly limited with standard errors that are only up to 20% smaller than for the one-step method.

To investigate the economic value of the above model, it is possible to compute so-called pricing errors (compare Cochrane, 1996). One can directly compute the average expected excess return according to the model, simply by replacing the population moments in (5.80) by the corresponding sample moments and using the estimated values for δ and γ. On the other hand the average excess returns on asset j can be directly computed from the data. In Figure 5.1, we plot the average excess returns against the predicted average excess returns, as well as a 45° line. We do this for the one-step estimator only because, as argued by Cochrane (1996), this estimator minimizes the vector of pricing errors of the 11 assets. Points on the 45° line indicate that the average pricing error is zero. Points above this line indicate that the return of the corresponding asset is underpredicted by the model. The figure confirms our idea that the economic performance of the model is somewhat disappointing. Clearly, the model is unable to fully capture the cross-sectional variation in expected excess returns. The two portfolios with the smallest firms have the highest mean excess return and are both above the 45° line. The model apparently does not solve the small-firm effect as the returns on these portfolios are underpredicted.

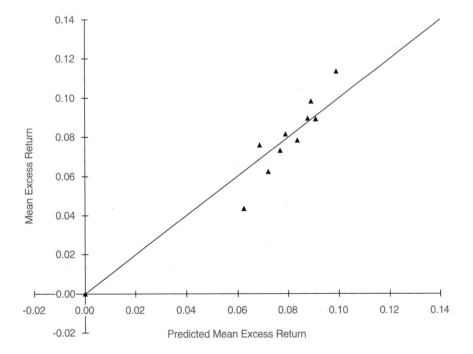

Figure 5.1 Actual versus predicted mean excess returns of size-based portfolios

Cochrane (1996) also presents a range of alternative asset pricing models that are estimated by GMM, which, in a number of cases, perform much better than the simple consumption-based model discussed here. Marquering and Verbeek (1999) extend the above model by including transaction costs and habit persistence in the utility function.

5.8 Concluding Remarks

This chapter has discussed a variety of models that can be headed under the term 'stochastic regressors'. Starting from a linear model with an endogenous regressor, we discussed instrumental variables estimation. It was shown how instrumental variables estimation exploits different moment conditions compared to the OLS estimator. If more moment conditions are imposed than unknown parameters, we can use a generalized instrumental variables estimator, which can also be derived in a GMM framework with an optimal weighting matrix. GMM was discussed in detail, with an application to intertemporal asset pricing models. In dynamic models one usually has the advantage that the choice of instruments is less suspect: lagged values can often be assumed to be uncorrelated with current innovations. The big advantage of GMM is that it can estimate the parameters in a model without having to solve the model analytically. That is, there is no need to write the model as $y = something + error\ term$. All one needs is conditions in terms of expectations, which are often derived directly from economic theory.

Exercises

Exercise 5.1 (Instrumental Variables)

Consider the following model

$$y_i = \beta_1 + \beta_2 x_{i2} + \beta_3 x_{i3} + \varepsilon_i, \quad i = 1, \ldots, N, \qquad (5.81)$$

where (y_i, x_{i2}, x_{i3}) are observed and have finite moments, and ε_i is an unobserved error term. Suppose this model is estimated by ordinary least squares. Denote the OLS estimator by b.

a. What are the *essential* conditions required for unbiasedness of b? What are the *essential* conditions required for consistency of b? Explain the difference between unbiasedness and consistency.

b. Show how the conditions for consistency can be written as moment conditions (if you have not done so already). Explain how a method of moments estimator can be derived from these moment conditions. Is the resulting estimator any different from the OLS one?

Now suppose that $\text{cov}\{\varepsilon_i, x_{i3}\} \neq 0$.

c. Give two examples of cases where one can expect a nonzero correlation between a regressor, x_{i3}, and the error ε_i.

d. In this case, is it possible to still make appropriate inferences based on the OLS estimator, while adjusting the standard errors appropriately?

e. Explain how an instrumental variable, z_i, say, leads to a new moment condition and, consequently, an alternative estimator for β.

f. Why does this alternative estimator lead to a smaller R^2 than the OLS one? What does this say of the R^2 as a measure for the adequacy of the model?

g. Why can we not choose $z_i = x_{i2}$ as an instrument for x_{i3}, even if $E\{x_{i2}\varepsilon_i\} = 0$? Would it be possible to use x_{i2}^2 as an instrument for x_{i3}?

Exercise 5.2 (Returns to Schooling – Empirical)

Consider the data used in Section 5.4, as available in SCHOOLING. The purpose of this exercise is to explore the role of parents' education as instruments to estimate the returns to schooling.

a. Estimate a reduced form for schooling, as reported in Table 5.2, but include mother's and father's education levels. What do these results indicate about the possibility of using parents' education as instruments?

b. Estimate the returns to schooling, on the basis of the same specification as in Section 5.4, using mother's and father's education as instruments (and age and age-squared as instruments for experience and its square).

c. Test the overidentifying restriction.

d. Re-estimate the model using also the lived near college dummy and test the two overidentifying restrictions.

e. Compare and interpret the different estimates on the returns to schooling from Table 5.3, and parts **b** and **d** of this exercise.

Exercise 5.3 (GMM)

An intertemporal utility maximization problem gives the following first order condition

$$E_t\left\{\delta\left(\frac{C_{t+1}}{C_t}\right)^{-\gamma}(1 + r_{t+1})\right\} = 1,$$

where E_t denotes the expectation operator conditional upon time t information, C_t denotes consumption in period t, r_{t+1} is the return on financial wealth, δ is a discount rate and γ is the coefficient of relative risk aversion. Assume that we have a time series of observations on consumption levels, returns and instrumental variables z_t.

a. Show how the above condition can be written as a set of *unconditional* moment conditions. Explain how we can estimate δ and γ consistently from these moment conditions.

b. What is the minimum number of moment conditions that is required? What do we (potentially) gain by having more moment conditions?

c. How can we improve the efficiency of the estimator for a given set of moment conditions? In which case does this not work?

d. Explain what we mean by 'overidentifying restrictions'. Is this a good or a bad thing?

e. Explain how the overidentifying restrictions test is performed. What is the null hypothesis that is tested? What do you conclude if the test rejects?

6 Maximum Likelihood Estimation and Specification Tests

In the previous chapter we paid attention to the generalized method of moments. In the GMM approach the model imposes assumptions about a number of expectations (moments) that involve observable data and unknown coefficients, which are exploited in estimation. In this chapter we consider an estimation approach that typically makes stronger assumptions, because it assumes knowledge of the entire distribution, not just of a number of its moments. If the distribution of a variable y_i conditional upon a number of variables x_i is known up to a small number of unknown coefficients, we can use this to estimate these unknown parameters by choosing them in such a way that the resulting distribution corresponds as well as possible, in a way to be defined more precisely below, to the observed data. This is, rather loosely formulated, the method of maximum likelihood.

In certain applications and models, distributional assumptions like normality are commonly imposed because estimation strategies that do not require such assumptions are complex or unavailable. If the distributional assumptions are correct, the maximum likelihood estimator is, under weak regularity conditions, consistent and asymptotically normal. Moreover, it fully exploits the assumptions about the distribution so that the estimator is asymptotically efficient. That is, alternative consistent estimators will have an asymptotic covariance matrix that is at least as large (in a matrix sense) as that of the maximum likelihood estimator.

This chapter starts with an introduction to maximum likelihood estimation. Section 6.1 describes the approach starting with some simple examples and concluding with some general results and discussion. Because the distributional assumptions are typically crucial for the consistency and efficiency of the maximum likelihood estimator, it is important to be able to test these assumptions. This is discussed in

Section 6.2, while Section 6.3 focuses on the implementation of the Lagrange multiplier tests for particular hypotheses, mostly in the context in the linear regression model. Section 6.4 explores the link with the generalized method of moments (GMM) to introduce quasi-maximum likelihood estimation and to extend the class of Lagrange multiplier tests to moment conditions tests. Knowledge of the issues in Section 6.1 is crucial for understanding Chapter 7 and some specific sections of Chapters 8, 9 and 10. The remaining sections of this chapter cover issues relating to specification tests and are somewhat more technical. They are a prerequisite for some specific sections of Chapter 7 that can be skipped without loss of continuity.

6.1   An Introduction to Maximum Likelihood

The starting point of maximum likelihood estimation is the assumption that the distribution of an observed phenomenon (the endogenous variable) is known, except for a finite number of unknown parameters. These parameters will be estimated by taking those values for them that give the observed values the highest probability, the highest likelihood. The **maximum likelihood** method thus provides a means of estimating a set of parameters characterizing a distribution, if we know, or assume we know, the form of this distribution. For example, we could characterize the distribution of some variable y_i (for given x_i) as normal with mean $\beta_1 + \beta_2 x_i$ and variance σ^2. This would represent the simple linear regression model with normal error terms.

6.1.1   Some Examples

The principle of maximum likelihood is most easily introduced in a discrete setting where y_i only has a finite number of outcomes. As an example, consider a large pool, filled with red and yellow balls. We are interested in the fraction p of red balls in this pool. To obtain information on p, we take a random sample of N balls (and do not look at all the other balls). Let us denote $y_i = 1$ if ball i is red and $y_i = 0$ if it is not. Then it holds by assumption[1] that $P\{y_i = 1\} = p$. Suppose our sample contains $N_1 = \sum_i y_i$ red and $N - N_1$ yellow balls. The probability of obtaining such a sample (in a given order) is given by

$$P\{N_1 \text{ red balls}, N - N_1 \text{ yellow balls}\} = p^{N_1}(1 - p)^{N - N_1}. \tag{6.1}$$

The expression in (6.1), interpreted as a function of the unknown parameter p, is referred to as the **likelihood function**. Maximum likelihood estimation for p implies that we choose a value for p such that (6.1) is maximal. This gives the maximum likelihood estimator $\hat{p}$. For computational purposes it is often more convenient to maximize the (natural) logarithm of (6.1), which is a monotone transformation. This gives the **loglikelihood function** defined as

$$\log L(p) = N_1 \log(p) + (N - N_1) \log(1 - p). \tag{6.2}$$

---

[1] We assume that sampling takes place with replacement. Alternatively, one can assume that the number of balls in the pool is infinitely large, such that previous draws do not affect the probability of drawing a red ball.

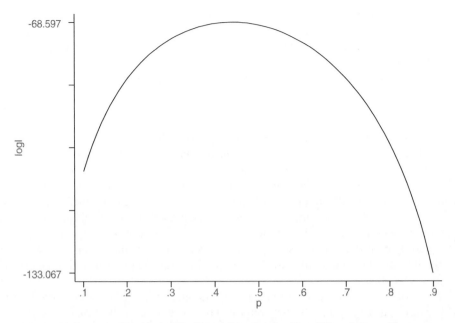

Figure 6.1 Sample loglikelihood function for $N = 100$ and $N_1 = 44$

For a sample of size 100 with 44 red balls ($N_1 = 44$), Figure 6.1 displays the loglikelihood function for values of p between 0.1 and 0.9. Maximizing (6.2) gives as first order condition

$$\frac{d \log L(p)}{dp} = \frac{N_1}{p} - \frac{N - N_1}{1 - p} = 0, \tag{6.3}$$

which, solving for p, gives the maximum likelihood (ML) estimator

$$\hat{p} = N_1/N. \tag{6.4}$$

The ML estimator thus corresponds with the sample proportion of red balls, and probably also corresponds with your best guess for p based on the sample that was drawn. In principle, we also need to check the second order condition to make sure that the solution we have corresponds to a maximum, although in this case it is obvious from Figure 6.1. This gives

$$\frac{d^2 \log L(p)}{dp^2} = -\frac{N_1}{p^2} - \frac{N - N_1}{(1 - p)^2} < 0, \tag{6.5}$$

showing, indeed, that we have found a maximum.

So the intuition of the maximum likelihood principle is as follows. From the (assumed) distribution of the data (e.g. y_i), we determine the likelihood of observing the sample that we happen to observe as a function of the unknown parameters that characterize the distribution. Next, we choose as our maximum likelihood estimates those values for the unknown parameters that give us the highest likelihood. It is clear that this approach makes sense in the above example. The usefulness of the maximum likelihood method is more general, as it can be shown that – under suitable regularity conditions – the maximum likelihood estimator is generally consistent for the true underlying parameters. The ML estimator has several other attractive properties, which we shall discuss below.

As a next illustration, consider the simple regression model

$$y_i = \beta_1 + \beta_2 x_i + \varepsilon_i, \tag{6.6}$$

where we make assumptions (A1)–(A4) from Chapter 2. These assumptions state that ε_i has mean zero, is homoskedastic, has no autocorrelation and is independent of all x_i ($i = 1, \ldots, N$). While these assumptions imply that $E\{y_i|x_i\} = \beta_1 + \beta_2 x_i$ and $V\{y_i|x_i\} = \sigma^2$, they do not impose a particular distribution. To enable maximum likelihood estimation we thus need to augment the above assumptions with an assumption about the shape of the distribution. The most common assumption is that ε_i is normal, as in assumption (A5) from Chapter 2. We can summarize these assumptions by saying that the error terms ε_i are normally and independently distributed (n.i.d.) with mean zero and variance σ^2, or $\varepsilon_i \sim NID(0, \sigma^2)$.

The probability of observing a particular outcome y for y_i is, however, zero for any y, because y_i has a continuous distribution. Therefore the contribution of observation i to the likelihood function is the value of the *density* function at the observed point y_i. For the normal distribution (see Appendix B) this gives

$$f(y_i|x_i; \beta, \sigma^2) = \frac{1}{\sqrt{2\pi\sigma^2}} \exp\left\{-\frac{1}{2}\frac{(y_i - \beta_1 - \beta_2 x_i)^2}{\sigma^2}\right\}, \tag{6.7}$$

where $\beta = (\beta_1, \beta_2)'$. Because of the independence assumption, the joint density of $y_1, \ldots, y_N$ (conditional on $X = (x_1, \ldots, x_N)'$) is given by

$$f(y_i, \ldots, y_N|X; \beta, \sigma^2) = \prod_{i=1}^{N} f(y_i|x_i; \beta, \sigma^2)$$

$$= \left(\frac{1}{\sqrt{2\pi\sigma^2}}\right)^N \prod_{i=1}^{N} \exp\left\{-\frac{1}{2}\frac{(y_i - \beta_1 - \beta_2 x_i)^2}{\sigma^2}\right\}. \tag{6.8}$$

The likelihood function is identical to the density function of $y_1, \ldots, y_N$ but it is considered as a function of the unknown parameters β, σ^2. Consequently, we can write down the loglikelihood function as

$$\log L(\beta, \sigma^2) = -\frac{N}{2}\log(2\pi\sigma^2) - \frac{1}{2}\sum_{i=1}^{N}\frac{(y_i - \beta_1 - \beta_2 x_i)^2}{\sigma^2}. \tag{6.9}$$

As the first term in this expression does not depend upon β, it is easily seen that maximizing (6.9) with respect to β_1 and β_2 corresponds to minimizing the residual sum of squares $S(\beta)$, as defined in Section 2.1. That is, the maximum likelihood estimators for β_1 and β_2 are identical to the OLS estimators. Denoting these estimators by $\hat{\beta}_1$ and $\hat{\beta}_2$, and defining the residuals $e_i = y_i - \hat{\beta}_1 - \hat{\beta}_2 x_i$, we can go on and maximize (6.9) with respect to σ^2. Substituting the ML solutions for β_1 and β_2 and differentiating[2] with respect to σ^2 we obtain the first order condition

$$-\frac{N}{2}\frac{2\pi}{2\pi\sigma^2} + \frac{1}{2}\sum_{i=1}^{N}\frac{e_i^2}{\sigma^4} = 0. \tag{6.10}$$

Solving this for σ^2 gives the maximum likelihood estimator for σ^2 as

$$\hat{\sigma}^2 = \frac{1}{N}\sum_{i=1}^{N} e_i^2. \tag{6.11}$$

This estimator is a consistent estimator for σ^2. It does not, however, correspond to the unbiased estimator for σ^2 that was derived from the OLS estimator (see Chapter 2), given by

$$s^2 = \frac{1}{N-K}\sum_{i=1}^{N} e_i^2,$$

where K is the number of regressors (including the intercept). The difference lies in the degrees of freedom correction in s^2. Because s^2 is unbiased, the ML estimator $\hat{\sigma}^2$ will be biased in finite samples. Asymptotically, $(N-K)/N$ converges to 1 and the bias disappears, so that the ML estimator is consistent, the degrees of freedom correction being a small sample issue.

In this particular example the maximum likelihood estimator for β happens to reproduce the OLS estimator and consequently has the small sample properties of the OLS estimator. The fact that the ML estimator for σ^2 deviates from the unbiased estimator s^2 indicates that this a not a general result. In small samples the latter estimator has better properties than the ML estimator. In many relevant cases, the ML estimator cannot be shown to be unbiased and its small sample properties are unknown. This means that in general the maximum likelihood approach can be defended only on asymptotic grounds, the ML estimator being consistent and asymptotically efficient. Furthermore, it is typically not possible to analytically solve for the ML estimator, except in a number of special cases (like those considered above).

If the error terms ε_i in this example are non-normal or heteroskedastic, the loglikelihood function given in (6.9) is incorrect, that is, does not correspond to the true distribution of y_i given x_i. In such a case the estimator derived from maximizing the incorrect loglikelihood function (6.9) is not the maximum likelihood estimator in a strict sense, and there is no guarantee that it will have good properties. In some particular cases consistency can still be achieved by maximizing an incorrect likelihood function, in which case it is common to refer to the estimator as a quasi-ML estimator. This example illustrates this point, because the (quasi-)ML estimator for β equals the OLS estimator b, which is consistent under much weaker conditions. Again this is not a general result and it is not appropriate in general to rely upon such an argument to defend the use of maximum likelihood. Section 6.4 presents some additional discussion on this issue.

---

[2] We shall consider σ^2 as an unknown parameter, so that we differentiate with respect to σ^2, not σ. The resulting estimator is invariant to this choice.

6.1.2 General Properties

To define the maximum likelihood estimator in a more general situation, suppose that interest lies in the conditional distribution of y_i given x_i. Let the density or probability mass function be given by $f(y_i|x_i; \theta)$, where θ is a K-dimensional vector of unknown parameters and assume that observations are mutually independent. In this situation the joint density or probability mass function of the sample $y_1, \ldots, y_N$ (conditional upon $X = (x_1, \ldots, x_N)')$ is given by[3]

$$f(y_1, \ldots, y_N|X; \theta) = \prod_{i=1}^{N} f(y_i|x_i; \theta).$$

The likelihood function for the available sample is then given by

$$L(\theta|y, X) = \prod_{i=1}^{N} L_i(\theta|y_i, x_i) = \prod_{i=1}^{N} f(y_i|x_i; \theta),$$

which is a function of θ. For several purposes it is convenient to employ the **likelihood contributions**, denoted by $L_i(\theta|y_i, x_i)$, which reflect how much observation i contributes to the likelihood function. The maximum likelihood estimator $\hat{\theta}$ for θ is the solution to

$$\max_{\theta} \log L(\theta) = \max_{\theta} \sum_{i=1}^{N} \log L_i(\theta), \tag{6.12}$$

where $\log L(\theta)$ is the loglikelihood function, and for simplicity we dropped the other arguments. The first order conditions of this problem imply that

$$\left. \frac{\partial \log L(\theta)}{\partial \theta} \right|_{\hat{\theta}} = \sum_{i=1}^{N} \left. \frac{\partial \log L_i(\theta)}{\partial \theta} \right|_{\hat{\theta}} = 0, \tag{6.13}$$

where $|_{\hat{\theta}}$ indicates that the expression is evaluated at $\theta = \hat{\theta}$. If the loglikelihood function is globally concave there is a unique global maximum and the maximum likelihood estimator is uniquely determined by these first order conditions. Only in special cases the ML estimator can be determined analytically. In general, numerical optimization is required (see Greene, 2000, Section 5.5, for a discussion). Fortunately, for many standard models efficient algorithms are available in recent software packages.

For notational convenience we shall denote the first derivatives of the individual loglikelihood contributions, also known as **scores**, as

$$s_i(\theta) \equiv \frac{\partial \log L_i(\theta)}{\partial \theta}, \tag{6.14}$$

so that the first order conditions state that

$$\sum_{i=1}^{N} s_i(\hat{\theta}) = 0.$$

---

[3] We use $f(.)$ as generic notation for a (multivariate) density or probability mass function.

This says that the sample averages of the K scores, evaluated at the ML estimate $\hat{\theta}$, should be zero.

Provided that the likelihood function is correctly specified, it can be shown under weak regularity conditions that the maximum likelihood estimator:

1. is **consistent** for θ (plim $\hat{\theta} = \theta$);
2. is **asymptotically efficient** (that is, asymptotically the ML estimator has the 'smallest' variance among all consistent asymptotically normal estimators);
3. is **asymptotically normally distributed**, according to

$$\sqrt{N}(\hat{\theta} - \theta) \rightarrow \mathcal{N}(0, V), \tag{6.15}$$

where V is the asymptotic covariance matrix.

The covariance matrix V is determined by the shape of the loglikelihood function and can be shown to equal

$$V = \left(-E\left\{ \frac{\partial^2 \log L_i(\theta)}{\partial\theta\,\partial\theta'} \right\} \right)^{-1}. \tag{6.16}$$

The term in brackets is the expected value of the matrix of second order derivatives and reflects the curvature of the loglikelihood function. Clearly, if the loglikelihood function is highly curved around its maximum, the second derivative is large, the variance is small and the maximum likelihood estimator is relatively accurate. If the function is less curved the variance will be larger. The symmetric matrix

$$I(\theta) \equiv -E\left\{ \frac{\partial^2 \log L_i(\theta)}{\partial\theta\,\partial\theta'} \right\} \tag{6.17}$$

is known as the (Fisher) **information matrix**. Loosely speaking, the information matrix summarizes the expected amount of information about θ contained in an arbitrary observation. Given the asymptotic efficiency of the maximum likelihood estimator, the inverse of the information matrix $I(\theta)^{-1}$ provides a lower bound on the asymptotic covariance matrix for any consistent asymptotically normal estimator for θ. The ML estimator is asymptotically efficient because it attains this bound, often referred to as the **Cramèr–Rao lower bound**.

In practice the covariance matrix V can be estimated consistently by replacing the expectations operator by a sample average and replacing the unknown coefficients by the maximum likelihood estimates. That is,

$$\hat{V}_H = \left(-\frac{1}{N} \sum_{i=1}^{N} \frac{\partial^2 \log L_i(\theta)}{\partial\theta\,\partial\theta'} \bigg|_{\hat{\theta}} \right)^{-1}, \tag{6.18}$$

where we take derivatives first and in the result replace the unknown θ by $\hat{\theta}$. The suffix H is used to stress that the estimator for V is based upon the Hessian matrix, the matrix of second derivatives.

If the likelihood function is correctly specified it can be shown that the matrix

$$J(\theta) \equiv E\{s_i(\theta)s_i(\theta)'\}, \tag{6.19}$$

with $s_i(\theta)$ defined in (6.14), is identical to the information matrix $I(\theta)$. We shall return to the possibility that the likelihood function is misspecified and that the matrices $I(\theta)$ and $J(\theta)$ are different in Section 6.4. For the moment, we shall use the notation $I(\theta)$ to reflect either definition. The result in (6.19) indicates that V can also be estimated from the first order derivatives of the loglikelihood function, as

$$\hat{V}_G = \left(\frac{1}{N} \sum_{i=1}^{N} s_i(\hat{\theta}) s_i(\hat{\theta})' \right)^{-1}, \tag{6.20}$$

where the suffix G reflects that the estimator employs the outer product of the gradients (first derivatives). This estimator for V was suggested by Berndt, Hall, Hall and Hausman (1974) and is sometimes referred to as the BHHH estimator. It is important to note that computation of the latter expression requires the individual likelihood contributions. In general the two covariance matrix estimates $\hat{V}_H$ and $\hat{V}_G$ will not be identical. The first estimator typically has somewhat better properties in small samples.

To illustrate the maximum likelihood principle, Subsection 6.1.3 again considers the simple example of the pool with balls, while Subsection 6.1.4 treats the linear regression model with normal errors. Chapter 7 provides more interesting models that typically require maximum likelihood estimation. The remainder of this chapter discusses issues relating to specification and misspecification tests. While this is not without importance, it is somewhat more technical and some readers may prefer to skip these sections on first reading and continue with Chapter 7. Section 6.4 also discusses the relationship between GMM estimation and maximum likelihood estimation in more detail and explains quasi-maximum likelihood estimation. This is mainly of theoretical importance, although it is of some relevance for Section 8.10, where models for conditional heteroskedasticity will be discussed.

6.1.3 An Example (Continued)

To clarify the general formulae in the previous subsection let us reconsider the example concerning the pool of red and yellow balls. In this model, the loglikelihood contribution of observation i can be written as

$$\log L_i(p) = y_i \log p + (1 - y_i) \log(1 - p),$$

with a first derivative

$$\frac{\partial \log L_i(p)}{\partial p} = \frac{y_i}{p} - \frac{1 - y_i}{1 - p}.$$

Note that the expected value of the first derivative is zero, using $E\{y_i\} = p$. The negative of the second derivative is

$$-\frac{\partial^2 \log L_i(p)}{\partial p^2} = \frac{y_i}{p^2} + \frac{1 - y_i}{(1 - p)^2},$$

which has an expected value of

$$E\left\{ -\frac{\partial^2 \log L_i(p)}{\partial p^2} \right\} = \frac{E\{y_i\}}{p^2} + \frac{1 - E\{y_i\}}{(1 - p)^2} = \frac{1}{p} + \frac{1}{1 - p} = \frac{1}{p(1 - p)}.$$

From this it follows that the asymptotic variance of the maximum likelihood estimator $\hat{p}$ is given by $V = p(1 - p)$ and we have that

$$\sqrt{N}(\hat{p} - p) \rightarrow \mathcal{N}(0, p(1 - p)).$$

This result can be used to construct confidence intervals or to test hypotheses. For example, the hypothesis H_0: $p = p_0$ can be tested using the test statistic

$$\frac{\hat{p} - p_0}{\sqrt{\hat{p}(1 - \hat{p})/N}}, \tag{6.21}$$

which – under the null hypothesis – has an asymptotic standard normal distribution. This is similar to the usual t-tests discussed in the context of the linear model. A 95% confidence interval is given by

$$\hat{p} - 1.96\sqrt{\hat{p}(1 - \hat{p})/N}, \quad \hat{p} + 1.96\sqrt{\hat{p}(1 - \hat{p})/N},$$

so that with a sample of 100 balls of which 44 are red ($\hat{p} = 0.44$), we can conclude with 95% confidence that p is between 0.343 and 0.537. When $N = 1000$ with 440 red balls, the interval reduces to $(0.409, 0.471)$. In this particular application it is clear that the normal distribution is an approximation based on large sample theory and will never hold in small samples. In any finite sample, $\hat{p}$ can only take a finite number of different outcomes in the range $[0, 1]$. In fact, in this example the small sample distribution of $N_1 = N\hat{p}$ is known to be binomial with parameters N and p, and this result could be employed instead.

6.1.4 The Normal Linear Regression Model

In this subsection we consider the linear regression model with normal i.i.d. errors (independent of all x_i). This is the model considered in Chapter 2 combined with assumptions (A1)–(A5). Writing

$$y_i = x_i'\beta + \varepsilon_i, \quad \varepsilon_i \sim NID(0, \sigma^2),$$

this imposes that (conditional upon the exogenous variables), y_i is normal with mean $x_i'\beta$ and a constant variance σ^2. Generalizing (6.9), the loglikelihood function for this model can be written as

$$\log L(\beta, \sigma^2) = \sum_{i=1}^{N} \log L_i(\beta, \sigma^2) = -\frac{N}{2}\log(2\pi\sigma^2) - \frac{1}{2}\sum_{i=1}^{N}\frac{(y_i - x_i'\beta)^2}{\sigma^2}. \tag{6.22}$$

The score vector is given by

$$s_i(\beta, \sigma^2) = \begin{pmatrix} \dfrac{\partial \log L_i(\beta, \sigma^2)}{\partial \beta} \\[2mm] \dfrac{\partial \log L_i(\beta, \sigma^2)}{\partial \sigma^2} \end{pmatrix} = \begin{pmatrix} \dfrac{(y_i - x_i'\beta)}{\sigma^2} x_i \\[2mm] -\dfrac{1}{2\sigma^2} + \dfrac{1}{2}\dfrac{(y_i - x_i'\beta)^2}{\sigma^4} \end{pmatrix},$$

while the maximum likelihood estimates $\hat{\beta}$, $\hat{\sigma}^2$ will satisfy the first order conditions

$$\sum_{i=1}^{N}\frac{(y_i - x_i'\hat{\beta})}{\hat{\sigma}^2} x_i = 0,$$

and

$$-\frac{N}{2\hat{\sigma}^2} + \frac{1}{2} \sum_{i=1}^{N} \frac{(y_i - x_i'\hat{\beta})^2}{\hat{\sigma}^4} = 0.$$

It is easily verified that the solutions to these equations are given by

$$\hat{\beta} = \left(\sum_{i=1}^{N} x_i x_i' \right)^{-1} \sum_{i=1}^{N} x_i y_i \quad \text{and} \quad \hat{\sigma}^2 = \frac{1}{N} \sum_{i=1}^{N} (y_i - x_i'\hat{\beta})^2.$$

The estimator for the vector of slope coefficients is identical to the familiar OLS estimator, while the estimator for the variance differs from the OLS value s^2 by dividing through N rather than $N - K$.

The information matrix is defined as $I(\beta, \sigma^2) = E\{s_i(\beta, \sigma^2) s_i(\beta, \sigma^2)'\}$. Using that for a normal distribution $E\{\varepsilon_i\} = 0$, $E\{\varepsilon_i^2\} = \sigma^2$, $E\{\varepsilon_i^3\} = 0$ and $E\{\varepsilon_i^4\} = 3\sigma^4$ (see Appendix B), it can be shown to equal

$$I(\beta, \sigma^2) = \begin{pmatrix} \sigma^{-2} E\{x_i x_i'\} & 0 \\ 0 & \frac{1}{2\sigma^4} \end{pmatrix}.$$

Because this information matrix is a block diagonal, its inverse is given by

$$I(\beta, \sigma^2)^{-1} = \begin{pmatrix} \sigma^2 E\{x_i x_i'\}^{-1} & 0 \\ 0 & 2\sigma^4 \end{pmatrix}.$$

From this it follows that $\hat{\beta}$ and $\hat{\sigma}^2$ are asymptotically normal and mutually independent according to

$$\sqrt{N}(\hat{\beta} - \beta) \to \mathcal{N}(0, \sigma^2 E\{x_i x_i'\}^{-1})$$
$$\sqrt{N}(\hat{\sigma}^2 - \sigma^2) \to \mathcal{N}(0, 2\sigma^4).$$

In small samples it thus holds approximately that

$$\hat{\beta} \sim \mathcal{N}(\beta, \sigma^2 E\{x_i x_i'\}^{-1}/N),$$

which can be estimated as

$$\hat{\beta} \sim \mathcal{N}\left(\beta, \hat{\sigma}^2 \left(\sum_{i=1}^{N} x_i x_i' \right)^{-1}\right).$$

Note that this corresponds quite closely to the results that are familiar for the OLS estimator.

6.2 Specification Tests

6.2.1 Three Test Principles

On the basis of the maximum likelihood estimator a large number of alternative tests can be constructed. Such tests are typically based upon one out of three different principles: the Wald, the likelihood ratio or the Lagrange multiplier principles.

Although any of the three principles can be used to construct a test for a given hypothesis, each of them has its own merits and advantages. The Wald test is used a number of times in the previous chapters and is generally applicable to any estimator that is consistent and asymptotically normal. The likelihood ratio (LR) principle provides an easy way to compare to alternative nested models, while the Lagrange multiplier (LM) tests allow one to test restrictions that are imposed in estimation. This makes the LM approach particularly suited for misspecification tests where a chosen specification of the model is tested for misspecification in several directions (like heteroskedasticity, non-normality, or omitted variables).

Consider again the general problem where we estimate a K-dimensional parameter vector θ by maximizing the loglikelihood function, i.e.

$$\max_{\theta} \log L(\theta) = \max_{\theta} \sum_{i=1}^{N} \log L_i(\theta).$$

Suppose that we are interested in testing one or more linear restrictions on the parameter vector $\theta = (\theta_1, \ldots, \theta_K)'$. These restrictions can be summarized as H_0: $R\theta = 9$ for some fixed J-dimensional vector 9, where R is a $J \times K$ matrix. It is assumed that the J rows of R are linearly independent, so that the restrictions are not in conflict with each other nor redundant. The three test principles can be summarized as follows:

1. **Wald test.** Estimate θ by maximum likelihood and check whether the difference $R\hat{\theta} - 9$ is close to zero, using its (asymptotic) covariance matrix. This is the idea that underlies the well-known t- and F-tests.
2. **Likelihood ratio test.** Estimate the model twice: once without the restriction imposed (giving $\hat{\theta}$) and once with the null hypothesis imposed (giving the **constrained maximum likelihood estimator** $\tilde{\theta}$, where $R\tilde{\theta} = 9$) and check whether the difference in loglikelihood values $\log L(\hat{\theta}) - \log L(\tilde{\theta})$ is significantly different from zero. This implies the comparison of an unrestricted and a restricted maximum of $\log L(\theta)$.
3. **Lagrange multiplier test.** Estimate the model with the restriction from the null hypothesis imposed (giving $\tilde{\theta}$) and check whether the first order conditions from the general model are significantly violated. That is, check whether $\partial \log L(\theta)/\partial \theta_{|\tilde{\theta}}$ is significantly different from zero.

While the three tests look at different aspects of the likelihood function, they are, in general, asymptotically equivalent (that is: the test statistics have the same asymptotic distribution, even if the null hypothesis is violated) and in some cases they even give the same numerical outcomes. Computation of the test statistics, however, is substantially different, so that most of the time we will choose the test that is most easily computed from the results that we have. For example, the Wald test requires estimating the model without the restriction imposed, while the Lagrange multiplier (LM) test requires only that the model is estimated under the null hypothesis. As a result, the LM test may be particularly attractive when relaxing the null hypothesis substantially complicates model estimation. It is also attractive when the number of different hypotheses one wants to test is large, as the model has to be estimated only

once. The likelihood ratio test requires the model to be estimated with and without
the restriction, but, as we shall see, is easily computed from the loglikelihood values.

The **Wald test** starts from the result that

$$\sqrt{N}(\hat{\theta} - \theta) \rightarrow \mathcal{N}(0, V),$$ (6.23)

from which it follows that the J-dimensional vector $R\hat{\theta}$ also has an asymptotic normal
distribution, given by (see Appendix B)

$$\sqrt{N}(R\hat{\theta} - R\theta) \rightarrow \mathcal{N}(0, RVR').$$ (6.24)

Under the null hypothesis $R\theta$ equals the known vector 9, so that we can construct a
test statistic by forming the quadratic form

$$\xi_W = N(R\hat{\theta} - 9)'[R\hat{V}R']^{-1}(R\hat{\theta} - 9),$$ (6.25)

where $\hat{V}$ is a consistent estimator for V (see above). Under H_0 this test statistic has a
Chi-squared distribution with J degrees of freedom, so that large values for ξ_W lead us
to reject the null hypothesis.

The **likelihood ratio test** is even simpler to compute, provided the model is estimated
with and without the restrictions imposed. This means that we have two different
estimators: the unrestricted ML estimator $\hat{\theta}$ and the constrained ML estimator $\tilde{\theta}$,
obtained by maximizing the loglikelihood function $\log L(\theta)$ subject to the restrictions
$R\theta = 9$. Clearly, maximizing a function subject to a restriction will not lead to a larger
maximum compared to the case without the restriction. Thus it follows that
$\log L(\hat{\theta}) - \log L(\tilde{\theta}) \geq 0$. If this difference is small, the consequences of imposing the
restrictions $R\theta = 9$ are limited, suggesting that the restrictions are correct. If the
difference is large, the restrictions are likely to be incorrect. The LR test statistic is
simply computed as

$$\xi_{LR} = 2[\log L(\hat{\theta}) - \log L(\tilde{\theta})],$$

which, under the null hypothesis, has a Chi-squared distribution with J degrees of
freedom. This shows that if we have estimated two specifications of a model we can
easily test the restrictive specification against the more general one by comparing
loglikelihood values. It is important to stress that the use of this test is only appropriate if the two models are nested (see Chapter 3). An attractive feature of the test
is that it is easily employed when testing nonlinear restrictions and that the result is
not sensitive to the way in which we formulate these restrictions. In contrast, the
Wald test can handle nonlinear restrictions but is sensitive to the way they are
formulated. For example, it will matter whether we test $\theta_k = 1$ or $\log \theta_k = 0$. See
Gregory and Veal (1985), Lafontaine and White (1986) or Phillips and Park (1988)
for a discussion.

6.2.2 Lagrange Multiplier Tests

Some of the tests discussed in the previous chapters, like the Breusch–Pagan test for
heteroskedasticity, are **Lagrange multiplier tests** (LM tests). To introduce the general
idea of an LM test, suppose the null hypothesis restricts some elements in
the parameter vector θ to equal a set of given values. To stress this, let us write

$\theta' = (\theta'_1, \theta'_2)$, where the null hypothesis now says that $\theta_2 = 9$, where θ_2 has dimension J. The term 'Lagrange multiplier' comes from the fact that it is implicitly based upon the value of the Lagrange multiplier in the constrained maximization problem. The first order conditions of the Lagrangian

$$H(\theta, \lambda) = \left[\sum_{i=1}^{N} \log L_i(\theta) - \lambda'(\theta_2 - 9) \right], \tag{6.26}$$

yield the constrained ML estimator $\tilde{\theta} = (\tilde{\theta}'_1, 9')'$ and $\tilde{\lambda}$. The vector $\tilde{\lambda}$ can be interpreted as a vector of shadow prices of the restrictions $\theta_2 = 9$. If the shadow prices are high, we would like to reject the restrictions. If they are close to zero, the restrictions are relatively 'innocent'. To derive a test statistic we would therefore like to consider the distribution of $\tilde{\lambda}$. From the first order conditions of (6.26) it follows that

$$\sum_{i=1}^{N} \frac{\partial \log L_i(\theta)}{\partial \theta_1} \bigg|_{\tilde{\theta}} = \sum_{i=1}^{N} s_{i1}(\tilde{\theta}) = 0 \tag{6.27}$$

and

$$\tilde{\lambda} = \sum_{i=1}^{N} \frac{\partial \log L_i(\theta)}{\partial \theta_2} \bigg|_{\tilde{\theta}} = \sum_{i=1}^{N} s_{i2}(\tilde{\theta}), \tag{6.28}$$

where the score vector $s_i(\theta)$ is decomposed into the subvectors $s_{i1}(\theta)$ and $s_{i2}(\theta)$, corresponding to θ_1 and θ_2, respectively. The result in (6.28) shows that the vector of Lagrange multipliers $\tilde{\lambda}$ equals the vector of first derivatives with respect to the restricted parameters θ_2, evaluated at the *constrained* estimator $\tilde{\theta}$. Consequently, the vector of shadow prices of the restrictions $\theta_2 = 9$ also has the interpretation of measuring the extent to which the first order conditions with respect to θ_2 are violated, if we evaluate them at the constrained estimates $\tilde{\theta} = (\tilde{\theta}'_1, 9')'$. As the first derivatives are also referred to as scores, the Lagrange multiplier test is also known as the **score test**.

To determine an appropriate test statistic, we exploit that it can be shown that the sample average $N^{-1}\tilde{\lambda}$ is asymptotically normal with covariance matrix

$$V_\lambda = I_{22}(\theta) - I_{21}(\theta)I_{11}(\theta)^{-1}I_{12}(\theta), \tag{6.29}$$

where $I_{jk}(\theta)$ are blocks in the information matrix $I(\theta)$, defined in (6.17), that is

$$I(\theta) = \begin{pmatrix} I_{11}(\theta) & I_{12}(\theta) \\ I_{21}(\theta) & I_{22}(\theta) \end{pmatrix},$$

where $I_{22}(\theta)$ is of dimension $J \times J$. Computationally, we can make use of the fact[4] that (6.29) is the inverse of the lower right $J \times J$ block of the inverse of $I(\theta)$,

$$I(\theta)^{-1} = \begin{pmatrix} I^{11}(\theta) & I^{12}(\theta) \\ I^{21}(\theta) & I^{22}(\theta) \end{pmatrix},$$

---

[4] This result is generally true and follows using partitioned inverses (see Davidson and MacKinnon, 1993, Appendix A; or Greene, 2000, Chapter 2).

that is $V_\lambda = I^{22}(\theta)^{-1}$. The Lagrange multiplier test statistic can be derived as

$$\xi_{LM} = N^{-1}\tilde{\lambda}'\hat{I}^{22}(\tilde{\theta})\tilde{\lambda}, \qquad (6.30)$$

which under the null hypothesis has an asymptotic Chi-squared distribution with J degrees of freedom, and where $\hat{I}(\tilde{\theta})$ denotes an estimate of the information matrix based upon the constrained estimator $\tilde{\theta}$. Only if $I_{12}(\theta) = 0$ and the information matrix is block diagonal it holds that $I^{22}(\theta) = I(\theta)_{22}^{-1}$. In general the other blocks of the information matrix are required to compute the appropriate covariance matrix of $N^{-1}\tilde{\lambda}$.

Computation of the LM test statistic is particularly attractive if the information matrix is estimated on the basis of the first derivatives of the loglikelihood function, as

$$\hat{I}_G(\tilde{\theta}) = \frac{1}{N} \sum_{i=1}^{N} s_i(\tilde{\theta})s_i(\tilde{\theta})', \qquad (6.31)$$

i.e. the average outer product of the vector of first derivatives, evaluated under the constrained ML estimates $\tilde{\theta}$. Using (6.27) and (6.28) we can write an LM test statistic as

$$\xi_{LM} = \sum_{i=1}^{N} s_i(\tilde{\theta})' \left(\sum_{i=1}^{N} s_i(\tilde{\theta})s_i(\tilde{\theta})' \right)^{-1} \sum_{i=1}^{N} s_i(\tilde{\theta}). \qquad (6.32)$$

Note that the first $K - J$ elements in the scores $s_i(\tilde{\theta})$ sum to zero because of (6.27). Nevertheless, these elements are generally important for computing the correct covariance matrix. Only in the case of block diagonality it holds that $I_{12}(\theta) = 0$ and the other block of the information matrix is irrelevant. An asymptotically equivalent version of the LM test statistic in the block diagonal case can be written as

$$\xi_{LM} = \sum_{i=1}^{N} s_{i2}(\tilde{\theta})' \left(\sum_{i=1}^{N} s_{i2}(\tilde{\theta})s_{i2}(\tilde{\theta})' \right)^{-1} \sum_{i=1}^{N} s_{i2}(\tilde{\theta}). \qquad (6.33)$$

The expression in (6.32) suggests an easy way to compute a Lagrange multiplier test statistic. Let us denote the $N \times K$ matrix of first derivatives as S, such that

$$S = \begin{pmatrix} s_1(\tilde{\theta})' \\ s_2(\tilde{\theta})' \\ \vdots \\ s_N(\tilde{\theta})' \end{pmatrix}. \qquad (6.34)$$

In the matrix S each row corresponds to an observation and each column corresponds to the derivative with respect to one of the parameters. Consequently, we can write

$$\sum_{i=1}^{N} s_i(\tilde{\theta}) = S'\iota,$$

where $\iota = (1, 1, 1, \ldots, 1)'$ of dimension N. Moreover

$$\sum_{i=1}^{N} s_i(\tilde{\theta}) s_i(\tilde{\theta})' = S'S.$$

This allows us to rewrite (6.32) as

$$\xi_{LM} = \iota' S(S'S)^{-1} S'\iota = N \frac{\iota' S(S'S)^{-1} S'\iota}{\iota'\iota}. \tag{6.35}$$

Now, consider an auxiliary regression of a column of ones upon the columns of the matrix S. From the standard expression for the OLS estimator, $(S'S)^{-1} S'\iota$, we obtain predicted values of this regression as $S(S'S)^{-1} S'\iota$. The explained sum of squares, therefore, is given by

$$\iota' S(S'S)^{-1} S'S(S'S)^{-1} S'\iota = \iota' S(S'S)^{-1} S'\iota,$$

while the total (uncentred) sum of squares of this regression is $\iota'\iota$. Consequently, it follows that one version of the Lagrange multiplier test statistic can be computed as

$$\xi_{LM} = NR^2, \tag{6.36}$$

where R^2 is the uncentred R^2 (see Section 2.4) of an auxiliary regression of a vector of ones upon the score vectors (in S).[5] Under the null hypothesis, the test statistic is asymptotically χ^2 distributed with J degrees of freedom, where J is the number of restrictions imposed upon θ. Note that the auxiliary regression should not include an intercept term.

The formulae in (6.32) or (6.36) provide one way of computing the Lagrange multiplier test statistic, often referred to as the **outer product gradient** (OPG) version of the LM test statistic (see Godfrey, 1988, p. 15). Unfortunately, tests based on the OPG estimate of the covariance matrix typically have small sample properties that are quite different from those asymptotic theory predicts. Several Monte Carlo experiments suggest that the OPG-based tests tend to reject the null hypothesis too often in cases where it happens to be true. That is, the actual size of the tests may be much larger than the asymptotic size (typically 5%). This means that one has to be careful in rejecting the null hypothesis when the test statistic exceeds the asymptotic critical value. See Davidson and MacKinnon (1993, p. 477) for additional discussion. Alternative ways are available to compute LM test statistics, for example using (6.30) and the matrix of second derivatives of the loglikelihood function, or on the basis of other auxiliary regressions. Some of these will be discussed in the next section.

Despite the above reservations, we shall focus our discussion mostly upon the NR^2 approach of the LM test. This is because computation is convenient as it requires only the first derivatives. A test for any hypothesis can easily be constructed in this approach, while the columns of S are often determined fairly easily on the basis of the estimation results. When implementing the OPG version of the test, it is recommended to check your programming by also running a regression of a vector

---

[5] If your software does not report uncentred R^2s, the same result is obtained by computing $N - RSS$, where RSS denotes the residual sum of squares.

of ones upon the columns in S that correspond to the unconstrained parameters. This should result in an R^2 of zero.

In Section 6.3 we discuss the implementation of the Lagrange multiplier principle to test for omitted variables, heteroskedasticity, autocorrelation and non-normality, all in the context of the linear regression model with normal errors. Chapter 7 will cover several applications of LM tests in different types of models. First, however, we shall consider our simple example again.

6.2.3 An Example (Continued)

Let us again consider the simple example concerning the pool of red and yellow balls. This example is particularly simple as it involves only one unknown coefficient. Suppose we are interested in testing the hypothesis $H_0: p = p_0$ for a given value p_0. The (unrestricted) maximum likelihood estimator was seen to equal

$$\hat{p} = \frac{1}{N} \sum_{i=1}^{N} y_i = \frac{N_1}{N},$$

while the constrained 'estimator' is simply $\tilde{p} = p_0$. The Wald test for H_0, in its quadratic form, is based upon the test statistic

$$\xi_W = N(\hat{p} - p_0)[\hat{p}(1 - \hat{p})]^{-1}(\hat{p} - p_0),$$

which is simply the square of (6.21).

For the likelihood ratio test we need to compare the maximum loglikelihood values of the unrestricted and the restricted model, that is

$$\log L(\hat{p}) = N_1 \log(N_1/N) + (N - N_1) \log(1 - N_1/N), \tag{6.37}$$

and

$$\log L(\tilde{p}) = N_1 \log(p_0) + (N - N_1) \log(1 - p_0).$$

The test statistic is simply computed as

$$\xi_{LR} = 2(\log L(\hat{p}) - \log L(\tilde{p})).$$

Finally, we consider the Lagrange multiplier test. With a single coefficient we obtain that the Lagrange multiplier $N^{-1}\tilde{\lambda}$ (expressed as a sample average) is asymptotically normal with variance $I(p) = [p(1 - p)]^{-1}$. Furthermore,

$$\tilde{\lambda} = \sum_{i=1}^{N} \frac{\partial \log L_i(p)}{\partial p} \bigg|_{p_0} = \frac{N_1}{p_0} - \frac{N - N_1}{1 - p_0}.$$

We can thus compute the LM test statistic as

$$\begin{aligned}
\xi_{LM} &= N^{-1}\tilde{\lambda}[p_0(1 - p_0)]\tilde{\lambda} \\
&= N^{-1}(N_1 - Np_0)[p_0(1 - p_0)]^{-1}(N_1 - Np_0) \\
&= N(\hat{p} - p_0)[p_0(1 - p_0)]^{-1}(\hat{p} - p_0).
\end{aligned}$$

This shows that in this case the LM test statistic is very similar to the Wald test statistic: the only difference is that the information matrix is estimated using the restricted estimator p_0 rather than the unrestricted estimator $\hat{p}$.

As an illustration, suppose that we have a sample of $N = 100$ balls, of which 44% are red. If we test the hypothesis that $p = 0.5$, we obtain Wald, LR and LM test statistics of 1.46, 1.44 and 1.44, respectively. The 5% critical value taken from the asymptotic Chi-squared distribution with one degree of freedom is 3.84, so that the null hypothesis is not rejected at the 5% level with each of the three tests.

6.3 Tests in the Normal Linear Regression Model

Let us again consider the normal linear regression model, as discussed in Subsection 6.1.4,

$$y_i = x_i'\beta + \varepsilon_i, \quad \varepsilon_i \sim NID(0, \sigma^2),$$

where ε_i is independent of x_i. Suppose we are interested in testing whether the current specification is misspecified. Misspecification could reflect the omission of relevant variables, the presence of heteroskedasticity or autocorrelation, or non-normality of the error terms. We can relatively easy test for such misspecifications using the Lagrange multiplier framework, where the current model is considered to be the restricted model and the ML estimates are the constrained ML estimates. We then consider more general models, that allow, e.g. for heteroskedasticity, and then test whether the current estimates significantly violate the first order conditions of the more general model.

6.3.1 Testing for Omitted Variables

The first specification test that we consider is testing for omitted variables. In this case, the more general model is

$$y_i = x_i'\beta + z_i'\gamma + \varepsilon_i,$$

where the same assumptions are made about ε_i as before, and z_i is a J-dimensional vector of explanatory variables, independent of ε_i. The null hypothesis states $H_0: \gamma = 0$. The first order conditions for the more general model imply that the following derivatives are all equal to zero:

$$\sum_{i=1}^{N} \frac{(y_i - x_i'\beta - z_i'\gamma)}{\sigma^2} x_i,$$

$$\sum_{i=1}^{N} \frac{(y_i - x_i'\beta - z_i'\gamma)}{\sigma^2} z_i,$$

and

$$-\frac{N}{2\sigma^2} + \frac{1}{2} \sum_{i=1}^{N} \frac{(y_i - x_i'\beta - z_i'\gamma)^2}{\sigma^4}.$$

Evaluating these derivatives at the (constrained) maximum likelihood estimates $\hat{\beta}, \hat{\sigma}^2$ (and $\gamma = 0$), while defining residuals $\hat{\varepsilon}_i = y_i - x_i'\hat{\beta}$ we can write the derivatives as

$$\sum_{i=1}^{N} \frac{\hat{\varepsilon}_i}{\hat{\sigma}^2} x_i \sum_{i=1}^{N} \frac{\hat{\varepsilon}_i}{\hat{\sigma}^2} z_i - \frac{N}{2\hat{\sigma}^2} + \frac{1}{2} \sum_{i=1}^{N} \frac{\hat{\varepsilon}_i^2}{\hat{\sigma}^4},$$

where the first and third expressions are zero by construction.[6] The Lagrange multiplier test should thus check whether $\sum_{i=1}^{N} \hat{\varepsilon}_i z_i / \hat{\sigma}^2$ differs significantly from zero. The LM test statistic can be computed as (6.35), where S has typical row

$$[\hat{\varepsilon}_i x_i' \quad \hat{\varepsilon}_i z_i']. \tag{6.38}$$

Because of the block diagonality of the information matrix, the derivatives with respect to σ^2 can be omitted here, although it would not be incorrect to include them in the matrix S as well. Furthermore, irrelevant proportionality factors are eliminated in S. This is allowed because such constants do not affect the outcome of (6.35). In summary, we compute the LM test statistic by regressing a vector of ones upon the (ML or OLS) residuals interacted with the included explanatory variables x_i and the omitted variables z_i, and multiplying the uncentred R^2 by the sample size N. Under the null hypothesis, the resulting test statistic NR^2 has an asymptotic Chi-squared distribution with J degrees of freedom. If z_i is taken to be a nonlinear function of x_i, this approach can straightforwardly be used to test the functional form of the model (against a well-defined alternative).

6.3.2 Testing for Heteroskedasticity

Now suppose that the variance of ε_i may not be constant, but a function of some variables z_i, typically a subset or function of x_i. This is formalized in equation (4.44) from Chapter 4 which says that

$$V\{\varepsilon_i\} = \sigma_i^2 = \sigma^2 h(z_i'\alpha), \tag{6.39}$$

where h is an unknown, continuously differentiable function (that does not depend on i), such that $h(.) > 0$, $h'(.) \neq 0$ and $h(0) = 1$, and where z_i is a J-dimensional vector of explanatory variables (not including a constant). The null hypothesis of homoskedastic errors corresponds to H_0: $\alpha = 0$ (and we have $V\{\varepsilon_i\} = \sigma^2$). The log-likelihood contribution for observation i in the more general model is given by

$$\log L_i(\beta, \alpha) = -\frac{1}{2}\log(2\pi) - \frac{1}{2}\log \sigma^2 h(z_i'\alpha) - \frac{1}{2}\frac{(y_i - x_i'\beta)^2}{\sigma^2 h(z_i'\alpha)}. \tag{6.40}$$

The score with respect to α is given by

$$\frac{\partial \log L_i(\beta, \alpha)}{\partial \alpha} = \left[-\frac{1}{2}\frac{1}{h(z_i'\alpha)} + \frac{1}{2}\frac{(y_i - x_i'\beta)^2}{\sigma^2 h(z_i'\alpha)^2} \right] \frac{\partial h(z_i'\alpha)}{\partial \alpha},$$

---

[6] These two expressions correspond to the first order conditions of the restricted model, and define $\hat{\beta}$ and $\hat{\sigma}^2$.

where

$$\frac{\partial h(z_i'\alpha)}{\partial \alpha} = h'(z_i'\alpha)z_i,$$

where h' is the derivative of h. If we evaluate this under the constrained ML estimates $\hat{\beta}$ and $\hat{\sigma}^2$ this reduces to

$$\left[-\frac{1}{2} + \frac{1}{2} \frac{(y_i - x_i'\hat{\beta})^2}{\hat{\sigma}^2} \right] \kappa z_i,$$

where $\kappa = h'(0) \neq 0$ is an irrelevant constant. This explains the surprising result that the test does not require us to specify the function h.

Because the information matrix is block diagonal with respect to β and (σ^2, α), the OPG-version of the Lagrange multiplier test for heteroskedasticitity is obtained by computing (6.35), where S has typical row

$$[\hat{\varepsilon}_i^2 - \hat{\sigma}^2 \quad (\hat{\varepsilon}_i^2 - \hat{\sigma}^2)z_i'],$$

where irrelevant proportionality factors are again eliminated. In the auxiliary regression we thus include the variables that we suspect to affect heteroskedasticity interacted with the squared residuals in deviation from the error variance estimated under the null hypothesis. With J variables in z_i the resulting test statistic NR^2 has an asymptotic Chi-squared distribution with J degrees of freedom (under the null hypothesis).

The above approach presents a way to compute the Breusch–Pagan test for heteroskedasticity corresponding to our general computation rule given in (6.35). There are alternative ways to compute (asymptotically equivalent) versions of the Breusch–Pagan test statistic, for example by computing N times the R^2 of an auxiliary regression of $\hat{\varepsilon}_i^2$ (the squared OLS or maximum likelihood residuals) on z_i and a constant. This was discussed in Chapter 4. See Engle (1984) or Godfrey (1988, Section 4.5) for additional discussion.

If the null hypothesis of homoskedasticity is rejected, one option is to estimate a more general model that allows for heteroskedasticity. This can be based upon (6,40), with a particular choice for $h(.)$, for example the exponential function. As heteroskedasticity, in this particular model, does not result in an inconsistent maximum likelihood (OLS) estimator for β, it is also appropriate to compute heteroskedasticity-consistent standard errors; see Chapter 4 and Section 6.4 below.

6.3.3 Testing for Autocorrelation

In a time-series context, the error term in a regression model may suffer from autocorrelation. Consider the linear model

$$y_t = x_t'\beta + \varepsilon_t, \quad t = 1, 2, \ldots, T,$$

with assumptions as stated above. The alternative hypothesis of first order autocorrelation states that

$$\varepsilon_t = \rho \varepsilon_{t-1} + v_t,$$

such that the null hypothesis corresponds to H_0: $\rho = 0$. If we rewrite the model as

$$y_t = x_t'\beta + \rho \varepsilon_{t-1} + v_t$$

it follows that testing for autocorrelation is similar to testing for an omitted variable, namely $\varepsilon_{t-1} = y_{t-1} - x_{t-1}'\beta$. Consequently, one can compute a version of the Lagrange multiplier test for autocorrelation using (6.35), where S has typical row

$$[\hat{\varepsilon}_t x_t' \quad \hat{\varepsilon}_t \hat{\varepsilon}_{t-1}]$$

and the number of observations is $T - 1$. If x_t does not contain a lagged dependent variable the information matrix is also diagonal with respect to β and (σ^2, ρ), and the scores with respect to β, corresponding to $\hat{\varepsilon}_t x_t'$ may be dropped from S. This gives a test statistic of

$$\xi_{LM} = \sum_{t=2}^{T} \hat{\varepsilon}_t \hat{\varepsilon}_{t-1} \left(\sum_{t=2}^{T} \hat{\varepsilon}_t^2 \hat{\varepsilon}_{t-1}^2 \right)^{-1} \sum_{t=2}^{T} \hat{\varepsilon}_t \hat{\varepsilon}_{t-1}.$$

Because under the null hypothesis ε_t and ε_{t-1} are independent,[7] it holds that $E\{\varepsilon_t^2\varepsilon_{t-1}^2\} = E\{\varepsilon_t^2\}E\{\varepsilon_{t-1}^2\}$. This indicates that an asymptotically equivalent test statistic is obtained by replacing $1/(T-1) \sum_t \hat{\varepsilon}_t^2 \hat{\varepsilon}_{t-1}^2$ by $(1/(T-1) \sum_t \hat{\varepsilon}_t^2)(1/(T-1) \sum_t \hat{\varepsilon}_{t-1}^2)$. This gives

$$\xi_{LM} = (T-1) \frac{\sum_{t=2}^{T} \hat{\varepsilon}_t \hat{\varepsilon}_{t-1} (\sum_{t=2}^{T} \hat{\varepsilon}_{t-1}^2)^{-1} \sum_{t=2}^{T} \hat{\varepsilon}_t \hat{\varepsilon}_{t-1}}{\sum_{t=2}^{T} \hat{\varepsilon}_t^2} = (T-1)R^2,$$

where R^2 is the R^2 of an auxiliary regression of the OLS or ML residual $\hat{\varepsilon}_t$ upon its lag $\hat{\varepsilon}_{t-1}$. This corresponds to the Breusch–Godfrey test for autocorrelation as discussed in Chapter 4. If x_t contains a lagged dependent variable, the appropriate auxiliary regression is of $\hat{\varepsilon}_t$ upon $\hat{\varepsilon}_{t-1}$ and x_t. Tests for p-th order autocorrelation are obtained by augmenting the rows of S with $\hat{\varepsilon}_t \hat{\varepsilon}_{t-2}$ up to $\hat{\varepsilon}_t \hat{\varepsilon}_{t-p}$, or – for the latter computation – by adding $\hat{\varepsilon}_{t-2}$ up to $\hat{\varepsilon}_{t-p}$ in the auxiliary regression explaining $\hat{\varepsilon}_t$. Engle (1984) and Godfrey (1988, Section 4.4) provide additional discussion.

6.4 Quasi-maximum Likelihood and Moment Conditions Tests

It is typically the case that maximum likelihood requires researchers to make full distributional assumptions, while the generalized method of moments (GMM) discussed in the previous chapter only makes assumptions about moments of the distribution. However, it is possible that the moment conditions employed in a GMM approach are based upon assumptions about the shape of the distribution as well. This allows us to re-derive the maximum likelihood estimator as a GMM estimator with moment conditions corresponding to the first order conditions of maximum likelihood. This is a useful generalization as it allows us to argue that in some cases the maximum likelihood estimator is consistent, even if the likelihood function is not entirely correct (but the first order conditions are). Moreover, it allows us to extend the class of Lagrange multiplier tests to (conditional) moment tests.

---

[7] Recall that under normality zero correlation implies independence (see Appendix B).

6.4.1 Quasi-maximum Likelihood

In this subsection we shall see that the maximum likelihood estimator can be interpreted as a GMM estimator by noting that the first order conditions of the maximum likelihood problem correspond to sample averages based upon theoretical moment conditions. The starting point is that it holds that

$$E\{s_i(\theta)\} = 0 \tag{6.41}$$

for the true K-dimensional parameter vector θ, under the assumption that the likelihood function is correct. The proof of this is relatively easy and instructive. If we consider the density function of y_i given x_i, $f(y_i|x_i; \theta)$, it holds by construction that (see Appendix B)

$$\int f(y_i|x_i; \theta) \, dy_i = 1,$$

where integration is over the support of y_i. Differentiating this with respect to θ gives

$$\int \frac{\partial f(y_i|x_i; \theta)}{\partial \theta} \, dy_i = 0.$$

Because

$$\frac{\partial f(y_i|x_i; \theta)}{\partial \theta} = \frac{\partial \log f(y_i|x_i; \theta)}{\partial \theta} f(y_i|x_i; \theta) = s_i(\theta) f(y_i|x_i; \theta)$$

it follows that

$$\int s_i(\theta) f(y_i|x_i; \theta) dy_i = E\{s_i(\theta)\} = 0,$$

where the first equality follows from the definition of the expectation operator.

Let us assume that θ is uniquely defined by these conditions. That is, there is only one vector θ that satisfies (6.41). Then (6.41) is a set of valid moment conditions and we can use the GMM approach to estimate θ. Because the number of parameters is equal to the number of moment conditions, this involves solving the first order conditions

$$\frac{1}{N} \sum_{i=1}^{N} s_i(\theta) = 0.$$

Of course this reproduces the maximum likelihood estimator $\hat{\theta}$. However, it shows that the resulting estimator is consistent for θ provided that (6.41) is correct, which may be weaker than the requirement that the entire distribution is correctly specified. In the linear regression model with normal errors, the first order conditions with respect to β are easily seen to correspond to

$$E\{(y_i - x_i'\beta)x_i\} = 0,$$

which corresponds to the set of moment conditions imposed by the OLS estimator. This explains why the maximum likelihood estimator in the normal linear regression model is consistent even if the distribution of ε_i is not normal.

If the maximum likelihood estimator is based upon the wrong likelihood function, but can be argued to be consistent on the basis of the validity of (6.41), the estimator is sometimes referred to as a **quasi-maximum likelihood estimator** or pseudo-maximum likelihood estimator (see White, 1982; or Gouriéroux, Monfort and Trognon, 1984). The asymptotic distribution of the quasi-ML estimator may differ from that of the ML estimator. In particular, the result in (6.16) may no longer be valid. Using our general formulae for the GMM estimator it is possible to derive the asymptotic covariance matrix of the quasi-ML estimator for θ, assuming that (6.41) is correct. Using (5.74)–(5.76), it follows that the quasi-maximum likelihood estimator $\hat{\theta}$ satisfies

$$\sqrt{N}(\hat{\theta} - \theta) \to \mathcal{N}(0, V)$$

where[8]

$$V = I(\theta)^{-1} J(\theta) I(\theta)^{-1}, \tag{6.42}$$

with

$$I(\theta) = E\left\{ -\frac{\partial s_i(\theta)}{\partial \theta'} \right\} = E\left\{ -\frac{\partial^2 \log L_i(\theta)}{\partial \theta \partial \theta'} \right\}$$

as defined in (6.17), and

$$J(\theta) = E\{s_i(\theta)s_i(\theta)'\},$$

as defined in (6.19). The covariance matrix in (6.42) generalizes the one in (6.16) and is correct whenever the quasi-ML estimator $\hat{\theta}$ is consistent. For example, in the case of the linear regression model estimating the covariance matrix on the basis of (6.42) would reproduce the heteroskedasticity-consistent covariance matrix as discussed in Subsection 4.3.4. Several software packages have the option to compute robust standard errors for the (quasi-)maximum likelihood estimator, based on the covariance matrix in (6.42).

The **information matrix test** (IM test) suggested by White (1982) tests the equality of the two $K \times K$ matrices $I(\theta)$ and $J(\theta)$ by comparing their sample counterparts. Because of the symmetry a maximum of $K(K-1)/2$ elements have to be compared, so that the degrees of freedom for the IM test is potentially very large. Depending on the shape of the likelihood function, the information matrix test checks for misspecification in a number of directions simultaneously (like functional form, heteroskedasticity, skewness and kurtosis). For additional discussion and computational issues, see Davidson and MacKinnon (1993, Section 16.9).

6.4.2 Conditional Moment Tests

The analysis in the previous subsection allows us to generalize the class of Lagrange multiplier tests to so-called **conditional moment tests** (CM tests), as suggested by Newey (1985) and Tauchen (1985). Consider a model characterized by (6.41)

$$E\{s_i(\theta)\} = 0,$$

---

[8] The covariance matrix maintains the assumption that observations are mutually independent.

where the (quasi-)ML estimator $\hat{\theta}$ satisfies

$$\frac{1}{N} \sum_{i=1}^{N} s_i(\hat{\theta}) = 0.$$

Now consider an hypothesis characterized by

$$E\{m_i(\theta)\} = 0, \tag{6.43}$$

where $m_i(\theta)$ is a J-dimensional function of the data and the unknown parameters in θ, just like $s_i(\theta)$. The difference is that (6.43) is not imposed in estimation. It is possible to test the validity of (6.43) by testing whether its sample counterpart

$$\frac{1}{N} \sum_{i=1}^{N} m_i(\hat{\theta}) \tag{6.44}$$

is close to zero. This can be done fairly easily by noting the resemblance between (6.44) and the scores of a more general likelihood function. Consequently, the OPG version of a moment conditions test for (6.43) can be computed by taking N times the uncentred R^2 of a regression of a vector of ones upon the columns of a matrix S, where S now has typical row

$$[s_i(\hat{\theta})' \quad m_i(\hat{\theta})'].$$

Under the null hypothesis that (6.43) is correct, the resulting test statistic has an asymptotic Chi-squared distribution with J degrees of freedom.

The above approach shows that the additional conditions that are tested do not necessarily have to correspond to scores of a more general likelihood function. A particular area where this approach is useful is when testing the hypothesis of normality.

6.4.3   Testing for Normality

Let us consider the linear regression model again with, under the null hypothesis, normal errors. For a continuously observed variable, normality tests usually check for skewness (third moment) and excess kurtosis (fourth moment), because the normal distribution implies that $E\{\varepsilon_i^3\} = 0$ and $E\{\varepsilon_i^4 - 3\sigma^4\} = 0$ (see Appendix B). If $E\{\varepsilon_i^3\} \neq 0$ the distribution of ε_i is not symmetric around zero. If $E\{\varepsilon_i^4 - 3\sigma^4\} > 0$ the distribution of ε_i is said to display **excess kurtosis**. This means that it has fatter tails than the normal distribution. Davidson and MacKinnon (1993, p. 63) provide graphical illustrations of these situations.

Given the discussion in the previous subsection, a test for normality can be obtained by running a regression of a vector of ones upon the columns of the matrix S, which now has typical row

$$[\hat{\varepsilon}_i x_i' \quad \hat{\varepsilon}_i^2 - \hat{\sigma}^2 \quad \hat{\varepsilon}_i^3 \quad \hat{\varepsilon}_i^4 - 3\hat{\sigma}^4],$$

where $\hat{\varepsilon}_i$ denotes the maximum likelihood (or OLS) residual, and then computing N times the uncentred R^2. Although non-normality of ε_i does not invalidate consistency of the OLS estimator nor its asymptotic normality, the above test is occasionally of interest. Finding that ε_i has a severely skewed distribution may indicate that it may be advisable to transform the dependent variable prior to estimation (for example, by considering log wages rather than wages itself). In Chapter 7 we shall see classes of models where normality is far more crucial.

A popular variant of the LM test for normality is the **Jarque–Bera test** (Jarque and Bera, 1980). The test statistic is computed as

$$\xi_{LM} = N\left[\frac{1}{6}\left(\frac{1}{N}\sum_{i=1}^{N}\hat{\varepsilon}_i^3/\hat{\sigma}^3\right)^2 + \frac{1}{24}\left(\frac{1}{N}\sum_{i=1}^{N}\hat{\varepsilon}_i^4/\hat{\sigma}^4 - 3\right)^2\right], \tag{6.45}$$

which is a weighted average of the squared sample moments corresponding to skewness and excess kurtosis, respectively. Under the null hypothesis, it is asymptotically distributed as a Chi-squared with two degrees of freedom; see Godfrey (1988, Sect. 4.7) for more details.

Exercises

Exercise 6.1 (The Normal Linear Regression Model)

Consider the following linear regression model

$$y_i = \beta_1 + \beta_2 x_i + \varepsilon_i,$$

where $\beta = (\beta_1, \beta_2)'$ is a vector of unknown parameters, and x_i is a one-dimensional observable variable. We have a sample of $i = 1, \ldots, N$ independent observations and assume that the error terms ε_i are $NID(0, \sigma^2)$, independent of all x_i. The density function of y_i (for a given x_i) is then given by

$$f(y_i|\beta, \sigma^2) = \frac{1}{\sqrt{2\pi\sigma^2}}\exp\left\{-\frac{1}{2}\frac{(y_i - \beta_1 - \beta_2 x_i)^2}{\sigma^2}\right\}.$$

a. Give an expression for the loglikelihood contribution of observation i, $\log L_i(\beta, \sigma^2)$. Explain why the loglikelihood function of the entire sample is given by

$$\log L(\beta, \sigma^2) = \sum_{i=1}^{N} \log L_i(\beta, \sigma^2).$$

b. Determine expressions for the two elements in $\partial \log L_i(\beta, \sigma^2)/\partial \beta$ and show that both have expectation zero for the true parameter values.

c. Derive an expression for $\partial \log L_i(\beta, \sigma^2)/\partial \sigma^2$ and show that it also has expectation zero for the true parameter values.

Suppose that x_i is a dummy variable equal to 1 for males and 0 for females, such that $x_i = 1$ for $i = 1, \ldots, N_1$ (the first N_1 observations) and $x_i = 0$ for $i = N_1 + 1, \ldots, N$.

d. Derive the first order conditions for maximum likelihood. Show that the maximum likelihood estimators for β are given by

$$\hat{\beta}_1 = \frac{1}{N - N_1}\sum_{i=N_1+1}^{N} y_i, \quad \hat{\beta}_2 = \frac{1}{N_1}\sum_{i=1}^{N_1} y_i - \hat{\beta}_1.$$

What is the interpretation of these two estimators? What is the interpretation of the true parameter values β_1 and β_2?

e. Show that

$$\partial^2 \log L_i(\beta, \sigma^2)/\partial\beta\,\partial\sigma^2 = \partial^2 \log L_i(\beta, \sigma^2)/\partial\sigma^2\partial\beta,$$

and show that it has expectation zero. What are the implications of this for the asymptotic covariance matrix of the ML estimator $(\hat{\beta}_1, \hat{\beta}_2, \hat{\sigma}^2)$?

f. Present two ways to estimate the asymptotic covariance matrix of $(\hat{\beta}_1, \hat{\beta}_2)'$ and compare the results.

g. Present an alternative way to estimate the asymptotic covariance matrix of $(\hat{\beta}_1, \hat{\beta}_2)'$ that allows ε_i to be heteroskedastic.

Suppose that we are interested in the hypothesis H_0: $\beta_2 = 0$ with alternative H_1: $\beta_2 \neq 0$. Tests can be based upon the likelihood ratio, Lagrange multiplier or Wald principle.

h. Explain what these three principles are.

i. Discuss for each of the three tests what is required to compute them.

Although the three test statistics have the same asymptotic Chi-squared distribution, it can be shown (see, e.g. Godfrey, 1988, Sect. 2.3) that in the above model it holds for any finite sample that

$$\xi_W \geq \xi_{LR} \geq \xi_{LM}.$$

j. Explain what is meant by the power of a test. What does this inequality tell us about the powers of the three tests? (Hint: if needed consult Chapter 2.)

k. Explain what is meant by the (actual) size of a test. What does the inequality tell us about the sizes of the three tests?

l. Would you prefer one of the three tests, knowing the above inequality?

Exercise 6.2 (The Poisson Regression Model)

Let y_i denote the number of times individual i buys tobacco in a given month. Suppose a random sample of N individuals is available, for which we observe values $0, 1, 2, 3, \ldots$. Let x_i be an observed characteristic of these individuals (e.g. gender). If we assume that, for given x_i, y_i has a Poisson distribution with parameter $\lambda_i = \exp\{\beta_1 + \beta_2 x_i\}$ (see, e.g. Greene, 2000, Sect. 19.9), the probability mass function of y_i conditional upon x_i is given by

$$P\{y_i = y | x_i\} = \frac{e^{-\lambda_i}\lambda_i^y}{y!}.$$

a. Write down the loglikelihood function for this so-called Poisson regression model.

b. Derive the score vector. Using that the Poisson distribution implies that $E\{y_i|x_i\} = \lambda_i$, show that the score has expectation zero.

c. Derive an expression for the information matrix $I(\beta_1, \beta_2)$. Use this to determine the asymptotic covariance matrix of the ML estimator and a consistent estimator for this matrix.

d. Describe how one can test for an omitted variable using the Lagrange multiplier framework. Which auxiliary regression is needed?

7 Models with Limited Dependent Variables

In practical applications one often has to cope with phenomena that are of a discrete or mixed discrete continuous nature. For example, one could be interested in explaining whether married women have a paid job (yes or no), or how many hours they work (zero or positive). If this type of variable has to be explained a linear regression model is generally inappropriate. In this chapter we consider alternative models that can be used to model discrete and discrete/continuous variables and pay attention to the estimation and interpretation of their parameters.

Although not exclusively, in many cases the problems analysed with this type of model are of a micro-economic nature, thus requiring data on individuals, households or firms. To stress this, we shall index all variables by i, running from 1 to sample size N. Section 7.1 starts with probably the simplest case of a limited dependent variable model, viz. a binary choice model. Extensions to multiple discrete outcomes are discussed in Section 7.2.[1] If the distribution of the endogenous variable is continuous with a probability mass at one or more discrete points, the use of tobit models is recommended. The standard tobit model is discussed in Section 7.3, while some extensions, including models with sample selection where a nonrandom proportion of the outcomes is not observed, are contained in Section 7.4. Because sample selection is a problem that often arises with micro data, Section 7.5 contains some additional discussion of the sample selection problem, mainly focusing on the identification problem and under what assumptions it can be solved. Throughout, a number of empirical illustrations is provided in subsections. Additional discussion of limited dependent variable models in econometrics can be found in two surveys by Amemiya (1981, 1984) and the monographs by Maddala (1983) and Lee (1996).

---

[1] This chapter does not cover the analyis of count data, where the endogenous variable is the frequency of a certain event (e.g. number of patents in a given year). Count data models are treated extensively in Cameron and Trivedi (1998).

7.1   Binary Choice Models

7.1.1   *Using Linear Regression?*

Suppose we want to explain whether a family possesses a car or not. Let the sole explanatory variable be the family income. We have data on N families ($i = 1, \ldots, N$), with observations on their income, x_{i2}, and whether or not they own a car. This latter element is described by the binary variable y_i, defined as

$$y_i = 1 \quad \text{if family } i \text{ owns a car}$$

$$y_i = 0 \quad \text{if family } i \text{ does not own a car.}$$

Suppose we would use a regression model to explain y_i from x_{i2} and an intercept term ($x_{i1} \equiv 1$). This linear model would be given by

$$y_i = \beta_1 + \beta_2 x_{i2} + \varepsilon_i = x_i'\beta + \varepsilon_i, \tag{7.1}$$

where $x_i = (x_{i1}, x_{i2})'$. It seems reasonable to make the standard assumption that $E\{\varepsilon_i|x_i\} = 0$ such that $E\{y_i|x_i\} = x_i'\beta$. This implies that

$$E\{y_i|x_i\} = 1.P\{y_i = 1|x_i\} + 0.P\{y_i = 0|x_i\}$$

$$= P\{y_i = 1|x_i\} = x_i'\beta. \tag{7.2}$$

Thus, the linear model implies that $x_i'\beta$ is a probability and should therefore lie between 0 and 1. This is only possible if the x_i values are bounded and if certain restrictions on β are satisfied. Usually this is hard to achieve in practice. In addition to this fundamental problem, the error term in (7.1) has a highly non-normal distribution and suffers from heteroskedasticity. Because y_i has only two possible outcomes (0 or 1), the error term, for a given value of x_i, has two possible outcomes as well. In particular, the distribution of ε_i can be summarized as

$$P\{\varepsilon_i = -x_i'\beta|x_i\} = P\{y_i = 0|x_i\} = 1 - x_i'\beta$$

$$P\{\varepsilon_i = 1 - x_i'\beta|x_i\} = P\{y_i = 1|x_i\} = x_i'\beta. \tag{7.3}$$

This implies that the variance of the error term is not constant but dependent upon the explanatory variables according to $V\{\varepsilon_i|x_i\} = x_i'\beta(1 - x_i'\beta)$. Note that the error variance also depends upon the model parameters β.

7.1.2   *Introducing Binary Choice Models*

To overcome the problems with the linear model, there exists a class of **binary choice models** (or univariate dichotomous models), designed to model the 'choice' between two discrete alternatives. These models essentially describe the probability that $y_i = 1$ directly, although they are often derived from an underlying latent variable model (see below). In general, we have

$$P\{y_i = 1|x_i\} = G(x_i, \beta) \tag{7.4}$$

for some function $G(.)$. This equation says that the probability of having $y_i = 1$ depends on the vector x_i containing individual characteristics. So, for example, the probability that a person owns a house depends on his income, education level, age and marital status. Or, from a different field, the probability that an insect survives a dose of poisonous insecticide depends upon the quantity x_i of the dose, and possibly some other characteristics. Clearly, the function $G(.)$ in (7.4) should take on values in the interval $[0, 1]$ only. Usually, one restricts attention to functions of the form $G(x_i, \beta) = F(x_i'\beta)$. As $F(.)$ also has to be between 0 and 1, it seems natural to choose F to be some distribution function. Common choices are the standard normal distribution function

$$F(w) = \Phi(w) = \int_{-\infty}^{w} \frac{1}{\sqrt{2\pi}} \exp\left\{-\frac{1}{2} t^2\right\} dt, \tag{7.5}$$

leading to the so-called **probit model**, and the standard logistic distribution function, given by

$$F(w) = L(w) = \frac{e^w}{1 + e^w}, \tag{7.6}$$

which results in the **logit model**. A third choice corresponds to a uniform distribution over the interval $[0, 1]$ with distribution function

$$F(w) = 0, w < 0;$$
$$F(w) = w, 0 \leq w \leq 1; \tag{7.7}$$
$$F(w) = 1, w > 1.$$

This results in the so-called **linear probability model**, which is similar to the regression model in (7.1), but the probabilities are set to 0 or 1 if $x_i'\beta$ exceeds the lower or upper limit, respectively. In fact, the first two models (probit and logit) are more common in applied work. Both a standard normal and a standard logistic random variable have an expectation of zero, while the latter has a variance of $\pi^2/3$ instead of 1. Because the two distribution functions are very similar if one corrects for this difference in scaling, the probit and logit model typically yield very similar results in empirical work.

Apart from their signs, the coefficients in these binary choice models are not easy to interpret directly. One way to interpret the parameters (and to ease comparison across different models) is to look at the derivative of the probability that y_i equals 1 with respect to the k-th element in x_i. For the three models above, we obtain:

$$\frac{\partial \Phi(x_i'\beta)}{\partial x_{ik}} = \phi(x_i'\beta)\beta_k;$$

$$\frac{\partial L(x_i'\beta)}{\partial x_{ik}} = \frac{e^{x_i'\beta}}{(1 + e^{x_i'\beta})^2} \beta_k;$$

$$\frac{\partial x_i'\beta}{\partial x_{ik}} = \beta_k; \text{(or 0)},$$

where $\phi(.)$ denotes the standard normal density function. Except for the last model, the effect of a change in x_{ik} depends upon the values of x_i. In all cases, however, the sign of the effect of a change in x_{ik} corresponds to the sign of its coefficient β_k.

7.1.3 An Underlying Latent Model

It is possible (but not necessary) to derive a binary choice model from underlying behavioural assumptions. This leads to a latent variable representation of the model, which is in common use even when such behavioural assumptions are not made. Let us look at the decision of a married female to have a paid job or not. The utility difference between having a paid job and not having one depends upon the wage that could be earned but also on other personal characteristics, like the woman's age and education, whether there are young children in the family, etc. Thus, for each person i we can write the utility difference between having a job and not having one as a function of observed characteristics, x_i say, and unobserved characteristics ε_i, say.[2] Assuming a linear additive relationship we obtain for the utility difference, denoted y_i^*,

$$y_i^* = x_i'\beta + \varepsilon_i. \tag{7.8}$$

Because y_i^* is unobserved, it is referred to as a **latent variable**. In this chapter, latent variables are indicated by an asterisk. Our assumption is that an individual chooses to work if the utility difference exceeds a certain threshold level, which can be set to zero without loss of generality. Consequently, we observe $y_i = 1$ (job) if and only if $y_i^* > 0$ and $y_i = 0$ (no job) otherwise. Thus we have

$$P\{y_i = 1\} = P\{y_i^* > 0\} = P\{x_i'\beta + \varepsilon_i > 0\} = P\{-\varepsilon_i \leq x_i'\beta\} = F(x_i'\beta), \tag{7.9}$$

where F denotes the distribution function of $-\varepsilon_i$, or, in the common case of a symmetric distribution, the distribution function of ε_i. Consequently, we have obtained a binary choice model, the form of which depends upon the distribution that is assumed for ε_i. As the scale of utility is not identified, a normalization on the distribution of ε_i is required. Usually this means that its variance is fixed at a given value. If a *standard* normal distribution is chosen one obtains the probit model, for the logistic one the logit model is obtained.

Although binary choice models in economics can often be interpreted as being derived from an underlying utility maximization problem, this is certainly not necessary. Usually, one defines the latent variable y_i^* directly, such that the probit model is fully described by

$$y_i^* = x_i'\beta + \varepsilon_i, \quad \varepsilon_i \sim NID(0, 1)$$
$$y_i = 1 \text{ if } y_i^* > 0 \tag{7.10}$$
$$= 0 \text{ if } y_i^* \leq 0,$$

where the ε_is are independent of all x_i. For the logit model, the normal distribution is replaced by the standard logistic one. Most commonly, the parameters in binary choice models (or limited dependent variable models in general) are estimated by the method of maximum likelihood.

7.1.4 Estimation

Given our general discussion of maximum likelihood estimation in Chapter 6, we can restrict attention to the form of the likelihood function here. In fact, this form is

---

[2] The error term ε_i is not to be confused with the one in the linear model (7.1).

rather simple as it follows immediately from the models given above. In general, the likelihood contribution of observation i with $y_i = 1$ is given by $P\{y_i = 1|x_i\}$ as a function of the unknown parameter vector β, and similarly for $y_i = 0$. The likelihood function for the entire sample is thus given by

$$\log L(\beta) = \prod_{i=1}^{N} P\{y_i = 1|x_i; \beta\}^{y_i} P\{y_i = 0|x_i; \beta\}^{1-y_i}, \qquad (7.11)$$

where we included β in the expressions for the probabilities to stress that the likelihood function is a function of β. As usual we prefer to work with the loglikelihood function. Substituting $P\{y_i = 1|x_i; \beta\} = F(x_i'\beta)$ we obtain

$$\log L(\beta) = \sum_{i=1}^{N} y_i \log F(x_i'\beta) + \sum_{i=1}^{N} (1 - y_i) \log(1 - F(x_i'\beta)). \qquad (7.12)$$

Substituting the appropriate form for F gives an expression that can be maximized with respect to β. As indicated above, the values of β and their interpretation depend upon the distribution function that is chosen. An empirical example in Subsection 7.1.6 will illustrate this.

It is instructive to consider the first order conditions of the maximum likelihood problem. Differentiating (7.12) with respect to β yields

$$\frac{\partial \log L(\beta)}{\partial \beta} = \sum_{i=1}^{N} \left[\frac{y_i - F(x_i'\beta)}{F(x_i'\beta)(1 - F(x_i'\beta))} f(x_i'\beta) \right] x_i = 0. \qquad (7.13)$$

where $f = F'$ is the derivative of the distribution function (so f is the density function). The term in square brackets is often referred to as the **generalized residual** of the model, and we shall see it re-appearing when discussing specification tests. It equals $f(x_i'\beta)/F(x_i'\beta)$ for the positive observations ($y_i = 1$) and $-f(x_i'\beta)/(1 - F(x_i'\beta))$ for the zero observations ($y_i = 0$). The first order conditions thus say that each explanatory variable should be orthogonal to the generalized residual (over the whole sample). This is comparable to the OLS first order conditions in (2.10), which state that the least squares residuals are orthogonal to each variable in x_i.

For the logit model we can simplify (7.13) to

$$\frac{\partial \log L(\beta)}{\partial \beta} = \sum_{i=1}^{N} \left[y_i - \frac{\exp(x_i'\beta)}{1 + \exp(x_i'\beta)} \right] x_i = 0. \qquad (7.14)$$

The solution of (7.14) is the maximum likelihood estimator $\hat{\beta}$. From this estimate we can estimate the probability that $y_i = 1$ for a given x_i as

$$\hat{p}_i = \frac{\exp(x_i'\hat{\beta})}{1 + \exp(x_i'\hat{\beta})}. \qquad (7.15)$$

Consequently, the first order conditions for the logit model imply that

$$\sum_{i=1}^{N} \hat{p}_i x_i = \sum_{i=1}^{N} y_i x_i. \qquad (7.16)$$

Thus, if x_i contains a constant term (and there is no reason why it should not), then the sum of the estimated probabilities is equal to $\sum_i y_i$ or the number of observations in the sample for which $y_i = 1$. In other words, the predicted frequency is equal to the actual frequency. Similarly, if x_i includes a dummy variable, say 1 for females, 0 for males, then the predicted frequency will be equal to the actual frequency for each gender group. Although a similar result does not hold exactly for the probit model, it does hold approximately by virtue of the similarity of the logit and probit model.

A look at the second order conditions of the ML problem, reveals that the matrix of second order derivatives is negative definite (assuming that the xs are not collinear). Consequently, the loglikelihood function is globally concave and convergence of the iterative maximum likelihood algorithm is guaranteed (and usually quite fast).

7.1.5 Goodness-of-fit

A goodness-of-fit measure is a summary statistic indicating the accuracy with which the model approximates the observed data, like the R^2 measure in the linear regression model. In the case in which the dependent variable is qualitative, accuracy can be judged either in terms of the fit between the calculated probabilities and observed response frequencies or in terms of the model's ability to forecast observed responses. Contrary to the linear regression model, there is no single measure for the goodness-of-fit in binary choice models and a variety of measures exists.

Often, goodness-of-fit measures are implicitly or explicitly based on comparison with a model that contains only a constant as explanatory variable. Let $\log L_1$ denote the maximum loglikelihood value of the model of interest and let $\log L_0$ denote the maximum value of the loglikelihood function when all parameters, except the intercept, are set to zero. Clearly, $\log L_1 \geq \log L_0$. The larger the difference between the two loglikelihood values, the more the extended model adds to the very restrictive model. (Indeed, a formal likelihood ratio test can be based on the difference between the two values.) A first goodness-of-fit measure is defined as (see Amemiya, 1981 for an extensive list)

$$pseudo R^2 = 1 - \frac{1}{1 + 2(\log L_1 - \log L_0)/N}, \qquad (7.17)$$

where N denotes the number of observations. An alternative measure is suggested by McFadden (1974),

$$McFadden R^2 = 1 - \log L_1 / \log L_0, \qquad (7.18)$$

sometimes referred to as the likelihood ratio index. Because the loglikelihood is the sum of log probabilities, it follows that $\log L_0 \leq \log L_1 < 0$, from which it is straightforward to show that both measures take on values in the interval $[0, 1]$ only. If all estimated slope coefficients are equal to zero we have $\log L_0 = \log L_1$, such that both R^2s are equal to zero. If the model would be able to generate (estimated) probabilities that correspond exactly to the observed values (that is $\hat{p}_i = y_i$ for all i), all probabilities in the loglikelihood would be equal to one, such that the loglikelihood would be exactly equal to zero. Consequently, the upper limit for the two measures above is obtained for $\log L_1 = 0$. The upper bound of 1 can therefore, in theory, only be attained by McFadden's measure; see Cameron and Windmeijer (1997) for a discussion of the properties of this and alternative measures.

To compute $\log L_0$ it is not necessary to estimate a probit or logit model with an intercept term only. If there is only a constant term in the model, the distribution function is irrelevant for the implied probabilities and the model essentially says $P\{y_i = 1\} = p$ for some unknown p. The ML estimator for p can easily be shown to be (see (6.4))

$$\hat{p} = N_1/N,$$

where $N_1 = \sum_i y_i$. That is, the estimated probability is equal to the proportion of ones in the sample. The maximum loglikelihood value is therefore given by (compare (6.37))

$$\log L_0 = \sum_{i=1}^{N} y_i \log(N_1/N) + \sum_{i=1}^{N} (1 - y_i) \log(1 - N_1/N)$$

$$= N_1 \log(N_1/N) + (N - N_1) \log(1 - N_1/N), \tag{7.19}$$

which can be directly computed from the sample size N and the sample frequency N_1. The value of $\log L_1$ should be given by your computer package.

An alternative way to evaluate the goodness-of-fit is comparing correct and incorrect predictions. To predict whether $y_i = 1$ or not, it seems natural to look at the estimated probability that follows from the model, which is given by $F(x_i'\hat{\beta})$. In general, one predicts that $y_i = 1$ if $F(x_i'\hat{\beta}) > 1/2$. Because $F(0) = 1/2$ for distributions that are symmetric around 0, this corresponds to $x_i'\hat{\beta} > 0$. Thus, the implied predictions are

$$\hat{y}_i = 1 \quad \text{if} \quad x_i'\hat{\beta} > 0$$

$$\hat{y}_i = 0 \quad \text{if} \quad x_i'\hat{\beta} \leq 0. \tag{7.20}$$

The proportion of incorrect predictions is now given by

$$wr_1 = \frac{1}{N} \sum_{i=1}^{N} (y_i - \hat{y}_i)^2.$$

As a benchmark, the outcome is again compared with the proportion of incorrect predictions based on the model with an intercept term only. It is easily seen that for this latter model we will predict a one for all observations if $\hat{p} = N_1/N > 1/2$ and a zero otherwise. The proportion of incorrect predictions is thus given by

$$wr_0 = 1 - \hat{p} \quad \text{if } \hat{p} > 0.5,$$

$$= \hat{p} \qquad \text{if } \hat{p} \leq 0.5.$$

A goodness-of-fit measure is finally obtained as

$$R_p^2 = 1 - \frac{wr_1}{wr_0}. \tag{7.21}$$

Because it is possible that the model predicts worse than the simple model one can have $wr_1 > wr_0$, in which case the R_p^2 becomes negative. Of course, this is not a good sign for the predictive quality of the model. Also note that $wr_0 \leq 1/2$, that is even the simplest model will predict at most half of the observations incorrectly. If in the sample 90% corresponds to $y_i = 1$, we even have $wr_0 = 0.1$. Consequently, in this case any binary choice model needs more than 90% correct predictions to beat the simple model. As a consequence, the proportion of correct predictions $(1 - wr_1)$ as such does not say much about the quality of the model. It could be 0.9 (90%) for a bad model.

7.1.6 Illustration: the Impact of Unemployment Benefits on Recipiency

As an illustration we consider a sample[3] of 4877 blue collar workers who lost their jobs in the US between 1982 and 1991, taken from a recent study by McCall (1995). Not all unemployed workers eligible for unemployment insurance (UI) benefits apply for it, probably due to the associated pecuniary and psychological costs. The percentage of eligible unemployed blue collar workers that actually applies for UI benefits is called the take-up rate, and it was only 68% in the available sample. It is therefore interesting to investigate what makes people decide not to apply.

The amount of UI benefits a person can receive depends upon the state of residence, the year of becoming unemployed, and his or her previous earnings. The replacement rate, defined as the ratio of weekly UI benefits to previous weekly earnings, varies from 33% to 54% with a sample average of 44%, and is potentially an important factor for an unemployed worker's choice to apply for unemployment benefits. Of course, other variables may influence the take-up rate as well. Due to personal characteristics, some people are more able than others to find a new job in a short period of time and will therefore not apply for UI benefits. Indicators of such personal characteristics are schooling, age, and, due to potential (positive or negative) discrimination in the labour market, racial and gender dummies. In addition, preferences and budgetary reasons, as reflected in the family situation, may be of importance. Due to the important differences in the state unemployment rates, the probability of finding a new job varies across states and we will therefore include the state unemployment rate in the analysis. The last type of variables that could be relevant relates to the reason why the job was lost. In the analysis we will include dummy variables for the reasons: slack work, position abolished, and end of seasonal work.

We estimate three different models, the results of which are presented in Table 7.1. The linear probability model is estimated by ordinary least squares, so no corrections for heteroskedasticity are made and no attempt is made to keep the implied probabilities between 0 and 1. The logit and probit model are both estimated by maximum likelihood. Because the logistic distribution has a variance of $\pi^2/3$, the estimates of β obtained from the logit model are roughly a factor $\pi/\sqrt{3}$ larger than those obtained from the probit model, acknowledging the small differences in the shape of the distributions. Similarly, the estimates for the linear probability model are quite different in magnitude and approximately four times as small as those for the logit model (except for the intercept term). Looking at the results in Table 7.1, we see that the signs of the coefficients are identical across the different specifications, while the

---

[3] The data for this illustration are available as BENEFITS.

Table 7.1 Binary choice models for applying for unemployment benefits (blue collar workers)

	LPM		Logit		Probit	
Variable	Estimate	s.e.	Estimate	s.e.	Estimate	s.e.
constant	−0.077	(0.122)	−2.800	(0.604)	−1.700	(0.363)
replacement rate	0.629	(0.384)	3.068	(1.868)	1.863	(1.127)
replacement rate^2	−1.019	(0.481)	−4.891	(2.334)	−2.980	(1.411)
age	0.0157	(0.0047)	0.068	(0.024)	0.042	(0.014)
age^2/10	−0.0015	(0.0006)	−0.0060	(0.0030)	−0.0038	(0.0018)
tenure	0.0057	(0.0012)	0.0312	(0.0066)	0.0177	(0.0038)
slack work	0.128	(0.014)	0.625	(0.071)	0.375	(0.042)
abolished position	−0.0065	(0.0248)	−0.0362	(0.1178)	−0.0223	(0.0718)
seasonal work	0.058	(0.036)	0.271	(0.171)	0.161	(0.104)
head of household	−0.044	(0.017)	−0.211	(0.081)	−0.125	(0.049)
married	0.049	(0.016)	0.242	(0.079)	0.145	(0.048)
children	−0.031	(0.017)	−0.158	(0.086)	−0.097	(0.052)
young children	0.043	(0.020)	0.206	(0.097)	0.124	(0.059)
live in SMSA	−0.035	(0.014)	−0.170	(0.070)	−0.100	(0.042)
non-white	0.017	(0.019)	0.074	(0.093)	0.052	(0.056)
year of displacement	−0.013	(0.008)	−0.064	(0.015)	−0.038	(0.009)
>12 years of school	−0.014	(0.016)	−0.065	(0.082)	−0.042	(0.050)
male	−0.036	(0.018)	−0.180	(0.088)	−0.107	(0.053)
state max. benefits	0.0012	(0.0002)	0.0060	(0.0010)	0.0036	(0.0006)
state unempl. rate	0.018	(0.003)	0.096	(0.016)	0.057	(0.009)
Loglikelihood			−2873.197		−2874.071	
Pseudo R^2			0.066		0.066	
McFadden R^2			0.057		0.057	
R_p^2	0.035		0.046		0.045	

statistical significance of the explanatory variables is also comparable. This is not an unusual finding. Qualitatively, the different models typically do not provide different answers.

For all specifications, the replacement rate has an insignificant positive coefficient, while its square is significantly negative. The ceteris paribus effect of the replacement rate will thus depend upon its value. For the probit model, for example, we can derive that the estimated marginal effect[4] of a change in the replacement rate (rr) equals the value of the normal density function multiplied by $1.863 − 2 \times 2.980rr$, which is negative for 85% of the observations in the sample. This is counterintuitive and suggests that other variables might be more important in explaining the take-up rate.

The dummy variable which indicates whether the job was lost because of slack work is highly significant in all specifications, which is not surprising given that these workers typically will find it hard to get a new job. Many other variables are statistically insignificant or only marginally significant. This is particularly troublesome as with this large number of observations a significance level of 1% or less may be more appropriate[5] than the traditional 5%. The two variables relating to the state of residence are statistically significant. The higher the state unemployment rate and the higher the maximum benefit level, the more likely it is that individuals apply for

---

[4] See Section 3.1 for the computation of marginal effects in the linear model.

[5] See the discussion on this issue in Section 2.5.7.

Table 7.2   Cross-tabulation of actual and predicted outcomes (logit model)

		$\hat{y}_i$		
		0	1	total
y_i	0	242	1300	1542
	1	171	3164	3335
	total	413	4464	4877

benefits, which is intuitively reasonable. The ceteris paribus effect of being married is estimated to be positive, while, somewhat surprisingly, being head of the household has a negative effect on the probability of take-up.

The fact that the models do not do a very good job in explaining the probability that someone applies for UI benefits is reflected in the goodness-of-fit measures that are computed. Usually, goodness-of-fit is fairly low for discrete choice models. In this application, the alternative goodness-of-fit measures indicate that the specified models perform between 3.5 and 6.6% better than a model that specifies the probability of take up to be constant. To elaborate upon this, let us consider the R_p^2 criterion for the logit model. If we generate predictions $\hat{y}_i$ on the basis of the estimated logit probabilities by predicting a one if the estimated probability is larger than 0.5 and a zero otherwise, we can produce the cross-tabulation in Table 7.2. The off-diagonal elements in this table indicate the number of observations for which the model's prediction is incorrect. It is clear that for the majority of individuals we predict that they will apply for UI benefits, while for 171 individuals we predict that they do not apply while in fact they do. The R_p^2 criterion can be computed directly from this table as

$$R_p^2 = 1 - \frac{171 + 1300}{1542},$$

where 1542 corresponds to the number of incorrect predictions from the naive model where the probability of take up is constant ($\hat{p} = 3335/4877$). The loglikelihood value for the latter model is given by

$$\log L_0 = 3335 \log \frac{3335}{4877} + 1542 \log \frac{1542}{4877} = -3046.187,$$

which allows us to compute the pseudo and McFadden R^2 measures.

7.1.7   Specification Tests in Binary Choice Models

Although maximum likelihood estimators have the property of being consistent, there is one important condition for this to hold: the likelihood function has to be correctly specified.[6] This means that we must be sure about the entire distribution that we impose upon our data. Deviations will cause inconsistent estimators and in binary

---

[6] We can relax this requirement somewhat to say that the first order conditions of the maximum likelihood problem should be valid (in the population). If this is the case, we can obtain consistent estimators even with the incorrect likelihood function. This is referred to as quasi-maximum likelihood estimation (see Section 6.4).

choice models this typically arises when the probability that $y_i = 1$ is misspecified as a function of x_i. Usually, such misspecifications are motivated from the latent variable model and reflect heteroskedasticity or non-normality (in the probit case) of ε_i. In addition, we may want to test for omitted variables without having to re-estimate the model. The optimal framework for such tests is the Lagrange multiplier (LM) framework as discussed in Section 6.2.

LM tests are based on the first order conditions from a more general model that specifies the alternative hypothesis, and check whether these are violated if we evaluate them at the parameter estimates of the current, restricted, model. Thus, if we want to test for J omitted variables z_i, we should evaluate whether

$$\sum_{i=1}^{N} \left[\frac{y_i - F(x_i'\hat{\beta})}{F(x_i'\hat{\beta})(1 - F(x_i'\hat{\beta}))} f(x_i'\hat{\beta}) \right] z_i \tag{7.22}$$

is significantly different from zero. Denoting the term in square brackets as the generalized residual, $\hat{\varepsilon}_i^G$, this means checking whether $\hat{\varepsilon}_i^G$ and z_i are correlated. As we have seen in Section 6.2, a simple way of computing the LM test statistic is obtained from a regression of a vector of ones upon the $K + J$ variables $\hat{\varepsilon}_i^G x_i'$ and $\hat{\varepsilon}_i^G z_i'$ and computing N times the uncentred R^2 (see Section 2.4) of this auxiliary regression. Under the null hypothesis that z_i enters the model with zero coefficients, the test statistic is asymptotically Chi-squared distributed with J degrees of freedom.

Heteroskedasticity of ε_i will cause the maximum likelihood estimators to be inconsistent and we can test for it fairly easily. Consider the alternative that the variance of ε_i depends upon exogenous variables[7] z_i as

$$V\{\varepsilon_i\} = kh(z_i'\alpha) \tag{7.23}$$

for some function $h > 0$ with $h(0) = 1$, $k = 1$ or $\pi^2/3$ (depending on whether we have a probit or logit model) and $h'(0) \neq 0$. The loglikelihood function would generalize to

$$\log L(\beta, \alpha) = \sum_{i=1}^{N} y_i \log F\left(\frac{x_i'\beta}{\sqrt{h(z_i'\alpha)}} \right) + \sum_{i=1}^{N} (1 - y_i) \log\left(1 - F\left(\frac{x_i'\beta}{\sqrt{h(z_i'\alpha)}} \right) \right). \tag{7.24}$$

The derivatives with respect to α, evaluated under the null hypothesis that $\alpha = 0$ are given by

$$\sum_{i=1}^{N} \left[\frac{y_i - F(x_i'\hat{\beta})}{F(x_i'\hat{\beta})(1 - F(x_i'\hat{\beta}))} f(x_i'\hat{\beta}) x_i'\hat{\beta} \right] \kappa z_i, \tag{7.25}$$

where κ is a constant that depends upon the form of h. Consequently, it is easy to test $H_0: \alpha = 0$ using the LM test by taking N times the uncentred R^2 of a regression of ones upon $\hat{\varepsilon}_i^G x_i'$ and $(\hat{\varepsilon}_i^G \cdot x_i'\hat{\beta}) z_i'$. Again, the test statistic is Chi-squared with J degrees of freedom (the dimension of z_i). Because of the normalization (the variance is not

---

[7] As the model describes the probability of $y_i = 1$ for a given set of x_i variables, the variables determining the variance of ε_i should be in this conditioning set as well. This means that z_i is a subset of (functions of) x_i. Note that it is possible that a priori restrictions on β are imposed to exclude some x_i variables from the 'mean' function $x_i'\beta$.

estimated), z_i should not include a constant. Also note that $\sum_i \hat{\varepsilon}_i^G \cdot x_i'\hat{\beta} = 0$ by construction because of the first order conditions. Although κ appears in the derivatives in (7.25), it is just a constant and therefore irrelevant in the computation of the test statistic. Consequently, the test for heteroskedasticity does not depend upon the form of the function $h(.)$, only upon the variables z_i that affect the variance (compare Newey, 1985). This is similar to the Breusch–Pagan test for heteroskedasticity in the linear regression model, as discussed in Subsections 4.4.3 and 6.3.2.

Finally, we discuss a normality test for the probit model. For a continuously observed variable, normality tests usually check for skewness (third moment) and excess kurtosis (fourth moment), that is they check whether $E\{\varepsilon_i^3\} = 0$ and $E\{\varepsilon_i^4 - 3\sigma^4\} = 0$ (compare Pagan and Vella, 1989). It is possible to derive tests for normality in the case with non-continuous observations in this way. Alternatively, and often equivalently, we can remain within the Lagrange Multiplier framework and specify an alternative distribution that is more general than the normal, and test the restrictions implied by the latter. A parametrization of non-normality is obtained by stating that ε_i has distribution function (compare Bera, Jarque and Lee, 1984, Ruud, 1984, or Newey, 1985)

$$P\{\varepsilon_i \leq t\} = \Phi(t + \gamma_1 t^2 + \gamma_2 t^3) \tag{7.26}$$

which characterizes the Pearson family of distributions (some restrictions on γ_1 and γ_2 apply). This class of distributions allows for skewness ($\gamma_1 \neq 0$) and excess kurtosis (fat tails) ($\gamma_2 \neq 0$) and reduces to the normal distribution if $\gamma_1 = \gamma_2 = 0$. Consequently, a test for normality is simply a test of two parametric restrictions. In the probit model the probability that $y_i = 1$ would more generally be described by

$$P\{y_i = 1 | x_i\} = \Phi(x_i'\beta + \gamma_1(x_i'\beta)^2 + \gamma_2(x_i'\beta)^3). \tag{7.27}$$

This shows that a test for normality, in this case, corresponds to a test for the omitted variables $(x_i'\beta)^2$ and $(x_i'\beta)^3$. Consequently, the test statistic for the null hypothesis $\gamma_1 = \gamma_2 = 0$ is easily obtained by running an auxiliary regression of ones upon $\hat{\varepsilon}_i^G x_i'$, $\hat{\varepsilon}_i^G (x_i'\hat{\beta})^2$ and $\hat{\varepsilon}_i^G (x_i'\hat{\beta})^3$ and computing N times R^2. Under the null, the test statistic is Chi-squared distributed with two degrees of freedom. The two additional terms in the regression correspond to skewness and kurtosis, respectively.

7.1.8 Relaxing Some Assumptions in Binary Choice Models

For a given set of x_i variables a binary choice model describes the probability that $y_i = 1$ as a function of these variables. There are several ways in which the restrictions imposed by the model can be relaxed. Almost without exception, these extensions are within the class of single index models in which there is one function of x_i that determines all probabilities (like $x_i'\beta$). First, it is straightforward, using the results of the previous subsection and analogous to linear regression models, to include nonlinear functions of x_i as additional explanatory variables. For example, if age is included in x_i, you could include age-squared as well.

Most extensions of binary choice models are motivated by the latent variable framework and involve relaxation of the distributional assumptions on the error term. For example, one could allow that the error term ε_i in (7.8) is heteroskedastic.

If the form of heteroskedasticity is known, say $V\{\varepsilon_i\} = \exp\{z_i'\alpha\}$, where z_i contains (functions of) elements in x_i and α is an unknown parameter vector, the essential change is that the probability that $y_i = 1$ also depends upon the error variance, that is

$$P\{y_i = 1 | x_i\} = F\left(x_i'\beta / \sqrt{\exp\{z_i'\alpha\}}\right),$$

The parameters in β and α can be estimated simultaneously by maximizing the loglikelihood function, as given in (7.24), with $h(.)$ as the exponential function. As in the standard homoskedastic case we have to impose a normalization restriction, which is done most easily by not including an intercept term in z_i. In this case $\alpha = 0$ corresponds to $V\{\varepsilon_i\} = 1$. Alternatively, one can set one of the β coefficients equal to 1 or -1, preferably one corresponding to a variable that is 'known' to have a nonzero effect on y_i, while not imposing a restriction on the variance of ε_i. This is a common normalization constraint when a semi-parametric estimator is employed.

It is also possible to estimate the parameter vector β **semi-parametrically**, that is without imposing distributional assumptions on the error ε_i, except that it has a median of zero and is independent of x_i. Although the interpretation of the β coefficients without a distribution function F is hard (if not impossible), its signs and significance are of interest. A well known method is referred to as Manski's **maximum score estimator** (Manski, 1975, 1985). Essentially, it tries to maximize the number of correct predictions based on (7.20). This is equivalent to minimizing the number of incorrect predictions $\sum_i (y_i - \hat{y}_i)^2$ with respect to β, where $\hat{y}_i$ is defined from (7.20). Because this objective function is not differentiable with respect to β, Manski describes a numerical algorithm to solve the maximization problem. Another problem is that the rate of convergence (to get consistency) is not $\sqrt{N}$, as usual, but less ($N^{1/3}$). To some extent, both problems are solved in Horowitz's smooth maximum score estimator (Horowitz, 1992), which is based on a smoothed version of the objective function above. Additional details and discussion can be found in Horowitz (1993, 1998), Lee (1996, Sect. 9.2), and Pagan and Ullah (1999, Chapter 7).

7.2 Multi-response Models

In many applications, the number of alternatives that can be chosen is larger than two. For example, we can distinguish the choice between full-time work, part-time work or not working, or the choice of a company to invest in Europe, Asia or the USA. Some quantitative variables can only be observed to lie in certain ranges. This may be because questionnaire respondents are unwilling to give precise answers, or are unable to do so, perhaps because of conceptual difficulties in answering the question. Examples of this are questions about income, the value of a house, or about job or income satisfaction. Multi-response models are developed to describe the probability of each of the possible outcomes as a function of personal or alternative specific characteristics. An important goal is to describe these probabilities with a limited number of unknown parameters and in a logically consistent way. For example, probabilities should lie between 0 and 1 and, over all alternatives, add up to one.

An important distinction exists between ordered response models and unordered models. An ordered response model is generally more parsimonious but can only be applied if there exists a logical ordering of the alternatives. The reason is that there is assumed to exist one underlying latent variable that drives the choice between the alternatives. In other words, the results will be sensitive to the ordering of the alternatives, so this ordering should make sense. Unordered models are not sensitive to the way in which the alternatives are numbered. In many cases, they can be based upon the assumption that each alternative has a random utility level and that individuals choose the alternative that yields highest utility.

7.2.1 Ordered Response Models

Let us consider the choice between M alternatives, numbered from 1 to M. If there is a logical ordering in these alternatives (for example, no car, 1 car, more than one car), a so-called **ordered response model** can be used. This model is also based on *one* underlying latent variable but with a different match from the latent variable, y_i^*, to the observed one ($y_i = 1, 2, \ldots, M$). Usually, one says that

$$y_i^* = x_i'\beta + \varepsilon_i \tag{7.28}$$

$$y_i = j \quad \text{if } \gamma_{j-1} < y_i^* \le \gamma_j, \tag{7.29}$$

for unknown γ_js with $\gamma_0 = -\infty$, $\gamma_1 = 0$ and $\gamma_M = \infty$. Consequently, the probability that alternative j is chosen is the probability that the latent variable y_i^* is between two boundaries γ_{j-1} and γ_j. Assuming that ε_i is i.i.d. standard normal results in the **ordered probit model**. The logistic distribution gives the **ordered logit model**. For $M = 2$ we are back at the binary choice model.

Consider an example from the labour supply literature. Suppose married females answer the question 'How much would you like to work?' in three categories 'not', 'part-time' and 'full-time'. According to neo-classical theory, desired labour supply, as measured by these answers, will depend upon preferences and a budget constraint. So variables related to age, family composition, husband's income and education level could be of importance. To model the outcomes, $y_i = 1$ (not working), $y_i = 2$ (part-time working) and $y_i = 3$ (full-time working), we note that there appears to be a logical ordering in these answers. To be precise, the question is whether it is reasonable to assume that there exists a single index $x_i'\beta$ such that higher values for this index correspond with, on average, larger values for y_i. If this is the case, we can write an ordered response model as

$$y_i^* = x_i'\beta + \varepsilon_i \tag{7.30}$$

$$y_i = 1 \quad \text{if } y_i^* \le 0,$$
$$ = 2 \quad \text{if } 0 < y_i^* \le \gamma, \tag{7.31}$$
$$ = 3 \quad \text{if } y_i^* > \gamma,$$

where we can loosely interpret y_i^* as 'willingness to work' or 'desired hours of work'. One of the boundaries is normalized to zero, which fixes the location, but we also need a normalization on the scale of y_i^*. The most natural one is that ε_i has a fixed variance. In the ordered probit model this means that ε_i is $NID(0, 1)$. The implied probabilities are obtained as

$$P\{y_i = 1|x_i\} = P\{y_i^* \leq 0|x_i\} = \Phi(-x_i'\beta),$$

$$P\{y_i = 3|x_i\} = P\{y_i^* > \gamma|x_i\} = 1 - \Phi(\gamma - x_i'\beta)$$

and

$$P\{y_i = 2|x_i\} = \Phi(\gamma - x_i'\beta) - \Phi(-x_i'\beta),$$

where γ is an unknown parameter that is estimated jointly with β. Estimation is based upon maximum likelihood, where the above probabilities enter the likelihood function. The interpretation of the β coefficients is in terms of the underlying latent variable model (for example, a positive β means that the corresponding variable increases a woman's willingness to work), or in terms of the effects on the respective probabilities, as we have seen above for the binary choice model. Suppose in the above model that the k-th coefficient, β_k, is positive. This means that the latent variable y_i^* increases if x_{ik} increases. Accordingly, the probability that $y_i = 3$ will increase, while the probability that $y_i = 1$ will decrease. The effect on the intermediate categories, however, is ambiguous; the probability that $y_i = 2$ may increase or decrease.

7.2.2 About Normalization

To illustrate the different normalization constraints that are required, let us consider a model where such constraints are not imposed. That is,

$$y_i^* = \beta_1 + x_i'\beta + \varepsilon_i, \quad \varepsilon_i \sim NID(0, \sigma^2).$$

$$y_i = 1 \quad \text{if } y_i^* \leq \gamma_1,$$

$$= 2 \quad \text{if } \gamma_1 < y_i^* \leq \gamma_2,$$

$$= 3 \quad \text{if } y_i^* > \gamma_2,$$

where the constant is taken out of the x_i vector. As we can only observe whether y_i is 1, 2 or 3, the only elements that the data can identify are the probabilities of these three events, for given values of x_i. Not accidentally, these are exactly the probabilities that enter the likelihood function. To illustrate this, consider the probability that $y_i = 1$ (given x_i), given by

$$P\{y_i = 1|x_i\} = P\{\beta_1 + x_i'\beta + \varepsilon_i \leq \gamma_1|x_i\} = \Phi\left(\frac{\gamma_1 - \beta_1}{\sigma} - x_i'\left(\frac{\beta}{\sigma}\right)\right),$$

which shows that varying β, β_1, σ and γ_1 does not lead a different probability as long as β/σ and $(\gamma_1 - \beta_1)/\sigma$ remain the same. This reflects an identification problem: different combinations of parameter values lead to the same loglikelihood value and there is no unique maximum. To circumvent this problem, normalization constraints are imposed. The standard model imposes that $\sigma = 1$ and $\gamma_1 = 0$, but it would also be possible, for example, to set $\sigma = 1$ and $\beta_1 = 0$. The interpretation of the coefficients is conditional upon a particular normalization constraint, but the probabilities are insensitive to it. In some applications, the boundaries correspond to observed values rather than unknown parameters and it is possible to estimate the variance of ε_i. This is illustrated in the next subsection.

7.2.3 Illustration: Willingness to Pay for Natural Areas

An interesting problem in public economics is how to determine the value of a good which is not traded. For example, what is the economic value of a public good like a forest or 'clean air'? In this subsection we consider an example from the contingent valuation literature. In this field surveys are used to elicit willingness to pay (WTP) values for a hypothetical change in the availability of some non-market good, e.g. a forest. Since the extensive study to measure the welfare loss to US citizens as a result of the massive oil spill due to the grounding of the oil tanker Exxon Valdez in the Gulf of Alaska (March 1989), the contingent valuation method plays an important role in measuring the benefits of a wide range of environmental goods.[8]

In this subsection, we consider a survey which has been conducted in 1997 in Portugal. The survey responses capture how much individuals are willing to pay to avoid the commercial and tourism development of the Alentejo Natural Park in southwest Portugal.[9] To find out what an individual's WTP is, it is not directly asked what amount a person would be willing to pay to preserve the park. Instead, each individual i in the sample is faced with a (potentially) different initial bid amount B_i^I and asked whether he would be willing to pay this amount or not. The interviewers used a so-called double-bounded procedure: each person is asked on a follow-up bid which is higher (lower) if the initial bid was accepted (rejected). For each respondent we thus have an initial bid B_i^I and one of the follow-up bids B_i^L or B_i^U, where $B_i^L < B_i^I < B_i^U$. Each person in the sample faced a random initial bid and the follow-up bid was dependent on this amount according to the following scheme:[10]

	Initial Bid	Increased Bid	Decreased Bid
Scheme 1	1200	3600	600
Scheme 2	2400	4800	1200
Scheme 3	4800	9600	2400
Scheme 4	9600	24 000	4800

A person's willingness to pay is unobserved and will be denoted by the latent variable B_i^*. To model how B_i^* varies with personal characteristics x_i we may want to specify a linear relationship

$$B_i^* = x_i'\beta + \varepsilon_i, \tag{7.32}$$

where ε_i is an unobserved error term, independent of x_i. Four possible outcomes can be observed, indexed by $y_i = 1, 2, 3, 4$. In particular,

$y_i = 1$ if both bids get rejected ($B_i^* < B_i^L$);
$y_i = 2$ if the first bid gets rejected and the second gets accepted ($B_i^L \leq B_i^* < B_i^I$);
$y_i = 3$ if the first gets accepted while the second gets rejected ($B_i^I \leq B_i^* < B_i^U$);
$y_i = 4$ if both bids get accepted ($B_i^* \geq B_i^U$).

---

[8] A non-technical discussion of contingent valuation is given in Portney (1994), Hanemann (1994) and Diamond and Hausman (1994).

[9] I am grateful to Paulo Nunes for providing the data used in this subsection. The data set employed here is available as WTP.

[10] The amounts are in escudos. Two hundred escudos is approximately 1 euro.

If we assume that ε_i is $NID(0, \sigma^2)$ the above setting corresponds to an ordered probit model. Because the boundaries B_i^L, B_i^I and B_i^U are observed, no normalization is needed on σ^2 and it can be estimated. Note that in this application the latent variable B_i^* has the clear interpretation of a person's willingness to pay, measured in escudos. Under the above assumptions, the probability of observing the last outcome ($y_i = 4$) is given by[11]

$$P\{y_i = 4|x_i\} = P\{x_i'\beta + \varepsilon_i \geq B_i^U|x_i\} = 1 - \Phi\left(\frac{B_i^U - x_i'\beta}{\sigma}\right). \qquad (7.33)$$

Similarly, the probability of observing the second outcome is

$$P\{y_i = 2|x_i\} = P\{B_i^L \leq x_i'\beta + \varepsilon_i < B_i^I|x_i\}$$

$$= \Phi\left(\frac{B_i^I - x_i'\beta}{\sigma}\right) - \Phi\left(\frac{B_i^L - x_i'\beta}{\sigma}\right). \qquad (7.34)$$

The other two probabilities can be derived along the same lines. These probabilities directly enter the loglikelihood function, maximization of which yields consistent estimators for β and σ^2.

The first model we estimate contains an intercept only. This is of interest as it can be interpreted as describing the (unconditional) distribution of the willingness to pay in the population. The second model includes three explanatory variables that may affect peoples' WTP, corresponding to age, gender and income. Consequently, we estimate two different models using maximum likelihood, one with an intercept only and one which includes age class (from 1 to 6), a female dummy and income class (ranging from 1 to 8). The results are presented in Table 7.3. In the subsample that we use, a total of $N = 312$ people were interviewed, of which 123 (39%) answered no to both bids, 18 answered no–yes, 113 yes–no and 58 answered yes to both questions.

From the model with an intercept only we see that the estimated average WTP is almost 3748 escudos (about 19 euro), with a fairly large standard deviation of 7722.4 escudos. Because we assumed that the distribution of B_i^* is normal, this implies that 31% of the population has a negative willingness to pay.[12] As this is not possible, we will reinterpret the latent variable as 'desired WTP', the actual WTP being the

Table 7.3   Ordered probit model for willingness to pay

Variable	I: intercept only Estimate	s.e.	II: with characteristics Estimate	s.e.
constant	3747.7	(499.4)	7058.2	(2116.6)
age class	—		−1386.6	(333.1)
female	—		−1036.7	(936.8)
income class	—		977.5	(381.9)
$\hat{\sigma}$	7722.4	(586.6)	7295.4	(549.7)
Loglikelihood	−409.00		−391.40	
Normality test (χ_2^2)	10.2758	($p = 0.006$)	3.9033	($p = 0.142$)

---

[11] As B_i^* is continuously distributed, the probability of each outcome is zero. This implies that the places of the equality signs in the inequalities are irrelevant.

[12] Note that $P\{B_i^* < 0\} = \Phi(-\mu/\sigma)$ if B_i^* is normally distributed with mean μ and standard deviation σ. Substituting the estimated values gives a probability of 0.31.

maximum of zero and the desired amount.[13] In this case, actual willingness to pay, given that it is positive, is described by a truncated normal distribution the expected value of which is estimated to be 7738 escudos.[14] The estimate for the expected WTP over the entire sample is then $7738.2 \times 0.69 = 5310$ escudos (about 27 euro), because 31% has a zero willingness to pay. Multiplying this by the total number of households in the population (about 3 million) produces an estimated total willingness to pay of about 80 million euro.

The inclusion of personal characteristics is not very helpful in eliminating the problem of negative values for B_i^*. Apparently, there is a relatively large group of people that says no to both bids, such that the imposed normal distribution generates substantial probability mass in the negative region. The explanatory variables that are included are age, in six brackets ($<29, 29–39, \ldots, >69$), a female dummy, and income (in 8 brackets). With the inclusion of these variables, the intercept term no longer has the same interpretation as before. Now, for example, the expected willingness to pay for a male in income class 1 ($<75\,000$ escudos) and age between 20 and 29 is $7058.2 - 1386.6 + 977.5 = 6649$ escudos, or, taking into account the censoring, 7366 escudos (about 37 euro). We see that the WTP significantly decreases with age and increases with income, while there is no statistical evidence of a gender effect.

As in the binary probit model, the assumption of normality is crucial here for consistency of the estimators as well as the interpretation of the parameter estimates (in terms of expected WTP). A test for normality can be computed within the Lagrange multiplier framework discussed in Section 6.2. As before, the alternative is that the appropriate distribution is within the Pearson family of distributions and a test for normality tests two parametric restrictions. Unfortunately, the analytical expressions are rather complicated and will not be presented here (see Glewwe, 1997). Under the null hypothesis of normality, the test statistics have a Chi-squared distribution with two degrees of freedom. The two statistics in the table indicate rejection of normality in the simple model with an intercept only, but do not lead to rejection of the model with individual characteristics.

7.2.4 Multinomial Models

In several cases, there is no natural ordering in the alternatives and it is not realistic to assume that there is a monotonic relationship between one underlying latent variable and the observed outcomes. Consider, for example, modelling the mode of transportation (bus, train, car, bicycle, walking). In such cases, an alternative framework has to be used to put some structure on the different probabilities. A common starting point is a random utility framework, in which the utility of each alternative is a linear function of observed characteristics (individual and/or alternative specific) plus an additive error term. Individuals are assumed to choose the alternative that has the highest utility. With appropriate distributional assumptions on these error terms, this approach leads to manageable expressions for the probabilities implied by the model.

To formalize this, suppose that there is a choice between M alternatives, indexed $j = 1, 2, \ldots, M$, noting that the order is arbitrary. Next, assume that the utility level

---

[13] This interpretation is similar to the one employed in tobit models. See below.

[14] If $y \sim \mathcal{N}(\mu, \sigma^2)$ we have that $E\{y|y > c\} = \mu + \sigma\lambda([c - \mu]/\sigma)$, where $\lambda(t) = \phi(-t)/\Phi(-t) \geq 0$. See Appendix B for details.

that individual i attaches to each of the alternatives is given by $U_{ij}, j = 1, 2, \ldots, M$. Then alternative j is chosen by individual i if it gives highest utility, that is if $U_{ij} = \max\{U_{i1}, \ldots, U_{iM}\}$. Of course, these utility levels are not observed and we need to make some additional assumptions to make this set-up operational. Let us assume that $U_{ij} = \mu_{ij} + \varepsilon_{ij}$, where μ_{ij} is a non-stochastic function of observables and a small number of unknown parameters, and ε_{ij} is an unobservable error term. From this, it follows that

$$
\begin{aligned}
P\{y_i = j\} &= P\{U_{ij} = \max\{U_{i1}, \ldots, U_{iM}\}\} \\
&= P\left\{\mu_{ij} + \varepsilon_{ij} > \max_{k=1, \ldots, J, k \neq j}\{\mu_{ik} + \varepsilon_{ik}\}\right\}.
\end{aligned}
\tag{7.35}
$$

To evaluate this probability, we need to be able to say something about the maximum of a number of random variables. In general, this is complicated, but a very convenient result arises if we can assume that all ε_{ij} are mutually independent with a so-called log Weibull distribution (also known as a Type I extreme value distribution). In this case, the distribution function of each ε_{ij} is given by

$$
F(t) = \exp\{-e^{-t}\},
\tag{7.36}
$$

which does not involve unknown parameters. Under these assumptions, it can be shown that

$$
P\{y_i = j\} = \frac{\exp\{\mu_{ij}\}}{\exp\{\mu_{i1}\} + \exp\{\mu_{i2}\} + \cdots + \exp\{\mu_{iM}\}}.
\tag{7.37}
$$

Notice that this structure automatically implies that $0 \leq P\{y_i = j\} \leq 1$ and that $\sum_{j=1}^{M} P\{y_i = j\} = 1$.

The distribution of ε_{ij} sets the scaling of utility (which is undefined) but not the location. To solve this, it is common to normalize one of the deterministic utility levels to zero, say $\mu_{i1} = 0$. Usually, μ_{ij} is assumed to be a linear function of observable variables, that may depend upon the individual (i), the alternative (j), or both. Thus we write $\mu_{ij} = x'_{ij}\beta$. With this we obtain

$$
P\{y_i = j\} = \frac{\exp\{x'_{ij}\beta\}}{1 + \exp\{x'_{i2}\beta\} + \cdots + \exp\{x'_{iM}\beta\}}, \quad j = 1, 2, \ldots, M.
\tag{7.38}
$$

This constitutes the so-called **multinomial logit model** or independent logit model; for details of the genesis of this model, see Greene (2000, Sect. 19.7). If there are only two alternatives ($M = 2$), it reduces to the standard binary logit model. The probability of an individual choosing alternative j is a simple expression of explanatory variables and coefficients β because of the convenient assumption made about the distribution of the unobserved errors. If, for example, we would have assumed that ε_{ij} were independent standard normals the probabilities would have involved $M - 1$ integrals,[15] which is computationally unattractive. As before, the multinomial

---

[15] The probability that a random variable x_j is the largest of a set of random variables $x_1, \ldots, x_M$ is the probability that $x_j - x_k \geq 0$ for $k = 1, \ldots, M, k \neq j$. This is an $M - 1$ dimensional subspace of $\mathbb{R}^M$ and the probability thus equals the integral of the joint density function of $x_1, \ldots, x_M$ over this $M - 1$ dimensional space. For moderate values of M, this is only tractable under very restrictive assumptions on the joint density of $x_1, \ldots, x_M$.

model is estimated by maximum likelihood, where the above probabilities enter the likelihood function.

Typical things to include in $x_{ij}'\beta$ are alternative specific characteristics. When explaining the mode of transportation, it may include variables like travelling time and costs, which may vary from one person to another. A negative β coefficient then means that the utility of an alternative is reduced if travelling time is increased. Consequently, if travelling time of one of the alternatives is reduced (while the other alternatives are not affected), this alternative will get a higher probability of being picked. Other things to include in $x_{ij}'\beta$ are personal characteristics (like age and gender), *with coefficients that are alternative-specific*. This could reveal, for example, that, ceteris paribus, men are more likely to travel by car than women.

Despite the attractiveness of the analytical expressions in the multinomial logit model, it has one big drawback, which is due to the assumption that all ε_{ij}s are independent. This implies that (conditional upon observed characteristics) utility levels of any two alternatives are independent. This is particularly troublesome if two or more alternatives are very similar. A typical example would be to decompose the category 'travel by bus', into 'travel by blue bus' and 'travel by red bus'. Clearly, we would expect that a high utility for a red bus implies a high utility for a blue bus. Another way to see the problem is to note that the probability ratio of two alternatives does not depend upon the nature of any of the other alternatives. Suppose that alternative 1 denotes travel by car and alternative 2 denotes travel by (blue) bus. Then the probability ratio (or odds ratio) is given by

$$\frac{P\{y_i = 2\}}{P\{y_i = 1\}} = \exp\{x_{i2}'\beta\} \tag{7.39}$$

irrespective of whether the third alternative is a red bus or a train. Clearly, this is something undesirable. McFadden (1974) called this property of the multinomial logit model **independence of irrelevant alternatives** (IIA). It is possible to relax the IIA property but this generally leads to (conceptually and computationally) more complicated models (see, for example, Amemiya, 1981, or Maddala, 1983). Therefore, the multinomial logit model is very frequently used in applied work.

Let us conclude this section with a small example from marketing, which involves stated preferences (rather than observed choices). Suppose that a number of respondents is asked to pick their preferred coffee-maker from a set of five, say, alternative combinations of characteristics (capacity, price, special filter (yes/no) and thermos flask (yes/no)). Typically, the combinations are not the same for all respondents. Let us refer to these characteristics as x_{ij}. To make sure that $\mu_{i1} = 0$, the x_{ij} are measured in differences from a reference coffee-maker, which without loss of generality corresponds to alternative 1. The probability that a respondent selects alternative j can be (assumed to be) described by a multinomial logit model, with

$$P\{y_i = j\} = \frac{\exp\{x_{ij}'\beta\}}{1 + \exp\{x_{i2}'\beta\} + \cdots + \exp\{x_{i5}'\beta\}}. \tag{7.40}$$

A positive β coefficient implies that people attach positive utility to the corresponding characteristic.

Under appropriate assumptions, the estimated model can be used to predict the probability of an individual choosing an alternative that is not yet on the market, provided this alternative is a (new) combination of existing characteristics. To illustrate this, suppose the current market for coffee-makers consists of two products: a machine for 10 cups without filter and thermos for 25 euro (z_1) and a machine for 15 cups with filter for 35 euro (z_2), while brand X is considering to introduce a new product: a machine for 12 cups with filter and thermos for 33 euro (z_3). If the respondents are representative for those who buy coffee-makers, the expected market share of this new product corresponds to the probability of preferring the new machine to the two existing ones, and could be estimated as

$$\frac{\exp\{(z_3 - z_1)'\hat{\beta}\}}{1 + \exp\{(z_2 - z_1)'\hat{\beta}\} + \exp\{(z_3 - z_1)'\hat{\beta}\}},$$

where $\hat{\beta}$ is the maximum likelihood estimate for β. In fact, it would be possible to select an optimal combination of characteristics in z_3 so as to maximize this estimated market share.[16]

7.3 Tobit Models

In certain applications, the dependent variable is continuous, but its range may be constrained. Most commonly this occurs when the dependent variable is zero for a substantial part of the population but positive (with many different outcomes) for the rest of the population. Examples are: expenditures on durable goods, hours of work, and the amount of foreign direct investment of a firm. Tobit models are particularly suited to model this type of variables. The original tobit model was suggested by James Tobin (Tobin, 1958), who analysed household expenditures on durable goods taking into account their non-negativity, while only in 1964 Arthur Goldberger referred to this model as a **tobit model**, because of its similarity to probit models. Since then, the original model has been generalized in many ways. In particular since the survey by Amemiya (1984), economists also refer to these generalizations as tobit models. In this section and the next we present the original tobit model and some of its extensions. More details can be found in Maddala (1983), Amemiya (1984) and Lee (1996).

7.3.1 The Standard Tobit Model

Suppose that we are interested in explaining the expenditures on tobacco of US households in a given year. Let y denote the expenditures on tobacco, while z denotes all other expenditures (both in US$). Total disposable income (or total expenditures)

---

[16] This example is clearly oversimplified. In marketing applications the property of independence of irrelevant alternatives is often considered unsatisfactory. Moreover, the model does not take into account observed and unobserved heterogeneity across consumers. See Louviere (1988) or Caroll and Green (1995) for some additional discussion.

is denoted by x. We can think of a simple utility maximization problem, describing the household's decision problem:

$$\max_{y,z} U(y,z) \tag{7.41}$$

$$y + z \leq x \tag{7.42}$$

$$y, z \geq 0. \tag{7.43}$$

The solution to this problem depends, of course, on the form of the utility function U. As it is unrealistic to assume that some households would spend all their money on tobacco, the corner solution $z = 0$ can be excluded a priori. However, the solution for y will be zero or positive and we can expect a corner solution for a large proportion of households. Let us denote the solution to (7.41)–(7.42) without the constraint in (7.43) as y^*. Under appropriate assumptions on U this solution will be linear in x. As economists we do not observe everything that determines the utility that a household attaches to tobacco. We account for this by allowing for unobserved heterogeneity in the utility function and thus for unobserved heterogeneity in the solution as well. Thus we write

$$y^* = \beta_1 + \beta_2 x + \varepsilon, \tag{7.44}$$

where ε corresponds to unobserved heterogeneity.[17] So, if there were no restrictions on y and consumers could spend any amount on tobacco, they would choose to spend y^*. The solution to the original, constrained problem, will therefore be given by

$$y = y^* \quad \text{if} \quad y^* > 0$$
$$y = 0 \quad \text{if} \quad y^* \leq 0 \tag{7.45}$$

So if a household would like to spend a negative amount y^*, it will spend nothing on tobacco. In essence, this gives us the **standard tobit model**, which we formalize as follows.

$$y_i^* = x_i'\beta + \varepsilon_i, \quad i = 1, 2, \ldots, N,$$
$$y_i = y_i^* \quad \text{if} \quad y_i^* > 0 \tag{7.46}$$
$$= 0 \quad \text{if} \quad y_i^* \leq 0,$$

where ε_i is assumed to be $NID(0, \sigma^2)$ and independent of x_i. Notice the similarity of this model with the standard probit model as given in (7.10); the difference is in the mapping from the latent variable to the observed variable. (Also note that we can identify the scaling here, so that we do not have to impose a normalization restriction.)

The model in (7.46) is also referred to as the **censored regression model**. It is a standard regression model, where all negative values are mapped to zeros. That is,

---

[17] Alternative interpretations of ε are possible. These may involve optimization errors of the household or measurement errors.

observations are censored (from below) at zero. The model thus describes two things. One is the probability that $y_i = 0$ (given x_i), given by

$$P\{y_i = 0\} = P\{y_i^* \leq 0\} = P\{\varepsilon_i \leq -x_i'\beta\}$$

$$= P\left\{\frac{\varepsilon_i}{\sigma} \leq -\frac{x_i'\beta}{\sigma}\right\} = \Phi\left(-\frac{x_i'\beta}{\sigma}\right) = 1 - \Phi\left(\frac{x_i'\beta}{\sigma}\right). \qquad (7.47)$$

The other is the distribution of y_i given that it is positive. This is a truncated normal distribution with expectation

$$E\{y_i|y_i > 0\} = x_i'\beta + E\{\varepsilon_i|\varepsilon_i > -x_i'\beta\} = x_i'\beta + \sigma\frac{\phi(x_i'\beta/\sigma)}{\Phi(x_i'\beta/\sigma)}. \qquad (7.48)$$

The last term in this expression denotes the conditional expectation of a mean-zero normal variable given that it is larger than $-x_i'\beta$ (see Appendix B). Obviously, this expectation is larger than zero. The result in (7.48) also shows why it is inappropriate to restrict attention to the positive observations only and estimate a linear model from this subsample: the conditional expectation of y_i no longer equals $x_i'\beta$, but also depends nonlinearly on x_i through $\phi(.)/\Phi(.)$.

The coefficients in the tobit model can be interpreted in a number of ways, depending upon one's interest. For example, the tobit model describes the probability of a zero outcome as

$$P\{y_i = 0\} = 1 - \Phi(x_i'\beta/\sigma).$$

This means that β/σ can be interpreted in a similar fashion as β in the probit model to determine the marginal effect of a change in x_{ik} upon the probability of observing a zero outcome (compare Subsection 7.1.2). That is,

$$\frac{\partial P\{y_i = 0\}}{\partial x_{ik}} = -\phi(x_i'\beta/\sigma)\frac{\beta_k}{\sigma}. \qquad (7.49)$$

Moreover, as shown in (7.48), the tobit model describes the expected value of y_i given that it is positive. This shows that the marginal effect of a change in x_{ik} upon the value of y_i, given the censoring, will be different from β_k. It will also involve the marginal change in the second term of (7.48), corresponding to the censoring. From (7.48) it follows that the expected value of y_i is given by[18]

$$E\{y_i\} = x_i'\beta\Phi(x_i'\beta/\sigma) + \sigma\phi(x_i'\beta/\sigma). \qquad (7.50)$$

From this it follows that the marginal effect on the expected value of y_i of a change in x_{ik} is given by[19]

$$\frac{\partial E\{y_i\}}{\partial x_{ik}} = \beta_k\Phi(x_i'\beta/\sigma). \qquad (7.51)$$

This tells us that the marginal effect of a change in x_{ik} upon the expected outcome y_i is given by the model's coefficient multiplied by the probability of having a positive

---

[18] Use that $E\{y\} = E\{y|y > 0\}P\{y > 0\} + 0$.

[19] This is obtained by differentiating with respect to x_{ik}, using the chain rule and using the functional form of ϕ. Several terms cancel out (compare Greene, 2000, Sect. 20.3).

outcome. If this probability is one for a particular individual, the marginal effect is simply β_k, as in the linear model. Finally, the marginal effect upon the latent variable is easily obtained as

$$\frac{\partial E\{y_i^*\}}{\partial x_{ik}} = \beta_k. \tag{7.52}$$

Unless the latent variable has a direct interpretation, which is typically not the case, it seems most natural to be interested in (7.51).

7.3.2 Estimation

Estimation of the tobit model is usually done through maximum likelihood. The contribution to the likelihood function of an observation either equals the probability mass (at the observed point $y_i = 0$) or the conditional density of y_i, given that it is positive, times the probability mass of observing $y_i > 0$. The loglikelihood function can thus be written as

$$\log L_1(\beta, \sigma^2) = \sum_{i \in I_0} \log P\{y_i = 0\} + \sum_{i \in I_1} [\log f(y_i|y_i > 0) + \log P\{y_i > 0\}]$$

$$= \sum_{i \in I_0} \log P\{y_i = 0\} + \sum_{i \in I_1} \log f(y_i), \tag{7.53}$$

where $f(.)$ is generic notation for a density function and the last equality follows from the definition of a conditional density.[20] The index sets I_0 and I_1 are defined as the sets of those indices corresponding to the zero and the positive observations, respectively. That is, $I_0 = \{i = 1, \ldots, N: y_i = 0\}$. Using the appropriate expressions for the normal distribution, we obtain

$$\log L_1(\beta, \sigma^2) = \sum_{i \in I_0} \log\left[1 - \Phi\left(\frac{x_i'\beta}{\sigma}\right)\right]$$

$$+ \sum_{i \in I_1} \log\left[\frac{1}{\sqrt{2\pi\sigma^2}} \exp\left\{-\frac{1}{2}\frac{(y_i - x_i'\beta)^2}{\sigma^2}\right\}\right]. \tag{7.54}$$

Maximization of (7.54) with respect to β and σ^2 yields the maximum likelihood estimates, as usual. Assuming that the model is correctly specified, this gives us consistent and asymptotically efficient estimators for both β and σ^2 (under mild regularity conditions).

The parameters in β have a double interpretation: one as the impact of a change in x_i on the probability of a non-zero expenditure, and one as the impact of a change in x_i on the level of this expenditure. Both effects thus automatically have the same sign. Although we motivated the tobit model above through a utility maximization framework, this is usually not the starting point in applied work: y_i^* could simply be interpreted as 'desired expenditures', with actual expenditures being equal to zero if the desired quantity is negative.

---

[20] Recall that $f(y|y > c) = f(y)/P\{y > c\}$ for $y > c$ and 0 otherwise (see Appendix B).

In some applications, observations are completely missing if $y_i^* \leq 0$. For example, our sample may be restricted to households with positive expenditures on tobacco only. In this case, we can still assume the same underlying structure but with a slightly different observation rule. This leads to the so-called **truncated regression model**. Formally, it is given by

$$y_i^* = x_i'\beta + \varepsilon_i, \quad i = 1, 2, \ldots, N, \tag{7.55}$$

$$y_i = y_i^* \quad \text{if} \quad y_i^* > 0$$

$$(y_i, x_i) \text{ not observed if } y_i^* \leq 0,$$

where, as before, ε_i is assumed to be $NID(0, \sigma^2)$ and independent of x_i. In this case we no longer have a **random sample** and we have to take this into account when making inferences (e.g. estimating β, σ^2). The likelihood contribution of an observation i is not just the density evaluated at the observed point y_i but the density at y_i conditional upon selection into the sample, i.e. conditional upon $y_i > 0$. The loglikelihood function for the truncated regression model is thus given by

$$\log L_2(\beta, \sigma^2) = \sum_{i \in I_1} \log f(y_i | y_i > 0) = \sum_{i \in I_1} [\log f(y_i) - \log P\{y_i > 0\}], \tag{7.56}$$

which, for the normal distribution, reduces to

$$\log L_2(\beta, \sigma^2) = \sum_{i \in I_1} \left\{ \log \left[\frac{1}{\sqrt{2\pi\sigma^2}} \exp \left\{ -\frac{1}{2} \frac{(y_i - x_i'\beta)^2}{\sigma^2} \right\} \right] - \log \Phi \left(\frac{x_i'\beta}{\sigma} \right) \right\}. \tag{7.57}$$

Although there is no need to observe what the characteristics of the individuals with $y_i = 0$ are, nor to know how many individuals are 'missing', we have to assume that they are unobserved only because their characteristics are such that $y_i^* \leq 0$. Maximizing $\log L_2$ with respect to β and σ^2 again gives consistent estimators. If observations with $y_i = 0$ are really missing it is the best one can do. However, even if observations with $y_i = 0$ are available, one could still maximize $\log L_2$ instead of $\log L_1$, that is, one could estimate a truncated regression model even if a tobit model would be applicable. It is intuitively obvious that the latter (tobit) approach uses more information and therefore will generally lead to more efficient estimators. In fact, it can be shown that the information contained in the tobit model combines that contained in the truncated regression model with that of the probit model describing the zero/non-zero decision. This fact follows easily from the result that the tobit loglikelihood function is the sum of the truncated regression and probit loglikelihood functions.

7.3.3 Illustration: Expenditures on Alcohol and Tobacco (Part 1)

In economics, (systems of) demand equations are often used to analyse the effect of, for example, income, tax or price changes on consumer demand. A practical problem that emerges is that expenditures on particular commodities may be zero, particularly if the goods are not aggregated into broad categories. While this typically occurs with durable goods, we shall concentrate on a different type of commodities here: alcoholic beverages and tobacco.

Starting from the assumption that a consumer maximizes his utility as a function of the quantities of the goods consumed, it is possible to derive (Marshallian) demand functions for each good as

$$q_j = g_j(x, p),$$

where q_j denotes the quantity of good j, x denotes total expenditures and p is a vector of prices of all relevant goods. The function g_j depends upon the consumer's preferences. In the empirical application we shall consider cross-sectional data where prices do not vary across observations. Therefore, p can be absorbed into the functional form to get

$$q_j = g_j^*(x).$$

This relationship is commonly referred to as an **Engel curve** (see, e.g. Deaton and Muellbauer, 1980, Chapter 1). From this, one can define the total expenditure elasticity of q_j, the quantity of good j that is consumed, as

$$\varepsilon_j = \frac{\partial g_j^*(x)}{\partial x} \frac{x}{q_j}.$$

This elasticity measures the relative effect of a 1% increase in total expenditures and can be used to classify goods into luxuries, necessities and inferior goods. A good is referred to as a luxury good if the quantity that is consumed increases more than proportionally with total expenditures ($\varepsilon_j > 1$), while it is a necessity if $\varepsilon_j < 1$. If the quantity of a good's purchase decreases when total expenditure increases, the good is said to be inferior, which implies that the elasticity ε_j is negative.

A convenient parametrization of the Engel curve is

$$w_j = \alpha_j + \beta_j \log x,$$

where $w_j = p_j q_j / x$ denotes the budget share of good j. It is a simple exercise to derive that the total expenditure elasticities for this functional form are given by

$$\varepsilon_j = 1 + \beta_j / w_j. \tag{7.58}$$

Recall that good j is a necessity if $\varepsilon_j < 1$ or $\beta_j < 0$, while a luxury good corresponds to $\beta_j > 0$.

Below we shall focus on two particular goods, alcoholic beverages and tobacco. Moreover, we explicitly focus on heterogeneity across households and the suffix i will be used to index observations on individual households. The Almost Ideal Demand System of Deaton and Muellbauer (1980, Section 3.4) implies Engel curves of the form

$$w_{ji} = \alpha_{ji} + \beta_{ji} \log x_i + \varepsilon_{ji},$$

where w_{ji} is household i's budget share of commodity j, and x_i denotes total expenditures. The parameters α_{ji} and β_{ji} may depend upon household characteristics, like family composition, age and education of the household head. The random terms ε_{ji} capture unobservable differences between households. Because β_{ji} varies over households, the functional form of the above Engel curve permits goods to be luxuries or necessities depending upon household characteristics.

When we consider expenditures on alcohol or tobacco, the number of zeroes is expected to be substantial. A first way to explain these zeroes is that they arise from corner solutions when the non-negativity constraint of the budget share ($w_{ji} \geq 0$) becomes binding. This means that households prefer not to buy alcoholic beverages or tobacco at current prices and income, but that a price decrease or income increase would (ultimately) change this. The discussion whether or not this is a realistic assumption is deferred to Subsection 7.4.4. As the corner solutions do not satisfy the first order conditions for an interior optimum of the underlying utility maximization problem, the Engel curve does not apply to observations with $w_{ji} = 0$. Instead, the Engel curve is assumed to describe the solution to the household's utility maximization problem if the non-negativity constraint is not imposed, a negative solution corresponding with zero expenditures on the particular good. This way, we can adjust the model to read

$$w_{ji}^* = \alpha_{ji} + \beta_{ji} \log x_i + \varepsilon_{ji},$$

$$w_{ji} = w_{ji}^* \quad \text{if } w_{ji}^* > 0$$

$$= 0 \quad \text{otherwise,}$$

which corresponds to a standard tobit model if it is assumed that $\varepsilon_{ji} \sim NID(0, \sigma^2)$ for a given good j. Atkinson, Gomulka and Stern (1990) use a similar approach to estimate an Engel curve for alcohol, but assume that ε_{ji} has a non-normal skewed distribution.

To estimate the above model, we employ data[21] from the Belgian household budget survey of 1995–1996, supplied by the National Institute of Statistics (NIS). The sample contains 2724 households for which expenditures on a broad range of goods are observed as well as a number of background variables, relating to, e.g. family composition and occupational status. In this sample, 62% of the households has zero expenditures on tobacco, while 17% does not spend anything on alcoholic beverages. The average budget shares, for the respective subsamples of positive expenditures, are 3.22% and 2.15%.

Below we shall estimate the two Engel curves for alcohol and tobacco separately. This means that we do not take into account the possibility that a binding non-negativity constraint on tobacco may also affect expenditures on alcohol, or vice versa. We shall assume that α_{ji} is a linear function of the age of the household head,[22] the number of adults in the household, and the numbers of children younger than 2 and 2 or older, while β_{ji} is taken to be a linear function of age and the number of adults. This implies that the products of log total expenditures with age and number of adults are included as explanatory variables in the tobit model. The estimation results for the standard tobit models are presented in Table 7.4.

For tobacco, there is substantial evidence that age is an important factor in explaining the budget share, both separately and in combination with total expenditures. For alcoholic beverages only the number of children and total expenditures are individually significant. As reported in the table, Wald tests for the hypothesis that

---

[21] I am grateful to the NIS for permission to use these data; available as TOBACCO.

[22] Age is measured in 10-year interval classes ranging from 0 (younger than 30) to 4 (60 or older).

Table 7.4 Tobit models for budget shares alcohol and tobacco

Variable	Alcoholic beverages		Tobacco	
	Estimate	s.e.	Estimate	s.e.
constant	−0.1592	(0.0438)	0.5900	(0.0934)
age class	0.0135	(0.0109)	−0.1259	(0.0242)
nadults	0.0292	(0.0169)	0.0154	(0.0380)
nkids ≥ 2	−0.0026	(0.0006)	0.0043	(0.0013)
nkids < 2	−0.0039	(0.0024)	−0.0100	(0.0055)
log x	0.0127	(0.0032)	−0.0444	(0.0069)
age × log x	−0.0008	(0.0088)	0.0088	(0.0018)
nadults × log x	−0.0022	(0.0012)	−0.0006	(0.0028)
$\hat{\sigma}$	0.0244	(0.0004)	0.0480	(0.0012)
Loglikelihood	4755.371		758.701	
Wald test (χ_7^2)	117.86	($p = 0.000$)	170.18	($p = 0.000$)

all coefficients, except the intercept term, are equal to zero, produce highly significant values for both goods. Under the null hypothesis, these test statistics, comparable with the F-statistic that is typically computed for the linear model (see Subsection 2.5.4), have an asymptotic Chi-squared distribution with 7 degrees of freedom.

If we assume that a household under consideration has a sufficiently large budget share to ignore changes in the second term of (7.48), the total expenditure elasticity can be computed on the basis of (7.58) as $1 + \beta_{ji}/w_{ji}$. It measures the total elasticity for those that consume alcohol and those that smoke, respectively. If we evaluate the above elasticities at the sample averages of those households that have positive expenditures, we obtain estimated elasticities[23] of 1.294 and 0.180, respectively. This indicates that alcoholic beverages are a luxury good, while tobacco is a necessity. In fact, the total expenditure elasticity of tobacco expenditures is fairly close to zero.

In this application the tobit model assumes that all zero expenditures are the result of corner solutions and that a sufficiently large change in income or relative prices would ultimately create positive expenditures for any household. In particular for tobacco this seems not really appropriate. Many people do not smoke because of, e.g. health or social reasons and would not smoke even if cigarettes were free. If this is the case, it seems more appropriate to model the decision to smoke or not as a process separate from the decision of how much to spend on it. The so-called tobit II model, one of the extensions of the tobit that will be discussed below, could be appropriate for this situation. Therefore, we shall come back to this example in Subsection 7.4.4 below.

7.3.4 Specification Tests in the Tobit Model

A violation of the distributional assumptions on ε_i will generally lead to inconsistent maximum likelihood estimators for β and σ^2. In particular non-normality and hetero-skedasticity are a concern. We can test for these alternatives, as well as for omitted variables, within the Lagrange multiplier framework. To start the discussion, first

---

[23] We first take averages and then compute the ratio.

note that the first order conditions of the loglikelihood $\log L_1$ with respect to β are given by

$$\sum_{i \in I_0} \frac{-\phi(x_i'\hat{\beta}/\hat{\sigma})}{1 - \Phi(x_i'\hat{\beta}/\hat{\sigma})} \, x_i + \sum_{i \in I_1} \frac{\hat{\varepsilon}_i}{\hat{\sigma}} \, x_i = \sum_{i=1}^{N} \hat{\varepsilon}_i^G x_i = 0, \qquad (7.59)$$

where we define the generalized residual $\hat{\varepsilon}_i^G$ as the scaled residual $\hat{\varepsilon}_i/\hat{\sigma} = (y_i - x_i'\hat{\beta})/\hat{\sigma}$ for the positive observations and as $-\phi(.)/(1 - \Phi(.))$, evaluated at $x_i'\hat{\beta}/\hat{\sigma}$, for the zero observations. Thus we obtain first order conditions that are of the same form as in the probit model or the linear regression model. The only difference is the definition of the appropriate (generalized) residual.

Because σ^2 is also a parameter that is estimated, we also need the first order condition with respect to σ^2 to derive the specification tests. Apart from an irrelevant scaling factor, this is given by

$$\sum_{i \in I_0} \frac{x_i'\hat{\beta}}{\hat{\sigma}} \frac{\phi(x_i'\hat{\beta}/\hat{\sigma})}{1 - \Phi(x_i'\hat{\beta}\hat{\sigma})} + \sum_{i \in I_1} \left(\frac{\hat{\varepsilon}_i^2}{\hat{\sigma}^2} - 1 \right) = \sum_{i=1}^{N} \hat{\varepsilon}_i^{G(2)} = 0, \qquad (7.60)$$

where we defined $\hat{\varepsilon}_i^{G(2)}$, a second order generalized residual. The first order condition with respect to σ^2 says that the sample average of $\hat{\varepsilon}_i^{G(2)}$ should be zero. It can be shown (see Gouriéroux et al., 1987) that the second order generalized residual is an estimate for $E\{\varepsilon_i^2/\sigma^2 - 1 | y_i, x_i\}$, just like the (first order) generalized residual $\hat{\varepsilon}_i^G$ is an estimate for $E\{\varepsilon_i/\sigma | y_i, x_i\}$. While it is beyond the scope of this text to derive this, it is intuitively reasonable: if ε_i cannot be determined from y_i, x_i and β, we replace the expressions by the conditional expected values given all we know about y_i^*, as reflected in y_i. This is simply the best guess of what we think the residual should be, given that we only know that it satisfies $\varepsilon_i < -x_i'\beta$.

From (7.59) it is immediately clear how we would test for J omitted variables z_i. As the additional first order conditions would imply that

$$\sum_{i=1}^{N} \hat{\varepsilon}_i^G z_i = 0,$$

we can simply do a regression of ones upon the $K + 1 + J$ variables $\hat{\varepsilon}_i^G x_i'$, $\hat{\varepsilon}_i^{G(2)}$, and $\hat{\varepsilon}_i^G z_i'$ and compute the test statistic as N times the uncentred R^2. The appropriate asymptotic distribution under the null hypothesis is a Chi-squared with J degrees of freedom.

A test for heteroskedasticity can be based upon the alternative that

$$V\{\varepsilon_i\} = \sigma^2 h(z_i'\alpha), \qquad (7.61)$$

where $h(.)$ is an unknown differentiable function with $h(0) = 1$ and $h(.) > 0$, and z_i is a J-dimensional vector of explanatory variables, not including an intercept term. The null hypothesis corresponds to $\alpha = 0$, implying that $V\{\varepsilon_i\} = \sigma^2$. The additional scores with respect to α, evaluated under the current set of parameters estimates $\hat{\beta}, \hat{\sigma}^2$ are easily obtained as $\kappa \hat{\varepsilon}_i^{G(2)} z_i'$, where κ is an irrelevant constant that depends upon h. Consequently, the LM test statistic for heteroskedasticity is easily obtained as N times the uncentred R^2 of a regression of ones upon the $K + 1 + J$ variables $\hat{\varepsilon}_i^G x_i'$,

$\hat{\varepsilon}_i^{G(2)}$, and $\hat{\varepsilon}_i^{G(2)} z_i'$. Note that also in this case the test statistic does not depend upon the form of h, only upon z_i.

If homoskedasticity is rejected, we can estimate the model with heteroskedastic errors if we specify a functional form for h, for example, $h(z_i'\alpha) = \exp\{z_i'\alpha\}$. In the loglikelihood function, we simply replace σ^2 by $\sigma^2 \exp\{z_i'\alpha\}$ and we estimate α jointly with the parameters β and σ^2. Alternatively, it is possible that heteroskedasticity is found because something else is wrong with the model. For example, the functional form may not be appropriate and nonlinear functions of x_i should be included. Also a transformation of the dependent variable could eliminate the heteroskedasticity problem. This explains, for example, why in many cases people specify a model for log wages rather than wages themselves.

Finally, we discuss a test for non-normality. This test can be based upon the framework of Pagan and Vella (1989) and implies a test of the following two conditional moment conditions that are implied by normality: $E\{\varepsilon_i^3/\sigma^3|x_i\} = 0$ and $E\{\varepsilon_i^4/\sigma^4 - 3|x_i\} = 0$, corresponding to the absence of skewness and excess kurtosis, respectively (see Section 6.4). Let us first consider the quantities $E\{\varepsilon_i^3/\sigma^3|y_i, x_i\}$ and $E\{\varepsilon_i^4/\sigma^4 - 3|y_i, x_i\}$, noting that taking expectations over y_i (given x_i) produces the two moments of interest. If $y_i > 0$ we can simply estimate the sample equivalents as $\hat{\varepsilon}_i^3/\hat{\sigma}^3$ and $\hat{\varepsilon}_i^4/\hat{\sigma}^4 - 3$, respectively, where $\hat{\varepsilon}_i = y_i - x_i'\hat{\beta}$. For $y_i = 0$ the conditional expectations are more complicated, but they can be computed using the following formulae (Lee and Maddala, 1985):

$$E\left\{\frac{\varepsilon_i^3}{\sigma^3}\middle|x_i, y_i = 0\right\} = \left[2 + \left(\frac{x_i'\beta}{\sigma}\right)^2\right] E\left\{\frac{\varepsilon_i}{\sigma}\middle|x_i, y_i = 0\right\} \tag{7.62}$$

$$E\left\{\frac{\varepsilon_i^4}{\sigma^4} - 3\middle|x_i, y_i = 0\right\} = 3E\left\{\frac{\varepsilon_i^2}{\sigma^2} - 1\middle|x_i, y_i = 0\right\} + \left(\frac{x_i'\beta}{\sigma}\right)^3 E\left\{\frac{\varepsilon_i}{\sigma}\middle|x_i, y_i = 0\right\}. \tag{7.63}$$

These two quantities can easily be estimated from the ML estimates $\hat{\beta}$ and $\hat{\sigma}^2$ and the generalized residuals $\hat{\varepsilon}_i^G$ and $\hat{\varepsilon}_i^{G(2)}$. Let us denote the resulting estimates as $\hat{\varepsilon}_i^{G(3)}$ and $\hat{\varepsilon}_i^{G(4)}$, respectively, such that

$$\hat{\varepsilon}_i^{G(3)} = \hat{\varepsilon}_i^3/\hat{\sigma}^3 \qquad \text{if } y_i > 0$$

$$= [2 + (x_i'\hat{\beta}/\hat{\sigma})^2]\hat{\varepsilon}_i^G \quad \text{otherwise}, \tag{7.64}$$

and

$$\hat{\varepsilon}_i^{G(4)} = \hat{\varepsilon}_i^4/\hat{\sigma}^4 - 3 \qquad \text{if } y_i > 0$$

$$= 3\hat{\varepsilon}_i^{G(2)} + (x_i'\hat{\beta}/\hat{\sigma})^3\hat{\varepsilon}_i^G \quad \text{otherwise}. \tag{7.65}$$

By the law of iterated expectations the null hypothesis of normality implies that (asymptotically) $E\{\hat{\varepsilon}_i^{G(3)}|x_i\} = 0$ and $E\{\hat{\varepsilon}_i^{G(4)}|x_i\} = 0$. Consequently, the conditional moment test for non-normality can be obtained by running a regression of a vector of ones upon the $K + 3$ variables $\hat{\varepsilon}_i^G x_i'$, $\hat{\varepsilon}_i^{G(2)}$, $\hat{\varepsilon}_i^{G(3)}$ and $\hat{\varepsilon}_i^{G(4)}$ and computing N times the uncentred R^2. Under the null hypothesis, the asymptotic distribution of the resulting test statistic is Chi-squared with 2 degrees of freedom.

Although the derivation of the different test statistics may seem complicated, their computation is relatively easy. They can be computed using an auxiliary regression after some straightforward computations involving the maximum likelihood estimates and the data. As consistency of the ML estimators crucially depends upon a correct specification of the likelihood function, testing for misspecification should be a standard routine in empirical work.

7.4 Extensions of Tobit Models

The standard tobit model imposes a structure which is often too restrictive: exactly the same variables affecting the probability of a non-zero observation determine the level of a positive observation and, moreover, with the same sign. This implies, for example, that those who are more likely to spend a positive amount are, on average, also those that spend more on a durable good. In this section, we shall discuss models that relax this restriction. Taking the specific example of holiday expenditures, it is conceivable that households with many children are less likely to have positive expenditures, while if a holiday is taken up, the expected level of expenditures for such households is higher.

Suppose that we are interested in explaining wages. Obviously, wages are only observed for people that are actually working, but for economic purposes we are often interested in (potential) wages not conditional upon this selection. For example: a change in some x variable may lower someone's wage such that he decides to stop working. Consequently, his wage would no longer be observed and the effect of this x variable could be underestimated from the available data. Because the sample of workers may not be a random sample of the population (of potential workers) – in particular one can expect that people with lower (potential) wages are more likely to be unemployed – this problem is often referred to as a **sample selection problem**.

7.4.1 The Tobit II Model

The traditional model to describe sample selection problems is the **tobit II model**,[24] also referred to as the **sample selection model**. In this context, it consists of a linear wage equation

$$w_i^* = x_{1i}'\beta_1 + \varepsilon_{1i}, \tag{7.66}$$

where x_{1i} denotes a vector of exogenous characteristics (age, education, gender,...) and w_i^* denotes person i's wage. The wage w_i^* is not observed for people that are not working (which explains the *). To describe whether a person is working or not a second equation is specified, which is of the binary choice type. That is,

$$h_i^* = x_{2i}'\beta_2 + \varepsilon_{2i}, \tag{7.67}$$

---

[24] This classification of tobit models is due to Amemiya (1984). The standard tobit model of Section 7.3 is then referred to as tobit I.

where we have the following observation rule:

$$w_i = w_i^*, \ h_i = 1 \quad \text{if } h_i^* > 0 \tag{7.68}$$

$$w_i \text{ not observed}, h_i = 0 \quad \text{if } h_i^* \le 0, \tag{7.69}$$

where w_i denotes person i's actual wage.[25] The binary variable h_i simply indicates working or not-working. The model is completed by a distributional assumption on the unobserved errors $(\varepsilon_{1i}, \varepsilon_{2i})$, usually a bivariate normal distribution with expectations zero, variances σ_1^2, σ_2^2, respectively, and a covariance σ_{12}. The model in (7.67) is, in fact, a standard probit model, describing the choice working or not working. Therefore, a normalization restriction is required and, as before, one usually sets $\sigma_2^2 = 1$. The choice to work is affected by the variables in x_{2i} with coefficients β_2. The equation (7.66) describes (potential) wages as a function of the variables in x_{1i} with coefficients β_1. The signs and magnitude of the β coefficients may differ across the two equations. In principle, the variables in x_1 and x_2 can be different, although one has to be very careful in this respect (see below). If we would impose that $x_{1i}'\beta_1 = x_{2i}'\beta_2$ and $\varepsilon_{1i} = \varepsilon_{2i}$, it is easily seen that we are back at the standard tobit model (tobit I).

The conditional expected wage, given that a person *is* working, is given by

$$
\begin{aligned}
E\{w_i|h_i = 1\} &= x_{1i}'\beta_1 + E\{\varepsilon_{1i}|h_i = 1\} \\
&= x_{1i}'\beta_1 + E\{\varepsilon_{1i}|\varepsilon_{2i} > -x_{2i}'\beta_2\} \\
&= x_{1i}'\beta_1 + \frac{\sigma_{12}}{\sigma_2^2} E\{\varepsilon_{2i}|\varepsilon_{2i} > -x_{2i}'\beta_2\} \\
&= x_{1i}'\beta_1 + \sigma_{12} \frac{\phi(x_{2i}'\beta_2)}{\Phi(x_{2i}'\beta_2)},
\end{aligned}
\tag{7.70}
$$

where the last equality uses $\sigma_2^2 = 1$ and the expression for the expectation of a truncated standard normal distribution, similar to that used in (7.49). The third equality uses that for two normal random variables $E\{\varepsilon_1|\varepsilon_2\} = (\sigma_{12}/\sigma_2^2)\varepsilon_2$. Appendix B provides more details on these results. Note that we can write $\sigma_{12} = \rho_{12}\sigma_1$, where ρ_{12} is the correlation coefficient between the two errors. Again, this shows the generality of the model in comparison with (7.49). It follows directly from (7.70) that the conditional expected wage equals $x_{1i}'\beta_1$ only if $\sigma_{12} = \rho_{12} = 0$. So, if the error terms from the two equations are uncorrelated, the wage equation can be estimated consistently by ordinary least squares. A sample selection bias in the OLS estimator arises if $\sigma_{12} \ne 0$. The term $\phi(x_{2i}'\beta_2)/\Phi(x_{2i}'\beta_2)$ is denoted $\lambda(x_{2i}'\beta_2)$ by Heckman (1979) and is therefore sometimes referred to as **Heckman's lambda**.

The crucial parameter which makes the sample selection model different from just a regression model and a probit model is the correlation coefficient (or covariance) between the two equations' error terms. If the errors are uncorrelated we could simply estimate the wage equation by OLS and ignore the selection equation (unless we are interested in it). Now, why can we expect correlation between the two error terms? Although the tobit II model can be motivated in different ways, we shall more or less

---

[25] In most applications the model is formulated in terms of *log* wages.

follow Gronau (1974) in his reasoning. Assume that the utility maximization problem of the individual (in Gronau's case: housewives) can be characterized by a **reservation wage** w_i^r (the value of time). An individual will work if the actual wage she is offered exceeds this reservation wage. The reservation wage of course depends upon personal characteristics, via the utility function and the budget constraint, so that we write (assume)

$$w_i^r = z_i'\gamma + \eta_i,$$

where z_i is a vector of characteristics and η_i is unobserved. Usually the reservation wage is not observed.

Now assume that the wage a person is offered depends on her personal characteristics (and some job characteristics) as in (7.66), i.e.

$$w_i^* = x_{1i}'\beta_1 + \varepsilon_{1i}.$$

If this wage is below w_i^r individual i is assumed not to work. We can thus write her labour supply decision as

$$h_i = 1 \quad \text{if } w_i^* - w_i^r > 0$$
$$= 0 \quad \text{if } w_i^* - w_i^r \leq 0$$

The inequality can be written in terms of observed characteristics and unobserved errors as

$$h_i^* \equiv w_i^* - w_i^r = x_{1i}'\beta_1 - z_i'\gamma + (\varepsilon_{1i} - \eta_i) = x_{2i}'\beta_2 + \varepsilon_{2i}, \tag{7.71}$$

by appropriately defining x_{2i} and ε_{2i}. Consequently, our simple economic model where labour supply is based on a reservation wage leads to a model of the tobit II form. A few things are worth noticing from (7.71). First, the offered wage influences the decision to work or not. This implies that the error term ε_{2i} involves the unobserved heterogeneity influencing the wage offer, i.e. involves ε_{1i}. If η_i is uncorrelated with ε_{1i}, the correlation between ε_{2i} and ε_{1i} is expected to be positive. Consequently, we can expect a sample selection bias in the least squares estimator from economic arguments. Second, the variables in x_{1i} are all included in x_{2i}, plus all variables in z_i that are not contained in x_{1i}. Economic arguments thus indicate that we should include in x_{2i} at least those variables which are contained in x_{1i}.

Let us repeat the statistical model, the tobit II model, for convenience, substituting y for w to stress generality.

$$y_i^* = x_{1i}'\beta_1 + \varepsilon_{1i} \tag{7.72}$$

$$h_i^* = x_{2i}'\beta_2 + \varepsilon_{2i} \tag{7.73}$$

$$y_i = y_i^*, h_i = 1 \quad \text{if } h_i^* > 0 \tag{7.74}$$

$$y_i \text{ not observed}, h_i = 0 \quad \text{if } h_i^* \leq 0, \tag{7.75}$$

where

$$\begin{pmatrix} \varepsilon_{1i} \\ \varepsilon_{2i} \end{pmatrix} \sim NID\left(\begin{pmatrix} 0 \\ 0 \end{pmatrix}, \begin{pmatrix} \sigma_1^2 & \sigma_{12} \\ \sigma_{12} & 1 \end{pmatrix} \right). \tag{7.76}$$

This model has two observed endogenous variables y_i and h_i. Statistically, it describes the joint distribution of y_i and h_i conditional upon the variables in *both* x_{1i} and x_{2i}. That is, (7.72) should describe the conditional distribution of y_i^* conditional upon *both* x_{1i} and x_{2i}. The only reason not to include a certain variable in x_{1i} which is included in x_{2i} is that we are confident that it has a zero coefficient in the wage equation. For example, there could be variables which affect reservation wages only but not the wage itself. Incorrectly omitting a variable from (7.72), while including it in (7.73), may seriously affect the estimation results and may lead to spurious conclusions of the existence of sample selection bias.

7.4.2 Estimation

For estimation purposes, the model can be thought of as consisting of two parts. The first part describes the binary choice problem. The contribution to the likelihood function is simply the probability of observing $h_i = 1$ or $h_i = 0$. The second part describes the distribution of the wage for those actually working, so that the likelihood contribution is $f(y_i|h_i = 1)$. We thus have for the loglikelihood function

$$\log L_3(\beta, \sigma_1^2, \sigma_{12}) = \sum_{i \in I_0} \log P\{h_i = 0\}$$

$$+ \sum_{i \in I_1} [\log f(y_i|h_i = 1) + \log P\{h_i = 1\}]. \qquad (7.77)$$

The binary choice part is standard; the only complicated part is the conditional distribution of y_i given $h_i = 1$. Therefore, it is more common to decompose the joint distribution of y_i and h_i differently, by using that

$$f(y_i|h_i = 1)P\{h_i = 1\} = P\{h_i = 1|y_i\}f(y_i). \qquad (7.78)$$

The last term on the right-hand side is simply the normal density function, while the first term is a probability from a conditional normal density function, characterized by (see Appendix B)

$$E\{h_i^*|y_i\} = x_{2i}'\beta_2 + \frac{\sigma_{12}}{\sigma_1^2}(y_i - x_{1i}'\beta_1)$$

$$V\{h_i^*|y_i\} = 1 - \sigma_{12}^2/\sigma_1^2$$

where the latter equality denotes the variance of h_i^* conditional upon y_i and given the exogenous variables. We thus write the loglikelihood as

$$\log L_3(\beta, \sigma_1^2, \sigma_{12}) = \sum_{i \in I_0} \log P\{h_i = 0\} + \sum_{i \in I_1} [\log f(y_i) + \log P\{h_i = 1|y_i\}] \qquad (7.79)$$

with the following equalities

$$P\{h_i = 0\} = 1 - \Phi(x'_{2i}\beta_2) \tag{7.80}$$

$$P\{h_i = 1|y_i\} = \Phi\left(\frac{x'_{2i}\beta_2 + (\sigma_{12}/\sigma_1^2)(y_i - x'_{1i}\beta_1)}{\sqrt{1 - \sigma_{12}^2/\sigma_1^2}}\right) \tag{7.81}$$

$$f(y_i) = \frac{1}{\sqrt{2\pi\sigma_1^2}} \exp\left\{-\frac{1}{2}(y_i - x'_{1i}\beta_1)^2/\sigma_1^2\right\}. \tag{7.82}$$

Maximization of $\log L_3(\beta, \sigma_1^2, \sigma_{12})$ with respect to the unknown parameters leads (under mild regularity conditions) to consistent and asymptotically efficient estimators, that have an asymptotic normal distribution.

In empirical work, the sample selection model is more often estimated in a two-step way. This is computationally simpler and it will also provide good starting values for the maximum likelihood procedure. The two-step procedure is due to Heckman (1979) and is based on the following regression (compare (7.70 above)

$$y_i = x'_{1i}\beta_1 + \sigma_{12}\lambda_i + \eta_i, \tag{7.83}$$

where

$$\lambda_i = \frac{\phi(x'_{2i}\beta_2)}{\Phi(x'_{2i}\beta_2)}.$$

The error term in this model equals $\eta_i = \varepsilon_{1i} - E\{\varepsilon_{1i}|x_i, h_i = 1\}$. Given the assumption that the distribution of ε_{1i} is independent of x_i (but not of h_i), η_i is uncorrelated with x_{1i} and λ_i by construction. This means that we could estimate β_1 and σ_{12} by running a least squares regression of y_i upon the original regressors x_{1i} and the additional variable λ_i. The fact that λ_i is not observed is not a real problem because the only unknown element in λ_i is β_2, which can be estimated consistently by probit maximum likelihood applied to the selection model. This means that in the regression (7.83) we replace λ_i by its estimate $\hat{\lambda}_i$ and OLS will still produce consistent estimators of β_1 and σ_{12}. In general, this two-step estimator will not be efficient, but it is computationally simple and consistent.

One problem with the two-step estimator is that routinely computed OLS standard errors are incorrect, unless $\sigma_{12} = 0$. This problem is often ignored because it is still possible to validly test the null hypothesis of no sample selection bias using a standard t-test on $\sigma_{12} = 0$. In general however, standard errors will have to be adjusted because η_i in (7.83) is heteroskedastic and because β_2 is estimated. See Greene (2000, Sect. 20.4) for details. If x_{1i} and x_{2i} are identical, the model is only identified through the fact that λ_i is a nonlinear function. Empirically, the two-step approach will therefore not work very well if there is little variation in λ_i and λ_i is close to being linear in x_{2i}. This is the subject of many Monte Carlo studies, a recent one being Leung and Yu (1996). The inclusion of variables in x_{2i} in addition to those in x_{1i} can be important for identification in the second step, although often there are no natural candidates and any choice is easily criticized. At the very least, some sensitivity analysis with respect to the imposed exclusion restrictions should be performed, to make sure that the λ term is not incorrectly picking up the effect of omitted variables.

The model that is estimated in the second step describes the conditional expected value of y_i given x_i and given that $h_i = 1$, for example the expected wage given that a person is working. This is information that is not directly provided if you estimate the model by maximum likelihood, although it can easily be computed from the estimates. Often, the expected value of y_i given x_i, not conditional upon $h_i = 1$, is the focus of interest and this is given by $x'_{1i}\beta_1$, which is also provided by the last regression. Predicting wages for an arbitrary person can thus be based upon (7.83), but should not include $\sigma_{12}\lambda(x'_{2i}\beta_2)$. A positive covariance σ_{12} indicates that there is unobserved heterogeneity that positively affects both wages and the probability of working. That is, those with a wage that is higher than expected are more likely to be working (conditional on a given set of x_i values).

The two-step estimator of the sample selection model is one of the most often used estimators in empirical micro-econometric work. There seems to be a strong belief that the inclusion of a λ correction term in a model eliminates all problems of selection bias. This is certainly not generally true. The presence of nonrandom selection induces a fundamental identification problem and, consequently, the validity of any solution will depend upon the validity of the assumptions that are made, which can only be partly tested. Section 7.5 below will pay more attention to sample selection bias and the implied identification problem.

7.4.3 Further Extensions

The structure of a model with one or more latent variables, normal errors and an observation rule mapping the unobserved endogenous variables into observed ones, can be used in a variety of applications. Amemiya (1984) characterizes several tobit models by the form of the likelihood function, because different structures may lead to models that are statistically the same. An obvious extension, resulting in the tobit III model, is the one where h_i^* in the above labour supply/wage equation model is partially observed as hours of work. In that case we observe

$$y_i = y_i^*, \quad h_i = h_i^* \quad \text{if } h_i^* > 0 \tag{7.84}$$

$$y_i \text{ not observed}, \quad h_i = 0 \quad \text{if } h_i^* \leq 0, \tag{7.85}$$

with the same underlying latent structure. Essentially, this says that the selection model is not of the probit type but of the standard tobit type. Applications using models of this and more complicated structures can often be found in labour economics, where one explains wages for different sectors, union/non-union members, etc. taking into account that sectoral choice is probably not exogenous but based upon potential wages in the two sectors, that labour supply is not exogenous, or both. Other types of selection models are also possible, including, for example, an ordered response model. See Vella (1998) for more discussion on this topic.

7.4.4 Illustration: Expenditures on Alcohol and Tobacco (Part 2)

In Subsection 7.3.3 we considered the estimation of Engel curves for alcoholic beverages and tobacco taking into account the problem of zero expenditures. The standard tobit model assumes that these zero expenditures are the result of corner

Table 7.5 Models for budget shares alcohol and tobacco, estimated by OLS using positive observations only

Variable	Alcoholic beverages		Tobacco	
	Estimate	s.e.	Estimate	s.e.
constant	0.0527	(0.0439)	0.4897	(0.0741)
age class	0.0078	(0.0110)	−0.0315	(0.0206)
nadults	−0.0131	(0.0163)	−0.0130	(0.0324)
nkids ≥ 2	−0.0020	(0.0006)	0.0013	(0.0011)
nkids < 2	−0.0024	(0.0023)	−0.0034	(0.0045)
$\log x$	−0.0023	(0.0032)	−0.0336	(0.0055)
$age \times \log x$	−0.0004	(0.0008)	0.0022	(0.0015)
$nadults \times \log x$	0.0008	(0.0012)	0.0011	(0.0023)
	$R^2 = 0.051$	$s = 0.0215$	$R^2 = 0.154$	$s = 0.0291$
	$N = 2258$		$N = 1036$	

solutions. That is, a household's budget constraint and preferences are such that the optimal budget shares of alcohol and tobacco, as determined by the first order conditions and in the absence of a non-negativity constraint, would be negative. As a consequence, the optimal allocation for the household is zero expenditures, which corresponds to a corner solution that is not characterized by the usual first order conditions. It can be disputed that this is a realistic assumption and this subsection considers some alternatives to the tobit I model. The alternatives are a simple OLS for the positive observations, possibly combined with a binary choice model that explains whether expenditures are positive or not, and a combined tobit II model that models budget shares jointly with the binary decision to consume or not.

Obviously one can think of reasons other than those implicit in the tobit model why households do not consume tobacco or alcohol. Because of social or health reasons, for example, many non-smokers would not smoke even if tobacco were available for free. This implies that whether or not we observe zero expenditures may be determined quite differently from the amount of expenditures for those that consume the good. Some commodities are possibly subject to abstention.[26] Keeping this in mind, we can consider alternative specifications to the tobit model. A first alternative is very simple and assumes that abstention is determined randomly in the sense that the unobservables that determine budget shares are independent of the decision to consume or not. If this is the case, we can simply specify an Engel curve that is valid for people that do not abstain and ignore the abstention decision. This would allow us to estimate the total expenditure elasticity for people that have a positive budget share, but would not allow us to analyse possible effects arising through a changing composition of the population with positive values. Statistically, this means that we can estimate the Engel curve simply by ordinary least squares but using only those observations that have positive expenditures. The results of this exercise are reported in Table 7.5. In comparison with the results for the tobit model, reported in Table 7.4, it is surprising that the coefficient for log total expenditures in the Engel curve for alcohol is negative and statistically not significantly different from zero. Estimating total expenditure elasticities, as defined in (7.58), on the basis of the OLS estimation results leads to values of 0.923 and 0.177, for alcohol and tobacco, respectively.

---

[26] Some authors refer to these goods as 'bads'.

Table 7.6 Probit models for abstention of alcohol and tobacco

Variable	Alcoholic beverages		Tobacco	
	Estimate	s.e.	Estimate	s.e.
constant	−15.882	(2.574)	8.244	(2.211)
age	0.6679	(0.6520)	−2.4830	(0.5596)
nadults	2.2554	(1.0250)	0.4852	(0.8717)
nkids ≥ 2	−0.0770	(0.0372)	0.0813	(0.0308)
nkids < 2	−0.1857	(0.1408)	−0.2117	(0.1230)
log(x)	1.2355	(0.1913)	−0.6321	(0.1632)
age × log(x)	−0.0448	(0.0485)	0.1747	(0.0413)
nadults × log(x)	−0.1688	(0.0743)	−0.0253	(0.0629)
blue collar	−0.0612	(0.0978)	0.2064	(0.0834)
white collar	0.0506	(0.0847)	0.0215	(0.0694)
Loglikelihood	−1159.865		−1754.886	
Wald test (χ_9^2) 173.18		($p = 0.000$)	108.91	($p = 0.000$)

The elasticities based on the OLS estimates are valid if abstention is determined on the basis of the observables in the model but not on the basis of the unobservables that are collected in the error term. Moreover they are conditional upon the fact that the household has positive expenditures. To obtain insight in what causes households to consume these two goods or not we can use a binary choice model, the most obvious choice being a probit model. If all zero expenditures are explained by abstention rather than by corner solutions, the probit model should include variables that determine preferences and should not include variables that determine the household's budget constraint. This is because in this case a changing budget constraint will never induce a household to start consuming alcohol or tobacco. This would imply that total expenditures and relative prices should not be included in the probit model. In the absence of price variation across households, total expenditures are an obvious candidate for exclusion from the probit model. However, it is conceivable that education level is an important determinant of abstention of alcohol or tobacco, while – unfortunately – no information about education is available in our sample. This is why we include total expenditures in the probit model, despite our reservations, but think of total expenditures as a proxy for education level, social status or other variables that affect household preferences. In addition to variables included in the Engel curve, the model for abstention also includes two dummy variables for blue and white collar workers.[27] It is assumed that these two variables do not affect the budget shares of alcohol and tobacco but only the decision to consume or not. As any exclusion restriction, this one can also be disputed and we shall return to this issue below when estimating a joint model for budget shares and abstention.

The estimation results for the two probit models are given in Table 7.6. For alcoholic beverages it appears that total expenditures, the number of adults in the household as well as the number of children older than two are statistically significant in explaining abstention. For tobacco, total expenditures, number of children older than two, age and being a blue collar worker are statistically important explanators for abstention. To illustrate the estimation results, consider a household consisting of

[27] The excluded category (reference group) includes inactive and self-employed people.

two adults, the head being a 35-year-old blue collar worker, and two children older than two. If the total expenditures of this artificial household are equal to the overall sample average, the implied estimated probabilities of a positive budget share of alcohol and tobacco are given by 86.8% and 51.7% respectively. A 10% increase in total expenditures changes these probabilities only marginally to 88.5% and 50.4%.

Assuming that the specification of the Engel curve and the abstention model are correct, the estimation results in Tables 7.5 and 7.6 are appropriate provided that the error term in the probit model is independent of the error term in the Engel curve. Correlation between these error terms invalidates the OLS results and would make a tobit II model more appropriate. Put differently, the two equation model that was estimated is a special case of a tobit II model in which the error terms in the respective equations are uncorrelated. It is possible to test for a nonzero correlation if we estimate the more general model. As discussed above, in the tobit II model it is very important which variables are included in which of the two equations. If the same variables are included in both equations, the model is only identified through the normality assumption that was imposed upon the error terms.[28] This is typically considered to be an undesirable situation. The exclusion of variables from the abstention model does not solve this problem. Instead, it is desirable to include variables in the abstention model of which we are confident that they do not determine the budget shares directly. The problem of finding such variables is similar to finding appropriate instruments with endogenous regressors (see Chapter 5) and we should be equally critical and careful in choosing them; our estimation results will critically depend upon the choice that we make. In the above abstention model the dummies for being a blue or white collar worker are included to take up this role. If we are confident that these variables do not affect budget shares directly, estimation of the tobit II model may be appropriate.

Using the two-step estimation procedure, as proposed by Heckman (1979), we can re-estimate the two Engel curves taking into account the sample selection problem due to possible endogeneity of the abstention decision. The results of this are presented in Table 7.7, where OLS is used but standard errors are adjusted to take into account heteroskedasticity and the estimation error in λ. For alcoholic beverages the inclusion of $\hat{\lambda}$ does not affect the results very much and we obtain estimates that are pretty close to those reported in Table 7.5. The t-statistic on the coefficient for $\hat{\lambda}$ does not allow us to reject the null hypothesis of no correlation, while the estimation results imply an estimated correlation coefficient (computed as the ratio of the coefficient for $\hat{\lambda}$ and the standard deviation of the error term $\hat{\sigma}_1$) of only -0.01. Computation of these correlation coefficients is important because the two-step approach may easily imply correlations outside the $[-1, 1]$ range, indicating that the tobit II model may not be appropriate, or indicating that some exclusion restrictions are not appropriate. Note that these estimation results imply that total expenditures have a significant impact on the probability of having positive expenditures on alcohol, but do not significantly affect the budget share of alcohol. For tobacco, on the other hand, we do find a significant impact of the sample selection term λ, with an implied estimated correlation coefficient of -0.31. Qualitatively, however, the results do not appear to

---

[28] To see this, note that the functional form of λ is determined by the distributional assumptions of the error term. See the discussion in Section 7.5 below.

Table 7.7 Two-step estimation of Engel curves for alcohol and tobacco (tobit II model)

Variable	Alcoholic beverages		Tobacco	
	Estimate	s.e.	Estimate	s.e.
constant	0.0543	(0.0487)	0.4516	(0.0735)
age class	0.0077	(0.0110)	−0.0173	(0.0206)
nadults	−0.0133	(0.0166)	−0.0174	(0.0318)
nkids	−0.0020	(0.0006)	0.0008	(0.0010)
nkids < 2	−0.0024	(0.0023)	−0.0021	(0.0045)
$\log(x)$	−0.0024	(0.0035)	−0.0301	(0.0055)
$age \times \log(x)$	−0.0004	(0.0008	0.0012	(0.0015)
$nadults \times \log(x)$	−0.0008	(0.0012)	−0.0041	(0.0023)
λ	−0.0002	(0.0028)	−0.0090	(0.0026)
$\hat{\sigma}_1$	0.0215	n.c.	0.0291	n.c.
Implied ρ	−0.01	n.c.	−0.31	n.c.
	$N = 2258$		$N = 1036$	

be very different from those in Table 7.5. The negative correlation coefficient indicates the existence of unobservable characteristics that positively affect the decision to smoke but negatively affect the budget share of tobacco. Let us, finally, compute the total expenditure elasticities of alcohol and tobacco on the basis of the estimation results in Table 7.7. Using similar computations as before, we obtain estimated elasticities of 0.920 and 0.243, respectively. Apparently and not surprisingly, tobacco is a necessary good for those that smoke. In fact, tobacco expenditures are close to being inelastic.

7.5 Sample Selection Bias

When the sample used in a statistical analysis is not randomly drawn from a larger population, selection bias may arise. That is, standard estimators and tests may result in misleading inferences. Because there are many situations where this may be the case, and the tobit II model not necessarily provides an adequate solution to it, some additional discussion of this problem is warranted.

At the general level, we can say that selection bias arises if the probability of a particular observation to be included in the sample depends upon the phenomenon we are explaining. There is a number of reasons why this may occur. First, it could be due to the sampling frame. For example, if you would interview people in the university restaurant and ask how often they visit it, those that go there every day are much more likely to end up in the sample than those that visit every two weeks. Second, **nonresponse** may result in selection bias. For example, people that refuse to report their income are typically those with relatively high or relatively low income levels. Third, it could be due to **self-selection** of economic agents. That is, individuals select themselves into a certain state, e.g. working, union member, public sector employment, in a nonrandom way on the basis of economic arguments. In general, those who benefit most from being in a certain state will be more likely to be in this state.

7.5.1 The Nature of the Selection Problem

Suppose we are interested in the conditional distribution of a variable y_i given a set of other (exogenous) variables x_i, that is $f(y_i|x_i)$. Usually, we will formulate this as a function of a limited number of parameters and interest lies in these parameters. Selection is indicated by a dummy variable r_i such that both y_i and x_i are observed if $r_i = 1$ and that either y_i is unobserved if $r_i = 0$, or both y_i and x_i are unobserved if $r_i = 0$.

All inferences ignoring the selection rule are (implicitly) conditional upon $r_i = 1$. Interest, however, lies in the conditional distribution of y_i given x_i but not given $r_i = 1$. We can thus say that the selection rule is **ignorable** (Rubin, 1976, Little and Rubin, 1987) if conditioning upon the outcome of the selection process has no effect. That is,

$$f(y_i|x_i, r_i = 1) = f(y_i|x_i). \tag{7.86}$$

If we are only interested in the conditional expectation of y_i given x_i, we can relax this to

$$E\{y_i|x_i, r_i = 1\} = E\{y_i|x_i\}. \tag{7.87}$$

A statement that is equivalent to (7.86) is that

$$P\{r_i = 1|x_i, y_i\} = P\{r_i = 1|x_i\}, \tag{7.88}$$

which says that the probability of selection into the sample should not depend upon y_i, given that it is allowed to depend upon the variables in x_i. This already shows some important results. First, selection bias does not arise if selection depends upon the exogenous variables only. Thus, if we are estimating a wage equation that has marital status on the right hand side, it does not matter if married people are more likely to end up in the sample than those who are not married. At a more general level, it follows that whether or not selection bias is a problem depends upon the distribution of interest.

If the selection rule it not ignorable, it should be taken into account when making inferences. As stressed by Manski (1989), a fundamental identification problem arises in this case. To see this, note that

$$E\{y_i|x_i\} = E\{y_i|x_i, r_i = 1\}P\{r_i = 1|x_i\} + E\{y_i|x_i, r_i = 0\}P\{r_i = 0|x_i\}. \tag{7.89}$$

If x_i is observed irrespective of r_i, it is possible to identify the probability that $r_i = 1$ as a function of x_i (using a binary choice model, for example). Thus, it is possible to identify $P\{r_i = 1|x_i\}$ and $P\{r_i = 0|x_i\}$, while $E\{y_i|x_i, r_i = 1\}$ is also identified (from the selected sample). However, since no information on $E\{y_i|x_i, r_i = 0\}$ is provided by the data, it is *not possible* to identify $E\{y_i|x_i\}$ without additional information or making additional (non-testable) assumptions. As Manski (1989) notes, in the absence of prior information, the selection problem is fatal for inference on $E\{y_i|x_i\}$.

If it is possible to restrict the range of possible values of $E\{y_i|x_i, r_i = 0\}$, it is possible to determine bounds on $E\{y_i|x_i\}$ that may be useful. To illustrate this, suppose we are interested in the unconditional distribution of y_i (so no x_i variables appear) and we happen to know that this distribution is normal with unknown mean μ and unit variance. If 10% is missing, the most extreme cases arise where these 10% are all in the left or all in the right tail of the distribution. Using properties of a truncated normal distribution,[29] one can derive that

$$-1.75 \leq E\{y_i|r_i = 0\} \leq 1.75,$$

so that

$$0.9E\{y_i|r_i = 1\} - 0.175 \leq E\{y_i\} \leq 0.9E\{y_i|r_i = 1\} + 0.175,$$

where $E\{y_i|r_i = 1\}$ can be estimated by the sample average in the selected sample. In this way, we can estimate an upper and lower bound for the unconditional mean of y_i, not making any assumptions about the selection rule. The price that we pay for this is that we need to make assumptions about the form of the distribution of y_i, which are not testable. If we shift interest in other aspects of the distribution of y_i, given x_i, rather than its mean, such assumptions may not be needed. For example, if we are interested in the *median* of the distribution we can derive upper and lower bounds from the probability of selection without assuming anything about the shape of the distribution.[30] Manski (1989, 1994) provides additional details and discussion of these issues.

A more common approach in applied work imposes additional structure on the problem to identify the quantities of interest. Let

$$E\{y_i|x_i\} = g_1(x_i) \tag{7.90}$$

and

$$E\{y_i|x_i, r_i = 1\} = g_1(x_i) + g_2(x_i), \tag{7.91}$$

which, as long as we do not make any assumptions about the functions g_1 and g_2, is not restrictive. Assumptions about the form of g_1 and g_2 are required to identify g_1, which is what we are interested in. The most common assumption is the **single index** assumption, which says that g_2 depends upon x_i only through a single index, $x_i'\beta_2$, say. This assumption is often motivated from a latent variable model:

$$y_i = g_1(x_i) + \varepsilon_{1i} \tag{7.92}$$

$$r_i^* = x_i'\beta_2 + \varepsilon_{2i} \tag{7.93}$$

$$r_i = 1 \quad \text{if } r_i^* > 0, \quad 0 \text{ otherwise}, \tag{7.94}$$

where $E\{\varepsilon_{1i}|x_i\} = 0$ and ε_{2i} is independent of x_i. Then it holds that

$$E\{y_i|x_i, r_i = 1\} = g_1(x_i) + E\{\varepsilon_{1i}|\varepsilon_{2i} > -x_i'\beta_2\}, \tag{7.95}$$

where the latter term depends upon x_i only through the single index $x_i'\beta_2$. Thus we can write

$$E\{y_i|x_i, r_i = 1\} = g_1(x_i) + g_2^*(x_i'\beta_2), \tag{7.96}$$

---

[29] For a standard normal variable y it holds that $P\{y > 1.28\} = 0.10$ and $E\{y|y > 1.28\} = \phi(1.28)/0.10 = 1.75$ (see Appendix B).

[30] Recall that the median of a random variable y is defined as the value m for which $P\{y \leq m\} = 0.5$ (see Appendix B). If 10% of the observations are missing we know that m is between the (theoretical) 40% and 60% quantiles of the observed distribution. That is, $m_1 \leq m \leq m_2$, with $P\{y \leq m_1|r = 1\} = 0.4$ and $P\{y \leq m_2|r = 1\} = 0.6$.

for some function g_2^*. Because β_2 can be identified from the selection process, provided observations on x_i are available irrespective of r_i, identification of g_1 is achieved by assuming that it does not depend upon one or more variables in x_i (while these variables have a nonzero coefficient in β_2). This means that exclusion restrictions are imposed upon g_1.

From (7.70), it is easily seen that the tobit II model constitutes a special case of the above framework, where $g_1(x_i) = x_i'\beta_1$ and g_2^* is given by $\sigma_{12}\phi(x_i'\beta_2)/\Phi(x_i'\beta_2)$. The assumption that ε_{1i} and ε_{2i} are i.i.d. jointly normal produces the functional form of g_2^*. Moreover, the restriction that g_1 is linear (while g_2^* is not) implies that the model is identified even in the absence of exclusion restrictions in $g_1(x_i)$. In practice though, empirical identification may benefit from imposing zero restrictions on β_1. When the distribution of ε_{1i} and ε_{2i} is not normal, (7.96) is still valid and this is what is exploited in many semi-parametric estimators of the sample selection model.

7.5.2 Semi-parametric Estimation of the Sample Selection Model

Although it is beyond the scope of this text to fully discuss semi-parametric estimators for limited dependent variable models, some intuitive discussion will be provided here. While semi-parametric estimators relax the joint normality assumption of ε_{1i} and ε_{2i} they generally maintain the single index assumption. That is, the conditional expectation of ε_{1i} given selection into the sample (and given the exogenous variables) depends upon x_i only through $x_i'\beta_2$. This requires that we can model the selection process in a fairly homogeneous way. If observations are missing for a variety of reasons, the single index assumption may no longer be appropriate. For example, individuals that do not have a job, may not be working because their reservation wage is too high (a supply side argument), as in the standard model, but also because employers are not interested in hiring them (a demand side argument). These two processes are not necessarily well described by a single index model.

The other crucial assumption in all semi-parametric approaches is that there is at least one variable that enters the selection equation $(x_i'\beta_2)$ that does not enter the equation of interest $g_1(x_i)$. This means that we need an exclusion restriction in g_1 in order to identify the model. This is obvious as we would never be able to separate g_1 from g_2^* if both depend upon the same set of variables and no functional form restrictions are imposed. Because a constant in g_1 cannot be distinguished from a constant in g_2^*, the constant term in the model will not be identified, which is not a problem if we are not interested in the intercept. If the intercept in g_1 is of interest, it can be estimated (Heckman, 1990, Andrews and Schafgans, 1998) from observations that are known to have values of g_2^* close to zero (individuals that have high values for $x_i'\beta_2$).

Most semi-parametric estimators are two-step estimators, just like Heckman's (1979). In the first step, the single index parameter β_2 is estimated semi-parametrically, that is, without imposing a particular distribution upon ε_{2i}. From this an estimate for the single index is constructed, so that in the second step the unknown function g_2^* is estimated jointly with g_1 (usually imposing some functional form upon g_1, like linearity). A simple way to approximate the unknown function $g_2^*(x_i'\beta_2)$ is the use of a series approximation, for example a polynomial in $x_i'\beta_2$. An alternative approach is based on the elimination of $g_2^*(x_i'\beta_2)$ from the model by considering differences between observations that have values of $x_i'\hat{\beta}_2$ that are similar.

All semi-parametric methods involve some additional regularity conditions and assumptions. An intuitive survey of alternative estimation methods for the sample selection model is given in Vella (1998). Pagan and Ullah (1999) provide more details. Empirical implementation is usually not straightforward; see Newey, Powell and Walker (1990) or Melenberg and van Soest (1993) for some applications.

Exercises

Exercise 7.1 (Binary Choice Models)

For a sample of 600 married females, we are interested in explaining participation in market employment from exogenous characteristics in x_i (age, family composition, education). Let $y_i = 1$ if person i has a paid job and 0 otherwise. Suppose we estimate a linear regression model

$$y_i = x_i'\beta + \varepsilon_i$$

by ordinary least squares.

a. Give two reasons why this is not really an appropriate model.

As an alternative, we could model the participation decision by a probit model.

b. Explain the probit model.

c. Give an expression for the loglikelihood function of the probit model.

d. How would you interpret a positive β coefficient for education in the probit model?

e. Suppose you have a person with $x_i'\beta = 2$. What is your prediction for her labour market status y_i? Why?

f. To what extent is a logit model different from a probit model?

Now assume that we have a sample of women that is not working ($y_i = 0$), part-time working ($y_i = 1$) or full-time working ($y_i = 2$).

g. Is it appropriate, in this case, to specify a linear model as $y_i = x_i'\beta + \varepsilon_i$?

h. What alternative model could be used instead, which exploits the information contained in part-time versus full-time working?

i. How would you interpret a positive β coefficient for education in this latter model?

j. Would it be appropriate to pool the two outcomes $y_i = 1$ and $y_i = 2$ and estimate a binary choice model? Why or why not?

Exercise 7.2 (Probit and Tobit Models)

To predict the demand for its new investment fund, a bank is interested in the question whether people invest part of their savings in risky assets. To this end, a tobit model is formulated of the following form

$$y_i^* = \beta_1 + \beta_2 x_{i2} + \beta_3 x_{i3} + \varepsilon_i,$$

where x_{i2} denotes a person's age, x_{i3} denotes income and the amount of savings invested in risky assets is given by

$$y_i = y_i^* \quad \text{if } y_i^* > 0$$
$$= 0 \quad \text{otherwise.}$$

It is assumed that ε_i is $NID(0, \sigma^2)$, independent of all explanatory variables.

Initially, the bank is only interested in the question whether a person is investing in risky assets, which is indicated by a discrete variable d_i, that satisfies

$$d_i = 1 \quad \text{if } y_i^* > 0$$
$$= 0 \quad \text{otherwise.}$$

a. Derive the probability that $d_i = 1$ as a function of $x_i = (1, x_{i2}, x_{i3})'$, according to the above model.

b. Show that the model that describes d_i is a probit model with coefficients $\gamma_1 = \beta_1/\sigma$, $\gamma_2 = \beta_2/\sigma$, $\gamma_3 = \beta_3/\sigma$.

c. Write down the loglikelihood function $\log L(\gamma)$ of the probit model for d_i. What are, in general, the properties for the maximum likelihood estimator $\hat{\gamma}$ for $\gamma = (\gamma_1, \gamma_2, \gamma_3)'$?

d. Give a general expression for the asymptotic covariance matrix of the ML estimator. Describe how it can be estimated in a given application.

e. Write down the first order condition with respect to γ_1 and use this to define the generalized residual of the probit model.

f. Describe how the generalized residual can be used to test the hypothesis that gender does not affect the probability of investing in risky assets. (Formulate the hypothesis first, describe how a test statistic can be computed and what the appropriate distribution or critical values are.) To what class does this test belong?

g. Explain why it is not possible to identify σ^2 using information on d_i and x_i only (as in the probit model).

h. It is possible to estimate $\beta = (\beta_1, \beta_2, \beta_3)'$ and σ^2 from the tobit model (using information on y_i). Write down the loglikelihood function of this model.

i. Suppose we are interested in the hypothesis that age does not affect the amount of risky savings. Formulate this hypothesis. Explain how this hypothesis can be tested using a likelihood ratio test.

j. It is also possible to test the hypothesis from **i** on the basis of the results of the probit model. Why would you prefer the test using the tobit results?

Exercise 7.3 (Tobit Models – Empirical)

Consider the data used in Subsections 7.3.3 and 7.4.4 to estimate Engel curves for alcoholic beverages and tobacco. In a recent paper, Banks, Blundell and Lewbel (1997) propose the Quadratic Almost Ideal Demand System, which implies quadratic Engel curves of the form

$$w_{ji} = \alpha_{ji} + \beta_{ji} \log x_i + \gamma_{ji} \log^2 x_i + \varepsilon_{ji}.$$

This form has the nice property that it allows goods to be luxuries at low income levels, while they can become necessities at higher levels of income (total expenditures). When answering the following questions, use the data from TOBACCO.

a. Re-estimate the standard tobit model for alcohol from Subsection 7.3.3. Refer to this as model A. Check that your results are the same as those in the text.

b. Extend model A by including the square of log total expenditures, and estimate it by maximum likelihood.

c. Test whether the quadratic term is relevant using a Wald test and a likelihood ratio test.

d. Compute the generalized residual for model A. Check that it has mean zero.

e. Compute the second-order generalized residual for model A, as defined in (7.60). Check that is has mean zero too.

f. Perform a Lagrange multiplier test in model A for the hypothesis that the quadratic term $\log^2 x$ is irrelevant.

g. Perform an LM test for heteroskedasticity in model A related to age and the number of adults.

h. Test for normality in model A.

Exercise 7.4 (Tobit Models)

A top university requires all students that apply to do an entry exam. Students that obtain a score of less than 100 are not admitted. For students that score above 100, the scores are registered, after which the university selects students from this group for admittance. We have a sample of 500 potential students that did their entry exam in 1996. For each student, we observe the result of the exam being:

- 'rejected', if the score is less than 100, or
- the score, if it is 100 or more.

In addition, we observe background characteristics of each candidate, including parents' education, gender and the average grade at high school.
   The dean is interested in the relationship between these background characteristics and the score for the entry exam. He specifies the following model

$$y_i^* = \beta_0 + x_i'\beta_1 + \varepsilon_i, \qquad \varepsilon_i \sim NID(0, \sigma^2)$$

$$y_i = y_i^* \qquad \text{if } y_i^* \geq 100$$

$$= \text{'rejected'} \quad \text{if } y_i^* < 100,$$

where y_i is the observed score of student i and x_i the vector of background characteristics (excluding an intercept).

a. Show that the above model can be written as the standard tobit model (tobit I).

b. First, the dean does a regression of y_i upon x_i and a constant (by OLS), using the observed scores of 100 and more ($y_i \geq 100$). Show that this approach does not lead to consistent or unbiased estimators for β_1.

c. Explain in detail how the parameter vector $\beta = (\beta_0, \beta_1')'$ can be estimated consistently, using the observed scores only.

d. Explain how you would estimate this model using all observations. Why is this estimator preferable to the one of **c**? (No proof or derivations are required.)

e. The dean considers specifying a tobit II model (a sample selection model). Describe this model. Is this model adequate for the above problem?

8 Univariate Time Series Models

One objective of analysing economic data is to predict or forecast the future values of economic variables. One approach to do this is to build a more or less structural econometric model, describing the relationship between the variable of interest with other economic quantities, to estimate this model using a sample of data, and to use it as the basis for forecasting and inference. Although this approach has the advantage of giving economic content to one's predictions, it is not always very useful. For example, it may be possible to adequately model the contemporaneous relationship between unemployment and the inflation rate, but as long as we cannot predict future inflation rates we are also unable to forecast future unemployment.

In this chapter we follow a different route: a pure time series approach. In this approach the current values of an economic variable are related to past values (either directly or indirectly). The emphasis is purely on making use of the information in past values of a variable for forecasting its future. In addition to producing forecasts, time series models also produce the distribution of future values, conditional upon the past, and can thus be used to evaluate the likelihood of certain events.

In this chapter we discuss the class of so-called ARIMA models that is developed to model time series processes. In Sections 8.1 and 8.2, we analyse the properties of these models and how they are related. An important issue is whether a time series process is stationary, which implies that the distribution of the variable of interest does not depend upon time. Nonstationarity can arise from different sources but an important one is the presence of so-called unit roots. Sections 8.3 and 8.4 discuss this problem and how one can test for this type of nonstationarity, while an empirical example concerning exchange rates and prices is provided in Section 8.5. In Section 8.6, we discuss how the parameters in the statistical models can be estimated, while Section 8.7 explains how an appropriate ARIMA model is chosen. Section 8.8 demonstrates how the resulting estimated univariate time series model can be used to forecast future values of an economic variable. To illustrate the use of such forecasts in an economic context, Section 8.9 analyses the expectations theory of the term structure of interest rates. Finally, Section 8.10 presents autoregressive conditional heteroskedasticity models that explain the variance of a series (of error terms) from its history.

The seminal work on the estimation and identification of ARIMA models is the monograph by Box and Jenkins (1976). Additional details and a discussion of more recent topics can be found in many textbooks on time series analysis. Mills (1990), Enders (1995) and Diebold (1998) are particularly suited for economists. At a more advanced level, Hamilton (1994) provides an excellent exposition.

8.1 Introduction

In general we consider a time series of observations on some variable, e.g. the unemployment rate, denoted as $Y_1, \ldots, Y_T$. These observations will be considered realizations of random variables that can be described by some stochastic process. It is the properties of this stochastic process that we try to describe by a relatively simple model. It will be of particular importance how observations corresponding to different time periods are related, so that we can exploit the dynamic properties of the series to generate predictions for future periods.

8.1.1 Some Examples

A simple way to model dependence between consecutive observations would be to state that Y_t is a constant mean μ plus the sum of a random variable ε_t and α times its value lagged one period, i.e.

$$Y_t = \mu + \varepsilon_t + \alpha \varepsilon_{t-1}, \quad \varepsilon_t \sim IID(0, \sigma^2), \tag{8.1}$$

where $IID(0, \sigma^2)$, as before, denotes independent drawings from the same distribution with expectation zero and variance σ^2. The innovation ε_t is not predictable from the history of the process and is therefore independent of $Y_{t-1}, Y_{t-2}, \ldots$. The process in (8.1) is referred to as a **moving average process** (MA process): apart from the mean μ, Y_1 is a weighted average of ε_1 and ε_0, Y_2 is a weighted average of ε_2 and ε_1, etc. In particular (8.1) is a first order moving average or $MA(1)$ process, because the maximum lag length is one. The values of Y_t are defined in terms of the unobservables ε_t, which are independently and identically distributed random variables. We will refer to the ε_t process as a **white noise process**. Unless indicated otherwise, ε_t will in this chapter always refer to such a process that is homoskedastic and exhibits no autocorrelation.

The model in (8.1) is a parsimonious way of describing a process for the Y_t series with certain properties. That is, the model in (8.1) implies restrictions on the time series properties of the series. In general, the joint distribution of all values of Y_t is characterized by the so-called **autocovariances**, the covariances between Y_t and one of its lags, Y_{t-k}. In the $MA(1)$ case we have

$$V\{Y_t\} = E\{(\varepsilon_t + \alpha \varepsilon_{t-1})^2\} = E\{\varepsilon_t^2\} + \alpha^2 E\{\varepsilon_{t-1}^2\} = (1 + \alpha^2)\sigma^2$$

$$\text{cov}\{Y_t, Y_{t-1}\} = E\{(\varepsilon_t + \alpha \varepsilon_{t-1})(\varepsilon_{t-1} + \alpha \varepsilon_{t-2})\} = \alpha E\{\varepsilon_{t-1}^2\} = \alpha \sigma^2$$

$$\text{cov}\{Y_t, Y_{t-2}\} = E\{(\varepsilon_t + \alpha \varepsilon_{t-1})(\varepsilon_{t-2} + \alpha \varepsilon_{t-3})\} = 0$$

or, in general,

$$\text{cov}\{Y_t, Y_{t-k}\} = 0, \quad \text{for } k = 2, 3, 4, \ldots$$

Consequently, if we consider the T-dimensional vector $Y = (Y_1, Y_2, \ldots, Y_T)'$ its covariance matrix is completely described by the assumptions in (8.1). That is, we can write

$$V\{Y\} = \Sigma,$$

where Σ is a $T \times T$ matrix, with elements $\text{cov}\{Y_t, Y_{t-k}\}$ on position $(t, t-k)$. It has $(1 + \alpha^2)\sigma^2$ on the diagonal and $\alpha\sigma^2$ just below and above the diagonal, while the remaining elements are zero. Thus, the simple moving average structure implies that observations that are two or more periods apart are uncorrelated. This may be much too restrictive and we may want to look for more general representations of a time series.

A generalization of (8.1) is given by

$$Y_t = \mu + \sum_{j=0}^{\infty} \alpha_j \varepsilon_{t-j}, \quad \alpha_0 \equiv 1, \quad \varepsilon_t \sim IID(0, \sigma^2). \tag{8.2}$$

Usually, the weights α_j in this infinite summation will decline when j increases and will converge to zero for 'infinite' j. This implies that the effects of the past upon today's values become increasingly smaller. We could assume, for example, that

$$\alpha_j = \theta^j \quad \text{for some } \theta, \quad |\theta| < 1. \tag{8.3}$$

In this case it holds that

$$Y_t = \mu + \sum_{j=0}^{\infty} \theta^j \varepsilon_{t-j}. \tag{8.4}$$

Because we can also write that $Y_{t-1} = \mu + \sum_{j=0}^{\infty} \theta^j \varepsilon_{t-j-1}$, it follows that

$$Y_t - \theta Y_{t-1} = \mu - \theta\mu + \sum_{j=0}^{\infty} \theta^j \varepsilon_{t-j} - \theta \sum_{j=0}^{\infty} \theta^j \varepsilon_{t-j-1}$$

$$= \mu - \theta\mu + \sum_{j=0}^{\infty} \theta^j \varepsilon_{t-j} - \sum_{j=1}^{\infty} \theta^j \varepsilon_{t-j} = \delta + \varepsilon_t, \tag{8.5}$$

where $\delta = \mu - \theta\mu$. Thus we have

$$Y_t = \delta + \theta Y_{t-1} + \varepsilon_t, \tag{8.6}$$

which, defining $y_t = Y_t - \mu$, we can write as

$$y_t = \theta y_{t-1} + \varepsilon_t, \quad \varepsilon_t \sim IID(0, \sigma^2). \tag{8.7}$$

The process in (8.7) is called a first order **autoregressive process** or $AR(1)$ process. It says that the current value y_t equals θ times its previous value plus an unpredictable component ε_t. We have seen processes like this before when discussing (first order) autocorrelation in the linear regression model. Writing the time series models in terms of y_t rather than Y_t is notationally more convenient, and we shall do so frequently in the rest of this chapter. One can allow for nonzero means by adding an intercept term to the models, which for moving average models corresponds to the mean μ of Y_t. For autoregressive models, the mean is a function of the intercept δ and the AR parameters. Recall that $V\{Y_t\} = V\{y_t\}$.

The dynamic properties of the y_t series can be determined using either (8.7) or (8.4). The latter is referred to as the moving average representation of the autoregressive process: the AR process in (8.7) is written as an infinite MA process. As we shall see, for some purposes one representation is more convenient than the other. The derivations based on (8.7) are easy if we impose that variances and autocovariances do not depend upon the index t. This is a so-called stationarity assumption and we return to it below. Writing

$$V\{y_t\} = V\{\theta y_{t-1} + \varepsilon_t\} = \theta^2 V\{y_{t-1}\} + V\{\varepsilon_t\}$$

and imposing that $V\{y_t\} = V\{y_{t-1}\}$, we obtain

$$V\{y_t\} = \frac{\sigma^2}{1 - \theta^2}. \tag{8.8}$$

It is clear from the resulting expression that we can only impose $V\{y_t\} = V\{y_{t-1}\}$ if $|\theta| < 1$, as was assumed before. Furthermore, we can determine that

$$\text{cov}\{y_t, y_{t-1}\} = E\{y_t y_{t-1}\} = E\{(\theta y_{t-1} + \varepsilon_t) y_{t-1}\} = \theta V\{y_{t-1}\} = \theta \frac{\sigma^2}{1 - \theta^2} \tag{8.9}$$

and, generally (for $k = 1, 2, 3, \ldots$),

$$\text{cov}\{y_t, y_{t-k}\} = \theta^k \frac{\sigma^2}{1 - \theta^2}. \tag{8.10}$$

Consequently, the covariance matrix Σ of the vector y is a full $T \times T$ matrix (provided $\theta \neq 0$). The (s, t) element is given by

$$\text{cov}\{y_s, y_t\} = \theta^{|s-t|} \frac{\sigma^2}{1 - \theta^2}. \tag{8.11}$$

As long as θ is nonzero, any two observations on y_t have a nonzero correlation, while this dependence is smaller (and potentially arbitrary close to zero) if the observations are further apart. Note that the covariance between y_t and y_{t-k} depends on k only, not on t. This reflects the stationarity of the process.

8.1.2 Stationarity and the Autocorrelation Function

A stochastic process is said to be **strictly stationary** if its properties are unaffected by a change of time origin; in other words, the joint probability distribution at any set of times is not affected by an arbitrary shift along the time axis. This implies that the distribution of y_1 is the same as that of any other value y_t, and also, e.g. that the covariances between y_t and y_{t-k} for any k do not depend upon t. Usually, we will only be concerned with the means, variances and covariances of the series, and it is sufficient to impose that these moments are independent of time, rather than the entire distribution. This is referred to as **weak stationarity** or covariance stationarity.

Formally, a process $\{Y_t\}$ is defined to be weakly stationary if for all t it holds that

$$E\{Y_t\} = \mu < \infty \tag{8.12}$$

$$V\{Y_t\} = E\{(Y_t - \mu)^2\} = \gamma_0 < \infty \tag{8.13}$$

$$\text{cov}\{Y_t, Y_{t-k}\} = E\{(Y_t - \mu)(Y_{t-k} - \mu)\} = \gamma_k, \quad k = 1, 2, 3, \ldots \tag{8.14}$$

In the sequel the term 'stationary' is taken to mean 'weakly stationary'. Conditions (8.12) and (8.13) require the process to have a constant finite mean and variance, while (8.14) states that the autocovariances of Y_t depend only upon the distance in time between the two observations. The mean, variances and autocovariances are thus independent of time. Strict stationarity is stronger[1] as it requires that the whole distribution is unaffected by a change in time horizon, not just the first and second order moments. Obviously, under joint normality the distribution is completely characterized by first and second order moments, and strict stationarity and weak stationarity are equivalent.

Under covariance stationarity, we can define the k-th order **autocovariance** γ_k as

$$\gamma_k = \text{cov}\{y_t, y_{t-k}\} = \text{cov}\{y_t, y_{t+k}\}, \tag{8.15}$$

which, for $k = 0$, gives the variance of y_t. As the autocovariances are not independent of the units in which the variables are measured, it is common to standardize by defining **autocorrelations** ρ_k as

$$\rho_k = \frac{\text{cov}\{y_t, y_{t-k}\}}{V\{y_t\}} = \frac{\gamma_k}{\gamma_0}. \tag{8.16}$$

Note that $\rho_0 = 1$, while $-1 \leq \rho_k \leq 1$. The autocorrelations considered as a function of k are referred to as the **autocorrelation function** (ACF) or, sometimes, the correlogram of the series y_t. The ACF plays a major role in modelling the dependencies among observations, because it characterizes the process describing the evolution of y_t over time. In addition to ρ_k, the process of y_t is described by its mean and its variance γ_0.

From the ACF we can infer the extent to which one value of the process is correlated with previous values and thus the length and strength of the memory of the process. It indicates how long (and how strongly) a shock in the process (ε_t) affects the values of y_t. For the two processes we have seen above, we have the following. For the $AR(1)$ process

$$y_t = \theta y_{t-1} + \varepsilon_t,$$

we have autocorrelation coefficients

$$\rho_k = \theta^k,$$

while for the $MA(1)$ process

$$y_t = \varepsilon_t + \alpha \varepsilon_{t-1},$$

---

[1] Strict stationarity does not necessarily imply that first and second moments are finite.

we have

$$\rho_1 = \frac{\alpha}{1+\alpha^2} \quad \text{and} \quad \rho_k = 0, k = 2, 3, 4, \ldots$$

Consequently, a shock in an $MA(1)$ process affects y_t in two periods only, while a shock in the $AR(1)$ process affects all future observations with a decreasing effect.

As an illustration, we generated several artificial time series according to a first order autoregressive process as well as a first order moving average process. The data for the simulated $AR(1)$ processes with parameter θ equal to 0.5 and 0.9 are depicted in Figure 8.1, combined with their autocorrelation functions. All series are standardized to have unit variance and zero mean. If we compare the AR series with $\theta = 0.5$ and $\theta = 0.9$, it appears that the latter process is smoother, that is, has a higher degree of persistence. This means that, after a shock, it takes longer for the series to return to its mean. The autocorrelation functions show an exponential decay in both cases, although it takes large lags for the ACF of the $\theta = 0.9$ series to become close to zero. For example, after 15 periods, the effect of a shock is still $0.9^{15} = 0.21$ of its original effect. For the $\theta = 0.5$ series, the effect at lag 15 is virtually zero.

The data and ACF for two simulated moving average processes, with $\alpha = 0.5$ and $\alpha = 0.9$, are displayed in Figure 8.2. The difference between the two is less pronounced than in the AR case. For both series, shocks only have an effect in two consecutive periods. This means that in the absence of new shocks, the series are back at their mean after two periods. The first order autocorrelation coefficients do not differ much, and are 0.40 and 0.50, respectively.

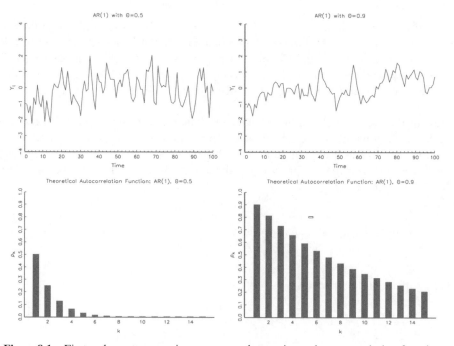

Figure 8.1   First order autoregressive processes: data series and autocorrelation functions

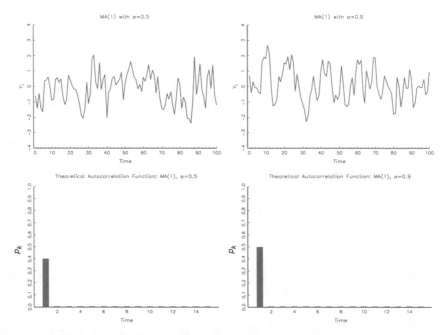

Figure 8.2   First order moving average processes: data series and autocorrelation functions

8.2   General ARMA Processes

8.2.1   Formulating ARMA Processes

In this section, we define more general autoregressive and moving average processes. First, we define a moving average process of order q, or in short an $MA(q)$ process, as

$$y_t = \varepsilon_t + \alpha_1 \varepsilon_{t-1} + \cdots + \alpha_q \varepsilon_{t-q}, \tag{8.17}$$

where ε_t is a white noise process. That is, the observed series y_t is a weighted combination of $q + 1$ white noise terms. An autoregressive process of order p, an $AR(p)$ process, is given by

$$y_t = \theta_1 y_{t-1} + \theta_2 y_{t-2} + \cdots + \theta_p y_{t-p} + \varepsilon_t. \tag{8.18}$$

Obviously, it is possible to combine the autoregressive and moving average specification into an $ARMA(p, q)$ model, which consists of an AR part of order p and an MA part of order q,

$$y_t = \theta_1 y_{t-1} + \cdots + \theta_p y_{t-p} + \varepsilon_t + \alpha_1 \varepsilon_{t-1} + \cdots + \alpha_q \varepsilon_{t-q}. \tag{8.19}$$

In fact, there is no fundamental difference between moving average and autoregressive processes. Under suitable conditions (see below) an AR model can be written as an MA model and vice versa. The order of one of these is usually quite long and the choice for an MA, AR or a combined ARMA representation is a matter of parsimony. For example, we have seen above that an $AR(1)$ model can be written as an $MA(\infty)$, a moving average model of infinite order. For certain purposes, the AR representation of the model is convenient, while for other purposes the MA representation is. This will become clear below.

Often it is convenient to use the **lag operator**, denoted by L (some authors use B, backshift operator). It is defined by

$$Ly_t = y_{t-1}. \tag{8.20}$$

Most of the time, the lag operator can be manipulated just as if it were a constant. For example,

$$L^2 y_t = L(Ly_t) = Ly_{t-1} = y_{t-2},$$

so that, more generally, $L^p y_t = y_{t-p}$ with $L^0 \equiv 1$. Operating L on a constant leaves the constant unaffected, e.g. $L\mu = \mu$. Using this lag operator allows us to write ARMA models in a concise way. For an $AR(1)$ model we can write

$$y_t = \theta L y_t + \varepsilon_t \tag{8.21}$$

or

$$(1 - \theta L)y_t = \varepsilon_t. \tag{8.22}$$

This says that a combination of y_t and its lag, with weights 1 and $-\theta$, equals a white noise process. Similarly, we can write a general $AR(p)$ as

$$\theta(L)y_t = \varepsilon_t, \tag{8.23}$$

where $\theta(L)$ is a polynomial of order p in the lag operator L, usually referred to as a **lag polynomial**, given by

$$\theta(L) = 1 - \theta_1 L - \theta_2 L^2 - \cdots - \theta_p L^p. \tag{8.24}$$

We can interpret a lag polynomial as a filter that, if applied to a time series, produces a new series. So the filter $\theta(L)$ applied to an $AR(p)$ process y_t produces a white noise process ε_t. It is relatively easy to manipulate lag polynomials. For example, transforming a series by two such polynomials one after the other, is the same as transforming the series once by a polynomial that is the product of the two original ones. This way, we can define the inverse of a filter, which is naturally given by the inverse of the polynomial. Thus the inverse of $\theta(L)$, denoted as $\theta^{-1}(L)$, is defined so as to satisfy $\theta^{-1}(L)\theta(L) = 1$. If $\theta(L)$ is a finite order polynomial in L, its inverse will be one of infinite order. For the $AR(1)$ case we find

$$(1 - \theta L)^{-1} = \sum_{j=0}^{\infty} \theta^j L^j \tag{8.25}$$

provided that $|\theta| < 1$. This is similar to the result that the infinite sum $\sum_{j=0}^{\infty} \theta^j$ equals $(1 - \theta)^{-1}$ if $|\theta| < 1$, while it does not converge for $|\theta| \geq 1$. In general, the inverse of a polynomial $\theta(L)$ exists if it satisfies certain conditions on its parameters, in which case we call $\theta(L)$ **invertible**. This is discussed in the next subsection. With (8.25) we can write the $AR(1)$ model as

$$(1 - \theta L)^{-1}(1 - \theta L)y_t = (1 - \theta L)^{-1}\varepsilon_t$$

or

$$y_t = \sum_{j=0}^{\infty} \theta^j L^j \varepsilon_t = \sum_{j=0}^{\infty} \theta^j \varepsilon_{t-j}, \tag{8.26}$$

which corresponds to (8.4) above.

Under appropriate conditions, the converse is also possible and we can write a moving average model in autoregressive form. Using the lag operator we can write the $MA(1)$ process as

$$y_t = (1 + \alpha L)\varepsilon_t$$

and the general $MA(q)$ process as

$$y_t = \alpha(L)\varepsilon_t$$

where

$$\alpha(L) = 1 + \alpha_1 L + \alpha_2 L^2 + \cdots + \alpha_q L^q. \tag{8.27}$$

Note that we have defined the polynomials such that the MA polynomial has plus signs, while the AR polynomial has minus signs. Now, if $\alpha^{-1}(L)$ exists, we can write that

$$\alpha^{-1}(L)y_t = \varepsilon_t, \tag{8.28}$$

which, in general, will be an AR model of infinite order. For the $MA(1)$ case, we use, similar to (8.25), that

$$(1 + \alpha L)^{-1} = \sum_{j=0}^{\infty} (-\alpha)^j L^j, \tag{8.29}$$

provided that $|\alpha| < 1$. Consequently, an $MA(1)$ model can be written as

$$y_t = \alpha \sum_{j=0}^{\infty} (-\alpha)^j y_{t-j-1} + \varepsilon_t. \tag{8.30}$$

A necessary condition for the infinite AR representation ($AR(\infty)$) to exist is that the MA polynomial is invertible, which, in the $MA(1)$ case, requires that $|\alpha| < 1$. Particularly for making predictions conditional upon an observed past, the AR representations are very convenient (see Section 8.8 below). The MA representations are often convenient to determine variances and covariances.

For a more parsimonious representation, we may want to work with an ARMA model that contains both an autoregressive and a moving average part. The general ARMA model can be written as

$$\theta(L)\dot{y}_t = \alpha(L)\varepsilon_t, \tag{8.31}$$

which (if the AR lag polynomial is invertible) can be written in $MA(\infty)$ representation as

$$y_t = \theta^{-1}(L)\alpha(L)\varepsilon_t, \tag{8.32}$$

or (if the MA lag polynomial is invertible) in infinite AR form as

$$\alpha^{-1}(L)\theta(L)y_t = \varepsilon_t. \tag{8.33}$$

Both $\theta^{-1}(L)\alpha(L)$ and $\alpha^{-1}(L)\theta(L)$ are lag polynomials of infinite length, with restrictions on the coefficients.

8.2.2 Invertibility of Lag Polynomials

As we have seen above, the first order lag polynomial $1 - \theta L$ is invertible if $|\theta| < 1$. In this section, we shall generalize this condition to higher order lag polynomials. Let us first consider the case of a second order polynomial, given by $1 - \theta_1 L - \theta_2 L^2$. Generally, we can find values ϕ_1 and ϕ_2 such that the polynomial can be written as

$$1 - \theta_1 L - \theta_2 L^2 = (1 - \phi_1 L)(1 - \phi_2 L). \tag{8.34}$$

It is easily verified that ϕ_1 and ϕ_2 can be solved for from[2] $\phi_1 + \phi_2 = \theta_1$ and $-\phi_1 \phi_2 = \theta_2$. The conditions for invertibility of the second order polynomial are just the conditions that both the first order polynomials $1 - \phi_1 L$ and $1 - \phi_2 L$ are invertible. Thus, the requirement for invertibility is that both $|\phi_1| < 1$ and $|\phi_2| < 1$.

These requirements can also be formulated in terms of the so-called **characteristic equation**

$$(1 - \phi_1 z)(1 - \phi_2 z) = 0. \tag{8.35}$$

This equation has two solutions, z_1 and z_2 say, referred to as the **characteristic roots**. The requirement $|\phi_i| < 1$ corresponds to $|z_i| > 1$. If any solution satisfies $|z_i| \leq 1$ the corresponding polynomial is non-invertible. A solution that equals unity is referred to as a **unit root**.

The presence of a unit root in the lag polynomial $\theta(L)$ can be detected relatively easy, without solving the characteristic equation, by noting that the polynomial $\theta(z)$ evaluated at $z = 1$ is zero if $\sum_{j=1}^{p} \theta_j = 1$. Thus, the presence of a first unit root can be verified by checking whether the sum of the polynomial coefficients equals one. If the sum exceeds one, the polynomial is not invertible.

As an example, consider the $AR(2)$ model

$$y_t = 1.2 y_{t-1} - 0.32 y_{t-2} + \varepsilon_t. \tag{8.36}$$

We can write this as

$$(1 - 0.8L)(1 - 0.4L) y_t = \varepsilon_t, \tag{8.37}$$

with characteristic equation

$$1 - 1.2z + 0.32 z^2 = (1 - 0.8z)(1 - 0.4z) = 0. \tag{8.38}$$

The solutions (characteristic roots) are $1/0.8$ and $1/0.4$, which are both larger than one. Consequently, the AR polynomial in (8.36) is invertible. Note that the $AR(1)$ model

$$y_t = 1.2 y_{t-1} + \varepsilon_t \tag{8.39}$$

describes a non-invertible AR process.

The issue whether or not the lag polynomials are invertible is important for several reasons. For moving average models, or more generally, models with a moving average component, invertibility of the MA polynomial is important for estimation and prediction. For models with an autoregressive part, the AR polynomial is invertible if and only if the process is stationary. Section 8.3 explores this last issue.

---

[2] It is possible that ϕ_1, ϕ_2 is a pair of complex numbers, for example if $\theta_1 = 0$ and $\theta_2 < 0$. In the text we shall ignore this possibility.

8.2.3 Common Roots

Decomposing the moving average and autoregressive polynomials into products of linear functions in L also shows the problem of **common roots** or **cancelling roots**. This means that the AR and the MA part of the model have a root that is identical and the corresponding linear functions in L cancel out. To illustrate this, let the true model be an $ARMA(2, 1)$ process, described by

$$(1 - \theta_1 L - \theta_2 L^2) y_t = (1 + \alpha L)\varepsilon_t.$$

Then, we can write this as

$$(1 - \phi_1 L)(1 - \phi_2 L) y_t = (1 + \alpha L)\varepsilon_t. \tag{8.40}$$

Now, if $\alpha = -\phi_1$, we can divide both sides by $(1 + \alpha L)$ to obtain

$$(1 - \phi_2 L) y_t = \varepsilon_t,$$

which is exactly the same as (8.40). Thus, in the case of one cancelling root, an $ARMA(p, q)$ model can be written equivalently as an $ARMA(p - 1, q - 1)$ model.

As an example, consider the model

$$y_t = y_{t-1} - 0.25 y_{t-2} + \varepsilon_t - 0.5\varepsilon_{t-1}, \tag{8.41}$$

which can be rewritten as

$$(1 - 0.5L)(1 - 0.5L) y_t = (1 - 0.5L)\varepsilon_t.$$

Clearly, this can be reduced to an $AR(1)$ model as

$$(1 - 0.5L) y_t = \varepsilon_t$$

or

$$y_t = 0.5 y_{t-1} + \varepsilon_t,$$

which describes exactly the same process as (8.41).

The problem of common roots illustrates why it may be problematic, in practice, to estimate an ARMA model with an AR and an MA part of a high order. The reason is that identification and estimation is hard if roots of the MA and AR polynomial are almost identical. In this case, a simplified $ARMA(p - 1, q - 1)$ model will yield an almost equivalent representation.

8.3 Stationarity and Unit Roots

Stationarity of a stochastic process requires that the variances and autocovariances are finite and independent of time. It is easily verified that finite order MA processes are stationary by construction, because they correspond to a weighted sum of a fixed number of stationary white noise processes. Of course, this result breaks down if we would allow the MA coefficients to vary over time, as in

$$y_t = \varepsilon_t + g(t)\varepsilon_{t-1}, \tag{8.42}$$

where $g(t)$ is some deterministic function of t. Now we have

$$E\{y_t^2\} = \sigma^2 + g^2(t)\sigma^2,$$

which is not independent of t. Consequently, the process in (8.42) is nonstationary.

Stationarity of autoregressive or ARMA processes is less trivial. Consider, for example, the $AR(1)$ process

$$y_t = \theta y_{t-1} + \varepsilon_t, \qquad (8.43)$$

with $\theta = 1$. Taking variances on both sides gives $V\{y_t\} = V\{y_{t-1}\} + \sigma^2$, which has no solution for the variance of the process consistent with stationarity, unless $\sigma^2 = 0$, in which case an infinity of solutions exists. The process in (8.43) is a first order autoregressive process with a unit root ($\theta = 1$), usually referred to as a **random walk**. The unconditional variance of y_t does not exist, i.e. is infinite and the process is nonstationary. In fact, for any value of θ with $|\theta| \geq 1$, (8.43) describes a nonstationary process.

We can formalize the above results as follows. The $AR(1)$ process is stationary if and only if the polynomial $1 - \theta L$ is invertible, that is, if the root of the characteristic equation $1 - \theta z = 0$ is larger than unity. This result is straightforwardly generalized to arbitrary ARMA models. The $ARMA(p, q)$ model

$$\theta(L)y_t = \alpha(L)\varepsilon_t \qquad (8.44)$$

corresponds to a stationary process if and only if the solutions $z_1, \ldots, z_p$ to $\theta(z) = 0$ are larger than one (in absolute value), that is when the AR polynomial is invertible. For example, the $ARMA(2, 1)$ process given by

$$y_t = 1.2y_{t-1} - 0.2y_{t-2} + \varepsilon_t - 0.5\varepsilon_{t-1} \qquad (8.45)$$

is nonstationary because $z = 1$ is a solution to $1 - 1.2z + 0.2z^2 = 0$.

A special case that is of particular interest arises when one root is exactly equal to one, while the other roots are larger than one. If this arises then we can write the process for y_t as

$$\theta^*(L)(1 - L)y_t = \theta^*(L)\Delta y_t = \alpha(L)\varepsilon_t, \qquad (8.46)$$

where $\theta^*(L)$ is an invertible polynomial in L of order $p - 1$. Because the roots of the AR polynomial are the solutions to $\theta^*(z)(1 - z) = 0$ there is one solution $z = 1$, or in other words a single unit root. Equation (8.46) thus shows that Δy_t can be described by a stationary ARMA model if the process for y_t has one unit root. Consequently, we can eliminate the nonstationarity by transforming the series into first differences (changes). Writing the process in (8.45) as

$$(1 - 0.2L)(1 - L)y_t = (1 - 0.5L)\varepsilon_t$$

shows that it implies that Δy_t is described by a stationary $ARMA(1, 1)$ process given by

$$\Delta y_t = 0.2\Delta y_{t-1} + \varepsilon_t - 0.5\varepsilon_{t-1}.$$

A series which becomes stationary after first differencing is said to be **integrated of order one**, denoted $I(1)$. If Δy_t is described by a stationary $ARMA(p, q)$ model, we say that y_t is described by an autoregressive *integrated* moving average (ARIMA) model of order $p, 1, q$, or in short an $ARIMA(p, 1, q)$ model.

First differencing quite often can transform a nonstationary series into a stationary one. In particular this may be the case for aggregate economic series or their natural logarithms. Note that when Y_t is, for example, the log of national income, ΔY_t corresponds to the income growth rate, which is not unlikely to be stationary.

Note that the AR polynomial is required to have an *exact* unit root. If the true model is an $AR(1)$ with $\theta = 1.01$, we have that $\Delta y_t = 0.01 y_{t-1} + \varepsilon_t$, which is nonstationary, as it depends upon the non-stationary process y_t. Consequently, an $AR(1)$ process with $\theta = 1.01$ is not integrated of order one.

In some cases, taking first differences is insufficient to obtain stationarity and another differencing step is required. In this case the stationary series is given by $\Delta(\Delta y_t) = \Delta y_t - \Delta y_{t-1}$, corresponding to the change in the growth rate for logarithmic variables. If a series must be differenced twice before it becomes stationary, then it is said to be **integrated of order** 2, denoted $I(2)$, and it must have two unit roots. Thus, a series y_t is $I(2)$ if Δy_t is non-stationary but $\Delta^2 y_t$ is stationary. A more formal definition of integration is given in Engle and Granger (1987), who also define higher orders of integration, which are not very relevant in economic applications. Thus, a time series integrated of order zero is stationary in levels, while for a time series integrated of order one, the first difference is stationary. A white noise series and a stable $AR(1)$ process are examples of $I(0)$ series, while a random walk process, as described by (8.43) with $\theta = 1$, is an example of an $I(1)$ series.

In the long-run, it can make a surprising amount of difference whether the series has an exact unit root or whether the root is slightly larger than one. It is the difference between being $I(0)$ and being $I(1)$. In general, the main differences between processes that are $I(0)$ and $I(1)$ can be summarized as follows. An $I(0)$ series fluctuates around its mean with a finite variance that does not depend on time, while an $I(1)$ series wanders widely. Typically, it is said that an $I(0)$ series is **mean reverting**, as there is a tendency in the long-run to return to its mean. Furthermore, an $I(0)$ series has a limited memory of its past behaviour (implying that the effects of a particular random innovation are only transitory), while an $I(1)$ process has an infinitely long memory (implying that an innovation will permanently affect the process). This last aspect becomes clear from the autocorrelation functions: for an $I(0)$ series the autocorrelations decline rapidly as the lag increases, while for the $I(1)$ process the estimated autocorrelation coefficients decay to zero only very slowly.

The last property makes the presence of a unit root an interesting question from an economic point of view. In models with unit roots, shocks (which may be due to policy interventions) have persistent effects that last forever, while in the case of stationary models, shocks can only have a temporary effect. Of course, the long-run effect of a shock is not necessarily of the same magnitude as the short-run effect. Consequently, starting in the early 1980s a vast amount of literature has appeared[3] on the presence of unit roots in many macro-economic time series, with – depending upon the particular technique applied – sometimes conflicting conclusions. The fact that the autocorrelations of a stationary series taper off or die out rapidly, may help in determining the degree of differencing needed to achieve stationarity (usually referred to as d). In addition, a number of formal unit root tests has been proposed in the recent literature, some of which we shall discuss in Section 8.4 below.

Empirical series where the choice between a unit root (non-stationarity) and a 'near unit root' (stationarity) is particularly ambiguous are interest rate series. The high degree of persistence in interest rates quite often makes the unit root hypothesis

---

[3] The most influential study is Nelson and Plosser (1982), which argues that many economic time series are better characterized by unit roots than by deterministic trends.

statistically not rejectable, although nonstationary interest rates do not seem to be very plausible from an *economic* point of view. The empirical example in Section 8.9 illustrates this issue.

8.4 Testing for Unit Roots

To introduce the testing procedures for a unit root we concentrate on autoregressive models. This may not be particularly restrictive since any ARMA model will always have an AR representation (provided the MA polynomial $\alpha(L)$ is invertible).

8.4.1 Testing for Unit Roots in a First Order Autoregressive Model

Let us consider, first of all, the $AR(1)$ process

$$y_t = \theta y_{t-1} + \varepsilon_t. \tag{8.47}$$

A test for a unit root is a test for $\theta = 1$ and it seems obvious to use the estimate $\hat{\theta}$ for θ from an ordinary least squares procedure (which is consistent, irrespective of the true value of θ) and the corresponding standard error to test the null hypothesis. However, as was shown in the seminal paper of Dickey and Fuller (1979), under the null that $\theta = 1$ the standard t-ratio does not have a t distribution, not even asymptotically. The reason for this is the non-stationarity of the process, invalidating standard results on the distribution of the OLS estimator $\hat{\theta}$ (as discussed in Chapter 2). For example, if $\theta = 1$ the variance of y_t, denoted by γ_0, is not defined (or, if you want, is infinitely large). For any finite sample size, however, a finite estimate of the variance for y_t will be obtained. To test the null hypothesis that $\theta = 1$ it is possible to use the standard t-statistic, given by

$$\hat{\tau} = \frac{\hat{\theta} - 1}{se(\hat{\theta})}, \tag{8.48}$$

where $se(\hat{\theta})$ denotes the usual OLS standard error. Critical values, however, have to be taken from the appropriate distribution, which under the null hypothesis of non-stationarity, is nonstandard. In particular, the distribution is skewed to the right so that critical values are smaller than those for (the normal approximation of) the t distribution. Using a 5% significance level in a one-tailed test of $H_0: \theta = 1$ (a unit root) against $H_1: |\theta| < 1$ (stationarity) the correct critical value is -1.95, rather than -1.65 for the normal approximation. Consequently, if you use the standard t tables you may reject a unit root too often. Selected percentiles of the appropriate distribution are published in several works by Dickey and Fuller. In Table 8.1 we present 1% and 5% critical values for this test, usually referred to as the **Dickey–Fuller test**, for a range of different samples sizes.

Usually, a slightly more convenient regression procedure is used. In this case the model is rewritten as

$$\Delta y_t = (\theta - 1)y_{t-1} + \varepsilon_t, \tag{8.49}$$

from which the t-statistic for $\theta - 1 = 0$ is identical to $\hat{\tau}$ above. The reason for this is that the least squares method is invariant to linear transformations of the model.

Table 8.1   1% and 5% critical values for Dickey–Fuller tests (Fuller, 1976, p. 373)

	No constant No trend		Constant No trend		Constant Trend	
Sample size	1%	5%	1%	5%	1%	5%
$T = 25$	−2.66	−1.95	−3.75	−3.00	−4.38	−3.60
$T = 50$	−2.62	−1.95	−3.58	−2.93	−4.15	−3.50
$T = 100$	−2.60	−1.95	−3.51	−2.89	−4.04	−3.45
$T = 250$	−2.58	−1.95	−3.46	−2.88	−3.99	−3.43
$T = 500$	−2.58	−1.95	−3.44	−2.87	−3.98	−3.42
$T = \infty$	−2.58	−1.95	−3.43	−2.86	−3.96	−3.41

Under the null hypothesis, y_t is described by a random walk, while under the alternative y_t is a first order autoregressive model with zero mean. If we consider the series Y_t that may have nonzero mean, it is appropriate to include a constant term in the Dickey–Fuller regressions. As the constant in a stationary $AR(1)$ model satisfies $\delta = (1 - \theta)\mu$, where μ is the mean of the series, the null hypothesis of a unit root also implies that the intercept term should be zero. The testing regression is thus

$$\Delta Y_t = \delta + (\theta - 1) Y_{t-1} + \varepsilon_t, \tag{8.50}$$

where the null hypothesis is the joint hypothesis H_0: $\delta = 0$, $\theta - 1 = 0$. Although it is possible to test these two restrictions jointly, it is easier (and more common) to test only that $\theta - 1 = 0$. The distribution of the t-ratio for this hypothesis, denoted $\hat{\tau}_\mu$, under the assumption that H_0 (the joint one) is correct, is also non-standard. The critical values for $\hat{\tau}_\mu$, also presented in Table 8.1, are smaller than those for $\hat{\tau}$. For large samples, the unit root hypothesis is rejected at the 5% level if $\hat{\tau}_\mu < -2.86$.

It is possible that (8.50) holds with $\theta = 1$ and a nonzero intercept $\delta \neq 0$. Because in this case δ cannot equal $(1 - \theta)\mu$, (8.50) cannot be derived from a pure $AR(1)$ model. This is seen by considering the resulting process

$$\Delta Y_t = \delta + \varepsilon_t, \tag{8.51}$$

which is known as a **random walk with drift**, where δ is the drift parameter. In the model for the level variable Y_t, δ corresponds to a linear time trend. Because (8.51) implies that $E\{\Delta Y_t\} = \delta$, it is the case that (for a given starting value Y_0) $E\{Y_t\} = Y_0 + \delta t$. This shows that the interpretation of the intercept term in (8.50) depends heavily upon the presence of a unit root. In the stationary case, δ reflects the non-zero mean of the series; in the unit root case, it reflects a **deterministic trend** in Y_t. Because in the latter case first differencing produces a stationary time series, the process for Y_t is referred to as **difference stationary**. In general, a difference stationary process is a process that can be made stationary by differencing.

It is also possible that nonstationarity is caused by the presence of a deterministic time trend in the process, rather than by the presence of a unit root. This happens when the $AR(1)$ model is extended to

$$Y_t = \delta + \theta Y_{t-1} + \gamma t + \varepsilon_t, \tag{8.52}$$

with $|\theta| < 1$ and $\gamma \neq 0$. In this case, we have a nonstationary process because of the linear trend γt. This nonstationarity can be removed by regressing Y_t upon a constant and t, and then considering the residuals of this regression, or by simply including t as additional variable in the model. The process for Y_t in this case is referred to as being **trend stationary**. Nonstationary processes may thus be characterized by the presence of a deterministic trend, like γt, a stochastic trend implied by the presence of a unit root, or both.

It is possible to test whether Y_t follows a random walk against the alternative that it follows the trend stationary process in (8.52). This can be tested by running the regression

$$\Delta Y_t = \delta + (\theta - 1)Y_{t-1} + \gamma t + \varepsilon_t. \tag{8.53}$$

The null hypothesis one would like to test is that the process is a random walk rather than trend stationary and corresponds to H_0: $\delta = \gamma = \theta - 1 = 0$. Instead of testing this joint hypothesis, it is quite common to use the t-ratio corresponding to $\hat{\theta} - 1$, denoted $\hat{\tau}_\tau$, assuming that the other restrictions in the null hypotheses are satisfied. Although the null hypothesis is still the same as in the previous two unit root tests, the testing regression is different and thus we have, again, a different distribution of the test statistic. The critical values for $\hat{\tau}_\tau$, given in the last two columns of Table 8.1, are still smaller than those for $\hat{\tau}_\mu$. In fact, with an intercept and a deterministic trend included the probability that $\hat{\theta} - 1$ is positive (given that the true value $\theta - 1$ equals zero) is negligibly small. It should be noted, however, that if the unit root hypothesis $\theta - 1 = 0$ is rejected, we cannot conclude that the process for Y_t is likely to be stationary. Under the alternative hypothesis γ may be nonzero so that the process for Y_t is not stationary (but only trend stationary).

The phrase Dickey–Fuller test, or simply DF test is used for any of the tests described above and can thus be based upon a regression with or without a constant and with or without a trend. Mostly, however, a constant term will be included in the regressions. It is important to stress that the unit root hypothesis corresponds to the *null* hypothesis. If we are unable to reject the presence of a unit root it does not necessarily mean that it is true. It could just be that there is insufficient information in the data to reject it. Of course, this is simply the general difference between accepting an hypothesis and not rejecting it. Because the long-run properties of the process depend crucially upon the imposition of a unit root or not, this is something to be aware of. Not all series for which we *cannot reject* the unit root hypothesis are necessarily integrated of order one.

To circumvent the problem that unit root tests often have low power, Kwiatskowski, Phillips, Schmidt and Shin (1992) propose an alternative test where stationarity is the null hypothesis and the existence of a unit root is the alternative. This test is usually referred to as the **KPSS test**. The basic idea is that a time series is decomposed into the sum of a deterministic time trend, a random walk and a stationary error term (typically not white noise). The null hypothesis (of trend stationarity) specifies that the variance of the random walk component is zero. The test is actually a Lagrange multiplier test (see Chapter 6) and computation of the test statistic is fairly simple. First, run an auxiliary regression of Y_t upon an intercept and a time trend t. Next, save the OLS residuals e_t and compute the partial sums $S_t = \sum_{s=1}^{t} e_s$ for all t. Then the test statistic is given by

$$KPSS = \sum_{t=1}^{T} S_t^2 / \hat{\sigma}^2,$$

where $\hat{\sigma}^2$ is an estimator for the error variance. This latter estimator $\hat{\sigma}^2$ may involve corrections for autocorrelation based on the Newey–West formula (see Chapter 4). The asymptotic distribution is non-standard, and Kwiatkowski *et al.* (1992) report a 5% critical value of 0.146. If the null hypothesis is stationarity rather than trend stationarity the trend term should be omitted from the auxiliary regression. The test statistic is then computed in the same fashion, but the 5% critical value is 0.463.

8.4.2 Testing for Unit Roots in Higher Order Autoregressive Models

A test for a single unit root in higher order AR processes can easily be obtained by extending the Dickey–Fuller test procedure. The general strategy is that lagged differences, such as $\Delta y_{t-1}, \Delta y_{t-2}, \ldots$, are included in the regression, such that its error term corresponds to white noise. This leads to the so-called **augmented Dickey–Fuller tests** (ADF tests), for which the same *asymptotic* critical values hold as those shown in Table 8.1.

Consider the $AR(2)$ model

$$y_t = \theta_1 y_{t-1} + \theta_2 y_{t-2} + \varepsilon_t, \tag{8.54}$$

which can be written in factorized form as

$$(1 - \phi_1 L)(1 - \phi_2 L) y_t = \varepsilon_t. \tag{8.55}$$

The stationarity condition requires that ϕ_1 and ϕ_2 are both less than one in absolute value, but if $\phi_1 = 1$ and $|\phi_2| < 1$, we have a single unit root, $\theta_1 + \theta_2 = 1$ and $\theta_2 = -\phi_2$. Equation (8.54) can be used to test the unit root hypothesis by testing $\theta_1 + \theta_2 = 1$, given $|\theta_2| < 1$. This is conveniently done be rewriting (8.54) as

$$\Delta y_t = (\theta_1 + \theta_2 - 1) y_{t-1} - \theta_2 \Delta y_{t-1} + \varepsilon_t. \tag{8.56}$$

The coefficients in (8.56) can be consistently estimated by ordinary least squares and the estimate of the coefficient for y_{t-1} provides a means for testing the null hypothesis $\pi \equiv \theta_1 + \theta_2 - 1 = 0$. The resulting t-ratio, $\hat{\pi}/se(\hat{\pi})$, has the same distribution as $\hat{\tau}$ above. In the spirit of the Dickey–Fuller procedure, one might add an intercept term or an intercept and a time trend to the test regression. Depending on which variant is used, the resulting test statistic has to be compared with a critical value taken from the appropriate row of Table 8.1.

This procedure can easily be generalized to the testing of a *single* unit root in an $AR(p)$ process. The trick is that any $AR(p)$ process can be written as

$$\Delta y_t = \pi y_{t-1} + c_1 \Delta y_{t-1} + \cdots + c_{p-1} \Delta y_{t-p+1} + \varepsilon_t, \tag{8.57}$$

with $\pi = \theta_1 + \cdots + \theta_p - 1$ and suitably chosen constants $c_1, \ldots, c_{p-1}$. As $\pi = 0$ implies $\theta(1) = 0$ it also implies that $z = 1$ is a solution to the characteristic equation $\theta(z) = 0$. Thus, as before, the hypothesis that $\pi = 0$ corresponds to a unit root and we can test it using the corresponding t-ratio. If the $AR(p)$ assumption is correct and under the null hypothesis of a unit root, the asymptotic distributions of the $\hat{\tau}$, $\hat{\tau}_\tau$ or $\hat{\tau}_\mu$ statistics, calculated from (8.57) (including, where appropriate, intercept and time trend) are the same as before. The small sample critical values are somewhat different from the tabulated ones and are provided by, for example, MacKinnon (1991).

Thus, when y_t follows an $AR(p)$ process, a test for a single unit root can be constructed from a regression of Δy_t on y_{t-1} and $\Delta y_{t-1}, \ldots, \Delta y_{t-p+1}$ by testing the significance of the 'level' variable y_{t-1} (using the one-sided appropriate critical values). It is interesting to note that under the null hypothesis of a single unit root, all variables in (8.57) are stationary, except y_{t-1}. Therefore, the equality in (8.57) can only make sense if y_{t-1} does not appear and $\pi = 0$, which explains intuitively why the unit root hypothesis corresponds to $\pi = 0$. The inclusion of the additional lags, in comparison to the standard Dickey–Fuller test, is done to make the error term in (8.57) asymptotically a white noise process, which is required for the distributional results to be valid. As it will generally be the case that p is unknown it is advisable to choose p fairly large. If too many lags are included this will somewhat reduce the power of the tests, but if too few lags are included the asymptotic distributions from the table are simply not valid, and the tests may lead to seriously biased conclusions. It is possible to use the model selection criteria discussed in Subsection 8.7.4 below, or statistical significance of the additional variables to select the lag length in the ADF tests.

A regression of the form (8.57) can also be used to test for a unit root in a general (invertible) ARMA model. Said and Dickey (1984) argue that when, theoretically, one lets the number of lags in the regression grow with the sample size (at a cleverly chosen rate), the same asymptotic distributions hold and the ADF tests are also valid for an ARMA model with a moving average component. The argument essentially is, as we have seen before, that any ARMA model (with invertible MA polynomial) can be written as an infinite autoregressive process. This explains why, when testing for unit roots, people usually do not worry about MA components.

Phillips and Perron (1988) have suggested an alternative to the augmented Dickey–Fuller tests. Instead of adding additional lags in the regressions to obtain an error term that has no autocorrelation, they stick to the original Dickey–Fuller regressions, but adjust the τ-statistics to take into account the (potential) autocorrelation pattern in the errors. These adjustments, based on corrections similar to those applied to compute Newey–West (HAC) standard errors (see Chapter 4), are quite complicated and will not be discussed here. The (asymptotic) critical values are again the same as those reported in Table 8.1. The Phillips–Perron test, sometimes referred to as a nonparametric test for a unit root, is, like the Said–Dickey (or ADF) test, applicable for general ARMA models (see Hamilton, 1994, pp. 506–515, for more details). Monte Carlo studies do not show a clear ranking of the two tests regarding their power (probability to reject the null if it is false) in finite samples.

If the ADF test does not allow rejection of the null hypothesis of one unit root, the presence of a second unit root may be tested by estimating the regression of $\Delta^2 y_t$ on $\Delta y_{t-1}, \Delta^2 y_{t-1}, \ldots, \Delta^2 y_{t-p+1}$, and comparing the t-ratio of the coefficient on Δy_{t-1} with the appropriate critical value from Table 8.1. Alternatively, the presence of two unit roots may be tested *jointly* by estimating the regression of $\Delta^2 y_t$ on $y_{t-1}, \Delta y_{t-1}, \Delta^2 y_{t-1}, \ldots, \Delta^2 y_{t-p+1}$, and computing the usual F-statistic for testing the joint significance of y_{t-1} and Δy_{t-1}. Again, though, this test statistic has a distribution under the null hypothesis of a double unit root that is not the usual F-distribution. Percentiles of this distribution are given by Hasza and Fuller (1979).

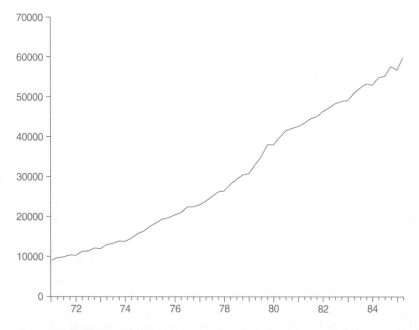

Figure 8.3 Quarterly UK disposable income, 1971:I–1985:II

8.4.3 Illustration: Quarterly Disposable Income

In this subsection we consider quarterly disposable income in the United Kingdom, over the quarters 1971:I to 1985:II, measured in million pounds and current prices ($T = 58$).[4] First, we plot the series in Figure 8.3. As could be expected, this shows a more or less monotonic growth pattern in the series, and it would be hard to argue that it is stationary. Using the above methodology we test for the presence of one or two unit roots in income. First, we estimate the standard Dickey–Fuller regression with an intercept, which gives

$$\Delta Y_t = \underset{(215.0)}{496.2} + \underset{(0.0064)}{0.0131}\ Y_{t-1} + e_t,$$

(8.58)

resulting in a DF test statistic of 2.064. As the appropriate critical value at the 5% level is -2.93, this does not allow us to reject the null hypothesis of a first unit root. However, we need to be sure that we included sufficient lags in this testing regression to make the error term white noise. Thus, it is advisable to perform a range of augmented Dickey–Fuller tests as well, implying that we add additional lags of ΔY_t to the right-hand side. Restricting attention to the test statistics, the results of this with up to 6 additional lags are as follows:

DF	$ADF(1)$	$ADF(2)$	$ADF(3)$	$ADF(4)$	$ADF(5)$	$ADF(6)$
2.064	2.693	1.648	1.792	0.712	0.564	0.912

---

[4] The data are available in the files INCOME.

Although the test statistics vary somewhat with the number of lags that is included, the conclusion does not change, and we cannot reject the presence of a first unit root.

If we impose a first unit root, we can test for the presence of a second unit root. This involves regressions of the form

$$\Delta^2 Y_t = \delta + \pi \Delta Y_{t-1} + c_1 \Delta^2 Y_{t-1} + \cdots + \varepsilon_t$$

and the null hypothesis corresponds to $\pi = 0$. The results are as follows:

DF	ADF(1)	ADF(2)	ADF(3)	ADF(4)	ADF(5)	ADF(6)
-8.904	-3.926	-3.768	-2.189	-1.856	-2.160	-2.075

For the lower order tests, the null hypothesis has to be rejected, but for ADF(3) to ADF(6) we can no longer reject the presence of a second unit root. If we look at the graph of the first differenced income series, as depicted in Figure 8.4, there does not seem any indication of a unit root. In fact, the results of the ADF tests show the danger of looking at the test statistics only and deciding that the null should be okay if the test does not reject. If we look at the results from the ADF regressions, we see that the standard errors for the θ coefficient are very large. This means that the tests do not have much power and that a lot of alternative hypotheses would also not be rejected (although they cannot be simultaneously true). For example, the ADF(4) test statistic is the ratio of an estimate for π of -0.491 with a large standard error of 0.265. It seems reasonable to conclude that quarterly disposable income, Y_t, has one unit root but not two. Below, in Subsection 8.7.5, we shall consider the problem of finding an appropriate ARMA model for ΔY_t.

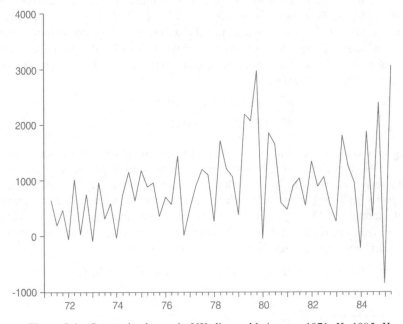

Figure 8.4 Quarterly change in UK disposable income 1971 : II–1985 : II

8.5   Illustration: Long-run Purchasing Power Parity (Part 1)

To illustrate the discussion above, we shall in this section pay attention to an empirical example concerning prices in two countries and the exchange rate between these countries. If two countries produce tradeable goods, and there are no impediments to international trade, such as tariffs or transaction costs, then the law of one price should hold, i.e.

$$S_t = P_t / P_t^*, \tag{8.59}$$

where S_t is the spot exchange rate (home currency price of a unit of foreign exchange), P_t is the (aggregate) price in the domestic country, and P_t^* is the price in the foreign country. In logarithms, we can write

$$s_t = p_t - p_t^*, \tag{8.60}$$

(where lower case letters denote natural logarithms). Condition (8.60), which is referred to as absolute **purchasing power parity** (absolute PPP), implies that an increase in the home price level should result in an equiproportionate rise in the exchange rate. Obviously this condition will never be satisfied in practice. Usually, PPP is seen as determining the exchange rate in the long-run. Below we shall analyse the question whether (8.60) is 'valid' in the long-run. A first necessary step for that is an analysis of the properties of the variables involved in (8.60).

Our empirical example concerns France and Italy over the period January 1981 until June 1996 ($T = 186$).[5] First we plot the two series for the log consumer price index in Figure 8.5. Clearly, this figure indicates non-stationarity of the two series,

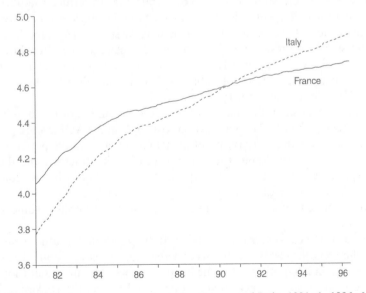

Figure 8.5   Log consumer price index France and Italy, 1981 : 1–1996 : 6

---

[5] Data available in the files PPP.

Table 8.2   Unit root tests for log price index France and Italy

Statistic	France (p_t^*)		Italy (p_t)	
	Without trend	With trend	Without trend	With trend
DF	−15.670	−9.462	−13.159	−8.403
ADF(1)	−7.147	−6.272	−6.378	−5.389
ADF(2)	−7.003	−6.933	−5.479	−5.131
ADF(3)	−4.964	−5.294	−4.407	−4.644
ADF(4)	−5.118	−6.077	−3.880	−4.289
ADF(5)	−4.115	−5.382	−3.692	−4.580
ADF(6)	−3.019	−3.919	−3.771	−5.474
ADF(7)	−3.183	−4.146	−3.260	−5.525
ADF(8)	−2.878	−3.728	−2.344	−4.529
ADF(9)	−2.688	−3.451	−2.039	−4.064
ADF(10)	−2.655	−3.591	−2.113	−3.742
ADF(11)	−2.408	−3.691	−1.687	−3.797
ADF(12)	−1.763	−2.908	−0.866	−2.997

while it is also clear that the two series have a different growth rate. Formal unit root tests can of course be obtained from regressions like (8.56) or (8.57). For p_t^*, the log of the French consumer price index, we obtain the following results, including a constant but no lagged differences in the model:

$$\Delta p_t^* = \underset{(0.0042)}{0.0694} - \underset{(0.0009)}{0.0146} \ p_{t-1}^* + e_t.$$

The Dickey–Fuller test statistic is −15.67, while the 5% critical value is −2.87, suggesting that the null hypothesis of a unit root should be rejected at any reasonable level of significance. However, it is quite likely that the simple $AR(1)$ model employed in this regression is too restrictive. Some software packages (like MicroFit) have the option of running a range of ADF tests simultaneously. This gives the results presented in the first two columns of Table 8.2. The critical values for the tests without trend are −2.877 and −3.435 for those with trend.[6]

The results clearly show the danger of testing for a unit root in a too restrictive model. Apparently, the 12th lag is important to include in the ADF regressions, which is not surprising given that we have monthly data and that seasonal patterns in prices are not uncommon. Thus, despite the fact that the majority of tests in the above table suggest rejection, we will not reject the hypothesis of a unit root when we consider the appropriate ADF test corresponding to 12 lags included in the regression. This choice can also be defended by looking at the graphs, which clearly show some source of nonstationarity.

For the log of the consumer price index in Italy, p_t, we find a rather similar set of results, as shown in the last two columns of Table 8.2. The conclusion is the same: we do not reject the null hypothesis that the log price series contains a unit root. For the log of the exchange rate, s_t, measured as Liras per FFranc, the Dickey–Fuller and

---

[6] The critical values change slightly from one row to the other. This is due to the change in the number of observations that is available to estimate the ADF regressions.

Table 8.3 Unit root tests for log exchange rate Italy–France

Statistic	Without trend	With trend
DF	−0.328	−1.900
ADF(1)	−0.361	−1.884
ADF(2)	−0.160	−1.925
ADF(3)	−0.291	−2.012
ADF(4)	−0.366	−2.026
ADF(5)	−0.463	−2.032
ADF(6)	−0.643	−2.262

augmented Dickey–Fuller tests give the results in Table 8.3, where we only report the ADF tests up to lag 6. The results here are quite clear. In none of the cases can we reject the null hypothesis of a unit root.

If purchasing power parity between France and Italy holds in the long-run, one can expect that short-run deviations, $s_t - (p_t - p_t^*)$, corresponding to the real exchange rate, are limited and do not wander widely. In other words, one can expect $s_t - (p_t - p_t^*)$ to be stationary. A test for PPP can thus be based on the analysis of the log real exchange rate $rs_t \equiv s_t - (p_t - p_t^*)$. The series is plotted in Figure 8.6, while the results for the augmented Dickey–Fuller tests for this variable are given in Table 8.4.

The results show that the null hypothesis of a unit root in rs_t (corresponding to non-stationarity) cannot be rejected. Consequently, there is no evidence for PPP to hold in this form. One reason why we may not be able to reject the null hypothesis is simply that our sample contains insufficient information, that is: our sample is too

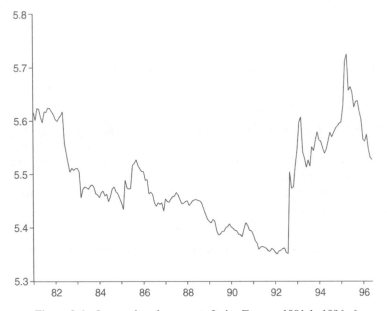

Figure 8.6 Log real exchange rate Italy–France, 1981:1–1996:6

Table 8.4 Unit root tests for log real exchange rate
Italy–France

Statistic	Without trend	With trend
DF	−1.930	−1.942
ADF(1)	−1.874	−1.892
ADF(2)	−1.930	−1.961
ADF(3)	−1.987	−2.022
ADF(4)	−1.942	−1.981
ADF(5)	−1.966	−2.005
ADF(6)	−2.287	−2.326

short and standard errors are simply too high to reject the unit root hypothesis. This is a problem often found in tests for purchasing power parity. A critical survey of this literature can be found in Froot and Rogoff (1996). In the next chapter, we shall also analyse whether some weaker form of PPP holds.

8.6 Estimation of ARMA Models

Suppose that we know that the data series $y_1, y_2, \ldots, y_T$ is generated by an ARMA process of order p, q. Depending upon the specification of the model, and the distributional assumptions we are willing to make, we can estimate the unknown parameters by ordinary or nonlinear least squares, or by maximum likelihood.

8.6.1 Least Squares

The least squares approach chooses the model parameters such that the residual sum of squares is minimal. This is particularly easy for models in autoregressive form. Consider the $AR(p)$ model

$$y_t = \theta_1 y_{t-1} + \theta_2 y_{t-2} + \cdots + \theta_p y_{t-p} + \varepsilon_t, \tag{8.61}$$

where ε_t is a white noise error term that is uncorrelated with anything dated $t-1$ or before. Consequently, we have that

$$E\{y_{t-j}\varepsilon_t\} = 0 \quad \text{for } j = 1, 2, 3, \ldots, p,$$

that is, error terms and explanatory variables are contemporaneously uncorrelated and OLS applied to (8.61) provides consistent estimators. Estimation of an autoregressive model is thus no different than that of a linear regression model with a lagged dependent variable.

For moving average models, estimation is somewhat more complicated. Suppose that we have an $MA(1)$ model

$$y_t = \varepsilon_t + \alpha \varepsilon_{t-1}.$$

Because ε_{t-1} is not observed, we cannot apply regression techniques here. In theory, ordinary least squares would minimize

$$S(\alpha) = \sum_{t=2}^{T} (y_t - \alpha \varepsilon_{t-1})^2.$$

A possible solution arises if we write ε_{t-1} in this expression as a function of observed y_ts. This is possible only if the MA polynomial is *invertible*. In this case we can use that

$$\varepsilon_{t-1} = \sum_{j=0}^{\infty} (-\alpha)^j y_{t-j-1}$$

(see above) and write

$$S(\alpha) = \sum_{t=2}^{T} \left(y_t - \alpha \sum_{j=0}^{\infty} (-\alpha)^j y_{t-j-1} \right)^2.$$

In practice, y_t is not observed for $t = 0, -1, \ldots$, so we have to cut off the infinite sum in this expression, to obtain an approximate sum of squares

$$\tilde{S}(\alpha) = \sum_{t=2}^{T} \left(y_t - \alpha \sum_{j=0}^{t-2} (-\alpha)^j y_{t-j-1} \right)^2. \tag{8.62}$$

Because asymptotically, if T goes to infinity, the difference between $S(\alpha)$ and $\tilde{S}(\alpha)$ disappears, minimizing (8.62) with respect to α gives a consistent estimator $\hat{\alpha}$ for α. Unfortunately, (8.62) is a high order polynomial in α and thus has very many local minima. Therefore, numerically minimizing (8.62) is complicated. However, as we know that $-1 < \alpha < 1$, a grid search (e.g., $-0.99, -0.98, -0.97, \ldots, 0.98, 0.99$) can be performed. The resulting nonlinear least squares estimator for α is consistent and asymptotically normal.

8.6.2 Maximum Likelihood

An alternative estimator for ARMA models is provided by maximum likelihood. This requires that an assumption is made about the distribution of ε_t, most commonly normality. Although the normality assumption is strong, the ML estimators are very often consistent even in cases where ε_t is not normal. Conditional upon an initial value the loglikelihood function can be written as

$$\log L(\alpha, \theta, \sigma^2) = -\frac{T-1}{2} \log(2\pi\sigma^2) - \frac{1}{2} \sum_{t=2}^{T} \varepsilon_t^2 / \sigma^2,$$

where ε_t is a function of the coefficients α and θ, y_t and its history. For an $AR(1)$ model it is $\varepsilon_t = y_t - \theta y_{t-1}$ and for the $MA(1)$ model we have

$$\varepsilon_t = y_t - \alpha \sum_{j=0}^{t-2} (-\alpha)^j y_{t-j-1} = \sum_{j=0}^{t-1} (-\alpha)^j y_{t-j}.$$

Both of the implied loglikelihood functions are conditional upon an initial value. For the $AR(1)$ case y_1 is treated as given, while for the $MA(1)$ case the initial condition is $\varepsilon_0 = 0$. The resulting estimators are therefore referred to as **conditional maximum likelihood** estimators. The conditional ML estimators for α and θ are easily seen to be identical to the least squares estimators.

The *exact* maximum likelihood estimator combines the conditional likelihood with the likelihood from the initial observations. In the $AR(1)$ case, for example, the following term is added to the loglikelihood:

$$-\frac{1}{2} \log(2\pi) - \frac{1}{2} \log[\sigma^2/(1 - \theta^2)] - \frac{1}{2} \frac{y_1^2}{\sigma^2/(1 - \theta^2)},$$

which follows from the fact that the marginal density of y_1 is normal with mean zero and variance $\sigma^2/(1 - \theta^2)$. For a moving average process the exact likelihood function is somewhat more complex. If T is large the way we treat the initial values has negligible impact, so that the conditional and exact maximum likelihood estimators are asymptotically equivalent in cases where the AR and MA polynomials are invertible. More details can be found in Hamilton (1994, Chapter 5).

It will be clear from the results above that estimating autoregressive models is simpler than estimating moving average models. Estimating ARMA models, that combine an autoregressive part with a moving average part, closely follows the lines of ML estimation of the MA parameters. As any (invertible) ARMA model can be approximated by an autoregressive model of infinite order, it has become more and more common practice to use autoregressive specifications instead of MA or ARMA ones, and allowing for a sufficient number of lags. Particularly if the number of observations is not too small this approach may work pretty well in practice. Of course, an MA representation of the same process may be more parsimonious. Another advantage of autoregressive models is that they are easily generalized to multivariate time series, where one wants to model a set of economic variables jointly. This leads to so-called **vector autoregressive models** (VAR) models, which are discussed in the next chapter.

8.7   Choosing a Model

Most of the time there are no economic reasons to choose a particular specification of the model. Consequently, to a large extent the data will determine which time series model is appropriate. Before estimating any model, it is common to estimate autocorrelation and partial autocorrelation coefficients directly from the data. Often this gives some idea about which model might be appropriate. After one or more models are estimated, their quality can be judged by checking whether the residuals are more or less white noise, and by comparing them with alternative specifications. These comparisons can be based on statistical significance tests or the use of particular model selection criteria.

8.7.1   The Autocorrelation Function

The autocorrelation function (ACF) describes the correlation between y_t and its lag y_{t-k} as a function of k. Recall that the k-th order autocorrelation coefficient is defined as

$$\rho_k = \frac{\text{cov}\{y_t, y_{t-k}\}}{V\{y_t\}} = \frac{\gamma_k}{\gamma_0}.$$

For the $MA(1)$ model we have seen that

$$\rho_1 = \frac{\alpha}{1 + \alpha^2}, \quad \rho_2 = 0, \quad \rho_3 = 0, \ldots,$$

that is, only the first autocorrelation coefficient is nonzero. For the $MA(2)$ model

$$y_t = \varepsilon_t + \alpha_1 \varepsilon_{t-1} + \alpha_2 \varepsilon_{t-2}$$

we have

$$E\{y_t^2\} = (1 + \alpha_1^2 + \alpha_2^2)\sigma^2$$

$$E\{y_t y_{t-1}\} = (\alpha_1 + \alpha_1 \alpha_2)\sigma^2$$

$$E\{y_t y_{t-2}\} = \alpha_2 \sigma^2$$

$$E\{y_t y_{t-k}\} = 0, \quad k = 3, 4, 5, \ldots$$

It follows directly from this that the ACF is zero after two lags. This is a general result for moving average models: for an $MA(q)$ model the ACF is zero after q lags.

The *sample* autocorrelation function gives the *estimated* autocorrelation coefficients as a function of k. The coefficient ρ_k can be estimated by[7]

$$\hat{\rho}_k = \frac{(1/(T-k)) \sum_{t=k+1}^{T} y_t y_{t-k}}{(1/T) \sum_{t=1}^{T} y_t^2} \tag{8.63}$$

That is, the population covariances in the ratio are replaced by their sample estimates. Alternatively, it can be estimated by regressing y_t upon y_{t-k}, which will give a slightly different estimator, because the summation in numerator and denominator will be over the same set of observations. Of course, it will usually not be the case that $\hat{\rho}_k$ is zero for an MA model of order $q < k$. But we can use $\hat{\rho}_k$ to test the hypothesis that $\rho_k = 0$. To do this, we can use the result that asymptotically

$$\sqrt{T}(\hat{\rho}_k - \rho_k) \to \mathcal{N}(0, v_k),$$

where

$$v_k = 1 + 2\rho_1^2 + 2\rho_2^2 + \cdots + 2\rho_q^2 \quad \text{if } q < k.$$

So, to test the hypothesis that the true model is $MA(0)$ versus the alternative that it is $MA(1)$, we can test $\rho_1 = 0$ by comparing the test statistic $\sqrt{T}\hat{\rho}_1$ with the critical values of a standard normal distribution. Testing $MA(k-1)$ versus $MA(k)$ is done by testing $\rho_k = 0$ and comparing the test statistic

$$\sqrt{T} \frac{\hat{\rho}_k}{\sqrt{1 + 2\hat{\rho}_1^2 + \cdots + 2\hat{\rho}_{k-1}^2}} \tag{8.64}$$

with critical values from the standard normal distribution. Typically, two-standard error bounds for $\hat{\rho}_k$ based on the estimated variance $1 + 2\hat{\rho}_1^2 + \cdots + 2\hat{\rho}_{k-1}^2$ are graphically displayed in the plot of the sample autocorrelation function (see the example in Subsection 8.7.5 below). The order of a moving average model can in

---

[7] Alternative consistent estimators are possible that have slightly different degrees of freedom corrections.

this way be determined from an inspection of the sample ACF. At least it will give us a reasonable value for q to start with and diagnostic checking, as discussed below, should indicate whether it is appropriate or not.

For autoregressive models the ACF is less helpful. For the $AR(1)$ model we have seen that the autocorrelation coefficients do not cut off at a finite lag length. Instead, they go to zero exponentially corresponding to $\rho_k = \theta^k$. For higher order autoregressive models, the autocorrelation function is more complex. Consider the general $AR(2)$ model

$$y_t = \theta_1 y_{t-1} + \theta_2 y_{t-2} + \varepsilon_t.$$

To derive the autocovariances, it is convenient to take the covariance of both sides with y_{t-k} to obtain

$$\mathrm{cov}\{y_t, y_{t-k}\} = \theta_1 \mathrm{cov}\{y_{t-1}, y_{t-k}\} + \theta_2 \mathrm{cov}\{y_{t-2}, y_{t-k}\} + \mathrm{cov}\{\varepsilon_t, y_{t-k}\}.$$

For $k = 0, 1, 2$, this gives

$$\gamma_0 = \theta_1 \gamma_1 + \theta_2 \gamma_2 + \sigma^2$$
$$\gamma_1 = \theta_1 \gamma_0 + \theta_2 \gamma_1$$
$$\gamma_2 = \theta_1 \gamma_1 + \theta_2 \gamma_0.$$

This set of equations, known as the **Yule–Walker equations**, can be solved for the autocovariances γ_0, γ_1 and γ_2 as a function of the model parameters θ_1, θ_2 and σ^2. The higher order covariances can be determined recursively from

$$\gamma_k = \theta_1 \gamma_{k-1} + \theta_2 \gamma_{k-2} \quad (k = 2, 3, \ldots),$$

which corresponds to a second order differential equation. Depending on θ_1 and θ_2 the patterns of the ACF can be very different. Consequently, in general only a real expert may be able to identify an $AR(2)$ process from the ACF pattern, let alone from the sample ACF pattern. An alternative source of information that is helpful, is provided by the *partial* autocorrelation function, discussed in the next subsection.

8.7.2 The Partial Autocorrelation Function

We now define the k-th order sample **partial autocorrelation coefficient** as the estimate for θ_k in an $AR(k)$ model. We denote this by $\hat{\theta}_{kk}$. So estimating

$$y_t = \theta_1 y_{t-1} + \varepsilon_t$$

gives us $\hat{\theta}_{11}$, while estimating

$$y_t = \theta_1 y_{t-1} + \theta_2 y_{t-2} + \varepsilon_t$$

yields $\hat{\theta}_{22}$, the estimated coefficient for y_{t-2} in the $AR(2)$ model. The partial autocorrelation $\hat{\theta}_{kk}$ measures the additional correlation between y_t and y_{t-k} after adjustments have been made for the intermediate values $y_{t-1}, \ldots, y_{t-k+1}$.

Obviously, if the true model is an $AR(p)$ process then estimating an $AR(k)$ model by OLS gives consistent estimators for the model parameters if $k \geq p$. Consequently, we have

$$\mathrm{plim}\,\hat{\theta}_{kk} = 0 \quad \text{if } k > p. \tag{8.65}$$

Moreover, it can be shown that the asymptotic distribution is standard normal, i.e.

$$\sqrt{T}(\hat{\theta}_{kk} - 0) \to \mathcal{N}(0,1) \quad \text{if } k > p. \tag{8.66}$$

Consequently, the partial autocorrelation coefficients (or the partial autocorrelation function (PACF)) can be used to determine the order of an AR process. Testing an $AR(k-1)$ model versus an $AR(k)$ model implies testing the null hypothesis that $\theta_{kk} = 0$. Under the null hypothesis that the model is $AR(k-1)$ the approximate standard error of $\hat{\theta}_{kk}$ based on (8.66) is $1/\sqrt{T}$, so that $\theta_{kk} = 0$ is rejected if $|\sqrt{T}\hat{\theta}_{kk}| > 1.96$. This way one can look at the PACF and test for which lags the partial autocorrelation coefficient differs from zero. For a genuine $AR(p)$ model the partial autocorrelations will be close to zero after the p-th lag.

For moving average models it can be shown that the partial autocorrelations do not have a cut off point but tail off to zero, just like the autocorrelations in an autoregressive model. In summary, an $AR(p)$ process is described by:

1. an ACF that is infinite in extent (it tails off).
2. a PACF that is (close to) zero for lags larger than p.

For a $MA(q)$ process we have that:

1. an ACF that is (close to) zero for lags larger than q.
2. a PACF that is infinite in extent (it tails off).

In the absence of any of these two situations, a combined ARMA model may provide a parsimonious representation of the data.

8.7.3 Diagnostic Checking

As a last step in the model-building cycle some checks on the model adequacy are required. Possibilities are doing a **residual analysis** and **overfitting** the specified model. For example, if an $ARMA(p, q)$ model is chosen (on the basis of the sample ACF and PACF), we could also estimate an $ARMA(p+1, q)$ and an $ARMA(p, q+1)$ model and test the significance of the additional parameters.

A residual analysis is usually based on the fact that the residuals of an adequate model should be approximately white noise. A plot of the residuals can be a useful tool in checking for outliers. Moreover, the estimated residual autocorrelations are usually examined. Recall that for a white noise series the autocorrelations are zero. Therefore the significance of the residual autocorrelations is often checked by comparing with approximate two standard error bounds $\pm 2/\sqrt{T}$. To check the overall acceptability of the residual autocorrelations, the Ljung–Box (1978) portmanteau test statistic,

$$Q_K = T(T+2) \sum_{k=1}^{K} \frac{1}{T-k} r_k^2 \tag{8.67}$$

is often used. Here, the r_k are the estimated autocorrelation coefficients of the residuals $\hat{\varepsilon}_t$ and K is a number chosen by the researcher. Values of Q for different K may be computed in a residual analysis. For an $ARMA(p, q)$ process (for y_t) the statistic Q_K is approximately Chi-squared distributed with $K - p - q$ degrees of freedom (under the null hypothesis that the $ARMA(p, q)$ is correctly specified). If a model is rejected at this stage, the model-building cycle has to be repeated. Note that this test only makes sense if $K > p + q$.

8.7.4 Criteria for Model Selection

Because economic theory does not provide any guidance to the appropriate choice of model, some additional criteria can be used to choose from alternative models that are acceptable from a statistical point of view. As a more general model will always provide a better fit (within the sample) than a restricted version of it, all such criteria provide a trade-off between goodness-of-fit and the number of parameters used to obtain that fit. For example, if an $MA(2)$ model would provide the same fit as an $AR(10)$ model, we would prefer the first as it is more parsimonious. As discussed in Chapter 3, a well known criterion is **Akaike's Information Criterion** (AIC) (Akaike, 1973). In the current context it is given by

$$AIC = \log \hat{\sigma}^2 + 2 \frac{p + q}{T}, \tag{8.68}$$

where $\hat{\sigma}^2$ is the estimated variance of ε_t. An alternative is Schwarz's **Bayesian Information Criterion** (SC, BIC or SBC), proposed by Schwarz (1978), which is given by

$$BIC = \log \hat{\sigma}^2 + 2 \frac{p + q}{T} \log T. \tag{8.69}$$

Both criteria are likelihood-based and represent a different trade-off between 'fit', as measured by the loglikelihood value, and 'parsimony', as measured by the number of free parameters, $p + q$. If a constant is included in the model, the number of parameters is increased to $p + q + 1$. Usually, the model with the smallest AIC or BIC value is preferred, although one can choose to deviate from this if the differences in criterion values are small for a subset of the models.

While the two criteria differ in their trade-off between fit and parsimony, the BIC criterion can be preferred because it has the property that it will almost surely select the true model, if $T \to \infty$, provided that the true model is in the class of $ARMA(p, q)$ models for relatively small values of p and q. The AIC criterion tends to result asymptotically in overparametrized models (see Hannan, 1980).

8.7.5 Illustration: Modelling Quarterly Disposable Income

In Subsection 8.4.3 we saw that the null hypothesis of a unit root in UK quarterly disposable income could not be rejected. Therefore, we shall in this section try to model the first differenced series, the change in income. The sample autocorrelation and partial autocorrelation function are presented in Figure 8.7. We see that both the autocorrelation and partial autocorrelation coefficients are significantly different from zero at lags one, two and four, while for the PACF a significant value is also found at lag 10. The relatively large (partial) autocorrelation at lag 4 can be explained from the quarterly nature of the data series.

From an inspection of the sample ACF and PACF, there is no obvious model that comes to mind. Because it could be argued that both ACF and PACF are zero after lag 4, the estimation of an $AR(4)$ or $MA(4)$ model could be considered. Given the

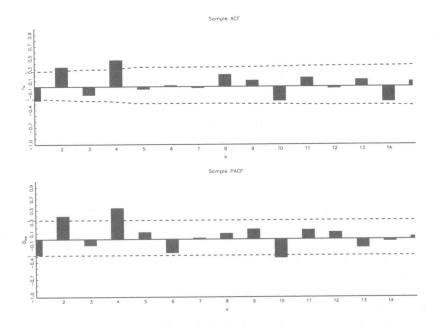

Figure 8.7 Sample ACF and PACF of change in quarterly income

significance of the 10th lag of the PACF, the $MA(4)$ specification is *a priori* slightly preferred. The two fourth order models are estimated after the mean has been subtracted from the observations, so that the intercept term can be excluded. All models are estimated by least squares. For the $AR(4)$ model we obtain:

$$\Delta y_t = -0.121\, \Delta y_{t-1} + 0.234\, \Delta y_{t-2} - 0.053\, \Delta y_{t-3} + 0.483\, \Delta y_{t-4} + \hat{\varepsilon}_t,$$
$$\quad\;\; (0.122) \qquad\quad (0.127) \qquad\quad (0.134) \qquad\quad (0.137) \qquad\qquad \hat{\sigma} = 632.926$$

$$Q_6 = 2.07\ (p = 0.354), \quad Q_{12} = 8.12\ (p = 0.422)$$
$$AIC = 901.888, \quad BIC = 910.060,$$

while the estimating the $MA(4)$ model produces:

$$\Delta y_t = 0.186\hat{\varepsilon}_{t-1} - 0.355\hat{\varepsilon}_{t-2} + 0.138\hat{\varepsilon}_{t-3} - 0.432\hat{\varepsilon}_{t-4} + \hat{\varepsilon}_t, \quad \hat{\sigma} = 656.387$$
$$\;\;(0.128) \qquad (0.129) \qquad (0.131) \qquad (0.132)$$

$$Q_6 = 1.70\ (p = 0.428), \quad Q_{12} = 9.24\ (p = 0.323)$$
$$AIC = 906.072, \quad BIC = 914.244.$$

For neither of the specifications we can reject the null hypothesis that the residuals correspond to a white noise process. The Ljung–Box statistics for the first $K = 6$ and 12 residual autocorrelations do not reject. The autoregressive specification provides a better fit to the data than the moving average one, although both specifications contain at least two insignificant lags.

It is interesting to see whether a more parsimonious model could provide almost the same fit (but with less parameters). Because the third order (partial) autocorrelation coefficient of Δy_t is very small, we consider fourth order AR and MA specifications but with the third lag excluded. This leads to the following autoregressive model:

$$\Delta y_t = -0.143 \, \Delta y_{t-1} + 0.241 \, \Delta y_{t-2} + 0.490 \, \Delta y_{t-4} + \hat{\varepsilon}_t, \quad \hat{\sigma} = 622.663$$
$$\quad (0.115) \qquad\quad (0.126) \qquad\quad (0.133)$$

$$Q_6 = 2.13 \; (p = 0.546), \quad Q_{12} = 7.88 \; (p = 0.546)$$

$$AIC = 900.074, \quad BIC = 906.203,$$

while the moving average model is given by:

$$\Delta y_t = 0.133 \, \hat{\varepsilon}_{t-1} - 0.336 \, \hat{\varepsilon}_{t-2} - 0.413 \, \hat{\varepsilon}_{t-4} + \hat{\varepsilon}_t, \quad \hat{\sigma} = 656.284$$
$$\quad (0.129) \qquad\quad (0.129) \qquad\quad (0.137)$$

$$Q_6 = 3.13 \; (p = 0.372), \quad Q_{12} = 10.62 \; (p = 0.303)$$

$$AIC = 905.060, \quad BIC = 911.189.$$

On the basis of the AIC and BIC criteria, both specifications can be preferred to their more general counterparts that include the third lag. The autoregressive model appears to provide a better fit, although two of its coefficients are individually not significantly different from zero (at the 5% level). Finally, we consider a fourth order AR model that only includes lags 2 and 4. This produces the following results:

$$\Delta y_t = 0.266 \, \Delta y_{t-2} + 0.513 \, \Delta y_{t-4} + \hat{\varepsilon}_t, \quad \hat{\sigma} = 626.791$$
$$\quad (0.126) \qquad\quad (0.133)$$

$$Q_6 = 4.62 \; (p = 0.329), \quad Q_{12} = 11.66 \; (p = 0.309)$$

$$AIC = 899.890, \quad BIC = 903.976.$$

Again both the AIC and BIC criteria would favour this more parsimonious model. Recall that the BIC criterion has a higher punishment for additional parameters compared to AIC. If now, we would consider dropping the second lag from the model, the resulting specification is no longer acceptable. In particular, the Ljung–Box statistics and the AIC and BIC criteria are given by

$$Q_6 = 12.03 \; (p = 0.034), \quad Q_{12} = 19.23 \; (p = 0.057)$$

$$AIC = 902.750, \quad BIC = 904.793.$$

Note that it has to be rejected that the model residuals are white noise, while AIC and BIC have increased again. We can thus conclude that the $AR(4)$ model with lags 2 and 4 included, provides an adequate description of the process for the change in quarterly income.

8.8   Predicting with ARMA Models

A main goal of building a time series model is predicting the future path of economic variables. It can be noted that ARMA models usually perform quite well in this respect and often outperform more complicated structural models. Of course, ARMA models do not provide any economic insight in one's predictions and are unable to forecast under alternative economic scenarios. In this section, we discuss the optimal predictor, which is simply the conditional expectation of a future value given the available information, and how it can be derived in ARMA models. Furthermore, we pay attention to forecast accuracy.

8.8.1 The Optimal Predictor

Suppose we are at time T and are interested in predicting y_{T+h}, the value of y_t h periods ahead. A predictor for y_{T+h} will be based on an **information set**, denoted $\mathcal{I}_T$, that contains the information that is available and potentially used at the time of making the forecast. Ideally it contains all the information that is observed and known at time T. In univariate time series modelling we will usually assume that the information set at any point t in time contains the value of y_t and all its lags. Thus we have

$$\mathcal{I}_T = \{y_{-\infty}, \ldots, y_{T-1}, y_T\}. \tag{8.70}$$

In general, the predictor $\hat{y}_{T+h|T}$ (the predictor for y_{T+h} as constructed at time T) is a function of (variables in) the information set $\mathcal{I}_T$. Our criterion for choosing a predictor from the many possible ones, is to minimize the expected quadratic prediction error

$$E\{(y_{T+h} - \hat{y}_{T+h|T})^2 | \mathcal{I}_T\}, \tag{8.71}$$

where $E\{.|\mathcal{I}_T\}$ denotes the conditional expectation given the information set $\mathcal{I}_T$. It is not very hard to show that the best predictor for y_{T+h} given the information set at time T is the conditional expectation of y_{T+h} given the information $\mathcal{I}_T$. We denote this optimal predictor as

$$y_{T+h|T} \equiv E\{y_{T+h} | \mathcal{I}_T\}. \tag{8.72}$$

Because the optimal predictor is a conditional expectation, it satisfies the usual properties of expectation operators. Most importantly, the conditional expectation of a sum is the sum of conditional expectations. Further, it holds that the conditional expectation of y_{T+h} given an information set $\mathcal{I}_T'$, where $\mathcal{I}_T'$ is a subset of $\mathcal{I}_T$ is at best as good as $y_{T+h|T}$ based on $\mathcal{I}_T$. In line with our intuition, it holds that the more information one uses to determine the predictor (the larger $\mathcal{I}_T$ is), the better the predictor is. For example, $E\{y_{T+h}|y_T, y_{T-1}, y_{T-2}, \ldots\}$ will usually be a better predictor than $E\{y_{T+h}|y_T\}$ or $E\{y_{T+h}\}$ (an empty information set).

To simplify things we shall, in the sequel, assume that the parameters in the ARMA model for y_t are known. In practice one would simply replace the unknown parameters by their consistent estimates. Now, how do we determine these conditional expectations when y_t follows an ARMA process? As a first example consider an $AR(1)$ process where

$$y_t = \theta y_{t-1} + \varepsilon_t.$$

So, for y_{T+1} it holds by assumption that

$$y_{T+1} = \theta y_T + \varepsilon_{T+1}.$$

Consequently,

$$y_{T+1|T} = E\{y_{T+1}|y_T, y_{T-1}, \ldots\} = \theta y_T + E\{\varepsilon_{T+1}|y_T, y_{T-1}, \ldots\} = \theta y_T, \tag{8.73}$$

where the latter equality follows from the fact that the white noise process is unpredictable. To predict two periods ahead ($h = 2$), we write

$$y_{T+2} = \theta y_{T+1} + \varepsilon_{T+2},$$

from which it follows that

$$E\{y_{T+2}|y_T, \, y_{T-1}, \ldots\} = \theta E\{y_{T+1}|y_T, \, y_{T-1}, \ldots\} = \theta^2 y_T. \tag{8.74}$$

In general, we obtain $y_{T+h|T} = \theta^h y_T$. Thus, the last observed value y_T contains all the information to determine the predictor for any future value. When h is large the predictor of y_{T+h} converges to 0 (the unconditional expectation of y_t), provided (of course) that $|\theta| < 1$. With a nonzero mean, the best predictor for Y_{T+h} is directly obtained as $\mu + y_{T+h|T} = \mu + \theta^h(Y_T - \mu)$. Note that this differs from $\theta^h Y_T$.

As a second example, consider an $MA(1)$ process, where

$$y_t = \varepsilon_t + \alpha \varepsilon_{t-1}.$$

Then we have

$$E\{y_{T+1}|y_T, \, y_{T-1}, \ldots\} = \alpha E\{\varepsilon_T|y_T, \, y_{T-1}, \ldots\} = \alpha \varepsilon_T,$$

where, implicitly, we assumed that ε_T is observed (contained in $\mathcal{I}_T$). This is an innocent assumption *provided the MA process is invertible*. In that case we can write

$$\varepsilon_T = \sum_{j=0}^{\infty} (-\alpha)^j y_{T-j}.$$

Consequently,

$$y_{T+1|T} = \alpha \sum_{j=0}^{\infty} (-\alpha)^j y_{T-j}. \tag{8.75}$$

Predicting two periods ahead gives

$$y_{T+2|T} = E\{\varepsilon_{T+2}|y_T, \, y_{T-1}, \ldots\} + \alpha E\{\varepsilon_{T+1}|y_T, \, y_{T-1}, \ldots\} = 0. \tag{8.76}$$

Predicting two periods ahead on the basis of an $MA(1)$ model is uninformative: the best predictor is simply the (unconditional) expected value of y_t, normalized at 0. This also follows from the autocorrelation function of the process, because the ACF is zero after one lag. That is, the 'memory' of the process is only one period.

For the general $ARMA(p, q)$ model,

$$y_t = \theta_1 y_{t-1} + \cdots + \theta_p y_{t-p} + \varepsilon_t + \alpha_1 \varepsilon_{t-1} + \cdots + \alpha_q \varepsilon_{t-q}$$

we can derive the following recursive formula to determine the optimal predictors:

$$y_{T+h|T} = \theta_1 y_{T+h-1|T} + \cdots + \theta_p y_{T+h-p|T} + \varepsilon_{T+h|T} + \alpha_1 \varepsilon_{T+h-1|T} + \cdots + \alpha_q \varepsilon_{T+h-q|T}, \tag{8.77}$$

where $\varepsilon_{T+K|T}$ is the optimal predictor for ε_{T+K} at time T, and

$$y_{T+k|T} = y_{T+k} \quad \text{if } k \leq 0$$

$$\varepsilon_{T+k|T} = 0 \quad \text{if } k > 0$$

$$\varepsilon_{T+k|T} = \varepsilon_{T+k} \quad \text{if } k \leq 0,$$

where the latter innovation can be solved from the autoregressive representation of the model. For this we have used the fact that the process is stationary and invertible, in which case the information set $\{y_T, y_{T-1}, \ldots\}$ is equivalent to $\{\varepsilon_T, \varepsilon_{T-1}, \ldots\}$. That is, if all ε_ts are known from $-\infty$ to T, then all y_ts are known from $-\infty$ to T and vice versa.

To illustrate this, consider an $ARMA(1,1)$ model, where

$$y_t = \theta y_{t-1} + \varepsilon_t + \alpha \varepsilon_{t-1},$$

such that

$$y_{T+1|T} = \theta y_{T|T} + \varepsilon_{T+1|T} + \alpha \varepsilon_{T|T} = \theta y_T + \alpha \varepsilon_T.$$

Using that (assuming invertibility)

$$y_t - \theta y_{t-1} = (1 + \alpha L)\varepsilon_t$$

can be rewritten as

$$\varepsilon_t = (1 + \alpha L)^{-1}(y_t - \theta y_{t-1}) = \sum_{j=0}^{\infty} (-\alpha)^j L^j (y_t - \theta y_{t-1}),$$

we can write for the one-period ahead predictor

$$y_{T+1|T} = \theta y_T + \alpha \sum_{j=0}^{\infty} (-\alpha)^j (y_{T-j} - \theta y_{T-j-1}). \tag{8.78}$$

Predicting two periods ahead gives

$$y_{T+2|T} = \theta y_{T+1|T} + \varepsilon_{T+2|T} + \alpha \varepsilon_{T+1|T} = \theta y_{T+1|T}. \tag{8.79}$$

Note that this does not equal $\theta^2 y_T$.

8.8.2 Prediction Accuracy

In addition to the prediction itself, it is important (sometimes even more important) to know how accurate this prediction is. To judge forecasting precision, we define the **prediction error** as $y_{T+h} - y_{T+h|T}$ and the expected quadratic prediction error as

$$C_h \equiv E\{(y_{T+h} - y_{T+h|T})^2\} = V\{y_{T+h}|\mathcal{I}_T\}, \tag{8.80}$$

where the latter step follows from the fact that $y_{T+h|T} = E\{y_{T+h}|\mathcal{I}_T\}$. Determining C_h, corresponding to the variance of the h-period ahead prediction error, is relatively easy with the moving average representation.

To start with the simplest case, consider an $MA(1)$ model. Then we have

$$C_1 = V\{y_{T+1}|y_T, y_{T-1}, \ldots\} = V\{\varepsilon_{T+1} + \alpha \varepsilon_T | \varepsilon_T, \varepsilon_{T-1}, \ldots\} = V\{\varepsilon_{T+1}\} = \sigma^2.$$

Alternatively, we explicitly solve for the predictor, which is $y_{T+1|T} = \alpha \varepsilon_T$ and determine the variance of $y_{T+1} - y_{T+1|T} = \varepsilon_{T+1}$, which gives the same result. For the two-period ahead predictor we have

$$C_2 = V\{y_{T+2}|y_T, y_{T-1}, \ldots\} = V\{\varepsilon_{T+2} + \alpha \varepsilon_{T+1} | \varepsilon_T, \varepsilon_{T-1}, \ldots\} = (1 + \alpha^2)\sigma^2.$$

As expected, the accuracy of the prediction decreases if we predict further into the future. It will not, however, increase any further if h is increased beyond 2. This becomes clear if we compare the expected quadratic prediction error with that of a simple unconditional predictor,

$$\hat{y}_{T+h|T} = E\{y_{T+h}\} = 0$$

(empty information set). For this predictor we have

$$C_h = E\{(y_{T+h} - 0)^2\} = V\{y_{T+h}\} = (1 + \alpha^2)\sigma^2.$$

Consequently, this gives an upper bound on the inaccuracy of the predictors. The $MA(1)$ model thus gives more efficient predictors only if one predicts one period ahead. More general ARMA models, however, will yield efficiency gains also in further ahead predictors.

Suppose the general model is $ARMA(p, q)$, which we write as an $MA(\infty)$ model, with α_j coefficients to be determined,

$$y_t = \sum_{j=0}^{\infty} \alpha_j \varepsilon_{t-j} \quad \text{with } \alpha_0 \equiv 1.$$

The h-period ahead predictor (in terms of ε_ts) is given by

$$y_{T+h|T} = E\{y_{T+h} | y_T, y_{T-1}, \ldots\} = \sum_{j=0}^{\infty} \alpha_j E\{\varepsilon_{T+h-j} | \varepsilon_T, \varepsilon_{T-1}, \ldots\} = \sum_{j=h}^{\infty} \alpha_j \varepsilon_{T+h-j},$$

such that

$$y_{T+h} - y_{T+h|T} = \sum_{j=0}^{h-1} \alpha_j \varepsilon_{T+h-j}.$$

Consequently, we have

$$E\{(y_{T+h} - y_{T+h|T})^2\} = \sigma^2 \sum_{j=0}^{h-1} \alpha_j^2. \tag{8.81}$$

This shows how the variances of the forecast errors can easily be determined from the coefficients in the moving average representation of the model. Recall that for the computation of the predictor, the autoregressive representation was most convenient.

As an illustration, consider the $AR(1)$ model where $\alpha_j = \theta^j$. The expected quadratic prediction errors are given by

$$C_1 = \sigma^2, \quad C_2 = \sigma^2(1 + \theta^2), \quad C_3 = \sigma^2(1 + \theta^2 + \theta^4),$$

etc. For h going to infinity, we have $C_\infty = \sigma^2(1 + \theta^2 + \theta^4 + \cdots) = \sigma^2/(1 - \theta^2)$, which is the unconditional variance of y_t and therefore the expected quadratic prediction error of a constant predictor $\hat{y}_{T+h|T} = E\{y_{T+h}\} = 0$. Consequently, the informational value contained in an $AR(1)$ process slowly decays over time. In the long-run the predictor equals the unconditional predictor, being the mean of the y_t series (as is the case in all stationary time series models). Note that for a random walk, with $\theta = 1$, the forecast error variance increases linearly with the forecast horizon.

In practical cases, the parameters in ARMA models will be unknown and we replace them by their estimated values. This introduces additional uncertainty in the predictors. Usually, however, this uncertainty is ignored. The motivation is that the additional variance that arises because of estimation error disappears asymptotically when the sample size T goes to infinity. In practice, the increase in the forecast error variance if one would take it into account is usually fairly small.

8.9 Illustration: The Expectations Theory of the Term Structure

Quite often, building a time series model is not a goal in itself, but a necessary ingredient in an economic analysis. To illustrate this, we shall in this section pay attention to the term structure of interest rates. The term structure has attracted considerable attention in both the macro-economics and the finance literature (see, for example, Pagan, Hall and Martin, 1996) and the expectations hypothesis plays a central role in many of these studies.

To introduce the problem, we consider an *n*-period discount bond, which is simply a claim to one dollar paid to you n periods from today. The (market) price at time t (today) of this discount bond is denoted as p_{nt}. The implied interest rate r_{nt} can then be solved from

$$p_{nt} = \frac{1}{(1 + r_{nt})^n}. \tag{8.82}$$

The **yield curve** describes r_{nt} as a function of its maturity n, and may vary from one period t to the other. This depicts the term structure of interest rates. Models for the term structure try to simultaneously model how the different interest rates are linked and how the yield curve moves over time.

The **pure expectations hypothesis**, in a linearized form, can be written as

$$r_{nt} = \frac{1}{n} \sum_{h=0}^{n-1} E\{r_{1,t+h} | \mathcal{I}_t\}, \tag{8.83}$$

where $\mathcal{I}_t$ denotes the information set containing all information available at time t. This says that the long term interest rate is the average of the expected short term rates over the same interval. The left-hand side of this can be interpreted as the certain yield of an *n*-period investment, while the right-hand side corresponds to the *expected*[8] yield from investing in one-period bonds over an *n*-period horizon. Thus, expected returns on bonds of different maturities are assumed to be equal.

The **expectations hypothesis**, in a more general form, allows for risk premia by assuming that expected returns on different bonds can differ by constants, which can depend on maturity but not on time. This extends (8.83) to

$$r_{nt} = \frac{1}{n} \sum_{h=0}^{n-1} E\{r_{1,t+h} | \mathcal{I}_t\} + \Phi_n, \tag{8.84}$$

---

[8] We impose *rational* expectations, which means that economic agents have expectations that correspond to mathematical expectations, conditional upon some information set.

where Φ_n denotes a risk or term premium that varies with maturity n. Instead of testing the expectations hypothesis in this form, which is the subject of many studies (see Campbell and Shiller, 1991), we shall look at a simple implementation of (8.84). Given that the term premia are constant, we can complete the model by making assumptions about the relevant information set $\mathcal{I}_t$ and the time series process of the one-period interest rate.

Let us assume, for simplicity, that

$$\mathcal{I}_t = \{r_{1t}, r_{1,t-1}, r_{1,t-2}, \ldots\},$$

such that the relevant information set contains the current and lagged short interest rates only. If r_{1t} can be described by an $AR(1)$ process,

$$r_{1t} - \mu = \theta(r_{1,t-1} - \mu) + \varepsilon_t,$$

with $0 < \theta \le 1$, the optimal s-period ahead predictor (see (8.74)) is given by

$$E\{r_{1,t+h}|\mathcal{I}_t\} = \mu + \theta^h(r_{1t} - \mu).$$

Substituting this into (8.84) results in

$$
\begin{aligned}
r_{n,t} &= \frac{1}{n}\sum_{h=0}^{n-1}[\mu + \theta^h(r_{1t} - \mu)] + \Phi_n \\
&= \mu + \left(\frac{1}{n}\sum_{h=0}^{n-1}\theta^h\right)(r_{1t} - \mu) + \Phi_n \\
&= \mu + \xi_n(r_{1t} - \mu) + \Phi_n,
\end{aligned}
\tag{8.85}
$$

where, for $0 < \theta < 1$,

$$\xi_n = \frac{1}{n}\sum_{h=0}^{n-1}\theta^h = \frac{1}{n}\frac{1-\theta^n}{1-\theta} < \xi_{n-1} < 1, \tag{8.86}$$

while for $\theta = 1$ we have $\xi_n = 1$ for each maturity n.

The rather simple model of the term structure in (8.85) implies that long rates depend linearly on short rates and that short rate changes have less impact on longer rates than shorter rates since ξ_n is decreasing with n if $0 < \theta < 1$. Note, for example, that

$$V\{r_{nt}\} = \xi_n^2 V\{r_{1t}\}, \tag{8.87}$$

which, with $0 < \theta < 1$, implies that short rates are more volatile than long rates. The result in (8.85) also implies that there is just one factor which drives interest rates at any maturity and thus one factor which shifts the term structure.

If all risk premia are zero ($\Phi_n = 0$) an inverted yield curve (with short rates exceeding long rates) occurs if the short rate is above its mean μ, which – when the distribution of ε_t is symmetric around zero (e.g. normal) – happens in 50% of the cases. The reason is that when the short rate is below its average, it is expected to increase to its average again, which increases the long rates. In practice, we see inverted yield curves

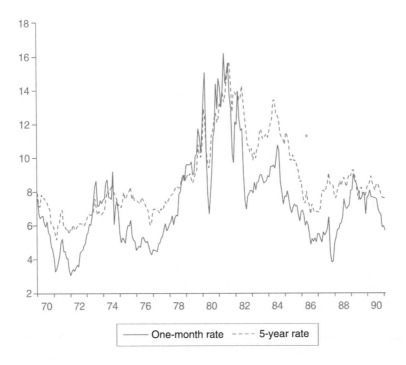

Figure 8.8   One month and 5-year interest rates (in %), 1970:1–1991:2

in less than 50% of the periods. For the United States,[9] for example, we displayed the one-month and the 5-year bond yields from January 1970 to February 1991 in Figure 8.8 ($T = 254$). Usually, the long rate is above the short rate, but there are a few periods of inversion where this is not the case, for example from June 1973 to March 1974.

Clearly the time series properties of the short-term interest rate are important for the cross-sectional relationships between the interest rates at different maturities. If the short rate follows an $AR(1)$ process we obtain the fairly simple expression in (8.85), for which we can note that the values of ξ_n are very sensitive to the precise value of θ, particularly for large maturities, if θ is close to unity. For more general time series processes, we obtain similar expressions but the result will not just involve the current short rate r_{1t}. Because the optimal predictor for an $AR(2)$ model, for example, depends upon the two last observations, an $AR(2)$ process for the short rate would give an expression similar to (8.85) that involves r_{1t} and $r_{1,t-1}$.

A debatable issue is that of stationarity. In many cases, the presence of a unit root in the short-term interest rate cannot be rejected *statistically*, but this does not necessarily mean that we have to accept the unit root hypothesis. *Economically*, it seems hard to defend non-stationarity of interest rates, although their persistence is known to be high. That is, even with stationarity it takes a very long time for the

---

[9] The data used in this section are taken from the McCulloch and Kwon data set (see McCulloch and Kwon, 1993). They are available in the files IRATES.

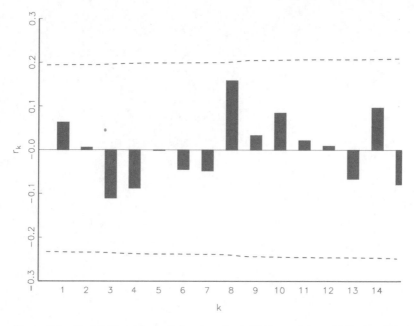

Figure 8.9 Residual autocorrelation function, $AR(1)$ model r_{1t}, 1970 : 1–1991 : 2

series to go back to its mean. Different authors make different judgements on this question and you will find empirical studies on the term structure of interest rates that choose either way. Let us first estimate an $AR(1)$ model for the one-month interest rate. Estimation by OLS gives (standard errors in parentheses):

$$r_{1t} = 0.350 + 0.951\ r_{1,t-1} + e_t, \quad \hat{\sigma} = 0.820. \tag{8.88}$$
$$\quad\ (0.152)\ \ (0.020)$$

The implied estimate for μ is $0.350/(1 - 0.951)$, which corresponds to approximately 7.2%, while the sample average is 7.3%. We can determine the Dickey–Fuller test statistic from this regression as $(0.951 - 1)/0.020 = -2.49$, which means that we cannot reject the null hypothesis of a unit root at the 5% nor the 10% level.[10] Because the $AR(1)$ model may be too restrictive, we also performed a number of augmented Dickey–Fuller tests with 1, 3 and 6 additional lags included. The resulting test statistics were: -2.63, -2.29 and -1.88, respectively. Only the first test implies a rejection at the 10% level. Thus, we find that a unit root in the short term interest rate cannot be rejected statistically. Despite this, we will not impose it a priori in the sequel.

The short term interest rate is surprisingly well described by the first order autoregressive process in (8.88). Estimating $AR(2)$ or $ARMA(1,1)$ specifications, for example, does not result in a significant improvement. The estimated autocorrelation function of the residuals of the $AR(1)$ model is given in Figure 8.9. It shows that we are unable to reject the null hypothesis that the error term in (8.88) is a white noise process.

---

[10] From Table 8.1, the appropriate critical values are -2.88 and -2.57, respectively.

Table 8.5 The term structure of interest rates

	Quarterly $n = 3$	Annual $n = 12$	5-year $n = 60$
value of ξ_n with $\theta = 0.95$	0.951	0.766	0.318
value of ξ_n with $\theta = 1$	1	1	1
OLS estimate of ξ_n	1.009	0.947	0.739
(standard error)	(0.009)	(0.017)	(0.028)
R^2 of regression	0.982	0.929	0.735

A way to test the expectations hypothesis is to regress a long interest rate on the short rate, that is

$$r_{nt} = \beta_1 + \beta_2 r_{1t} + u_t. \tag{8.89}$$

If (8.85) is taken to be literally true, the error term in this regression should be negligibly small (that is, the R^2 should be rather close to unity) and the true value of β_2 should equal ξ_n. The results of these regressions for maturities $n = 3$, 12 and 60 are given in Table 8.5. Given the high sensitivity of ξ_n with respect to θ, which was not significantly different from one, the estimated values for ξ_n do not, a priori, seem in conflict with the time series model for the short rate. It must be said, however, that the R^2 of the regression with the 5-year bond yield is fairly low. This implies that other factors affect the long term yield in addition to the short rate. One explanation is time variation in the risk premium Φ_n. Alternatively, the presence of measurement errors in the interest rates may reduce their cross-sectional correlations.

At a more general level, the above example illustrates the delicate dependence of long-run forecasts on the imposition of a unit root. While the estimated value of 0.95 is not significantly different from one, imposing the unit root hypothesis would imply that interest rates follow a random walk and that the forecast for *any* future period is the last observation, in this case 5.68%. Using $\theta = 0.95$, the optimal forecast 10 periods ahead is 6.3%, while the forecast for a 5-year horizon is virtually identical to the unconditional mean of the series, 7.2%.

8.10 Autoregressive Conditional Heteroskedasticity

In financial time series one often observes what is referred to as **volatility clustering**. In this case big shocks (residuals) tend to be followed by big shocks in either direction, and small shocks tend to follow small shocks. For example, stock markets are typically characterized by periods of high volatility and more 'relaxed' periods of low volatility. This is particularly true at high frequencies, for example with daily or weekly returns, but less clear at lower frequencies. One way to model such patterns is to allow the variance of ε_t to depend upon its history.

8.10.1 ARCH and GARCH Models

The seminal paper in this area is Engle (1982), which proposes the concept of **auto-regressive conditional heteroskedasticity (ARCH)**. It says that the variance of the error term at time t depends upon the squared error terms from previous periods. The most simple form is

$$\sigma_t^2 \equiv E\{\varepsilon_t^2 | \mathcal{I}_{t-1}\} = \varpi + \alpha \varepsilon_{t-1}^2, \tag{8.90}$$

where $\mathcal{I}_{t-1}$ denotes the information set, typically including ε_{t-1} and its entire history. This specification is called an **ARCH(1)** process. To ensure that $\sigma_t^2 \geq 0$ irrespective of ε_{t-1}^2 we need to impose that $\varpi \geq 0$ and $\alpha \geq 0$. The ARCH(1) model says that when a big shock happens in period $t-1$ it is more likely that ε_t has a large (absolute) value as well. That is, when ε_{t-1}^2 is large, the variance of the next innovation ε_t is also large.

The specification in (8.90) does not imply that the process for ε_t is nonstationary. It just says that the squared values ε_t^2 and ε_{t-1}^2 are correlated. The *unconditional* variance of ε_t is given by

$$\sigma^2 = E\{\varepsilon_t^2\} = \varpi + \alpha E\{\varepsilon_{t-1}^2\}$$

and has a stationary solution

$$\sigma^2 = \frac{\varpi}{1 - \alpha} \tag{8.91}$$

provided that $0 \leq \alpha < 1$. Note that the unconditional variance does not depend upon t.

The ARCH(1) model is easily extended to an **ARCH(p)** process, which we can write as

$$\sigma_t^2 = \varpi + \alpha_1 \varepsilon_{t-1}^2 + \alpha_2 \varepsilon_{t-2}^2 + \cdots + \alpha_p \varepsilon_{t-p}^2 = \varpi + \alpha(L)\varepsilon_{t-1}^2, \tag{8.92}$$

where $\alpha(L)$ is a lag polynomial of order $p-1$. To ensure that the conditional variance is non-negative ϖ and the coefficients in $\alpha(L)$ must be non-negative. To ensure that the process is stationary it is also required that $\alpha(1) < 1$. The effect of a shock j periods ago on current volatility is determined by the coefficient α_j. In an ARCH(p) model, old shocks of more than p periods ago have no effect on current volatility.

The presence of ARCH errors in a regression or autoregressive model does not invalidate OLS estimation. It does imply, however, that more efficient (nonlinear) estimators exist than OLS. More importantly, it may be of interest to predict future variances, for example, because they correspond to the riskiness of an investment. Consequently, it is relevant to test for the presence of ARCH effects and, if needed, to estimate the model allowing for it. Testing for p-th order autoregressive heteroskedasticity can be done along the lines of the Breusch–Pagan test for heteroskedasticity discussed in Chapter 4. It suffices to run an auxiliary regression of squared OLS residuals e_t^2 upon lagged squares $e_{t-1}^2, \ldots, e_{t-p}^2$ and a constant and compute T times the R^2. Under the null hypothesis of homoskedasticity ($\alpha_1 = \cdots = \alpha_p = 0$) the resulting test statistic asymptotically follows a Chi-squared distribution with p degrees of freedom. In other words, testing homoskedasticity against the alternative that the errors follow an ARCH(p) process is very simple.

ARCH models have been generalized in many different ways. A useful variant, proposed by Bollerslev (1986), is the generalized ARCH or **GARCH** model. In its general form, a GARCH(p, q) model can be written as

$$\sigma_t^2 = \varpi + \sum_{j=1}^{p} \alpha_j \varepsilon_{t-j}^2 + \sum_{j=1}^{q} \beta_j \sigma_{t-j}^2 \tag{8.93}$$

or

$$\sigma_t^2 = \varpi + \alpha(L)\varepsilon_{t-1}^2 + \beta(L)\sigma_{t-1}^2, \tag{8.94}$$

where $\alpha(L)$ and $\beta(L)$ are lag polynomials. In practice a GARCH(1, 1) specification often performs very well. It can be written as

$$\sigma_t^2 = \varpi + \alpha\varepsilon_{t-1}^2 + \beta\sigma_{t-1}^2, \tag{8.95}$$

which has only three unknown parameters to estimate. Non-negativity of σ_t^2 requires that ϖ, α and β are non-negative. If we define the surprise in squared returns as $v_t \equiv \varepsilon_t^2 - \sigma_t^2$, the GARCH(1, 1) process can be rewritten as

$$\varepsilon_t^2 = \varpi + (\alpha + \beta)\varepsilon_{t-1}^2 + v_t - \beta v_{t-1},$$

which shows that the squared errors follow an $ARMA(1, 1)$ process. While the error v_t is uncorrelated over time (because it is a surprise term), it does exhibit heteroskedasticity. The root of the autoregressive part is $\alpha + \beta$, so that stationarity requires that $\alpha + \beta < 1$. Values of $\alpha + \beta$ close to unity imply that the persistence in volatility is high.[11] Noting that,[12] under stationarity, $E\{\varepsilon_{t-1}^2\} = E\{\sigma_{t-1}^2\} = \sigma^2$, the unconditional variance of ε_t can be written as

$$\sigma^2 = \varpi + \alpha\sigma^2 + \beta\sigma^2$$

or

$$\sigma^2 = \frac{\varpi}{1 - \alpha - \beta}. \tag{8.96}$$

We can recursively substitute lags of (8.95) into itself to obtain

$$\sigma_t^2 = \varpi(1 + \beta + \beta^2 + \cdots) + \alpha(\varepsilon_{t-1}^2 + \beta\varepsilon_{t-2}^2 + \beta^2\varepsilon_{t-3}^2 + \cdots)$$

$$= \frac{\varpi}{1 - \beta} + \alpha\sum_{j=1}^{\infty} \beta^{j-1}\varepsilon_{t-j}^2, \tag{8.97}$$

which shows that the GARCH(1,1) specification is equivalent to an infinite order ARCH model with geometrically declining coefficients. It implies that the effect of a shock on current volatility decreases over time. Consequently, a GARCH specification may provide a parsimonious alternative to a higher order ARCH process. Equation (8.97) can also be rewritten as

$$\sigma_t^2 - \sigma^2 = \alpha\sum_{j=1}^{\infty} \beta^{j-1}(\varepsilon_{t-j}^2 - \sigma^2), \tag{8.98}$$

which is convenient for forecasting.

Many alternative specifications to model conditional volatility are proposed in the literature, corresponding to a variety of different acronyms (see Bollerslev, Chou and Kroner, 1992; Bera and Higgins, 1993; Bollerslev, Engle and Nelson, 1994; or Diebold and Lopez, 1995, for a review). An important restriction of the ARCH and

---

[11] The integrated GARCH(1,1) or IGARCH(1,1) process arises when $\alpha + \beta = 1$ and volatility shocks have a permanent effect (see Engle and Bollerslev, 1986).

[12] The equality that follows only holds if ε_t does not exhibit autocorrelation.

GARCH specifications above is their symmetry: only the absolute value of the innovations matters, not their sign. That is, a big negative shock has the same impact on future volatility as a big positive shock of the same magnitude. An interesting extension is towards asymmetric volatility models, in which good news and bad news have a different impact on future volatility. Note that the distinction between good and bad news is more sensible for stock markets than for exchange rates, where agents typically are on both sides of the market. That is, good news for one agent may be bad news for another.

An asymmetric model should allow for the possibility that an unexpected drop in price ('bad news') has a larger impact on future volatility than an unexpected increase in price ('good news') of similar magnitude. A fruitful approach to capture such asymmetries is provided by Nelson's (1990) **exponential GARCH** or **EGARCH** model, given by

$$\log \sigma_t^2 = \varpi + \beta \log \sigma_{t-1}^2 + \gamma \frac{\varepsilon_{t-1}}{\sigma_{t-1}} + \alpha \frac{|\varepsilon_{t-1}|}{\sigma_{t-1}}, \qquad (8.99)$$

where α, β and γ are constant parameters. Because the level $\varepsilon_{t-1}/\sigma_{t-1}$ is included, the EGARCH model is asymmetric as long as $\gamma \neq 0$. When $\gamma < 0$, positive shocks generate less volatility than negative shocks ('bad news'). It is possible to extend the EGARCH model by including additional lags. Note that we can rewrite (8.99) as

$$\log \sigma_t^2 = \varpi + \beta \log \sigma_{t-1}^2 + (\gamma + \alpha) \frac{\varepsilon_{t-1}}{\sigma_{t-1}} \quad \text{if } \varepsilon_{t-1} > 0$$

$$= \varpi + \beta \log \sigma_{t-1}^2 + (\gamma - \alpha) \frac{\varepsilon_{t-1}}{\sigma_{t-1}} \quad \text{if } \varepsilon_{t-1} < 0.$$

The logarithmic transformation guarantees that variances will never become negative. Typically, one would expect that $\gamma + \alpha > 0$ while $\gamma < 0$.

Engle and Ng (1993) characterize a range of alternative models for conditional volatility by a so-called **news impact curve**, which describes the impact of the last return shock (news) on current volatility (keeping all information dated $t - 2$ or before constant and fixing all lagged conditional variances at the unconditional variance σ^2). Compared to GARCH(1, 1) the EGARCH model has an asymmetric news impact curve (with a larger impact for negative shocks). Moreover, because the effect upon σ_t^2 is exponential, rather than quadratic, the news impact curve of the EGARCH model typically has larger slopes (see Engle and Ng, 1993).

Financial theory tells us that certain sources of risk are priced by the market. That is, assets with more 'risk' may provide higher average returns to compensate it. If σ_t^2 is an appropriate measure of risk, the conditional variance may enter the conditional mean function of y_t. One variant of the **ARCH-in-mean** or **ARCH-M** model of Engle, Lilien and Roberts (1987) specifies that

$$y_t = x_t'\theta + \delta\sigma_t^2 + \varepsilon_t,$$

where ε_t is described by an ARCH(p) process (with conditional variance σ_t^2). Campbell, Lo and MacKinlay (1997, Section 12.2) provide additional discussion on the links between ARCH-M models and asset pricing models, like the CAPM discussed in Section 2.7.

8.10.2 Estimation and Prediction

There are different approaches to the estimation of conditional volatility models. Let us assume that ε_t is the error term of a model like[13] $y_t = x_t'\theta + \varepsilon_t$, where x_t may include lagged values of y_t. As a special case x_t is just a constant. Furthermore, let the conditional variance of ε_t be described by an ARCH(p) process. Now, if we make assumptions about the (conditional) distribution of ε_t we can estimate the model by maximum likelihood. To see how, let

$$\varepsilon_t = \sigma_t v_t \quad \text{with} \quad v_t \sim NID(0,1).$$

This implies that *conditional* upon the information in $\mathcal{I}_t$ the innovation ε_t is normal with mean zero and variance σ_t^2. It does not imply, however, that the *unconditional* distribution of ε_t is normal, because σ_t becomes a random variable if we do not condition upon $\mathcal{I}_t$. Typically, the unconditional distribution has fatter tails than a normal one. From this, we can write down the conditional distribution of y_t as

$$f(y_t|x_t,\mathcal{I}_t) = \frac{1}{\sqrt{2\pi\sigma_t^2}} \exp\left\{-\frac{1}{2}\left(\varepsilon_t^2/\sigma_t^2\right)\right\}$$

where $\sigma_t^2 = \varpi + \alpha_1\varepsilon_{t-1}^2 + \cdots + \alpha_p\varepsilon_{t-p}^2$ and $\varepsilon_t = y_t - x_t'\theta$. From this, the loglikelihood function can be determined as the sum over all t of the log of the above expression, substituting the appropriate expressions for σ_t^2 and ε_t. The result can be maximized in the usual way with respect to θ, $\alpha_1,\ldots,\alpha_p$ and ϖ. Imposing the stationarity condition ($\sum_{j=1}^p \alpha_j < 1$) and the non-negativity condition ($\alpha_j \geq 0$ for all j) may be difficult in practice, so that large values for p are not recommended.

Even if v_t does not have a standard normal distribution, the above maximum likelihood procedure may provide consistent estimators for the model parameters, even though the likelihood function is incorrectly specified. The reason is that under some fairly weak assumptions, the first order conditions of the maximum likelihood procedure are also valid when v_t is not normally distributed. This is referred to as **quasi-maximum likelihood estimation** (see Section 6.4). Some adjustments have to be made, however, for the computation of the standard errors (see Hamilton, 1994, p. 663 for details).

A computationally simpler approach would be feasible GLS (see Chapter 4). In this case, θ is first estimated consistently by applying OLS. Second, a regression is done of the squared OLS residuals e_t^2 upon $e_{t-1}^2,\ldots,e_{t-p}^2$ and a constant. This is the same regression that was used for the heteroskedasticity test described above. The fitted values from this regression are estimates for σ_t^2 and can be used to transform the model and compute a weighted least squares (EGLS) estimator for θ. This approach only works well if the fitted values for σ_t^2 are all strictly positive. Moreover, it does not provide asymptotically efficient estimators for the ARCH parameters.

Forecasting the conditional variance from an ARCH(p) model is straightforward. To see this, rewrite the model 'in deviations from means' as

$$\sigma_t^2 - \sigma^2 = \alpha_1(\varepsilon_{t-1}^2 - \sigma^2) + \cdots + \alpha_p(\varepsilon_{t-p}^2 - \sigma^2)$$

---

[13] To avoid confusion with the GARCH parameters, the regression coefficients are referred to as θ.

with $\sigma^2 = \varpi/(1 - \alpha_1 \cdots - \alpha_p)$. Assuming for notational convenience that the model parameters are known, the one-period ahead forecast follows as

$$\sigma_{t+1|t}^2 \equiv E\{\varepsilon_{t+1}^2 | \mathcal{I}_t\} = \sigma^2 + \alpha_1(\varepsilon_t^2 - \sigma^2) + \cdots + \alpha_p(\varepsilon_{t-p+1}^2 - \sigma^2).$$

This is analogous to predicting from an $AR(p)$ model for y_t as discussed in Section 8.8. Forecasting the conditional volatility more than one period ahead can be done using the recursive formula

$$\sigma_{t+h|t}^2 \equiv E\{\varepsilon_{t+h}^2 | \mathcal{I}_t\} = \sigma^2 + \alpha_1(\sigma_{t+h-1|t}^2 - \sigma^2) + \cdots + \sigma_p(\sigma_{t+h-p|t}^2 - \sigma^2),$$

where $\sigma_{t+j|t}^2 = \varepsilon_{t+j}^2$ if $j \leq 0$. The h-period ahead forecast converges to the unconditional variance σ^2 if h becomes large (assuming that $\alpha_1 + \cdots + \alpha_p < 1$).

For a GARCH model prediction and estimation can take place along the same lines if we use (8.97), (8.98) or a higher order generalization. For example, the one-period ahead forecast for a GARCH(1,1) model is given by

$$\sigma_{t+1|t}^2 = \sigma^2 + (\alpha + \beta)(\sigma_t^2 - \sigma^2)$$

where $\sigma_t^2 = \sigma^2 + \alpha \sum_{j=1}^{\infty} \beta^{j-1}(\varepsilon_{t-j}^2 - \sigma^2)$. The h-period ahead forecast can be written as

$$\sigma_{t+h|t}^2 = \sigma^2 + (\alpha + \beta)^h(\sigma_t^2 - \sigma^2),$$

which shows that the volatility forecasts converge to the unconditional variance at a rate $\alpha + \beta$. For EGARCH models estimation can also be done by maximum likelihood, although simple closed-form expressions for multi-period forecasts are not available. Empirically the likelihood function for an EGARCH model is more difficult to maximize and problems of nonconvergence occasionally occur.

8.10.3   Illustration: Volatility in Daily Exchange Rates

To illustrate some of the volatility models discussed above, we consider a series of daily exchange rates between the US$ and the Deutsche Mark (DM) from 1 January 1980 to 21 May 1987. Excluding days for which no prices our quoted (New Year's day etc.), this results in a total of $T = 1867$ observations. As (log) exchange rates are to a rough approximation described by a random walk, we consider a model where y_t is the change in the log exchange rate and the conditional mean only includes an intercept. The series for y_t is plotted in Figure 8.10, which shows the existence of periods with low volatility and periods with high volatility.

The OLS residuals e_t of regressing y_t upon a constant correspond, of course, with y_t minus its sample average. On the basis of these residuals we can perform tests for ARCH effects, by regressing e_t^2 upon a constant and p of its lags. A test of homoskedasticity against ARCH(1) errors produces a test statistic (computed as T times the R^2 of the auxiliary regression) of 21.77, which is highly significant for a Chisquared distribution with one degree of freedom. Similarly, we can test against ARCH(6) errors with a statistic of 83.46, which also results in a clear rejection of the homoskedasticity assumption.

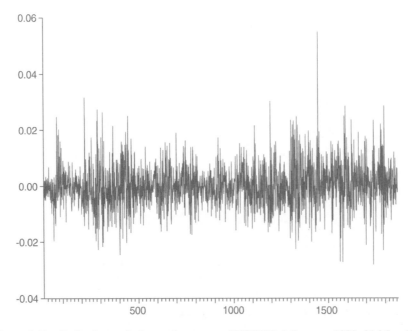

Figure 8.10   Daily change in log exchange rate US$/DM, 2 January 1980–21 May 1987

The following three models are estimated: an ARCH(6), a GARCH(1, 1) and a standard exponential GARCH model[14] (EGARCH(1, 1)) and we present the results in Table 8.6. All specifications are estimated by maximum likelihood assuming that the conditional distribution of the errors is normal. The results for the ARCH(6) specification show that all 6 lags have a significant and positive effect. Moreover, the coefficients do not appear to decrease to zero very quickly. The more parsimonious GARCH(1, 1) model also indicates that the effect of lagged shocks dies out only very slowly. The estimated value of $\alpha + \beta$ is 0.976, so that the estimated process is close to being nonstationary. For the exponential GARCH model we do not find evidence of asymmetry as the γ coefficient has a t-ratio of only -1.37. As indicated above, this is not an unusual finding for exchange rates. The large coefficient for $\log \sigma_t^2$ also reflects the high degree of persistence in exchange rate volatility.

To compare the alternative volatility models, Figure 8.11 plots the estimated standard deviations $\hat{\sigma}_t$ as implied by the parameter estimates. To minimize the impact of initial conditions and to appreciate the differences across models we only present results for the five months of 1987. The graph shows that the volatility implied by the ARCH(6) specification is less smooth than those for the GARCH(1, 1) and EGARCH(1, 1) models. Apparently, six lags are insufficient to capture the persistence of volatility.

---

[14] Standard software for these models is available, for example in MicroFit or EViews. Depending on the optimization routine, starting values and convergence criteria used by these programs, the estimation results may be slightly different.

Table 8.6 GARCH estimates for change in log exchange rate US$/DM

	ARCH(6)	GARCH(1,1)		EGARCH
constant	0.000	0.016		−0.483
	(0.000)	(0.005)		(0.090)
ε_{t-1}^2	0.091	0.110	$|\varepsilon_{t-1}|/\sigma_t$	0.215
	(0.027)	(0.016)		(0.026)
ε_{t-2}^2	0.080	—		
	(0.025)			
ε_{t-3}^2	0.123	—		
	(0.029)			
ε_{t-4}^2	0.138	—		
	(0.033)			
ε_{t-5}^2	0.123	—		
	(0.029)			
ε_{t-6}^2	0.102	—		
	(0.030)			
σ_{t-1}^2	—	0.868	$\log(\sigma_{t-1}^2)$	0.968
		(0.018)		(0.009)
			$\varepsilon_{t-1}/\sigma_t$	−0.017
				(0.013)

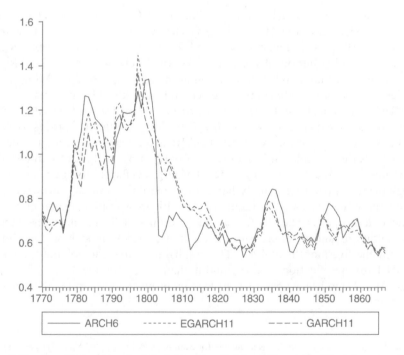

Figure 8.11 Conditional standard deviations implied by different models, 1 January–21 May 1987

8.11   What about Multivariate Models?

This chapter has concentrated on a more or less pure statistical approach of fitting an adequate time series model (from the class of ARMA models) to an observed time series. This is what we referred to as univariate time series modelling. In real life, it is obvious that many economic variables are related to each other. This, however, does not imply that a pure time series analysis is wrong. Building structural models in which variables are linked to each other (often based on economic theory) is a different branch. It gives insight into the interrelationships between variables and *how* a certain policy (shock) affects the economy (not just what its final effect is). Of course, these advantages do require a 'correct' representation of the underlying economy. In the time series approach, one is more concerned with predicting future values, including future uncertainty (variances). To this end, (in univariate time series analysis) only the history of the variable under concern is taken into account. As said before, from the predictive point of view, a pure time series approach often outperforms a more structural approach.

To illustrate the relationships, assume that the following regression model describes the relationship between two variables y_t and x_t,

$$y_t = \beta x_t + \varepsilon_t,$$

where ε_t is a white noise error term. If x_t can be described by some ARMA model, then y_t is the sum of an ARMA process and a white noise process and will therefore also follow an ARMA process. For example, if x_t can be described by a first order moving average model

$$x_t = u_t + \alpha u_{t-1},$$

where u_t is a white noise error independent of ε_t, then we can write

$$y_t = \beta u_t + \alpha \beta u_{t-1} + \varepsilon_t.$$

From this, we can easily derive that the autocovariances of y_t are $V\{y_t\} = \sigma_\varepsilon^2 + \beta^2(1 + \alpha^2)\sigma_u^2$, $\text{cov}\{y_t, y_{t-1}\} = \beta^2 \alpha \sigma_u^2$ and $\text{cov}\{y_t, y_{t-k}\} = 0$ for $k = 2, 3, \ldots$. Consequently, y_t follows a first order moving average process, with parameters that can be solved from the above covariances. Thus, the fact that two variables are related does not imply that a pure times series approach is invalid.

In the next chapter, we shall extend the univariate time series approach to a multivariate setting. This allows us to consider the time series properties of a number of series simultaneously, along with their short-run and long-run dependencies.

Exercises

Exercise 8.1   (ARMA Models and Unit Roots)

A researcher uses a sample of 200 quarterly observations on Y_t, the number (in 1000s) of unemployed persons, to model the time series behaviour of the series and to generate predictions. First, he computes the sample autocorrelation function, with the following results:

k	1	2	3	4	5	6	7	8	9	10
$\hat{\rho}_k$	0.83	0.71	0.60	0.45	0.44	0.35	0.29	0.20	0.11	−0.01

a. What do we mean by the sample autocorrelation function? Does the above pattern indicate that an autoregressive or moving average representation is more appropriate? Why?

Next, the sample partial autocorrelation function is determined. It is given by

k	1	2	3	4	5	6	7	8	9	10
$\hat{\theta}_{kk}$	0.83	0.16	−0.09	0.05	0.04	−0.05	0.01	0.10	−0.03	−0.01

b. What do we mean by the sample partial autocorrelation function? Why is the first partial autocorrelation equal to the first autocorrelation coefficient (0.83)?

c. Does the above pattern indicate that an autoregressive or moving average representation is more appropriate? Why?

The researcher decides to estimate, as a first attempt, a first order autoregressive model given by

$$Y_t = \delta + \theta Y_{t-1} + \varepsilon_t. \tag{8.100}$$

The estimated value for θ_1 is 0.83 with a standard error of 0.07.

d. Which estimation method is appropriate for estimating the $AR(1)$ model? Explain why it is consistent.

e. The researcher wants to test for a unit root. What is meant by 'a unit root'? What are the implications of the presence of a unit root? Why are we interested in it? (Give statistical or economic reasons.)

f. Formulate the hypothesis of a unit root and perform a unit root test based on the above regression.

g. Perform a test for the null hypothesis that $\theta = 0.90$.

Next, the researcher extends the model to an $AR(2)$, with the following results (standard errors in parentheses):

$$Y_t = \begin{array}{ccc} 50.0 & + \ 0.74 \ Y_{t-1} & + \ 0.16 \ Y_{t-2} + \hat{\varepsilon}_t. \\ (5.67) & (0.07) & (0.07) \end{array} \tag{8.101}$$

h. Would you prefer the $AR(2)$ model to the $AR(1)$ model? How would you check whether an $ARMA(2, 1)$ model may be more appropriate?

i. What do the above results tell you about the validity of the unit root test of **f**?

j. How would you test for the presence of a unit root in the $AR(2)$ model?

k. From the above estimates, compute an estimate for the average number of unemployed $E\{Y_t\}$.

l. Suppose the last two quarterly unemployment levels for 1996-III and 1996-IV were 550 and 600, respectively. Compute predictions for 1997-I and 1997-II.

m. Can you say anything sensible about the predicted value for the quarter 2023-I? (And its accuracy?)

Exercise 8.2   (Modelling Daily Returns–Empirical)

In the files SP500 daily returns on the S&P 500 index are available from January 1981 to April 1991 ($T = 2783$). Returns are computed as first differences of the log of the S&P 500 US stock price index.

a. Plot the series and determine the sample autocorrelation and partial autocorrelation function.

b. Estimate an $AR(1)$ up to $AR(7)$ model and test the individual and joint significance of the AR coefficients. Why would a significance level of 1% or less be more appropriate than the usual 5%?

c. Perform Ljung–Box tests on residual autocorrelation in these seven models for $K = 6$ (when appropriate), 12 and 18.

d. Compare AIC and BIC values. Use them, along with the results of the statistical tests, to choose a preferred specification.

For the next questions use your preferred specification.

e. Save the residuals of your model and test against p-th order autoregressive heteroskedasticity (choose several alternative values for p).

f. Re-estimate your model allowing for ARCH(p) errors (where p is chosen on the basis of the above tests). Compare the estimates with those of the test regressions.

g. Re-estimate your model allowing for GARCH(1,1) errors. Is there any indication of nonstationarity?

h. Re-estimate your model allowing for EGARCH errors. (Be sure to check that the program has converged.) Is there any evidence for asymmetry?

9 Multivariate Time Series Models

In the previous chapter we considered models for the stochastic process of a single economic time series. One reason why it may be more interesting to consider several series simultaneously is that it may improve forecasts. For example, the history of a second variable, X_t say, may help forecasting future values of Y_t. It is also possible that particular values of X_t are associated with particular movements in the Y_t variable. For example, oil price shocks may be helpful in explaining gasoline consumption. In addition to the forecasting issue, this also allows us to consider 'what if' questions. For example, what is the expected future development of gasoline consumption if oil prices are decreasing by 10% over the next couple of years?

In this chapter we consider multivariate time series models. In Section 9.1, we shall consider explaining one variable from its own past including current or lagged values of a second variable. This way, the dynamic effects of a change in X_t upon Y_t can be modelled and estimated. To apply standard estimation or testing procedures in a dynamic time series model, it is typically required that the various variables are stationary, since the majority of econometric theory is built upon the assumption of stationarity. For example, regressing a nonstationary variable Y_t upon a nonstationary variable X_t may lead to a so-called **spurious regression**, in which estimators and test statistics are misleading. The use of nonstationary variables not necessarily results in invalid estimators. An important exception arises when two or more $I(1)$ variables are **cointegrated**, that is, if there exists a particular linear combination of these *nonstationary* variables which is *stationary*. In such cases a long-run relationship between these variables exists. Often, economic theory suggests the existence of such long-run or equilibrium relationships, for example, purchasing power parity or the quantity theory of money. The existence of a long-run relationship also has its implications for the short-run behaviour of the $I(1)$ variables, because there has to be some mechanism that drives the variables to their long-run equilibrium relationship. This mechanism is modelled by an **error-correction mechanism**, in which the 'equilibrium error' also drives the short-run dynamics of the series. Section 9.2 introduces the concept of cointegration and relates it to error-correction models in the context where only two variables are involved. In Section 9.3 an empirical illustration is provided on purchasing power parity, which can be characterized as corresponding to a long-run cointegrating relationship.

Another starting point of multivariate time series analysis is the multivariate generalization of the ARMA processes of Chapter 8. This is the topic of Section 9.4, where particular emphasis is placed on **vector autoregressive models** (VARs). The existence of cointegrating relationships between the variables in the VAR has important implications on the way it can be estimated and represented. Section 9.5 discusses how hypotheses regarding the number of cointegrating relationships can be tested, and how an error-correction model representing the data can be estimated. Finally, Section 9.6 concludes with an empirical illustration.

There exists a fairly large number of recent textbooks on time series analysis that discuss cointegration, vector autoregressions and error-correction models. For economists attractive choices are Mills (1990), Enders (1995), Harris (1995), and Franses (1998). More technical detail is provided in, for example, Banerjee, Dolado, Galbraith and Hendry (1993), Hamilton (1994), Johansen (1995) and Boswijk (1999). Most of these texts also discuss topics that are not covered in this chapter, including structural VARs, Granger causality, seasonality and structural breaks.

9.1 Dynamic Models with Stationary Variables

Considering an economic time series in isolation and applying techniques from the previous chapter to model it, may provide good forecasts in many cases. It does not, however, allow us to determine what the effects are of, for example, a change in a policy variable. To do so, it is possible to include additional variables in the model. Let us consider two (stationary) variables[1] Y_t and X_t, and assume that it holds that

$$Y_t = \delta + \theta Y_{t-1} + \phi_0 X_t + \phi_1 X_{t-1} + \varepsilon_t. \tag{9.1}$$

As an illustration, we can think of Y_t as 'company sales' and X_t as 'advertising', both in month t. If we assume that ε_t is a white noise process, independent of $X_t, X_{t-1}, \ldots$ and $Y_{t-1}, Y_{t-2}, \ldots$, the above relation is sometimes referred to as an **autoregressive distributed lag** model.[2] To estimate it consistently, we can simply use ordinary least squares.

The interesting element in (9.1) is that it describes the dynamic effects of a change in X_t upon current and future values of Y_t. Taking partial derivatives, we can derive that the immediate response is given by

$$\partial Y_t / \partial X_t = \phi_0. \tag{9.2}$$

---

[1] In line with the previous chapter we use capital letters to denote the original series and small letters for deviations from the mean.

[2] More details can be found in, for example, Davidson and MacKinnon (1993, Sect. 19.4) or Johnston and Dinardo (1997, Chapter 8).

Sometimes this is referred to as the **impact multiplier**. An increase in X with one unit has an immediate impact on Y of ϕ_0 units. The effect after one period is

$$\partial Y_{t+1}/\partial X_t = \theta \partial Y_t/\partial X_t + \phi_1 = \theta\phi_0 + \phi_1, \tag{9.3}$$

and after two periods

$$\partial Y_{t+2}/\partial X_t = \theta \partial Y_{t+1}/\partial X_t = \theta(\theta\phi_0 + \phi_1) \tag{9.4}$$

and so on. This shows that after the first period, the effect is decreasing if $|\theta| < 1$. Imposing this so-called stability condition allows us to determine the long-run effect of a unit change in X_t. It is given by the **long-run multiplier** (or equilibrium multiplier)

$$\phi_0 + (\theta\phi_0 + \phi_1) + \theta(\theta\phi_0 + \phi_1) + \cdots = \phi_0 + (1 + \theta + \theta^2 + \cdots)(\theta\phi_0 + \phi_1) = \frac{\phi_0 + \phi_1}{1 - \theta}. \tag{9.5}$$

This says that if advertising X_t increases with one unit, the expected cumulative increase in sales is given by $(\phi_0 + \phi_1)/(1 - \theta)$. If the increase in X_t is permanent, the long-run multiplier also has the interpretation of the expected long-run permanent increase in Y_t. From (9.1) the long-run equilibrium relation between Y and X can be seen to be (imposing $E\{Y_t\} = E\{Y_{t-1}\}$)

$$E\{Y_t\} = \delta + \theta E\{Y_t\} + \phi_0 E\{X_t\} + \phi_1 E\{X_t\} \tag{9.6}$$

or

$$E\{Y_t\} = \frac{\delta}{1 - \theta} + \frac{\phi_0 + \phi_1}{1 - \theta} E\{X_t\}, \tag{9.7}$$

which presents an alternative derivation of the long-run multiplier. We shall write (9.7) shortly as $E\{Y_t\} = \alpha + \beta E\{X_t\}$, with obvious definitions of α and β.

There is an alternative way to formulate the autoregressive distributed lag model from (9.1). Subtracting Y_{t-1} from both sides of (9.1) and some rewriting gives

$$\Delta Y_t = \delta - (1 - \theta)Y_{t-1} + \phi_0 \Delta X_t + (\phi_0 + \phi_1)X_{t-1} + \varepsilon_t$$

or

$$\Delta Y_t = \phi_0 \Delta X_t - (1 - \theta)[Y_{t-1} - \alpha - \beta X_{t-1}] + \varepsilon_t. \tag{9.8}$$

This formulation is an example of an **error-correction model**. It says that the change in Y_t is due to the current change in X_t plus an error-correction term. If Y_{t-1} is above the equilibrium value that corresponds to X_{t-1}, that is if the 'equilibrium error' in square brackets is positive, an additional negative adjustment in Y_t is generated. The speed of adjustment is determined by $1 - \theta$, which is the adjustment parameter. Assuming stability ensures that $1 - \theta > 0$.

It is also possible to consistently estimate the error-correction model by least squares. Because the residual sum of squares that is minimized with (9.8) is the same as that of (9.1), the resulting estimates are numerically identical.[3]

Both the autoregressive distributed lag model in (9.1) and the error-correction model in (9.8) assume that the values of X_t can be treated as given, that is, as being

---

[3] The model in (9.8) can be estimated by nonlinear least squares or by OLS after reparametrization and solving for the original parameters from the resulting estimates. The results are the same.

uncorrelated with the equations' error terms. Essentially this says that (9.1) is appropriately describing the expected value of Y_t given its own history and conditional upon current and lagged values of X_t. If X_t is simultaneously determined with Y_t and $E\{X_t\varepsilon_t\} \neq 0$, OLS in either (9.1) or (9.8) would be inconsistent. The typical solution in this context is to consider a bivariate model for both Y_t and X_t (see Section 9.5 below).

Special cases of the model in (9.1) can be derived from alternative models, that have some economic interpretation. For example, let Y_t^* denote the optimal or desired level of Y_t and assume that

$$Y_t^* = \alpha + \beta X_t + \eta_t, \tag{9.9}$$

for some unknown coefficients α and β, and where η_t is an error term independent of $X_t, X_{t-1}, \ldots$. The actual value Y_t differs from Y_t^* because adjustment to its optimal level corresponding to X_t is not immediate. Suppose that the adjustment is only partial in the sense that

$$Y_t - Y_{t-1} = (1 - \theta)(Y_t^* - Y_{t-1}) \tag{9.10}$$

where $0 < \theta < 1$. Substituting (9.9) we obtain

$$Y_t = Y_{t-1} + (1 - \theta)\alpha + (1 - \theta)\beta X_t - (1 - \theta)Y_{t-1} + (1 - \theta)\eta_t$$
$$= \delta + \theta Y_{t-1} + \phi_0 X_t + \varepsilon_t, \tag{9.11}$$

where $\delta = (1 - \theta)\alpha$, $\phi_0 = (1 - \theta)\beta$ and $\varepsilon_t = (1 - \theta)\eta_t$. This is a special case of (9.1) as it does not include X_{t-1}. The model given by (9.9) and (9.10) is referred to as a **partial adjustment model**.

The autoregressive distributed lag model in (9.1) can be easily generalized. Restricting attention to two variables only, we can write a general form as

$$\theta(L)Y_t = \delta + \phi(L)X_t + \varepsilon_t, \tag{9.12}$$

where

$$\theta(L) = 1 - \theta_1 L - \cdots - \theta_p L^p$$
$$\phi(L) = \phi_0 + \phi_1 L + \cdots + \phi_q L^q$$

are two lag polynomials. Note that the constant in $\phi(L)$ is not restricted to be one. Assuming that $\theta(L)$ is invertible (see Subsection 8.2.2), we can write

$$Y_t = \theta^{-1}(1)\delta + \theta^{-1}(L)\phi(L)X_t + \theta^{-1}(L)\varepsilon_t. \tag{9.13}$$

The coefficients in the lag polynomial $\theta^{-1}(L)\phi(L)$ describe the dynamic effects of X_t upon current and future values of Y_t. The long-run effect of X_t is obtained as

$$\theta^{-1}(1)\phi(1) = \frac{\phi_0 + \phi_1 + \cdots + \phi_q}{1 - \theta_1 - \cdots - \theta_p}, \tag{9.14}$$

which generalizes the result above. Recall from Subsection 8.2.2 that invertibility of $\theta(L)$ requires that $\theta_1 + \theta_2 + \cdots + \theta_p < 1$, which guarantees that the denominator in (9.14) is nonzero.

A special case arises if $\theta(L) = 1$, so that the model in (9.13) does not contain any lags of Y_t. This is referred to as a distributed lag model. Sometimes restrictions are imposed upon the ϕ_j coefficients to reduce collinearity problems and to save degrees of freedom (see Greene, 2000, Sect. 17.2, or Judge et al., 1988, Sect. 17.3, for a discussion).

As long as it can be assumed that the error term ε_t is a white noise process, or – more generally – is stationary and independent of $X_t, X_{t-1}, \ldots$ and $Y_{t-1}, Y_{t-2}, \ldots$, the distributed lag models can be estimated consistently by ordinary least squares. Problems may arise, however, if along with Y_t and X_t the implied ε_t is also non-stationary. This is discussed in the next section.

9.2 Models with Nonstationary Variables

9.2.1 Spurious Regressions

The assumption that the Y_t and X_t variables are stationary is crucial for the properties of standard estimation and testing procedures. To show consistency of the OLS estimator, for example, we typically use the result that when the sample size increases, sample (co)variances converge to population (co)variances. Unfortunately, when the series are nonstationary the latter (co)variances are ill-defined because the series are not fluctuating around a constant mean.

As an illustration, consider two variables, Y_t and X_t, generated by two independent random walks,

$$Y_t = Y_{t-1} + \varepsilon_{1t}, \qquad \varepsilon_{1t} \sim IID(0, \sigma_1^2) \tag{9.15}$$

$$X_t = X_{t-1} + \varepsilon_{2t}, \qquad \varepsilon_{2t} \sim IID(0, \sigma_2^2) \tag{9.16}$$

where ε_{1t} and ε_{2t} are mutually independent. There is nothing in this data generating mechanism that leads to a relationship between Y_t and X_t. A researcher, unfamiliar with these processes, may want to estimate a regression model explaining Y_t from X_t and a constant,[4]

$$Y_t = \alpha + \beta X_t + \varepsilon_t. \tag{9.17}$$

The results from this regression are likely to be characterized by a fairly high R^2 statistic, highly autocorrelated residuals and a significant value for β. This phenomenon is the well-known problem of nonsense or **spurious regressions** (see Granger and Newbold, 1974). In this case, two independent nonstationary series are spuriously related due to fact that they are both trended. As argued by Granger and Newbold, in these situations, characterized by a high R^2 and a low Durbin–Watson (dw) statistic, the usual t- and F-tests on the regression parameters may be very misleading. The reason for this is that the distributions of the conventional test statistics are very different from those derived under the assumption of stationarity. In particular, as shown by Phillips (1986), the OLS estimator does not converge in probability as the sample size increases, the t- and F-test statistics do not have well-defined asymptotic distributions, and the dw statistic converges to zero. The reason is that with Y_t and X_t being $I(1)$ variables, the error term ε_t will also be a nonstationary $I(1)$ variable.

---

[4] To ensure consistent notation throughout this chapter, the constant term is denoted by α and the slope coefficient by β. It will be clear from what follows that the role of the constant is often fundamentally different from the slope coefficients when variables are nonstationary.

Table 9.1 Spurious regression: OLS involving two independent random walks

Dependent variable: Y

Variable	Estimate	Standard error	t-ratio
constant	3.9097	0.2462	15.881
X	−0.4435	0.0473	−9.370

$s = 3.2698 \quad R^2 = 0.3072 \quad \bar{R}^2 = 0.3037 \quad F = 87.7987 \quad dw = 0.1331$

To illustrate the spurious regression result, we generated two series of 200 observations[5] according to (9.15) and (9.16) with normal error terms, starting with $Y_0 = X_0 = 0$ and setting $\sigma_1^2 = \sigma_2^2 = 1$. The results of a standard OLS regression of Y_t upon X_t and a constant are presented in Table 9.1. While the parameter estimates in this table would be completely different from one simulation to the next, the t-ratios, R^2 and dw statistic show a very typical pattern: using the usual significance levels both the constant term and X_t are highly significant, the R^2 of 31% seems reasonable, while the Durbin–Watson statistic is extremely low. (Remember from Chapter 4 that values close to 2 correspond to the null hypothesis of no autocorrelation.) *Estimation results like this should not be taken seriously.* Because both Y_t and X_t contain a stochastic trend, the OLS estimator tends to find a significant correlation between the two series, even if they are completely unrelated. Statistically, the problem is that ε_t is nonstationary.

If lagged values of both the dependent and independent variables are included in the regression, as in (9.1), no spurious regression problem arises because there exist parameter values (viz. $\theta = 1$ and $\phi_0 = \phi_1 = 0$) such that the error term ε_t is $I(0)$, even if Y_t and/or X_t are $I(1)$. In this case the OLS estimator is consistent for all parameters. Thus, including lagged values in the regression is sufficient to solve many of the problems associated with spurious regression (see Hamilton, 1994, p. 562).

9.2.2 Cointegration

An important exception to the results in the previous subsection arises when there exists a particular relationship between the two nonstationary series. Consider again the two random walk series Y_t and X_t, but suppose that there is indeed a (linear) relationship between Y_t and X_t. This is reflected in the proposition that there exists some value β such that $Y_t - \beta X_t$ is $I(0)$, although Y_t and X_t are both $I(1)$. In such a case it is said that Y_t and X_t are **cointegrated**. Although the relevant asymptotic theory is nonstandard, it can be shown that one can consistently estimate β from an OLS regression of Y_t on X_t as in (9.17). In fact, in this case, the OLS estimator b is said to be **super consistent** for β, because it converges to β at a much faster rate than with conventional asymptotics. In the standard case, we have that $\sqrt{T}(b - \beta)$ is asymptotically normal and we say that b is $\sqrt{T}$-consistent for β. In the cointegration case, $\sqrt{T}(b - \beta)$ is degenerate, which means that b converges to β at such a fast rate that the difference $b - \beta$, multiplied by an increasing $\sqrt{T}$ factor, still converges to zero. Instead, the appropriate asymptotic distribution is the one of $T(b - \beta)$. Consequently, conventional inference procedures do not apply.

---

[5] These simulated series are available in SPURIOUS.

The intuition behind the super consistency result is quite straightforward. Suppose the estimated regression model is

$$Y_t = a + bX_t + e_t. \qquad (9.18)$$

For the true value of β, $Y_t - \beta X_t$ is $I(0)$. Clearly, for $b \neq \beta$, the OLS residual e_t will be nonstationary and hence will have a very large variance in any finite sample. For $b = \beta$, however, the estimated variance of e_t will be much smaller. Since ordinary least squares chooses a and b to minimize the sample variance of e_t, it is extremely good in finding an estimate close to β.

If Y_t and X_t are both $I(1)$ and there exists a β such that $Z_t = Y_t - \beta X_t$ is $I(0)$, Y_t and X_t are cointegrated, with β being called the cointegrating parameter, or, more generally, $(1, -\beta)'$ being called the **cointegrating vector**. When this occurs, a special constraint operates on the long-run components of Y_t and X_t. Since both Y_t and X_t are $I(1)$, they will be dominated by 'long wave' components, but Z_t, being $I(0)$, will not be: Y_t and βX_t must therefore have long-run components that virtually cancel out to produce Z_t.

This idea is related to the concept of a **long-run equilibrium**. Suppose that such an equilibrium is defined by the relationship

$$Y_t = \alpha + \beta X_t. \qquad (9.19)$$

Then $z_t = Z_t - \alpha$ is the 'equilibrium error', which measures the extent to which the value of Y_t deviates from its 'equilibrium value' $\alpha + \beta X_t$. If z_t is $I(0)$, the equilibrium error is stationary and fluctuating around zero. Consequently, the system will, on average, be in equilibrium. However, if Y_t and X_t are not cointegrated and, consequently, z_t is $I(1)$, the equilibrium error can wander widely and zero-crossings would be very rare. Under such circumstances, it does not make sense to refer to $Y_t = \alpha + \beta X_t$ as a long-run equilibrium. Consequently, the presence of a cointegrating vector can be interpreted as the presence of a long-run equilibrium relationship.

From the discussion above, it is obvious that it is important to distinguish cases where there is a cointegrating relationship between Y_t and X_t and spurious regression cases. Suppose we know from previous results that Y_t and X_t are integrated of order one, and suppose we estimate the 'cointegrating regression'

$$Y_t = \alpha + \beta X_t + \varepsilon_t. \qquad (9.20)$$

If Y_t and X_t are cointegrated the error term in (9.20) is $I(0)$. If not, ε_t will be $I(1)$. Hence, one can test for the presence of a cointegrating relationship by testing for a unit root in the OLS residuals e_t from (9.20). It seems that this can be done by using the Dickey–Fuller tests of the previous section. For example, one can run the regression,

$$\Delta e_t = \gamma_0 + \gamma_1 e_{t-1} + u_t \qquad (9.21)$$

and test whether $\gamma_1 = 0$ (a unit root). There is, however, an additional complication in testing for unit roots in OLS residuals rather than in observed time series. Because the OLS estimator 'chooses' the residuals in the cointegrating regression (9.20) to have as small a sample variance as possible, even if the variables are not cointegrated, the OLS estimator will make the residuals 'look' as stationary as possible. Thus using standard DF or ADF tests we may reject the null hypothesis of nonstationarity too often. As a result, the appropriate critical values are more negative than those for the

Table 9.2 Asymptotic critical values residual unit root tests for cointegration (with constant term) (Davidson and MacKinnon, 1993)

Number of variables (incl. Y_t)	Significance level		
	1%	5%	10%
2	−3.90	−3.34	−3.04
3	−4.29	−3.74	−3.45
4	−4.64	−4.10	−3.81
5	−4.96	−4.42	−4.13

standard Dickey–Fuller tests and are presented in Table 9.2. If e_t is not appropriately described by a first order autoregressive process, one should add lagged values of Δe_t to (9.21), leading to the augmented Dickey–Fuller (ADF) tests, with the same asymptotic critical values. This test can be extended to test for cointegration between three or more variables. If more than a single X_t variable is included in the cointegrating regression, the critical values shift further to the left. This is reflected in the additional rows in Table 9.2.

An alternative test for cointegration is based on the usual Durbin–Watson statistic from (9.20). Note that the presence of a unit root in ε_t asymptotically corresponds with a zero value for the *dw* statistic. Thus under the null hypothesis of a unit root, the appropriate test is whether *dw* is significantly larger than *zero*. Unfortunately, critical values for this test, commonly referred to as the **Cointegrating Regression Durbin–Watson test** or **CRDW test** (see Sargan and Bhargava, 1983), depend upon the process that generated the data. When the data are generated by a random walk, 5% critical values are given in Table 9.3 for a number of different sample sizes. Note that when T goes to infinity, and Y_t and X_t are not cointegrated, the *dw* statistic converges to zero (in probability).

Note that the cointegration tests discussed here test the presence of a unit root in regression residuals. This implies that the null hypothesis of a unit root corresponds to *no* cointegration. So, if we cannot reject the presence of a unit root in the OLS residuals, this implies that we *cannot reject* that Y_t and X_t are *not* cointegrated. Alternatively, we would reject the presence of a unit root and thus that the two variables are not cointegrated.

If Y_t and X_t are cointegrated, OLS applied to (9.20) produces a super consistent estimator of the cointegrating vector, even if short-run dynamics are incorrectly omitted. The reason for this is that the nonstationarity asymptotically dominates all forms of misspecification in the stationary part of (9.20). Thus, incomplete short-run dynamics, autocorrelation in ε_t, omitted (stationary) variables, endogeneity

Table 9.3 5% Critical values CRDW tests for cointegration (Banerjee *et al.*, 1993)

Number of variables (incl. Y_t)	Number of observations		
	50	100	200
2	0.72	0.38	0.20
3	0.89	0.48	0.25
4	1.05	0.58	0.30
5	1.19	0.68	0.35

of X_t are all problems in the stationary part of the regression which can be neglected (that is, are of lower order) when looking at the asymptotic distribution of the super consistent estimator b. Thus, asymptotically[6] it is never necessary to include, e.g. seasonal dummy variables in the cointegrating regression. One can even interchange the role of Y_t and X_t and estimate

$$X_t = \alpha^* + \beta^* Y_t + u_t^*, \qquad (9.22)$$

to get super consistent estimates of $\alpha^* = -\alpha/\beta$ and $\beta^* = 1/\beta$. It is important to note that this would not occur if Y_t and X_t were stationary, in which case the distinction between endogenous and exogenous variables is crucial. For example, if (Y_t, X_t) is i.i.d. bivariate normal with expectations zero, variances σ_y^2, σ_x^2 and covariance σ_{xy}, the conditional expectation of Y_t given X_t equals $\sigma_{xy}/\sigma_x^2 X_t = \beta X_t$ and the conditional expectation of X_t given Y_t is $\sigma_{xy}/\sigma_y^2 Y_t = \beta^* Y_t$ (see Appendix B). Note that $\beta^* \neq 1/\beta$, unless Y_t and X_t are perfectly correlated ($\sigma_{xy} = \sigma_x \sigma_y$). As perfect correlation also implies that the R^2 equals unity, this also suggests that the R^2 obtained from a cointegrating regression should be quite high (as it converges to one if the sample size increases).

Although the existence of a long-run relationship between two variables is of interest, it may be even more relevant to analyse the short-run properties of the two series. This can be done using the result that the presence of a cointegrating relationship implies that there exists an error-correction model that describes the short-run dynamics consistently with the long-run relationship.

9.2.3   Cointegration and Error-correction Mechanisms

The Granger representation theorem (Granger, 1983; Engle and Granger, 1987) states that if a set of variables are cointegrated, then there exists a valid **error-correction representation** of the data. Thus, if Y_t and X_t are both $I(1)$ and have a cointegrating vector $(1, -\beta)'$, there exists an error-correction representation, with $Z_t = Y_t - \beta X_t$, of the form

$$\theta(L)\Delta Y_t = \delta + \phi(L)\Delta X_{t-1} - \gamma Z_{t-1} + \alpha(L)\varepsilon_t, \qquad (9.23)$$

where ε_t is white noise[7] and where $\theta(L)$, $\phi(L)$ and $\alpha(L)$ are polynomials in the lag operator L (with $\theta_0 \equiv 1$). Let us consider a special case of (9.23),

$$\Delta Y_t = \delta + \phi_1 \Delta X_{t-1} - \gamma(Y_{t-1} - \beta X_{t-1}) + \varepsilon_t, \qquad (9.24)$$

where the error term has no moving average part and the systematic dynamics are kept as simple as possible. Intuitively, it is clear why the Granger representation theorem should hold. If Y_t and X_t are both $I(1)$ but have a long-run relationship, there must be some force which pulls the equilibrium error back towards zero. The error-correction model does exactly this: it describes how Y_t and X_t behave in the

---

[6] It must be mentioned that Monte Carlo studies indicate that in small samples the bias in the estimated cointegrating relation may be substantial, despite the super consistency property (see Banerjee *et al.*, 1993, Sect. 7.4). Typically, these biases are small if the R^2 of the cointegrating regression is close to unity. A large number of alternative estimators has been proposed in the literature (see Hargreaves, 1994, for a review).

[7] The white noise term ε_t is assumed to be independent of both $Y_{t-1}, Y_{t-2}, \ldots$ and $X_{t-1}, X_{t-2}, \ldots$.

short-run consistent with a long-run cointegrating relationship. If the cointegrating parameter β is known, all terms in (9.24) are $I(0)$ and no inferential problems arise: we can estimate it by OLS in the usual way.

When $\Delta Y_t = \Delta X_{t-1} = 0$ we obtain the 'no change' steady state equilibrium

$$Y_t - \beta X_t = \frac{\delta}{\gamma}, \tag{9.25}$$

which corresponds with (9.19) if $\alpha = \delta/\gamma$. In this case the error-correction model can be written as

$$\Delta Y_t = \phi_1 \Delta X_{t-1} - \gamma(Y_{t-1} - \alpha - \beta X_{t-1}) + \varepsilon_t, \tag{9.26}$$

where the constant is only present in the long-run relationship. If, however, the error-correction model (9.24) contains a constant that equals $\delta = \alpha\gamma + \lambda$, with $\lambda \neq 0$, this implies deterministic trends in both Y_t and X_t and the long-run equilibrium corresponds to a steady state growth path with $\Delta Y_t = \Delta X_{t-1} = \lambda/(1 - \phi_1)$. Recall from Chapter 8 that a nonzero intercept in a univariate ARMA model with a unit root also implies that the series has a deterministic trend.

In some cases it makes sense to assume that the cointegrating vector is known a priori (e.g. when the only sensible equilibrium is $Y_t = X_t$). In that case, inferences in (9.23) or (9.24) can be made in a standard way. If β is unknown, the cointegrating vector can be estimated (super) consistently from the cointegrating regression (9.20). Consequently, with standard $\sqrt{T}$ asymptotics, one can ignore the fact that β is estimated and apply conventional theory to the estimation of the parameters in (9.23).

Note that the precise lag structure in (9.23) is not specified by the theorem, so we probably need to do some specification analysis in this direction. Moreover, the theory is symmetric in its treatment of Y_t and X_t, so that there should also exist an error-correction representation with ΔX_t as the left-hand side variable. Because at least one of the variables has to adjust to deviations from the long-run equilibrium, at least one of the adjustment parameters γ in the two error-correction equations has to be nonzero. If X_t does not adjust to the equilibrium error (has a zero adjustment parameter), it is weakly exogenous for β (as defined by Engle, Hendry and Richard, 1983). This means that we can include ΔX_t in the right hand side of (9.24) without affecting the error-correction term $-\gamma(Y_{t-1} - \beta X_{t-1})$. That is, we can condition upon X_t in the error-correction model for Y_t (see Section 9.5 below).

The representation theorem also holds conversely, i.e. if Y_t and X_t are both $I(1)$ and have an error-correction representation, then they are necessarily cointegrated. It is important to realize that the concept of cointegration can be applied to (non-stationary) integrated time series only. If Y_t and X_t are $I(0)$ the generating process can always be written in an error-correction form (see Section 9.1).

9.3 Illustration: Long-run Purchasing Power Parity (Part 2)

In the previous chapter, we introduced the topic of purchasing power parity (PPP), which requires the exchange rate between two currencies to equal the ratio of the two countries' price levels. In logarithms, absolute PPP can be written as

$$s_t = p_t - p_t^*, \tag{9.27}$$

where s_t is the log of the spot exchange rate, p_t the log of domestic prices and p_t^* the log of foreign prices. Few proponents of PPP would argue for a strict adherence to PPP. Rather, PPP is usually seen as determining the exchange rate in the long-run, whilst a variety of other factors, such as trading restrictions, productivity and preference changes, may influence the exchange rate in conditions of disequilibrium. Consequently, (9.27) is viewed as an equilibrium or cointegrating relationship.

Using monthly observations for France and Italy from January 1981 until June 1996, as before, we are thus looking for a cointegrating relationship between p_t, p_t^* and s_t. In Section 8.5 we already concluded that nonstationarity of the real exchange rate $rs_t \equiv s_t - p_t + p_t^*$ could not be rejected. This implies that $(1, -1, 1)'$ is rejected as a cointegrating vector. In this section we test whether another cointegrating relationship exists, initially using only two variables: s_t, the log exchange rate and $ratio_t \equiv p_t - p_t^*$, the log of the price ratio. Intuitively, such relationship would imply that a change in relative prices corresponds to a less than (or more than) proportionate change in the exchange rate, while imposing symmetry. The corresponding cointegrating regression is

$$s_t = \alpha + \beta ratio_t + \varepsilon_t, \tag{9.28}$$

where $\beta = 1$ corresponds to (9.27). Note that p_t and p_t^* are not based on prices but price indices. Therefore, one may expect that the constant in (9.28) is different from zero. Consequently, we can only test for relative PPP instead of absolute PPP.

The evidence in Section 8.5 suggested that s_t was $I(1)$. For the log price ratio, $ratio_t$, the results of the (augmented) Dickey–Fuller tests are given in Table 9.4. Clearly, we cannot reject the null hypothesis of a unit root in $ratio_t$, a conclusion which is in line with what can be inferred from the graph in Figure 8.5.

We are now ready to estimate the cointegrating regression and test for cointegration between s_t and $p_t - p_t^*$. First, we estimate (9.28) by ordinary least squares. This gives the results in Table 9.5. The test for the existence of a cointegrating relationship is a test for stationarity of the residuals in this regression. We can test for a unit root in the residuals by means of the CRDW test, based on the Durbin–Watson statistic. Clearly, the value of 0.055 is not significant at any reasonable level of significance and consequently, we cannot reject the null hypothesis of a unit root in the residuals. Instead of the CRDW test we can also apply the augmented Dickey–Fuller tests, the results of which are given in Table 9.6. The appropriate 5% critical value is -3.37

Table 9.4   Unit root tests for log price ratio Italy vs. France

Statistic	Without trend	With trend
DF	−1.563	−2.692
ADF(1)	−0.993	−2.960
ADF(2)	−1.003	−2.678
ADF(3)	−1.058	−3.130
ADF(4)	−1.014	−2.562
ADF(5)	−1.294	−2.493
ADF(6)	−2.015	−3.096

Table 9.5 OLS results

Dependent variable: s_t (log exchange rate)

Variable	Estimate	Standard error	t-ratio
constant	5.4872	0.00678	809.706
$ratio_t = p_t - p_t^*$	0.9822	0.05133	19.136

$s = 0.0860$ $R^2 = 0.6656$ $\bar{R}^2 = 0.6638$ $F = 366.191$ $dw = 0.0555$ $T = 186$

Table 9.6 ADF (cointegration) tests of residuals

DF	−1.904		
ADF(1)	−1.850	ADF(4)	−1.910
ADF(2)	−1.896	ADF(5)	−1.946
ADF(3)	−1.952	ADF(6)	−2.249

(see Table 9.2). Again, the null hypothesis of a unit root cannot be rejected and, consequently, there is no evidence in the data that the spot exchange rate and the price ratio are cointegrated. This conclusion corresponds with that in, e.g. Corbae and Ouliaris (1988), who conclude that there is no long-run tendency for exchange rates and relative prices to settle down on an equilibrium track.

A potential explanation for this rejection is that the restriction imposed, viz. that p_t and p_t^* enter (9.28) with coefficient β and $-\beta$, respectively, is invalid, due to, for example, transportation costs or measurement error. We can estimate (9.28) with unconstrained coefficients, so that we can test the existence of a more general co-integrating relationship between the three variables, s_t, p_t and p_t^*. However, when we consider more than two-dimensional systems, the number of cointegrating relation-ships may be more than one. For example, there may be two different cointegrating relationships between three $I(1)$ variables, which makes that analysis somewhat more complicated than in the two-dimensional case. Section 9.5 will pay attention to the more general case.

When there exists only one cointegrating vector, we can estimate the cointegrating relationship, as before, by regressing one variable upon the other variables. This does require, however, that the cointegrating vector involves the left-hand side variable of this regression, because its coefficient is implicitly normalized to minus one. In our example, we regress s_t upon p_t and p_t^* to obtain the results reported in Table 9.7. The ADF tests on the residuals produce the results in Table 9.8, where the appropriate 5% critical value is −3.77 (see Table 9.2). Again, we have to conclude that we cannot reject the null hypothesis that there is no cointegrating relationship between the log exchange rate and the log price indices of France and Italy. It does not seem to be the

Table 9.7 OLS results

Dependent variable: s_t (log exchange rate)

Variable	Estimate	Standard error	t-ratio
constant	12.5092	0.5170	24.194
p_t	3.0964	0.1508	19.372
p_t^*	−4.6291	0.2710	−17.085

$s = 0.0609$ $R^2 = 0.8335$ $\bar{R}^2 = 0.8316$ $F = 357.902$ $dw = 0.1525$ $T = 186$

Table 9.8 ADF (cointegration) tests of residuals

DF	-2.806		
ADF(1)	-3.159	ADF(4)	-2.863
ADF(2)	-2.964	ADF(5)	-2.923
ADF(3)	-2.872	ADF(6)	-2.918

case that some (weak) form of purchasing power parity holds for these two countries. Of course, it could be the case that our sample period is just not long enough to find sufficient evidence for a cointegrating relationship. This seems to be in line with what people find in the literature. With longer samples, up to a century or more, the evidence is more in favour of some long-run tendency to PPP (see the survey in Froot and Rogoff, 1994).

9.4 Vector Autoregressive Models

The autoregressive moving average models of the previous chapter can be readily extended to the multivariate case, in which the stochastic process that generates the time series of a *vector* of variables is modelled. The most common approach is to consider a **vector autoregressive** model (**VAR**). A VAR describes the dynamic evolution of a number of variables from their common history. If we consider two variables, Y_t and X_t, say, the VAR consists of two equations. A first order VAR would be given by

$$Y_t = \delta_1 + \theta_{11} Y_{t-1} + \theta_{12} X_{t-1} + \varepsilon_{1t} \tag{9.29}$$

$$X_t = \delta_2 + \theta_{21} Y_{t-1} + \theta_{22} X_{t-1} + \varepsilon_{2t}, \tag{9.30}$$

where ε_{1t} and ε_{2t} are two white noise processes (independent of the history of Y and X) that may be correlated. If, for example, $\theta_{12} \neq 0$ it means that the history of X helps explaining Y. The system (9.29)–(9.30) can be written as

$$\begin{pmatrix} Y_t \\ X_t \end{pmatrix} = \begin{pmatrix} \delta_1 \\ \delta_2 \end{pmatrix} + \begin{pmatrix} \theta_{11} & \theta_{12} \\ \theta_{21} & \theta_{22} \end{pmatrix} \begin{pmatrix} Y_{t-1} \\ X_{t-1} \end{pmatrix} + \begin{pmatrix} \varepsilon_{1t} \\ \varepsilon_{2t} \end{pmatrix} \tag{9.31}$$

or, with appropriate definitions, as

$$\vec{Y}_t = \delta + \Theta_1 \vec{Y}_{t-1} + \vec{\varepsilon}_t, \tag{9.32}$$

where $\vec{Y}_t = (Y_t, X_t)'$ and $\vec{\varepsilon}_t = (\varepsilon_{1t}, \varepsilon_{2t})'$. This extends the first order autoregressive model from Chapter 8 to the more dimensional case. In general, a $VAR(p)$ model for a k-dimensional vector $\vec{Y}_t$ is given by

$$\vec{Y}_t = \delta + \Theta_1 \vec{Y}_{t-1} + \cdots + \Theta_p \vec{Y}_{t-p} + \vec{\varepsilon}_t, \tag{9.33}$$

where each Θ_j is a $k \times k$ matrix and $\vec{\varepsilon}_t$ is a k-dimensional vector of white noise terms with covariance matrix Σ. As in the univariate case, we can use the lag operator to define a matrix lag polynomial

$$\Theta(L) = I_k - \Theta_1 L - \cdots - \Theta_p L^p,$$

where I_k is the k-dimensional identity matrix, so that we can write the VAR as

$$\Theta(L) \vec{Y}_t = \delta + \vec{\varepsilon}_t.$$

The matrix lag polynomial is a $k \times k$ matrix where each element corresponds to a p-th order polynomial in L. Extensions to vectorial ARMA models (VARMA) can be obtained by premultiplying $\vec{\varepsilon}_t$ with a (matrix) lag polynomial.

The VAR model implies univariate ARMA models for each of its components. The advantages of considering the components simultaneously include that the model may be more parsimonious and includes less lags, and that more accurate forecasting is possible, because the information set is extended to also include the history of the other variables. From a different perspective, Sims (1980) has advocated the use of VAR models instead of structural simultaneous equations models because the distinction between endogenous and exogenous variables does not have to be made a priori, and 'arbitrary' constraints to ensure identification are not required (see, e.g. Canova, 1995 for a discussion). Like a reduced form a VAR is always identified.

The expected value of $\vec{Y}_t$ can be determined if we impose stationarity. This gives

$$E\{\vec{Y}_t\} = \delta + \Theta_1 E\{\vec{Y}_t\} + \cdots + \Theta_p E\{\vec{Y}_t\}$$

or

$$\mu = E\{\vec{Y}_t\} = (I - \Theta_1 - \cdots - \Theta_p)^{-1}\delta = \Theta(1)^{-1}\delta,$$

which shows that stationarity will require that the $k \times k$ matrix $\Theta(1)$ is invertible.[8] For the moment we shall assume that this is the case. As before, we can subtract the mean and consider $\vec{y}_t = \vec{Y}_t - \mu$, for which we have that

$$\vec{y}_t = \Theta_1 \vec{y}_{t-1} + \cdots + \Theta_p \vec{y}_{t-p} + \vec{\varepsilon}_t. \tag{9.34}$$

We can use the VAR model for forecasting in a straightforward way. For forecasting from the end of the sample period (period T), the relevant information set now includes the vectors $\vec{y}_T, \vec{y}_{T-1}, \ldots$, and we obtain for the optimal one-period ahead forecast

$$\vec{y}_{T+1|T} = E\{\vec{y}_{T+1}|\vec{y}_T, \vec{y}_{T-1}, \ldots\} = \Theta_1 \vec{y}_T + \cdots + \Theta_p \vec{y}_{T-p+1}. \tag{9.35}$$

The one-period ahead forecast error variance is simply $V\{\vec{y}_{T+1}|\vec{y}_T, \vec{y}_{T-1}, \ldots\} = \Sigma$. Forecasts more than one period ahead can be obtained recursively. For example,

$$\vec{y}_{T+2|T} = \Theta_1 \vec{y}_{T+1|T} + \cdots + \Theta_p \vec{y}_{T-p+2}$$

$$= \Theta_1(\Theta_1 \vec{y}_T + \cdots + \Theta_p \vec{y}_{T-p+1}) + \cdots + \Theta_p \vec{y}_{T-p+2}. \tag{9.36}$$

To estimate a vector autoregressive model we can simply use ordinary least squares equation by equation[9], which is consistent because the white noise terms are assumed to be independent of the history of $\vec{y}_t$. From the residuals of each of the k equations, $e_{1t}, \ldots, e_{kt}$, we can estimate the (i, j)-element in Σ as[10]

$$\hat{\sigma}_{ij} = \frac{1}{T - p} \sum_{t=p+1}^{T} e_{it} e_{jt}, \tag{9.37}$$

---

[8] Recall from Chapter 8 that in the $AR(p)$ case stationarity requires that $\theta(1) \neq 0$, so that $\theta(1)^{-1}$ exists.

[9] Because the explanatory variables are the same for each equation, a system estimator, like SUR (see Greene, 2000, Sect. 15.4), provides the same estimates as OLS applied to each equation separately. If different restrictions are imposed upon the equations, SUR estimation will be more efficient than OLS, though OLS remains consistent.

[10] Assuming that observations are available from $t = 1, \ldots, T$, the number of useful observations is $T - p$. Note that a degrees of freedom correction can be applied, as in the linear regression model (see Chapter 2).

so that

$$\hat{\Sigma} = \frac{1}{T-p} \sum_{t=p+1}^{T} \vec{e}_t \vec{e}_t', \tag{9.38}$$

where $\vec{e}_t = (e_{1t}, \ldots, e_{kt})'$.

Determining the lag length p in an empirical application is not always easy and univariate autocorrelation or partial autocorrelation functions will not help; see Canova (1995) for a discussion. A reasonable strategy is to estimate a VAR model for different values of p and then select on the basis of the Akaike or Schwarz information criteria, as discussed in Chapters 3 and 8, or on the basis of statistical significance.

If $\Theta(1)$ is invertible, it means that we can write the vector autoregressive model as a vector moving average model (VMA) by premultiplying with $\Theta(L)^{-1}$. This is similar to deriving the moving average representation of a univariate autoregressive model. This gives

$$\vec{Y}_t = \Theta(1)^{-1}\delta + \Theta(L)^{-1}\vec{\varepsilon}_t = \mu + \Theta(L)^{-1}\vec{\varepsilon}_t, \tag{9.39}$$

which describes each element in $\vec{Y}_t$ as a weighted sum of all current and past shocks in the system. Writing $\Theta(L)^{-1} = I_k + A_1 L + A_2 L^2 + \cdots$, we have that

$$\vec{Y}_t = \mu + \vec{\varepsilon}_t + A_1\vec{\varepsilon}_{t-1} + A_2\vec{\varepsilon}_{t-2} + \cdots \tag{9.40}$$

If the white noise vector $\vec{\varepsilon}_t$ increases by a vector d, the effect upon $\vec{Y}_{t+s}$ ($s > 0$) is given by $A_s d$. Thus the matrix

$$A_s = \frac{\partial \vec{Y}_{t+s}}{\partial \vec{\varepsilon}_t'} \tag{9.41}$$

has the interpretation that its (i, j)-element measures the effect of a one-unit increase in ε_{it} upon $Y_{j,t+s}$. If only the first element ε_{1t} of $\vec{\varepsilon}_t$ changes, the effects are given by the first column of A_s. The dynamic effects upon the j-th variable of such a one-unit increase are given by the elements in the first column and j-th row of $I_k, A_1, A_2, \ldots$. A plot of these elements as a function of s is called the **impulse-response function**. It measures the response of $Y_{j,t+s}$ to an impulse in Y_{1t}, keeping constant all other variables dated t and before. Although it may be hard to derive expressions for the elements in $\Theta(L)^{-1}$, the impulse-responses can be determined fairly easily by simulation methods (see Hamilton, 1994).

If $\Theta(1)$ is not invertible it cannot be the case that all variables in $\vec{Y}_t$ are stationary $I(0)$ series. At least one stochastic trend must be present. In the extreme case where we have k independent stochastic trends, all k variables are integrated of order one, while no cointegrating relationships exist. In this case $\Theta(1)$ is equal to a null matrix. The intermediate cases are more interesting: the rank of the matrix $\Theta(1)$ equals the number of linear combinations of variables in $\vec{Y}_t$ that are $I(0)$, that is determines the number of cointegrating vectors. This is the topic of the next section.

9.5   Cointegration: The Multivariate Case

When more than two variables are involved, cointegration analysis is somewhat more complex, because the cointegrating vector generalizes to a **cointegrating space**, the dimension of which is not known a priori. That is, when we have a set of k $I(1)$ variables, there may exist up to $k - 1$ independent linear relationships that are $I(0)$, while any linear combination of these relationships is – by construction – also $I(0)$. This implies that individual cointegrating vectors are no longer statistically identified; only the space spanned by these vectors is. Ideally, vectors in the cointegrating space can be found that have an economic interpretation and can be interpreted as representing long-run equilibria.

9.5.1   Cointegration in a VAR

If the variables of interest are stacked in the k-dimensional vector $\vec{Y}_t$, the elements of which are assumed to be $I(1)$, there may be different vectors β such that $Z_t = \beta' \vec{Y}_t$ is $I(0)$. That is, there may be more than one cointegrating vector β. It is clearly possible for several equilibrium relations to govern the long-run behaviour of the k variables. In general, there can be $r \leq k - 1$ linearly independent cointegrating vectors[11], which are gathered together into the $k \times r$ **cointegrating matrix**[12] β. By construction, the rank of the matrix[13] β is r, which will be called the **cointegrating rank** of $\vec{Y}_t$. This means that each element in the r-dimensional vector $\vec{Z}_t = \beta' \vec{Y}_t$ is $I(0)$, while each element in the k-dimensional vector $\vec{Y}_t$ is $I(1)$.

The Granger representation theorem (Engle and Granger, 1987) directly extends to this more general case and claims that if $\vec{Y}_t$ is cointegrated, there exists a valid error-correction representation of the data. While there are different ways to derive and describe such a representation, we shall here start from the vector autoregressive model for $\vec{Y}_t$ introduced in the previous section:

$$\vec{Y}_t = \delta + \Theta_1 \vec{Y}_{t-1} + \cdots + \Theta_p \vec{Y}_{t-p} + \vec{\varepsilon}_t \tag{9.42}$$

or

$$\Theta(L) \vec{Y}_t = \delta + \vec{\varepsilon}_t. \tag{9.43}$$

For the case with $p = 3$ we can write this as

$$\Delta \vec{Y}_t = \delta + (\Theta_1 + \Theta_2 - I_k) \vec{Y}_{t-1} - \Theta_2 \Delta \vec{Y}_{t-1} + \Theta_3 \vec{Y}_{t-3} + \vec{\varepsilon}_t$$
$$= \delta + (\Theta_1 + \Theta_2 + \Theta_3 - I_k) \vec{Y}_{t-1} - \Theta_2 \Delta \vec{Y}_{t-1} - \Theta_3 (\Delta \vec{Y}_{t-1} + \Delta \vec{Y}_{t-2}) + \vec{\varepsilon}_t,$$

or

$$\Delta \vec{Y}_t = \delta + \Gamma_1 \Delta \vec{Y}_{t-1} + \Gamma_2 \Delta \vec{Y}_{t-2} + (\Theta_1 + \Theta_2 + \Theta_3 - I_k) \vec{Y}_{t-1} + \vec{\varepsilon}_t,$$

---

[11] The existence of k cointegrating relationships between the k elements in $\vec{Y}_t$ would imply that there exist k independent linear combinations that are $I(0)$, such that, necessarily, all individual elements in $\vec{Y}_t$ must be $I(0)$. Clearly, this is in conflict with the definition of cointegration as a property of $I(1)$ variables, and it follows that $r \leq k - 1$.

[12] We follow the convention in the cointegration literature to denote the cointegrating *matrix* by a Greek lower case β.

[13] See Appendix A for the definition of the rank of a matrix.

where $\Gamma_1 = -\Theta_2 - \Theta_3$ and $\Gamma_2 = -\Theta_3$. Similarly, we can write for general values of p that[14]

$$\Delta \vec{Y}_t = \delta + \Gamma_1 \Delta \vec{Y}_{t-1} + \cdots + \Gamma_{p-1} \Delta \vec{Y}_{t-p-1} + \Pi \vec{Y}_{t-1} + \vec{\varepsilon}_t, \qquad (9.44)$$

where the 'long-run matrix'

$$\Pi \equiv -\Theta(1) = -(I_k - \Theta_1 - \cdots - \Theta_p) \qquad (9.45)$$

determines the long-run dynamic properties of $\vec{Y}_t$.[15] This equation is a direct generalization of the regressions used in the augmented Dickey–Fuller test. Because $\Delta \vec{Y}_t$ and $\vec{\varepsilon}_t$ are stationary (by assumption), it must be the case that $\Pi \vec{Y}_{t-1}$ in (9.44) is also stationary. This could reflect three different situations. First, if all elements in $\vec{Y}_t$ are integrated of order one and no cointegrating relationships exists, it must be the case that $\Pi = 0$ and (9.44) presents a (stationary) VAR model for $\Delta \vec{Y}_t$. Second, if all elements in $\vec{Y}_t$ are stationary $I(0)$ variables, the matrix $\Pi = -\Theta(1)$ must be of full rank and invertible so that we can write a vector moving average representation $\vec{Y}_t = \Theta^{-1}(L)(\delta + \vec{\varepsilon}_t)$. Third, if Π is of rank r $(0 < r < k)$ the elements in $\Pi \vec{Y}_{t-1}$ are linear combinations that are stationary. If the variables in $\vec{Y}_t$ are $I(1)$, these linear combinations must correspond to cointegrating vectors. This intermediate case is the most interesting one. If Π has a reduced rank of $r \le k - 1$, this means that there are r independent linear combinations of the k elements in $\vec{Y}_t$ that are stationary, that is: there exist r cointegrating relationships. Note that the existence of k cointegrating relationships is impossible: if k independent linear combinations produce stationary series, all k variables themselves must be stationary.

If Π has reduced rank it can be written as the product of a $k \times r$ matrix γ and an $r \times k$ matrix β' that both have rank r.[16] That is, $\Pi = \gamma \beta'$. Substituting this produces the model in error-correction form

$$\Delta \vec{Y}_t = \delta + \Gamma_1 \Delta \vec{Y}_{t-1} + \cdots + \Gamma_{p-1} \Delta \vec{Y}_{t-p+1} + \gamma \beta' \vec{Y}_{t-1} + \vec{\varepsilon}_t. \qquad (9.46)$$

The linear combinations $\beta' \vec{Y}_{t-1}$ present the r cointegrating relationships. The coefficients in γ measure how the elements in $\Delta \vec{Y}_t$ are adjusted to the r 'equilibrium errors' $\vec{Z}_{t-1} = \beta' \vec{Y}_{t-1}$. Thus, (9.46) is a generalization of (9.24) and is referred to as a **vector error-correction model (VECM)**.

If we take expectations in the error-correction model we can derive that

$$(I - \Gamma_1 - \cdots - \Gamma_{p-1}) E\{\Delta \vec{Y}_t\} = \delta + \gamma E\{\vec{Z}_{t-1}\}. \qquad (9.47)$$

There is no deterministic trend in any of the variables if $E\{\Delta \vec{Y}_t\} = 0$. Under the assumption that the matrix $(I - \Gamma_1 - \cdots - \Gamma_{p-1})$ is nonsingular, this requires that $\delta + \gamma E\{\vec{Z}_{t-1}\} = 0$ (compare Subsection 9.2.3), where $E\{\vec{Z}_{t-1}\}$ corresponds to the vector of intercepts in the cointegrating relations. If we impose this restriction,

---

[14] It is possible to rewrite the VAR such that any of the lags appears in levels on the right-hand side, with the same coefficients in the 'long run matrix' Π. For comparison with the univariate case, we choose for inclusion of the first lag.

[15] In the univariate case, the long-run properties are determined by $\theta(1)$, where $\theta(L)$ is the AR polynomial (see Chapter 8).

[16] This means that the r columns in γ are linearly independent, and that the r rows in β' are independent (see Appendix A).

intercepts appear in the cointegrating relationships only, and we can rewrite the error-correction model to include $\vec{z}_t = \vec{Z}_{t-1} - E\{\vec{Z}_{t-1}\}$ and have no intercepts, i.e.

$$\Delta \vec{Y}_t = \Gamma_1 \Delta \vec{Y}_{t-1} + \cdots + \Gamma_{p-1} \Delta \vec{Y}_{t-p+1} + \gamma(-\alpha + \beta' \vec{Y}_{t-1}) + \vec{\varepsilon}_t,$$

where α is an r-dimensional vector of constants, satisfying $E\{\beta' \vec{Y}_{t-1}\} = E\{\vec{Z}_{t-1}\} = \alpha$. As a result, all terms in this expression have mean zero and no deterministic trends exists.

If we add one common constant to the vector error-correction model, we obtain

$$\Delta \vec{Y}_t = \lambda + \Gamma_1 \Delta \vec{Y}_{t-1} + \cdots + \Gamma_{p-1} \Delta \vec{Y}_{t-p+1} + \gamma(-\alpha + \beta' \vec{Y}_{t-1}) + \vec{\varepsilon}_t,$$

where λ is a k-dimensional vector with identical elements λ_1. Now the long-run equilibrium corresponds to a steady state growth path with growth rates for all variables given by

$$E\{\Delta \vec{Y}_t\} = (I - \Gamma_1 - \cdots - \Gamma_{p-1})^{-1} \lambda.$$

The deterministic trends in each Y_{jt} are assumed to cancel out in the long-run, so that no deterministic trend is included in the error-correction term. We can go as far as allowing for $k - r$ separate deterministic trends that cancel out in the cointegrating relationships, in which case we are back at specification (9.46) without restrictions on δ. In this case, δ is capturing r intercept terms in the long-run relationships and $k - r$ different deterministic trends in the variables in $\vec{Y}_t$. If there would be more than $k - r$ separate deterministic trends, they cannot cancel out in $\beta' \vec{Y}_{t-1}$ and we should include a deterministic trend in the cointegrating equations. See Harris (1995, p. 96) for additional discussion and some alternatives.

9.5.2 Example: Cointegration in a Bivariate VAR

As an example, consider the case where $k = 2$. In this case the number of cointegrating vectors may be zero or one ($r = 0, 1$). Let us consider a first order (nonstationary) VAR for $\vec{Y}_t = (Y_t, X_t)'$. That is,

$$\begin{pmatrix} Y_t \\ X_t \end{pmatrix} = \begin{pmatrix} \theta_{11} & \theta_{12} \\ \theta_{21} & \theta_{22} \end{pmatrix} \begin{pmatrix} Y_{t-1} \\ X_{t-1} \end{pmatrix} + \begin{pmatrix} \varepsilon_{1t} \\ \varepsilon_{2t} \end{pmatrix},$$

where, for simplicity, we did not include intercept terms. The matrix Π is given by

$$\Pi = -\Theta(1) = \begin{pmatrix} \theta_{11} - 1 & \theta_{12} \\ \theta_{21} & \theta_{22} - 1 \end{pmatrix}.$$

This matrix is a zero matrix if $\theta_{11} = \theta_{22} = 1$ and $\theta_{12} = \theta_{21} = 0$. This corresponds to the case where Y_t and X_t are two random walks. The matrix Π has reduced rank if

$$(\theta_{11} - 1)(\theta_{22} - 1) - \theta_{21}\theta_{12} = 0. \tag{9.48}$$

If this is the case,

$$\beta' = (\theta_{11} - 1 \quad \theta_{12})$$

is a cointegrating vector (where we chose an arbitrary normalization) and we can write

$$\Pi = \gamma\beta' = \begin{pmatrix} 1 \\ \theta_{21}/(\theta_{11} - 1) \end{pmatrix} (\theta_{11} - 1 \quad \theta_{12}).$$

Using this, we can write the model in error-correction form. First, write

$$\begin{pmatrix} Y_t \\ X_t \end{pmatrix} = \begin{pmatrix} Y_{t-1} \\ X_{t-1} \end{pmatrix} + \begin{pmatrix} \theta_{11} - 1 & \theta_{12} \\ \theta_{21} & \theta_{22} - 1 \end{pmatrix} \begin{pmatrix} Y_{t-1} \\ X_{t-1} \end{pmatrix} + \begin{pmatrix} \varepsilon_{1t} \\ \varepsilon_{2t} \end{pmatrix}.$$

Next, we rewrite this as

$$\begin{pmatrix} \Delta Y_t \\ \Delta X_t \end{pmatrix} = \begin{pmatrix} 1 \\ \theta_{21}/(\theta_{11} - 1) \end{pmatrix} ((\theta_{11} - 1) Y_{t-1} + \theta_{12} X_{t-1}) + \begin{pmatrix} \varepsilon_{1t} \\ \varepsilon_{2t} \end{pmatrix}. \tag{9.49}$$

The error-correction form is thus quite simple, as it excludes any dynamics. Note that both Y_t and X_t adjust to the equilibrium error, because $\theta_{21} = 0$ is excluded. (Also note that $\theta_{21} = 0$ would imply $\theta_{11} = \theta_{22} = 1$ and no cointegration.)

The fact that the linear combination $Z_t = (\theta_{11} - 1) Y_t + \theta_{12} X_t$ is $I(0)$ also follows from this result. Note that we can write

$$\Delta Z_t = (\theta_{11} - 1 \quad \theta_{12}) \begin{pmatrix} 1 \\ \theta_{21}/(\theta_{11} - 1) \end{pmatrix} Z_{t-1} + (\theta_{11} - 1 \quad \theta_{12}) \begin{pmatrix} \varepsilon_{1t} \\ \varepsilon_{2t} \end{pmatrix}$$

or (using (9.48)):

$$Z_t = Z_{t-1} + (\theta_{11} - 1 + \theta_{22} - 1)Z_{t-1} + v_t = (\theta_{11} + \theta_{22} - 1)Z_{t-1} + v_t,$$

where $v_t = (\theta_{11} - 1)\varepsilon_{1t} + \theta_{12}\varepsilon_{2t}$ is a white noise error term. Consequently, Z_t is described by a stationary $AR(1)$ process unless $\theta_{11} = 1$ and $\theta_{22} = 1$, which was excluded.

9.5.3 *Testing for Cointegration*

If it is known that there exists at most one cointegrating vector, a simple approach to test for the existence of cointegration is the Engle–Granger approach described in Section 9.2.2. It requires running a regression of Y_{1t} (being the first element of $\vec{Y}_t$) on the other $k - 1$ variables $Y_{2t}, \ldots, Y_{kt}$ and testing for a unit root in the residuals. This can be done using the ADF tests on the OLS residuals applying the critical values from Table 9.2. If the unit root hypothesis is rejected, the hypothesis of no-cointegration is also rejected. In this case, the static regression gives consistent estimates of the cointegrating vector, while in a second stage, the error-correction model can be estimated using the estimated cointegrating vector from the first stage.

There are some problems with this Engle–Granger approach. First, the results of the tests are sensitive to the left-hand side variable of the regression, that is, to the normalization applied to the cointegrating vector. Second, if the cointegrating vector happens not to involve Y_{1t} but only $Y_{2t}, \ldots, Y_{kt}$, the test is not appropriate and the cointegrating vector will not be consistently estimated by a regression of Y_{1t} upon $Y_{2t}, \ldots, Y_{kt}$. Third, it is possible that more than one cointegrating relationship exists between the variables $Y_{1t}, \ldots, Y_{kt}$. If, for example, two distinct cointegrating relationships exist, OLS typically estimates a linear combination of them (see Hamilton, 1994, p. 590). Fortunately, as the null hypothesis for the cointegration tests is that there is *no* cointegration, the tests are still appropriate for their purpose.

An alternative approach that does not suffer from these drawbacks was proposed by Johansen (1988), who developed a maximum likelihood estimation procedure, which also allows one to test for the number of cointegrating relations. The details of the Johansen procedure are very complex and we shall only focus on a few aspects. Further details can be found in Johansen and Juselius (1990) and Johansen (1991), or in textbooks like Banerjee *et al.* (1993, Chapter 8); Hamilton (1994, Chapter 20); Johansen (1995, Chapter 11) and Stewart and Gill (1998, Sections 9.4 and 9.5). The starting point of the Johansen procedure is the VAR representation of $\vec{Y}_t$ given in (9.44) and reproduced here:

$$\Delta \vec{Y}_t = \delta + \Gamma_1 \Delta \vec{Y}_{t-1} + \cdots + \Gamma_{p-1} \Delta \vec{Y}_{t-p-1} + \Pi \vec{Y}_{t-1} + \vec{\varepsilon}_t, \tag{9.50}$$

where $\vec{\varepsilon}_t$ is $NID(0, \Sigma)$. Note that the use of maximum likelihood requires us to impose a particular distribution for the white noise terms. Assuming that $\vec{Y}_t$ is a vector of $I(1)$ variables, while r linear combinations of $\vec{Y}_t$ are stationary, we can write

$$\Pi = \gamma \beta', \tag{9.51}$$

where, as before, γ and β are of dimension $k \times r$. Again, β denotes the matrix of cointegrating vectors, while γ represents the matrix of weights with which each co-integrating vector enters each of the $\Delta \vec{Y}_t$ equations. The approach of Johansen is based on the estimation of the system (9.50) by maximum likelihood, while imposing the restriction in (9.51) for a given value of r.

The first step in the Johansen approach involves testing hypotheses about the rank of the long-run matrix Π, or – equivalently – the number of columns in β. For a given r, it can be shown (see, e.g. Hamilton, 1994, Sect. 20.2) that the ML estimate for β equals the matrix containing the r eigenvectors corresponding to the r largest (estimated) eigenvalues of a $k \times k$ matrix that can be estimated fairly easily using an OLS package. Let us denote the (theoretical) eigenvalues of this matrix in decreasing order as $\lambda_1 \geq \lambda_2 \geq \cdots \geq \lambda_k$. If there are r cointegrating relationships (and Π has rank r) it must be the case that $\log(1 - \lambda_j) = 0$ for the smallest $k - r$ eigenvalues, that is for $j = r+1, r+2, \ldots, k$. We can use the (estimated) eigenvalues, say $\hat{\lambda}_1 > \hat{\lambda}_2 > \cdots > \hat{\lambda}_k$, to test hypotheses about the rank of Π. For example, the hypothesis $H_0 : r \leq r_0$ versus the alternative $H_1 : r_0 < r \leq k$, can be tested using the statistic

$$\lambda_{\text{trace}}(r_0) = -T \sum_{j=r_0+1}^{k} \log(1 - \hat{\lambda}_j). \tag{9.52}$$

This test is the so-called **trace test**. It checks whether the smallest $k - r_0$ eigenvalues are significantly different from zero. Furthermore, we can test $H_0 : r \leq r_0$ versus the more restrictive alternative $H_1 : r = r_0 + 1$ using

$$\lambda_{\text{max}}(r_0) = -T \log(1 - \hat{\lambda}_{r_0+1}). \tag{9.53}$$

This alternative test is called the **maximum eigenvalue test**, as it is based on the estimated $(r_0 + 1)$th largest eigenvalue.

The two tests described here are actually likelihood ratio tests (see Chapter 6), but do not have the usual Chi-squared distributions. Instead, the appropriate distributions are multivariate extensions of the Dickey–Fuller distributions. As with the

Table 9.9 Critical values Johansen's LR tests for cointegration (Pesaran, Shin and Smith, 2000)

	λ_{trace}-statistic $H_0: r \leq r_0$ vs $H_1: r > r_0$		λ_{max}-statistic $H_0: r \leq r_0$ vs $H_1: r = r_0 + 1$	
$k - r_0$	5%	10%	5%	10%
Case 1: restricted intercepts in VAR (in cointegrating relations only)				
1	9.16	7.53	9.16	7.53
2	20.18	17.88	15.87	13.81
3	34.87	31.93	22.04	19.86
4	53.48	49.95	28.27	25.80
5	75.98	71.81	34.40	31.73
Case 2: unrestricted intercepts in VAR				
1	8.07	6.50	8.07	6.50
2	17.86	15.75	14.88	12.98
3	31.54	28.78	21.12	19.02
4	48.88	45.70	27.42	24.99
5	70.49	66.23	33.64	31.02

unit root tests, the percentiles of the distributions depend on the fact whether a constant (and a time trend) are included. Critical values for two cases are presented in Table 9.9. Case 1 assumes that there are no deterministic trends and includes r intercepts in the cointegrating relationships. Case 2 is based on the inclusion of k unrestricted intercepts in the VAR, which implies $k - r$ separate deterministic trends and r intercepts in the cointegration vectors. The critical values depend upon $k - r_0$, the number of nonstationary components under the null hypothesis. Note that when $k - r_0 = 1$ the two test statistics are identical and thus have the same distribution.

It is important to realize that the parameters γ and β are not uniquely identified in the sense that different combinations of γ and β can produce the same matrix $\Pi = \gamma\beta'$. This is because $\gamma\beta' = \gamma P P^{-1} \beta'$ for any invertible $r \times r$ matrix P. In other words, what the data can determine is the space spanned by the columns of β, the cointegration space, and the space spanned by γ. Consequently, the cointegrating vectors in β have to be normalized in some way to obtain unique cointegrating relationships. Often, it is hoped that these relationships have a sensible economic interpretation.

9.5.4 Illustration: Long-run Purchasing Power Parity (Part 3)

In this section, we reconsider the above example concerning long-run purchasing power parity. We shall analyse the existence of one or more cointegrating relationships between the three variables s_t, p_t and p_t^*, using Johansen's technique described in the previous section. This is a standard option available in, for example, MicroFit.

The first step in this procedure is the determination of p, the maximum order of the lags in the autoregressive representation given in (9.42). It appears that, in general, too few lags in the model leads to rejection of the null hypotheses too easily, while too many lags in the model decreases the power of the tests. This indicates that there is some optimal lag length. In addition to p, we have to decide upon whether to include a time trend in (9.42) or not. In the absence of a time trend, an intercept is automatically

Table 9.10   Maximum eigenvalue tests for cointegration

Null hypothesis	Alternative	λ_{max}-statistic	5% critical value
H_0: $r = 0$	H_1: $r = 1$	65.509	22.04
H_0: $r \leq 1$	H_1: $r = 2$	22.032	15.87
H_0: $r \leq 2$	H_1: $r = 3$	6.371	9.16

lag length $p = 3$ intercepts included $T = 183$
Estimated eigenvalues: 0.3009, 0.1134, 0.0342

included in the cointegrating relationship(s). Let us, more or less arbitrarily, consider the case with $p = 3$ excluding a time trend. The first step in Johansen's procedure yields the results[17] in Table 9.10. These results present the estimated eigenvalues $\hat{\lambda}_1, \ldots, \hat{\lambda}_k$ ($k = 3$) in descending order. Recall that each nonzero eigenvalue corresponds to a cointegrating vector. A range of test statistics based on these estimated eigenvalues is given as well. These results indicate that:

1. The null hypothesis of no cointegration ($r = 0$) has to be rejected at a 5% level, when tested against the hypothesis of one cointegrating vector ($r = 1$), because 65.5 exceeds the critical value of 22.04.
2. The null hypothesis of zero or one cointegrating vector ($r \leq 1$) also has to be rejected against the alternative of two cointegrating relationships ($r = 2$).
3. The null hypothesis of two or less cointegrating vectors cannot be rejected against the alternative of $r = 3$. Recall that $r = 3$ corresponds to stationarity of each of the three series, which was also rejected by the univariate unit root tests.

From these results we have to choose the number of cointegrating vectors. Given our previous results it is somewhat surprising that Johansen's tests seem to indicate the presence of two cointegrating relationships. In the first Engle–Granger steps, we could not reject no-cointegration in any of the cases we considered. A possible explanation for this finding may be that the number of lags in the VAR is too small. Similar to what we found before with the univariate unit root tests on p_t and p_t^*, the inclusion of too few lags may lead to the wrong conclusion that the series are stationary, or – in this case – are cointegrated.[18] Table 9.11 shows what happens if we repeat the above procedure with a lag length of $p = 12$, motivated by the fact that we have monthly data.

What is quite clear from these results is that the evidence in favour of one or two cointegrating vectors is much weaker than before. The first test that considers the null hypothesis of no cointegration ($r = 0$) versus the alternative of one cointegrating

Table 9.11   Maximum eigenvalue tests for cointegration

Null hypothesis	Alternative	λ_{max}-statistic	5% critical value
H_0: $r = 0$	H_1: $r = 1$	19.521	22.04
H_0: $r \leq 1$	H_1: $r = 2$	16.437	15.87
H_0: $r \leq 2$	H_1: $r = 3$	6.180	9.16

lag length $p = 12$ intercepts included $T = 174$
Estimated eigenvalues: 0.1061, 0.0901, 0.0349

---

[17] The results in this subsection are obtained by MicroFit 4.0, Oxford University Press.
[18] Note, for example, that the 'cointegrating' vector $(0, 0, 1)'$ corresponds to stationarity of the last element.

Table 9.12 Johansen estimation results

Estimated cointegrating vector

Variable		Normalized
s_t	−0.092	1.000
p_t	−1.354	6.347
p_t^*	0.058	−14.755

Based on VAR with $p = 12$

relationship ($r = 1$) does not lead to rejection of the null. The second test though, implies a marginal rejection of the hypothesis of the existence of zero or one cointegrating vectors. Suppose we continue our analysis despite our reservations, while we decide that the number of cointegrating vectors is equal to one ($r = 1$). The next part of the results consists of the estimated cointegrating vector β, presented in Table 9.12. The normalized cointegrating vector is given in the third column and corresponds to

$$s_t = 6.347p_t - 14.755p_t^*, \tag{9.54}$$

which does not seem to correspond to an economically interpretable long-run relationship.

As the conclusion that there exists one cointegrating relationship between our three variables is most probably incorrect, we do not pursue this example any further. To appropriately test for long-run purchasing power parity via the Johansen procedure, we will probably need longer time series. Alternatively, some authors use several sets of countries simultaneously and apply panel data cointegration techniques (see Chapter 10). Another problem may lie in measuring the two price indices in an accurate way, comparable across the two countries.

9.6 Illustration: Money Demand and Inflation

One of the advantages of cointegration in multivariate time series models is that it may help improving forecasts. The reason is that forecasts from a cointegrated system are tied together by virtue of the existence of one or more long-run relationships. Typically, this advantage is realized when forecasting over medium or long horizons (compare Engle and Yoo, 1987). Hoffman and Rasche (1996) and Lin and Tsay (1996) empirically examine the forecast performance in a cointegrated system. In this section, based on the Hoffman and Rasche study, we consider an empirical example concerning a five-dimensional vector process. The empirical work is based on quarterly data for the United States from 1954:1 to 1994:4 ($T = 164$) for the following variables:[19]

m_t: log of real M1 money balances
$infl_t$:   quarterly inflation rate (in % per year)
cpr_t: commercial paper rate
y_t: log real GDP (in billions of 1987 dollars)
tbr_t: treasury bill rate

---

[19] The data are available in the files MONEY.

The commercial paper rate and the treasury bill rate are considered as risky and risk-free returns on a quarterly horizon, respectively. The series for M1 and GDP are seasonally adjusted. Although one may dispute the presence of a unit root in some of these series, we shall follow Hoffman and Rasche (1996) and assume that these five variables are all well described by an $I(1)$ process.

A priori one could think of three possible cointegrating relationships governing the long-run behaviour of these variables. First, we can specify an equation for *money demand* as

$$m_t = \alpha_1 + \beta_{14}y_t + \beta_{15}tbr_t + \varepsilon_{1t},$$

where β_{14} denotes the income elasticity and β_{15} the interest rate elasticity. It can be expected that β_{14} is close to unity, corresponding to a unitary income elasticity, and that $\beta_{15} < 0$. Second, if *real* interest rates are stationary we can expect that

$$infl_t = \alpha_2 + \beta_{25}tbr_t + \varepsilon_{2t}$$

corresponds to a cointegrating relationship with $\beta_{25} = 1$. This is referred to as the Fisher relation, where we are using actual inflation as a proxy for expected inflation.[20] Third, it can be expected that the risk premium, as measured by the difference between the commercial paper rate and the treasury bill rate, is stationary, so that a third cointegrating relationship is given by

$$cpr_t = \alpha_3 + \beta_{35}tbr_t + \varepsilon_{3t}$$

with $\beta_{35} = 1$.

Before proceeding to the vector process of these five variables, let us consider the OLS estimates of the above three regressions. These are presented in Table 9.13. To ease comparison with later results the lay out stresses that the left-hand side variables are included in the cointegrating vector (if it exists) with a coefficient of -1. Note that the OLS standard errors are inappropriate if the variables in the regression are integrated. Except for the risk premium equation, the R^2s are not close to unity, which is an informal requirement for a cointegrating regression. The Durbin–Watson statistics are small and if the critical values from Table 9.3 are appropriate,

Table 9.13 Univariate cointegrating regressions by OLS (standard errors in parentheses), intercept estimates not reported

	Money demand	Fisher equation	Risk premium
m_t	−1	0	0
$infl_t$	0	−1	0
cpr_t	0	0	−1
y_t	0.423	0	0
	(0.016)		
tbr_t	−0.031	0.558	1.038
	(0.002)	(0.053)	(0.010)
R^2	0.815	0.409	0.984
dw	0.199	0.784	0.705
$ADF(6)$	−3.164	−1.888	−3.975

---

[20] The real interest rate is defined as the nominal interest rate minus the *expected* inflation rate.

we would reject the null hypothesis of no cointegration at the 5% level for the last two equations but not for the money demand equation. Recall that the critical values in Table 9.3 are based on the assumption that all series are random walks, which may by correct for interest rate series but may be incorrect for money supply and GDP. Alternatively, we can test for a unit root in the residuals of these regressions by the augmented Dickey–Fuller tests. The results are not very sensitive to the number of lags that is included and the test statistics for 6 lags are reported in Table 9.13. The 5% asymptotic critical value from Table 9.2 is given by -3.77 for the regression involving three variables and -3.37 for the regressions with two variables. Only for the risk premium equation we can thus reject the null hypothesis of no cointegration.

The empirical evidence for the existence of the suggested cointegrating relationships between the five variables is somewhat mixed. Only for the risk premium equation we find an R^2 close to unity, a sufficiently high Durbin–Watson statistic and a significant rejection of the ADF test for a unit root in the residuals. For the two other regressions there is little reason to reject the null hypothesis of no cointegration. Potentially this is caused by the lack of power of the tests that we employ, and it is possible that a multivariate vector analysis provides stronger evidence for the existence of cointegrating relationships between these five variables. Some additional information is provided if we plot the residuals from these three regressions. If the regressions correspond to cointegration these residuals can be interpreted as long-run equilibrium errors and should be stationary and fluctuating around zero. For the three regressions, the residuals are displayed in Figures 9.1, 9.2 and 9.3, respectively. Although a visual inspection of these graphs is ambiguous, the residuals of the money demand and risk premium regressions could be argued to be stationary on the basis of these graphs. For the Fisher equation, the current sample period provides less evidence of mean reversion.

The first step in the Johansen approach involves testing for the cointegrating rank r. To compute these tests we need to choose the maximum lag length p in the vector autoregressive model. Choosing p too small will invalidate the tests and choosing p

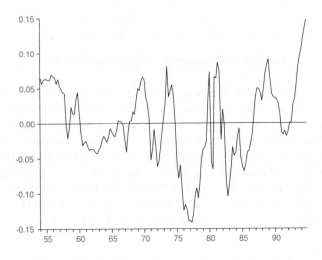

Figure 9.1   Residuals of money demand regression

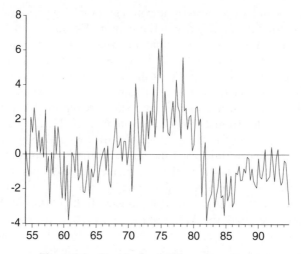

Figure 9.2   Residuals of Fisher regression

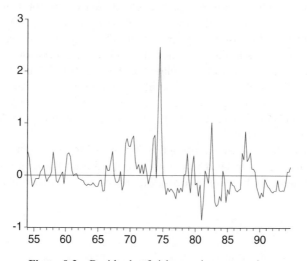

Figure 9.3   Residuals of risk premium regression

too large may result in a loss of power. In Table 9.14 we present the results[21] of the cointegrating rank tests for $p = 5$ and $p = 6$. The results show that there is some sensitivity with respect to the choice of the maximum lag length in the vector auto-regressions, although qualitatively the conclusion changes only marginally. At the 5% level all tests reject the null hypotheses of none or one cointegrating relationship. The tests for the null hypothesis that $r = 2$ only reject at the 5% level, albeit marginally, if we choose $p = 6$ and use the trace test statistic. As before, we need to choose the cointegrating rank r from these results. The most obvious choice is $r = 2$, although one could consider $r = 3$ as well (see Hoffman and Rasche, 1996).

---

[21] The results reported in this table are obtained from MicroFit 4.0; critical values taken from Table 9.9.

Table 9.14   Trace and maximum eigenvalue tests for cointegration

Null hypothesis	Alternative	Test statistic		5% critical value
		$p = 5$	$p = 6$	
λ_{trace}-statistic				
$H_0: r = 0$	$H_1: r \geq 1$	108.723	127.801	75.98
$H_0: r \leq 1$	$H_1: r \geq 2$	59.189	72.302	53.48
$H_0: r \leq 2$	$H_1: r \geq 3$	29.201	35.169	34.87
$H_0: r \leq 3$	$H_1: r \geq 4$	13.785	16.110	20.18
λ_{max}-statistic				
$H_0: r = 0$	$H_1: r = 1$	49.534	55.499	34.40
$H_0: r \leq 1$	$H_1: r = 2$	29.988	37.133	28.27
$H_0: r \leq 2$	$H_1: r = 3$	15.416	19.059	22.04
$H_0: r \leq 3$	$H_1: r = 4$	9.637	11.860	15.87

intercepts included $T = 164$

If we restrict the rank of the long-run matrix to be equal to two we can estimate the cointegrating vectors and the error-correction model by maximum likelihood, following the Johansen procedure. Recall that statistically the cointegrating vectors are not individually defined, only the space spanned by these vectors is. To identify individual cointegrating relationships we thus need to normalize the cointegrating vectors somehow. When $r = 2$ we need to impose two normalization constraints on each cointegrating vector. Note that in the cointegrating regressions in Table 9.13 a number of constraints are imposed a priori, including a -1 for the right-hand side variables and zero restrictions on some of the other variables' coefficients. In the current case we need to impose two restrictions and, assuming that the money demand and risk premium relationships are the most likely candidates, we shall impose that m_t and cpr_t have coefficients of $-1, 0$ and $0, -1$, respectively. Economically, we expect that $infl_t$ does not enter in any of the cointegrating vectors. With these two restrictions, the cointegrating vectors are estimated by maximum likelihood, jointly with the coefficients in the vector error-correction model. The results for the cointegrating vectors are presented in Table 9.15.

The cointegrating vector for the risk premium equation corresponds closely to our a priori expectations, with the coefficients for $infl_t$, y_t and tbr_t being insignificantly

Table 9.15   ML estimates of cointegrating vectors (after normalization) based on VAR with $p = 6$ (standard errors in parentheses), intercept estimates not reported

	Money demand	Risk premium
m_t	-1	0
$infl_t$	-0.023	0.041
	(0.006)	(0.031)
cpr_t	0	-1
y_t	0.425	-0.037
	(0.033)	(0.173)
tbr_t	-0.028	1.017
	(0.005)	(0.026)

loglikelihood value: 808.2770

different from zero, zero and one, respectively. For the vector corresponding to the money demand equation $infl_t$ appears to enter the equation significantly. Recall that m_t corresponds to *real* money demand, which should normally not depend upon the inflation rate. The coefficient estimate of -0.023 implies that, ceteris paribus, *nominal* money demand $(m_t + infl_t)$ increases somewhat less than proportionally with the inflation rate.

It is possible to test our a priori cointegrating vectors by using likelihood ratio tests. These tests require that the model is re-estimated imposing some additional restrictions on the cointegrating vectors. This way we can test the following hypotheses:[22]

$$H_0^a: \beta_{12} = 0, \quad \beta_{14} = 1;$$

$$H_0^b: \beta_{22} = \beta_{24} = 0, \quad \beta_{25} = 1; \text{ and}$$

$$H_0^c: \beta_{12} = \beta_{22} = \beta_{24} = 0, \quad \beta_{14} = \beta_{25} = 1,$$

where β_{12} denotes the coefficient for $infl_t$ in the money demand equation and β_{22} and β_{24} are the coefficients for inflation and GDP in the risk premium equation, respectively. The loglikelihood values for the complete model, estimated imposing H_0^a, H_0^b and H_0^c, respectively, are given by 782.3459, 783.7761 and 782.3196. The likelihood ratio test statistics, defined as twice the difference in loglikelihood values, for the three null hypotheses are thus given by 51.86, 49.00 and 51.91. The asymptotic distributions under the null hypotheses of the test statistics are the usual Chi-squared distributions, with degrees of freedom given by the number of restrictions that is tested (see Chapter 6). Compared with the Chi-squared critical values with 3, 2 or 5 degrees of freedom, each of the hypotheses is clearly rejected.

As a last step we consider the vector error-correction model for this system. This corresponds to a VAR of order $p - 1 = 5$ for the first-differenced series, with the inclusion of two error-correction terms in each equation, one for each cointegrating vector. Note that the number of parameters estimated in this vector error-correction model is well above 100, so we shall concentrate on a limited part of the results only. The two error-correction terms are given by

$$ecm1_t = -m_t - 0.023infl_t + 0.425y_t - 0.028tbr_t + 3.362;$$

$$ecm2_t = -cpr_t + 0.041infl_t + -0.037y_t + 1.017tbr_t + 0.687.$$

The adjustment coefficients in the 5×2 matrix γ, with their associated standard errors are reported in Table 9.16. The long-run money demand equation contributes significantly to the short-run movements of both money demand and income. The short-run behaviour of money demand, inflation and the commercial paper rate appears to be significantly affected by the long-run risk premium relationship. There is no statistical evidence that the treasury bill rate adjusts to any deviation from long-run equilibria, so that it could be treated as weakly exogenous.

---

[22] The tests here are actually overidentifying restrictions tests (see Chapter 5). We interpret them as regular hypotheses tests taking the a priori restrictions in Table 9.15 as given.

Table 9.16 Estimated matrix of adjustment coefficients (standard errors in parentheses), * indicates significance at the 5% level

Equation	Error-correction term	
	$ecm1_{t-1}$	$ecm2_{t-1}$
Δm_t	0.0276*	0.0090*
	(0.0104)	(0.0024)
$\Delta infl_t$	1.4629	−1.1618*
	(2.3210)	(0.5287)
Δcpr_t	−2.1364	0.6626*
	(1.1494)	(0.2618)
Δy_t	0.0687*	−0.0013
	(0.0121)	(0.0028)
Δtbr_t	−1.2876	0.3195
	(1.0380)	(0.2365)

9.7 Concluding Remarks

The literature on cointegration and related issues is of a recent date and still expanding. In this chapter we have been fairly brief on some topics, while other topics have been left out completely. Fortunately, there exists a substantial number of specialized textbooks on the topic that provide a more extensive coverage. Examples of relatively non-technical textbooks are Mills (1990); Enders (1995); Harris (1995) and Franses (1998). More technical discussion is available in Lütkepohl (1991); Cuthbertson, Hall and Taylor (1992); Banerjee *et al.* (1993); Hamilton (1994); Johansen (1995); and Boswijk (1999).

Exercises

Exercise 9.1 (Cointegration Theory)

a. Assume that the two series y_t and x_t are $I(1)$ and assume that both $y_t - \beta_1 x_t$ and $y_t - \beta_2 x_t$ are $I(0)$. Show that this implies that $\beta_1 = \beta_2$, showing that there can be only one unique cointegrating parameter.

b. Explain intuitively why the Durbin–Watson statistic in a regression of the $I(1)$ variables y_t upon x_t is informative about the question of cointegration between y_t and x_t.

c. Explain what is meant by 'super consistency'.

d. Consider three $I(1)$ variables y_t, x_t and z_t. Assume that y_t and x_t are cointegrated, and that x_t and z_t are cointegrated. Does this imply that y_t and z_t are also cointegrated? Why (not)?

Exercise 9.2   (Cointegration)

Consider the following very simple relationship between aggregate savings S_t and aggregate income Y_t.

$$S_t = \alpha + \beta Y_t + \varepsilon_t, \quad t = 1, \ldots, T. \tag{9.55}$$

For some country this relationship is estimated by OLS over the years 1946–1995 $(T = 50)$. The results are given in Table 9.17.

Table 9.17   Aggregate savings explained from aggregate income; OLS results

Variable	Coefficient	Standard error	t-ratio
constant	38.90	4.570	8.51
income	0.098	0.009	10.77

$T = 50$ $s = 22.57$ $R^2 = 0.93$ $dw = 0.70$

Assume, for the moment, that the series S_t and Y_t are *stationary*. (Hint: if needed consult Chapter 4 for the first set of questions.)

a. How would you interpret the coefficient estimate of 0.098 for the income variable?

b. Explain why the results indicate that there may be a problem of positive autocorrelation. Can you give arguments why, in economic models, positive autocorrelation is more likely than negative autocorrelation?

c. What are the effects of autocorrelation on the properties of the OLS estimator? Think about unbiasedness, consistency and the BLUE property.

d. Describe two different approaches to handle the autocorrelation problem in the above case. Which one would you prefer?

From now on, assume that S_t and Y_t are nonstationary $I(1)$ series.

e. Are there indications that the relationship between the two variables is 'spurious'?

f. Explain what we mean by 'spurious regressions'.

g. Are there indications that there is a cointegrating relationship between S_t and Y_t?

h. Explain what we mean by a 'cointegrating relationship'.

i. Describe two different tests that can be used to test the null hypothesis that S_t and Y_t are not cointegrated.

j. How do you interpret the coefficient estimate of 0.098 under the hypothesis that S_t and Y_t are cointegrated?

k. Are there reasons to correct for autocorrelation in the error term when we estimate a cointegrating regression?

l. Explain intuitively why the estimator for a cointegrating parameter is super consistent.

m. Assuming that S_t and Y_t are cointegrated, describe what we mean by an error-correction mechanism. Give an example. What do we learn from it?

n. How can we consistently estimate an error-correction model?

Exercise 9.3   (Cointegration – Empirical)

In the files INCOME we find quarterly data on UK nominal consumption and income, for 1971:1 to 1985:2 ($T = 58$). Part of these data was used in Chapter 8.

a. Test for a unit root in the consumption series using several augmented Dickey–Fuller tests.

b. Perform a regression by OLS explaining consumption from income. Test for cointegration using two different tests.

c. Perform a regression by OLS explaining income from consumption. Test for cointegration.

d. Compare the estimation results and R^2s from the last two regressions.

e. Determine the error-correction term from one of the two regressions and estimate an error-correction model for the change in consumption. Test whether the adjustment coefficient is zero.

f. Repeat the last question for the change in income. What do you conclude?

10 Models Based on Panel Data

A panel data set contains repeated observations over the same units (individuals, households, firms), collected over a number of periods. Although panel data are typically collected at the micro-economic level, it has become more and more practice to pool individual time series of a number of countries or industries and analyse them simultaneously. The availability of repeated observations on the same units allows economists to specify and estimate more complicated and more realistic models than a single cross-section or a single time series would do. The disadvantages are more of a practical nature: because we repeatedly observe the same units, it is usually no longer appropriate to assume that different observations are independent. This may complicate the analysis, particularly in nonlinear and dynamic models. Furthermore, panel data sets very often suffer from missing observations. Even if these observations are missing in a random way (see below), the standard analysis has to be adjusted.

This chapter provides an introduction to the analysis of panel data. A simple linear panel data model is presented in Section 10.1 and some advantages compared to cross-sectional or time series data are discussed in the context of this model. Section 10.2 pays attention to the so-called fixed effects and random effects models, and discusses issues relating to the choice between these two basic models. An empirical illustration is provided in Section 10.3. The introduction of a lagged dependent variable in the linear model complicates consistent estimation, and, as will be discussed in Section 10.4, instrumental variables procedures or GMM provide interesting alternatives. Section 10.5 provides an empirical example on the estimation of short- and long-run wage elasticities of labour demand. Other complications arise when the model of interest involves limited dependent variables. Panel data extensions of logit, probit and tobit models are discussed in Section 10.6. Finally, we discuss the problems associated with incomplete panels and selection bias in Section 10.7. Extensive discussions of the econometrics of panel data can be found in Hsiao (1986), Baltagi (1995) and Mátyás and Sevestre (1996).

10.1   Advantages of Panel Data

An important advantage of panel data compared to time series or cross-sectional data sets is that it allows identification of certain parameters or questions, without the need to make restrictive assumptions. For example, panel data make it possible to analyse *changes* on an *individual* level. Consider a situation in which the average consumption level rises with 2% from one year to another. Panel data can identify whether this rise is the result of, for example, an increase of 2% for all individuals or an increase of 4% for approximately one half of the individuals and no change for the other half (or any other combination). That is, panel data are not only suitable to model or explain why individual units behave differently but also to model why a given unit behaves differently at different time periods (for example, because of a different past).

We shall, in the sequel, index all variables by an i for the individual[1] ($i = 1, \ldots, N$) and a t for the time period ($t = 1, \ldots, T$). In very general terms, we could specify a linear model as

$$y_{it} = x'_{it}\beta_{it} + \varepsilon_{it},$$

where β_{it} measures the partial effects of x_{it} in period t for unit i. Of course, this model is much too general to be useful, and we need to put more structure on the coefficients β_{it}. The standard assumption, used in many empirical cases, is that β_{it} is constant for all i and t, except – possibly - the intercept term. This could be written as

$$y_{it} = \alpha_i + x'_{it}\beta + \varepsilon_{it}, \qquad (10.1)$$

where x_{it} is a K-dimensional vector of explanatory variables, *not including a constant*.[2] This means that the effects of a change in x are the same for all units and all periods, but that the average level for unit i may be different from that for unit j. The α_i thus capture the effects of those variables that are peculiar to the i-th individual and that are constant over time. In the standard case, ε_{it} is assumed to be independent and identically distributed over individuals and time, with mean zero and variance σ_ε^2. If we treat the α_i as N fixed unknown parameters, the model in (10.1) is referred to as the standard **fixed effects model**.

An alternative approach assumes that the intercepts of the individuals are different but that they can be treated as drawings from a distribution with mean μ and variance σ_α^2. The essential assumption here is that these drawings are independent of the explanatory variables in x_{it} (see below). This leads to the **random effects model**, where the individual effects α_i are treated as random. The error term in this model consists of two components: a time-invariant component[3] α_i and a remainder component ε_{it} that is uncorrelated over time.[4] It can be written as

$$y_{it} = \mu + x'_{it}\beta + \alpha_i + \varepsilon_{it}, \qquad (10.2)$$

where μ denotes the intercept term.

---

[1] While we refer to the cross-sectional units as individuals, they could also refer to other units like firms, countries, industries, households or assets.

[2] The elements in β are indexed as β_1 to β_K, where the first element – unlike the previous chapters - does not refer to the intercept.

[3] In the random effects model, the α_is are redefined to have a zero mean.

[4] The model is sometimes referred to as a (one-way) error components model.

The possibility of treating the α_is as fixed parameters has some great advantages, but also some disadvantages. Most panel data models are estimated under either the fixed effects or the random effects assumption and we shall discuss this extensively in Section 10.2. First, the next two subsections discuss some potential advantages of panel data in more detail.

10.1.1 Efficiency of Parameter Estimators

Because panel data sets are typically larger than cross-sectional or time series data sets, and explanatory variables vary over two dimensions (individuals and time) rather than one, estimators based on panel data are quite often more accurate than from other sources. Even with identical sample sizes, the use of a panel data set will often yield more efficient estimators than a series of independent cross-sections (where different units are sampled in each period). To illustrate this, consider the following special case of the random effects model in (10.2) where we only include time dummies, i.e.

$$y_{it} = \mu_t + \alpha_i + \varepsilon_{it}, \tag{10.3}$$

where each μ_t is an unknown parameter corresponding to the population mean in period t. Suppose we are not interested in the mean μ_t in a particular period, but in the change of μ_t from one period to another. In general the variance of the efficient estimator for $\mu_t - \mu_s$ ($s \neq t$), $\hat{\mu}_t - \hat{\mu}_s$, is given by

$$V\{\hat{\mu}_t - \hat{\mu}_s\} = V\{\hat{\mu}_t\} + V\{\hat{\mu}_s\} - 2 \operatorname{cov}\{\hat{\mu}_t, \hat{\mu}_s\} \tag{10.4}$$

with $\hat{\mu}_t = 1/N \sum_{i=1}^{N} y_{it}$ ($t = 1, \ldots, T$). Typically, if a panel data set is used the covariance between $\hat{\mu}_t$ and $\hat{\mu}_s$ will be positive, in particular – if the random effects assumptions of model (10.2) hold – equal σ_α^2/N. However, if two independent cross-sectional data sets are used different periods will contain different individuals so $\hat{\mu}_t$ and $\hat{\mu}_s$ will have zero covariance. In other words, if one is interested in changes from one period to another, a panel will yield more efficient estimators than a series of cross-sections.

Note however that the reverse is also true, in the sense that repeated cross-sections will be more informative than a panel when one is interested in a sum or average of μ_t over several periods. At a more intuitive level, panel data may provide better information because the *same* individuals are repeatedly observed. On the other hand, having the same individuals rather than different ones may imply less variation in the explanatory variables and thus relatively inefficient estimators. A comprehensive analysis on the choice between a pure panel, a pure cross-section and a combination of these two data sources, is provided in Nijman and Verbeek (1990). Their results indicate that when exogenous variables are included in the model and one is interested in the parameters which measure the effects of these variables, a panel data set will typically yield more efficient estimators than a series of cross-sections with the same number of observations.

10.1.2 Identification of Parameters

A second advantage of the availability of panel data is that it reduces identification problems. Although this advantage may come under different headings, in many cases it involves identification in the presence of endogenous regressors or measurement error, robustness to omitted variables and the identification of individual dynamics.

Let us start with an illustration of the last of these. There are two alternative explanations for the often observed phenomenon that individuals who have experienced an event in the past are more likely to experience that event in the future. The first explanation is that the fact that an individual has experienced the event changes his preferences, constraints, etc., in such a way that he is more likely to experience that event in the future. The second explanation says that individuals may differ in unobserved characteristics which influence the probability of experiencing the event (but are not influenced by the experience of the event). Heckman (1978) terms the former explanation true state dependence and the latter spurious state dependence. A well-known example concerns the 'event' of being unemployed. The availability of panel data will ease the problem of distinguishing between true and spurious state dependence, because individual histories are observed and can be included in the model.

Omitted variable bias arises if a variable that is correlated with the included variables is excluded from the model. A classical example is the estimation of production functions (Mundlak, 1961). In many cases, especially in the case of small firms, it is desirable to include management quality as an input in the production function. In general however, management quality is unobservable. Suppose that a production function of the Cobb–Douglas type is given by

$$y_{it} = \mu + x'_{it}\beta + m_i\beta_{K+1} + \varepsilon_{it} \tag{10.5}$$

where y_{it} denotes log output, x_{it} is a K-dimensional vector of log inputs, both for firm i at time t, and m_i denotes the management quality for firm i (which is assumed to be constant over time). The unobserved variable m_i is expected to be negatively correlated with the other inputs in x_{it}, since a high quality management will probably result in a more efficient use of inputs. Therefore, unless $\beta_{K+1} = 0$, deletion of m_i from (10.5) will lead to biased estimates of the other parameters in the model. If panel data are available this problem can be resolved by introducing a firm specific effect $\alpha_i = \mu + m_i\beta_{K+1}$ and considering this as a fixed unknown parameter. Note that without additional information it is not possible to identify β_{K+1}; a restriction that identifies β_{K+1} is the imposition of constant returns to scale.[5]

In a similar way, a fixed time effect can be included in the model to capture the effect of all (observed and unobserved) variables that do not vary over the individual units. This illustrates the proposition that panel data can reduce the effects of omitted variable bias, or – in other words – estimators from a panel data set may be more robust for an incomplete model specification.

Finally, in many cases panel data will provide 'internal' instruments for regressors that are endogenous or subject to measurement error. That is, transformations of the original variables can often be argued to be uncorrelated with the model's error term and correlated with the explanatory variables themselves and no external instruments are needed. For example, if x_{it} is correlated with α_i, it can be argued that $x_{it} - \bar{x}_i$, where $\bar{x}_i$ is the time-average for individual i, is uncorrelated with α_i and provides a valid instrument for x_{it}. More generally, estimating the model under the fixed effects

---

[5] Constant returns to scale implies that $\beta_{K+1} = 1 - (\beta_1 + \cdots + \beta_K)$.

assumption eliminates α_i from the error term and, consequently, eliminates all endogeneity problems relating to it. This will be illustrated in the next section. An extensive discussion of the benefits and limitations of panel data is provided in Hsiao (1985).

10.2 The Static Linear Model

In this section we discuss the static linear model in a panel data setting. We start with two basic models, the fixed effects and the random effects model, and subsequently discuss the choice between the two, as well as alternative procedures that could be considered to be somewhere between a fixed effects and a random effects treatment.

10.2.1 The Fixed Effects Model

The fixed effects model is simply a linear regression model in which the intercept terms vary over the individual units i, i.e.

$$y_{it} = \alpha_i + x_{it}'\beta + \varepsilon_{it}, \quad \varepsilon_{it} \sim IID(0, \sigma_\varepsilon^2), \tag{10.6}$$

where it is usually assumed that all x_{it} are independent of all ε_{it}. We can write this in the usual regression framework by including a dummy variable for each unit i in the model. That is,

$$y_{it} = \sum_{j=1}^{N} \alpha_j d_{ij} + x_{it}'\beta + \varepsilon_{it}, \tag{10.7}$$

where $d_{ij} = 1$ if $i = j$ and 0 elsewhere. We thus have a set of N dummy variables in the model. The parameters $\alpha_1, \ldots, \alpha_N$ and β can be estimated by ordinary least squares in (10.7). The implied estimator for β is referred to as the **least squares dummy variable (LSDV) estimator**. It may, however, be numerically unattractive to have a regression model with so many regressors. Fortunately one can compute the estimator for β in a simpler way. It can be shown that exactly the same estimator for β is obtained if the regression is performed in deviations from individual means. Essentially, this implies that we eliminate the individual effects α_i first by transforming the data. To see this, first note that

$$\bar{y}_i = \alpha_i + \bar{x}_i'\beta + \bar{\varepsilon}_i, \tag{10.8}$$

where $\bar{y}_i = T^{-1}\sum_t y_{it}$ and similarly for the other variables. Consequently, we can write

$$y_{it} - \bar{y}_i = (x_{it} - \bar{x}_i)'\beta + (\varepsilon_{it} - \bar{\varepsilon}_i). \tag{10.9}$$

This is a regression model in deviations from individual means and does not include the individual effects α_i. The transformation that produces observations in deviation from individual means, as in (10.9), is called the **within transformation**. The OLS estimator for β obtained from this transformed model is often called the **within estimator** or **fixed effects estimator**, and it is exactly identical to the LSDV estimator described above. It is given by

$$\hat{\beta}_{FE} = \left(\sum_{i=1}^{N} \sum_{t=1}^{T} (x_{it} - \bar{x}_i)(x_{it} - \bar{x}_i)' \right)^{-1} \sum_{i=1}^{N} \sum_{t=1}^{T} (x_{it} - \bar{x}_i)(y_{it} - \bar{y}_i). \tag{10.10}$$

If it is assumed that *all* x_{it} are independent of *all* ε_{it} (compare assumption (A2) from Chapter 2), the fixed effects estimator can be shown to be unbiased for β. If, in addition, normality of ε_{it} is imposed, $\hat{\beta}_{FE}$ also has a normal distribution. For consistency,[6] it is required that

$$E\{(x_{it} - \bar{x}_i)\varepsilon_{it}\} = 0 \qquad (10.11)$$

(compare assumption (A7) in Chapters 2 and 5). Sufficient for this is that x_{it} is uncorrelated with ε_{it} and that $\bar{x}_i$ has no correlation with the error term. These conditions are in turn implied by

$$E\{x_{it}\varepsilon_{is}\} = 0 \quad \text{for all } s, t, \qquad (10.12)$$

in which case we call x_{it} **strictly exogenous**. A strictly exogenous variable is not allowed to depend upon current, future and past values of the error term. In some applications this may be restrictive. Clearly, it excludes the inclusion of lagged dependent variables in x_{it}, but any x_{it} variable which depends upon the history of y_{it} would also violate the condition. For example, if we are explaining labour supply of an individual, we may want to include years of experience in the model, while quite clearly experience depends upon the person's labour history.

With explanatory variables independent of all errors, the N intercepts are estimated unbiasedly as

$$\hat{\alpha}_i = \bar{y}_i - \bar{x}_i'\hat{\beta}_{FE}, \quad i = 1, \ldots, N.$$

Under assumption (10.11) these estimators are consistent for the fixed effects α_i provided T goes to infinity. The reason why $\hat{\alpha}_i$ is inconsistent for fixed T is clear: when T is fixed the individual averages $\bar{y}_i$ and $\bar{x}_i$ do not converge to anything if the number of individuals increases.

The covariance matrix for the fixed effects estimator $\hat{\beta}_{FE}$, assuming that ε_{it} is i.i.d. across individuals and time with variance σ_ε^2, is given by

$$V\{\hat{\beta}_{FE}\} = \sigma_\varepsilon^2 \left(\sum_{i=1}^{N} \sum_{t=1}^{T} (x_{it} - \bar{x}_i)(x_{it} - \bar{x}_i)' \right)^{-1}. \qquad (10.13)$$

Unless T is large, using the standard OLS estimate for the covariance matrix based upon the within regression in (10.9) will underestimate the true variance. The reason is that in this transformed regression the error covariance matrix is singular (as the T transformed errors of each individual add up to zero) and the variance of $\varepsilon_{it} - \bar{\varepsilon}_i$ is $(T-1)/T\sigma_\varepsilon^2$ rather than σ_ε^2. A consistent estimator for σ_ε^2 is obtained as the within residual sum of squares divided by $N(T-1)$. That is,

$$\hat{\sigma}_\varepsilon^2 = \frac{1}{N(T-1)} \sum_{i=1}^{N} \sum_{t=1}^{T} (y_{it} - \hat{\alpha}_i - x_{it}'\hat{\beta}_{FE})^2$$

$$= \frac{1}{N(T-1)} \sum_{i=1}^{N} \sum_{t=1}^{T} (y_{it} - \bar{y}_i - (x_{it} - \bar{x}_i)'\hat{\beta}_{FE})^2. \qquad (10.14)$$

---

[6] Unless stated otherwise, we consider in this chapter consistency for the number of individuals N going to infinity. This corresponds with the common situation that we have panels with large N and small T.

It is possible to apply the usual degrees of freedom correction in which case K is subtracted from the denominator. Note that using the standard OLS covariance matrix in model (10.7) with N individual dummies is reliable, because the degrees of freedom correction involves N additional unknown parameters corresponding to the individual intercept terms. Under weak regularity conditions, the fixed effects estimator is asymptotically normal, so that the usual inference procedures can be used (like t and Wald tests).

Essentially, the fixed effects model concentrates on differences 'within' individuals. That is, it is explaining to what extent y_{it} differs from $\bar{y}_i$ and does not explain why $\bar{y}_i$ is different from $\bar{y}_j$. The parametric assumptions about β on the other hand, impose that a change in x has the same (ceteris paribus) effect, whether it is a change from one period to the other or a change from one individual to the other. When interpreting the results, however, from a fixed effects regression, it may be important to realize that the parameters are identified only through the within dimension of the data.

10.2.2 The Random Effects Model

It is commonly assumed in regression analysis that all factors that affect the dependent variable, but that have not been included as regressors, can be appropriately summarized by a random error term. In our case, this leads to the assumption that the α_i are random factors, independently and identically distributed over individuals. Thus we write the random effects model as

$$y_{it} = \mu + x'_{it}\beta + \alpha_i + \varepsilon_{it}, \quad \varepsilon_{it} \sim IID(0, \sigma_\varepsilon^2); \alpha_i \sim IID(0, \sigma_\alpha^2), \tag{10.15}$$

where $\alpha_i + \varepsilon_{it}$ is treated as an error term consisting of two components: an individual specific component, that does not vary over time, and a remainder component, that is assumed to be uncorrelated over time. That is, all correlation of the error terms over time is attributed to the individual effects α_i. It is assumed that α_i and ε_{it} are mutually independent and independent of x_{js} (for all j and s). This implies that the OLS estimator for μ and β from (10.15) is unbiased and consistent. The error components structure implies that the composite error term $\alpha_i + \varepsilon_{it}$ exhibits a particular form of autocorrelation (unless $\sigma_\alpha^2 = 0$). Consequently, routinely computed standard errors for the OLS estimator are incorrect and a more efficient (GLS) estimator can be obtained by exploiting the structure of the error covariance matrix.

To derive the GLS estimator,[7] first note that for individual i all error terms can be stacked as $\alpha_i \iota_T + \varepsilon_i$, where $\iota_T = (1, 1, \ldots, 1)'$ of dimension T and $\varepsilon_i = (\varepsilon_{i1}, \ldots, \varepsilon_{iT})'$. The covariance matrix of this vector is (see Hsiao, 1986, p. 34)

$$V\{\alpha_i \iota_T + \varepsilon_i\} = \Omega = \sigma_\alpha^2 \iota_T \iota_T' + \sigma_\varepsilon^2 I_T, \tag{10.16}$$

where I_T is the T-dimensional identity matrix. This can be used to derive the generalized least squares (GLS) estimator for the parameters in (10.15). For each individual, we can transform the data by premultiplying the vectors $y_i = (y_{i1}, \ldots, y_{iT})'$ etc. by Ω^{-1}, which is given by

$$\Omega^{-1} = \sigma_\varepsilon^{-2} \left[I_T - \frac{\sigma_\alpha^2}{\sigma_\varepsilon^2 + T\sigma_\alpha^2} \iota_T \iota_T' \right],$$

---

[7] It may be instructive to re-read the general introduction to GLS estimation in Section 4.2.

which can also be written as

$$\Omega^{-1} = \sigma_\varepsilon^{-2}\left[\left(I_T - \frac{1}{T}\iota_T\iota_T'\right) + \psi\frac{1}{T}\iota_T\iota_T'\right],$$

where

$$\psi = \frac{\sigma_\varepsilon^2}{\sigma_\varepsilon^2 + T\sigma_\alpha^2}.$$

Noting that $I_T - (1/T)\iota_T\iota_T'$ transforms the data in deviations from individual means and $(1/T)\iota_T\iota_T'$ takes individual means, the GLS estimator for β can be written as

$$\hat{\beta}_{GLS} = \left(\sum_{i=1}^{N}\sum_{t=1}^{T}(x_{it} - \bar{x}_i)(x_{it} - \bar{x}_i)' + \psi T\sum_{i=1}^{N}(\bar{x}_i - \bar{x})(\bar{x}_i - \bar{x})'\right)^{-1}$$

$$\times \left(\sum_{i=1}^{N}\sum_{t=1}^{T}(x_{it} - \bar{x}_i)(y_{it} - \bar{y}_i) + \psi T\sum_{i=1}^{N}(\bar{x}_i - \bar{x})(\bar{y}_i - \bar{y})\right), \qquad (10.17)$$

where $\bar{x} = (1/(NT))\sum_{i,t}x_{it}$ denotes the overall average of x_{it}. It is easy to see that for $\psi = 0$ the fixed effects estimator arises. Because $\psi \to 0$ if $T \to \infty$, it follows that the fixed and random effects estimators are equivalent for large T. If $\psi = 1$, the GLS estimator is just the OLS estimator (and Ω is diagonal). From the general formula for the GLS estimator it can be derived that

$$\hat{\beta}_{GLS} = \Delta\hat{\beta}_B + (I_k - \Delta)\hat{\beta}_{FE},$$

where

$$\hat{\beta}_B = \left(\sum_{i=1}^{N}(\bar{x}_i - \bar{x})(\bar{x}_i - \bar{x})'\right)^{-1}\sum_{i=1}^{N}(\bar{x}_i - \bar{x})(\bar{y}_i - \bar{y})$$

is the so-called **between estimator** for β. It is the OLS estimator in the model for individual means

$$\bar{y}_i = \mu + \bar{x}_i'\beta + \alpha_i + \bar{\varepsilon}_i, \quad i = 1,\dots,N. \qquad (10.18)$$

The matrix Δ is a weighting matrix and is proportional to the inverse of the covariance matrix of $\hat{\beta}_B$ (see Hsiao, 1986, p. 36, for details). That is, the GLS estimator is a matrix-weighted average of the between estimator and the within estimator, where the weight depends upon the relative variances of the two estimators. (The more accurate one gets the higher the weight.)

The between estimator ignores any information within individuals. The GLS estimator, under the current assumptions, is the optimal combination of the within estimator and the between estimator, and is therefore more efficient then either of these two estimators. The OLS estimator (with $\psi = 1$) is also a linear combination of the two estimators, but not the efficient one. Thus, GLS will be more efficient than OLS, as usual. If the explanatory variables are independent of all ε_{it} and all α_i, the GLS estimator is unbiased. It is a consistent estimator for N or T or both tending to infinity if in addition to (10.11) it also holds that $E\{\bar{x}_i\varepsilon_{it}\} = 0$ and most importantly that

$$E\{\bar{x}_i\alpha_i\} = 0. \qquad (10.19)$$

Note that these conditions are also required for the between estimator to be consistent.

An easy way to compute the GLS estimator is obtained by noting that it can be determined as the OLS estimator in a transformed model (compare Chapter 4), given by

$$(y_{it} - \vartheta \bar{y}_i) = \mu(1 - \vartheta) + (x_{it} - \vartheta \bar{x}_i) + u_{it}, \tag{10.20}$$

where $\vartheta = 1 - \psi^{1/2}$. The error term in this transformed regression is i.i.d. over individuals and time. Note again that $\psi = 0$ corresponds to the within estimator ($\vartheta = 1$). In general, a fixed proportion ϑ of the individuals means is subtracted from the data to obtain this transformed model ($0 \leq \vartheta \leq 1$).

Of course, the variance components σ_α^2 and σ_ε^2 are unknown in practice. In that case we can use the feasible GLS estimator (EGLS), where the unknown variances are consistently estimated in a first step. The estimator for σ_ε^2 is easily obtained from the within residuals, as given in (10.14). For the between regression the error variance is $\sigma_\alpha^2 + (1/T)\sigma_\varepsilon^2$, which we can estimate consistently by

$$\hat{\sigma}_B^2 = \frac{1}{N} \sum_{i=1}^N (\bar{y}_i - \hat{\mu}_B - \bar{x}_i' \hat{\beta}_B)^2, \tag{10.21}$$

where $\hat{\mu}_B$ is the between estimator for μ. From this, a consistent estimator for σ_α^2 follows as

$$\hat{\sigma}_\alpha^2 = \hat{\sigma}_B^2 - \frac{1}{T} \hat{\sigma}_\varepsilon^2. \tag{10.22}$$

Again, it is possible to adjust this estimator by applying a degrees of freedom correction, implying that the number of regressors $K + 1$ is subtracted in the denominator of (10.21) (see Hsiao, 1986, p. 38; or Baltagi, 1995, p. 15). The resulting EGLS estimator is referred to as the **random effects estimator** for β (and μ), denoted below as $\hat{\beta}_{RE}$.

Under weak regularity conditions, the random effects estimator is asymptotically normal. Its covariance matrix is given by

$$V\{\hat{\beta}_{RE}\} = \sigma_\varepsilon^2 \left(\sum_{i=1}^N \sum_{t=1}^T (x_{it} - \bar{x}_i)(x_{it} - \bar{x}_i)' + \psi T \sum_{i=1}^N (\bar{x}_i - \bar{x})(\bar{x}_i - \bar{x})' \right)^{-1}, \tag{10.23}$$

which shows that the random effects estimator is more efficient than the fixed effects estimator as long as $\psi > 0$. The gain in efficiency is due to the use of the between variation in the data ($\bar{x}_i - \bar{x}$). The covariance matrix in (10.23) is routinely estimated by the OLS expressions in the transformed model (10.20).

In summary, we have seen a range of estimators for the parameter vector β. The basic two are:

1. The **between estimator**, exploiting the between dimension of the data (differences between individuals), determined as the OLS estimator in a regression of individual averages of y on individual averages of x (and a constant). Consistency, for $N \to \infty$, requires that $E\{\bar{x}_i \alpha_i\} = 0$ and $E\{\bar{x}_i \bar{\varepsilon}_i\} = 0$. Typically this means that the explanatory variables are strictly exogenous and uncorrelated with the individual specific effect α_i.

2. The **fixed effects (within) estimator**, exploiting the within dimension of the data (differences within individuals), determined as the OLS estimator in a regression in deviations from individual means. It is consistent for β for $T \to \infty$ or $N \to \infty$, provided that $E\{(x_{it} - \bar{x}_i)\varepsilon_{it}\} = 0$. Again this requires the x-variables to be strictly exogenous, but it does not impose any restrictions upon the relationship between α_i and x_{it}.

The other two estimators are:

3. The **OLS estimator**, exploiting both dimensions (within and between) but not efficiently. Determined (of course) as OLS in the original model. Consistency for $T \to \infty$ or $N \to \infty$ requires that $E\{x_{it}(\varepsilon_{it} + \alpha_i)\} = 0$. This requires the explanatory variables to be uncorrelated with α_i but does not impose that they are strictly exogenous. It suffices that x_{it} and ε_{it} are contemporaneously uncorrelated.
4. The **random effects (EGLS) estimator**, combining the information from the between and within dimensions in an efficient way. It is consistent for $T \to \infty$ or $N \to \infty$ under the combined conditions of 1 and 2. It can be determined as a weighted average of the between and within estimator or as the OLS estimator in a regression where the variables are transformed as $y_{it} - \hat{\vartheta}\bar{y}_i$, where $\hat{\vartheta}$ is an estimate for $\vartheta = 1 - \psi^{1/2}$ with $\psi = \sigma_\varepsilon^2/(\sigma_\varepsilon^2 + T\sigma_\alpha^2)$.

10.2.3 Fixed Effects or Random Effects?

Whether to treat the individual effects α_i as fixed or random is not an easy question to answer. It can make a surprising amount of difference in the estimates of the β parameters in cases where T is small and N is large. When only a few observations are available for each individual it is very important to make the most efficient use of the data. The most common view is that the discussion should not be about the 'true nature' of the effects α_i. The appropriate interpretation is that the fixed effects approach is conditional upon the values for α_i. That is, it essentially considers the distribution of y_{it} given α_i, where the α_is can be estimated. This makes sense intuitively if the individuals in the sample are 'one of a kind', and cannot be viewed as a random draw from some underlying population. This interpretation is probably most appropriate when i denotes countries, (large) companies or industries, and predictions we want to make are for a particular country, company or industry. Inferences are thus with respect to the effects that are in the sample.

In contrast, the random effects approach is not conditional upon the individual α_is, but 'integrates them out'. In this case, we are usually not interested in the particular value of some person's α_i; we just focus on arbitrary individuals that have certain characteristics. The random effects approach allows one to make inference with respect to the population characteristics. One way to formalize this is noting that the random effects model states that

$$E\{y_{it}|x_{it}\} = x_{it}'\beta, \tag{10.24}$$

while the fixed effects model estimates

$$E\{y_{it}|x_{it}, \alpha_i\} = x_{it}'\beta + \alpha_i. \tag{10.25}$$

Note that the β coefficients in these two conditional expectations are the same only if $E\{\alpha_i|x_{it}\} = 0$. To summarize this, a first reason why one may prefer the fixed effects estimator is that some interest lies in α_i, which makes sense if the number of units is relatively small and of a specific nature. That is, identification of individual units is important.

However, even if we are interested in the larger population of individual units, and a random effects framework seems appropriate, the fixed effects estimator may be preferred. The reason for this is that it may be the case that α_i and x_{it} are correlated, in which case the random effects approach, ignoring this correlation, leads to inconsistent estimators. We saw an example of this above, where α_i included management quality and was argued to be correlated with the other inputs included in the production function. The problem of correlation between the individual effects α_i and the explanatory variables in x_{it} can be handled by using the fixed effects approach, which essentially eliminates the α_i from the model, and thus eliminates any problems that they may cause.

Hausman (1978) has suggested a test for the null hypothesis that x_{it} and α_i are uncorrelated. The general idea of a **Hausman test** is that two estimators are compared: one which is consistent under both the null and alternative hypothesis and one which is consistent (and typically efficient) under the null hypothesis only. A significant difference between the two estimators indicates that the null hypothesis is unlikely to hold. In the present case, assume that $E\{\varepsilon_{it}x_{is}\} = 0$ for all s, t, so that the fixed effects estimator $\hat{\beta}_{FE}$ is consistent for β irrespective of the question whether x_{it} and α_i are uncorrelated, while the random effects estimator $\hat{\beta}_{RE}$ is consistent and efficient only if x_{it} and α_i are not correlated. Let us consider the difference vector $\hat{\beta}_{FE} - \hat{\beta}_{RE}$. To evaluate the significance of this difference, we need its covariance matrix. In general this would require us to estimate the covariance between $\hat{\beta}_{FE}$ and $\hat{\beta}_{RE}$, but because the latter estimator is efficient under the null hypothesis, it can be shown that (under the null)

$$V\{\hat{\beta}_{FE} - \hat{\beta}_{RE}\} = V\{\hat{\beta}_{FE}\} - V\{\hat{\beta}_{RE}\}. \tag{10.26}$$

Consequently, we can compute the Hausman test statistic as

$$\xi_H = (\hat{\beta}_{FE} - \hat{\beta}_{RE})'[\hat{V}\{\hat{\beta}_{FE}\} - \hat{V}\{\hat{\beta}_{RE}\}]^{-1}(\hat{\beta}_{FE} - \hat{\beta}_{RE}), \tag{10.27}$$

where the $\hat{V}$s denote estimates of the true covariance matrices. Under the null hypothesis, which implicitly says that $\text{plim}(\hat{\beta}_{FE} - \hat{\beta}_{RE}) = 0$, the statistic ξ_H has an asymptotic Chi-squared distribution with K degrees of freedom, where K is the number of elements in β.

The Hausman test thus tests whether the fixed effects and random effects estimator are significantly different. Computationally, this is relatively easy because the covariance matrix satisfies (10.26). An important reason why the two estimators would be different is the existence of correlation between x_{it} and α_i, although other sorts of misspecification may also read to rejection (we shall see an example of this below). A practical problem when computing (10.27) is that the covariance matrix in square brackets may not be positive definite in finite samples, such that its inverse cannot be computed. As an alternative, it is possible to test for a subset of the elements in β.

10.2.4 Goodness-of-fit

The computation of goodness-of-fit measures in panel data applications is somewhat uncommon. One reason is the fact that one may attach different importance to explaining the within and between variation in the data. Another reason is that the usual R^2 or adjusted R^2 criteria are only appropriate if the model is estimated by OLS.

Our starting point here is the definition of the R^2 in terms of the squared correlation coefficient between actual and fitted values, as presented in Section 2.4. This definition has the advantage that it produces values within the $[0, 1]$ interval, irrespective of the estimator that is used to generate the fitted values. Recall that it corresponds to the standard definition of the R^2 (in terms of sums of squares) if the model is estimated by OLS (provided that an intercept term is included). In the current context, the total variation in y_{it} can be written as the sum of the within variation and the between variation, that is

$$\frac{1}{NT} \sum_{i,t} (y_{it} - \bar{y})^2 = \frac{1}{NT} \sum_{i,t} (y_{it} - \bar{y}_i)^2 + \frac{1}{N} \sum_i (\bar{y}_i - \bar{y})^2, \tag{10.28}$$

where $\bar{y}$ denotes the overall sample average. Now, we can define alternative versions of an R^2 measure, depending upon the dimension of the data that we are interested in.

For example, the fixed effects estimator is chosen to explain the within variation as well as possible, and thus maximizes the 'within R^2' given by

$$R^2_{within}(\hat{\beta}_{FE}) = \text{corr}^2\{\hat{y}_{it}^{FE} - \hat{y}_i^{FE}, \ y_{it} - \bar{y}_i\}, \tag{10.29}$$

where $\hat{y}_{it}^{FE} - \hat{y}_i^{FE} = (x_{it} - \bar{x}_i)'\hat{\beta}_{FE}$ and corr^2 denotes the squared correlation coefficient. The between estimator, being an OLS estimator in the model in terms of individual means, maximizes the 'between R^2', which we define as

$$R^2_{between}(\hat{\beta}_B) = \text{corr}^2\{\hat{y}_i^B, \ \bar{y}_i\}, \tag{10.30}$$

where $\hat{y}_i^B = \bar{x}_i'\hat{\beta}_B$. The OLS estimator maximizes the overall goodness-of-fit and thus the overall R^2, which is defined as

$$R^2_{overall}(\hat{\beta}) = \text{corr}^2\{\hat{y}_{it}, \ y_{it}\}, \tag{10.31}$$

with $\hat{y}_{it} = x_{it}'b$. It is possible to define within, between and overall R^2s for an arbitrary estimator $\hat{\beta}$ for β by using as fitted values $\hat{y}_{it} = x_{it}'\hat{\beta}$, $\hat{y}_i = (1/T)\sum_t \hat{y}_{it}$ and $\hat{y} = (1/(NT))\sum_{i,t} \hat{y}_{it}$, where the intercept terms are omitted (and irrelevant).[8] For the fixed effects estimator this ignores the variation captured by the $\hat{\alpha}_i$s. If we would take into account the variation explained by the N estimated intercepts $\hat{\alpha}_i$, the fixed effects model perfectly fits the between variation. This is somewhat unsatisfactory though, as it is hard to argue that the fixed effects $\hat{\alpha}_i$ *explain* the variation between individuals, they just capture it. Put differently, if we ask ourselves: why does individual i consume on average more than another individual, the answer provided by $\hat{\alpha}_i$ is simply: because it is individual i. Given this argument, and because the $\hat{\alpha}_i$s are often not computed, it seems appropriate to ignore this part of the model.

Taking the definition in terms of the squared correlation coefficients, the three measures above can be computed for any of the estimators that we considered. If

---

[8] These definitions correspond to the R^2 measures as computed in Stata 5.0.

we take the random effects estimator, which is (asymptotically) the most efficient estimator if the assumptions of the random effects model are valid, the within, between and overall R^2s are necessarily smaller than for the fixed effects, between and OLS estimator, respectively. This, again, stresses that goodness-of-fit measures are not adequate to choose between alternative estimators. They provide, however, possible criteria for choosing between alternative (potentially non-nested) specifications of the model.

10.2.5 Alternative Instrumental Variables Estimators

The fixed effects estimator eliminates anything that is time-invariant from the model. This may be a high price to pay for allowing the x-variables to be correlated with the individual specific heterogeneity α_i. For example, we may be interested in the effect of time-invariant variables (like gender) on a person's wage. Actually, there is no need to restrict attention to the fixed and random effects assumptions only, as it is possible to derive instrumental variables estimators that can be considered to be in between a fixed and random effects approach.

To see this, let us first of all note that we can write the fixed effects estimator as

$$\hat{\beta}_{FE} = \left(\sum_{i=1}^{N} \sum_{t=1}^{T} (x_{it} - \bar{x}_i)(x_{it} - \bar{x}_i)' \right)^{-1} \sum_{i=1}^{N} \sum_{t=1}^{T} (x_{it} - \bar{x}_i)(y_{it} - \bar{y}_i)$$

$$= \left(\sum_{i=1}^{N} \sum_{t=1}^{T} (x_{it} - \bar{x}_i)x_{it}' \right)^{-1} \sum_{i=1}^{N} \sum_{t=1}^{T} (x_{it} - \bar{x}_i)y_{it}. \tag{10.32}$$

Writing the estimator like this shows that it has the interpretation of an instrumental variables estimator[9] for β in the model

$$y_{it} = \mu + x_{it}'\beta + \alpha_i + \varepsilon_{it},$$

where each explanatory variable is instrumented by its value in deviation from the individual specific mean. That is, x_{it} is instrumented by $x_{it} - \bar{x}_i$. Note that $E\{(x_{it} - \bar{x}_i)\alpha_i\} = 0$ by construction (if we take expectations over i and t), so that the IV estimator is consistent provided $E\{(x_{it} - \bar{x}_i)\varepsilon_{it}\} = 0$, which is implied by the strict exogeneity of x_{it}. Clearly, if a particular element in x_{it} is known to be uncorrelated with α_i there is no need to instrument it; that is, this variable can be used as its own instrument. This route may also allow us to estimate the effect of time-invariant variables.

To describe the general approach, let us consider a linear model with four groups of explanatory variables (Hausman and Taylor, 1981)

$$y_{it} = \mu + x_{1,it}'\beta_1 + x_{2,it}'\beta_2 + w_{1i}'\gamma_1 + w_{2i}'\gamma_2 + \alpha_i + \varepsilon_{it}, \tag{10.33}$$

where the x-variables are time-varying and the w-variables are time-invariant. The variables with index 1 are assumed to be uncorrelated with both α_i and all ε_{is}. The variables $x_{2,it}$ and w_{2i} are correlated with α_i but not with any ε_{is}. Under these assumptions, the fixed effects estimator would be consistent for β_1 and β_2, but would

---

[9] It may be instructive to re-read Section 5.3 for a general discussion of instrumental variables estimation.

not identify the coefficients for the time-invariant variables. Moreover, it is inefficient because $x_{1,it}$ is needlessly instrumented. Hausman and Taylor (1981) suggest to estimate (10.33) by instrumental variables using the following variables as instruments: $x_{1,it}, w_{1i}$ and $x_{2,it} - \bar{x}_{2i}, \bar{x}_{1i}$. That is, the exogenous variables serve as their own instruments, $x_{2,it}$ is instrumented by its deviation from individual means (as in the fixed effects approach) and w_{2i} is instrumented by the individual average of $x_{1,it}$. Obviously, identification requires that the number of variables in $x_{1,it}$ is at least as large as that in w_{2i}. The resulting estimator, the **Hausman–Taylor estimator**, allows us to estimate the effect of time-invariant variables, even though the time-varying regressors are correlated with α_i. If the time-invariant variables are believed to be also correlated with α_i they need to be instrumented as well and we require that sufficient time-varying variables are included that have no correlation with α_i. Of course, it is a straightforward extension to include additional instruments in the procedure that are not based on variables included in the model. This is what one is forced to do in the cross-sectional case, where no transformations are available that can be argued to produce valid instruments. The strong advantage of the Hausman–Taylor approach is that one does not have to use external instruments. With sufficient assumptions instruments can be derived within the model. Despite this important advantage, the Hausman–Taylor estimator plays a surprisingly minor role in current empirical work.

Hausman and Taylor also show that the instrument set is equivalent to using $x_{1,it} - \bar{x}_{1i}, x_{2,it} - \bar{x}_{2i}$ and $x_{1,it}, w_{1i}$. This follows directly from the fact that taking different linear combinations of the original instruments does not affect the estimator. Hausman and Taylor also show how the nondiagonal covariance matrix of the error term in (10.33) can be exploited to improve the efficiency of the estimator. Nowadays, this would typically be handled in a GMM framework, as we shall see in the next section (see Arellano and Bover, 1995).

Two subsequent papers try to improve upon the efficiency of the Hausman–Taylor instrumental variables estimator by suggesting a larger set of instruments. Amemiya and MaCurdy (1986) also suggest the use of the *time-invariant* instruments $x_{1,i1} - \bar{x}_{1i}$ up to $x_{1,iT} - \bar{x}_{1i}$. This requires that $E\{(x_{1,it} - \bar{x}_{1i})\alpha_i\} = 0$ for *each* t. This assumption makes sense if the correlation between α_i and $x_{1,it}$ is due to a time-invariant component in $x_{1,it}$, such that $E\{x_{1,it}\alpha_i\}$ for a given t does not depend upon t. Breusch, Mizon and Schmidt (1989) nicely summarize this literature and suggest as additional instruments the use of the time-invariant variables $x_{2,i1} - \bar{x}_{2i}$ up to $x_{2,iT} - \bar{x}_{2i}$.

10.2.6 Alternative Error Structures

Both the random effects and the fixed effects models assume that the presence of α_i captures all correlation between the unobservables in different time periods. That is, ε_{it} is assumed to be uncorrelated over individuals and time. Provided that the x_{it} variables are strictly exogenous, the presence of autocorrelation in ε_{it} does not result in inconsistency of the standard estimators. It does, however, invalidate the standard errors and resulting tests, just as we saw in Chapter 4. Moreover, it implies that the estimators are no longer efficient. For example, if the true covariance matrix Ω does not satisfy (10.16), the random effects estimator no longer corresponds to the feasible

GLS estimator for β. As we know, the presence of heteroskedasticity in ε_{it} or – for the random effects model – in α_i, has similar consequences.

One way to avoid misleading inferences, without the need to impose alternative assumptions on the structure of the covariance matrix Ω, is the use of the OLS estimator for β, while adjusting its standard errors for general forms of heteroskedasticity and autocorrelation. Consider the following model[10]

$$y_{it} = x_{it}'\beta + u_{it}, \tag{10.34}$$

without the assumption that u_{it} has an error components structure. Consistency of the OLS estimator

$$b = \left(\sum_{i=1}^{N}\sum_{t=1}^{T} x_{it}x_{it}'\right)^{-1} \sum_{i=1}^{N}\sum_{t=1}^{T} x_{it}y_{it} \tag{10.35}$$

for β requires that

$$E\{x_{it}u_{it}\} = 0. \tag{10.36}$$

Assuming that error terms of different individuals are uncorrelated ($E\{u_{it}u_{js}\} = 0$ for all $i \neq j$), the OLS covariance matrix can be estimated by a variant of the Newey–West estimator from Chapter 4, given by

$$\hat{V}\{b\} = \left(\sum_{i=1}^{N}\sum_{t=1}^{T} x_{it}x_{it}'\right)^{-1} \sum_{i=1}^{N}\sum_{t=1}^{T}\sum_{s=1}^{T} \hat{u}_{it}\hat{u}_{is}x_{it}x_{is}' \left(\sum_{i=1}^{N}\sum_{t=1}^{T} x_{it}x_{it}'\right)^{-1}, \tag{10.37}$$

where $\hat{u}_{it}$ denotes the OLS residual. This estimator allows for general forms of heteroskedasticity as well as autocorrelation (within a given individual). If heteroskedasticity is excluded a priori, the middle matrix in (10.37) can be replaced by

$$\sum_{i=1}^{N}\sum_{t=1}^{T}\sum_{s=1}^{T} \left(\frac{1}{N}\sum_{i=1}^{N} \hat{u}_{it}\hat{u}_{is}\right) x_{it}x_{is}', \tag{10.38}$$

where $(1/N)\sum_{i=1}^{N} \hat{u}_{it}\hat{u}_{is}$ is a consistent estimator for $\Omega_{ts} = E\{u_{it}u_{is}\}$.

If u_{it} has a time-invariant component α_i that might be correlated with the explanatory variables, the fixed effects estimator would be more appropriate than OLS and a similar correction for heteroskedasticity and autocorrelation (in ε_{it}) can be employed (Arellano, 1987). The resulting expression is similar to (10.37) but replaces each x_{it} with its within transformation $x_{it} - \bar{x}_i$ and the OLS residual by the within residual (see Baltagi, 1995, p. 13).

If one is willing to make specific assumptions about the form of heteroskedasticity or autocorrelation, it is possible to derive more efficient estimators than OLS or fixed effects, by exploiting the structure of the error covariance matrix using a feasible GLS or maximum likelihood approach. An overview of a number of such estimators, which are typically computationally unattractive, is provided in Baltagi (1995, Chapter 5). Kmenta (1986) suggests a relatively simple feasible GLS estimator that allows for first order autocorrelation in u_{it} combined with individual specific hetero-

---

[10] For notational convenience, the constant is assumed to be included in x_{it}.

skedasticity, but does not allow for a time-invariant component in u_{it} (see Baltagi, 1996).

10.2.7 Testing for Heteroskedasticity and Autocorrelation

Most of the tests that can be used for heteroskedasticity or autocorrelation in the random effects model are computationally burdensome. For the fixed effects model, which is essentially estimated by OLS, things are relatively less complex. Fortunately, as the fixed effects estimator can be applied even if we make the random effects assumption that α_i is i.i.d. and independent of the explanatory variables, the tests for the fixed effects model can also be used in the random effects case.

A fairly simple test for autocorrelation in the fixed effects model is based upon the Durbin–Watson test discussed in Chapter 4. The alternative hypothesis is that

$$\varepsilon_{it} = \rho \varepsilon_{i,t-1} + v_{it}, \tag{10.39}$$

where v_{it} is i.i.d. across individuals and time. This allows for autocorrelation over time with the restriction that each individual has the same autocorrelation coefficient ρ. The null hypothesis under test is $H_0 : \rho = 0$ against the one-sided alternative $\rho < 0$ or $\rho > 0$. Let $\hat{\varepsilon}_{it}$ denote the *residuals from the within regression* (10.9) or – equivalently – from (10.7). Then Bhargava, Franzini and Narendranathan (1983) suggest the following generalization of the Durbin–Watson statistic

$$dw_p = \frac{\sum_{i=1}^{N} \sum_{t=2}^{T} (\hat{\varepsilon}_{it} - \hat{\varepsilon}_{i,t-1})^2}{\sum_{i=1}^{N} \sum_{t=1}^{T} \hat{\varepsilon}_{it}^2}. \tag{10.40}$$

Using similar derivations as Durbin and Watson, the authors are able to derive lower and upper bounds on the true critical values that depend upon N, T, and K only. Unlike the true time series case, the inconclusive region for the panel data Durbin–Watson test is very small, particularly when the number of individuals in the panel is large. In Table 10.1 we present some selected lower and upper bounds for the true 5% critical values that can be used to test against the alternative of positive autocorrelation. The numbers in the table confirm that the inconclusive regions are small and also indicate that the variation with K, N or T is limited. In a model with three explanatory variables estimated over 6 time periods, we reject $H_0 : \rho = 0$ at the 5% level if dw_p is smaller than 1.859 for $N = 100$ and 1.957 for $N = 1000$, both against the one-sided alternative of $\rho > 0$. For panels with very large N, Bhargava *et al.* suggest simply to test if the computed statistic dw_p is less than two, when testing against positive autocorrelation. Because the fixed effects estimator is also consistent in the random effects

Table 10.1 5% lower and upper bounds panel Durbin–Watson test (Bhargava *et al.*, 1983)

		N = 100		N = 500		N = 1000	
		d_L	d_U	d_L	d_U	d_L	d_U
$T = 6$	$K = 3$	1.859	1.880	1.939	1.943	1.957	1.959
	$K = 9$	1.839	1.902	1.935	1.947	1.954	1.961
$T = 10$	$K = 3$	1.891	1.904	1.952	1.954	1.967	1.968
	$K = 9$	1.878	1.916	1.949	1.957	1.965	1.970

model, it is also possible to use this panel data Durbin–Watson test in the latter model.

To test for heteroskedasticity in ε_{it}, we can again use the fixed effects residuals $\hat{\varepsilon}_{it}$. The auxiliary regression of the test regresses the squared within residuals $\hat{\varepsilon}_{it}^2$ upon a constant and the J variables z_{it} that we think may affect heteroskedasticity. This is a variant of the Breusch–Pagan test[11] for heteroskedasticity discussed in Chapter 4. Its alternative hypothesis is that

$$V\{\varepsilon_{it}\} = \sigma^2 h(z_{it}'\alpha), \tag{10.41}$$

where h is an unknown continuously differentiable function with $h(0) = 1$, so that the null hypothesis that is tested is given by H_0: $\alpha = 0$. Under the null hypothesis, the test statistic, computed as $N(T-1)$ times the R^2 of the auxiliary regression, will have an asymptotic Chi-squared distribution, with J degrees of freedom. An alternative test can be computed from the residuals of the between regression, and is based upon N times the R^2 of an auxiliary regression of the between residuals upon $\bar{z}_i$ or, more generally, upon $z_{i1}, \ldots, z_{iT}$. Under the null hypothesis of homoskedastic errors, the test statistic has an asymptotic Chi-squared distribution, with degrees of freedom equal to the number of variables included in the auxiliary regression (excluding the intercept). The alternative hypothesis of the latter test is less well-defined.

10.3 Illustration: Explaining Individual Wages

In this section we shall apply a number of the above estimators when estimating an individual wage equation. The data[12] are taken from the Youth Sample of the National Longitudinal Survey held in the USA, and comprise a sample of 545 full-time working males who have completed their schooling by 1980 and then followed over the period 1980–1987. The males in the sample are young, with an age in 1980 ranging from 17 to 23, and entered the labour market fairly recently, with an average of 3 years of experience in the beginning of the sample period. The data and specifications we choose are similar to those in Vella and Verbeek (1998). Log wages are explained from years of schooling, years of experience and its square, dummy variables for being a union member, working in the public sector and being married and two racial dummies.

The estimation results[13] for the between estimator, based upon individual averages, and the within estimator, based upon deviations from individual means, are given in the first two columns of Table 10.2. First of all, it should be noted that the fixed effects or within estimator eliminates any time-invariant variables from the model. In this case, it means that the effects of schooling and race are wiped out. The differences between the two sets of estimates seems substantial, and we shall come back to this below. In the next column the OLS results are presented applied to the random effects model, where the *standard errors are not adjusted for the error components structure*.

---

[11] In a panel data context, the term Breusch–Pagan test is usually associated with a Lagrange Multiplier test in the random effects model for the null hypothesis that there are no individual specific effects ($\sigma_\alpha^2 = 0$); see Baltagi (1995, Sect. 4.2.1). In applications, this test almost always rejects the null hypothesis.

[12] The data used in this section are available as MALES.

[13] The estimation results in this section are obtained by Stata 5.0.

Table 10.2 Estimation results wage equation, males 1980–1987 (standard errors in parentheses)

Dependent variable: log(*wage*)

Variable	Between	Fixed effects	OLS	Random effects
constant	0.490	—	−0.034	−0.104
	(0.221)		(0.065)	(0.111)
schooling	0.095	—	0.099	0.101
	(0.011)		(0.005)	(0.009)
experience	−0.050	0.116	0.089	0.112
	(0.050)	(0.008)	(0.010)	(0.008)
experience^2	0.0051	−0.0043	−0.0028	−0.0041
	(0.0032)	(0.0006)	(0.0007)	(0.0006)
union member	0.274	0.081	0.180	0.106
	(0.047)	(0.019)	(0.017)	(0.018)
married	0.145	0.045	0.108	0.063
	(0.041)	(0.018)	(0.016)	(0.017)
black	−0.139	—	−0.144	−0.144
	(0.049)		(0.024)	(0.048)
hispanic	0.005	—	0.016	0.020
	(0.043)		(0.021)	(0.043)
public sector	−0.056	0.035	0.004	0.030
	(0.109)	(0.039)	(0.037)	(0.036)
within R^2	0.0470	0.1782	0.1679	0.1776
between R^2	0.2196	0.0006	0.2027	0.1835
overall R^2	0.1371	0.0642	0.1866	0.1808

The last column presents the random effects EGLS estimator. As discussed in Subsection 10.2.2, the variances of the error components α_i and ε_{it} can be estimated from the within and between residuals. In particular, we have $\hat{\sigma}_B^2 = 0.1209$ and $\hat{\sigma}_\varepsilon^2 = 0.1234$. From this, we can consistently estimate σ_α^2 as $\hat{\sigma}_\alpha^2 = 0.1209 - 0.1234/8 = 0.1055$. Consequently, the factor ψ is estimated as

$$\hat{\psi} = \frac{0.1234}{0.1234 + 8 \times 0.1055} = 0.1276,$$

leading to $\hat{\vartheta} = 1 - \hat{\psi}^{1/2} = 0.6428$. This means that the EGLS estimator can be obtained from a transformed regression where 0.64 times the individual mean is subtracted from the original data. Recall that OLS imposes $\vartheta = 0$ while the fixed effects estimator employs $\vartheta = 1$. Note that both the OLS and the random effects estimates are in between the between and fixed effects estimates.

If the assumptions of the random effects model are satisfied, all four estimators in Table 10.2 are consistent, the random effects estimator being the most efficient one. If, however, the individual effects α_i are correlated with one or more of the explanatory variables, the fixed effects estimator is the only one that is consistent. This hypothesis can be tested by comparing the between and within estimators, or the within and random effects estimators, which leads to tests that are equivalent. The simplest one to perform is the Hausman test discussed in Subsection 10.2.3, based upon the latter comparison. The test statistic takes a value of 31.75 and reflects the differences in the coefficients on experience, experience squared and the union, married and public sector dummies. Under the null hypothesis, the statistic follows a Chi-squared distribution with 5 degrees of freedom, so that we have to reject the null at any reasonable level of significance.

Marital status is a variable that is likely to be correlated with the unobserved heterogeneity in α_i. Typically one would not expect an important *causal* effect of being married upon one's wage, so that the marital dummy is typically capturing other (unobservable) differences between married and unmarried workers. This is confirmed by the results in the table. If we eliminate the individual effects from the model and consider the fixed effects estimator the effect of being married reduces to 4.5%, while for the between estimator, for example, it is almost 15%. Note that the effect of being married in the fixed effects approach is identified only through people that change marital status over the sample period. Similar remarks can be made for the effect of union status upon a person's wage. Recall, however, that all estimators assume that the explanatory variables are uncorrelated with the idiosyncratic error term ε_{it}. If such correlations would exist, even the fixed effects estimator would be inconsistent. Vella and Verbeek (1998) concentrate on the impact of endogenous union status on wages for this group of workers and consider alternative, more complicated, estimators.

The goodness-of-fit measures confirm that the fixed effects estimator results in the largest within R^2 and thus explains the within variation as well as possible. The OLS estimator maximizes the usual (overall) R^2, while the random effects estimator results in reasonable R^2s in all dimensions. Recall that the standard errors of the OLS estimator are misleading as they do not take into account the correlation across different error terms. The correct standard errors for the OLS estimator should be larger than those for the efficient EGLS estimator that exploits these correlations.

10.4 Dynamic Linear Models

Among the major advantages of panel data is the ability to model individual dynamics. Many economic models suggest that current behaviour depends upon past behaviour (persistence, habit formation, partial adjustment, etc.), so in many cases we would like to estimate a dynamic model on an individual level. The ability to do so is unique for panel data.

10.4.1 An Autoregressive Panel Data Model

Consider the linear dynamic model with exogenous variables and a lagged dependent variable, that is

$$y_{it} = x_{it}'\beta + \gamma y_{i,t-1} + \alpha_i + \varepsilon_{it},$$

where it is assumed that ε_{it} is $IID(0, \sigma_\varepsilon^2)$. In the static model, we have seen arguments of consistency (robustness) and efficiency for choosing between a fixed or random effects treatment of the α_i. In a dynamic model the situation is substantially different, because $y_{i,t-1}$ will depend upon α_i, irrespective of the way we treat α_i. To illustrate the problems that this causes, we first consider the case where there are no exogenous variables included and the model reads

$$y_{it} = \gamma y_{i,t-1} + \alpha_i + \varepsilon_{it}, \quad |\gamma| < 1. \tag{10.42}$$

Assume that we have observations on y_{it} for periods $t = 0, 1, \dots, T$.

The fixed effects estimator for γ is given by

$$\hat{\gamma}_{FE} = \frac{\sum_{i=1}^{N} \sum_{t=1}^{T} (y_{it} - \bar{y}_i)(y_{i,t-1} - \bar{y}_{i,-1})}{\sum_{i=1}^{N} \sum_{t=1}^{T} (y_{i,t-1} - \bar{y}_{i,-1})^2}, \tag{10.43}$$

where $\bar{y}_i = 1/T \sum_{t=1}^{T} y_{it}$ and $\bar{y}_{i,-1} = 1/T \sum_{t=1}^{T} y_{i,t-1}$. To analyse the properties of $\hat{\gamma}_{FE}$ we can substitute (10.42) into (10.43) to obtain

$$\hat{\gamma}_{FE} = \gamma + \frac{(1/(NT)) \sum_{i=1}^{N} \sum_{t=1}^{T} (\varepsilon_{it} - \bar{\varepsilon}_i)(y_{i,t-1} - \bar{y}_{i,-1})}{(1/(NT)) \sum_{i=1}^{N} \sum_{t=1}^{T} (y_{i,t-1} - \bar{y}_{i,-1})^2}. \tag{10.44}$$

This estimator, however, is biased and inconsistent for $N \to \infty$ and fixed T, as the last term in the right-hand side of (10.44) does not have expectation zero and does not converge to zero if N goes to infinity. In particular, it can be shown that (see Nickell, 1981; or Hsiao, 1986, p. 74)

$$\plim_{N \to \infty} \frac{1}{NT} \sum_{i=1}^{N} \sum_{t=1}^{T} (\varepsilon_{it} - \bar{\varepsilon}_i)(y_{i,t-1} - \bar{y}_{i,-1}) = -\frac{\sigma_\varepsilon^2}{T^2} \cdot \frac{(T-1) - T\gamma + \gamma^T}{(1-\gamma)^2} \neq 0. \tag{10.45}$$

Thus, for fixed T we have an inconsistent estimator. Note that this inconsistency is not caused by anything we assumed about the α_is, as these are eliminated in estimation. The problem is that the within transformed lagged dependent variable is correlated with the within transformed error. If $T \to \infty$, (10.45) converges to 0 so that the fixed effects estimator is consistent for γ if both $T \to \infty$ and $N \to \infty$.

One could think that the asymptotic bias for fixed T is quite small and therefore not a real problem. This is certainly not the case, as for finite T the bias can hardly be ignored. For example, if the true value of γ equals 0.5, it can easily be computed that (for $N \to \infty$)

$$\plim \hat{\gamma}_{FE} = -0.25 \quad \text{if } T = 2$$
$$\plim \hat{\gamma}_{FE} = -0.04 \quad \text{if } T = 3$$
$$\plim \hat{\gamma}_{FE} = 0.33 \quad \text{if } T = 10,$$

so even for moderate values of T the bias is substantial. Fortunately, there are relatively easy ways to avoid these biases.

To solve the inconsistency problem, we first of all start with a different transformation to eliminate the individual effects α_i, in particular we take first differences. This gives

$$y_{it} - y_{i,t-1} = \gamma(y_{i,t-1} - y_{i,t-2}) + (\varepsilon_{it} - \varepsilon_{i,t-1}), \quad t = 2, \ldots, T. \tag{10.46}$$

If we estimate this by OLS we do not get a consistent estimator for γ because $y_{i,t-1}$ and $\varepsilon_{i,t-1}$ are, by definition, correlated, even if $T \to \infty$. However, this transformed specification suggests an instrumental variables approach. For example, $y_{i,t-2}$ is correlated with $y_{i,t-1} - y_{i,t-2}$ but not with $\varepsilon_{i,t-1}$, unless ε_{it} exhibits autocorrelation (which we excluded by assumption). This suggests an instrumental variables estimator[14] for γ as

$$\hat{\gamma}_{IV} = \frac{\sum_{i=1}^{N} \sum_{t=2}^{T} y_{i,t-2}(y_{it} - y_{i,t-1})}{\sum_{i=1}^{N} \sum_{t=2}^{T} y_{i,t-2}(y_{i,t-1} - y_{i,t-2})}. \tag{10.47}$$

---

[14] See Section 5.3 for a general introduction to instrumental variables estimation.

A necessary condition for consistency of this estimator is that

$$\text{plim} \frac{1}{N(T-1)} \sum_{i=1}^{N} \sum_{t=2}^{T} (\varepsilon_{it} - \varepsilon_{i,t-1}) y_{i,t-2} = 0 \qquad (10.48)$$

for either T, or N, or both going to infinity. The estimator in (10.47) was one of the estimators proposed by Anderson and Hsiao (1981). They also proposed an alternative, where $y_{i,t-2} - y_{i,t-3}$ is used as an instrument. This gives

$$\hat{\gamma}_{IV}^{(2)} = \frac{\sum_{i=1}^{N} \sum_{t=3}^{T} (y_{i,t-2} - y_{i,t-3})(y_{it} - y_{i,t-1})}{\sum_{i=1}^{N} \sum_{t=3}^{T} (y_{i,t-2} - y_{i,t-3})(y_{i,t-1} - y_{i,t-2})}, \qquad (10.49)$$

which is consistent (under regularity conditions) if

$$\text{plim} \frac{1}{N(T-2)} \sum_{i=1}^{N} \sum_{t=3}^{T} (\varepsilon_{it} - \varepsilon_{i,t-1})(y_{i,t-2} - y_{i,t-3}) = 0. \qquad (10.50)$$

Consistency of both of these estimators is guaranteed by the assumption that ε_{it} has no autocorrelation.

Note that the second instrumental variables estimator requires an additional lag to construct the instrument, such that the effective number of observations used in estimation is reduced (one sample period is 'lost'). The question which estimator one should choose is not really an issue. A method of moments approach can unify the estimators and eliminate the disadvantages of reduced sample sizes. A first step in this approach is to note that

$$\text{plim} \frac{1}{N(T-1)} \sum_{i=1}^{N} \sum_{t=2}^{T} (\varepsilon_{it} - \varepsilon_{i,t-1}) y_{i,t-2} = E\{(\varepsilon_{it} - \varepsilon_{i,t-1}) y_{i,t-2}\} = 0 \qquad (10.51)$$

is a moment condition (compare Chapter 5). Similarly,

$$\text{plim} \frac{1}{N(T-2)} \sum_{i=1}^{N} \sum_{t=3}^{T} (\varepsilon_{it} - \varepsilon_{i,t-1})(y_{i,t-2} - y_{i,t-3})$$

$$= E\{(\varepsilon_{it} - \varepsilon_{i,t-1})(y_{i,t-2} - y_{i,t-3})\} = 0 \qquad (10.52)$$

is a moment condition. Both IV estimators thus impose one moment condition in estimation. It is well known that imposing more moment conditions increases the efficiency of the estimators (provided the additional conditions are valid, of course). Arellano and Bond (1991) suggest that the list of instruments can be extended by exploiting additional moment conditions and letting their number vary with t. To do this, they keep T fixed. For example, when $T = 4$, we have

$$E\{(\varepsilon_{i2} - \varepsilon_{i1}) y_{i0}\} = 0$$

as the moment condition for $t = 2$. For $t = 3$, we have

$$E\{(\varepsilon_{i3} - \varepsilon_{i2}) y_{i1}\} = 0,$$

but it also holds that

$$E\{(\varepsilon_{i3} - \varepsilon_{i2}) y_{i0}\} = 0.$$

For period $t = 4$, we have three moment conditions and three valid instruments

$$E\{(\varepsilon_{i4} - \varepsilon_{i3})y_{i0}\} = 0$$
$$E\{(\varepsilon_{i4} - \varepsilon_{i3})y_{i1}\} = 0$$
$$E\{(\varepsilon_{i4} - \varepsilon_{i3})y_{i2}\} = 0.$$

All these moment conditions can be exploited in a GMM framework. To introduce the GMM estimator define for general sample size T,

$$\Delta\varepsilon_i = \begin{pmatrix} \varepsilon_{i2} - \varepsilon_{i1} \\ \cdots \\ \varepsilon_{i,T} - \varepsilon_{i,T-1} \end{pmatrix} \tag{10.53}$$

as the vector of transformed error terms, and

$$Z_i = \begin{pmatrix} [y_{i0}] & 0 & \cdots & 0 \\ 0 & [y_{i0}, y_{i1}] & & 0 \\ \vdots & & \ddots & 0 \\ 0 & \cdots & 0 & [y_{i0}, \ldots, y_{i,T-2}] \end{pmatrix} \tag{10.54}$$

as the matrix of instruments. Each row in the matrix Z_i contains the instruments that are valid for a given period. Consequently, the set of all moment conditions can be written concisely as

$$E\{Z_i'\Delta\varepsilon_i\} = 0. \tag{10.55}$$

Note that these are $1 + 2 + 3 + \cdots + T - 1$ conditions. To derive the GMM estimator, write this as

$$E\{Z_i'(\Delta y_i - \gamma\Delta y_{i,-1})\} = 0. \tag{10.56}$$

Because the number of moment conditions will typically exceed the number of unknown coefficients, we estimate γ by minimizing a quadratic expression in terms of the corresponding sample moments (compare Chapter 5), that is

$$\min_{\gamma} \left[\frac{1}{N}\sum_{i=1}^{N} Z_i'(\Delta y_i - \gamma\Delta y_{i,-1}) \right]' W_N \left[\frac{1}{N}\sum_{i=1}^{N} Z_i'(\Delta y_i - \gamma\Delta y_{i,-1}) \right], \tag{10.57}$$

where W_N is a symmetric positive definite weighting matrix.[15] Differentiating this with respect to γ and solving for γ gives

$$\hat{\gamma}_{GMM} = \left(\left(\sum_{i=1}^{N}\Delta y_{i,-1}'Z_i \right) W_N \left(\sum_{i=1}^{N}Z_i'\Delta y_{i,-1} \right) \right)^{-1}$$
$$\times \left(\sum_{i=1}^{N}\Delta y_{i,-1}'Z_i \right) W_N \left(\sum_{i=1}^{N}Z_i'\Delta y_i \right). \tag{10.58}$$

---

[15] The suffix N reflects that W_N can depend upon the sample size N and does not reflect the dimension of the matrix.

The properties of this estimator depend upon the choice for W_N, although it is consistent as long as W_N is positive definite, for example, for $W_N = I$, the identity matrix.

The **optimal weighting matrix** is the one that gives the most efficient estimator, i.e. that gives the smallest asymptotic covariance matrix for $\hat{\gamma}_{GMM}$. From the general theory of GMM in Chapter 5, we know that the optimal weighting matrix is (asymptotically) proportional to the inverse of the covariance matrix of the sample moments. In this case, this means that the optimal weighting matrix should satisfy

$$\underset{N\to\infty}{\text{plim}} \ W_N = V\{Z_i'\Delta\varepsilon_i\}^{-1} = E\{Z_i'\Delta\varepsilon_i\Delta\varepsilon_i'Z_i\}^{-1}. \tag{10.59}$$

In the standard case where no restrictions are imposed upon the covariance matrix of ε_i, this can be estimated using a first-step consistent estimator of γ and replacing the expectation operator by a sample average. This gives

$$\hat{W}_N^{opt} = \left(\frac{1}{N}\sum_{i=1}^N Z_i'\Delta\hat{\varepsilon}_i\Delta\hat{\varepsilon}_i'Z_i\right)^{-1}, \tag{10.60}$$

where $\Delta\hat{\varepsilon}_i$ is a residual vector from a first-step consistent estimator, for example using $W_N = I$.

The general GMM approach does not impose that ε_{it} is i.i.d. over individuals and time, and the optimal weighting matrix is thus estimated without imposing these restrictions. Note, however, that the absence of autocorrelation was needed to guarantee the validity of the moment conditions. Instead of estimating the optimal weighting matrix unrestrictedly, it is also possible (and potentially advisable in small samples) to impose the absence of autocorrelation in ε_{it}, combined with a homoskedasticity assumption. Noting that under these restrictions

$$E\{\Delta\varepsilon_i\Delta\varepsilon_i'\} = \sigma_\varepsilon^2 G = \sigma_\varepsilon^2 \begin{pmatrix} 2 & -1 & 0 & \cdots \\ -1 & 2 & \ddots & 0 \\ 0 & \ddots & \ddots & -1 \\ \vdots & & 0 & -1 & 2 \end{pmatrix}, \tag{10.61}$$

the optimal weighting matrix can be determined as

$$W_N^{opt} = \left(\frac{1}{N}\sum_{i=1}^N Z_i'GZ_i\right)^{-1}. \tag{10.62}$$

Note that this matrix does not involve unknown parameters, so that the optimal GMM estimator can be computed in one step if the original errors ε_{it} are assumed to be homoskedastic and exhibit no autocorrelation.

In general, the GMM estimator for γ is asymptotically normal with its covariance matrix given by

$$\text{plim}\left(\left(\frac{1}{N}\sum_{i=1}^N \Delta y_{i,-1}'Z_i\right)\left(\frac{1}{N}\sum_{i=1}^N Z_i'\Delta\varepsilon_i\Delta\varepsilon_i'Z_i\right)^{-1}\left(\frac{1}{N}\sum_{i=1}^N Z_i'\Delta y_{i,-1}\right)\right)^{-1}. \tag{10.63}$$

This follows from the more general expressions in Section 5.6. With i.i.d. errors the middle term reduces to

$$\sigma_\varepsilon^2 W_N^{opt} = \sigma_\varepsilon^2 \left(\frac{1}{N} \sum_{i=1}^{N} Z_i' G Z_i \right)^{-1}.$$

10.4.2 Dynamic Models with Exogenous Variables

If the model also contains exogenous variables, we have

$$y_{it} = x_{it}'\beta + \gamma y_{i,t-1} + \alpha_i + \varepsilon_{it}, \tag{10.64}$$

which can also be estimated by the generalized instrumental variables or GMM approach. Depending upon the assumptions made about x_{it}, different sets of additional instruments can be constructed. If the x_{it} are *strictly exogenous* in the sense that they are uncorrelated with any of the ε_{is} error terms, we also have that

$$E\{x_{is}\Delta\varepsilon_{it}\} = 0 \quad \text{for each } s, t, \tag{10.65}$$

so that $x_{i1}, \ldots, x_{iT}$ can be added to the instruments list for the first-differenced equation in each period. This would make the number of rows in Z_i quite large. Instead, almost the same level of information may be retained when the first-differenced x_{it}s are used as their own instruments.[16] In this case, we impose the moment conditions

$$E\{\Delta x_{it}\Delta\varepsilon_{it}\} = 0 \quad \text{for each } t \tag{10.66}$$

and the instrument matrix can be written as

$$Z_i = \begin{pmatrix} [y_{i0}, \Delta x_{i2}'] & 0 & \cdots & 0 \\ 0 & [y_{i0}, y_{i1}, \Delta x_{i3}'] & & 0 \\ \vdots & & \ddots & 0 \\ 0 & \cdots & 0 & [y_{i0}, \ldots, y_{i,T-2}, \Delta x_{iT}'] \end{pmatrix}. \tag{10.67}$$

If the x_{it} variables are not strictly exogenous but **predetermined**, in which case current and lagged x_{it}s are uncorrelated with current error terms, we only have that $E\{x_{it}\varepsilon_{is}\} = 0$ for $s \geq t$. In this case, only $x_{i,t-1}, \ldots, x_{i1}$ are valid instruments for the first differenced equation in period t. Thus, the moment conditions that can be imposed are

$$E\{x_{it-j}\Delta\varepsilon_{it}\} = 0 \quad \text{for } j = 1, \ldots, t-1 \text{ (for each } t). \tag{10.68}$$

In practice, a combination of strictly exogenous and predetermined x-variables may occur rather than one of these two extreme cases. The matrix Z_i should then be adjusted accordingly. Baltagi (1995, Chapter 8) provides additional discussion and examples.

Arellano and Bover (1995) provide a framework to integrate the above approach with the instrumental variables estimators of Hausman and Taylor (1981) and others

---

[16] We give up potential efficiency gains if some x_{it} variables help 'explaining' the lagged endogenous variables.

discussed in Subsection 10.2.5. Most importantly, they discuss how information in levels can also be exploited in estimation. That is, in addition to the moment conditions presented above, it is also possible to exploit the presence of valid instruments for the levels equation (10.64) or its average over time (the between regression). This is of particular importance when the γ coefficient is close to unity; see also Blundell and Bond (1998).

10.4.3 Unit Roots and Cointegration

The recent literature exhibits an increasing integration of techniques and ideas from time series analysis, like unit roots and cointegration, into the area of panel data modelling. The underlying reason for this development is that researchers increasingly realize that cross-sectional information is a useful additional source of information that should be exploited. To analyse the effect of a certain policy measure, for example adopting a road tax or a pollution tax, it may be more fruitful to compare with other countries than to try to extract information about these effects only from the country's own history. Pooling data from different countries may also help to overcome the problem that sample sizes of time series are fairly small, so that tests regarding long-run properties are not very powerful.

A number of recent articles discuss problems of unit roots, spurious regressions and cointegration in panel data. It should be stressed that these concepts are *long-run* concepts and typically lead to inferential problems if T tends to infinity. In many cases keeping T fixed and letting N go to infinity circumvents such problems, at least theoretically.

The crucial issue in analysing the time series on a number of units simultaneously is that of heterogeneity. As long as we consider each time series individually, and the series is of sufficient length, there is nothing wrong with applying the time series techniques from Chapters 8 and 9. However, if we pool different series, we have to be aware of the possibility that their processes not all have the same characteristics or are described by the same parameters. For example, it is conceivable that y_{it} is stationary for country 1 but integrated of order one for country 2. Assuming that all variables involved are $I(1)$, suppose that in each country i the variables y_{it} and x_{it} are cointegrated with parameter β_i. In that case $y_{it} - \beta_i x_{it}$ is $I(0)$ for each i, but there does not exist a common cointegrating parameter β that makes $y_{it} - \beta x_{it}$ stationary for all i (unless β_i is identical for all countries). Similarly, there is no guarantee that the cross-sectional averages $\bar{y}_t = (1/N)\sum_i y_{it}$ and $\bar{x}_t$ are cointegrated, even if all underlying individual series are cointegrated.

To illustrate some of the issues involved, consider the autoregressive model

$$y_{it} = \alpha_i + \gamma_i y_{i,t-1} + \varepsilon_{it},$$

which we can write as

$$\Delta y_{it} = \alpha_i + \pi_i y_{i,t-1} + \varepsilon_{it},$$

where $\pi_i = \gamma_i - 1$. The null hypothesis that all series have a unit root then becomes H_0: $\pi_i = 0$ for all i. The alternative hypothesis could be that all series are stationary with the same mean-reversion parameter, i.e. H_1: $\pi_i = \pi < 0$ for all i. This is implicit in the approaches of Levin and Lin (1992), Quah (1994) and Harris and Tzavalis

(1999). A less restrictive alternative specifies that H_1: $\pi_i < 0$ for all i, which allows π_i to be different across groups, and is used by Im, Pesaran and Shin (1997). Alternative test statistics are derived along with their asymptotic distributions if N, T or both go to infinity, but the discussion of them is beyond the scope of this text. In any case, the central hypothesis is that the time series of *all* individual units have a unit root against the alternative that *all* time series are stationary. One could therefore criticize the above approaches by saying that it is plausible that there is a nonzero probability that one or more individuals are stationary while all others have a unit root or vice versa. In this case, neither the null nor the alternative hypothesis is satisfied and it is unclear whether we would wish our test to reject or not. Another technical issue is the possibility of cross-sectional dependence between the ε_{it}s from different countries, which invalidates a number of the proposed tests.

Robertson and Symons (1992) and Pesaran and Smith (1995) stress the importance of parameter heterogeneity in dynamic panel data models and analyse the potentially severe biases that may arise from handling it in an inappropriate manner. Such biases are particularly misleading in a nonstationary world as the relationships between the individual series may be completely destroyed. Results on panel data tests for spurious regressions and cointegration are relatively limited; see Kao (1999) and Phillips and Moon (1999) for some recent work.

10.5   Illustration: Wage Elasticities of Labour Demand

In this section we consider a model that explains labour demand of firms from wages, output, lagged labour demand and some other variables. Our goal is to derive estimates for the short- and long-run wage elasticities of labour demand in Belgium. The data and models are taken from Konings and Roodhooft (1997), who use a panel of more than 3000 large Belgian firms over the period 1986–1994. The static demand for labour is given by

$$\log L_{it} = \beta_1 + \beta_2 \log w_{it} + \beta_3 \log r_{it} + \beta_4 \log Y_{it} + \beta_5 \log w_{jt} + u_{it},$$

where L_{it} denotes desired employment of firm i in period t (labour demand), w_{it} and r_{it} the unit cost of labour and capital, respectively, and Y_{it} denotes the output level. The last variable w_{jt} denotes the industry average of the real wage. This relationship is interpreted as a long-run result, as it ignores costs of adjustment.

For the short-run Konings and Roodhooft experiment with alternative dynamic specifications. The simplest one assumes that

$$\log L_{it} = \beta_1 + \beta_2 \log w_{it} + \beta_3 \log r_{it} + \beta_4 \log Y_{it} + \beta_5 \log w_{jt} + \gamma \log L_{i,t-1} + u_{it}.$$

In estimation, r_{it} is approximated by the capital stock K_{it}, and Y_{it} by value added. The dynamic model that we estimate is then given by

$$\log L_{it} = \beta_1 + \beta_2 \log w_{it} + \beta_3 \log K_{it} + \beta_4 \log Y_{it} + \beta_5 \log w_{jt} + \gamma \log L_{i,t-1} + \alpha_i + \varepsilon_{it},$$

where it is assumed that the error term consists of two components. The component α_i denotes unobserved firm specific time-invariant heterogeneity. First differencing this equation, as in the previous section, eliminates α_i but does not result in an equation that can be estimated consistently by OLS. First, there is correlation between $\Delta \log L_{i,t-1}$ and $\Delta \varepsilon_{it}$ (as above). Second, it is by no means obvious that the factor costs are exogenously given. In particular for the labour costs w_{it}, several alternative situations can be thought of in which wages are determined simultaneously with employment. For example, trade unions may bargain with employers over wages and employment. Thus, we can expect that

$$E\{\Delta \log w_{it} \Delta \varepsilon_{it}\} \neq 0.$$

Therefore, $\Delta \log w_{it}$ is also instrumented in estimation. Valid instruments are given by $\log w_{i,t-2}, \log w_{i,t-3}, \ldots$, similar to the instruments for $\Delta \log L_{i,t-1}$. The number of available instruments thus increases with t.

In Table 10.3 we present the estimation results of the static and dynamic model discussed above. This is a subset of the results in Konings and Roodhooft (1997), who also consider models with additional lags of the other variables. The first column gives the estimates for the static (long-run) labour demand function. The wage is treated as endogenous and instrumented as indicated above. In the second column, lagged labour demand is included, which is also instrumented in the manner described above. Both specifications also include regional and time dummies. To test the model against a non-specified alternative we can use the overidentifying restrictions tests, as discussed in Chapter 5. The test statistics of 29.7 and 51.66 have to be compared with the critical values from a Chi-squared distribution with 15 and 29 degrees of freedom, respectively. With p-values of 0.013 and 0.006 the overidentifying restrictions are, at the 1% level, on the boundary of being rejected for both specifications. The significance of the lagged dependent variable (standard errors are given in parentheses), suggests that the dynamic specification should be preferred.

The estimated short-run wage elasticity from the last column is -0.66, while the long-run elasticity is $-0.66/(1 - 0.60) = -1.6$, which is close to the estimate of -1.78 from the static long-run model. Both of these estimates are quite high. For example, they suggest that in the long run a 1% wage increase results in a 1.6% decrease in labour demand. These estimates are much higher than was initially believed based on macro-economic time series data. Apparently, the possibility to correct for observed and unobserved firm heterogeneity has a substantial impact on the estimates. A potential problem of the results in Table 10.3 lies in the way the data are constructed.

Table 10.3 Estimation results labour demand equation (Konings and Roodhooft, 1997)

Dependent variable: $\log L_{it}$				
Variables	Static model		Dynamic model	
$\log L_{i,t-1}$	–		0.60	(0.045)
$\log Y_{it}$	0.021	(0.009)	0.008	(0.005)
$\log w_{it}$	−1.78	(0.60)	−0.66	(0.19)
$\log w_{jt}$	0.16	(0.07)	0.054	(0.033)
$\log K_{it}$	0.08	(0.011)	0.078	(0.006)
overidentifying restr. test	29.7	($p = 0.013$)	51.66	($p = 0.006$)
	($df = 15$)		($df = 29$)	
number of observations	10599		10599	

First, the panel is unbalanced (see Section 10.7 below), while the model ignores changes in labour demand due to firms that enter or leave the sample (for example, because of financial distress). In addition, employment is measured as the mean number of employees in a given year, while wages (unit labour costs) are computed as total labour costs divided by the number of employees. Clearly, this ignores the problem of a reduction in average labour time per worker, which may have taken place in this decade. For example, if a firm replaces one full-time worker by two part-time workers, employment increases while labour costs decrease. In reality however, no real changes have taken place. See Konings and Roodhooft (1997) for additional discussion.

10.6 Models with Limited Dependent Variables

Panel data are relatively often used in micro-economic problems where the models of interest involve nonlinearities. Discrete or limited dependent variables are an important phenomenon in this area, and their combination with panel data usually complicates estimation. The reason is that with panel data it can usually not be argued that different observations on the same unit are independent. Correlations between different error terms typically complicate the likelihood functions of such models and therefore complicate their estimation. In this section we discuss the estimation of panel data logit, probit and tobit models. More details on panel data models with limited dependent variables can be found in Maddala (1987).

10.6.1 Binary Choice Models

As in the cross-sectional case, the binary choice model is usually formulated in terms of an underlying latent model. Typically, we write[17]

$$y_{it}^* = x_{it}'\beta + \alpha_i + \varepsilon_{it}, \tag{10.69}$$

where we observe $y_{it} = 1$ if $y_{it}^* > 0$ and $y_{it} = 0$ otherwise. For example, y_{it} may indicate whether person i is working in period t or not. Let us assume that the idiosyncratic error term ε_{it} has a symmetric distribution with distribution function $F(.)$, i.i.d. across individuals and time and independent of all x_{is}. Even in this case the presence of α_i complicates estimation, both when we treat them as fixed unknown parameters and when we treat them as random error terms.

If we treat α_i as fixed unknown parameters, we are essentially including N dummy variables in the model. The loglikelihood function is thus given by (compare (7.12))

$$\log L(\beta, \alpha_1, \ldots, \alpha_N) = \sum_{i,t} y_{it} \log F(\alpha_i + x_{it}'\beta)$$

$$+ \sum_{i,t} (1 - y_{it}) \log\left[1 - F(\alpha_i + x_{it}'\beta)\right]. \tag{10.70}$$

Maximizing this with respect to β and α_i $(i = 1, \ldots, N)$ results in consistent estimators *provided that the number of time periods T goes to infinity.* For fixed T and

---

[17] To simplify the notation we shall assume that x_{it} includes a constant, whenever appropriate.

$N \to \infty$, the estimators are inconsistent. The reason is that for fixed T, the number of parameters grows with sample size N and we have what is known as an 'incidental parameters' problem. That is, any α_i can only be estimated consistently if we have a growing number of observations for individual i, thus if we have T tending to infinity. In general, the inconsistency of $\hat{\alpha}_i$ for fixed T will carry over to the estimator for β.

The incidental parameters problem, where the number of parameters increases with the number of observations, arises in any fixed effects model, including the linear one. For the linear case, however, it was possible to eliminate the α_i s, such that β could be estimated consistently, even though all the α_i parameters could not. For most non-linear models however, the inconsistency of $\hat{\alpha}_i$ leads to inconsistency of the other parameter estimators as well. Also note that from a practical point of view, the estimation of more than N parameters may not be very attractive if N is fairly large.

Although it is possible to transform the *latent* model such that the individual effects α_i are eliminated, this does not help in this context because there is no mapping from, for example, $y_{it}^* - y_{i,t-1}^*$, to observables like $y_{it} - y_{i,t-1}$. An alternative strategy is the use of **conditional maximum likelihood** (see Andersen, 1970; or Chamberlain, 1980). In this case, we consider the likelihood function conditional upon a set of statistics t_i that are sufficient for α_i. This means that conditional upon t_i an individual's likelihood contribution no longer depends upon α_i, but still depends upon the other parameters β. In the panel data binary choice model, the existence of a sufficient statistic depends upon the functional form of F, that is, depends upon the distribution of ε_{it}.

At the general level let us write the joint density or probability mass function of $y_{i1}, \ldots, y_{iT}$ as $f(y_{i1}, \ldots, y_{iT} | \alpha_i, \beta)$, which depends upon the parameters β and α_i. If a sufficient statistic t_i exists, this means that there exists a statistic t_i such that $f(y_{i1}, \ldots, y_{iT} | t_i, \alpha_i, \beta) = f(y_{i1}, \ldots, y_{iT} | t_i, \beta)$ and so does not depend upon α_i. Consequently, we can maximize the **conditional likelihood function**, based upon $f(y_{i1}, \ldots, y_{iT} | t_i, \beta)$ to get a consistent estimator for β. Moreover, we can use all the distributional results from Chapter 6 if we replace the loglikelihood by the conditional loglikelihood function. For the *linear* model with normal errors, a sufficient statistic for α_i is $\bar{y}_i$. That is, the conditional distribution of y_{it} given $\bar{y}_i$ does not depend upon α_i, and maximizing the conditional likelihood function can be shown to reproduce the fixed effects estimator for β. Unfortunately, this result does not automatically extend to nonlinear models. For the probit model, for example, it has been shown that no sufficient statistic for α_i exists. This means that we cannot estimate a fixed effects probit model consistently for fixed T.

10.6.2 The Fixed Effects Logit Model

For the fixed effects logit model, the situation is different. In this model $t_i = \bar{y}_i$ is a sufficient statistic for α_i and consistent estimation is possible by conditional maximum likelihood. It should be noted that the conditional distribution of $y_{i1}, \ldots, y_{iT}$ is degenerate if $t_i = 0$ or $t_i = 1$. Consequently, such individuals do not contribute to the conditional likelihood and should be discarded in estimation. Put differently, their behaviour would be completely captured by their individual effect α_i. This means that only individuals that change status at least once are relevant for estimating β. To illustrate the fixed effects logit model, we consider the case with $T = 2$.

Conditional upon $t_i = 1/2$, the two possible outcomes are $(0, 1)$ and $(1, 0)$. The conditional probability of the first outcome is

$$P\{(0,1)|t_i = 1/2, \alpha_i, \beta\} = \frac{P\{(0,1)|\alpha_i, \beta\}}{P\{(0,1)|\alpha_i, \beta\} + P\{1,0)|\alpha_i, \beta\}}. \tag{10.71}$$

Using that

$$P\{(0,1)|\alpha_i, \beta\} = P\{y_{i1} = 0|\alpha_i, \beta\} P\{y_{i2} = 1|\alpha_i, \beta\}$$

with[18]

$$P\{y_{i2} = 1|\alpha_i, \beta\} = \frac{\exp\{\alpha_i + x'_{i2}\beta\}}{1 + \exp\{\alpha_i + x'_{i2}\beta\}},$$

it follows that the conditional probability is given by

$$P\{(0,1)|t_i = 1/2, \alpha_i, \beta\} = \frac{\exp\{(x_{i2} - x_{i1})'\beta\}}{1 + \exp\{(x_{i2} - x_{i1})'\beta\}}, \tag{10.72}$$

which indeed does not depend upon α_i. Similarly,

$$P\{(1,0)|t_i = 1/2, \alpha_i, \beta\} = \frac{1}{1 + \exp\{(x_{i2} - x_{i1})'\beta\}}. \tag{10.73}$$

This means that we can estimate the fixed effect logit model for $T = 2$ using a standard logit with $x_{i2} - x_{i1}$ as explanatory variables and the change in y_{it} as the endogenous event (1 for a positive change, 0 for a negative one). Note that in this fixed effects binary choice model it is even more clear than in the linear case that the model is only identified through the 'within dimension' of the data; individuals who do not change status are simply discarded in estimation as they provide no information whatsoever about β. For the case with larger T it is a bit more cumbersome to derive all the necessary conditional probabilities, but in principle it is a straightforward extension of the above case (see Chamberlain, 1980 or Maddala, 1987). Chamberlain (1980) also discusses how the conditional maximum likelihood approach can be extended to the multinomial logit model.

If it can be assumed that the α_i are independent of the explanatory variables in x_{it}, a random effects treatment seems more appropriate. This is most easily achieved in the context of a probit model.

10.6.3 The Random Effects Probit Model

Let us start with the latent variable specification

$$y^*_{it} = x'_{it}\beta + u_{it}, \tag{10.74}$$

with

$$\begin{aligned} y_{it} &= 1 \quad \text{if } y^*_{it} > 0 \\ y_{it} &= 0 \quad \text{if } y^*_{it} \leq 0, \end{aligned} \tag{10.75}$$

where u_{it} is an error term with mean zero and unit variance, independent of $(x_{i1}, \ldots, x_{iT})$. To estimate β by maximum likelihood we will have to complement this with an assumption about the joint distribution of $u_{i1}, \ldots, u_{iT}$. The likelihood contribution of individual i is the (joint) probability of observing the T outcomes

---

[18] See (7.6) in Chapter 7 for the logistic distribution function.

$y_{i1}, \ldots, y_{iT}$. This joint probability is determined from the joint distribution of the latent variables $y_{i1}^*, \ldots, y_{iT}^*$ by integrating over the appropriate intervals. In general, this will thus imply T integrals, which in estimation are typically to be computed numerically. When $T = 4$ or more, this makes maximum likelihood estimation infeasible. It is possible to circumvent this 'curse of dimensionality' by using simulation-based estimators, as discussed in, for example, Keane (1993) and Weeks (1995). Their discussion is beyond the scope of this text.

Clearly, if it can be assumed that all u_{it} are independent, we have that $f(y_{i1}, \ldots, y_{iT} | x_{i1}, \ldots, x_{iT}, \beta) = \prod_t f(y_{it} | x_{it}, \beta)$, which involves T one-dimensional integrals only (as in the cross-sectional case). If we make an error components assumption, and assume that $u_{it} = \alpha_i + \varepsilon_{it}$, where ε_{it} is independent over time (and individuals), we can write the joint probability as

$$f(y_{i1}, \ldots, y_{iT} | x_{i1}, \ldots, x_{iT}, \beta) = \int_{-\infty}^{\infty} f(y_{i1}, \ldots, y_{iT} | x_{i1}, \ldots, x_{iT}, \alpha_i, \beta) f(\alpha_i) d\alpha_i$$

$$= \int_{-\infty}^{\infty} \left[\prod_t f(y_{it} | x_{it}, \alpha_i, \beta) \right] f(\alpha_i) d\alpha_i, \qquad (10.76)$$

which requires numerical integration over one dimension. This is a feasible specification that allows the error terms to be correlated across different periods, albeit in a restrictive way. The crucial step in (10.76) is that conditional upon α_i the errors from different periods are independent.

In principle arbitrary assumptions can be made about the distributions of α_i and ε_{it}. For example, one could assume that ε_{it} is i.i.d. normal while α_i has a logistic distribution. However, this may lead to distributions for $\alpha_i + \varepsilon_{it}$ that are nonstandard. For example, the sum of two logistically distributed variables in general does not have a logistic distribution. This implies that individual probabilities, like $f(y_{it} | x_{it}, \beta)$, are hard to compute, and do not correspond to a cross-sectional probit or logit model. Therefore, it is more common to start from the joint distribution of $u_{i1}, \ldots, u_{iT}$. The multivariate logistic distribution has the disadvantage that all correlations are restricted to be $1/2$ (see Maddala, 1987), so that it is not very attractive in practice. Consequently, the most common approach is to start from a multivariate normal distribution, which leads to the **random effects probit model**.

Let us assume that the joint distribution of $u_{i1}, \ldots, u_{iT}$ is normal with zero means and variances equal to 1 and $\text{cov}\{u_{it}, u_{is}\} = \sigma_\alpha^2, s \neq t$. This corresponds to assuming that α_i is $NID(0, \sigma_\alpha^2)$ and ε_{it} is $NID(0, 1 - \sigma_\alpha^2)$. Recall that as in the cross-sectional case we need a normalization on the errors' variances. The normalization chosen here implies that the error variance in a given period is unity, such that the estimated β coefficients are directly comparable to estimates obtained from estimating the model from one wave of the panel using cross-sectional probit maximum likelihood. For the random effects probit model, the expressions in the likelihood function are given by

$$f(y_{it} | x_{it}, \alpha_i, \beta) = \Phi\left(\frac{x_{it}'\beta + \alpha_i}{\sqrt{1 - \sigma_\alpha^2}}\right) \qquad \text{if } y_{it} = 1$$

$$= 1 - \Phi\left(\frac{x_{it}'\beta + \alpha_i}{\sqrt{1 - \sigma_\alpha^2}}\right) \qquad \text{if } y_{it} = 0, \qquad (10.77)$$

where Φ denotes the cumulative density function of the standard normal distribution. The density of α_i is given by

$$f(\alpha_i) = \frac{1}{\sqrt{2\pi\sigma_\alpha^2}} \exp\left\{-\frac{1}{2}\frac{\alpha_i^2}{\sigma_\alpha^2}\right\}. \tag{10.78}$$

The integral in (10.76) has to be computed numerically, which can be done using the algorithm described in Butler and Moffitt (1982). Several software packages (for example, LIMDEP and Stata) have standard routines for estimating the random effects probit model.

It can be shown (Robinson, 1982) that ignoring the correlations across periods and estimating the β coefficients using standard probit maximum likelihood on the pooled data is consistent, though inefficient. Moreover, routinely computed standard errors are incorrect. Nevertheless, these values can be used as initial estimates in an iterative maximum likelihood procedure based on (10.76).

10.6.4 Tobit Models

The random effects tobit model is very similar to the random effects probit model, the only difference is in the observation rule. Consequently, we can be fairly brief here. Let us start with

$$y_{it}^* = x_{it}'\beta + \alpha_i + \varepsilon_{it}, \tag{10.79}$$

while

$$\begin{aligned} y_{it} &= y_{it}^* \quad \text{if } y_{it}^* > 0 \\ y_{it} &= 0 \quad \text{if } y_{it}^* \le 0. \end{aligned} \tag{10.80}$$

We make the usual random effects assumption that α_i and ε_{it} are i.i.d. normally distributed, independent of $x_{i1}, \ldots, x_{iT}$, with zero means and variances σ_α^2 and σ_ε^2, respectively. Using f as generic notation for a density or probability mass function, the likelihood function can be written as in (10.76),

$$f(y_{i1}, \ldots, y_{iT}|x_{i1}, \ldots, x_{iT}, \beta) = \int_{-\infty}^{\infty} \prod_t f(y_{it}|x_{it}, \alpha_i, \beta) f(\alpha_i) d\alpha_i,$$

where $f(\alpha_i)$ is given by (10.78) and $f(y_{it}|x_{it}, \alpha_i, \beta)$ is given by

$$\begin{aligned} f(y_{it}|x_{it}, \alpha_i, \beta) &= \frac{1}{\sqrt{2\pi\sigma_\varepsilon^2}} \exp\left\{-\frac{1}{2}\frac{(y_{it} - x_{it}'\beta - \alpha_i)^2}{\sigma_\varepsilon^2}\right\} \quad &\text{if } y_{it} > 0 \\ &= 1 - \Phi\left(\frac{x_{it}'\beta + \alpha_i}{\sigma_\varepsilon}\right) \quad &\text{if } y_{it} = 0. \end{aligned} \tag{10.81}$$

Note that the latter two expressions are similar to the likelihood contributions in the cross-sectional case, as discussed in Chapter 7. The only difference is the inclusion of α_i in the conditional mean.

In a completely similar fashion, other forms of censoring can be considered, to obtain, for example, the random effects ordered probit model. In all cases, the integration over α_i has to be done numerically.

It is possible to consistently estimate a tobit model as well as a truncated regression model with fixed effects, using the generalized method of moments exploiting the moment conditions given by Honoré (1992) or Honoré (1993) for the dynamic model. These estimators are semi-parametric in the sense that no assumptions are required on the shape of the distribution function of ε_{it}.

10.6.5 Dynamics and the Problem of Initial Conditions

The possibility of including a lagged dependent variable in the above models is of economic interest. For example, suppose we are explaining whether or not an individual is unemployed over a number of consecutive months. It is typically the case that individuals who have a longer history of being unemployed are less likely to leave the state of unemployment. As discussed in the introductory section of this chapter there are two explanations for this: an individual with a longer unemployment history may be discouraged in looking for a job or may (for whatever reason) be less attractive for an employer to hire. This is referred to as **state dependence**: the longer you are in a certain state the less likely you are to leave it. Alternatively, it is possible that **unobserved heterogeneity** is present such that individuals with certain unobserved characteristics are less likely to leave unemployment. The fact that we observe a spurious state dependence in the data is simply due to a selection mechanism: the long-term unemployed have certain unobservable (time-invariant) characteristics that make it less likely for them to find a job anyhow. In the binary choice models discussed above, the individual effects α_i capture the unobserved heterogeneity. If we include a lagged dependent variable, we can distinguish between the above two explanations.

Let us consider the random effect probit model, although similar results hold for the random effects tobit case. Suppose the latent variable specification is changed into

$$y_{it}^* = x_{it}'\beta + \gamma y_{i,t-1} + \alpha_i + \varepsilon_{it}, \tag{10.82}$$

with $y_{it} = 1$ if $y_{it}^* > 0$ and 0 otherwise. In this model $\gamma > 0$ indicates positive state dependence: the ceteris paribus probability that $y_{it} = 1$ is larger if $y_{i,t-1}$ is also one. Let us consider maximum likelihood estimation of this dynamic random effects probit model, making the same distributional assumptions as before. In general terms, the likelihood contribution of individual i is given by[19]

$$f(y_{i1}, \ldots, y_{iT} | x_{i1}, \ldots, x_{iT}, \beta)$$

$$= \int_{-\infty}^{\infty} f(y_{i1}, \ldots, y_{iT} | x_{i1}, \ldots, x_{iT}, \alpha_i, \beta) f(\alpha_i) d\alpha_i$$

$$= \int_{-\infty}^{\infty} \left[\prod_{t=2}^{T} f(y_{it} | y_{i,t-1}, x_{it}, \alpha_i, \beta) \right] f(y_{i1} | x_{i1}, \alpha_i, \beta) f(\alpha_i) d\alpha_i, \tag{10.83}$$

---

[19] For notational convenience, the time index is defined such that the first observation is (y_{i1}, x_{i1}').

where

$$f(y_{it}|y_{i,t-1}, x_{it}, \alpha_i, \beta) = \Phi\left(\frac{x_{it}'\beta + \gamma y_{i,t-1} + \alpha_i}{\sqrt{1 - \sigma_\alpha^2}}\right) \qquad \text{if } y_{it} = 1$$

$$= 1 - \Phi\left(\frac{x_{it}'\beta + \gamma y_{i,t-1} + \alpha_i}{\sqrt{1 - \sigma_\alpha^2}}\right) \qquad \text{if } y_{it} = 0.$$

This is completely analogous to the static case and $y_{i,t-1}$ is simply included as an additional explanatory variable. However, the term $f(y_{i1}|x_{i1}, \alpha_i, \beta)$ in the likelihood function may cause problems. It gives the probability of observing $y_{i1} = 1$ or 0 without knowing the previous state but conditional upon the unobserved heterogeneity term α_i.

If the initial value is exogenous in the sense that its distribution does not depend upon α_i, we can put the term $f(y_{i1}|x_{i1}, \alpha_i, \beta) = f(y_{i1}|x_{i1}, \beta)$ outside the integral. In this case, we can simply consider the likelihood function conditional upon y_{i1} and ignore the term $f(y_{i1}|x_{i1}, \beta)$ in estimation. The only consequence may be a loss of efficiency if $f(y_{i1}|x_{i1}, \beta)$ provides information about β. This approach would be appropriate if the initial state is necessarily the same for all individuals or if it is randomly assigned to individuals. An example of the first situation is given in Nijman and Verbeek (1992), who model nonresponse with respect to consumption and the initial period refers to the month before the panel and no nonresponse was necessarily observed.

However, it may be hard to argue in many applications that the initial value y_{i1} is exogenous and does not depend upon a person's unobserved heterogeneity. In that case we would need an expression for $f(y_{i1}|x_{i1}, \alpha_i, \beta)$ and this is problematic. If the process that we are estimating has been going on for a number of periods before the current sample period, $f(y_{i1}|x_{i1}, \alpha_i, \beta)$ is a complicated function that depends upon person i's unobserved history. This means that it is typically impossible to derive an expression for the marginal probability $f(y_{i1}|x_{i1}, \alpha_i, \beta)$ that is consistent with the rest of the model. Heckman (1981) suggests an approximate solution to this **initial conditions problem** that seems to work reasonably well in practice. It requires an approximation for the marginal probability of the initial state by a probit function using as much pre-sample information as available, without imposing restrictions between its coefficients and the structural β and γ parameters. Vella and Verbeek (1999) provide an illustration of this approach in a dynamic random effects tobit model. The impact of the initial conditions diminishes if the number of sample periods T increases, so one may decide to ignore the problem when T is fairly large.

10.7 Incomplete Panels and Selection Bias

Because of a variety of reasons, empirical panel data sets are often incomplete. For example, after a few waves of the panel people may refuse cooperation, households may not be located again or have split up, firms may have finished business or have merged with another firm, or investment funds may be closed down. On the other hand, firms may enter business at a later stage, refreshment samples may have been drawn to compensate attrition, or the panel may be collected as a rotating panel. In a rotating panel, each period a fixed proportion of the units is replaced. A consequence of all these events is that the resulting panel data set is no longer rectangular. If the total number of individuals equals N and the number of time periods is T then the total number of observations is substantially smaller than NT.

A first consequence of working with an incomplete panel is a computational one. Most of the expressions for the estimators given above are no longer appropriate if observations are missing. A simple 'solution' is to discard any individual from the panel that has incomplete information and to work with the completely observed units only. In this approach estimation uses the **balanced sub-panel** only. This is computationally attractive, but potentially highly inefficient: a substantial amount of information may be 'thrown away'. This loss in efficiency can be prevented by using all observations including those on individuals that are not observed in all T periods. This way, one uses the **unbalanced panel**. In principle this is straightforward, but computationally it requires some adjustments to the formulae in the previous sections. We shall discuss some of these adjustments in Subsection 10.7.1. Fortunately, most software that can handle panel data also allows for unbalanced data.

Another potential and even more serious consequence of using incomplete panel data is the danger of **selection bias**. If individuals are incompletely observed because of an endogenous reason, the use of either the balanced sub-panel or the unbalanced panel may lead to biased estimators and misleading tests. To elaborate upon this, suppose that the model of interest is given by

$$y_{it} = x_{it}'\beta + \alpha_i + \varepsilon_{it}. \tag{10.84}$$

Furthermore, define the indicator variable r_{it} ('response') as $r_{it} = 1$ if (x_{it}, y_{it}) is observed and 0 otherwise. The observations on (x_{it}, y_{it}) are **missing at random** if r_{it} is independent of α_i and ε_{it}. This means that conditioning upon the outcome of the selection process does not affect the conditional distribution of y_{it} given x_{it}. If we want to concentrate upon the balanced sub-panel, the conditioning is upon $r_{i1} = \cdots = r_{iT} = 1$ and we require that r_{it} is independent of α_i and $\varepsilon_{i1}, \ldots, \varepsilon_{iT}$. In these cases, the usual consistency properties of the estimators are not affected if we restrict attention to the available or complete observations only. If selection depends upon the equations' error terms the OLS, random effects and fixed effects estimators may suffer from selection bias (compare Chapter 7). Subsection 10.7.2 provides additional details on this issue, including some simple tests. In cases with selection bias, alternative estimators have to be used, which are typically computationally unattractive. This is discussed in Subsection 10.7.3. Additional details and discussion on incomplete panels and selection bias can be found in Verbeek and Nijman (1992, 1996).

10.7.1 Estimation with Randomly Missing Data

The expressions for the fixed and random effects estimators are easily extended to the unbalanced case. The fixed effects estimator, as before, can be determined as the OLS estimator in the linear model where each individual has its own intercept term. Alternatively, the resulting estimator for β can be obtained directly by applying OLS to the within transformed model, where now all variables are in deviation from the mean *over the available observations*. Individuals that are observed only once provide no information on β and should be discarded in estimation. Defining 'available means' as[20]

$$\bar{y}_i = \frac{\sum_{t=1}^{T} r_{it} y_{it}}{\sum_{t=1}^{T} r_{it}}; \quad \bar{x}_i = \frac{\sum_{t=1}^{T} r_{it} x_{it}}{\sum_{t=1}^{T} r_{it}},$$

the fixed effects estimator can be concisely written as

$$\hat{\beta}_{FE} = \left(\sum_{i=1}^{N} \sum_{t=1}^{T} r_{it}(x_{it} - \bar{x}_i)(x_{it} - \bar{x}_i)' \right)^{-1} \sum_{i=1}^{N} \sum_{t=1}^{T} r_{it}(x_{it} - \bar{x}_i)(y_{it} - \bar{y}_i). \quad (10.85)$$

That is, all sums are simply over the available observations only.

In a similar way, the random effects estimator can be generalized. The random effects estimator for the unbalanced case can be obtained from

$$\hat{\beta}_{GLS} = \left(\sum_{i=1}^{N} \sum_{t=1}^{T} r_{it}(x_{it} - \bar{x}_i)(x_{it} - \bar{x}_i)' + \sum_{i=1}^{N} \psi_i T_i (\bar{x}_i - \bar{x})(\bar{x}_i - \bar{x})' \right)^{-1}$$

$$\times \left(\sum_{i=1}^{N} \sum_{t=1}^{T} r_{it}(x_{it} - \bar{x}_i)(y_{it} - \bar{y}_i) + \sum_{i=1}^{N} \psi_i T_i (\bar{x}_i - \bar{x})(\bar{y}_i - \bar{y}) \right), \quad (10.86)$$

where $T_i = \sum_{t=1}^{T} r_{it}$ denotes the number of periods individual i is observed and

$$\psi_i = \frac{\sigma_\varepsilon^2}{\sigma_\varepsilon^2 + T_i \sigma_\alpha^2}.$$

Alternatively, it is obtained from OLS applied to the following transformed model

$$(y_{it} - \vartheta_i \bar{y}_i) = \mu(1 - \vartheta_i) + (x_{it} - \vartheta_i \bar{x}_i) + u_{it}, \quad (10.87)$$

where $\vartheta_i = 1 - \psi_i^{1/2}$. Note that the transformation applied here is individual specific as it depends upon the number of observations for individual i.

Essentially, the more general formulae for the fixed effects and random effects estimators are characterized by the fact that all summations and means are over the available observations only and that T_i replaces T. Completely analogous adjustments apply to the expressions for the covariance matrices of the two estimators given in (10.13) and (10.23). Consistent estimators for the unknown variances σ_α^2 and σ_ε^2 are given by

$$\hat{\sigma}_\varepsilon^2 = \frac{1}{\sum_{i=1}^{N} T_i - N} \sum_{i=1}^{N} \sum_{t=1}^{T} r_{it} \left(y_{it} - \bar{y}_i - (x_{it} - \bar{x}_i)' \hat{\beta}_{FE} \right)^2 \quad (10.88)$$

and

$$\hat{\sigma}_\alpha^2 = \frac{1}{N} \sum_{i=1}^{N} \left[(\bar{y}_i - \bar{x}_i' \hat{\beta}_B)^2 - \frac{1}{T_i} \hat{\sigma}_\varepsilon^2 \right], \quad (10.89)$$

respectively, where $\hat{\beta}_B$ is the between estimator for β (computed as the OLS estimator in (10.18), where the means now reflect 'available means'). Because the efficiency of the estimators for σ_α^2 and σ_ε^2 asymptotically has no impact on the efficiency of the random effects estimator, it is possible to use computationally simpler estimators for

---

[20] We assume that $\sum_{t=1}^{T} r_{it} \geq 1$, i.e. each individual is observed at least once.

σ_α^2 and σ_ε^2 that are consistent. For example, one could use the standard estimators computed from the residuals obtained from estimating with the balanced sub-panel only, and then use (10.86) or (10.87) to compute the random effects estimator.

10.7.2 Selection Bias and Some Simple Tests

In addition to the usual conditions for consistency of the random effects and fixed effects estimator, based on either the balanced sub-panel or the unbalanced panel, it was assumed above that the response indicator variable r_{it} was independent of all unobservables in the model. This assumption may be unrealistic. For example, explaining the performance of mutual funds may suffer from the fact that funds with a bad performance are less likely to survive (Ter Horst, Nijman and Verbeek, 1998), analysing the effect of an income policy experiment may suffer from biases if people that benefit less from the experiment are more likely to drop out of the panel (Hausman and Wise, 1979), or estimating the impact of the unemployment rate on individual wages may be disturbed by the possibility that people with relatively high wages are more likely to leave the labour market in case of increasing unemployment (Keane, Moffitt and Runkle, 1988).

If r_{it} depends upon α_i or ε_{it}, **selection bias** may arise in the standard estimators (see Chapter 7). This means that the distribution of y given x and conditional upon selection (into the sample) is different from the distribution of y given x (which is what we are interested in). For consistency of the fixed effects estimator it is now required that

$$E\{(x_{it} - \bar{x}_i)\varepsilon_{it}|r_{i1}, \ldots, r_{iT}\} = 0. \tag{10.90}$$

This means that the fixed effects estimator is inconsistent if the fact whether an individual is in the sample or not tells us something about the expected value of the error term that is related with x_{it}. Clearly, if (10.11) holds and r_{it} is independent of α_i and all ε_{is} (for given x_{is}), the above condition is satisfied. Note that sample selection may depend upon α_i without affecting consistency of the fixed effects estimator for β. In fact, ε_{it} may even depend upon r_{it} as long as their relationship is time-invariant (see Verbeek and Nijman, 1992, 1996 for additional details).

In addition to (10.90), the conditions for consistency of the random effects estimator are now given by $E\{\bar{x}_i\varepsilon_{it}|r_{i1}, \ldots, r_{iT}\} = 0$ and

$$E\{\bar{x}_i\alpha_i|r_{i1}, \ldots, r_{iT}\} = 0. \tag{10.91}$$

This does not allow the expected value of either error component to depend on the selection indicators. If individuals with certain values for their unobserved heterogeneity α_i are less likely to be observed in some wave of the panel, this will typically bias the random effects estimator. Similarly, if individuals with certain shocks ε_{it} are more likely to drop out, the random effects estimator is typically inconsistent. Note that because the fixed effects estimator allows selection to depend upon α_i and upon ε_{it} in a time-invariant way, it is more robust against selection bias than the random effects estimator. Another important observation made by Verbeek and Nijman (1992) is that estimators from the unbalanced panel do not necessarily suffer less from selection bias than those from the balanced sub-panel. In general, the selection biases in the estimators from the unbalanced and balanced samples need not be the same, and their relative magnitude is not known a priori.

Verbeek and Nijman (1992) suggest a number of simple tests for selection bias based upon the above observations. First, as the conditions for consistency state that the error terms should – in one sense or another – not depend upon the selection indicators, one can test this by simply including some function of $r_{i1}, \ldots, r_{iT}$ in the model and checking its significance. Clearly, the null hypothesis says that whether an individual was observed in any of the periods 1 to T should not give us any information about his unobservables in the model. Obviously, adding r_{it} to the model in (10.84) leads to multicollinearity as $r_{it} = 1$ for all observations in the sample. Instead, one could add functions of $r_{i1}, \ldots, r_{iT}$, like $r_{i,t-1}$, $c_i = \prod_{t=1}^{T} r_{it}$ or $T_i = \sum_{t=1}^{T} r_{it}$, indicating whether unit i was observed in the previous period, whether he was observed over all periods, and the total number of periods i is observed, respectively. Note that in the balanced sub-panel all variables are identical for all individuals and thus incorporated in the intercept term. Verbeek and Nijman (1992) suggest that the inclusion of c_i and T_i may provide a reasonable procedure to check for the presence of selection bias. Note that this requires that the model is estimated under the random effects assumption, as the within transformation would wipe out both c_i and T_i. Of course, if the tests do not reject, there is no reason to accept the null hypothesis of no selection bias, because the power of the tests may be low.

Another group of tests is based upon the idea that the four different estimators, random effects and fixed effects, using either the balanced sub-panel or unbalanced panel, usually all suffer differently from selection bias. A comparison of these estimators may therefore give an indication for the likelihood of selection bias. Although any pair of estimators can be compared (see Verbeek and Nijman, 1992, or Baltagi, 1995, Section 10.5), it is known that fixed effects and random effects estimators may be different for other reasons than selection bias (see Subsection 10.2.3). Therefore, it is most natural to compare either the fixed effects or the random effects estimator using the balanced sub-panel, with its counterpart using the unbalanced panel. If different samples, selected on the basis of $r_{i1}, \ldots, r_{iT}$, lead to significantly different estimators, it must be the case that the selection process tells us something about the unobservables in the model. That is, it indicates the presence of selection bias. As the estimators using the unbalanced panel are efficient within a particular class of estimators, we can use the result of Hausman again and derive a test statistic based upon the random effects estimator as (compare (10.27))

$$\xi_{RE} = (\hat{\beta}_{RE}^{B} - \hat{\beta}_{RE}^{U})'[\hat{V}\{\hat{\beta}_{RE}^{B}\} - \hat{V}\{\hat{\beta}_{RE}^{U}\}]^{-1}(\hat{\beta}_{RE}^{B} - \hat{\beta}_{RE}^{U}), \qquad (10.92)$$

where the $\hat{V}$ denote estimates of the covariance matrices and the superscripts B and U refer to the balanced and unbalanced sample, respectively. Similarly, a test based on the two fixed effects estimators can be derived. Under the null hypothesis, the test statistic follows a Chi-squared distribution with K degrees of freedom. Note that the implicit null hypothesis for the test is that $\text{plim}(\hat{\beta}_{RE}^{B} - \hat{\beta}_{RE}^{U}) = 0$. If this is approximately true and the two estimators suffer similarly from selection bias, the test has no power.[21] Again, it is possible to test for a subset of the elements in β.

---

[21] The test suggested here is not a real Hausman test because none of the estimators is consistent under the alternative hypothesis. This does not invalidate the test as such but may result in limited power in certain directions.

10.7.3 Estimation with Nonrandomly Missing Data

As in the cross-sectional case (see Section 7.5), selection bias introduces an identification problem. As a result, it is not possible to consistently estimate the model parameters in the presence of selection bias, unless additional assumptions are imposed. As an illustration, let us assume that the selection indicator r_{it} can be explained by a random effects probit model, that is

$$r_{it}^* = z_{it}'\gamma + \xi_i + \eta_{it}, \tag{10.93}$$

where $r_{it} = 1$ if $r_{it}^* > 0$ and 0 otherwise, and z_{it} is a (well-motivated) vector of exogenous variables that includes x_{it}. The model of interest is given by

$$y_{it} = x_{it}'\beta + \alpha_i + \varepsilon_{it}. \tag{10.94}$$

Let us assume that the error components in the two equations have a joint normal distribution. This is a generalization of the cross-sectional sample selection model considered in Subsection 7.4.1. The effect of sample selection in (10.94) is reflected in the expected values of the unobservables, conditional upon the exogenous variables and the selection indicators, that is

$$E\{\alpha_i | z_{i1}, \ldots, z_{iT}, r_{i1}, \ldots, r_{iT}\} \tag{10.95}$$

and

$$E\{\varepsilon_{it} | z_{i1}, \ldots, z_{iT}, r_{i1}, \ldots, r_{iT}\}. \tag{10.96}$$

It can be shown (Verbeek and Nijman, 1992) that (10.96) is time-invariant if $\text{cov}\{\varepsilon_{it}, \eta_{it}\} = 0$ or if $z_{it}'\gamma$ is time-invariant. This is required for consistency of the fixed effects estimator. Further, (10.95) is zero if $\text{cov}\{\alpha_i, \xi_i\} = 0$, while (10.96) is zero if $\text{cov}\{\varepsilon_{it}, \eta_{it}\} = 0$ so that the random effect estimator is consistent if the unobservables in the primary equation and the selection equation are uncorrelated.

Estimation in the more general case is relatively complicated. Hausman and Wise (1979) consider a case where the panel has two periods and attrition only takes place in the second period. In the more general case, using maximum likelihood to estimate the two equations simultaneously requires numerical integration over two dimensions (to integrate out the two individual effects). Nijman and Verbeek (1992), and Vella and Verbeek (1999) present alternative estimators based upon the two-step estimation method for the cross-sectional sample selection model. Essentially, the idea is that the terms in (10.95) and (10.96), apart from a constant, can be determined from the probit model in (10.93), so that estimates of these terms can be included in the primary equation. Wooldridge (1995) presents some alternative estimators based on somewhat different assumptions.

Exercises

Exercise 10.1 (Linear Model)

Consider the following simple panel data model

$$y_{it} = x_{it}\beta + \alpha_i^* + \varepsilon_{it}, \quad i = 1, \ldots, N, \quad t = 1, \ldots, T, \tag{10.97}$$

where β is one-dimensional, and where it is assumed that

$$\alpha_i^* = \bar{x}_i\lambda + \alpha_i, \quad \text{with} \quad \alpha_i \sim NID(0, \sigma_\alpha^2), \quad \varepsilon_{it} \sim NID(0, \sigma_\varepsilon^2),$$

mutually independent and independent of all x_{it}s, where $\bar{x}_i = (1/T)\sum_{t=1}^{T} x_{it}$.

The parameter β in (10.97) can be estimated by the fixed effects (or within) estimator given by

$$\hat{\beta}_{FE} = \frac{\sum_{i=1}^{N}\sum_{t=1}^{T}(x_{it} - \bar{x}_i)(y_{it} - \bar{y}_i)}{\sum_{i=1}^{N}\sum_{t=1}^{T}(x_{it} - \bar{x}_i)^2}.$$

As an alternative, the correlation between the error term $\alpha_i^* + \varepsilon_{it}$ and x_{it} can be handled by an instrumental variables approach.

a. Give an expression for the IV estimator $\hat{\beta}_{IV}$ for β in (10.97) using $x_{it} - \bar{x}_i$ as an instrument for x_{it}. Show that $\hat{\beta}_{IV}$ and $\hat{\beta}_{FE}$ are identical.

Another way to eliminate the individual effects α_i^* from the model is obtained by taking first differences. This results in

$$y_{it} - y_{i,t-1} = (x_{it} - x_{i,t-1})\beta + (\varepsilon_{it} - \varepsilon_{i,t-1}), \quad i = 1,\ldots,N, \quad t = 2,\ldots,T. \quad (10.98)$$

b. Denote the OLS estimator based on (10.98) by $\hat{\beta}_{FD}$. Show that $\hat{\beta}_{FD}$ is identical to $\hat{\beta}_{IV}$ and $\hat{\beta}_{FE}$ if $T = 2$. This identity does no longer hold for $T > 2$. Which of the two estimators would you prefer in that case? Explain. (Note: for additional discussion see Verbeek, 1995.)

c. Consider the between estimator $\hat{\beta}_B$ for β in (10.97). Give an expression for $\hat{\beta}_B$ and show that it is unbiased for $\beta + \lambda$.

d. Finally, suppose we substitute the expression for α_i^* into (10.97), giving

$$y_{it} = x_{it}\beta + \bar{x}_i\lambda + \alpha_i + \varepsilon_{it}, \quad i = 1,\ldots,N, \quad t = 1,\ldots,T. \quad (10.99)$$

The vector $(\beta, \lambda)'$ can be estimated by GLS (random effects) based on (10.99). It can be shown that the implied estimator for β is identical to $\hat{\beta}_{FE}$. Does this imply that there is no real distinction between the fixed effects and random effects approaches? (Note: for additional discussion see Hsiao, 1986, Sect. 3.4.2a.)

Exercise 10.2 (Hausman–Taylor Model)

Consider the following linear panel data model

$$y_{it} = x_{1,it}'\beta_1 + x_{2,it}'\beta_2 + w_{1,i}'\gamma_1 + w_{2,i}'\gamma_2 + \alpha_i + \varepsilon_{it}, \quad (10.100)$$

where $w_{k,i}$ are time-invariant and $x_{k,it}$ are time-varying explanatory variables. The variables with index 1 ($x_{1,it}$ and $w_{1,i}$) are strictly exogenous in the sense that $E\{x_{1,it}\alpha_i\} = 0$, $E\{x_{1,is}\varepsilon_{it}\} = 0$ for all s, t, $E\{w_{1,i}\alpha_i\} = 0$ and $E\{w_{1,i}\varepsilon_{it}\} = 0$. It is also assumed that $E\{w_{2,i}\varepsilon_{it}\} = 0$ and that the usual regularity conditions (for consistency and asymptotic normality) are met.

a. Under which additional assumptions would OLS applied to (10.100) provide a consistent estimator for $\beta = (\beta_1, \beta_2)'$ and $\gamma = (\gamma_1, \gamma_2)'$?

b. Consider the fixed effects (within) estimator. Under which additional assumption(s) would it provide a consistent estimator for β?

c. Consider the OLS estimator for β based upon a regression in first differences. Under which additional assumption(s) will this provide a consistent estimator for β?

d. Discuss one or more alternative consistent estimators for β and γ if it can be assumed that $E\{x_{2,is}\varepsilon_{it}\} = 0$ (for all s, t), and $E\{w_{2,i}\varepsilon_{it}\} = 0$. What are the restrictions, in this case, on the number of variables in each of the categories?

e. Discuss estimation of β if $x_{2,it}$ equals $y_{i,t-1}$.

f. Discuss estimation of β if $x_{2,it}$ includes $y_{i,t-1}$.

g. Would it be possible to estimate both β and γ consistently if $x_{2,it}$ includes $y_{i,t-1}$? If so, how? If not, why not? (Make additional assumptions, if necessary.)

Exercise 10.3 (Dynamic and Binary Choice Models)

Consider the following dynamic wage equation

$$w_{it} = x_{it}'\beta + \gamma w_{i,t-1} + \alpha_i + \varepsilon_{it}, \tag{10.101}$$

where w_{it} denotes an individual's log hourly wage rate and x_{it} is a vector of personal and job characteristics (age, schooling, gender, industry, etc.).

a. Explain in words why OLS applied to (10.101) is inconsistent.

b. Also explain why the fixed effects estimator applied to (10.101) is inconsistent for $N \to \infty$ and fixed T, but consistent for $N \to \infty$ and $T \to \infty$. (Assume that ε_{it} is i.i.d.)

c. Explain why the results from **a** and **b** also imply that the random effects (GLS) estimator in (10.101) is inconsistent for fixed T.

d. Describe a simple consistent (for $N \to \infty$) estimator for β, γ, assuming that α_i and ε_{it} are i.i.d. and independent of all x_{it}s.

e. Describe a more efficient estimator for β, γ under the same assumptions.

In addition to the wage equation, assume there is a binary choice model explaining whether an individual is working or not. Let $r_{it} = 1$ if individual i was working in period t and zero otherwise. Then the model can be described as

$$r_{it}^* = z_{it}'\delta + \xi_i + \eta_{it}$$
$$r_{it} = 1 \quad \text{if } r_{it}^* > 0 \tag{10.102}$$
$$= 0 \quad \text{otherwise,}$$

where z_{it} is a vector of personal characteristics. Assume that $\xi_i \sim NID(0, \sigma_\xi^2)$ and $\eta_{it} \sim NID(0, 1 - \sigma_\xi^2)$, mutually independent and independent of all z_{it}s. The model in (10.102) can be estimated by maximum likelihood.

f. Give an expression for the probability that $r_{it} = 1$ given z_{it} and ξ_i.

g. Use the expression from **f** to obtain a computationally tractable expression for the likelihood contribution of individual i.

h. Explain why it is not possible to treat the ξ_is as fixed unknown parameters and estimate δ consistently (for fixed T) from this fixed effects probit?

From now on, assume that the appropriate wage equation is static and given by (10.101) with $\gamma = 0$.

i. What are the consequences for the random effects estimator in (10.101) if η_{it} and ε_{it} are correlated? Why?

j. What are the consequences for the fixed effects estimator in (10.101) if ξ_i and α_i are correlated (while η_{it} and ε_{it} are not)? Why?

A Vectors and Matrices

At occasional places in this text use is made of results from linear algebra. This Appendix is meant to review the concepts that are used. More details can be found in textbooks on linear algebra or, for example, Chapter 2 of Greene (2000) or Appendix A of Davidson and MacKinnon (1993). Some of the more complex topics are used in a limited number of places in the text. For example, eigenvalues and the rank of a matrix only play a role in Chapter 9, while the rules of differentiation are only needed in Chapters 2 and 5.

A.1 Terminology

In this book a **vector** is always a *column* of numbers, denoted

$$a = \begin{pmatrix} a_1 \\ a_2 \\ \vdots \\ a_n \end{pmatrix}.$$

The **transpose** of a vector, denoted $a' = (a_1, a_2, \ldots, a_n)$ is a row of numbers, sometimes called a row vector. A **matrix** is a rectangular array of numbers. Of dimension $n \times k$, it can be written as

$$A = \begin{pmatrix} a_{11} & a_{12} & \cdots & a_{1k} \\ a_{21} & a_{22} & & \\ & & \ddots & \\ a_{n1} & a_{n2} & \cdots & a_{nk} \end{pmatrix}.$$

The first index of the element a_{ij} refers to i-th row, the second index to the j-th column. Denoting the vector in the j-th column of this matrix by a_j, it is seen that A consists of k vectors a_1 to a_k, which we can denote as

$$A = [a_1 \quad a_2 \quad \ldots \quad a_k].$$

The symbol $'$ denotes the **transpose** of a matrix or vector, obtained as

$$A' = \begin{pmatrix} a_{11} & a_{21} & \cdots & a_{n1} \\ a_{12} & a_{22} & & a_{n2} \\ & & \ddots & \vdots \\ a_{1k} & & \cdots & a_{nk} \end{pmatrix}.$$

The columns of A are the rows of A' and vice versa. A matrix is **square** if $n = k$. A square matrix A is **symmetric** if $A = A'$. A square matrix A is called a **diagonal** matrix if $a_{ij} = 0$ for all $i \neq j$. Note that a diagonal matrix is symmetric by construction. The **identity matrix** I is a diagonal matrix with all diagonal elements equal to one.

A.2 Matrix Manipulations

If two matrices or vectors have the same dimensions they can be **added** or **subtracted**. Let A and B be two matrices of dimension $n \times k$ with typical elements a_{ij} and b_{ij}, respectively. Then $A + B$ has typical element $a_{ij} + b_{ij}$, while $A - B$ has typical element $a_{ij} - b_{ij}$. It easily follows that $A + B = B + A$ and $(A + B)' = A' + B'$.

A matrix A of dimension $n \times k$ and a matrix B of dimension $k \times m$ can be **multiplied** to produce a matrix of dimension $n \times m$. Let us consider the special case of $k = 1$ first. Then $A = a'$ is a row vector and $B = b$ is a column vector. Then we define

$$AB = a'b = (a_1, a_2, \ldots, a_n)' \begin{pmatrix} b_1 \\ b_2 \\ \vdots \\ b_n \end{pmatrix} = a_1 b_1 + a_2 b_2 + \cdots + a_n b_n.$$

We call $a'b$ the **inner product** of the vectors a and b. Note that $a'b = b'a$. Two vectors are called **orthogonal** if $a'b = 0$. For any vector a, except the null vector, we have that $a'a > 0$. The **outer product** of a vector a is aa', which is of dimension $n \times n$.

Another special case arises for $m = 1$, in which case A is an $n \times k$ matrix and $B = b$ is a vector of dimension k. Then $c = Ab$ is also a vector, but of dimension n. It has typical elements

$$c_i = a_{i1} b_1 + a_{i2} b_2 + \cdots + a_{ik} b_k,$$

which is the inner product between the vector obtained from the i-th row of A and the vector b.

When $m > 1$, B is a matrix and $C = AB$ is a matrix of dimension $n \times m$ with typical elements

$$c_{ij} = a_{i1} b_{1j} + a_{i2} b_{2j} + \cdots + a_{ik} b_{kj},$$

being the inner products between the vectors obtained from the i-th row of A and the j-th column of B. Note that this can only make sense if the number of columns in A equals the number of rows in B.

As an example, consider

$$A = \begin{pmatrix} 1 & 2 & 3 \\ 4 & 5 & 0 \end{pmatrix}, \quad B = \begin{pmatrix} 1 & 2 \\ 3 & 4 \\ 0 & 5 \end{pmatrix}$$

and

$$AB = \begin{pmatrix} 7 & 25 \\ 19 & 28 \end{pmatrix}.$$

It is important to note that $AB \neq BA$. Even if AB exists, BA may not be defined because the dimensions of B and A do not match. If A is of dimension $n \times k$ and B is of dimension $k \times n$, then AB exists and has dimension $n \times n$, while BA exists with dimension $k \times k$. In the above example, we have

$$BA = \begin{pmatrix} 9 & 12 & 3 \\ 19 & 26 & 9 \\ 20 & 25 & 0 \end{pmatrix}.$$

For the transpose of a product of two matrices, it holds that

$$(AB)' = B'A'.$$

From this (and $(A')' = A$) it follows that both $A'A$ and AA' exist and are symmetric. Finally, multiplying a scalar and a matrix is the same as multiplying each element in the matrix by this scalar. That is, for a scalar c we have that cA has typical element ca_{ij}.

A.3 Properties of Matrices and Vectors

If we consider a number of vectors a_1 to a_k we can take a **linear combination** of these vectors. With scalar weights $c_1, \ldots, c_k$ this produces the vector $c_1 a_1 + c_2 a_2 + \cdots + c_k a_k$, which we can shortly write as Ac, where, as before, $A = [a_1 \cdots a_k]$ and $c = (c_1, \ldots, c_k)'$.

A set of vectors is **linearly dependent** if any of the vectors can be written as a linear combination of the others. That is, if there exists values for $c_1, \ldots, c_k$, not all zero, such that $c_1 a_1 + c_2 a_2 + \cdots + c_k a_k = 0$ (the null vector). Equivalently, a set of vectors is **linearly independent** if the only solution to

$$c_1 a_1 + c_2 a_2 + \cdots + c_k a_k = 0$$

is

$$c_1 = c_2 = \cdots = c_k = 0.$$

That is, if the only solution to $Ac = 0$ is $c = 0$.

If we consider all possible vectors that can be obtained as linear combinations of the vectors $a_1, \ldots, a_k$, these vectors form a **vector space**. If the vectors $a_1, \ldots, a_k$ are linearly dependent, we can reduce the number of vectors without changing this vector space. The minimal number of vectors needed to span a vector space is called the

dimension of that space. This way, we can define the **column space** of a matrix as the space spanned by its columns, and the **column rank** of a matrix as the dimension of its column space. Clearly, the column rank can never exceed the number of columns. A matrix is of **full column rank** if the column rank equals the number of columns. The **row rank** of a matrix is the dimension of the space spanned by the rows of the matrix. In general, it holds that the row rank and the column rank of a matrix are equal, so we can unambiguously define the **rank of a matrix**. Note that this does not imply that a matrix that is of full column rank is automatically of full row rank (this only holds if the matrix is square).

A useful result in regression analysis is that for any A

$$rank(A) = rank(A'A) = rank(AA').$$

A.4   Inverse Matrices

A matrix B, if it exists, is the **inverse** of a matrix A if $AB = I$ and $BA = I$. A necessary requirement for this is that A is a *square* matrix and has *full rank*, in which case A is also called **invertible** or **nonsingular**. In this case, we can define $B = A^{-1}$, and

$$AA^{-1} = I \qquad \text{and} \qquad A^{-1}A = I.$$

Note that the definition implies that $A = B^{-1}$. Thus we have that $(A^{-1})^{-1} = A$. If A^{-1} does not exist, we say that A is **singular**. Analytically, the inverse of a diagonal matrix and a 2×2 matrix are easily obtained. For example,

$$\begin{pmatrix} a_{11} & 0 & 0 \\ 0 & a_{22} & 0 \\ 0 & 0 & a_{33} \end{pmatrix}^{-1} = \begin{pmatrix} a_{11}^{-1} & 0 & 0 \\ 0 & a_{22}^{-1} & 0 \\ 0 & 0 & a_{33}^{-1} \end{pmatrix}$$

and

$$\begin{pmatrix} a_{11} & a_{12} \\ a_{21} & a_{22} \end{pmatrix}^{-1} = \frac{1}{a_{11}a_{22} - a_{12}a_{21}} \begin{pmatrix} a_{22} & -a_{12} \\ -a_{21} & a_{11} \end{pmatrix}.$$

If $a_{11}a_{22} - a_{12}a_{21} = 0$ the 2×2 matrix A is singular: its columns are linearly dependent, and so are its rows. We call $a_{11}a_{22} - a_{12}a_{21}$ the determinant of this 2×2 matrix (see below).

Suppose we are asked to solve $Ac = d$ for given A and d, where A is of dimension $n \times n$ and both c and d are n-dimensional vectors. This is a system of n linear equations with n unknowns. If A^{-1} exists, we can write

$$A^{-1}Ac = c = A^{-1}d$$

to obtain the solution. If A is not invertible, the system of linear equations has linear dependencies. There are two possibilities. Either more than one vector c satisfies $Ac = d$, so no unique solution exists; or the equations are inconsistent, so there is no solution to the system. If d is the null vector, only the first possibility remains.

It is straightforward to derive that

$$(A^{-1})' = (A')^{-1}$$

and

$$(AB)^{-1} = B^{-1}A^{-1}.$$

(assuming that both inverse matrices exist).

A.5 Idempotent Matrices

A special class of matrices is that of symmetric and idempotent matrices. A matrix P is symmetric if $P' = P$ and **idempotent** if $PP = P$. A symmetric idempotent matrix P has the interpretation of a **projection matrix**. This means that the projection vector Px is in the column space of P, while the residual vector $x - Px$ is orthogonal to any vector in the column space of P.

A projection matrix which projects upon the column space of a matrix A can be constructed as $P = A(A'A)^{-1}A'$. Clearly, this matrix is symmetric and idempotent. Projecting twice upon the same space should leave the result unaffected so we should have $PPx = Px$, which follows directly. The residual from the projection is $x - Px = (I - A(A'A)^{-1}A')x$, so that $M = I - A(A'A)^{-1}A'$ is also a projection matrix with $MP = PM = 0$ and $MM = M = M'$. Thus the vectors Mx and Px are orthogonal.

An interesting projecting matrix (used in Chapter 10) is $Q = I - (1/n)\iota\iota'$, where ι is an n-dimensional vector of ones (so that $\iota\iota'$ is a matrix of ones). The diagonal elements in this matrix are $1 - 1/n$ and all off-diagonal elements are $-1/n$. Now Qx is a vector containing x in deviation from its mean. A vector of means is produced by the transformation matrix $P = (1/n)\iota\iota'$. Note that $PP = P$ and $QP = 0$.

The only nonsingular projection matrix is the identity matrix. All other projection matrices are singular, each having rank equal to the dimension of the space upon which they project.

A.6 Eigenvalues and Eigenvectors

Let A be a symmetric $n \times n$ matrix. Consider the following problem of finding combinations of a vector c (other than the null vector) and a scalar λ that satisfy

$$Ac = \lambda c.$$

In general, there are n solutions $\lambda_1, \ldots, \lambda_n$, called the **eigenvalues** (characteristic roots) of A, corresponding with n vectors $c_1, \ldots, c_n$, called the **eigenvectors** (characteristic vectors). If c_1 is a solution then so is kc_1 for any constant k, so the eigenvectors are defined up to a constant. The eigenvectors of a symmetric matrix are orthogonal, that is $c_i'c_j = 0$ for all $i \neq j$.

If an eigenvalue is zero, the corresponding vector c satisfies $Ac = 0$, which implies that A is not of full rank and thus singular. Thus a singular matrix has at least one zero eigenvalue. In general, the rank of a symmetric matrix corresponds to the number of nonzero eigenvalues.

A symmetric matrix is called **positive definite** if all its eigenvalues are positive. It is called **positive semi-definite** if all its eigenvalues are non-negative. A positive definite matrix is invertible. If A is positive definite, it holds for any vector x (not the null vector) that

$$x'Ax > 0.$$

The reason is that any vector x can be written as a linear combination of the eigenvectors as $x = d_1c_1 + \cdots + d_nc_n$ for scalars $d_1, \ldots, d_n$, and we can write

$$x'Ax = (d_1c_1 + \cdots + d_nc_n)'A(d_1c_1 + \cdots + d_nc_n)$$
$$= \lambda_1 d_1^2 c_1'c_1 + \cdots + \lambda_n d_n^2 c_n'c_n > 0.$$

Similarly, for a positive semi-definite matrix A we have that for any vector x

$$x'Ax \geq 0.$$

The **determinant** of a symmetric matrix equals the product of its n eigenvalues. The determinant of a positive definite matrix is positive. A symmetric matrix is singular if the determinant is zero (i.e. if one of the eigenvalues is zero).

A.7 Differentiation

Let x be an n-dimensional column vector. If c is also an n-dimensional column vector, $c'x$ is a scalar. Let us consider $c'x$ as a function of the vector x. Then, we can consider the vector of derivatives of $c'x$ with respect to each of the elements in x, that is

$$\frac{\partial c'x}{\partial x} = c.$$

This is a column vector of n derivatives, the typical element being c_i. More generally, we have for a vectorial function Ax (where A is a matrix) that

$$\frac{\partial Ax}{\partial x} = A'.$$

The element in column i, row j of this matrix is the derivative of the j-th element in the function Ax with respect to x_i.

Further,

$$\frac{\partial x'Ax}{\partial x} = 2Ax$$

for a symmetric matrix A. If A is not symmetric, we have

$$\frac{\partial x'Ax}{\partial x} = (A + A')x.$$

All these results follow from collecting the results from an element-by-element differentiation.

A.8 Some Least Squares Manipulations

Let $x_i = (x_{i1}, x_{i2}, \ldots, x_{iK})'$ with $x_{i1} \equiv 1$ and $\beta = (\beta_1, \beta_2, \ldots, \beta_K)'$. Then

$$x_i'\beta = \beta_1 + \beta_2 x_{i2} + \cdots + \beta_K x_{iK}.$$

The matrix

$$\sum_{i=1}^{N} x_i x_i' = \sum_{i=1}^{N} \begin{pmatrix} x_{i1} \\ x_{i2} \\ \vdots \\ x_{iK} \end{pmatrix} (x_{i1}, \ x_{i2}, \ldots, x_{iK})$$

$$= \begin{pmatrix} \sum_{i=1}^{N} x_{i1}^2 & \sum_{i=1}^{N} x_{i2} x_{i1} & \cdots & \sum_{i=1}^{N} x_{iK} x_{i1} \\ \vdots & \sum_{i=1}^{N} x_{i2}^2 & & \\ \vdots & & \ddots & \vdots \\ \sum_{i=1}^{N} x_{i1} x_{iK} & & \cdots & \sum_{i=1}^{N} x_{iK}^2 \end{pmatrix}$$

is a $K \times K$ symmetric matrix containing sums of squares and cross-products. The vector

$$\sum_{i=1}^{N} x_i y_i = \begin{pmatrix} \sum_{i=1}^{N} x_{i1} y_i \\ \sum_{i=1}^{N} x_{i2} y_i \\ \vdots \\ \sum_{i=1}^{N} x_{iK} y_i \end{pmatrix}$$

has length K, so that the system

$$\left(\sum_{i=1}^{N} x_i x_i' \right) b = \sum_{i=1}^{N} x_i y_i$$

is a system of K equations with K unknowns (in b). If $\sum_{i=1}^{N} x_i x_i'$ is invertible a unique solution exists. Invertibility requires that $\sum_{i=1}^{N} x_i x_i'$ is of full rank. If it is not full rank, a nonzero K-dimensional vector c exists such that $x_i'c = 0$ for each i and a linear dependence exists between the columns/rows of the matrix $\sum_{i=1}^{N} x_i x_i'$.

With matrix notation, the $N \times K$ matrix X is defined as

$$X = \begin{pmatrix} x_{11} & x_{12} & \cdots & x_{1K} \\ \vdots & \vdots & \ddots & \vdots \\ x_{N1} & x_{N2} & \cdots & x_{NK} \end{pmatrix}$$

and $y = (y_1, y_2, \ldots, y_N)'$. From this it is easily verified that

$$X'X = \sum_{i=1}^{N} x_i x_i'$$

and

$$X'y = \sum_{i=1}^{N} x_i y_i.$$

The matrix $X'X$ is not invertible if the matrix X is not of full rank. That is, if a linear dependence exists between the columns of X ('regressors').

B Statistical and Distribution Theory

This Appendix briefly reviews some statistical and distribution theory that is used in this text. More details can be found in, for example, Greene (2000, Chapter 3) or Davidson and MacKinnon (1993, Appendix B).

B.1 Discrete Random Variables

A **random variable** is a variable that can take different outcomes depending upon 'the state of nature'. For example, the outcome of throwing once with a dice is random, with possible outcomes 1, 2, 3, 4, 5, and 6. Let us denote an arbitrary random variable by Y. If Y denotes the outcome of the dice experiment (and the dice is fair and thrown randomly), the **probability** of each outcome is 1/6. We can denote this as

$$P\{Y = y\} = 1/6 \quad \text{for } y = 1, 2, \ldots, 6.$$

The function which links possible outcomes (in this case $y = 1, 2, \ldots, 6$) to the corresponding probabilities is the **probability mass function** or, more generally, the probability distribution function. We can denote it by

$$f(y) = P\{Y = y\}.$$

Note that $f(y)$ is not a function of the random variable Y, but of all its possible outcomes.

The function $f(y)$ has the property that if we sum it over all possible outcomes the result is one. That is

$$\sum_j f(y_j) = 1.$$

The **expected value** of a discrete random variable is a weighted average of all possible outcomes, where the weights correspond to the probability of that particular outcome. We denote

$$E\{Y\} = \sum_j y_j f(y_j).$$

Note that $E\{Y\}$ does not necessarily correspond to one of the possible outcomes. In the dice experiment, for example, the expected value is 3.5.

A distribution is **degenerate** if it is concentrated in one point only, that is if $P\{Y = y\} = 1$ for one particular value of y and zero for all other values.

B.2 Continuous Random Variables

A **continuous random variable** can take an infinite number of different outcomes, for example, any value in the interval $[0, 1]$. In this case each individual outcome has a probability of zero. Instead of a probability mass function, we define the **probability density function** $f(y) \geq 0$ as

$$P\{a \leq Y \leq b\} = \int_a^b f(y)dy.$$

In a graph, $P\{a \leq Y \leq b\}$ is the area under the function $f(y)$ between the points a and b. Taking the integral of $f(y)$ over all possible outcomes gives

$$\int_{-\infty}^{\infty} f(y)dy = 1.$$

If Y takes values within a certain range only, it is implicitly assumed that $f(y) = 0$ anywhere outside this range.

We can also define the **cumulative density function** (cdf) as

$$F(y) = P\{Y \leq y\} = \int_{-\infty}^{y} f(t)dt,$$

such that $f(y) = F'(y)$ (the derivative). The cumulative density function has the property that $0 \leq F(y) \leq 1$, and is monotonically increasing, i.e.

$$F(y) \geq F(x) \quad \text{if } y > x.$$

It easily follows that $P\{a \leq Y \leq b\} = F(b) - F(a)$.

The **expected value** or **mean** of a continuous random variable, often denoted as μ, is defined as

$$\mu = E\{Y\} = \int_{-\infty}^{\infty} yf(y)dy.$$

Other measures of location are the **median**, which is the value m for which we have

$$P\{Y \leq m\} \geq 1/2 \quad \text{and} \quad P\{Y \geq m\} \leq 1/2.$$

So 50% of the observations is below the median and 50% above. The **mode** is simply the value for which $f(y)$ takes its maximum. It is not often used in econometric applications.

A distribution is **symmetric** around its mean if $f(\mu - y) = f(\mu + y)$. In this case the mean and the median of the distribution are identical.

B.3 Expectations and Moments

If Y and X are random variables and a and b are constants, then it holds that

$$E\{aY + bX\} = aE\{Y\} + bE\{X\},$$

showing that the expectation is a linear operator. Similar results do not necessarily hold if we consider a nonlinear transformation of a random variable. For a nonlinear function g, it does *not* hold in general that $E\{g(Y)\} = g(E\{Y\})$. If g is concave $(g''(Y) < 0)$, **Jensen's inequality** says that

$$E\{g(Y)\} \le g(E\{Y\}).$$

For example, $E\{\log Y\} \le \log E\{Y\}$. The implication of this is that we cannot determine the expected value of a function of Y from the expected value of Y only. Of course, it holds by definition that

$$E\{g(Y)\} = \int_{-\infty}^{\infty} g(y) f(y) dy.$$

The **variance** of a random variable, often denoted by σ^2, is a measure of the dispersion of the distribution. It is defined as

$$\sigma^2 = V\{Y\} = E\{(Y - \mu)^2\}$$

and equals the expected quadratic deviation from the mean. It is sometimes called the **second central moment**. A useful result is that

$$E\{(Y - \mu)^2\} = E\{Y^2\} - 2E\{Y\}\mu + \mu^2 = E\{Y^2\} - \mu^2,$$

where $E\{Y^2\}$ is the second moment. If Y has a discrete distribution, its variance is determined as

$$V\{Y\} = \sum_j (y_j - \mu)^2 f(y_j),$$

where j indexes the different outcomes. For a continuous distribution we have

$$V\{Y\} = \int_{-\infty}^{\infty} (y - \mu)^2 f(y) dy.$$

Using these definitions it is easily verified that

$$V\{aY + b\} = a^2 V\{Y\},$$

where a and b are arbitrary constants. Often we will also use the **standard deviation** of a random variable, denoted σ, defined as the square root of the variance. The standard deviation is expressed in the same units as Y.

In most cases the distribution of a random variable is not completely described by its mean and variance, and we can define the **k-th central moment** as

$$E\{(Y - \mu)^k\}, \quad k = 1, 2, 3, \ldots$$

In particular, the third central moment is a measure for **skewness**, where a value of 0 indicates a symmetric distribution, and the fourth central moment measures **kurtosis**. It is a measure of the thickness of the tails of the distribution.

B.4 Multivariate Distributions

The **joint density function** of two random variables Y and X, denoted $f(y, x)$, is defined by

$$P\{a_1 < Y < b_1,\ a_2 < X < b_2\} = \int_{a_1}^{b_1} \int_{a_2}^{b_2} f(y, x)\, dy\, dx.$$

If Y and X are **independent**, it holds that $f(y, x) = f(y)f(x)$, such that

$$P\{a_1 < Y < b_1,\ a_2 < X < b_2\} = P\{a_1 < Y < b_1\}P\{a_2 < X < b_2\}.$$

In general, the **marginal distribution** of Y is characterized by the density function

$$f(y) = \int_{-\infty}^{\infty} f(y, x)\, dx.$$

This implies that the expected value of Y is given by

$$E\{Y\} = \int_{-\infty}^{\infty} yf(y)\, dy = \int_{-\infty}^{\infty} \int_{-\infty}^{\infty} yf(y, x)\, dx\, dy.$$

The **covariance** between Y and X is a measure of *linear* dependence between the two variables. It is defined as

$$\sigma_{xy} = \mathrm{cov}\{Y, X\} = E\{(Y - \mu_y)(X - \mu_x)\},$$

where $\mu_y = E\{Y\}$ and $\mu_x = E\{X\}$. The **correlation coefficient** is given by the covariance standardized by the two standard deviations, that is

$$\rho_{yx} = \frac{\mathrm{cov}\{Y, X\}}{\sqrt{V\{Y\}V\{X\}}} = \frac{\sigma_{xy}}{\sigma_x \sigma_y}.$$

The correlation coefficient is always between -1 and 1 and is not affected by the scaling of the variables. If $\mathrm{cov}\{Y, X\} = 0$, Y and X are said to be **uncorrelated**. When a, b, c, d are constants, it holds that

$$\mathrm{cov}\{aY + b,\ cX + d\} = ac\,\mathrm{cov}\{Y, X\}.$$

Further,

$$\mathrm{cov}\{aY + bX,\ X\} = a\,\mathrm{cov}\{Y, X\} + b\,\mathrm{cov}\{X, X\} = a\,\mathrm{cov}\{Y, X\} + bV\{X\}.$$

It also follows that two variables Y and X are perfectly correlated ($\rho_{yx} = 1$) if $Y = aX$ for some nonzero value of a. If Y and X are correlated, the variance of a linear function of Y and X depends upon their covariance. In particular,

$$V\{aY + bX\} = a^2 V\{Y\} + b^2 V\{X\} + 2ab\,\mathrm{cov}\{Y, X\}.$$

If we consider a K-dimensional vector of random variables, $\vec{Y} = (Y_1, \ldots, Y_K)'$, we can define its expectation vector as

$$E\{\vec{Y}\} = \begin{pmatrix} E\{Y_1\} \\ \vdots \\ E\{Y_K\} \end{pmatrix}$$

and its variance-covariance matrix (or simply **covariance matrix**) as

$$V\{\vec{Y}\} = \begin{pmatrix} V\{Y_1\} & \cdots & \operatorname{cov}\{Y_1, Y_K\} \\ \vdots & \ddots & \vdots \\ \operatorname{cov}\{Y_K, Y_1\} & \cdots & V\{Y_K\} \end{pmatrix}.$$

Note that this matrix is symmetric. If we consider one or more linear combinations of the elements in $\vec{Y}$, say $R\vec{Y}$, where R is of dimension $J \times K$, it holds that

$$V\{R\vec{Y}\} = RV\{\vec{Y}\}R'.$$

B.5 Conditional Distributions

A conditional distribution describes the distribution of a variable, say Y, given the outcome of another variable X. For example, if we throw with two die, X could denote the outcome of the first dice and Y could denote the total of the two die. Then we could be interested in the distribution of Y conditional upon the outcome of the first dice. For example, what is the probability of throwing 7 in total if the first dice had an outcome of 3. Or an outcome of 3 or less? The conditional distribution is implied by the joint distribution of the two variables. We define

$$f(y|X = x) = f(y|x) = \frac{f(y, x)}{f(x)}.$$

If Y and X are independent, it immediately follows that $f(y|x) = f(y)$. From the above definition it follows that

$$f(y, x) = f(y|x)f(x),$$

which says that the joint distribution of two variables can be decomposed in the product of a conditional distribution and a marginal distribution. Similarly, we can write

$$f(y, x) = f(x|y)f(y).$$

The **conditional expectation** of Y given $X = x$ is the expected value of Y from the conditional distribution. That is,

$$E\{Y|X = x\} = E\{Y|x\} = \int yf(y|x)dy.$$

The conditional expectation is a function of x, unless Y and X are independent.
Similarly, we can define the conditional variance as

$$V\{Y|x\} = \int (y - E\{Y|x\})^2 f(y|x)dy,$$

which can be written as
$$V\{Y|x\} = E\{Y^2|x\} - (E\{Y|x\})^2.$$

It holds that
$$V\{Y\} = E_x\{V\{Y|X\}\} + V_x\{E\{Y|X\}\},$$

where E_x and V_x denote the expected value and variance, respectively, based upon the marginal distribution of X. The terms $V\{Y|X\}$ and $E\{Y|X\}$ are functions of the random variable X and therefore random variables themselves.

Let us consider the relationship between two random variables Y and X, where $E\{Y\} = 0$. Then it follows that Y and X are **uncorrelated** if
$$E\{YX\} = \text{cov}\{Y, X\} = 0.$$

If Y is **conditional mean independent** of X it means that
$$E\{Y|X\} = E\{Y\} = 0.$$

This is stronger than zero correlation because $E\{Y|X\} = 0$ implies that $E\{Yg(X)\} = 0$ for any function g. If Y and X are **independent** this is again stronger and it implies that
$$E\{g_1(Y)g_2(X)\} = E\{g_1(Y)\}E\{g_2(X)\}$$

for arbitrary functions g_1 and g_2. It is easily verified that this implies conditional mean independence and zero correlation. Note that $E\{Y|X\} = 0$ does not necessarily imply that $E\{X|Y\} = 0$.

B.6 The Normal Distribution

In econometrics the **normal distribution** plays a central role. The density function for a normal distribution with mean μ and variance σ^2 is given by
$$f(y) = \frac{1}{\sqrt{2\pi\sigma^2}} \exp\left\{ -\frac{1}{2}\frac{(y-\mu)^2}{\sigma^2} \right\},$$

which we write as $Y \sim \mathcal{N}(\mu, \sigma^2)$. It is easily verified that the normal distribution is symmetric. A standard normal distribution is obtained for $\mu = 0$ and $\sigma = 1$. Note that the standardized variable $(Y - \mu)/\sigma$ is $\mathcal{N}(0, 1)$ if $Y \sim \mathcal{N}(\mu, \sigma^2)$. The density of a standard normal distribution, typically denoted by ϕ, is given by
$$\phi(y) = \frac{1}{\sqrt{2\pi}} \exp\left\{ -\frac{1}{2}y^2 \right\}.$$

A useful property of a normal distribution is that a linear function of a normal variable is also normal. That is, if $Y \sim \mathcal{N}(\mu, \sigma^2)$ then
$$aY + b \sim \mathcal{N}(a\mu + b, a^2\sigma^2).$$

The cumulative density function of the normal distribution does not have a closed form expression. We have
$$P\{Y \le y\} = P\left\{ \frac{Y-\mu}{\sigma} \le \frac{y-\mu}{\sigma} \right\} = \Phi\left(\frac{y-\mu}{\sigma} \right) = \int_{-\infty}^{(y-\mu)/\sigma} \phi(t)dt,$$

where Φ denotes the cdf of the standard normal distribution. Note that $\Phi(y) = 1 - \Phi(-y)$ due to the symmetry.

The symmetry also implies that the third central moment of a normal distribution is zero. It can be shown that the fourth central moment of a normal distribution is given by

$$E\{(Y - \mu)^4\} = 3\sigma^4.$$

Note that this implies that $E\{Y^4\} = 4\sigma^4$. Typically these properties of the third and fourth central moments are exploited in tests against non-normality.

If (Y, X) have a **bivariate normal distribution** with mean vector $\mu = (\mu_y, \mu_x)'$ and covariance matrix

$$\Sigma = \begin{pmatrix} \sigma_y^2 & \sigma_{yx} \\ \sigma_{yx} & \sigma_x^2 \end{pmatrix},$$

denoted $(Y, X)' \sim \mathcal{N}(\mu, \Sigma)$, the joint density function is given by

$$f(y, x) = f(y|x)f(x),$$

where both the **conditional density** of Y given X and the **marginal density** of X are normal. The conditional density function is given by

$$f(y|x) = \frac{1}{\sqrt{2\pi\sigma_{y|x}^2}} \exp\left\{ -\frac{1}{2} \frac{(y - \mu_{y|x})^2}{\sigma_{y|x}^2} \right\},$$

where $\mu_{y|x}$ is the **conditional expectation** of Y given X, given by

$$\mu_{y|x} = \mu_y + (\sigma_{yx}/\sigma_x^2)(x - \mu_x),$$

and $\sigma_{y|x}^2$ is the conditional variance of Y given X,

$$\sigma_{y|x}^2 = \sigma_y^2 - \sigma_{yx}^2/\sigma_x^2 = \sigma_y^2(1 - \rho_{yx}^2),$$

with ρ_{yx} denoting the correlation coefficient between Y and X. These results have some important implications. First, if two (or more) variables have a joint normal distribution, all marginal distributions and conditional distributions are also normal. Second, the conditional expectation of one variable given the other(s) is a linear function (with an intercept term). Third, if $\rho_{yx} = 0$ it follows that $f(y|x) = f(y)$ so that

$$f(y, x) = f(y)f(x),$$

and Y and X are independent. Thus, if Y and X have a joint normal distribution with zero correlation then they are automatically independent. Recall that in general independence is a stronger requirement than uncorrelatedness.

Another important result is that a linear function of normal variables is also normal, that is, if $(Y, X)' \sim \mathcal{N}(\mu, \Sigma)$ then

$$aY + bX \sim \mathcal{N}(a\mu_y + b\mu_x,\ a^2\sigma_y^2 + b^2\sigma_x^2 + 2ab\sigma_{yx}).$$

These results can be generalized to a general K-variate normal distribution. If the K-dimensional vector $\vec{Y}$ has a normal distribution with mean vector μ and covariance matrix Σ, that is

$$\vec{Y} \sim \mathcal{N}(\mu, \Sigma),$$

it holds that the distribution of $R\vec{Y}$, where R is a $J \times K$ matrix, is a J-variate normal distribution, given by

$$R\vec{Y} \sim \mathcal{N}(R\mu, R\Sigma R').$$

In models with limited dependent variables we often encounter forms of **truncation**. If Y has density $f(y)$, the distribution of Y truncated from below at a given point c ($Y \geq c$) is given by

$$f(y|Y \geq c) = \frac{f(y)}{P\{Y \geq c\}} \quad \text{if } y \geq c \quad \text{and 0 otherwise.}$$

If Y is a standard normal variable, the truncated distribution of $Y \geq c$ has mean

$$E\{Y|Y \geq c\} = \lambda_1(c),$$

where

$$\lambda_1(c) = \frac{\phi(c)}{1 - \Phi(c)},$$

and variance

$$V\{Y|Y \geq c\} = 1 - \lambda_1(c)[\lambda_1(c) - c].$$

If the distribution is truncated from above ($Y \leq c$) it holds that

$$E\{Y|Y \leq c\} = \lambda_2(c),$$

with

$$\lambda_2(c) = \frac{-\phi(c)}{\Phi(c)}.$$

If Y has a normal density with mean μ and variance σ^2 the truncated distribution $Y \geq c$ has mean

$$E\{Y|Y \geq c\} = \mu + \sigma\lambda_1(c^*) \geq \mu$$

where $c^* = (c - \mu)/\sigma$, and, similarly,

$$E\{Y|Y \leq c\} = \mu + \sigma\lambda_2(c^*) \leq \mu.$$

When (Y, X) have a bivariate normal distribution, as above, we obtain that

$$E\{Y|X \geq c\} = \mu_y + (\sigma_{yx}/\sigma_x^2)[E\{X|X \geq c\} - \mu_x]$$
$$= \mu_y + (\sigma_{yx}/\sigma_x)\lambda_1(c^*).$$

More details can be found in Maddala (1983, Appendix).

B.7 Related Distributions

Besides the normal distribution several other distributions are important. First, we define the **Chi-squared distribution** as follows. If $Y_1, \ldots, Y_J$ is a set of independent standard normal variables, it holds that

$$\xi = \sum_{j=1}^{J} Y_j^2$$

has a Chi-squared distribution with J degrees of freedom. We denote $\xi \sim \chi_J^2$. More generally, if $Y_1, \ldots, Y_J$ is a set of independent normal variables with mean μ and variance σ^2, if follows that

$$\xi = \sum_{j=1}^{J} \frac{(Y_j - \mu)^2}{\sigma^2}$$

is Chi-squared with J degrees of freedom. Most generally, if $\vec{Y} = (Y_1, \ldots, Y_J)'$ is a vector of random variables that has a joint normal distribution with mean vector μ and (nonsingular) covariance matrix Σ, it follows that

$$\xi = (\vec{Y} - \mu)' \Sigma^{-1} (\vec{Y} - \mu) \sim \chi_J^2.$$

If ξ has a Chi-squared distribution with J degrees of freedom it holds that $E\{\xi\} = J$ and $V\{\xi\} = 2J$.

Next, we consider the t **distribution** (or Student distribution). If X has a standard normal distribution, $X \sim \mathcal{N}(0, 1)$, and $\xi \sim \chi_J^2$ and if X and ξ are independent, the ratio

$$t = \frac{X}{\sqrt{\xi/J}}$$

has a t distribution with J degrees of freedom. Like the standard normal distribution, the t distribution is symmetric around zero, but it has fatter tails, particularly for small J. If J approaches infinity, the t distribution approaches the normal distribution.

If $\xi_1 \sim \chi_{J_1}^2$ and $\xi_2 \sim \chi_{J_2}^2$ and if ξ_1 and ξ_2 are independent, it follows that the ratio

$$f = \frac{\xi_1/J_1}{\xi_2/J_2}$$

has an F **distribution** with J_1 and J_2 degrees of freedom in numerator and denominator, respectively. It easily follows that the inverse ratio

$$\frac{\xi_2/J_2}{\xi_1/J_1}$$

also has an F distribution, but with J_2 and J_1 degrees of freedom, respectively. The F distribution is thus the distribution of the ratio of two independent Chi-squared distributed variables, divided by their respective degrees of freedom. When $J_1 = 1$, ξ_1 is a squared normal variable, say $\xi_1 = X^2$, and it follows that

$$t^2 = \left(\frac{X}{\sqrt{\xi_2/J_2}} \right)^2 = \frac{\xi_1}{\xi_2/J_2} = f \sim F_{J_2}^1.$$

Thus, with one degree of freedom in the numerator, the F distribution is just the square of a t distribution. If J_2 is large, the distribution of

$$J_1 f = \frac{\xi_1}{\xi_2/J_2}$$

is well approximated by a Chi-squared distribution with J_1 degrees of freedom. For large J_2 the denominator is thus negligible.

Finally, we consider the **lognormal distribution**. If $\log Y$ has a normal distribution with mean μ and variance σ^2 then $Y > 0$ has a so-called lognormal distribution. The lognormal density is often used to describe the population distribution of (labour) income or the distribution of asset returns (see Campbell, Lo and MacKinlay, 1997). While $E\{\log Y\} = \mu$, it holds that

$$E\{Y\} = \exp\left\{\mu + \frac{1}{2}\sigma^2\right\}$$

(compare Jensen's inequality above).

Bibliography

Akaika, H. (1973), Information Theory and an Extension of the Maximum Likelihood Principle. In: B. N. Petrov and F. Cszaki, eds., *Second International Symposium on Information Theory*, Akademiai Kiado, Budapest, 267–281.

Amemiya, T. (1981), Qualitative Response Models: A Survey, *Journal of Economic Literature*, 19, 1483–1536.

Amemiya, T. (1984), Tobit Models: A Survey, *Journal of Econometrics*, 24, 3–61.

Amemiya, T. and MaCurdy, T. (1986), Instrumental-Variable Estimation of an Error-Components Model, *Econometrica*, 54, 869–881.

Andersen, E. B. (1970), Asymptotic Properties of Conditional Maximum Likelihood Estimation, *Journal of the Royal Statistical Society, Series B*, 32, 283–301.

Anderson, T. W. and Hsiao, C. (1981), Estimation of Dynamic Models with Error Components, *Journal of the American Statistical Association*, 76, 598–606.

Andrews, D. W. K. and Schafgans, M. A. (1998), Semiparametric Estimation of the Intercept of a Sample Selection Model, *Review of Economic Studies*, 63, 497–517.

Anglin, P. M. and Gençay, R. (1996), Semiparametric Estimation of a Hedonic Price Function, *Journal of Applied Econometrics*, 11, 633–648.

Angrist, J. D. and Krueger, A. B. (1991), Does Compulsory School Attendance Affect Schooling and Earnings?, *Quarterly Journal of Economics*, 106, 979–1014.

Arellano, M. (1987), Computing Robust Standard Errors for Within-Groups Estimators, *Oxford Bulletin of Economics and Statistics*, 49, 431–434.

Arellano, M. and Bond, S. (1991), Some Tests of Specification for Panel Data: Monte Carlo Evidence and an Application to Employment Equations, *Review of Economic Studies*, 58, 277–294.

Arellano, M. and Bover, O. (1995), Another Look at the Instrumental Variable Estimation of Error-Components Models, *Journal of Econometrics*, 68, 29–51.

Atkinson, A. B., Gomulka, J. and Stern, N. H. (1990), Spending on Alcohol: Evidence from the Family Expenditure Survey 1970–1983, *Economic Journal*, 100, 808–827.

Baltagi, B. H. (1995), *Econometric Analysis of Panel Data*, John Wiley and Sons, New York.

Baltagi, B. H. (1996), Specification Issues. In: L. Mátyás and P. Sevestre, eds., *The Econometrics of Panel Data. A Handbook of the Theory with Applications*, 2nd revised edition, Kluwer Academic Publishers, Dordrecht, 293–306.

Banerjee, A., Dolado, J., Galbraith, J. W. and Hendry, D. F. (1993), *Co-Integration, Error-Correction, and the Econometric Analysis of Non-Stationary Data*, Oxford University Press.

Banks, J., Blundell, R. and Lewbel, A. (1997), Quadratic Engel Curves and Consumer Demand, *Review of Economics and Statistics*, 74, 527–539.

Banz, R. (1981), The Relation between Returns and Market Value of Common Stocks, *Journal of Financial Economics*, 9, 3–18.

Bera, A. K. and Higgins, M. L. (1993), ARCH Models: Properties, Estimation and Testing, *Journal of Economic Surveys*, 7, 305–366.

Bera, A. K., Jarque, C. M. and Lee, L. F. (1984), Testing the Normality Assumption in Limited Dependent Variable Models, *International Economic Review*, 25, 563–578.

Berndt, E. R. (1991), *The Practice of Econometrics, Classic and Contemporary*, Addison-Wesley, Reading.

Berndt, E. R., Hall, B. H., Hall, R. E. and Hausman, J. A. (1974), Estimation and Inference in Nonlinear Structural Models, *Annals of Economic and Social Measurement*, 3, 653–665.

Bhargava, A., Franzini, L. and Narendranathan, W. (1983), Serial Correlation and the Fixed Effects Model, *Review of Economic Studies*, 49, 533–549.

Blundell, R. and Bond, S. (1998), Initial Conditions and Moment Restrictions in Dynamic Panel Data Models, *Journal of Econometrics*, 87, 115–143.

Bollerslev, T. (1986), Generalized Autoregressive Conditional Heteroskedasticity, *Journal of Econometrics*, 31, 307–327.

Bollerslev, T., Chou, R. Y. and Kroner, K. F. (1992), ARCH Modeling in Finance. A Review of the Theory and Empirical Evidence, *Journal of Econometrics*, 52, 5–59.

Bollerslev, T., Engle, R. F. and Nelson, D. B. (1994), ARCH Models. In: R. F. Engle and D. L. McFadden, eds., *Handbook of Econometrics, Volume IV*, Elsevier Science, Amsterdam, 2961–3038.

Boswijk, H. P. (1999), *Asymptotic Theory for Integrated Processes*, Oxford University Press, Oxford.

Box, G. E. P. and Jenkins, G. M. (1976), *Time Series Analysis: Forecasting and Control*, revised edition, Holden-Day.

Breusch, T. (1978), Testing for Autocorrelation in Dynamic Linear Models, *Australian Economic Papers*, 17, 334–355.

Breusch, T. and Pagan, A. (1980), A Simple Test for Heteroskedasticity and Random Coefficient Variation, *Econometrica*, 47, 1287–1294.

Breusch, T., Mizon, G. and Schmidt, P. (1989), Efficient Estimation Using Panel Data, *Econometrica*, 57, 695–700.

Butler, J. S. and Moffitt, R. (1982), A Computationally Efficient Quadrature Procedure for the One-Factor Multinomial Probit Model, *Econometrica*, 50, 761–764.

Cameron, A. C. and Trivedi, P. K. (1998), *Regression Analysis of Count Data*, Cambridge University Press.

Cameron, A. C. and Windmeijer, F. A. G. (1997), An *R*-squared Measure of Goodness of Fit for Some Common Nonlinear Regression Models, *Journal of Econometrics*, 77, 329–342.

Campbell, J. Y. and Shiller, R. (1991), Yield Spreads and Interest Rate Movements: A Bird's Eye View, *Review of Economic Studies*, 58, 495–514.

Campbell, J. Y., Lo, A. W. and MacKinlay, A. C. (1997), *The Econometrics of Financial Markets*, Princeton University Press, Princeton.

Canova, F. (1995), The Economics of VAR Models. In: K. D. Hoover, ed., *Macroeconometrics: Developments, Tensions and Prospects*, Kluwer Academic Publishers, Boston, 57–97.

Card, D. (1995), Using Geographical Variation in College Proximity to Estimate the Return to Schooling. In: L. N. Christofides, E. K. Grant and R. Swidinsky, eds., *Aspects of Labour Market Behaviour: Essays in Honour of John Vanderkamp*, University of Toronto Press, Toronto, 201–222.

Card, D. (1999), The Causal Effect of Education on Earnings. In: O. Ashenfelter and D. Card, eds., *Handbook of Labor Economics, Volume IIIA*, Elsevier Science, Amsterdam.

Carhart, M. M. (1997), On Persistence in Mutual Fund Performance, *Journal of Finance*, 52, 57–82.

Carroll, J. D. and Green, P. E. (1995), Psychometric Methods in Marketing Research: Part 1 Conjoint Analysis, *Journal of Marketing Research*, 32, 385–391.

Chamberlain, G. (1980), Analysis of Covariance with Qualitative Data, *Review of Economic Studies*, 47, 225–238.

Charemza, W. W. and Deadman, D. F. (1992), *New Directions in Econometric Practice. General to Specific Modelling, Cointegration and Vector Autoregression*, Edward Elgar, Aldershot.

Cochrane, D. and Orcutt, G. (1949), Application of Least Squares Regression to Relationships Containing Autocorrelated Error Terms, *Journal of the American Statistical Association*, 44, 32–61.

Cochrane, J. H. (1996), A Cross-Sectional Test of an Investment-Based Asset Pricing Model, *Journal of Political Economy*, 104, 572–621.

Corbae D. and Ouliaris, S. (1988), Cointegration and Tests of Purchasing Power Parity, *Review of Economics and Statistics*, 70, 508–511.

Cuthbertson K., Hall, S. G. and Taylor, M. P. (1992), *Applied Econometric Techniques*, Philip Allan, Hemel Hempstead.

Davidson, R. and MacKinnon, J. G. (1981), Several Tests for Model Specification in the Presence of Alternative Hypotheses, *Econometrica*, 49, 781–793.

Davidson, R. and MacKinnon, J. G. (1993), *Estimation and Inference in Econometrics*, Oxford University Press.

Deaton, A. and Muellbauer, J. (1980), *Economics and Consumer Behavior*, Cambridge University Press, Cambridge.

Diamond, P. A. and Hausman, J. A. (1994), Contingent Valuation: Is Some Number Better than No Number?, *Journal of Economics Perspectives*, 8, 45–64.

Dickey, D. A. and Fuller, W. A. (1979), Distribution of the Estimators for Autoregressive Time Series with a Unit Root, *Journal of the American Statistical Association*, 74, 427–431.

Diebold, F. X. (1998), *Forecasting*, South-Western College Publishing, Cincinnati, Ohio.

Diebold, F. X. and Lopez, J. A. (1995), Modeling Volatility Dynamics. In: K. D. Hoover, ed., *Macroeconometrics: Developments, Tensions and Prospects*, Kluwer Academic Publishers, Boston, 427–466.

Durbin, J. and Watson, G. (1950), Testing for Serial Correlation in Least Squares Regression – I, *Biometrika*, 37, 409–428.

Eicker, F. (1967), Limit Theorems for Regressions with Unequal and Dependent Errors. In: L. LeCam and J. Neyman, eds., *Proceedings of the Fifth Berkeley Symposium on Mathematical Statistics and Probability*, University of California Press, Berkeley, 59–82.

Elton, E. J. and Gruber, M. J. (1995), *Modern Portfolio Theory and Investment Analysis*, 5th edition, John Wiley and Sons, New York.

Enders, W. (1995), *Applied Econometric Time Series*, John Wiley and Sons, New York.

Engle, R. F. (1982), Autoregressive Conditional Heteroskedasticity with Estimates of the Variance of United Kingdom Inflation, *Econometrica*, 50, 987–1007.

Engle, R. F. (1984), Wald, Likelihood Ratio and Lagrange Multiplier Tests in Econometrics. In: Z. Griliches and M. D. Intriligator, eds., *Handbook of Econometrics, Volume II*, Elsevier Science, Amsterdam, 775–826.

Engle, R. F. and Bollerslev, T. (1986), Modelling the Persistence of Conditional Variances, *Econometric Reviews*, 5, 1–50.

Engle, R. F. and Granger, C. W. J. (1987), Cointegration and Error Correction: Representation, Estimation and Testing, *Econometrica*, 55, 251–276.

Engle, R. F. and Ng, V. K. (1993), Measuring and Testing the Impact of News on Volatility, *Journal of Finance*, 48, 1749–1778.

Engle, R. F. and Yoo, B. S. (1987), Forecasting and Testing in Co-Integrated Systems, *Journal of Econometrics*, 35, 143–159.

Engle, R. F., Hendry, D. F. and Richard, J.-F. (1983), Exogeneity, *Econometrica*, 51, 277–304.

Engle, R. F., Lilien, D. M. and Robins, R. P. (1987), Estimating Time Varying Risk Premia in the Term Structure: The ARCH-M Model, *Econometrica*, 55, 591–407.

Fama, E. F. (1970), Efficient Capital Markets: A Review of the Theory and Empirical Work, *Journal of Finance*, 25, 383–417.

Fama, E. F. and French, K. R. (1988), Permanent and Temporary Components of Stock Prices, *Journal of Political Economy*, 81, 246–273.

Frankel, J. (1993), *On Exchange Rates*, MIT Press, Cambridge.

Franses, P. H. B. F. (1998), *Time Series Models for Business and Economic Forecasting*, Cambridge University Press, Cambridge.

Froot, K. A. and Rogoff, K. (1996), Perspectives on PPP and Long-run Exchange Rates. In: S. Grossman and K. Rogoff, eds., *Handbook of International Economics, Volume III*, Elsevier Science, Amsterdam.

Fuller, W. A. (1976), *Introduction to Statistical Time-Series*, John Wiley & Sons, New York.

Glewwe, P. (1997), A Test of the Normality Assumption in the Ordered Probit Model, *Econometric Reviews*, 16, 1–19.

Godfrey, L. (1978), Testing against General Autoregressive and Moving Average Error Models when the Regressors Include Lagged Dependent Variables, *Econometrica*, 46, 1293–1302.

Godfrey, L. (1988), *Misspecification Tests in Econometrics. The Lagrange Multiplier Principle and Other Approaches*, Cambridge University Press, Cambridge.

Goldfeld, S. and Quandt, R. (1965), Some Tests for Homoskedasticity, *Journal of the American Statistical Association*, 60, 539–547.

Gouriéroux, C., Monfort, A. and Trognon, A. (1984), Pseudo-maximum Likelihood Methods: Theory, *Econometrica*, 42, 681–700.

Gouriéroux, C., Monfort, A., Renault, E. and Trognon, A. (1987), Generalized Residuals, *Journal of Econometrics*, 34, 5–32.

Granger, C. W. J. (1983), Co-Integrated Variables and Error-Correcting Models, *Unpublished Discussion Paper 83-13*, University of California, San Diego.

Granger, C. W. J. and Newbold, P. (1974), Spurious Regressions in Econometrics, *Journal of Econometrics*, 35, 143–159.

Greene, W. H. (1997), *Econometric Analysis*, 3rd edition, Prentice Hall.

Greene, W. H. (2000), *Econometric Analysis*, 4th edition, Prentice Hall.

Gregory, A. W. and Veall, M. R. (1985), On Formulating Wald Tests of Nonlinear Restrictions, *Econometrica*, 53, 1465–1468.

Griliches, Z. (1977), Estimating the Returns to Schooling: Some Econometric Problems, *Econometrica*, 45, 1–22.

Gronau, R. (1974), Wage Comparisons: A Selectivity Bias, *Journal of Political Economy*, 82, 1119–1143.

Hall, A. (1993), Some Aspects of Generalized Method of Moments Estimation. In: G. S. Maddala, C. R. Rao and H. D. Vinod, eds., *Handbook of Statistics, Volume XI*, Elsevier Science, Amsterdam, 393–417.

Hamilton, J. D. (1994), *Time Series Analysis*, Princeton University Press, Princeton.

Hanemann, W. M. (1994), Valueing the Environment through Contingent Valuation, *Journal of Economic Perspectives*, 8, 19–44.

Hannan, E. J. (1980), The Estimation of the Order of an ARMA Process, *Annals of Statistics*, 8, 1071–1081.

Hansen, L. P. (1982), Large Sample Properties of Generalized Method of Moments Estimators, *Econometrica*, 50, 1029–1054.

Hansen, L. P. and Singleton, K. (1982), Generalized Instrumental Variables Estimation of Nonlinear Rational Expectations Models, *Econometrica*, 50, 1269–1286.

Hargreaves, C. P. (1994), A Review of Methods of Estimating Cointegrating Relationships. In: C. P. Hargreaves, ed., *Nonstationary Time Series Analsysis and Cointegration*, Oxford University Press, Oxford.

Harris, R. D. F. and Tzavalis, E. (1999), Inference for Unit Roots in Dynamic Panels Where the Time Dimension is Fixed, *Journal of Econometrics*, 91, 201–226.

Harris, R. I. D. (1995), *Using Cointegration Analysis in Econometric Modelling*, Prentice Hall–Harvester Wheatsheaf, London.

Hasza, D. P. and Fuller, W. A. (1979), Estimation for Autoregressive Processes with Unit Roots, *Annals of Statistics*, 7, 1106–1120.

Hausman, J. A. (1978), Specification Tests in Econometrics, *Econometrica*, 46, 1251–1271.

Hausman, J. A. and Taylor, W. E. (1981), Panel Data and Unobservable Individual Effects, *Econometrica*, 49, 1377–1398.

Hausman, J. A. and Wise, D. A. (1979), Attrition Bias in Experimental and Panel Data: The Gary Income Maintenance Experiment, *Econometrica*, 47, 455–473.

Heckman, J. J. (1978), Simple Statistical Models for Discrete Panel Data Developed and Applied to Test the Hypothesis of True State Dependence against the Hypothesis of Spurious State Dependence, *Annales de l'INSEE*, 30/31, 227–269.

Heckman, J. J. (1979), Sample Selection Bias as a Specification Error, *Econometrica*, 47, 153–161.

Heckman, J. J. (1981), The Incidental Parameters Problem and the Problem of Initial Conditions in Estimating a Discrete Time–Discrete Data Stochastic Process. In: C. F. Manski and D. F. McFadden, eds., *Structural Analysis of Discrete Data with Econometric Applications*, MIT Press, Cambridge, 179–195.

Heckman, J. J. (1990), Varieties of Selection Bias, *American Economic Review*, 80, 313–318.

Hildreth, C. and Lu, J. (1960), Demand Relations with Autocorrelated Disturbances, Technical Bulletin No. 276, Michigan State University.

Hoffman, D. L. and Rasche, R. H. (1996), Assessing Forecast Performance in a Cointegrated System, *Journal of Applied Econometrics*, 11, 495–517.

Honoré, B. E (1992), Trimmed LAD and Least Squares Estimation of Truncated and Censored Regression Models with Fixed Effects, *Econometrica*, 60, 533–565.

Honoré, B. E (1993), Orthogonality Conditions for Tobit Models with Fixed Effects and Lagged Dependent Variables, *Journal of Econometrics*, 59, 35–61.

Horowitz, J. L. (1992), A Smoothed Maximum Score Estimator for the Binary Response Model, *Econometrica*, 60, 505–531.

Horowitz, J. L. (1993), Semiparametric and Nonparametric Estimation of Quantile Response Models. In: G. S. Maddala, C. R. Rao and H. D. Vinod, eds., *Handbook of Statistics, Volume XI*, Elsevier Science, Amsterdam.

Horowitz, J. L. (1998), *Semiparametric Methods in Econometrics*, Springer-Verlag, New York.

Hsiao, C. (1985), Benefits and Limitations of Panel Data, *Econometric Reviews*, 4, 121–174.

Hsiao, C. (1986), *Analysis of Panel Data*, Cambridge University Press.

Im, K., Pesaran, M. H. and Shin, Y. (1997), Testing for Unit Roots in Heterogeneous Panels, Discussion Paper, Department of Applied Economics, University of Cambridge, Cambridge.

Isard, P. (1995), *Exchange Rate Economics*, Cambridge University Press.

Jarque, C. M. and Bera, A. K. (1980), Efficient Tests for Normality, Homoskedasticity and Serial Independence of Regressions Residuals, *Economics Letters*, 6, 255–259.

Johansen, S. (1988), Statistical Analysis of Cointegration Vectors, *Journal of Economic Dynamics and Control*, 12, 231–254.

Johansen, S. (1991), Estimation and Hypothesis Testing of Cointegrating Vectors in Gaussian Vector Autoregressive Models, *Econometrica*, 59, 1551–1580.

Johansen, S. (1995), Likelihood-Based Inference in Cointegrated Vector Autoregressive Models, Oxford University Press, Oxford.

Johansen, S. and Juselius, K. (1990), Maximum Likelihood Estimation and Inference on Cointegration – with Applications to the Demand for Money, *Oxford Bulletin of Economics and Statistics*, 52, 169–210.

Johnston, J. and Dinardo, J. (1997), *Econometric Methods*, 4th edition, McGraw-Hill, New York.

Judge, G. G., Hill, R. C., Griffiths, W. E., Lütkepohl, H. and Lee, T. S. (1988), *Introduction to the Theory and Practice of Econometrics*, 2nd edition, John Wiley and Sons, New York.

Kao, C. (1999), Spurious Regression and Residual-Based Tests for Cointegration in Panel Data, *Journal of Econometrics*, 90, 1–44.

Keane, M. P. (1993), Simulation Estimation for Panel Data Models with Limited Dependent Variables. In: G. S. Maddala, C. R. Rao and H. D. Vinod, eds., *Handbook of Statistics, Volume XI*, Elsevier Science, Amsterdam, 545–571.

Keane, M. P., Moffitt, R. and Runkle, D. (1988), Real Wages over the Business Cycle: Estimating the Impact of Heterogeneity with Micro Data, *Journal of Political Economy*, 96, 1232–1266.

Kmenta, J. (1986), *Elements of Econometrics*, MacMillan, New York.

Konings, J. and Roodhooft, F. (1997), How Elastic is the Demand for Labour in Belgian Enterprises? Results from Firm Level Panel Data, 1986–1994, *De Economist*, 145, 229–241.

Kwiatkowski, D., Phillips, P. C. B., Schmidt, P. and Shin, Y. (1992), Testing the Null Hypothesis of Stationarity Against the Alternative of a Unit Root: How Sure Are We That Economic Time Series Have a Unit Root? *Journal of Econometrics*, 54, 159–178.

Lafontaine, F. and White, K. J. (1986), Obtaining Any Wald Statistic You Want, *Economics Letters*, 21, 35–40.

Leamer, E. (1978), *Specification Searches*, John Wiley and Sons, New York.

Lee, L. F. and Maddala, G. S. (1985), The Common Structure of Tests for Selectivity Bias, Serial Correlation, Heteroskedasticity and Non-Normality in the Tobit Model, *International Economic Review*, 26, 1–20.

Lee, M. J. (1996), *Methods of Moments and Semiparametric Econometrics for Limited Dependent Variable Models*, Springer-Verlag, New York.

Leung, S. F. and Yu, S. (1996), On the Choice Between Sample Selection and Two-Part Models, *Journal of Econometrics*, 72, 197–229.

Levin, A. and Lin, C.-F. (1993), Unit Root Tests in Panel Data: New Results, Discussion Paper, Department of Economics, University of San Diego.

Lin, J.-L. and Tsay, R. S. (1996), Co-Integration Constraint and Forecasting: An Empirical Examination, *Journal of Applied Econometrics*, 11, 519–538.

Little, R. J. A. and Rubin, D. B. (1987), *Statistical Analysis with Missing Data*, John Wiley and Sons, New York.

Ljung, G. M. and Box, G. E. P. (1978), On a Measure of Lack of Fit in Time Series Models, *Biometrika*, 65, 297–303.

Lo, A. and MacKinlay, C. (1990), Data-Snooping Biases in Tests of Financial Asset Pricing Models, *Review of Financial Studies*, 3, 431–468.

Louviere, J. J. (1988), Conjoint Analysis Modeling of Stated Preferences. A Review of Theory, Methods, Recent Developments and External Validity, *Journal of Transport Economics and Policy*, 22, 93–119.

Lovell, M. C. (1983), Data Mining, *Review of Economics and Statistics*, 65, 1–12.

Lütkepohl, H. (1991), *Introduction to Multiple Time Series Analysis*, Springer-Verlag, Berlin.

MacKinnon, J. G. (1991), Critical Values for Cointegration Tests. In: R. F. Engle and C. W. J. Granger, eds., *Long-Run Economic Relationships: Readings in Cointegration*, Oxford University Press, 267–276.

MacKinnon, J. G., White, H. and Davidson, R. (1983), Test for Model Specification in the Presence of Alternative Hypotheses: Some Further Results, *Journal of Econometrics*, 21, 53–70.

Maddala, G. S. (1983), *Limited-Dependent and Qualitative Variables in Econometrics*, Cambridge University Press, Cambridge.

Maddala, G. S. (1987), Limited Dependent Variable Models Using Panel Data, *The Journal of Human Resources*, 22, 307–338.

Maddala, G. S. (1992), *Introduction to Econometrics*, 2nd edition, Prentice-Hall, Englewood Cliffs.

Manski, C. F. (1975), Maximum Score Estimation of the Stochastic Utility Model of Choice, *Journal of Econometrics*, 3, 205–228.

Manski, C. F. (1985), Semiparametric Analysis of Discrete Response, *Journal of Econometrics*, 27, 313–333.

Manski, C. F. (1989), Anatomy of the Selection Problem, *The Journal of Human Resources*, 24, 243–260.

Manski, C. F. (1994), The Selection Problem. In: C. A. Sims, ed., *Advances in Econometrics, Sixth World Congress, Volume I*, Cambridge University Press, Cambridge, 143–170.

Marquering W. and Verbeek, M. (1999), An Empirical Analysis of Intertemporal Asset Pricing Models with Transactions Costs and Habit Persistence, *Journal of Empirical Finance*, 6, 243–265.

Mátyás, L. and Sevestre, P. (1996), eds., *The Econometrics of Panel Data. A Handbook of the Theory with Applications*, 2nd revised edition, Kluwer Academic Publishers, Dordrecht.

McCall, B. P. (1995), The Impact of Unemployment Insurance Benefit Levels on Recipiency, *Journal of Business and Economic Statistics*, 13, 189–198.

McCulloch, J. H. and Kwon, H. C. (1993), *U.S. Term Structure Data, 1947–1991*, Ohio State working paper 93–6, Ohio State University, Columbus, OH.

McFadden, D. F. (1974), Conditional Logit Analysis of Qualitative Choice Behavior. In: P. Zaremba, ed., *Frontiers in Econometrics*, Academic Press, New York, 105–142.

Mehra, R. and Prescott, E. (1985), The Equity Premium: A Puzzle, *Journal of Monetary Economics*, 15, 145–161.

Melenberg, B. and van Soest, A. (1993), Semiparametric Estimation of the Sample Selection Model, CentER Discussion Paper 9334, Tilburg University.

Mills, T. C. (1990), *Time Series Techniques for Economists*, Cambridge University Press, Cambridge.

Mizon, G. E. (1984), The Encompassing Approach in Econometrics. In: K. F. Wallis and D. F. Hendry, eds., *Quantitative Economics and Econometric Analysis*, Basil Blackwell, Oxford, 135–172.

Mizon, G. E. and Richard, J. F. (1986), The Encompassing Principle and its Application to Testing Non-Nested Hypotheses, *Econometrica*, 54, 657–678.

Mundlak, Y. (1961), Empirical Production Function Free of Management Bias, *Journal of Farm Economics*, 43, 44–46.

Nelson. C. R. and Plosser, C. I. (1982), Trends and Random Walks in Macro-economic Time Series: Some Evidence and Implications, *Journal of Monetary Economics*, 10, 139–162.

Nelson, D. (1990), Conditional Heteroskedasticity in Asset Returns: A New Approach, *Econometrica*, 59, 347–370.

Newey, W. K. (1985), Maximum Likelihood Specification Testing and Conditional Moment Tests, *Econometrica*, 53, 1047–1070.

Newey, W. K. and West, K. (1987), A Simple Positive Semi-Definite, Heteroskedasticity and Autocorrelation Consistent Covariance Matrix, *Econometrica*, 55, 703–708.

Newey, W. K., Powell, J. L. and Walker, J. R. (1990), Semiparametric Estimation of Selection Models: Some Empirical Results, *American Economic Review*, 80, 324–328.

Nickell, S. (1981), Biases in Dynamic Models with Fixed Effects, *Econometrica*, 49, 1417–1426.

Nijman, Th. E. (1990), Estimation of Models Containing Unobserved Rational Expectations. In: F. van der Ploeg, ed., *Advanced Lectures in Quantative Economics*, Academic Press, London.

Nijman, Th. E. and Verbeek, M. (1990), Estimation of Time Dependent Parameters in Linear Models Using Cross Sections, Panels or Both, *Journal of Econometrics*, 46, 333–346.

Nijman, Th. E. and Verbeek, M. (1992), Nonresponse in Panel Data: The Impact on Estimates of a Life Cycle Consumption Function, *Journal of Applied Econometrics*, 7, 243–257.

Pagan, A. and Ullah, A. (1999), *Nonparametric Economics*, Cambridge University Press, Cambridge.

Pagan, A. and Vella, F. (1989), Diagnostic Tests for Models Based on Individual Data: A Survey, *Journal of Applied Econometrics*, 4, S29–S59.

Pagan, A., Hall, A. D. and Martin, V. (1996), Modeling the Term Structure. In: G. S. Maddala and C. R. Rao, eds., *Handbook of Statistics, Volume XIV*, Elsevier Science, Amsterdam, 91–118.

Pesaran, M. H. and Smith, R. (1995), Estimation of Long-Run Relationships from Dynamic Heterogeneous Panels, *Journal of Econometrics*, 68, 79–113.

Pesaran, M. H., Shin, Y. and Smith, R. J. forthcoming, Structural Analysis of Vector Error Correction Models with Exogenous $I(1)$ Variables, *Journal of Econometrics*.

Phillips, P. C. B. (1986), Understanding Spurious Regressions in Econometrics, *Journal of Econometrics*, 33, 311–340.

Phillips, P. C. B. and Moon, H. R. (1999), Linear Regression Limit Theory for Nonstationary Panel Data, *Econometrica*, 67, 1057–1111.

Phillips, P. C. B. and Park, J. Y. (1988), On the Formulation of Wald Tests of Nonlinear Restrictions, *Econometrica*, 56, 1065–1083.

Phillips, P. C. B. and Perron, P. (1988), Testing for a Unit Root in Time Series Regression, *Biometrika*, 75, 335–346.

Portney, P. R. (1994), The Contingent Valuation Debate: Why Should Economists Care?, *Journal of Economic Perspectives*, 8, 3–18.

Prais, S. and Winsten, C. (1954), Trend Estimation and Serial Correlation, Cowles Commission Discussion Paper 383, Chicago.

Quah, D. (1994), Exploiting Cross-Section Variation for Unit Root Inference in Dynamic Data, *Economics Letters*, 44, 9–19.

Ramsey, J. B. (1969), Tests for Specification Errors in Classical Linear Least Squares Regression Analysis, *Journal of the Royal Statistical Society B*, 32, 350–371.

Robertson, D. and Symons, J. (1992), Some Strange Properties of Panel Data Estimators, *Journal of Applied Econometrics*, 7, 175–189.

Robinson, P. M. (1982), On the Asymptotic Properties of Estimators of Models Containing Limited Dependent Variables, *Econometrica*, 50, 27–41.

Rosen, S. (1974), Hedonic Prices and Implicit Markets: Product Differentiation in Perfect Competition, *Journal of Political Economy*, 82, 34–55.

Rubin, D. B. (1976), Inference and Missing Data, *Biometrika*, 63, 581–592.

Ruud, P. A. (1984), Test of Specification in Econometrics, *Econometric Reviews*, 3, 211–242.

Said, S. E. and Dickey, D. A. (1984), Testing for Unit Roots in Autoregressive Moving Average Models of Unknown Order, *Biometrika*, 71, 599–607.

Sargan, J. D. and Bhargava, A. S. (1983), Testing Residuals from Least Squares Regression for Being Generated by the Gaussian Random Walk, *Econometrica*, 51, 213–248.

Savin, N. E. and White, K. J. (1977), The Durbin–Watson Test for Serial Correlation with Extreme Sample Sizes or Many Regressors, *Econometrica*, 45, 1989–1996.

Schwarz, G. (1978), Estimating the Dimension of a Model, *Annals of Statistics*, 6, 461–464.

Sims, C. A. (1980), Macroeconomics and Reality, *Econometrica*, 48, 1–48.

Stewart, J. and Gill, L. (1998), *Econometrics*, 2nd edition, Prentice Hall, London.

Stoll, H. R. and Whaley, R. E. (1993), *Futures and Options. Theory and Applications*, South-Western Publishing Co., Cincinnati, Ohio.

Sullivan, R., Timmermann, A. and White, H. (1998), Dangers of Data-Driven Inference: The Case of Calendar Effects in Stock Returns, *Discussion Paper*, University of California, San Diego.

Tauchen, G. E. (1985), Diagnostic Testing and Evaluation of Maximum Likelihood Models, *Journal of Econometrics*, 30, 415–443.

Ter Horst, J. R., Nijman, Th. E. and Verbeek, M. (1998), Eliminating Biases in Evaluating Mutual Fund Performance from a Survivorship Free Sample, CentER Discussion Paper 9855, CentER, Tilburg University.

Theil, H. (1953), Repeated Least Squares Applied to Complete Equation Systems, mimeo, Central Planning Bureau, The Hague.

Tobin, J. (1958), Estimation of Relationships for Limited Dependent Variables, *Econometrica*, 26, 24–36.

Vella, F. (1998), Estimating Models with Sample Selection Bias: A Survey, *Journal of Human Resources*, 33, 127–169.

Vella, F. and Verbeek, M. (1998), Whose Wages Do Unions Raise? A Dynamic Model of Unionism and Wage Rate Determination for Young Men, *Journal of Applied Econometrics*, 13, 163–183.

Vella, F. and Verbeek, M. (1999), Two-Step Estimation of Panel Data Models with Censored Endogenous Variables and Selection Bias, *Journal of Econometrics*, 90, 239–263.

Verbeek, M. (1995), Alternative Transformations to Eliminate Fixed Effects, *Econometric Reviews*, 14, 205–211.

Verbeek, M. and Nijman, Th. E. (1992), Testing for Selectivity Bias in Panel Data Models, *International Economic Review*, 33, 681–703.

Verbeek, M. and Nijman, Th. E. (1996), Incomplete Panels and Selection Bias. In: L. Mátyás, and P. Sevestre, eds., *The Econometrics of Panel Data. A Handbook of the Theory with Applications*, 2nd revised edition, Kluwer Academic Publishers, Dordrecht, 449–490.

Wallis, K. F. (1979), *Topics in Applied Econometrics*, 2nd edition, Basil Blackwell, Oxford.

Weeks, M. (1995), Circumventing the Curse of Dimensionality in Applied Work Using Computer Intensive Methods, *Economic Journal*, 105, 520–530.

White, H. (1980), A Heteroskedasticity-Consistent Covariance Matrix Estimator and a Direct Test for Heteroskedasticity, *Econometrica*, 48, 817–838.

White, H. (1982), Maximum Likelihood Estimation of Misspecified Models, *Econometrica*, 50, 1–25.

Wooldridge, J. (1995), Selection Corrections for Panel Data Models under Conditional Mean Independence Assumptions, *Journal of Econometrics*, 68, 115–132.

Index

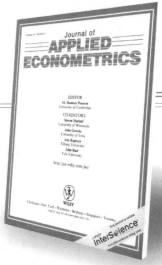